Windows Presentation Foundation Development Cookbook

100 recipes to build rich desktop client applications on Windows

Kunal Chowdhury

BIRMINGHAM - MUMBAI

Windows Presentation Foundation Development Cookbook

Commissioning Editor: Merint Mathew
Acquisition Editor: Nitin Dasan
Content Development Editor: Akshada Iyer
Technical Editor: Supriya Thabe
Copy Editor: Safis Editing
Project Coordinator: Prajakta Naik
Proofreader: Safis Editing
Indexer: Aishwarya Gangawane
Graphics: Jisha Chirayil
Production Coordinator: Shantanu Zagade

First published: February 2018

Production reference: 1210218

Published by Packt Publishing Ltd.
Livery Place
35 Livery Street
Birmingham
B3 2PB, UK.

ISBN 978-1-78839-980-7

www.packtpub.com

Contributors

About the author

Kunal Chowdhury has been a Microsoft MVP since 2010. He is a renowned public speaker, an active blogger (by passion), and a software engineer (technical lead) by profession. Over the years, he has acquired profound knowledge of various Microsoft products and helped developers throughout the world with his deep knowledge and experience.

He has authored the book *Mastering Visual Studio 2017* and written many articles, tips, and tricks on his technical blog (kunal-chowdhury [DOT] com) for developers and consumers. You can follow him on Twitter at @kunal2383 and become one of his fans on social media.

I would like to thank my wife, Manika Paul Chowdhury, and my parents for their continuous support throughout the period of writing this book. I would also like to thank the publisher and reviewers for their valuable feedback. Lastly, thanks to all my friends and colleagues who helped me to learn all that I have gathered over the years.

About the reviewer

Alvin Ashcraft is a developer living near Philadelphia. He has spent his 23-year career building software with C#, Visual Studio, WPF, ASP.NET, and more. He has been awarded, nine times, a Microsoft MVP. You can read his daily links for .NET developers on his blog, *the Morning Dew*. He works as a principal software engineer for Allscripts, building healthcare software. He has previously been employed with software companies, including Oracle. He has reviewed titles for Packt Publishing, such as *Mastering ASP.NET Core 2.0*, *Mastering Entity Framework Core 2.0*, and *Learning ASP.NET Core 2.0*.

I would like to thank wonderful wife, Stelene, and our three amazing daughters for their support. They were very understanding when I was reading and reviewing these chapters on evenings and weekends to help deliver a useful, high-quality book for WPF developers.

Packt is searching for authors like you

If you're interested in becoming an author for Packt, please visit `authors.packtpub.com` and apply today. We have worked with thousands of developers and tech professionals, just like you, to help them share their insight with the global tech community. You can make a general application, apply for a specific hot topic that we are recruiting an author for, or submit your own idea.

Table of Contents

Preface

Along with Windows 1.0, in the year 1985, Microsoft introduced Graphics Device Interface (GDI) and the USER subsystem in order to build a Windows-based Graphical User Interface (GUI). In 1990, OpenGL came into picture to create 2D and 3D graphics on Windows and non-Windows systems. In 1995, Microsoft presented another technology, called DirectX, to create high-performance 2D/3D graphics. Later, GDI+ was introduced to add alpha blending and gradient brush support on top of the existing GDI.

In 2002, Microsoft introduced .NET Framework. Along with this, Windows Forms was also introduced to build User Interface (UI) for Windows using C# and Visual Basic languages. It was built on top of GDI+, and hence, it still had the limitations of the GDI+ and USER subsystems.

Over the years, Microsoft decided to bring a new technology to build rich UIs for Windows-based applications, which not only helped the users (developers and designers) to escape the limitations of GDI/GDI+ and USER subsystems, but also helped them to improve their productivity when building desktop-based applications.

In November 2006, along with .NET 3.0, Windows Presentation Foundation (WPF) was introduced to provide the developers a unified programming model to build dynamic, data-driven desktop applications for Windows. It came with a broad set of features to create a graphical subsystem to render rich UIs using various controls, layouts, graphics, resources, and more, considering the application and the security of the data. As it was first shipped as part of the .NET Framework 3.0, the first release was called WPF 3.0.

WPF is a resolution-independent framework that uses a vector-based rendering engine using an XML-based language called XAML (pronounced Zammel), to create modern user experiences that provided a declarative model for application programming. Using this, you can easily customize the controls and add skins to it to get a better representation of the application's UI.

As WPF was different than classic Windows Forms, as it uses XAML, data binding, templates, styles, animations, documents, and more, initially it got little attention. However, later, it started gaining a lot of popularity and attraction. Many updated versions were released to add more functionality to it to make it robust and powerful.

In this book, we will cover a set of recipes that will show you how to perform common tasks using WPF. Starting with WPF fundamentals, we will cover standard controls, layouts, panels, data bindings, custom controls, user controls, styles, templates, triggers, and animations and later move on to the uses of resources, MVVM patterns, WCF services, debugging, threading, and WPF interoperabilities, to make sure you understand the foundation properly.

The examples given in this book are simple, easy to understand, and provide you with a what you need to learn and master the skills that you need to build desktop applications using WPF. By the time you reach the end of this book, you will be proficient enough with deep knowledge about each of the chapters that it covers. Although this book has covered most of the important topics, there will always be some topics that no books can completely cover. You will definitely enjoy reading this book, as there are lots of graphical and textual steps to help you gain confidence working with Windows Presentation Foundation.

Who this book is for

The book is intended for developers who are relatively new to Windows Presentation Foundation (WPF) or those who have been working with WPF for some time, but want to get a deeper understanding of its foundation and concepts to gain practical knowledge. Basic knowledge of C# and Visual Studio is assumed.

What this book covers

`Chapter 1`, *WPF Fundamentals*, focuses on WPF's architecture, application types, and XAML syntax, terminologies, and explains how to install WPF Workload with Visual Studio 2017 to create your first application targeting Windows Presentation Foundation. It will cover the navigation mechanisms, various dialog boxes, building ownership between multiple windows, and then proceed toward creating a single instance application. This chapter will then cover how to pass arguments to WPF application and how to handle unhandled exceptions thrown in WPF.

`Chapter 2`, *Using WPF Standard Controls*, provides you with an in-depth knowledge to help you learn about various common control parts of WPF. This chapter will begin with TextBlock, Label, TextBox, and Image controls, and then continue with 2D shapes, Tooltip, standard menu, Context Menu, Radio buttons, and CheckBox controls. This chapter will also cover how to work with Progress Bar, Slider, Calendar, ListBox, ComboBox, StatusBar, and Toolbar panel.

`Chapter 3`, *Layouts and Panels*, gives you quick tour of the standard layout and panels. This chapter will cover how to use the panels to create proper layouts. It will also cover implementing the drag and drop feature in brief.

`Chapter 4`, *Working with Data Bindings*, discusses the important concept of data binding and how to use it in WPF. It also discusses CLR properties, dependency properties, attached properties, converters, and data operations (such as sorting, grouping, and filtering). The step-by-step approaches will guide you to be proficient with all types of data bindings.

`Chapter 5`, *Using Custom Controls and User Controls*, provides the basic building blocks you need to create custom controls and user controls that you can reuse in various places. You will also learn how to customize the control template using custom properties and events from the custom controls and user controls.

`Chapter 6`, *Using Styles, Templates, and Triggers*, provides a deep insight into the styles and templates of a control, followed by various triggers that you can use to perform some operations or UI changes directly from the XAML, without using any C# code.

`Chapter 7`, *Using Resources and MVVM Patterns*, begins by demonstrating various ways to use and manage binary resources, logical resources, and static resources. It will then continue with the Model View ViewModel (MVVM) pattern to build a WPF application by writing less code in the code behind file. The MVVM pattern is introduced with some examples to show how you can build command bindings.

`Chapter 8`, *Working with Animations*, provides a tour to the animation capabilities in WPF and discusses how to use various transforms and animations and apply effects to animations.

`Chapter 9`, *Using WCF Services*, makes it easy for you to understand the *ABC* of WCF services and explains how to create, host, and consume them in a WPF application.

`Chapter 10`, *Debugging and Threading*, discusses WPF's support for debugging the XAML application UI using the Live Visual Tree and Live Property Explorer. This chapter helps you to create asynchronous operations so that the application UI is always responsive.

`Chapter 11`, *Interoperability with Win32 and WinForm*, focuses on understanding the interoperability of WPF with Win32 and Windows Forms. In this chapter, you will learn how to host an element from one technology (WPF/WinForm) to other technology (WinForm/WPF), followed by calling Win32 APIs and embedding ActiveX controls in a WPF application.

To get the most out of this book

This book assumes that the reader has knowledge of .NET Framework and C# (at least C# version 3.0, but C# 7.0 or higher version is preferable) and has working experience of Visual Studio 2015 or higher (Visual Studio 2017 is preferable). Basic knowledge of WPF and XAML has been assumed.

Download the example code files

You can download the example code files for this book from your account at `www.packtpub.com`. If you purchased this book elsewhere, you can visit `www.packtpub.com/support` and register to have the files emailed directly to you.

You can download the code files by following these steps:

1. Log in or register at `www.packtpub.com`.
2. Select the **SUPPORT** tab.
3. Click on **Code Downloads & Errata**.
4. Enter the name of the book in the **Search** box and follow the onscreen instructions.

Once the file is downloaded, please make sure that you unzip or extract the folder using the latest version of:

- WinRAR/7-Zip for Windows
- Zipeg/iZip/UnRarX for Mac
- 7-Zip/PeaZip for Linux

The code bundle for the book is also hosted on GitHub at `https://github.com/PacktPublishing/Windows-Presentation-Foundation-Development-Cookbook`. In case there's an update to the code, it will be updated on the existing GitHub repository.

We also have other code bundles from our rich catalog of books and videos available at `https://github.com/PacktPublishing/`. Check them out!

Download the color images

We also provide a PDF file that has color images of the screenshots/diagrams used in this book. You can download it here: `https://www.packtpub.com/sites/default/files/downloads/WindowsPresentationFoundationDevelopmentCookbook_ColorImages.pdf`.

Conventions used

There are a number of text conventions used throughout this book.

`CodeInText`: Indicates code words in text, database table names, folder names, filenames, file extensions, pathnames, dummy URLs, user input, and Twitter handles. Here is an example: "The Presentation Core layer, part of `presentationcore.dll`, provides you with the wrapper around the Media Integration Library."

A block of code is set as follows:

```
<Button>
  <Button.Background>
    <SolidColorBrush Color="Red" />
  </Button.Background>
</Button>
```

Any command-line input or output is written as follows:

```
svcutil.exe http://localhost:59795/Services/EmployeeService.svc?wsdl
```

Bold: Indicates a new term, an important word, or words that you see onscreen. For example, words in menus or dialog boxes appear in the text like this. Here is an example: "To build WPF applications targeting the .NET Framework, select the **.NET desktop development** workload."

Warnings or important notes appear like this.

Tips and tricks appear like this.

Get in touch

Feedback from our readers is always welcome.

General feedback: Email `feedback@packtpub.com` and mention the book title in the subject of your message. If you have questions about any aspect of this book, please email us at `questions@packtpub.com`.

Errata: Although we have taken every care to ensure the accuracy of our content, mistakes do happen. If you have found a mistake in this book, we would be grateful if you would report this to us. Please visit `www.packtpub.com/submit-errata`, selecting your book, clicking on the Errata Submission Form link, and entering the details.

Piracy: If you come across any illegal copies of our works in any form on the Internet, we would be grateful if you would provide us with the location address or website name. Please contact us at `copyright@packtpub.com` with a link to the material.

If you are interested in becoming an author: If there is a topic that you have expertise in and you are interested in either writing or contributing to a book, please visit `authors.packtpub.com`.

Reviews

Please leave a review. Once you have read and used this book, why not leave a review on the site that you purchased it from? Potential readers can then see and use your unbiased opinion to make purchase decisions, we at Packt can understand what you think about our products, and our authors can see your feedback on their book. Thank you!

For more information about Packt, please visit `packtpub.com`.

1
WPF Fundamentals

In this chapter, we will cover the following recipes:

- Installing WPF Workload with Visual Studio 2017
- Creating WPF applications
- Creating and navigating from one window to another
- Creating and navigating from one page to another
- Creating a dialog box
- Creating ownership between windows
- Creating a single instance application
- Passing arguments to WPF applications
- Handling unhandled exceptions

Introduction

The **Windows Presentation Foundation** (**WPF**) provides developers with a unified programming model to build dynamic, data-driven desktop applications for Windows. It was first released in 2006 along with .NET 3.0. It is part of the .NET Framework itself.

WPF is a graphical subsystem, for rendering rich **user interfaces** (UIs), and is a resolution-independent framework that uses a vector-based rendering engine in the **Extensible Application Markup Language** (**XAML**) to create stunning user interfaces. It supports a broad set of features that includes application models, controls, layouts, graphics, resources, security, and more.

The runtime libraries for it to execute have been included with Windows since Windows Vista and Windows Server 2008. If you are using Windows XP with SP2/SP3 and Windows Server 2003, you can optionally install the necessary libraries.

To begin learning the different recipes of WPF, you should have a clear understanding of the basic foundations. In this chapter, we will start with the architecture and syntaxes, and will guide you in creating a building block.

The WPF Architecture

WPF uses a layered architecture that includes managed, unmanaged, and the core APIs in five different layers called **Presentation Framework**, **Presentation Core**, **Common Language Runtime**, **Media Integration Library**, and **OS Core**. The programming model is exposed through the managed code.

In the following diagram, you can see a clear picture of the architecture:

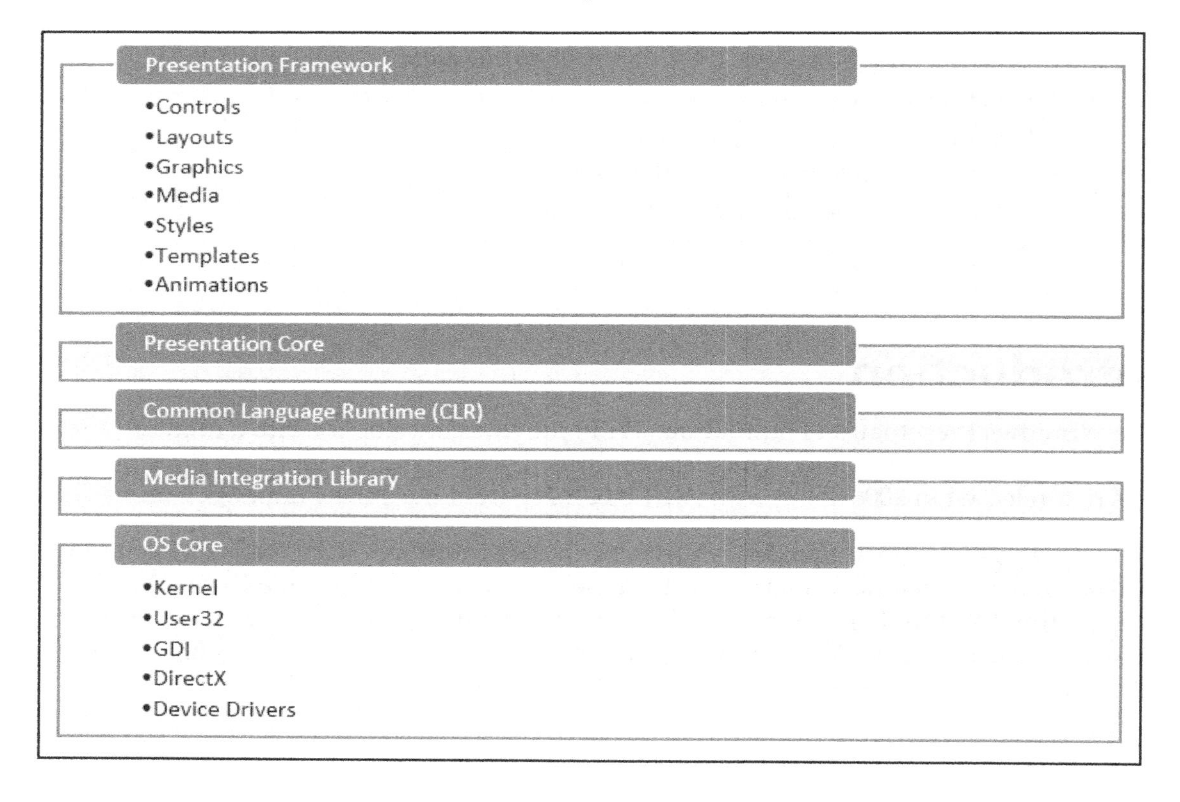

Presentation Framework

The **Presentation Framework**, which is part of `presentationframework.dll`, provides the basic required components (such as controls, layouts, graphics, media, styles, templates, animations, and more) to start building the UIs of your WPF applications. It is part of the managed layer.

Presentation Core

The **Presentation Core** layer, part of `presentationcore.dll`, provides you with the wrapper around the **Media Integration Library** (**MIL**). It present you with the public interfaces to access the MIL Core and the Visual System to develop the Visual Tree. It contains visual elements and rendering instructions to build applications for Windows using the XAML tools. This is also part of the managed code.

Common Language Runtime

Common Language Runtime, commonly known as the **CLR** and part of the managed layer, provides you with several features to build robust applications covering **common type system** (**CTS**), error handling, memory management, and more.

Media Integration Library

The **Media Integration Library (MIL)**, which resides in `milcore.dll`, is part of the unmanaged layer used to display all graphics rendered through the DirectX engine. It provides you with basic support for 2D and 3D surfaces, and allows you to access the unmanaged components to enable tight integrations with DirectX. It also enables you to gain performance while rendering instructions from the Visual System to the **Common Language Runtime** (**CLR**).

OS Core

Just after the MIL, the next layer is the **OS Core**, which provides you with access to the low-level APIs to handle the core components of the operating system. This layer includes Kernel, User32, DirectX, GDI, and device drivers.

Types of WPF applications

Though WPF is mainly used for desktop applications, you can also create web-based applications. Thus, WPF applications can be of two types:

- Desktop-based executables (EXE)
- Web-based applications (XBAP)

The desktop applications are the normal `.exe` executables, which you normally run on any of your Windows-based systems, whereas the web-based applications are the `.xbap` files that can be deployed in web servers and can run inside any supported browser. The .NET Framework is mandatory to run any of these application types.

When you run a WPF application, it starts in two threads. The UI thread uses the `System.Threading.DispatcherObject` to create the messaging system and that maintains the UI operations queue. Just like the Win32 message pumping, it performs the UI operation based on the priority set for it.

The other thread is the background thread, which is used to handle the rendering engine being managed by WPF. It picks up a copy of the visual tree and performs actions to show the visual components in the Direct3D surface. Then it calls the UI elements to determine the size and arranges the child elements by their parents.

The XAML overview

XAML stands for **Extensible Application Markup Language**. It is an XML-based markup language that is used to declaratively create the UI of any XAML-based application, such as **Windows Platform Foundation** (**WPF**), **Universal Windows Platform** (**UWP**), and **Xamarin.Forms**. You can create visible UI elements in a declarative XAML syntax to design the rich UI and then write the code behind to perform a runtime logic.

Microsoft recently introduced **XAML Standards**, which is a specification that defines a standard XAML vocabulary, which will allow the supported frameworks to share common XAML-based UI definitions.

You can learn more about this specification by visiting GitHub here: `http://aka.ms/xamlstandard`.

Though it is not mandatory to use the XAML markup to create a UI, it has been widely accepted as the smart option for the creation of the entire application's UI, as it makes things easier to create. You can create the UI by writing C# or VB.NET code too, but that makes it more difficult and tougher to maintain. Also, that makes it difficult for the designers to work independently.

Designing an application UI using XAML is as easy as writing an XML node with a few optional attributes. Attributes are used to set additional styles, behaviors, and properties. To create a simple button in the UI, you can just write `<Button />` in your XAML file. Similarly, you can just write `<TextBox />` to create a user-input box.

Additionally, you can add more details to the controls. For example, to add a label to a button, use its `Content` property, and to set its dimension, use the `Height` and `Width` property, as shown in the following code:

```
<Button Content="Click Here" />
<Button Height="36" Width="120" />
```

In general, when you add XAML pages to your WPF application project, it compiles along with the project and produces a binary file in what is known as **Binary Application Markup Language** (**BAML**). The final output of the project (that is, the assembly file) contains this BAML file as a resource. When the application loads into the memory, the BAML is then parsed at runtime.

You can also load an XAML into memory and directly render it on the UI. But, in this case, if it has any XAML syntax errors, it will throw those in runtime. If you compare the performance with the first process, the latter is slower, as it renders the entire XAML syntax onto UI.

Here's a flow diagram, that demonstrates the ways to load and render/parse the XAML UI:

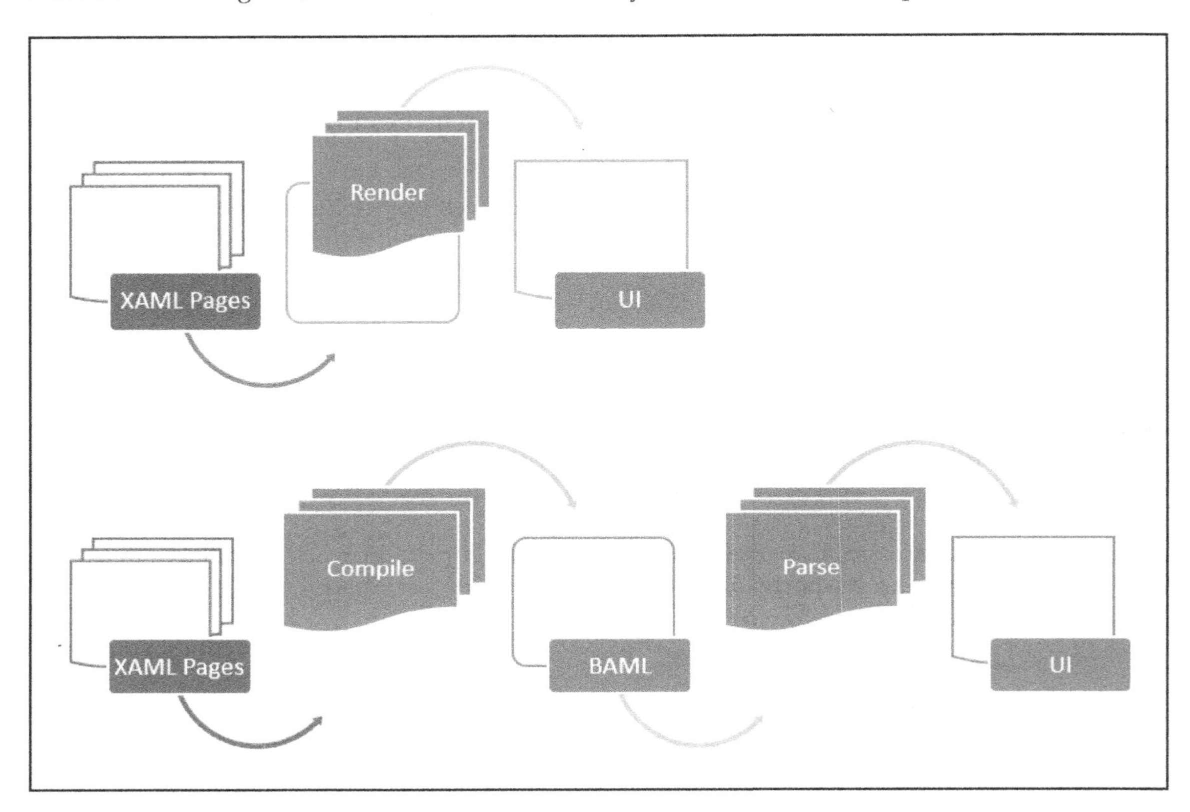

XAML syntax terminologies

XAML uses some syntax terminologies to define an element in the UI and create the instance of it. Before you start working on it, you must understand the different terminologies that it offers. Let's have a look at a few of them.

Object element syntax

Each instance of a type is defined using proper XAML syntax to create an object element in the UI. Each of these object elements starts with a left angular bracket (<) and defines the name of the element. You can optionally prefix the namespace when it is defined outside the default scope. You can use a self-closing angular bracket (/>) or a right angular bracket (>) to close the object element definition. If the object element does not have any child elements, the self-closing angular bracket is used. For example, (`<Button Content="Click Here" />`) uses a self-closing angular bracket. If you write the same with a child element, it closes with an end tag (`<Button>Click Here</Button>,`) as shown.

When you define the object element in an XAML page, the instruction to create the instance of the element gets generated and it creates the instance by calling the constructor of the element when you load it in memory.

Property Attribute syntax

You can define one or more properties to an element. These are done by writing an attribute called **Property Attribute syntax** to the element. It starts with the name of the property and an assignment operator (=), followed by the value within quotes. The following example demonstrates how easy it is to define a button element to have a label as its content, and how to set its dimension in UI:

```
<Button Content="Click Here" />
<Button Content="Click Here" Width="120" Height="30" />
```

Property Element syntax

This is another type of XAML syntax that allows you to define the property as an element. This is often used when you cannot assign the value of the property within quotes. If we take the previous example, the text `Click Here` can be assigned to the button content easily. But, when you have another element or a composite property value, you cannot write those within the quotes. For this, XAML introduces **Property Element syntax** to help you to define the property value easily.

It starts with `<element.PropertyName>` and ends with `</element.PropertyName>`. The following example demonstrates how to assign a color to a button background with a `SolidColorBrush` object:

```
<Button>
  <Button.Background>
     <SolidColorBrush Color="Red" />
  </Button.Background>
</Button>
```

Content syntax

This is another type of XAML syntax that is used to set the content of a UI element. It can be set as the value of child elements. The following example demonstrates how to set the text content property of a `Border` control to hold a `Button` control as its `child` element:

```
<Border>
  <Border.Child>
    <Button Content="Click Here" />
  </Border.Child>
</Border>
```

While using **Content syntax**, you should remember the following points:

- The value of a `Content` property must be contiguous
- You cannot define an XAML `Content` property twice within a single instance

Thus, the following is invalid as it will throw XAML error:

```
<Border>
    <Border.Child>
        <Button Content="Button One" />
    </Border.Child>
    <Border.Child>
        <Button Content="Button Two" />
    </Border.Child>
</Border>
```

Collection syntax

When you need to define a collection of elements to the parent root, the **Collection syntax** is used to make it easy to read. For example, to add elements inside `StackPanel`, we use its `Children` property, as shown in the following code:

```
<StackPanel>
  <StackPanel.Children>
     <Button Content="Button One" />
     <Button Content="Button Two" />
  </StackPanel.Children>
</StackPanel>
```

This can be also written as follows, and the parser knows how to create and assign the elements to `StackPanel`:

```
<StackPanel>
  <Button Content="Button One" />
  <Button Content="Button Two" />
</StackPanel>
```

Event Attribute syntax

When you add a button, you need to associate an event listener to it, to perform some operation. The same is applicable for adding other controls and UI layouts. The XAML allows you to use the **Event Attribute syntax** to define events for a specific XAML object element.

The syntax looks like a property attribute, but it is used to associate the event listener to the element. The following example demonstrates how to assign the click event to a button control:

```
<Button Content="Click Here" Click="OnButtonClicked" />
```

The associated event gets generated from the code behind the XAML page, where you can perform the real action. Here is the code snippet for the event implementation of the preceding button-click event:

```
void OnButtonClicked (object sender, RoutedEventArgs e)
{
    // event implementation
}
```

Installing WPF Workload with Visual Studio 2017

As we have learned the basic concepts of WPF Architecture and XAML syntax, we can start to learn different recipes to build applications for Windows using the XAML tools for WPF. But, before that, let's install the required workload/components for **Visual Studio 2017**. If you are using prior versions of Visual Studio, this step will be different.

Getting ready

To install the required components for building WPF applications, run the Visual Studio 2017 installer. If you don't have the installer, you can go to `https://www.visualstudio.com/downloads` and download the correct edition. Let's download the **Visual Studio Community 2017** edition as it is a fully featured IDE and available free for students, open source, and individual developers.

How to do it...

Once you have downloaded the Visual Studio 2017 installer, follow these steps to install the correct workload:

1. Once you have run the installer, it will show you the following screen. Click on **Continue**:

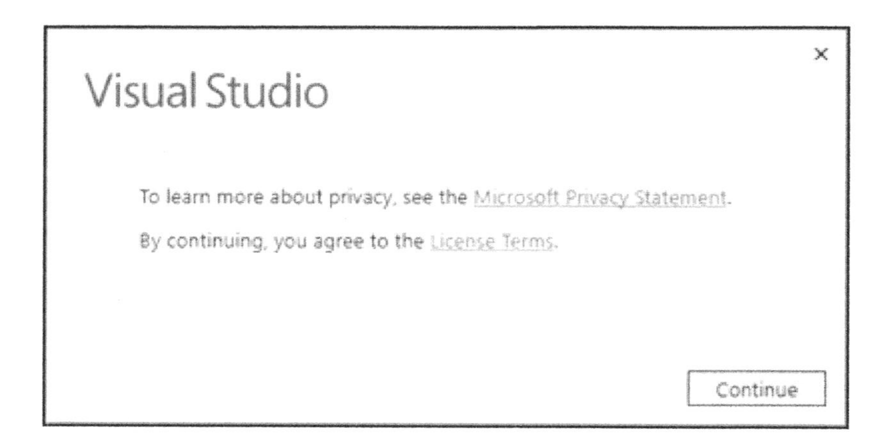

2. Wait for a few minutes to let the installer prepare itself for the installation process. A progress bar will show you the status of the current progress:

3. Then the following screen will pop up, where it will ask you to select the **workloads** or **components** that you want to install:

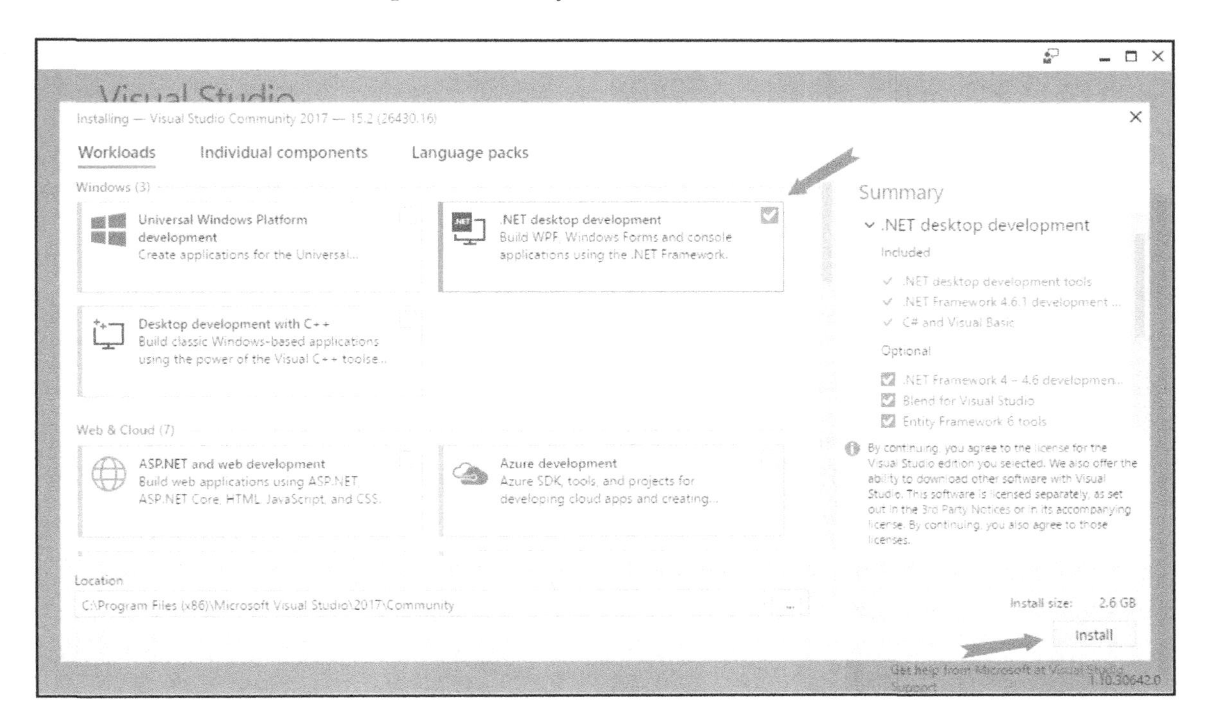

4. To build WPF applications targeting .NET Framework, select the **.NET desktop development** workload, as shown in the preceding screenshot.
5. Click on the **Install** button to continue with the installation.
6. The following screen will be displayed, showing the status of the installation. It will take some time, based on your internet bandwidth, as it's going to download the required components, based on your selection, from the Microsoft servers and install them one by one:

7. Once the installation has completed, you may have to restart your system for the changes to take effect. In this case, a popup will appear on the screen, asking you to reboot your PC.

Once you have installed the **.NET desktop development component** and restarted your system, you are good to go with building your first WPF application.

Creating WPF applications

The WPF development platform supports a broad set of features that includes UI controls, layouts, resources, graphics, data binding, application model, and more. Before using each of those features, you need to create the WPF project using Visual Studio.

The goal of this recipe is to create a WPF project and learn the basic project structure and components. Let's start building our first WPF application using the **XAML tools**.

Getting ready

To get started with the WPF application development, you must have Visual Studio running on your system with the required components already installed on it.

How to do it...

Follow these steps to create your first WPF application:

1. Inside your Visual Studio IDE, navigate to the **File** | **New** | **Project...** menu as shown in the following screenshot:

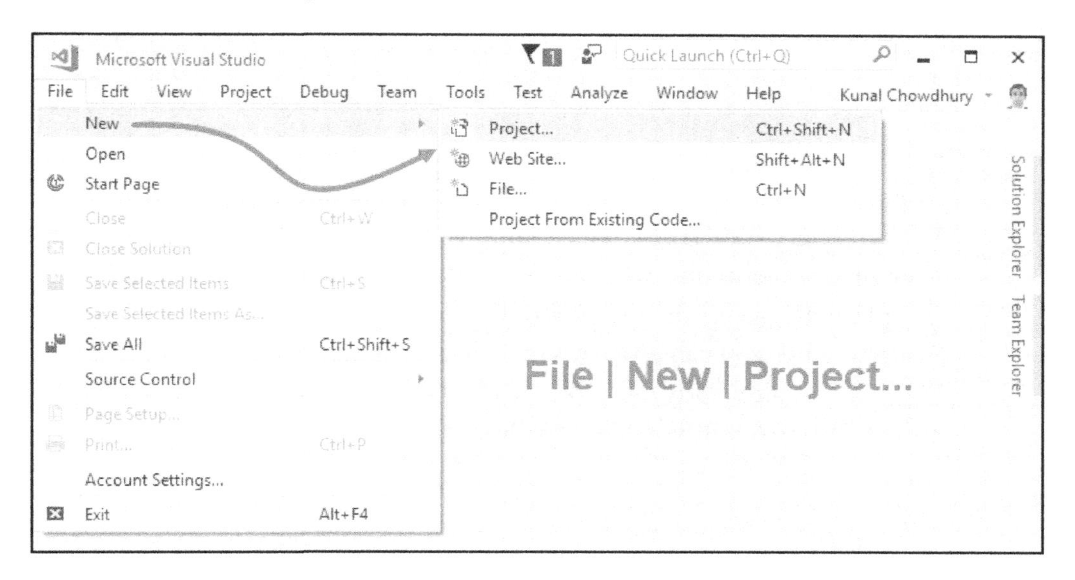

2. This will open the **New Project** dialog on the screen. You can alternatively open it by pressing the keyboard shortcut *Ctrl* + *Shift* + *N*.
3. In the **New Project** dialog, navigate to **Installed** | **Templates** | **Visual C#** | **Windows Classic Desktop**, as shown in the left-hand side of the following screenshot:

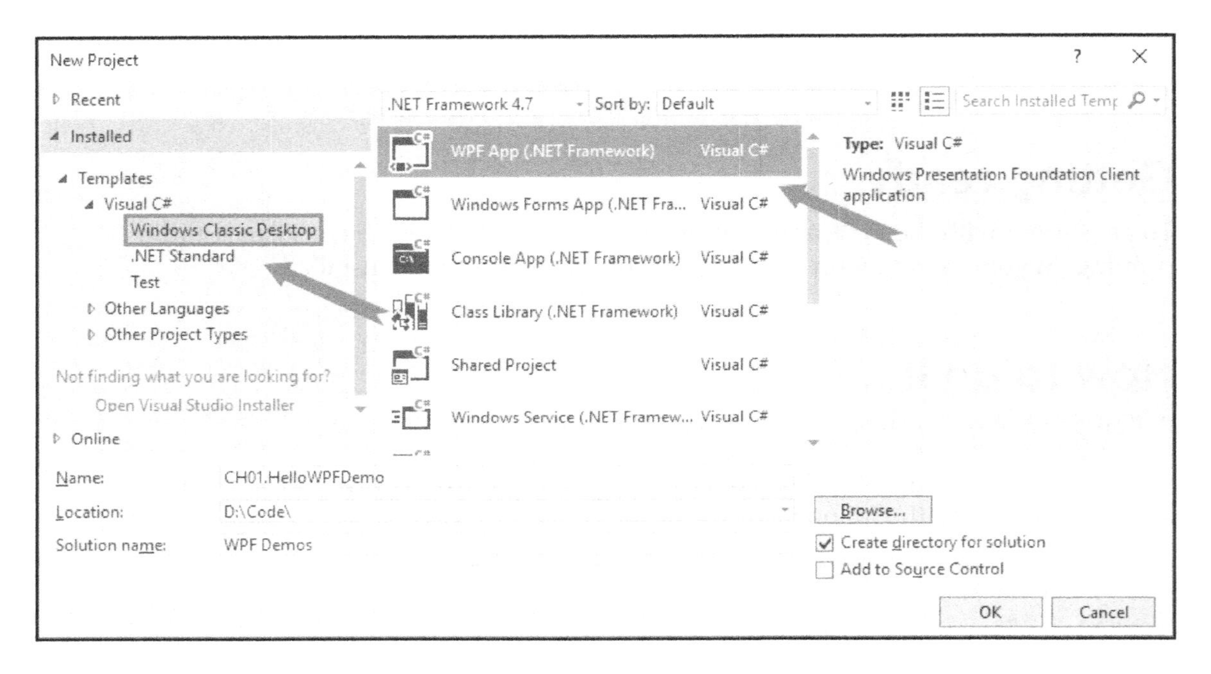

4. In the right-hand side panel, first select the **.NET Framework** that you want your application to target. We have selected **.NET Framework 4.7** here.
5. Then select **WPF App (.NET Framework)**, from the available list of templates.
6. Give a name (in our case, it is `CH01.HelloWPFDemo`) to the project.
7. Optionally, select the location of the project, where you want to create it.
8. Optionally, you can also provide a different name for the **Solution**.
9. When you are ready, click on the **OK** button to let Visual Studio create the project based on the template that you have selected.

Once the project has been created, Visual Studio will open the **Solution Explorer**, which lists the project with all the default files created on it. The project structure will look like the following screenshot:

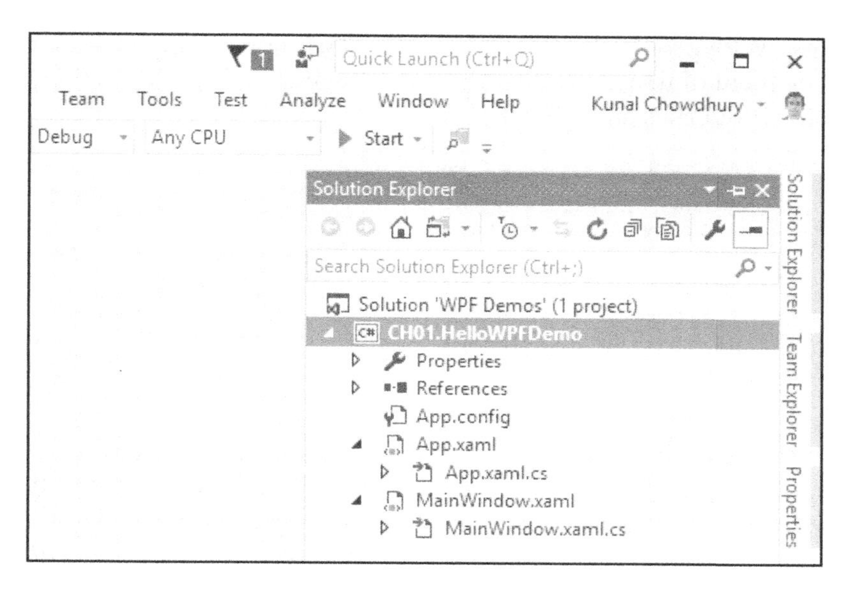

There's more...

Each WPF application project created by Visual Studio using the default template consists of the following files:

- `App.config`: This is the configuration file of your WPF application. By default, it contains the following lines that describe the supported runtime version for the application to run. This contains exactly the same runtime version that we selected during the project creation:

```
<?xml version="1.0" encoding="utf-8" ?>
  <configuration>
    <startup>
      <supportedRuntime
       version="v4.0"sku=".NETFramework,Version=v4.7" />
    </startup>
  </configuration>
```

The `config` file can also contain application settings and other configuration settings that you want to use/refer in your application.

- `App.xaml`: Visual Studio automatically creates the `App.xaml` file when you create a WPF project. It is the declarative starting point of your application. The root element of this file is the `Application` instance, which defines application specific properties and events:

```
<Application x:Class="CH01.HelloWPFDemo.App"
  xmlns="http://schemas.microsoft.com/winfx
  /2006/xaml/presentation"
  xmlns:x="http://schemas.microsoft.com/winfx/2006/xaml"
  xmlns:local="clr-namespace:CH01.HelloWPFDemo"
  StartupUri="MainWindow.xaml">
<Application.Resources>
</Application.Resources>
</Application>
```

The instance of the `Application` class defines the `Window` or a `Page` that's going to be the startup UI, and is registered with the `StartupUri` property. In the preceding code, (`StartupUri="MainWindow.xaml"`) states that the `MainWindow.xaml` page will get loaded, once you run the application.

The application instance can also hold global/application-level resources (such as, **Style**, **Template**, and **Converter**) that can be used globally throughout the application.

- `App.xaml.cs`: This is the code-behind class file of the `App.xaml` and extends the `Application` class of the framework to write application-specific code. You can use this file to subscribe to the events such as `Startup`, `UnhandledException` to perform common operations:

```
namespace CH01.HelloWPFDemo
{
    /// <summary>
    /// Interaction logic for App.xaml
    /// </summary>
    public partial class App : Application
    {
    }
}
```

This class is often used to manipulate command-line parameters and load different XAML pages based on that.

- `MainWindow.xaml`: This is the default UI page that Visual Studio generates on creation of the WPF project. It is the page that gets registered as the `StartupUri` in `App.xaml`. The root element of this page is `Window` and it contains a `Grid` layout by default. Here is the default code snippet:

```
<Window x:Class="CH01.HelloWPFDemo.MainWindow"
  xmlns=
   "http://schemas.microsoft.com/winfx/2006/xaml/presentation"
   xmlns:x="http://schemas.microsoft.com/winfx/2006/xaml"
   Title="MainWindow" Height="350" Width="525">
  <Grid>
  </Grid>
</Window>
```

The `x:Class` attribute defines the associated partial class where the UI logic is being written. You can modify this XAML to provide a fresh look to your application start page. Various UI controls and layouts are going to be covered in the later chapters of this book.

- `MainWindow.xaml.cs`: This is the code-behind class of `MainWindow.xaml` and contains the logic related to UI operations. In general, developers write implementations of various UI operations in this class.

Whenever you add any UI elements to an XAML page, the control gets registered internally in a partial class file that has `.g.i.cs` as the extension. For example, if you add a control in the `MainWindow.xaml` file, it gets registered in the `MainWindow.g.i.cs` residing in the `obj` folder. If you open the file, you can observe the entire loading process inside the `InitializeComponent()` method.

Creating and navigating from one window to another

In WPF standalone applications, a window is used to host the UI elements to enable users to interact with the UI and data. The base class `Window` provides all the APIs to create and interact with the Window UI.

In WPF applications, the generic window layout is divided into multiple parts. Here is a screenshot of a basic window, containing its various parts:

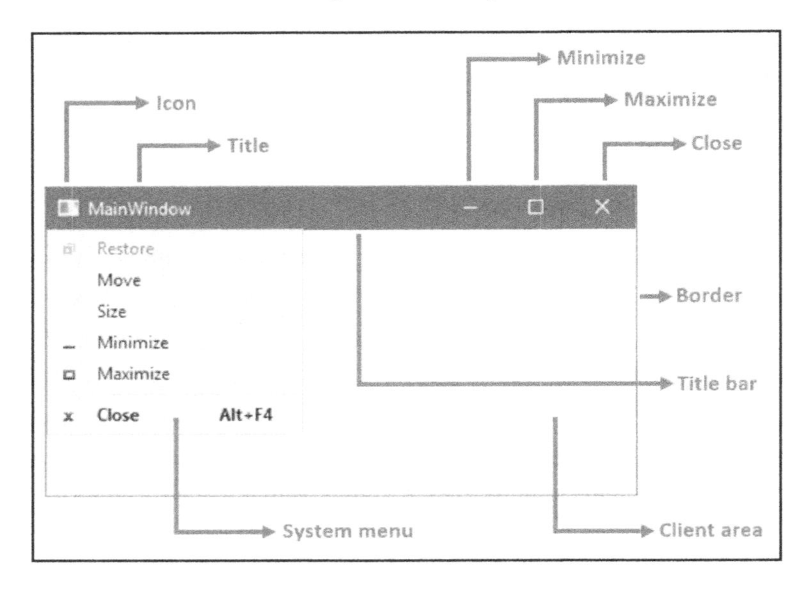

The various parts of the window are as mentioned here:

- The outer part of the window is a **Border**, which you can utilize to enable the resizing option:
    - The outer border can contain a **resizing grip**, which enables you to resize the window diagonally
- The window contains a **Title bar** at the top, which consists of the following parts:
    - An **Icon** to provide a unique brand to your application window
    - A **Title**, showing the identifiable name of the window
    - A small panel, containing **Minimize**, **Maximise/Restore**, and **Close** buttons
    - A **System menu** with menu items to allow users to perform **Minimize**, **Maximize/ Restore**, **Mov**e, **Size**, and **Close** operations on the window
- A **client area** for the developers to add application/window specific layouts and controls

Getting ready

To get started with this recipe, open your Visual Studio instance and create a WPF project called `CH01.WindowDemo` based on the **WPF App (.NET Framework)** template. Once the project has been created, it will have files called `MainWindow.xaml` and `MainWindow.xaml.cs`, along with the other default files.

Let's get started with creating a new window in the same project and invoke a button to open the new window from the `MainWindow`.

How to do it...

To create a new window, follow these simple steps:

1. Open the **Solution Explorer** and right-click on the project node.
2. From the right-click context menu, navigate to **Add** | **Window...** as shown in the following screenshot:

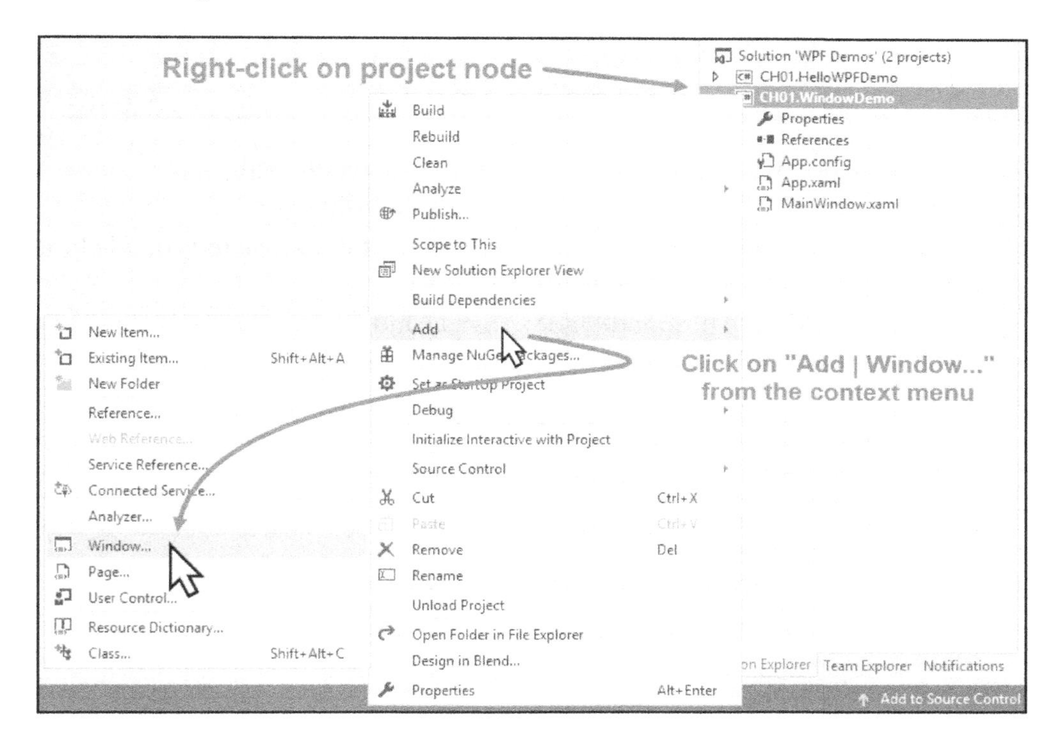

3. The following Add New Item dialog will appear on the screen:

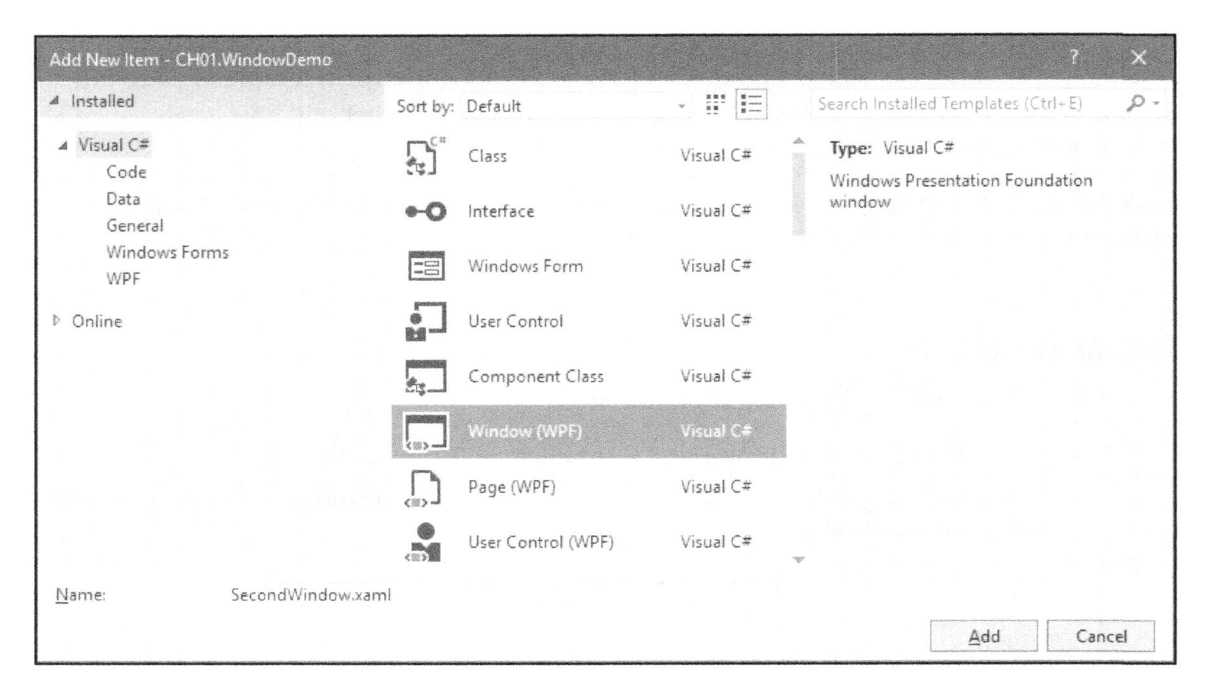

4. Make sure that the selected template is **Window (WPF)**. Give it a name, `SecondWindow.xaml`, and click the **Add** button.
5. This will create the `SecondWindow.xaml` file and its associated code-behind file `SecondWindow.xaml.cs` in the project directory.
6. Open the XAML file (`SecondWindow.xaml`) and replace the entire contents with the following XAML code:

```
<Window x:Class="CH01.WindowDemo.SecondWindow"
  xmlns=
    "http://schemas.microsoft.com/winfx/2006/xaml/presentation"
    xmlns:x="http://schemas.microsoft.com/winfx/2006/xaml"
    Title="Second Window" Height="200" Width="300">
    <Grid>
        <TextBlock Text="Second Window Instance"
                   HorizontalAlignment="Center"
                   VerticalAlignment="Center"
                   FontSize="16"/>
    </Grid>
</Window>
```

7. Now open the `MainWindow.xaml` file to add a button into it. Replace the entire `<Grid> </Grid>` block, with the following XAML code:

```
<Grid>
    <Button Content="Open Second Window"
            Height="30" Width="150"
            Click="OnSecondWindowButtonClicked"/>
</Grid>
```

8. Now we need to add the implementation for the button-click event. Simply open the `MainWindow.xaml.cs` file and add the following lines of code inside the class definition:

```
private void OnSecondWindowButtonClicked(object sender,
RoutedEventArgs e)
{
    var window = new SecondWindow();
    window.Show();
}
```

9. Now, when you run the application, you will see that the **MainWindow** opens on the screen, containing a button labeled **Open Second Window**. Clicking on this button opens the second window on the screen that has text content of **Second Window Instance**. Here's the screenshot for your reference:

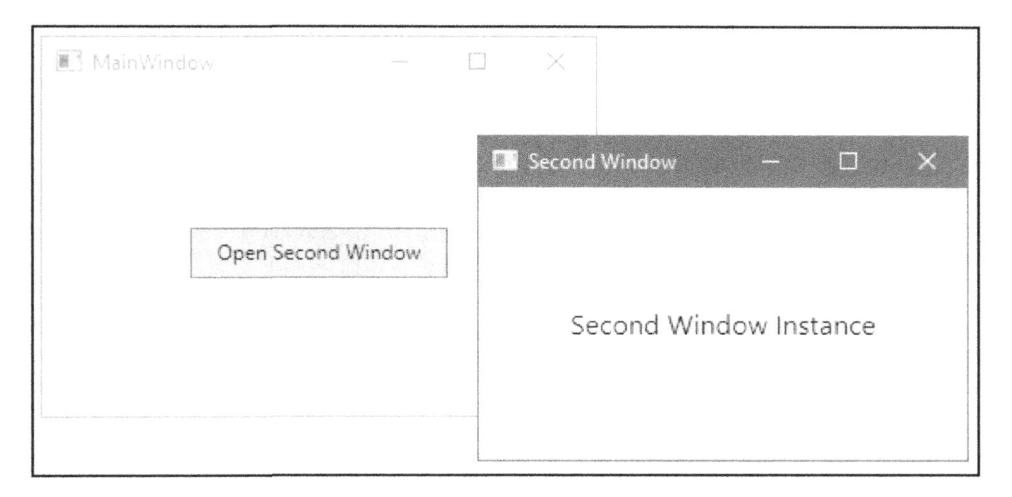

Please note that if you click the button again, it will create another instance of the second window because it's modeless.

How it works...

When you create the instance of the `Window` class, it will not become visible to the user. It only becomes visible when you call the `Show()` method, which returns the handle to the originated caller without waiting for the window to close.

When you call the `Show()` method, it basically creates a modeless window, and hence you can interact with other windows within the same application when the same is already open. The `Window` class also exposes a method called `ShowDialog()`, which creates a model window and prevent users from interacting with other windows of the application. We will discuss the more later in this chapter, in the *Creating a dialog box* section.

There's more...

The `Window` class provides you with a bunch of properties, methods, and events to customize the look of the window, and perform specific operations or to be notified of the current context. To ask the client area to support transparency, set the `AllowsTransparency` property of the window to `true`. This is often useful when you want to create a custom-shaped window or a skinned theme.

You can change the default icon of the window by setting the `Icon` property and enable/disable the window resizing by setting the `ResizeMode` property. You can also set the window title, startup location, window state, window style, and taskbar visibility by settings the `Title`, `WindowStartupLocation`, `WindowState`, `WindowStyle`, and `ShowInTaskbar` properties, respectively.

Not only these but you can bring the window to the foreground by calling its `Activate()` method and close the window by calling the `Close()` method available in the `Window` class. Sometimes, when you want to hide the window instead of quitting it completely, you can utilize the `Hide()` method to make the window hidden and bring it back again by calling the `Show()` method on the same instance.

The class also exposes some events to notify you of the current contextual information. You can use the `Activated`, `Deactivated`, `Closing`, `Closed`, and `StateChanged`, events in your code to get such notifications.

Creating and navigating from one page to another

The WPF application supports a browser style navigation mechanism, which can be used in both standalone applications as well as in XBAP applications. To implement it, WPF provides the `Page` class to encapsulate the `Page` content that can be navigated to and hosted by the browser, a `NavigationWindow` and/or a `Frame`.

Getting ready

To get started with this recipe to build an application that supports navigations mechanisms from one WPF page to another, open the Visual Studio IDE and create a project based on the **WPF App (.NET Framework)** template. Give it a name (in our case, it's `CH01.PageDemo`).

How to do it...

Once you have created your project based on the **WPF App (.NET Framework)** template, follow these steps to add pages to your project and integrate them with the `NavigationService`:

1. Right-click on the project node where you want to create the pages.

2. As shown in this screenshot, navigate to **Add** | **Page...** from the context menu:

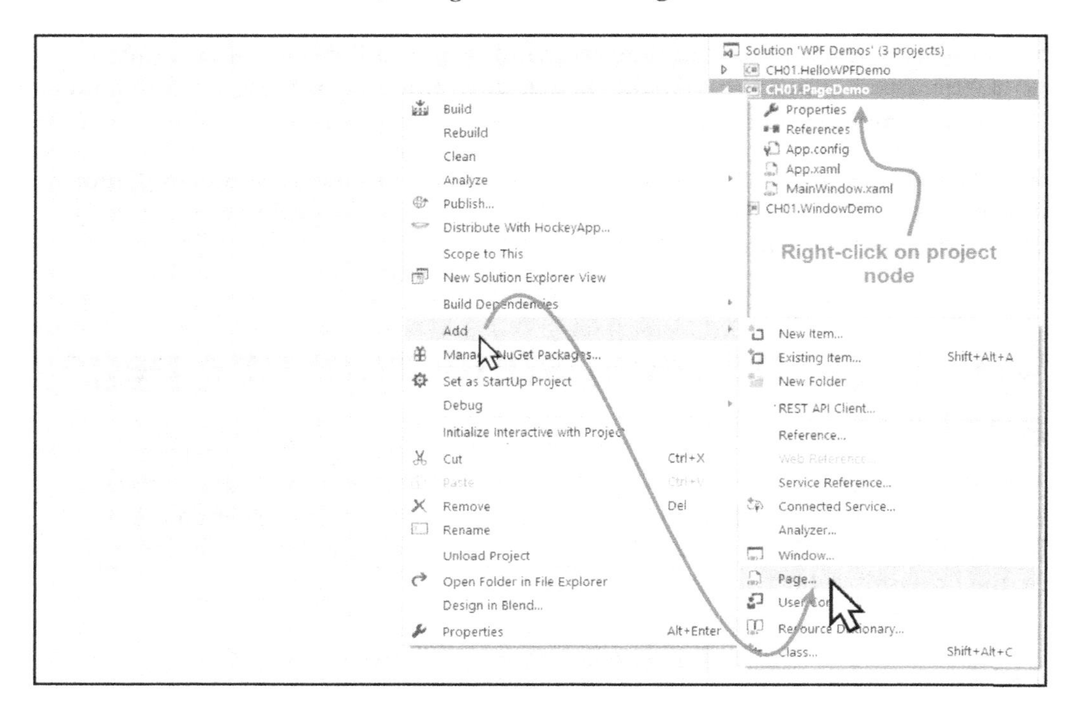

3. This will open the following **Add New Item** dialog window, where the item titled **Page (WPF)** is already selected. Give it a name, `Page1.xaml` and click **Add**. It will create the `Page1.xaml` and the associated code-behind file `Page1.xaml.cs` in your project:

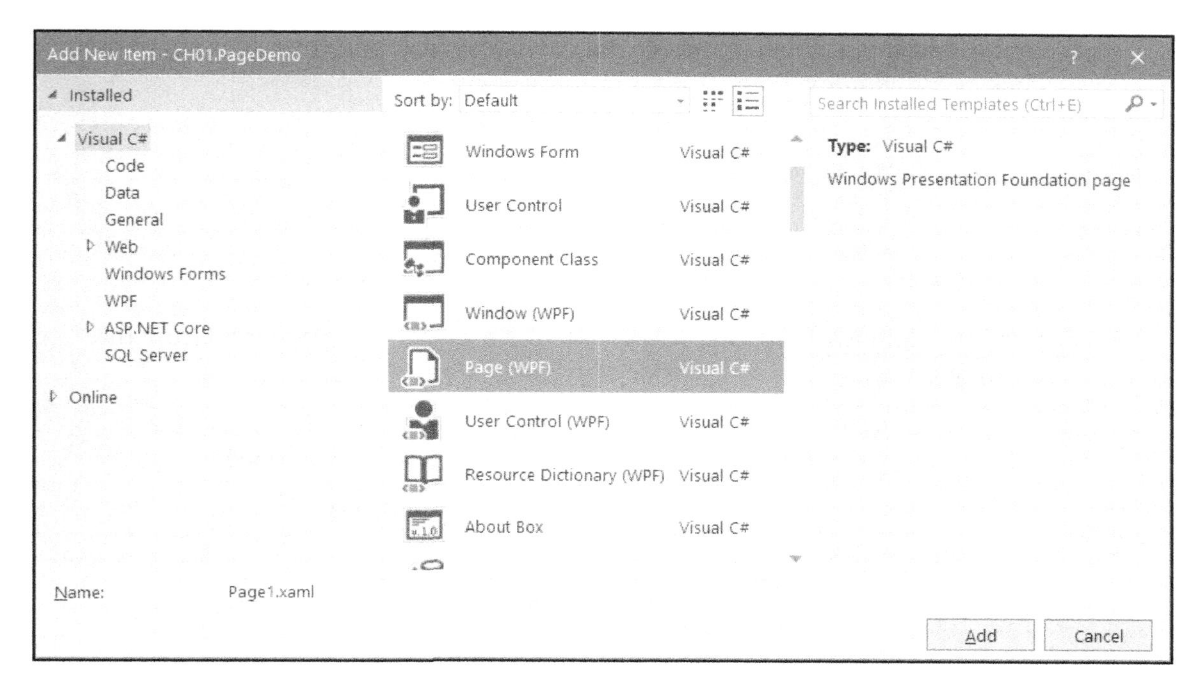

4. Now follow the same steps, 1 to 3, to create another page `Page2.xaml`, which will add both the XAML and associated C# code-behind file into the project.
5. Open the `Page1.xaml` file and replace the `Grid` with the following XAML:

```
<Grid>
    <TextBlock Text="This is Page 1" FontSize="20"
               HorizontalAlignment="Center"
               VerticalAlignment="Center"/>
    <Button Content="Next" Height="30" Width="120"
            Margin="20"
            HorizontalAlignment="Right"
            VerticalAlignment="Bottom"
            Click="OnNextButtonClicked"/>
</Grid>
```

6. In the associated code-behind file (`Page1.xaml.cs`), add the following button-click event handler:

```
private void OnNextButtonClicked(object sender,
 RoutedEventArgs e)
{
  NavigationService.Navigate(new Uri("Page2.xaml",
   UriKind.Relative));
}
```

7. Similarly, add the following XAML into the `Page2.xaml` page, replacing the existing `Grid`:

```
<Grid>
    <TextBlock Text="This is Page 2" FontSize="20"
               HorizontalAlignment="Center"
               VerticalAlignment="Center"/>
    <Button Content="Previous" Height="30" Width="120"
            Margin="20"
            HorizontalAlignment="Right"
            VerticalAlignment="Bottom"
            Click="OnPreviousButtonClicked"/>
</Grid>
```

8. Add the following button-click event handler into the `Page2.xaml.cs` file:

```
private void OnPreviousButtonClicked(object sender,
RoutedEventArgs e)
{
    if (NavigationService.CanGoBack)
    {
        NavigationService.GoBack();
    }
}
```

9. Now open the `MainWindow.xaml` file and replace the XAML content with the following:

```
<NavigationWindow x:Class="CH01.PageDemo.MainWindow"
  xmlns=
   "http://schemas.microsoft.com/winfx/2006/xaml/presentation"
    xmlns:x="http://schemas.microsoft.com/winfx/2006/xaml"
    Title="MainWindow" Height="350" Width="525"
    Source="Page1.xaml">

</NavigationWindow>
```

10. Now open the `MainWindow.xaml.cs` file and change its base class to `NavigationWindow`, instead of `Window`.
11. Run the application, which will open the following screen containing **Page 1**:

12. Clicking on the **Next** button will navigate you to **Page 2**, as shown here, which contains the activated navigational button automatically provided by the WPF Framework:

13. Now, if you click on the **Previous** button or the **back** button in the navigation panel, it will navigate you to **Page 1**.

How it works...

The `NavigationWindow`, which is defined in the `MainWindow.xaml` page, provides the basic mechanism to support the content navigation. The `Source` attribute (`Source="Page1.xaml"`), defined as `URI`, asks `NavigationWindow` to load the mentioned page (`Page1.xaml`) by default.

When you click on the **Next** button of `Page1`, the `NavigationService.Navigate` method executes, passing the `URI` of the page that you want to load next. The navigation buttons automatically activate based on the history of the navigation that you performed.

In `Page2`, when you click on the **Previous** button, it first checks whether the `NavigationService` has an immediate history item to navigate you to a previous page. If it finds a previous page, it then automatically navigates you to the desired page by calling the `NavigationService.GoBack()` method call. In this case, you don't have to pass the `URI` of the page.

There's more...

`NavigationService` offers a variety of properties, methods, and events to perform navigation mechanisms on your page content. `CanGoBack()` and `CanGoForward()` return a `Boolean` value indicating whether there is at least one entry in the back and forward navigation history, respectively. The method `GoBack()` navigates you to the most recent entry from back navigation history, whereas the `GoForward()` method navigates you to the forward navigation history, if there's one available.

To refresh the current content, you can call the `Refresh()` method. The `StopLoading()` method stops the current execution from downloading/loading the content part of the current navigation context. You can also programmatically add or remove an entry from the navigation history. The `AddBackEntry` method takes a parameter for the `CustomContentState` object to add the entry into the back-navigation history. The `RemoveBackEntry()` method removes the most recent entry from the back-navigation history.

Events such as `Navigating`, `Navigated`, `NavigationFailed`, `NavigationStopped`, `NavigationProgress`, and `LoadCompleted` are there to notify you of the various statuses of the current navigation process. Use them wisely, based on your requirements.

Creating a dialog box

A dialog box is also a kind of window, and is generally used to get some inputs from the user or to show a message to the user. It uses a model window to prevent users from interacting with other windows of the same application when it is already open. In this recipe, we will learn how to create a model dialog and use the common dialog boxes that the framework provides.

Getting ready

To get started with building and using dialog boxes in a WPF application, open your Visual Studio IDE and create a new WPF project, calling it `CH01.DialogBoxDemo`.

How to do it...

Follow these steps to create the dialog window and invoke it from the `MainWindow` to show a message to the user:

1. Open the **Solution Explorer** and right-click on the project node.
2. From the context menu, select **Add** | **Window...** to open the **Add New Item** dialog.
3. Making sure that the **Window (WPF)** template is selected, give it the name `MessageDialog`, and click **Add** to continue. This will create `MessageDialog.xaml` and `MessageDialog.xaml.cs` files in the project.
4. Open the `MessageDialog.xaml` file and replace the entire XAML content with the following:

```
<Window x:Class="CH01.DialogBoxDemo.MessageDialog"
 xmlns=
   "http://schemas.microsoft.com/winfx/2006/xaml/presentation"
    xmlns:x="http://schemas.microsoft.com/winfx/2006/xaml"
    ShowInTaskbar="False" WindowStyle="SingleBorderWindow"
    Title="Message" Height="150" Width="400"
    FontSize="14" Topmost="True" ResizeMode="NoResize">
    <Grid>
       <TextBlock TextWrapping="Wrap" Margin="8"
        Text="Thank you for reading 'Windows Presentation
        Foundation Cookbook'. Click 'OK' to continue next."/>
        <StackPanel Orientation="Horizontal"
                    VerticalAlignment="Bottom"
                    HorizontalAlignment="Right"
                    Margin="4">
            <Button Content="OK" Width="60" Height="30"
                    Margin="4" IsDefault="True"
                    Click="OnOKClicked"/>
            <Button Content="Cancel" Width="60" Height="30"
                    Margin="4" IsCancel="True"
                    Click="OnCancelClicked"/>
        </StackPanel>
    </Grid>
</Window>
```

5. Open the `MessageDialog.xaml.cs` file, and add the following event implementations for the **OK** button and **Cancel** button:

```
private void OnOKClicked(object sender, RoutedEventArgs e)
{
    DialogResult = true;
}

private void OnCancelClicked(object sender, RoutedEventArgs e)
{
    DialogResult = false;
}
```

6. Now open the `MainWindow.xaml` page and replace the `Grid` with the following XAML content:

```
<Grid>
    <ListBox x:Name="result" Height="100" Margin="8"
             HorizontalAlignment="Stretch"
             VerticalAlignment="Top" />
    <Button Content="Show Message" Width="150" Height="30"
            VerticalAlignment="Bottom" Margin="8"
            Click="OnShowMessageButtonClicked"/>
</Grid>
```

7. Go to the code-behind file, `MainWindow.xaml.cs`, and add the button event implementation as shared in the following code section:

```
private void OnShowMessageButtonClicked(object sender,
RoutedEventArgs e)
{
    var messageDialog = new MessageDialog();
    var dialogResult = messageDialog.ShowDialog();

    if (dialogResult == true)
    {
        result.Items.Add("You clicked 'OK' button.");
    }
    else if (dialogResult == false)
    {
        result.Items.Add("You clicked 'Cancel' button.");
    }
}
```

8. Now run the application. The visible window will have a button labeled **Show Message**. Click on it to invoke the message dialog window that we have created:

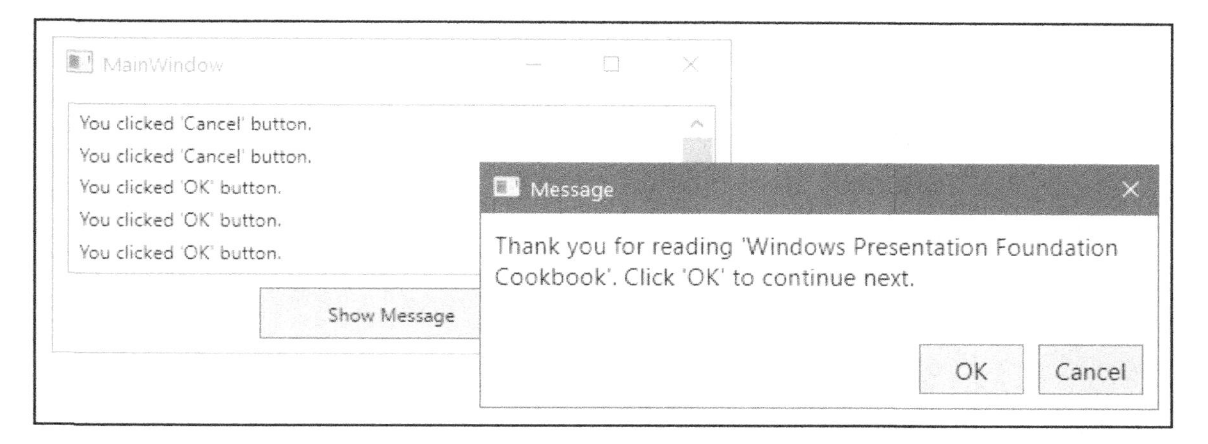

9. Click on the **Cancel** button, which will add **You clicked 'Cancel' button** text into the list present in the **MainWindow**.
10. Launch the message window again and click on the **OK** button. This will add **You clicked 'OK' button** in the list.

How it works...

When you call the `ShowDialog()` method of the `Window` instance, it opens it as a model dialog and waits until the user provides an input to it. In this case, the user input is the interaction with the **OK** and **Cancel** button. When you click the **OK** button, the associated event handler assigns `true` to the `DialogResult` property and returns to the caller. Similarly, the **Cancel** button event handler, assigns `false` to the `DialogResult` property and returns.

Based on the return value of the `ShowDialog()` method, which actually returns the value of `DialogResult`, you can decide whether the user clicked the **OK** or **Cancel** button.

The dialog window has been customized by setting the following properties to the `Window` instance:

- The `ShowInTaskbar` property has been set to `False` to prevent the window from being visible in the Taskbar.
- The `WindowStyle` property has been set to `SingleBorderWindow` to add a thin border to the window, removing the minimize and maximize buttons from the title bar.
- The `Topmost` property has been set to `True` to keep it always visible on top of other windows. This is optional, but good to have.
- The `ResizeMode` property has been set to `NoResize` to prevent the user from resizing the dialog window.

There's more...

The operating system provides some reusable dialog boxes, which provide a user experience consistent with the version of the operating system in which the application is running. The experience also stays consistent across all applications to provide a unique interface for performing common operations such as opening files, saving files, printing files, color selection, and more.

WPF provides these reusable, common dialog boxes as managed wrapper classes, encapsulating the core implementation. This reduces the extra effort creating and managing the common operations.

Using the open file dialog

To open files in your WPF application, you can use the managed wrapper class `OpenFileDialog`, which is present under the `Microsoft.Win32` namespace. You just have to create the instance and call the `ShowDialog()` method by optionally setting a few properties for UI customization.

A basic open file dialog looks like the following screenshot, providing you with an option to select one or more files to open:

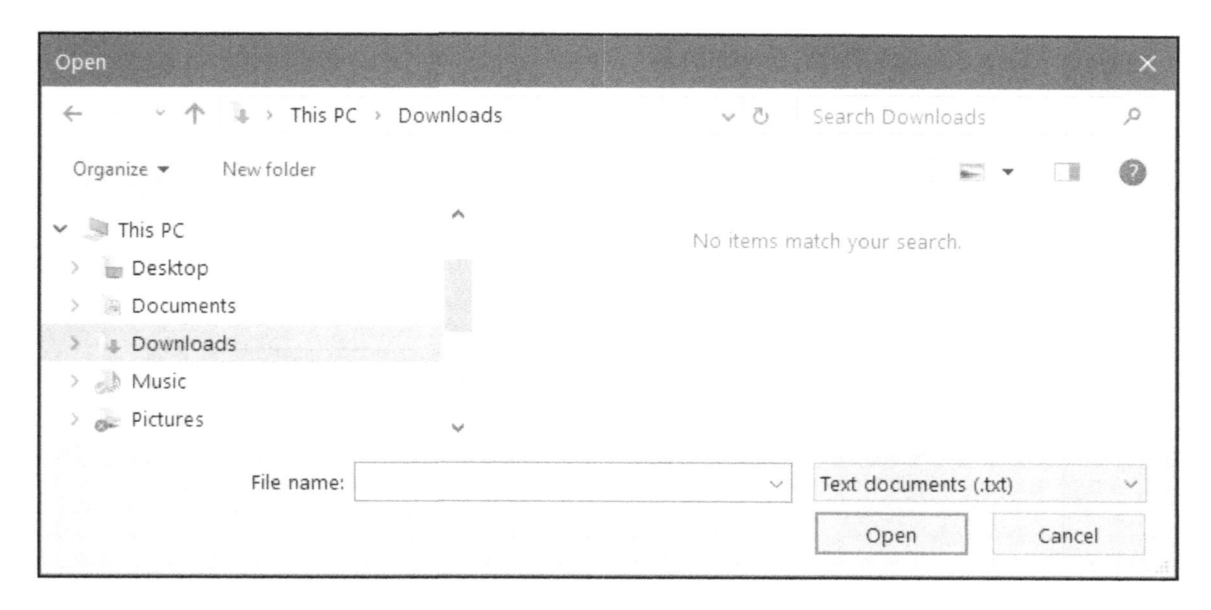

The following code snippet demonstrates how to initiate the open file dialog by optionally filling the file-extension filter:

```
private void OnOpenButtonClicked(object sender, RoutedEventArgs e)
{
    var openfileDialog = new OpenFileDialog
    {
        Filter = "Text documents (.txt) | *.txt | Log files (.log) |
        *.log"
    };

    var dialogResult = openfileDialog.ShowDialog();
    if (dialogResult == true)
    {
        var fileName = openfileDialog.FileName;
    }
}
```

The `dialogResult` returned by the `ShowDialog()` method tells us whether the operation was performed successfully. Based on that, you can call the instance of the file dialog to get more details about the selected file.

Using the save file dialog

Along with the `OpenFileDialog` interface, the `Microsoft.Win32` namespace also provides the `SaveFileDialog` managed wrapper to perform file saving operations from your WPF application. Similar to the open file dialog, you need to create the instance of it by optionally filling its various properties to finally call the `ShowDialog()` method.

The save file dialog looks like the following screenshot, where you can provide a name to save as a file:

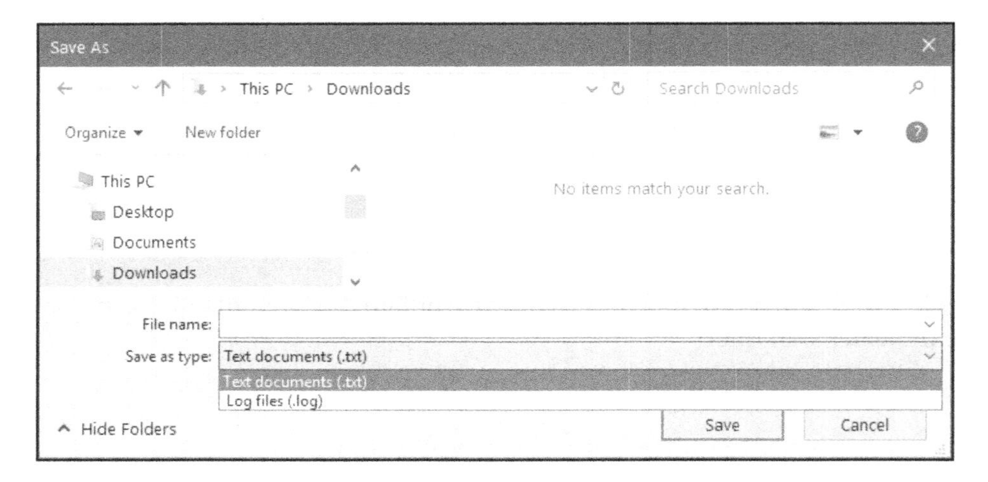

Optionally, you can set the extension filter, default file name, and other properties before launching the dialog window, as shown in the following code snippet:

```
private void OnSaveButtonClicked(object sender, RoutedEventArgs e)
{
    var saveFileDialog = new SaveFileDialog
    {
        Filter = "Text documents (.txt) | *.txt | Log files (.log)
|
          *.log"
    };

    var dialogResult = saveFileDialog.ShowDialog();
    if (dialogResult == true)
    {
        var fileName = saveFileDialog.FileName;
    }
}
```

Based on the `dialogResult` returned by the `ShowDialog()` call you can decide whether the save was successful and retrieve more information about the saved file from the file dialog instance.

Using the print dialog

The managed wrapper `PrintDialog` is also present in the `Microsoft.Win32` namespace, and provides you with the interface to call the operating system's printer properties and perform the `print` operation. The dialog gives you the option to **Select Printer**, configure the printing preferences, and select the page range and other parameters, as shown in the following screenshot:

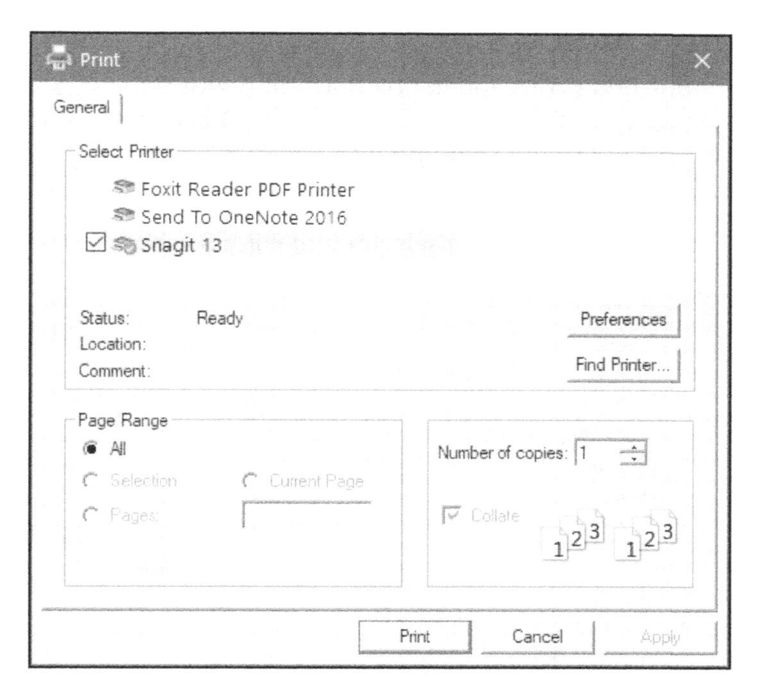

To invoke the same, just create the instance of the `PrintDialog` and call its `ShowDialog()` method. You can optionally set page range, printable area, and other properties. If the `dialogResult` returned by the `ShowDialog()` method is set to `true`, it confirms that the printing job has been queued up successfully, and based on that you can perform the next set of actions.

Here's the code snippet for your reference:

```
private void OnPrintButtonClicked(object sender, RoutedEventArgs e)
{
    var printDialog = new PrintDialog();
    var dialogResult = printDialog.ShowDialog();

    if (dialogResult == true)
    {
        // perform the print operation
    }
}
```

Other common dialogs

WPF also provides some other common dialog boxes to perform the selection of various formatting options, such as font, font style, font size, text effects, and color. You can use the `FontDialog` and `ColorDialog`, present under the `System.Windows.Forms` namespace, to add support for the font and color selections, respectively.

Here's the screenshot presenting the font selector and color selector dialogs:

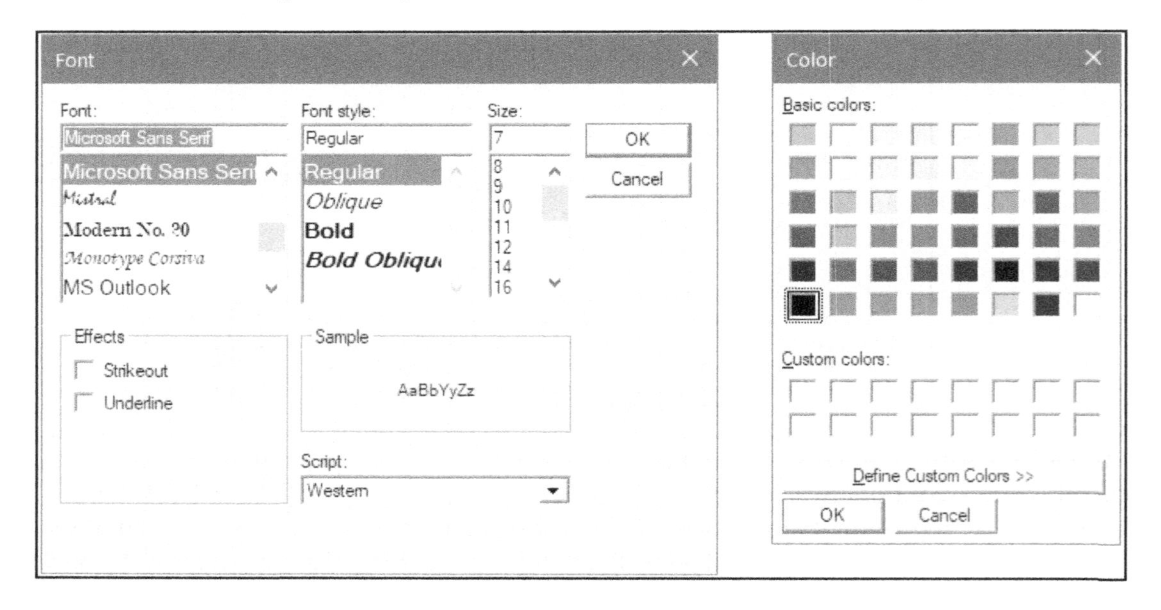

Creating ownership between windows

In the WPF application, the window objects that you create are independent of each other by default. But, sometimes, you may want to create an owner-owned relationship between them. For example, the toolbox window that you generally see in your Visual Studio IDE and/or in a Photoshop application.

When you set an owner of a window, it acts according to the owner instance. For example, if you minimize or close the owner window, the other window under the owner-owned relationship automatically minimizes or closes according to its owner.

Let's begin creating this recipe to have an owner-owned relationship between two windows.

Getting ready

To get started with this recipe, open your Visual Studio IDE and create a new WPF project called `CH01.OwnershipDemo`.

How to do it...

Perform the following steps to create a `ToolBox` window and assign its ownership to the `MainWindow`, so that it can act according to its owner:

1. Right-click on the project node and select **Add** | **Window...** from the context menu. The **Add New Item** dialog will be shown on the screen.
2. Select **Window (WPF)** from the available list, give it the name `ToolBox`, and click **Add** to continue. This will add `ToolBox.xaml` and `ToolBox.xaml.cs` into your project.
3. Open the `ToolBox.xaml` file and replace its content with the following XAML code:

```
<Window x:Class="CH01.OwnershipDemo.ToolBox"
  xmlns=
   "http://schemas.microsoft.com/winfx/2006/xaml/presentation"
    xmlns:x="http://schemas.microsoft.com/winfx/2006/xaml"
    SizeToContent="WidthAndHeight"
    ResizeMode="NoResize"
    Title="ToolBox">
    <StackPanel Margin="10">
```

```
            <Button Content="Bold" Width="70" Margin="4"/>
            <Button Content="Italics" Width="70" Margin="4"/>
            <Button Content="Underlined" Width="70"
                    Margin="4"/>
        </StackPanel>
    </Window>
```

4. Now open the `App.xaml` page and remove the property attribute `StartupUri`, defined as (`StartupUri="MainWindow.xaml"`) from it.
5. Go to its code-behind file `App.xaml.cs` and override the `OnStartup` event. We need to modify the implementation according to our needs. Replace the entire `OnStartup` event handler with the following code block:

```
protected override void OnStartup(StartupEventArgs e)
{
    base.OnStartup(e);

    var mainWindow = new MainWindow();
    mainWindow.Show(); // must show before setting it
    as owner of some other window

    var toolBox = new ToolBox { Owner = mainWindow };
    toolBox.Show();
}
```

6. Run the application to see the relationship between the two windows. The windows will look like the following screenshot:

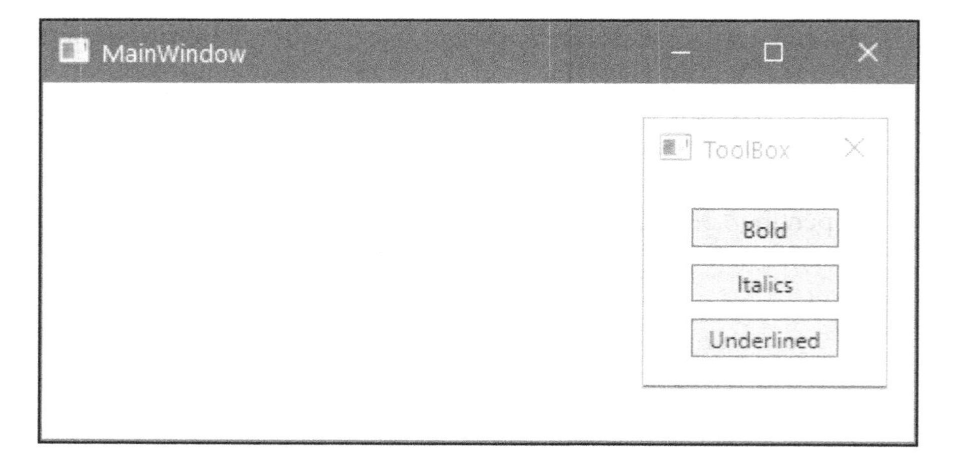

7. Drag the **ToolBox** window and you can see that you are able to move it outside the **MainWindow**. Now perform some operations, such as minimizing and closing, on the **MainWindow**, and you will see that the **ToolBox** window also acts according to its owner.

How it works...

By default, the owner of every `Window` object is set to null, and thus each window is independent of the other. But, when you set its owner, it follows the owner-owned relationship and acts with the owner window.

`Window` ownership is not a feature of WPF, but a capability of the Win32 user API and, accessible from a WPF application.

There's more...

Make sure you display the owner window first, before setting it as the owner of some other window, otherwise the system will throw an `InvalidOperationException`:

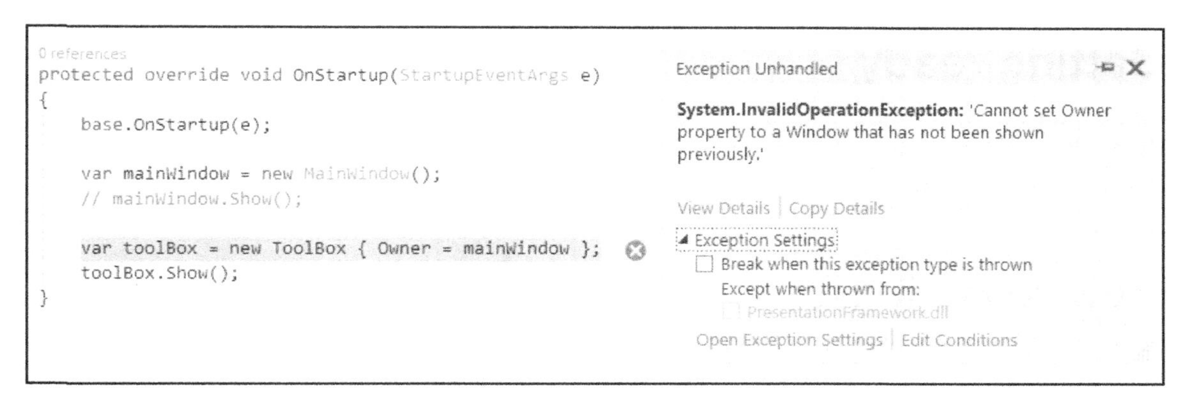

Some points to note about window ownership:

- The window that has an ownership relationship with another window always appears on top of that owner
- You can drag the window outside the owner window
- When you minimize or close the owner, the other window, which is related to it, will follow the owner and minimize or close respectively

- By default, the window in a relationship gets displayed in the taskbar, but when you minimize the owner, it gets removed from the taskbar
- When you want to break the relationship, just set the `Owner` property to `null`

Creating a single instance application

When you build applications for Windows, there are many reasons why you would want to restrict users from launching multiple instances of your application. Some common examples are installers, uninstallers, update utilities, media applications, utility tools, and so on.

In a normal application, when you launch the app, it creates a Windows process, and allocates its own memory space and resources. But, when you don't want to create multiple instances of the process for a single application that is already running, you want to silently quit the new instance and bring the running process into the foreground.

In this recipe, we will learn how to achieve this using **Mutex** (**Mutual Exclusion**) and unmanaged code.

Getting ready

To get started with this, open your Visual Studio instance and create a new project based on the WPF application template. During the project creation, give it the name `CH01.SingleInstanceDemo`.

How to do it...

Once the WPF project has been created, follow these steps to create a single instance of the WPF application:

1. Run the application by pressing the *CTRL* + *F5* key combination. This will launch one instance of the application.

2. Press *CTRL* + *F5* multiple times to launch multiple instances of the application. Now it's time to make the application a single instance application:

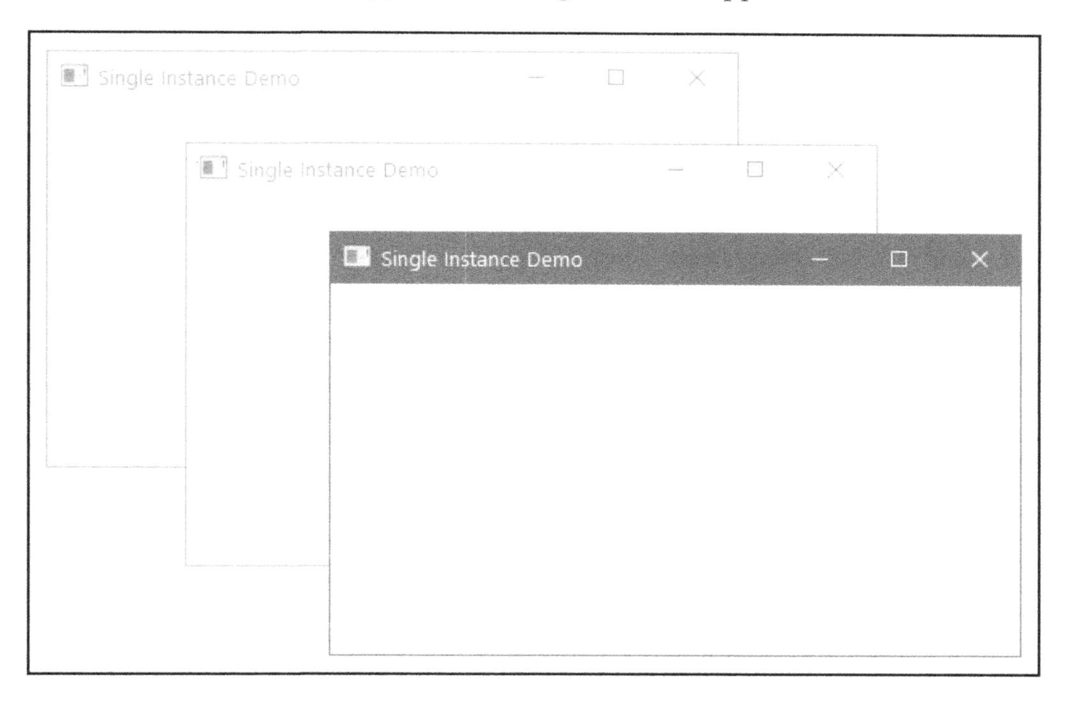

3. Close all the running processes and then follow the next steps to implement the single instance behavior.
4. Open the `MainWindow.xaml` and add the window title to `Single Instance Demo`. Here you can find the entire XAML code:

```
<Window x:Class="CH01.SingleInstanceDemo.MainWindow"
  xmlns=
    "http://schemas.microsoft.com/winfx/2006/xaml/presentation"
     xmlns:x="http://schemas.microsoft.com/winfx/2006/xaml"
     Title="Single Instance Demo"
     Height="250" Width="400">
    <Grid>
    </Grid>
</Window>
```

5. Open the `App.xaml.cs` file and override the base implementation of the `OnStartup` method.
6. Change the code of the `OnStartup` method so that it looks like the following code:

```
protected override void OnStartup(StartupEventArgs e)
{
  base.OnStartup(e);

  var mutex = new Mutex(true, "SingleInstanceDemo",
  out bool isNewInstance);
  if (!isNewInstance)
  {
    MessageBox.Show("Application instance is
     already running!");
    Shutdown();
  }
}
```

7. Add the `System.Threading` namespace declaration, so that the Mutex can be discoverable. The Mutex resides in the aforesaid namespace.
8. Now compile the project to make sure that there are no compiler errors.
9. Press *CTRL* + *F5*, which will run the first instance of the application.
10. Now return to the Visual Studio, without closing the application, and then hit *CTRL* + *F5*. This time, instead of launching the application UI, an **Application instance is already running!** message will pop up on the screen. Clicking **OK** will close the message.
11. Press *CTRL* + *F5* again. Observe that no second instance of the UI is visible on the screen.

How it works...

It's a trick to handle the application to have only a single instance. The **Mutex** (**Mutual Exclusion**) object is used to define the instance with a unique name. Here we called it `SingleInstanceDemo`. The Boolean `out` parameter returns whether the current calling thread has been granted the initial ownership of the `mutex` object.

A **Mutex** object is a synchronization object, which is generally used to synchronize access to a shared resource, so that only one thread can access that resource at a single point in time.

For the first instance of the application, it will be granted as the initial ownership. When the second instance runs, the calling thread will not get the initial ownership because the `mutex` object with the same name, `SingleInstanceDemo`, already exists and is running.

So, the Boolean value of `isNewInstance` will be `false` and the message box will get displayed on the screen. The second instance of the application is still running at that moment and calls the `Shutdown()` method when you click on the **OK** button to close the message box.

Thus, the second instance will be removed from the process list. The first instance will continue running on the system.

There's more...

There could be a scenario where the application is running in a background process and the user tries to relaunch the application. In such a scenario, instead of showing a message to the user, you may want to activate the already running application and show its UI.

You can do this by changing a bit of the existing code and integrating an unmanaged code call. To do so, open the `App.xaml.cs` file once again and follow these steps:

1. Add the following `using namespace` into the file: `System.Runtime.InteropServices`.
2. Then, you need to add the following unmanaged code declaration from the `user32.dll` to the `App.xaml.cs` file:

```
[DllImport("user32", CharSet = CharSet.Unicode)]
static extern IntPtr FindWindow(string cls, string win);

[DllImport("user32")]
static extern IntPtr SetForegroundWindow(IntPtr hWnd);
```

3. Add the following method to activate the already running window, provided that the title of the window is static. In our case, it is **Single Instance Demo**, modified in the `MainWindow.xaml` page:

```
private static void ActivateWindow()
{
    var otherWindow = FindWindow(null, "Single Instance Demo");
    if (otherWindow != IntPtr.Zero)
    {
        SetForegroundWindow(otherWindow);
    }
}
```

4. Now, instead of calling the `MessageBox`, call the `ActivateWindow()` method in the `OnStartup`. Here, you can find this new code:

```
protected override void OnStartup(StartupEventArgs e)
{
    base.OnStartup(e);

    var mutex = new Mutex(true,
     "SingleInstanceDemo",
     out bool isNewInstance);
    if (!isNewInstance)
    {
        // MessageBox.Show("Application instance is
           already running!");
        ActivateWindow();
        Shutdown();
    }
}
```

5. Now run the application. It will launch the `MainWindow` titled **Single Instance Demo** on the screen.
6. Return to Visual Studio. This will put the application window in the background. Now run the application once again by pressing the keyboard shortcut *CTRL* + *F5*. This time, instead of running a different instance to show the UI, it will activate the existing window and push the running application to foreground.

It's not mandatory that the application window must always have a static title. In such cases, it will become more complex to handle said scenario.

Passing arguments to WPF applications

The command-line arguments are used to take optional parameters or values from the user, while launching the application. These are generally used to perform specific commands on the application from the outside.

In this recipe, we will learn how to pass command-line arguments to a WPF application.

Getting ready

To get started, open the Visual Studio IDE and create a WPF application project called `CH01.CommandLineArgumentDemo`.

How to do it...

Now follow these steps to let the application support command line arguments and perform actions based on those:

1. Open the `MainWindow.xaml` to add a `TextBlock` into the `Grid` panel. Replace the entire XAML content with the following lines:

```
<Window x:Class="CH01.CommandLineArgumentDemo.MainWindow"
  xmlns=
   "http://schemas.microsoft.com/winfx/2006/xaml/presentation"
    xmlns:x="http://schemas.microsoft.com/winfx/2006/xaml"
    Title="Main Window" Height="200" Width="400">
    <Grid>
        <TextBlock Text="This is 'Main Window'
          of the application."
            HorizontalAlignment="Center"
            VerticalAlignment="Center"
            FontSize="18" />
    </Grid>
</Window>
```

2. Create a new window in the project by right-clicking on the project node and then following the context menu path **Add** | **Window...** to open the **Add New Item** dialog window. Give it the name `OtherWindow` and click the **Add** button. This will add `OtherWindow.xaml` and `OtherWindow.xaml.cs` into the project.

3. Now open the `OtherWindow.xaml` and change its UI to have different text. Let's replace the entire XAML code with the following lines:

```
<Window x:Class="CH01.CommandLineArgumentDemo.OtherWindow"
xmlns=
  "http://schemas.microsoft.com/winfx/2006/xaml/presentation"
   xmlns:x="http://schemas.microsoft.com/winfx/2006/xaml"
   Title="Other Window" Height="200" Width="400">
    <Grid>
        <TextBlock Text="This is 'Other Window' of the
          application."
            HorizontalAlignment="Center"
            VerticalAlignment="Center"
            FontSize="18" />
    </Grid>
</Window>
```

4. Now open the `App.xaml` and remove the `StartupUri="MainWindow.xaml"`. This has been done to control the launch of the proper window, based on the argument passed to the application.
5. Open the `App.xaml.cs` and override its `OnStartup` method to retrieve the arguments passed to it and open the desired window based on that. Let's add the following code implementation for the `OnStartup` method:

```
protected override void OnStartup(StartupEventArgs e)
{
    base.OnStartup(e);

    var args = e.Args;
    if (args.Contains("/other"))
    {
        new OtherWindow().Show();
    }
    else
    {
        new MainWindow().Show();
    }
}
```

6. Now build the project. Navigate to the `bin\Debug` folder and launch a **Command Window** in that location. Alternatively, you can launch a **Command Window** (**cmd.exe**) and navigate to the `bin\Debug` path, where your application is available.

7. In the console window, enter the name of the application without passing any arguments to it, as shown in the following command:

```
CH01.CommandLineArgumentDemo.exe
```

8. This will launch the `MainWindow` of our application, with this screen:

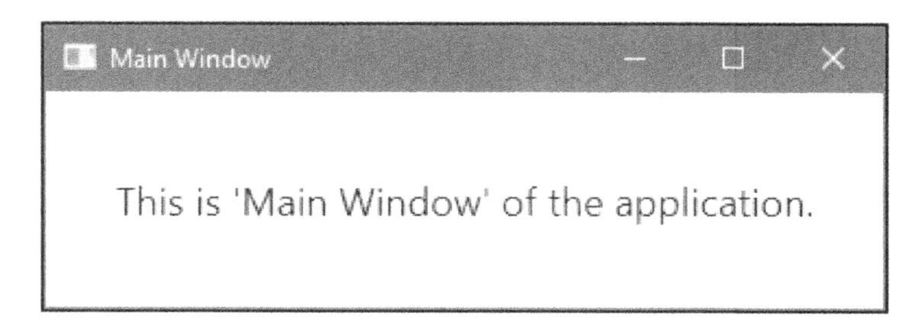

9. Close the application window and, from the console window, enter the application name by specifying the `/other` argument to it, as shown in the following command:

```
CH01.CommandLineArgumentDemo.exe /other
```

10. This will launch the `OtherWindow` of the application, instead of the `MainWindow`:

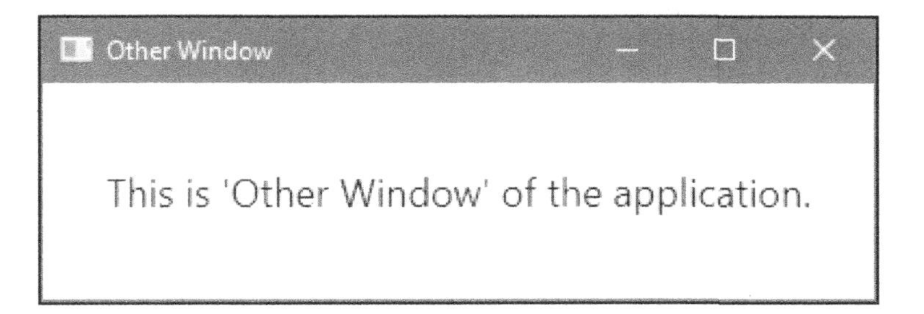

How it works...

The `OnStartup(StartupEventArgs e)` method signature contains `StartupEventArgs` as a method parameter. It contains a property, `Args`, that returns a string array of the command line arguments that were passed to the application. If no command line arguments were passed, the string array will have zero items in it.

Now, by checking the condition, we launch the desired window that we want to show to the user. You can also take arguments such that the application launches in normal mode, maximized mode, or minimized. You can also use it to open the application as hidden, in some specific cases.

There's more...

As we have seen how to launch the WPF application from the command line by passing the arguments, let's learn how to do this from Visual Studio itself to launch it in debug mode.

To pass a command line argument to your WPF application from Visual Studio in debug mode, right-click on the project node and click **Properties** from the context menu entry. This will open the project properties. Now navigate to the **Debug** tab. Please refer to the following screenshot:

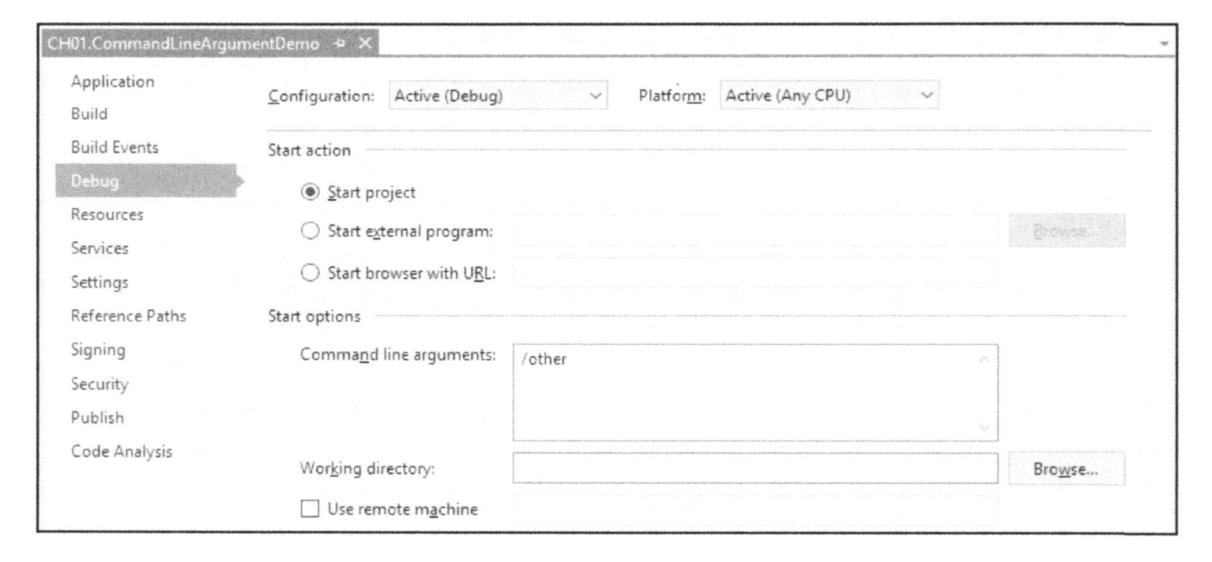

Under **Start options**, enter `/other` as the command line arguments. Now run the application in debug mode by pressing *F5*. You will see that the `OtherWindow` opens on the screen. To launch the `MainWindow`, just remove the `/other` argument from the project properties mentioned earlier and run the application again. This time you will see that the `MainWindow` opens instead of the `OtherWindow`.

Handling unhandled exceptions

Exception handling is a vital part of software development. When an exception occurs at runtime, due to any error in the code, we handle those with a `try {} catch {}` block. The `try {}` block contains the code where the exception occurred; the `catch {}` block knows how to handle that, based on the type of the exception. After the exception has been handled, the normal execution of the program continues without affecting the application.

Though, in most of the cases we handle, there could be cases that may go unnoticed and come into the picture at runtime. Such an unhandled exception crashes the application. In this recipe, we will learn how to catch the unhandled exceptions in the WPF application and close the application properly.

Getting ready

To get started, open the Visual Studio IDE. Now create a new project, based on the WPF Application template, and call it `CH01.UnhandledExceptionDemo`.

How to do it...

Let's start the demonstration by following these steps:

1. Open the `MainWindow.xaml` page, and add two radio buttons and one button on it. The first radio button will cause an exception handled in a `try {} catch {}` block, whereas the second radio button will throw an exception that will go unhandled. Add the following code into your `MainWindow.xaml`:

```
<Window x:Class="CH01.UnhandledExceptionDemo.MainWindow"
  xmlns=
    "http://schemas.microsoft.com/winfx/2006/xaml/presentation"
     xmlns:x="http://schemas.microsoft.com/winfx/2006/xaml"
     Title="UnhandledException Demo"
     Height="120" Width="400">
    <Grid Margin="10">
        <StackPanel Orientation="Vertical">
            <RadioButton x:Name="radioOne" GroupName="type"
                  Content="Handle in Try/Catch Block"
                  IsChecked="True" Margin="4"/>
            <RadioButton x:Name="radioTwo" GroupName="type"
                  Content="Handle in Unhandled Block"
                  IsChecked="False" Margin="4"/>
```

```
            </StackPanel>
            <Button Content="Throw Exception"
                    Width="120" Height="30"
                    VerticalAlignment="Top"
                    HorizontalAlignment="Right"
                    Margin="10"
                    Click="OnThrowExceptionClicked"/>
        </Grid>
    </Window>
```

2. Open the `MainWindow.xaml.cs` file to add the button-click event handler. Add the following code block inside the class:

```
private void OnThrowExceptionClicked(object sender,
RoutedEventArgs e)
{
    if (radioOne.IsChecked == true)
    {
        try { throw new Exception("Demo Exception"); }
        catch (Exception ex)
        {
            MessageBox.Show("'" + ex.Message +
                  "' handled in Try/Catch block");
        }
    }
    else
    {
        throw new Exception("Demo Exception");
    }
}
```

3. Go to the `App.xaml.cs` file and override the `OnStartup` method to have the application level `DispatcherUnhandledException` event registered as shown in the following code:

```
protected override void OnStartup(StartupEventArgs e)
{
    base.OnStartup(e);

    DispatcherUnhandledException += OnUnhandledException;
}
```

4. Add the `DispatcherUnhandledException` event handler into the `App.xaml.cs` and handle the exception as shown in the following code, but with an empty code block:

```
private void OnUnhandledException(object sender,
DispatcherUnhandledExceptionEventArgs e)
{

}
```

5. Let's build and run the application. You will see the following UI on the screen:

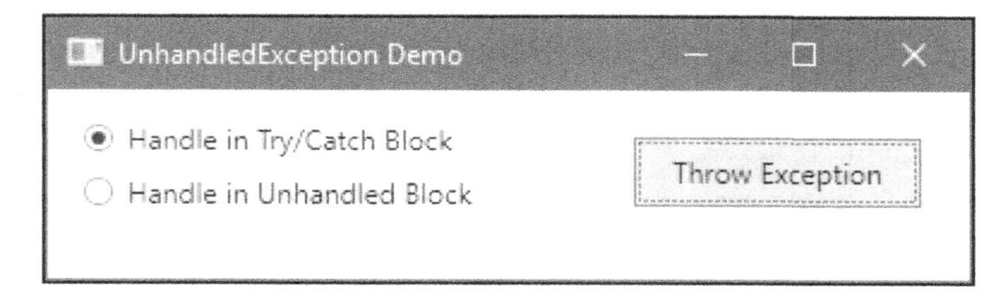

6. It will have two radio selectors and one button in the application window. When the first radio button is checked and you click on the **Throw Exception** button, it will generate an exception in a `try {}` block, which will then immediately be handled by the associated `catch {}` block without crashing the application. The following message box will be shown on the UI:

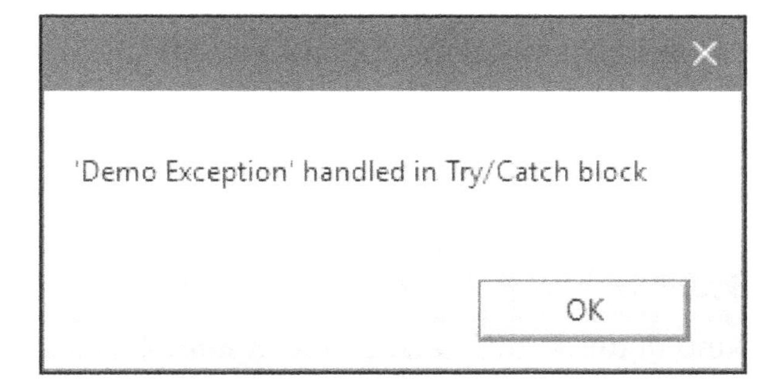

7. For the second radio button, when checked, if you click on the **Throw Exception** button, the exception will go unhandled and will be caught in the `App.xaml.cs` file, under the `OnUnhandledException` event, and the application will crash:

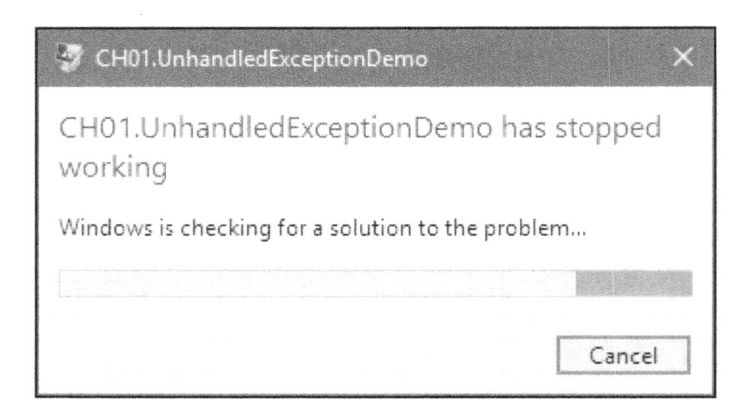

8. Open the `App.xaml.cs` once again and modify the `OnUnhandledException` event implementation, as follows, to handle the thrown exception:

```
private void OnUnhandledException(object sender,
DispatcherUnhandledExceptionEventArgs e)
{
    e.Handled = true;
}
```

9. Now run the application once again, check the second radio button and click on the button. You will notice that the application will not crash this time.
10. Click the **Throw Exception** button multiple times. The application will continue as-is, without causing any crash of the UI.

How it works...

When you handle this kind of uncaught/unhandled exception by specifying `e.Handled = true`, your application will not crash and will continue running. The best part of catching an unhandled exception is logging the unknown/unhandled errors, so that you can investigate the root cause behind these exceptions and fix them in future builds.

When there's a critical error, you can restart the application programmatically from this block.

There's more...

You can also use the `AppDomain.CurrentDomain.UnhandledException` event handler to catch any unhandled exceptions, but you won't be able to handle it in a way to continue running the application. When used, you can log the error and terminate/restart the application.

Unhandled exceptions handled in the `DispatcherUnhandledException` event, by specifying `e.Handled = true` will not route to the `AppDomain.CurrentDomain.UnhandledException`.

2

Using WPF Standard Controls

In this chapter, we will cover the following recipes:

- Using the `TextBlock` control to add plain text
- Using `Label` to add other controls in text
- Providing a user option to input text
- Adding images in your application UI
- Working with ready-to-use 2D shapes
- Adding tooltips to show additional information
- Adding a standard menu to the WPF application
- Providing extra functionalities using the context menu
- Adding user options with radio buttons and checkboxes
- Working with the progress bar control
- Using the `Slider` control to pick a numeric value
- Using the calendar control in your application
- Listing items in a `ListBox` control
- Providing options to select from a ComboBox
- Adding a status bar to your window
- Adding a toolbar panel to perform quick tasks

Introduction

Every UI Framework must provide the standard controls to design the application UI and **Windows Presentation Foundation** (**WPF**) is one of them. WPF provides a set of standard controls and UI elements such as `TextBlock`, `TextBox`, `Button`, `Image`, various shapes, `ProgressBar`, `Slider`, various menus, `Toolbar`, `ListBox`, `ComboBox`, `DataGrid`, and more.

As you can see from the following diagram, UI controls can be of two types—**ItemsControl** and **ContentControl**, which inherit from `Control` class. All the panels available in WPF share the same base class `Panel`. The `Control` and `Panel` class have the base **FrameworkElement**, which again inherits from the **UIElement**. It has the base class as the **DependencyObject** and the superbase as the **Object**:

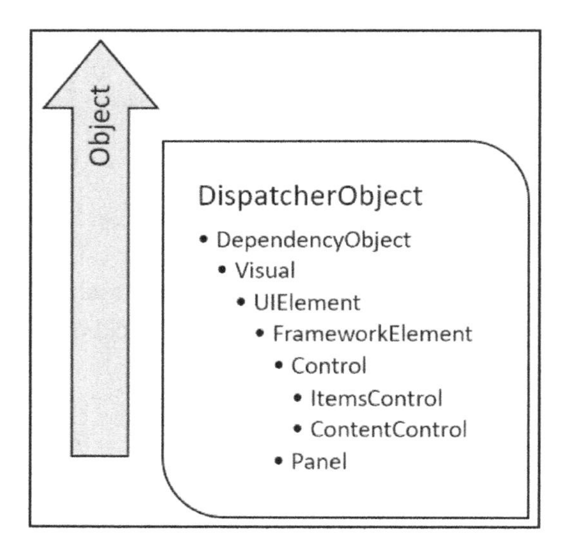

Every control has some common set of properties exposed. This includes `FontFamily`, `FontSize`, `FontStyle`, `Foreground`, `Background`, `BorderBrush`, `BorderThickness`, and more. Every framework element exposes additional properties such as `Width`, `MaxWidth`, `MinWidth`, `ToolTip`, `Height`, `Name`, `Language`, `Margin`, and more. When using any element in the UI, you will use these common properties to set the UIElement's style and other parameters.

Using the TextBlock control to add plain text

The `TextBlock` control in WPF is a lightweight UI element, which is used to display text content to the screen. Almost everywhere, you will use this element in your application UI to display plain text in a single line or a multiline format. To add simple plain text, you can either write `<TextBlock Text="Text message" />` or `<TextBlock>Text message</TextBlock>` in your XAML page.

In this recipe, we will explore more about this UI element.

Getting ready

To get started, open your Visual Studio IDE, and create a new WPF project called `CH02.TextBlockDemo`.

How to do it...

Now open the `MainWindow.xaml`, and follow these steps to add `TextBlock` control with various formatting options:

1. First, change the pre-existing `Grid` panel to a `StackPanel`.
2. Now add the following two `TextBlock` controls to it, which will have plain text in them:

```
<TextBlock Text="1. This is a TextBlock control, with 'Text'
   property" Margin="10 5" />
<TextBlock Margin="10 5">
   2. This is a TextBlock control, having text as Content
</TextBlock>
```

3. Add the following XAML to have a few more `TextBlock` controls, with some basic text formatting applied to them:

```
<TextBlock Text="3. This is a TextBlock control, having text
           formatting"
           FontWeight="Bold"
           FontStyle="Italic"
           TextDecorations="Underline"
           Foreground="Red"
           Margin="10 5" />
<TextBlock Text="4. TextBlock with different FontFamily"
```

```
                FontFamily="Lucida Handwriting"
                FontSize="16" Foreground="Blue"
                Margin="10 5" />
     <TextBlock Text="5. This is a TextBlock control,
                having long text
                content, wrapped automatically using
                'TextWrapping' property."
                TextWrapping="Wrap"
                Margin="10 5" />
     <TextBlock Text="6. This is a TextBlock control,
                having long text content, trimmed
                automatically using
                'TextTrimming' property."
                TextTrimming="CharacterEllipsis"
                Margin="10 5" />
```

4. Let's build the project and run it. You will see the following UI on the screen:

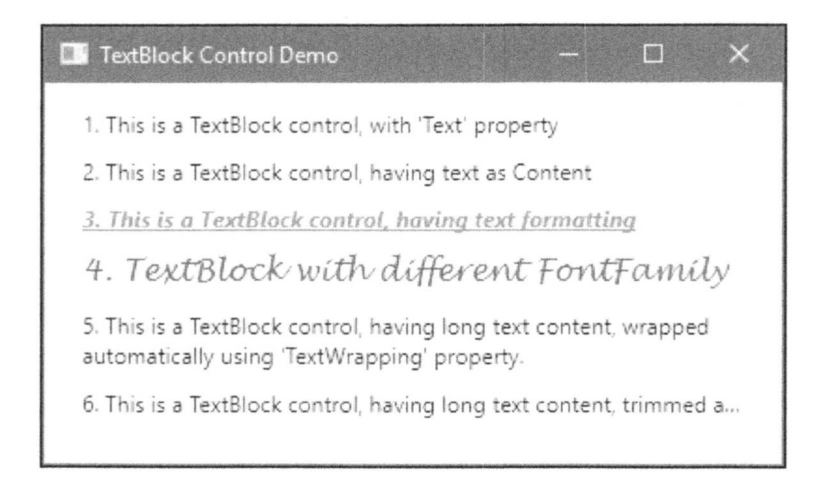

How it works...

For the first two `TextBlock` controls, the UI will have a plain text on it. The third `TextBlock` control will have **Bold**, **Italic**, and **Underline** applied to it, by specifying the `FontWeight`, `FontStyle`, and `TextDecoration` properties of the control. Also, the foreground color of it has been set to *red*, by specifying the `Foreground` property.

You can also set a different font to your `TextBlock` control. Use the `FontFamily` property to set it. As you can see, the fourth `TextBlock` control has a **Lucida Handwriting** font applied to it.

When you have a long text, which is not viewable in a single line, you can either wrap it to multiline or trim it, based on the available space. `TextWrapping="Wrap"`, in the fifth `TextBlock` spans it to multiline. Try making the window bigger or smaller, and you will see that the `TextBlock` automatically adjusts itself to match the available space, whereas, the text of the sixth `TextBlock` control trims with the `TextTrimming` property set to character ellipsis (three dots at the end). This says that more text is available but it has been `cropped.`

As an alternative to `CharacterEllipsis`, you may use `WordEllipsis`, which will trim the text at the end of the last possible word, instead of the last possible character.

There's more...

The `TextBlock` control also supports inline formatting. Just like HTML tags, you can surround a text content with `Bold`, `Italic`, and `Underline` tags to format it, as shown in the following XAML code:

```
<TextBlock Margin="10, 5">
    7. TextBlock with <Bold>Bold</Bold>, <Italic>Italics</Italic>,
<Underline>Underlined</Underline> text
</TextBlock>
```

You can also add a line break to a text content, like this:

```
<TextBlock Margin="10, 5">
    8. TextBlock with LineBreak<LineBreak/> in between the text
</TextBlock>
```

The following XAML code demonstrates how to add a hyperlink element to a `TextBlock` control that matches the style of your Windows theme:

```
<TextBlock Margin="10, 5">
    9. TextBlock with a <Hyperlink
NavigateUri="http://www.kunal-chowdhury.com">Hyperlink</Hyperlink>
text in it
</TextBlock>
```

The `NavigateUri` property is used to define the URL that you wish to navigate to.

You can use the `Span` element to set the style of individual text content that includes font style, size, foreground color, and so on. It also allows you to specify other inline elements inside it. The `Run` element allows you to style a text content using all the available properties of the `Span` element. The following example demonstrates how easy it is to use the `Span` and `Run` elements inside a `TextBlock` control:

```
<TextBlock Margin="10, 5"
    TextWrapping="Wrap">
    10. This is a <Span><Bold>TextBlock</Bold></Span> control, with
<Span Foreground="Brown">Span</Span> Elements and <Run
TextDecorations="Underline">Run</Run> commands in it
</TextBlock>
```

The `Span` element may contain other inline elements, but a `Run` element can contain only plain text.

Running the preceding example will result in the following output:

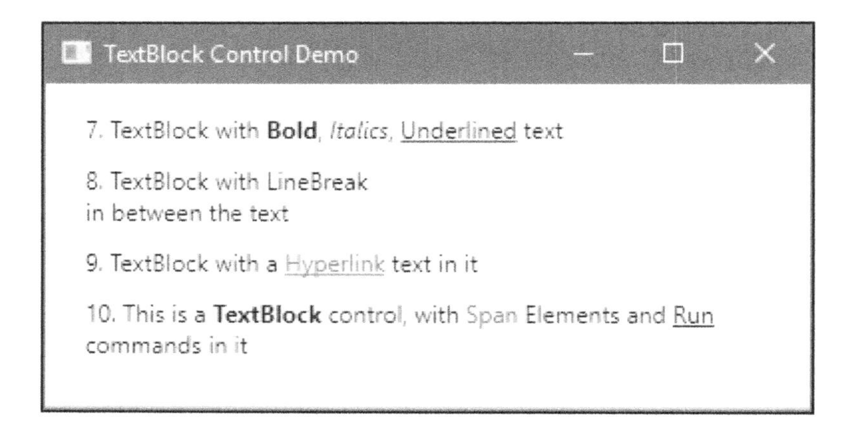

Using Label to add other controls in text

The `Label` control is another way of representing text in WPF application. It looks like what `TextBlock` control offers, but instead of having only text support, it can also host any kind of other controls. It exposes the `Content` property to host text and other controls.

In this recipe, we will explore how to use the `Label` control in a WPF.

Getting ready

To get started with this control, open Visual Studio to create an application based on the WPF project template and call it `CH02.LabelDemo`.

How to do it...

Once the project gets created, follow these simple steps to add text in your application UI, using the `Label` control:

1. Open the `MainWindow.xaml` file to change the application UI.
2. Replace the existing `Grid` panel with the following XAML code:

```
<StackPanel Margin="10 10 10 20">
    <Label Content="1. This is a Label control" />
    <Label Content="2. A Label control with text formatting"
           FontWeight="Bold" Foreground="Red"
           FontStyle="Italic"/>
    <Label>
        <StackPanel Orientation="Horizontal">
           <TextBlock Text="3. A Rectangle" />
           <Rectangle Width="20" Height="20" Fill="Red"
           Margin="10 0" />
           <TextBlock Text="inside a Label control" />
        </StackPanel>
    </Label>
</StackPanel>
```

3. Now build and run the application. You will see the following output on the screen:

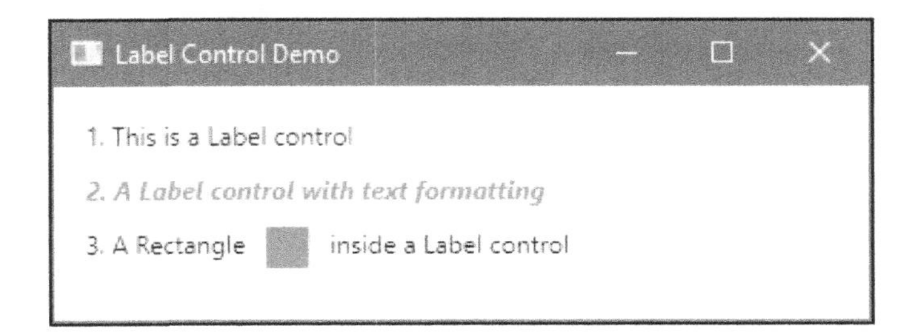

How it works...

The first control added in the `StackPanel` is a very basic label, which has plain text as its `Content` property. The second `Label` control also contains plain text, but has various formatting (such as, `FontWeight`, `Foreground`, and `FontStyle`) applied to it to give it a bold, italic, and red color look to its style.

As the `Label` control derives from `System.Windows.Controls.ContentControl`, it also supports adding other controls to its content. The third label added to the UI is a little different than the previous two examples. It not only contains text, but also other controls, such as `StackPanel`, `TextBlock`, and a `Rectangle`, owing to its `Content` property.

In the preceding example, for the third label, the `TextBlock` control is used to hold the actual text content, and `StackPanel` is used as a panel control to hold both the `TextBlock` and the `Rectangle`.

A point to remember is that `Label` is heavier than a `TextBlock`. So, when you need to render a plain text on the UI, prefer `TextBlock` only.

There's more...

In Windows and other operating systems, it's a widespread practice to access the controls in a window by holding the *Alt* key and then pressing a character defined as its access key. For example, to open the **File** menu of any Windows application, we use *Alt* + *F*. Here, the character *F* is the access key, which gets invoked when we press *Alt*.

Let's learn how to add an access key to labels in the WPF application, using the `Label` control. Create a new project called `CH02.LabelAccessKeyDemo`, open the `MainWindow.xaml` page, and replace the default `Grid` by a `StackPanel`. Now add two labels and two textboxes inside the `StackPanel`, as follows:

```
<StackPanel Margin="10 10 10 20">
    <Label Content="Enter _Username:"
           Target="{Binding ElementName=txbUsername}" />
    <TextBox x:Name="txbUsername" Margin="6 0" />

    <Label Content="Enter _Password:"
           Target="{Binding ElementName=txbPassword}" />
    <TextBox x:Name="txbPassword" Margin="6 0" />
</StackPanel>
```

Now run the application. Press *Alt* + *U* to activate the access key for the first label, and place the focus on the `txbUsername` field. Press *Alt* + *P* to automatically focus on the `txbPassword` field:

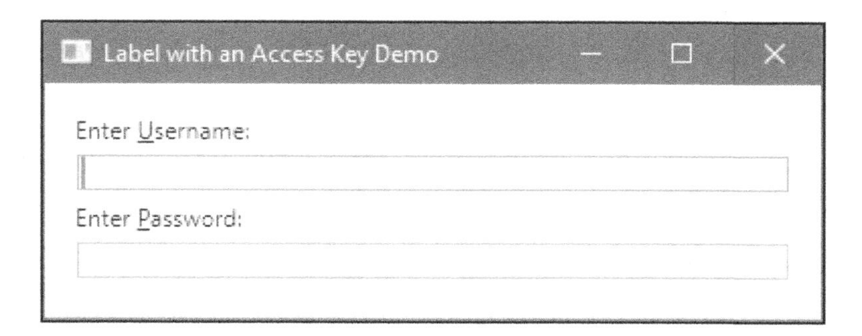

The Windows Form application uses "`&`" as its access key specifier, but in the WPF application it's a little different, as it uses XML notation to create the UI. So, in the WPF application, if you want to add an access key specifier to labels, you need to specify _ (underscore) before the character which you want to highlight.

For example, adding _ before the `U` in **Username**, activates the said label when *Alt* + *U* is pressed. It's a similar case for the **Password** field, in the preceding example.

The frequently used practice is to use the first character that's not already used as an access key of another control. But, on a need basis, you can specify any character part of the label content.

The `Target` property of the `Label` control passes the instruction to the designated control to activate automatically when the access key gets triggered by the user. The `ElementName` property, which is present in the binding (`Target="{Binding ElementName=txbPassword}"`), tells the name of the control where you want to send the activation instruction.

Providing a user option to input text

The `TextBox` control in WPF is used to allow the user to input plain text in a single line or multiline format. A single-line textbox is the commonly used control for form inputs; whereas the multiline textbox is used like an editor.

Getting ready

Open your Visual Studio IDE, and create a new project named `CH02.TextBoxDemo`, based on the WPF application template.

How to do it...

Once the project gets created, follow the mentioned steps to play with some of the `TextBox` properties:

1. Open the `MainWindow.xaml` page, and replace the default `Grid` with a `StackPanel` so that we can add the controls in a stacked fashion.
2. Now add five `TextBox` controls inside the `StackPanel`, and set various properties, as follows:

```
<StackPanel Margin="10 10 10 20">
        <TextBox Height="30" Margin="10 5"
                 Text="Hello"/>
        <TextBox Text="Hello WPF!"
                 FontSize="18" Foreground="Blue"
                 FontWeight="Bold"
                 Height="30" Margin="10 5"/>
        <TextBox Text="This is a 'ReadOnly' TextBox control"
                 IsReadOnly="True" Height="30" Margin="10 5"/>
        <TextBox Text="This is a 'Disabled' TextBox control"
                 IsEnabled="False" Height="30" Margin="10 5"/>
        <TextBox TextWrapping="Wrap" AcceptsReturn="True"
                 Height="60" VerticalScrollBarVisibility="Auto"
                 Margin="10 5">
            This is multiline textbox.
            User can press 'Enter' key to move to next line.
        </TextBox>
    </StackPanel>
```

3. Run the application so that it has the following UI on the screen:

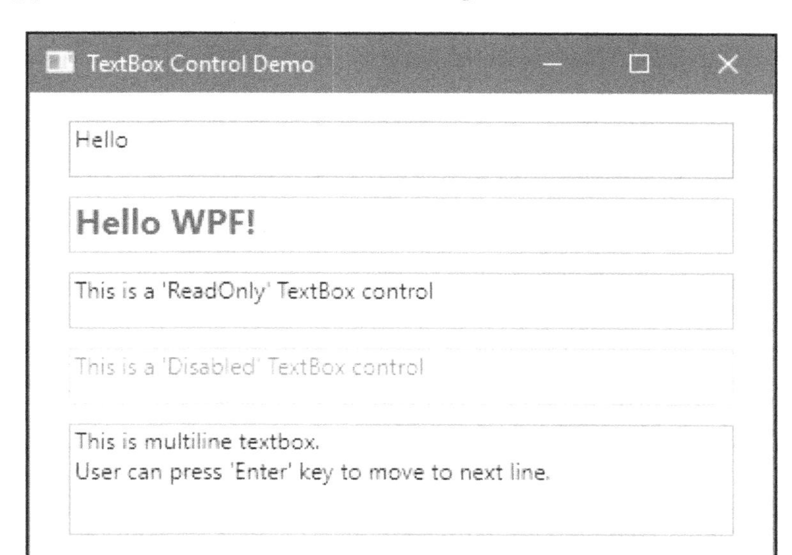

How it works...

The first `TextBox` control, which we added to the `StackPanel`, is the simplest one, and when it is rendered in the UI, it contains empty text. The user can enter any plain text here. You can also specify text from code, by using the `Text` property, as shown in the second control.

You can also define a range of styles for the text of the `TextBox` control. As shown in the second control, we specified `FontSize`, `Foreground`, `FontWeight`. You can specify other properties too, as part of any control.

The third one is a `ReadOnly` textbox, which you can define by setting the `IsReadOnly` property value to `True`. When you want to disable a `TextBox`, set its `IsEnabled` property to `False`, as shown in the fourth example.

The fifth example demonstrates how easy it is to define a multiline textbox. Just set its `AcceptsReturn` property to `True` and `TextWrapping` to `Wrap`. The control will behave like a multiline text editor.

There's more...

When you are using `TextBox` as a multiline text-input control, don't forget to set its `VerticalScrollBarVisibility`. This will allow your user to scroll the text content. As shown in the last example, set it to `Auto` to make it enabled on demand, based on its content.

Windows Clipboard support

The `TextBox` control automatically supports the **Windows Clipboard**. Right-click on it to see the context menu pop up in the screen with common clipboard functions, such as **Select all**, **Cut**, **Copy**, and **Paste**. Along with these functions, it also supports the common keyboard shortcuts for clipboard operations, **undo/redo**, by default.

Adding spellcheck support

The attached `SpellCheck.IsEnabled` property allows you to add spellcheck support to the `TextBox` control. Set it to `True` to enable it. Let's add a multiline textbox in the UI with this feature enabled:

```
<TextBox TextWrapping="Wrap" AcceptsReturn="True"
         Height="60" VerticalScrollBarVisibility="Auto"
         SpellCheck.IsEnabled="True"
         Margin="10 5" />
```

Now run the application to have a window with a multiline text-input field in the UI. Enter some text with some spelling mistakes. You will see that the wrongly spelled words get highlighted with red underline. Right-click on it to see a context menu, which suggests words from the dictionary.

As shown in the following screenshot, select the one that is best suited in this context:

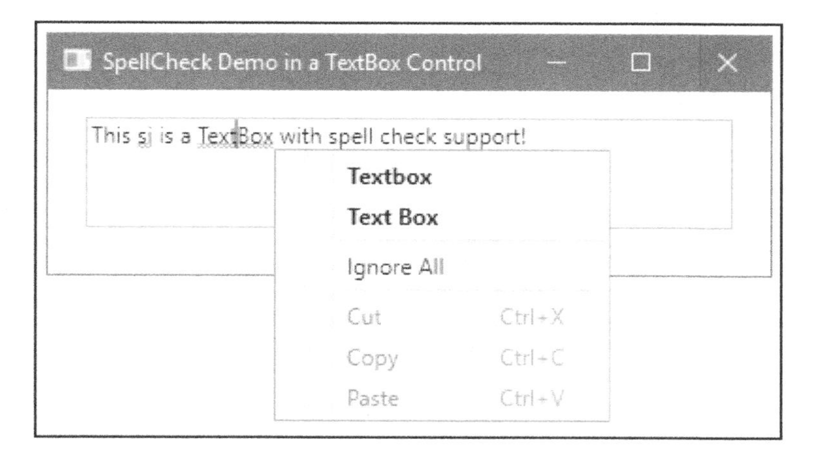

Adding images to your application UI

Images are used to create a UI that looks good, with a background, icons, and thumbnails, and they convey more information to the user. In WPF, the `Image` element is used to display images. Let's take a look at this.

Getting ready

To get started with images in WPF, launch your Visual Studio IDE and create a WPF project called `CH02.ImageDemo`, and add an image called `demoImage.jpg`.

How to do it...

Let's follow these steps to add images in the `MainWindow.xaml` page:

1. Open the `MainWindow.xaml` page, and replace the existing `Grid` with a `StackPanel`. Set its `Orientation` property to `Horizontal` so that the items added to this panel stack themselves horizontally.
2. Add four images to the `StackPanel`, and set their `Source` property to `demoImage.jpg`, which is available within the project directory.

3. Set the width and the height of each image to `100`.
4. For the first image, set its `Stretch` property to `None`.
5. For the second image, set its `Stretch` property to `Fill`.
6. For the third and fourth images, set their `Stretch` property to `Uniform` and `UniformToFill`, respectively.
7. Here's the complete XAML code, to which you can refer:

```
<StackPanel Orientation="Horizontal">
    <Image Source="demoImage.jpg"
           Stretch="None"
           Width="100" Height="100"
           Margin="10 10 5 10" />
    <Image Source="demoImage.jpg"
           Stretch="Fill"
           Width="100" Height="100"
           Margin="10 10 5 10" />
    <Image Source="demoImage.jpg"
           Stretch="Uniform"
           Width="100" Height="100"
           Margin="10 10 5 10" />
    <Image Source="demoImage.jpg"
           Stretch="UniformToFill"
           Width="100" Height="100"
           Margin="10 10 5 10" />
</StackPanel>
```

8. Let's build and run the application. You will see the following output in the application UI:

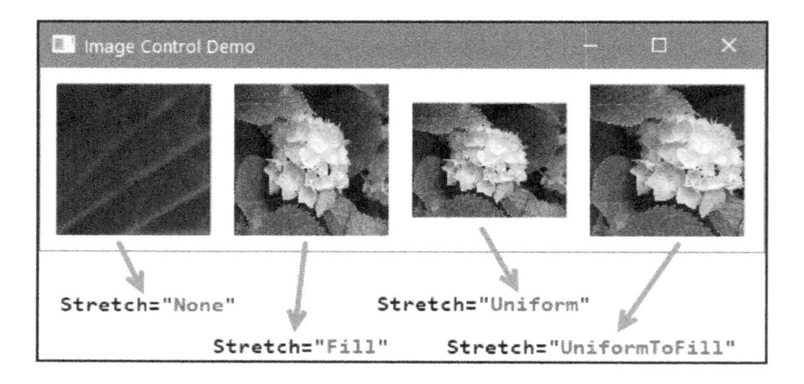

How it works...

In XAML, the `Source` property of the `Image` control is the path of the image file that you want to display. When you access the same from code, it's a `BitmapImage`.

The `Stretch` property of an image describes how it should be stretched to fill the destination. For the first image, that we set as `Stretch= "None"`, it preserves the original size of the image. When you set it as `Fill`, for the second image in the example, the content is resized to fill the destination dimensions without preserving its aspect ratio.

For the third and fourth image, setting it to `Uniform` and `UniformToFill`, respectively, set its content resized to fit in the destination dimensions while preserving its native aspect ratio. But for the fourth case, if the aspect ratio of the destination image differs from the source, the source content is clipped to fit in the destination dimensions.

The default value of the image `Stretch` property is `Uniform`. That means, when you add an image to the UI, by default, it sets its content resized to fit in the destination dimensions.

There's more...

You can also set an image in XAML by creating a `BitmapImage` instance and assigning it to its `Source` property. The `BitmapImage` instance exposes the `UriSource` property to set the image path. Here's an example of how to set the image source in XAML, using the `BitmapImage` element:

```
<Image>
    <Image.Source>
        <BitmapImage UriSource="demoImage.jpg" />
    </Image.Source>
</Image>
```

You can also rotate an image by setting the `Rotation` property of `BitmapImage`. It contains four values `Rotate0`, `Rotate90`, `Rotate180`, and `Rotate270`. Here's an example to demonstrate how to rotate an image by 180 degrees:

```
<Image>
    <Image.Source>
        <BitmapImage UriSource="demoImage.jpg"
                     Rotation="Rotate180"/>
    </Image.Source>
</Image>
```

Additionally, you can also use the `StretchDirection` property of an `Image` control. The value indicates how the image is scaled. There are three values `UpOnly`, `DownOnly`, and `Both`. The content scales upward, downward, or in both directions, based on the size of the image content.

Working with ready-to-use 2D shapes

In WPF, a `Shape` is an `UIElement` that enables you to draw a 2D shape in your application. There are a couple of ready-to-use shapes already provided by WPF, and they are as follows:

- Rectangle
- Ellipse
- Line
- Polyline
- Polygon
- Path

All of these `UIElements` expose some common properties to draw the shape. The `Stroke` and `StrokeThickness` properties describe the color and the thickness to draw the shape's outline. The `Fill` property describes the color used to decorate the interior of the shape.

In this recipe, we will learn how to create various shapes.

Getting ready

Let's begin with creating a new project. Open your Visual Studio, and create a WPF project called `CH02.ShapesDemo`. As we will be creating multiple shapes, we will be using the `UniformGrid` panel to host the shapes in this demonstration. You can learn more about this panel in the next chapter.

How to do it...

Follow these steps to create various shapes in your application:

1. Open your `MainWindow.xaml` file, and replace the existing `Grid` panel with `UniformGrid`. Set its maximum columns count to `3`, by setting its `Column` property.
2. Let's add our first shape, a `Rectangle`. Add the following XAML code inside the `UniformGrid`:

```
<Rectangle Width="200" Height="100"
           Stroke="DarkBlue" StrokeThickness="5"
           Fill="SkyBlue" Margin="10 5" />
```

3. Now let's add an `Ellipse`, which you can change to a circle by setting the same value to its `Height` and `Width` properties. Add the following code to create the ellipse:

```
<Ellipse Width="200" Height="100"
         Stroke="DarkBlue" StrokeThickness="5"
         Fill="SkyBlue" Margin="10 5" />
```

4. To add a `Line` in the panel, add the following XAML:

```
<Line X1="10" Y1="80" X2="190" Y2="20"
      Stroke="DarkBlue" StrokeThickness="5"
      Margin="10 5" />
```

5. `Polyline` is a series of connected straight lines. Add the following XAML to easily create a polyline shape, where the line is being drawn based on the data points provided in the `Points` property:

```
<Polyline Points="10,60 60,180 100,20 180,80 120,140"
          Stroke="DarkBlue" StrokeThickness="5"
          Margin="10 5" />
```

6. Similarly, you can add a `Polygon` shape to the UI. Add the following code inside the `UniformGrid` to draw the shape:

```
<Polygon Points="10,60 60,180 100,20 180,80 120,140"
         Fill="SkyBlue" Stroke="DarkBlue"
         StrokeThickness="5" Margin="10 5" />
```

7. To add a `Path` shape control, add the following XAML code:

```
<Path Data="M10,60 60,180 C100,20 180,80 120,140"
      Stroke="DarkBlue" StrokeThickness="5"
      Margin="10 5" />
```

8. Now let's build your project and run the application. You will see the following shapes on the screen, as we have added the preceding code:

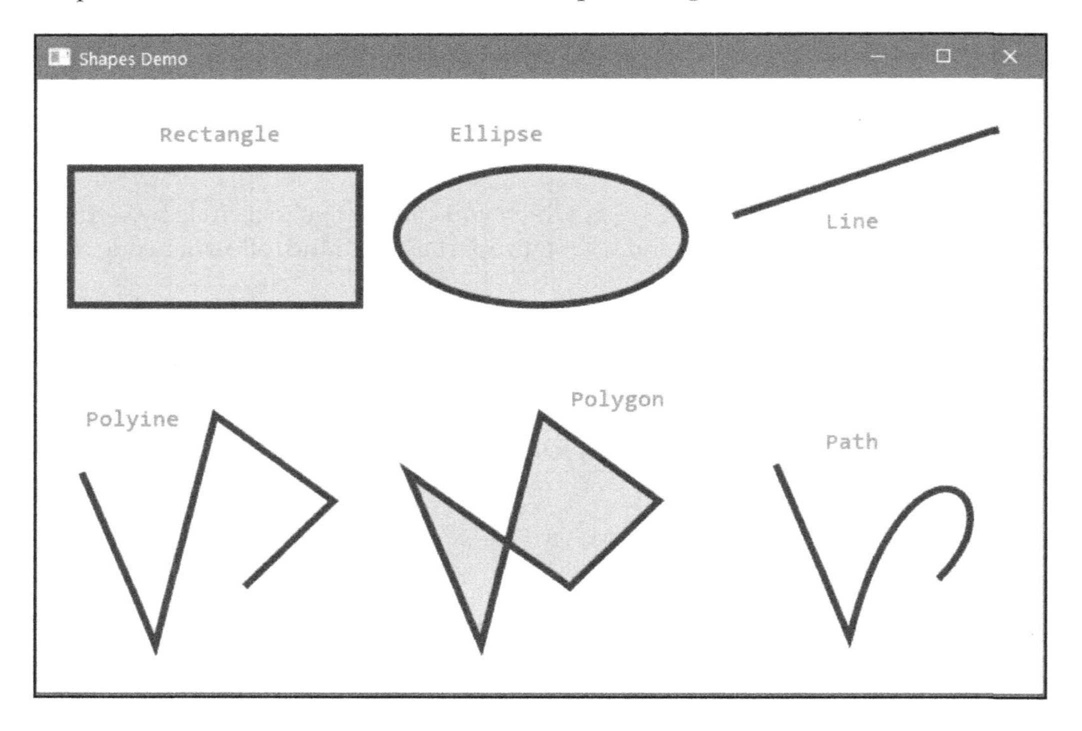

How it works...

A rectangular shape is being drawn by setting the `Height` and `Width` properties of the `Rectangle` class, along with the stroke color and the thickness of it. To create a square, you can use this shape by setting its dimension properly.

In the second example, a circular shape has been drawn using the `Ellipse` control. It uses the same property sets to create the shape. To make it a complete circle, set its `Height` and `Width` to the same value.

If you want to draw a straight line in the UI, use the `Line` class. It exposes four properties to draw the line. Set the `X1` and `Y1` properties to mark the starting point; set `X2` and `Y2` properties to mark the ending point of the line. In the preceding example, a line has been drawn from the (`10,80`) coordinate point to the (`190,20`) coordinate point.

In the fourth example, we have seen how to create a series of connected straight lines using the `Polyline` shape control. You need to set the (*X*, *Y*) coordinate points of the lines in its `Points` property. In the preceding example, it creates the shape connecting the following coordinate points (`10,60`), (`60,180`), (`100,20`), (`180,80`), and (`120,140`).

`Polygon` also uses the same concept to draw a series of lines, but it completes the connected series of lines to draw a closed shape.

Using the `Path` control, in the sixth example, you can draw a series of connected lines and curves. The `Data` property is used to set the geometry that specifies the shape to be drawn. The data points always start with `M` to begin drawing the lines. In any part, if you want to create a curve, prefix the character `C` at that point.

There's more...

The `PathGeometry` objects are used to draw lines, curves, arcs, and complex shapes. WPF provides two classes to describe the geometric paths using the mini language **Path Markup Syntax**.

You can learn more about it here:
`http://bit.ly/path-markup-syntax`

If you want to draw simple shapes, you can use the `EllipseGeometry`, `LineGeometry`, and `RectangleGeometry` objects. Composite geometries are created by `GeometryGroup` and to create combine geometries, use the `CombineGeometry`.

Let's take the following example to demonstrate a complex path geometry using a `PathSegmentCollection` of three segments:

```
<Path Stroke="DarkBlue" StrokeThickness="5">
    <Path.Data>
        <PathGeometry>
            <PathGeometry.Figures>
                <PathFigureCollection>
                    <PathFigure StartPoint="10,100">
                        <PathFigure.Segments>
                            <PathSegmentCollection>
                                <ArcSegment Point="40,80" />
                                <BezierSegment Point1="100,300"
                                               Point2="100,-100"
                                               Point3="200,150" />
                                <BezierSegment Point1="100,200"
                                               Point2="200,-10"
                                               Point3="100,150" />
                            </PathSegmentCollection>
                        </PathFigure.Segments>
                    </PathFigure>
                </PathFigureCollection>
            </PathGeometry.Figures>
        </PathGeometry>
    </Path.Data>
</Path>
```

The collection consists of one `ArcSegment` and two `BeizerSegments` to set the geometry points to draw the following shape, but you can also add additional segments, such as `LineSegment`, `PolyBeizerSegment`, `PolyLineSegment`, `PolyQuadraticBeizerSegment`, and `QuadraticBeizerSegment` to create a more complex path:

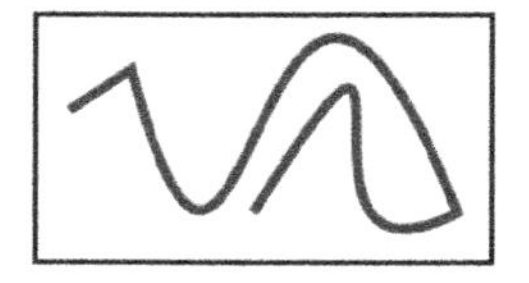

Note that all shapes are stretchable. You can use the `Stretch` property to define a shape's stretching behavior. If you set it to `None`, the `Shape` object will not be stretchable. If you set it to `Fill`, `Uniform`, or `UniformToFill`, the `Shape` content will be stretched to fill the space with or without preserving the aspect ratio.

Adding tooltips to show additional information

Tooltips are used to show additional information about a specific control or a link when hovering your mouse over it. The `FrameworkElement` class exposes a property named `Tooltip`, which you can find on all the controls available in WPF.

In this recipe, we will learn how to work with the tooltips in WPF. We will also cover how to design a tooltip using other controls.

Getting ready

Open your Visual Studio IDE and create a new WPF application project called `CH02.TooltipDemo`.

How to do it...

Open the `MainWindow.xaml` page, and then follow these steps to add simple tooltips to the UI:

1. First, replace the default `Grid` with a `StackPanel`, and set its `Orientation` property to `Horizontal` to have some horizontally stacked items.
2. Add three buttons to the `StackPanel`, and set their `ToolTip` property. To add a show duration of the tooltip, set its `ToolTipService.ShowDuration` attached property to a value in milliseconds. You can use the following XAML as a reference:

```
<StackPanel Orientation="Horizontal"
            HorizontalAlignment="Center"
            Margin="20">
    <Button Content="New" Width="60" Height="30"
            ToolTip="Create a New file"
            Margin="4" />
    <Button Content="Open" Width="60" Height="30"
            ToolTip="Open a file"
            ToolTipService.ShowDuration="2000"
            Margin="4" />
    <Button Content="Save" Width="60" Height="30"
            ToolTip="Clicking on this button,
            saves the file to disk"
```

```
                        Margin="4" />
            </StackPanel>
```

3. Run the application, and hover over the buttons to see the tooltip pop up on the screen, as shown in the following screenshot:

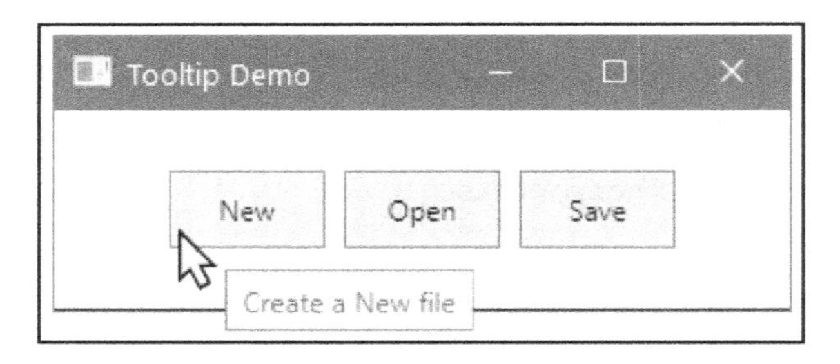

How it works...

The `ToolTip` property, when set in any WPF control, gets visible when you hover over the control. Apart from this, the `ToolTipService` class has a bunch of attached properties to help you set various behaviors of the tooltip.

Like the second example, as shown earlier, if you hover over the `Open` button, the `Tooltip` property will be visible on screen for 2 seconds. This is because we set the `ShowDuration` property of the `ToolTipService` to `2000` milliseconds (2 seconds).

You can also use the `ToolTipService.ShowOnDisabled` property to show or hide a `Tooltip` on an element that is disabled. The `HasDropShadow` property of the class ensures whether the `Tooltip` will have a shadow on it.

There's more...

As the `ToolTip` property is of `object` type, you can assign anything to it, including various UI controls. Hence, it helps you to customize the UI of the tooltip with a much richer experience.

Let's modify the `Tooltip` property of the third button in the preceding example. Place a few `TextBlock` and `Border` controls in a `StackPanel` to design the UI, as shared in the following XAML code snippet:

```
<Button Content="Save" Width="60" Height="30"
    Margin="4">
    <Button.ToolTip>
        <StackPanel>
            <TextBlock FontWeight="Bold"
                       Text="Save File" />
            <TextBlock Text="Clicking on this button,
                       saves the file to disk"
                       FontSize="10" />
            <Border BorderBrush="Silver"
                    BorderThickness="0,1,0,0"
                    Margin="0 4" />
            <TextBlock FontStyle="Italic"
                       FontSize="9"
                       Text="Press F1 for more help" />
        </StackPanel>
    </Button.ToolTip>
</Button>
```

When you run the application, hover over the third button to see the customized UI of the tooltip for that button, as shown in the following screenshot:

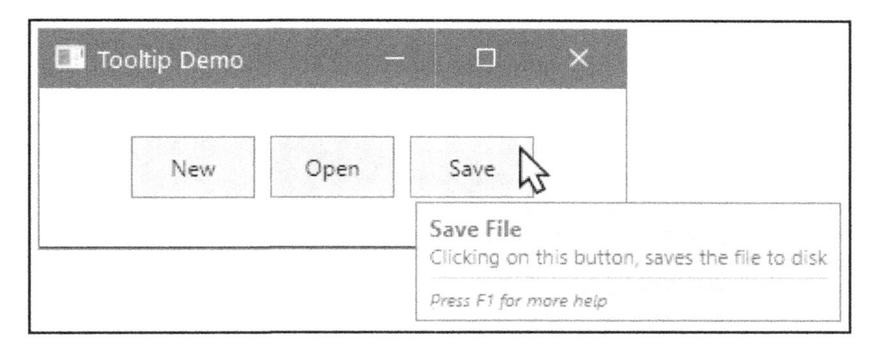

The `ToolTipService` class also exposes a few additional properties, such as `HorizontalOffset` and `VerticalOffset` to position `Tooltip` in a specific position on the screen.

Adding a standard menu to the WPF application

One of the most common parts of WPF applications is the menu, as it gives various options within a very little space. WPF comes with a control named `Menu`, to hold items named `MenuItem`.

Let's learn more about this menu control and how to add it to Windows applications.

Getting ready

Open your Visual Studio, and create a new WPF project called `CH02.MenuDemo`.

How to do it...

Follow these steps to add menus to your WPF application:

1. Open the `MainWindow.xaml` page, and replace the default `Grid` with a `DockPanel`. We will discuss more about this panel in the next chapter.
2. Now add the `Menu` control inside the `DockPanel`. This will create the base to hold all the menu items.
3. You can then add root-level menu items and sub-menu items in a hierarchical fashion, as shown in the following code snippet:

```
<DockPanel>
    <Menu>
        <MenuItem Header="File">
            <MenuItem Header="New" />
            <MenuItem Header="Open" />
            <MenuItem Header="Save" />
            <Separator />
            <MenuItem Header="Exit" />
        </MenuItem>
        <MenuItem Header="Edit">
            <MenuItem Header="Undo" />
            <MenuItem Header="Redo" />
        </MenuItem>
    </Menu>
</DockPanel>
```

4. Run the application to see the following window containing the added menu items:

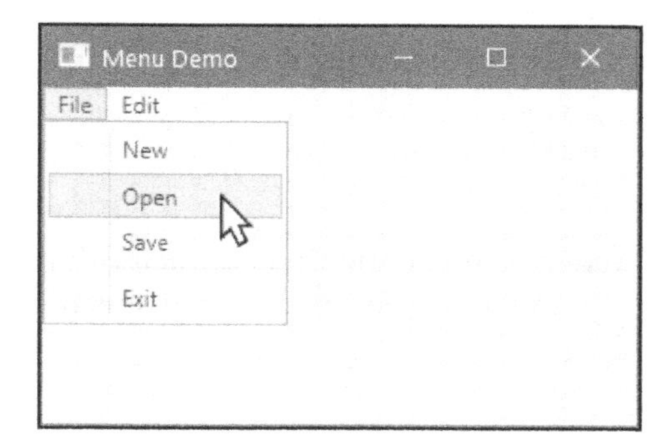

How it works...

When you add the first menu item under the `<Menu>` tag, it creates the root-level menu item; for example, **File** menu, **Edit** menu. Each root menu item can contain one or more hierarchical sub-menu items. In the preceding example, the **File** menu contains four sub-menu items.

The header property of the `MenuItem` is used to add the label of each item. When you want to add a separator, you can do so by adding the `<Separator />` tag, as shown in the preceding example. A separator does not need any `Header` content.

There's more...

You can further customize a menu entry to have an icon, a check-mark, a shortcut key, or a keyboard access specifier. Let's discuss each of them.

Adding an access key to menus

It's a general practice to access application menus by holding the *Alt* key and then pressing the character defined as its access key. For example, to open the **File** menu of any Windows application, we use *Alt* + *F*, and to access the **File** | **New** menu, we use *Alt* + *F*, *N*. Here, the character *F* and *N* are used as access keys that are invoked when we press *Alt*.

In the WPF application, you need to specify _ (underscore) before the character you want to highlight as the access key. For example, adding _ before the `F` in **File** menu header content activates the said menu when *Alt* + *F* is pressed:

```
<MenuItem Header="_File">
      <MenuItem Header="_New" />
      <MenuItem Header="_Open" />
</MenuItem>
```

The frequently used practice is to use the first character that's not already used as an access key of another control. But, on a need basis, you can specify any character part of the label content.

Adding icons to menus

You can add icons to menus to give a better look to the application's menu items. The `MenuItem` element contains a property named `Icon` to add an image icon or a Unicode character as an icon to it.

Let's add a Unicode character to add an icon for the **Open** and **Save** menu items:

```
<MenuItem Header="_Open" Icon="&#x1F4C2;" />
<MenuItem Header="_Save" Icon="&#x1F4BE;" />
```

Run the application now to see the icons added to the said menus, as shown in the following screenshot:

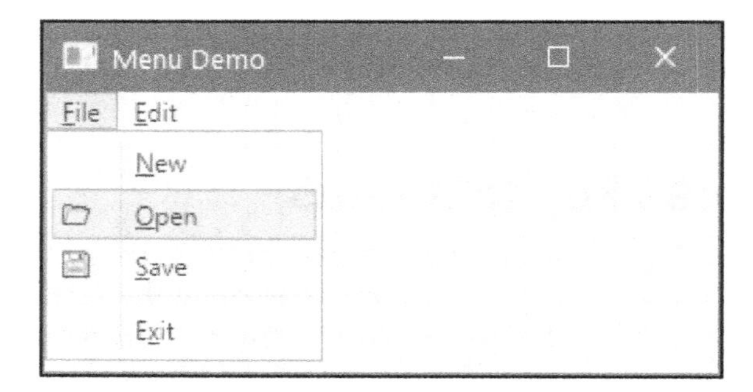

Adding checkable menu items

You can add checkable menu items too. The WPF menu item exposes two properties to handle this. The `IsCheckable` property tells the menu item that it can handle **check/uncheck** options. When `IsCheckable` is set to `True`, it sets to the **check/uncheck** icon on an alternate click of that menu item.

You can also programmatically **check/uncheck** a menu item. Set its `IsChecked` property to `True` or `False`. Make sure to set `IsCheckable="True"`. Let's add the following menu item, under the **Edit** menu:

```
<MenuItem Header="Save _settings on exit"
          IsCheckable="True" IsChecked="True" />
```

Adding click-event handlers to menus

Menus are not just to add to the application; you need to perform some actions on the menu with a click by adding the `Click` event handler, as shown in the following code snippet:

```
<MenuItem Header="E_xit" Click="OnExitMenuClicked" />
```

In the code behind, implement the handler, as shown in the following code:

```
private void OnExitMenuClicked(object sender, RoutedEventArgs e)
{
    MessageBox.Show("'Exit' menu item clicked!");
    Environment.Exit(0);
}
```

This will first show a message box and then exit the application when the user clicks on the **Exit** menu item.

Providing extra functionalities using the context menu

The context menu provides a vital role in any Windows applications offering additional functionalities to the user, within that context. This is often done relevant to a single control or a window.

When you right-click on a control or a window, you can provide a popup context menu to the user, to perform single-click actions. WPF provides a `ContextMenu` property to all framework elements to hold a `ContextMenu`, having hierarchical `MenuItems`.

Consider this recipe to learn more about adding a context menu in your WPF application.

Getting ready

Create a new project named `CH02.ContextMenuDemo`, using the WPF application project template of Visual Studio.

How to do it...

Follow these steps to add a context menu to a `TextBlock` control. The same steps can be followed to add a context menu to any of the controls inheriting `FrameworkElement`:

1. Open the `MainWindow.xaml` file to modify the application UI.
2. Replace the entire `Grid` block with the following XAML code:

```
<Grid>
    <TextBlock Text="Right-click on me to open Context Menu!"
        Margin="10">
        <TextBlock.ContextMenu>
            <ContextMenu>
                <MenuItem Header="Menu item 1" />
                <MenuItem Header="Menu item 2"
                    InputGestureText="Ctrl + R, Ctrl + G"/>
                <Separator />
                <MenuItem Header="Menu item 3"
                          IsCheckable="True"
                          IsChecked="True" />
            </ContextMenu>
        </TextBlock.ContextMenu>
    </TextBlock>
</Grid>
```

3. Run the application. You will see a text saying **Right-click on me to open Context Menu!**.

4. Right-click on the window. You will see the following context menu pop up on the screen:

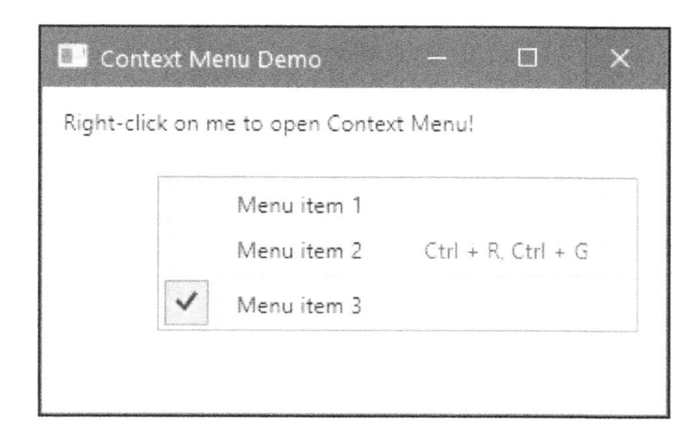

How it works...

As you see from the preceding example, each `FrameworkElement` exposes a property named `ContextMenu`, which can hold a `ContextMenu` item. Just like the menu, as we learnt in the previous recipe, the context menu can also hold multiple items as `MenuItem`, and each menu item can again hold one or more menu items to make the context menu hierarchical.

Labels of menu items are assigned by setting its `Header` property. You can also set icons for each menu item, by assigning an image or a Unicode character to its `Icon` property. If you have binded a command to the menu, you can assign the shortcut key text as `InputGestureText` property.

Additionally, you can create checkable context menu items. As shown in the **Menu item 3**, you can set the `IsCheckable` property to `True`, to make the menu checkable. Then you can use the `IsCheck` property to show/hide the check mark on it.

To add a separator between a group of context menu items, you can use the `<Separator />` tag, as shown in the preceding example.

Adding user options with radio buttons and checkboxes

Radio buttons and check boxes have a vital role in Windows Application Development. They are mostly used to provide the user an option to select from a group of items. Radio buttons allow you to select one from a group of options, whereas a checkbox allows you to toggle an option.

In this recipe, we will learn how to use `RadioButton` and `CheckBox` controls in the WPF application.

Getting ready

To get started, open your Visual Studio IDE, and create a new project named `CH02.OptionSelectorsDemo`. Make sure you select the WPF application project template.

How to do it...

Open the `MainWindow.xaml` page, and follow these steps to add a set of radio buttons and checkbox controls to it:

1. First, replace the default `Grid` panel with a `StackPanel` to hold items stacked vertically.
2. Now add the following `StackPanel` with a set of radio buttons with a `GroupName="rdoGroup1"`:

```
<StackPanel Orientation="Horizontal">
    <RadioButton GroupName="rdoGroup1"
                 Content="Radio 1"
                 IsChecked="True"
                 Margin="4" />
    <RadioButton GroupName="rdoGroup1"
                 Content="Radio 2"
                 Margin="4" />
    <RadioButton GroupName="rdoGroup1"
                 Content="Radio 3"
                 Margin="4" />
</StackPanel>
```

3. Add another set of radios, with the `GroupName="rdoGroup2"`, in a horizontally placed `StackPanel`, and add it to the root `StackPanel`:

```
<StackPanel Orientation="Horizontal">
    <RadioButton GroupName="rdoGroup2"
                 Content="Radio 1"
                 Margin="4" />
    <RadioButton GroupName="rdoGroup2"
                 Content="Radio 2"
                 IsChecked="True"
                 Margin="4" />
    <RadioButton GroupName="rdoGroup2"
                 Content="Radio 3"
                 Margin="4" />
</StackPanel>
```

4. Now place the following `CheckBox` controls in a horizontal `StackPanel` and add it to the root:

```
<StackPanel Orientation="Horizontal">
    <CheckBox Content="Checkbox 1"
              IsChecked="True"
              Margin="4" />
    <CheckBox Content="Checkbox 2"
              IsChecked="True"
              Margin="4" />
    <CheckBox Content="Checkbox 3"
              Margin="4" />
</StackPanel>
```

5. Run the application, which will give you the following output on screen:

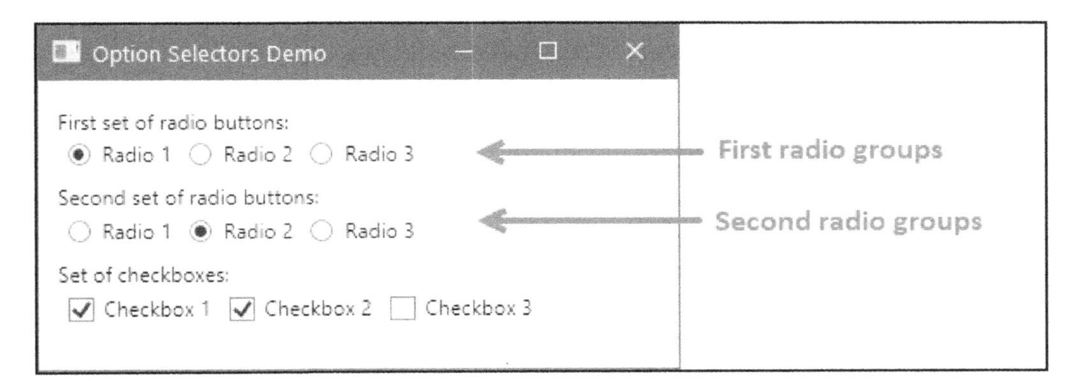

6. Select a few of the radio and checkbox controls to feel the behavior.

How it works...

The first set of radio button controls are placed in a group with the same name `rdoGroup1`. When a group name is set to a set of radio buttons, the selection follows that. The first radio button in that group is by default selected, by setting its `IsChecked` property to `True`. If you select any other radio button within that group, the previous selection resets to unchecked status.

The same is true for the second group too, but selection of one group does not affect the other group. So, when you check one radio button from the first group, it will not uncheck the radio buttons from the other group.

This is not the same for `CheckBox` controls. `Checkbox` controls allow you to have many checked items. When you select a checkbox, it can just toggle from one state to another.

Both the radio button and checkbox control expose the `IsChecked` property to return a Boolean value to tell whether the control is checked or unchecked.

There's more...

To disable the radio button or the checkbox control, set its `IsEnabled` property to `False`. Both the controls expose two events—`Checked` and `Unchecked`. When you register the events, the `Checked` event of the control will trigger when you check that. Similarly, the `Unchecked` event will trigger when you uncheck that.

Working with the progress bar control

When you perform a lengthy task in the background, you probably would like to add a progress indicator in your application UI to give a visual indication that some work is in progress. WPF provides us with a control name, `ProgressBar`, to show a percentage value of the work between 0% to 100%, in general.

In this recipe, we will learn about the progress bar control and its various properties.

Getting ready

Let's open the Visual Studio and create a new WPF application project. Name it `CH02.ProgressBarDemo`.

How to do it...

Once the project gets created, follow these steps to add a progress indicator to the application's UI:

1. Open the `MainWindow.xaml`, and replace the existing `Grid` panel with a `StackPanel`, so that, we can add our controls stacked vertically.
2. As shown in the following code snippet, add three `ProgressBar` controls in the `StackPanel`:

```
<StackPanel Margin="10">
    <TextBlock Text="Progress Indicator set at: 20%" />
    <ProgressBar Height="30"
                 Margin="0 4"
                 Minimum="0"
                 Maximum="100"
                 Value="20" />
    <TextBlock Text="Progress Indicator set at: 70%" />
    <ProgressBar Height="30"
                 Margin="0 4"
                 Minimum="0"
                 Maximum="100"
                 Value="70" />
    <TextBlock Text="Progress Indicator set at:
     Indeterminate" />
    <ProgressBar Height="30"
                 Margin="0 4"
                 Minimum="0"
                 Maximum="100"
                 IsIndeterminate="True" />
</StackPanel>
```

3. Set the `Minimum` and `Maximum` properties of both the three controls to `0` (zero) and `100` (hundred) respectively.

4. As shared in the preceding XAML code snippet, set the `Value` of the first progress bar to `20`, and the second progress bar to `70`.
5. Set the `IsIndeterminate` property of the third progress bar to `True`.
6. Now run the application. You will see the following output for the XAML code we shared earlier:

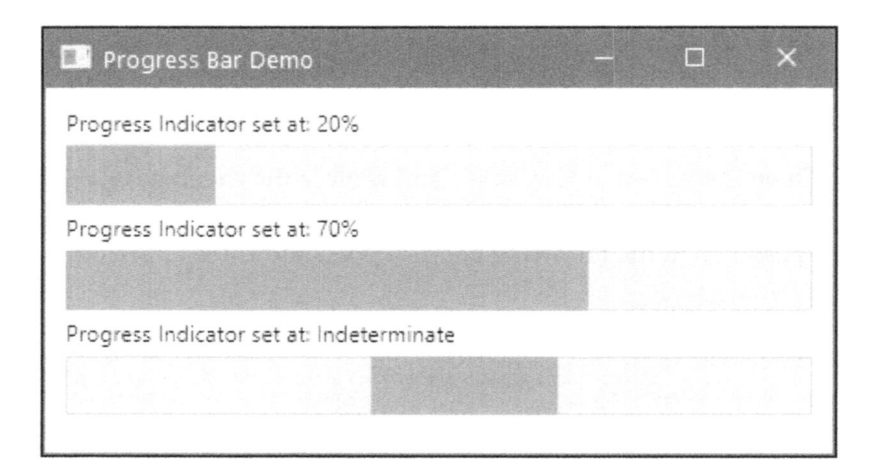

How it works...

The value of the first progress indicator is set to `20`, whereas the second progress indicator is set to `70`. This denotes that the 20% and 70% job is done respectively. As and when you progress with the task, you can just increment the value to have the visual indication of the progress in the UI, with the `ProgressBar` control.

For the third `ProgressBar` control, in the preceding example, it's a bit different. When you are unsure about the total job to be done, you can set its `IsIndeterminate` property to `True`, as shown in the preceding screenshot. When your job is done, you can stop the indeterminate state and set its `Value` to 100.

Using the Slider control to pick a numeric value

The `Slider` control is used to pick a numeric value by dragging a thumb button along a horizontal or vertical line. This is often used to provide a visualization of a playing video and as a volume indicator.

WPF provides us a control named `Slider` to quickly implement this in your application UI, and, with a lot of properties for various configurations. Let's learn more about it, in this recipe.

Getting ready

First, create a project named `CH02.SliderDemo`, based on the WPF application template.

How to do it...

Integration of the slider in WPF is very easy. Just place `<Slider />` in your XAML page, and it will start working. But to customize it further, let's follow these steps:

1. Open the `MainWindow.xaml` page, and replace the default `Grid` with a `StackPanel`.
2. Now add a `Slider` and a `TextBlock` control inside the `StackPanel`, as shown in the following XAML snippet:

```
<StackPanel Margin="10">
    <Slider x:Name="slider"
            Minimum="0" Maximum="100"
            Value="25"
            SmallChange="1"
            LargeChange="5" />
    <TextBlock Margin="4">
        <Run Text="Current slider value: " />
        <Run Text="{Binding Value, ElementName=slider}" />
    </TextBlock>
</StackPanel>
```

3. Run the application. You will see a `Slider` control in the UI, along with a text that shows the current value, which is set to `25`. Move the slider thumb to right, and it will show you the currently selected value. In our demonstration, it's now `65`, as shown in the following screenshot:

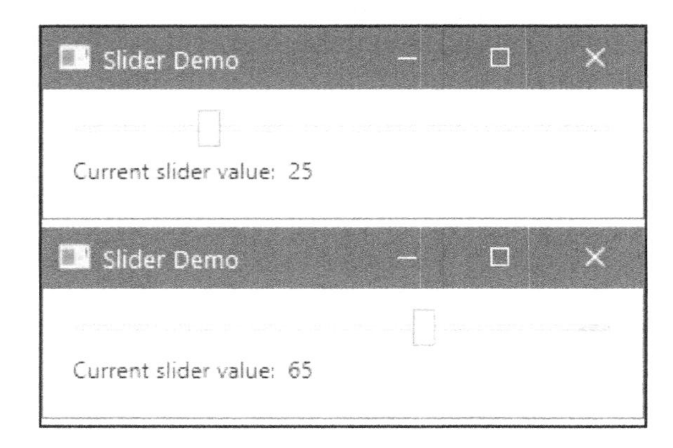

How it works...

It works based on the current value. The property named `Value`, provides us with an integer, which denotes the current position. You can programmatically set it to move the slider thumb to a smaller or larger value.

The `Minimum` and `Maximum` properties denote the minimum and maximum value that the slider can accept. In our example, we set it to `0` (zero) and `100` (hundred), respectively.

The other control, `TextBlock`, in our example code, has a data binding to the `Value` property of the slider that we have in the XAML. It displays the current value of the slider in a plain text format.

There's more...

You can also enable the tick display in a slider control, to provide a better indication of the thumb placement. Use the `TickPlacement` property to turn on the tick markers. It has four values `None`, `TopLeft`, `BottomRight`, and `Both`. Let's add `TickPlacement="BottomRight"` in our previous slider control.

The `TickFrequency` property is used to set the range of possible values between `0` and `100`. Let's add `TickFrequency="20"` to our code and then run the application again. You will see the following screen:

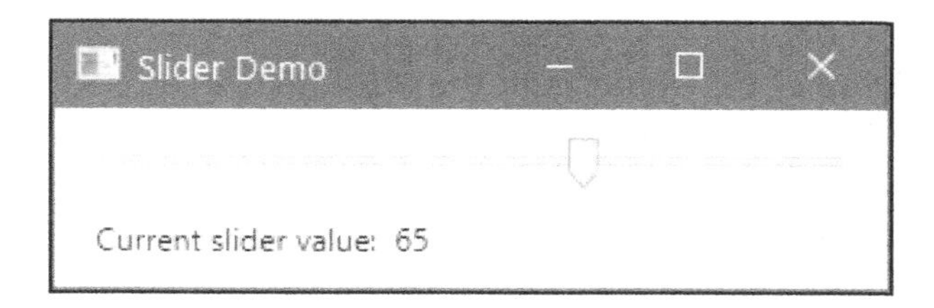

As shown in the preceding screenshot, you can see that some dots are added to the bottom of the slider. They represent the tick. As we have added `TickFrequency` as `20`, it divided the entire slider range to `100/20 = 5` sections.

In general, moving the slider will not snap to the tick. Thus, you will observe the thumb placed between ticks. Use the `IsSnapToTickEnabled` property and set it to `True`, to make sure that the thumb always stays on the tick marker only. In this case, dragging the slider will move the thumb based on the tick frequency count.

Using the Calendar control in your application

The `Calendar` control, part of the `System.Windows.Controls` namespace, allows you to create a visual calendar in WPF applications. It allows you to select a date or a collection of dates. As it inherits from the `Control` class, all common properties and events from `Control` class are available to it.

In this recipe, we will learn more about `Calendar` control and how to use that.

Getting ready

To get started with this recipe, let's create a WPF application project named `CH02.CalendarDemo`.

How to do it...

Follow these steps to add the basic controls to the main window:

1. Open the `MainWindow.xaml` page.
2. Inside the default `Grid` panel, add the tag `<Calendar />` to create the basic calendar control in the application UI.
3. To retrieve the date selected by the user, register the `SelectedDatesChanged` event to it, as shown in the following code snippet:

```
<Grid Margin="10">
    <Calendar SelectedDatesChanged="OnSelectedDateChanged"
      HorizontalAlignment="Left" />
</Grid>
```

4. Add the associated event handler (`OnSelectedDateChanged`) in the code-behind class (`MainWindow.xaml.cs`), as shown in the following code, to retrieve the selected date and show it in a message box:

```
private void OnSelectedDateChanged(object sender,
 SelectionChangedEventArgs e)
{
    MessageBox.Show("You selected: " +
      ((DateTime)e.AddedItems[0]).ToString("dd-MMM-yyyy"));
}
```

5. Let's run the application. You will see the following UI on the screen:

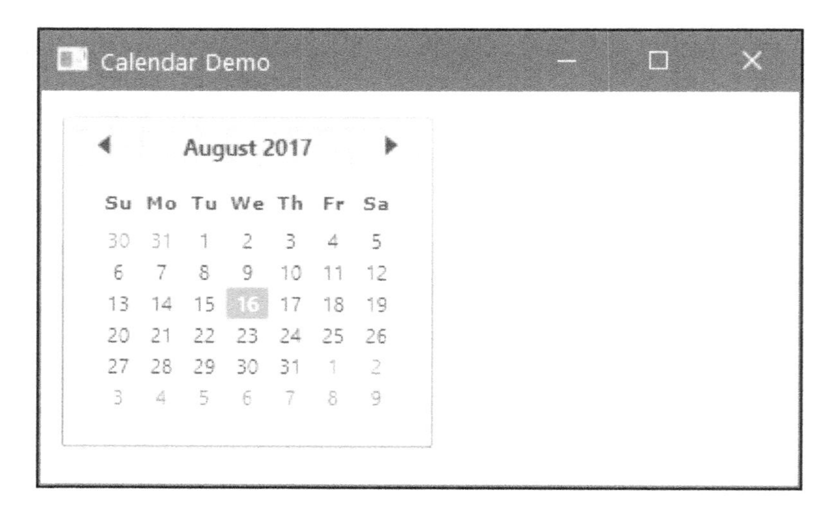

6. Once you select a date from the calendar, the selected date will be shown in a message box, like this:

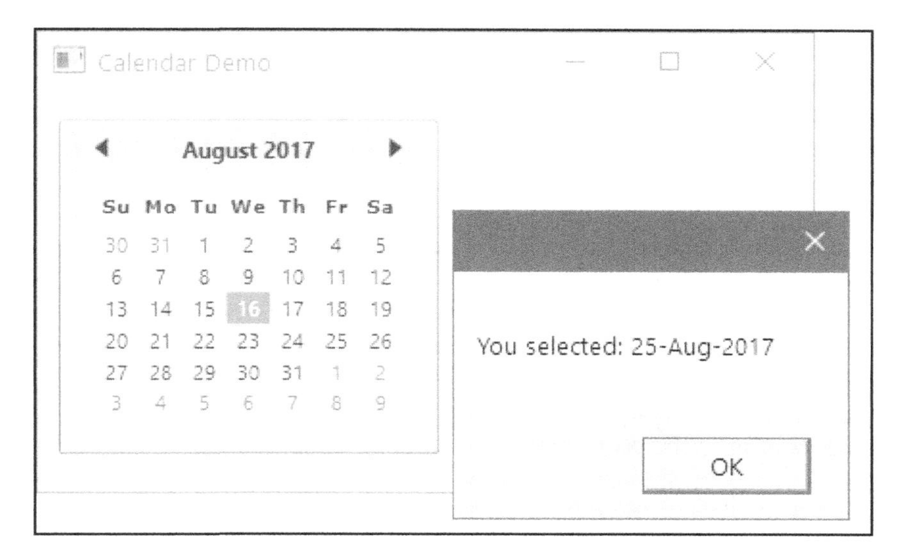

7. Select a different date. This will show the message to the UI with the newly selected date.

How it works...

WPF `Calendar` control provides you with the basic UI to begin the calendar integration in your application. The top two arrow-heads, allow you to navigate back and forth to other months and select the desired date from the calendar.

The navigation also supports year view and decade view, so, you can select the desired year and month very easily. Click on the month name (in our case, it's **August 2017**) present at the top, to navigate to the year view. When you are in the year view, it will show you the Jan–Dec month range, and clicking on the year will navigate you to the decade view where you can select the desired year.

There's more...

The `Calendar` control exposes many properties and events for you to customize the behavior and look of the control. Let's discuss this further.

The SelectionModes property

The `SelectionMode` property allows you to get or set the value indicating what kind of selections are allowed on the calendar. There are four values available, named `None`, `SingleDate`, `SingleRange`, and `MultipleRange`. The `enum` value `SingleDate` is default, and allows you to select only a single date. But when you want multi-selection, set it as `MultipleRange`:

```
<Calendar SelectionMode="MultipleRange" />
```

The DisplayDate property

The `Calendar` control allows you to set the start and end display dates. The `DisplayDate` property represents the current date to display; whereas, setting the `DisplayDateStart` and `DisplayDateEnd` properties limits you to select only the dates from the period ranging from the start date to the end date.

The following XAML code demonstrates how to set the `DisplayDate`, `DisplayDateStart`, and `DisplayDateEnd` properties in `Calendar` control:

```
<Calendar SelectionMode="MultipleRange"
          DisplayDateStart="8/10/2017"
          DisplayDateEnd="8/21/2017"
          DisplayDate="8/16/2017" />
```

Run the application now to see the following output:

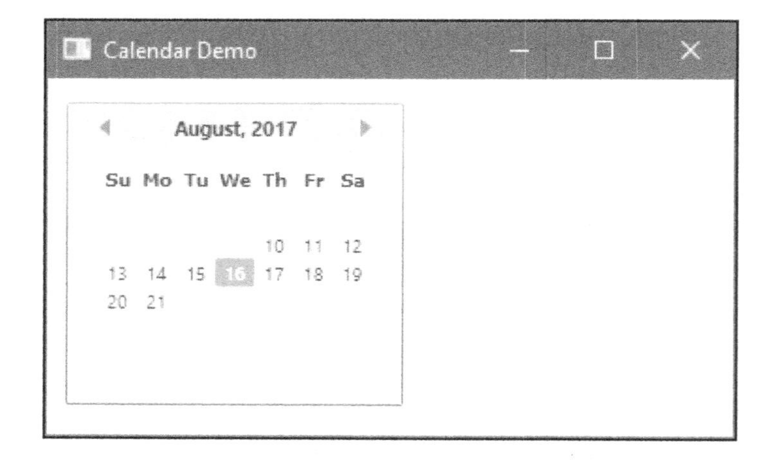

The DisplayMode property

The `DisplayMode` property allows you to select the format of the calendar, which can be a month, a year, or a decade. When you launch a basic calendar, by default, it shows the month view:

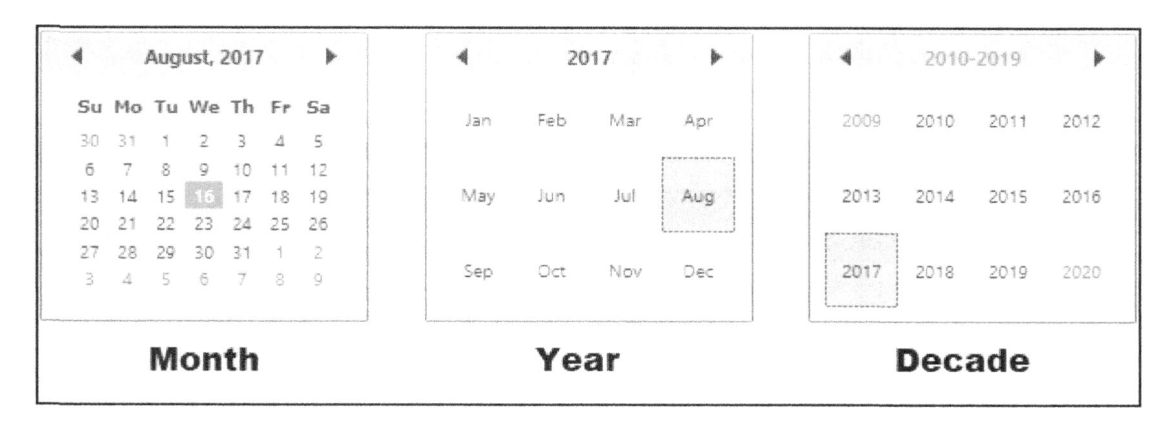

But a user can easily navigate from month to year to decade by clicking the header text of the `Calendar` control.

To change the display mode from code, you can set the `DisplayMode` property to `Month`, `Year`, or `Decade`:

```
<Calendar DisplayMode="Month" /> <!-- default mode -->
<Calendar DisplayMode="Year" />
<Calendar DisplayMode="Decade" />
```

The user can initiate the downward transitions by clicking any of the calendar cells, and they can easily navigate from decade to year to month and select the correct date.

The BlackoutDates property

You can choose ranges of dates to be non-selectable despite being displayed. You can implement the same by using the calendar's `BlackoutDates` property, which takes a collection of `CalendarDateRange` objects.

The following `Calendar` control will block the date range from August 1st, 2017 to August 8th, 2017, and August 21st, 2017 to August 31st, 2017:

```
<Calendar>
    <Calendar.BlackoutDates>
        <CalendarDateRange Start="8/1/2017" End="8/8/2017" />
        <CalendarDateRange Start="8/21/2017" End="8/31/2017" />
    </Calendar.BlackoutDates>
</Calendar>
```

All non-selection dates are marked by a cross, as shown in the following screenshot:

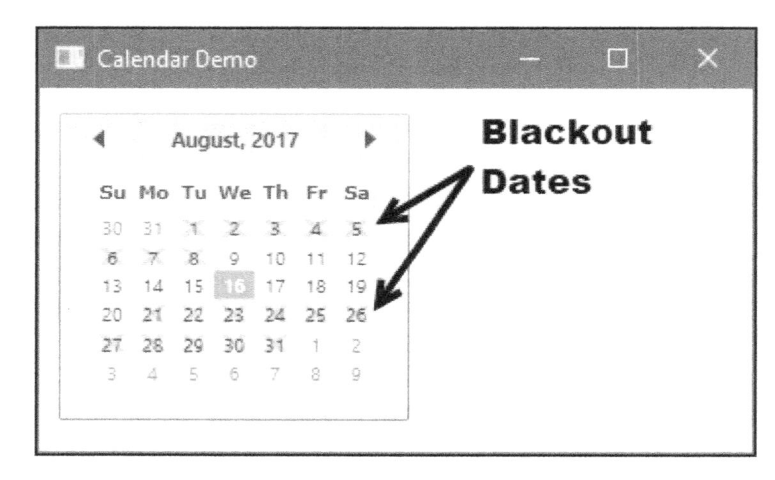

Listing items in a Listbox control

In WPF, the `ListBox` control is used to display a list of items. Users can select one or more items from the list, depending on the `SelectionMode` specified.

In this recipe, we are going to learn how to create a `ListBox` control and use it in WPF applications.

Getting ready

Open your Visual Studio IDE and create a new WPF application project, called `CH02.ListBoxDemo`.

How to do it...

Adding a `ListBox` control in the UI is as easy as writing a `<ListBox />` tag in any XAML page. But to hold the data in it, you will have to use its properties properly. Follow these steps to add a `ListBox` control with some static data:

1. Open the `MainWindow.xaml` page of the WPF project.
2. Under the default `Grid` panel, add the `<ListBox></ListBox>` tag to add the control.
3. Add a few `ListBoxItem` inside the control, as shared here:

```
<ListBox x:Name="lstBox"
         Width="120" Height="85"
         Margin="10 10 20 5">
    <ListBoxItem Content="Item 1" />
    <ListBoxItem Content="Item 2" IsSelected="True" />
    <ListBoxItem Content="Item 3" />
    <ListBoxItem Content="Item 4" />
    <ListBoxItem Content="Item 5" />
</ListBox>
```

4. Add two buttons labelled + and - to perform the `add` and `delete` operations on the said `Listbox` control. Register the `Click` event of both the buttons:

```
<StackPanel Orientation="Horizontal"
            HorizontalAlignment="Center">
    <Button Content="+"
            Width="20" Height="20"
            Margin="0 0 4 0"
            Click="OnAddItemClicked" />
    <Button Content="-"
            Width="20" Height="20"
            Margin="0 0 4 0"
            Click="OnDeleteItemClicked" />
</StackPanel>
```

5. In the code-behind file, `MainWindow.xaml.cs`, implement the button-click event handler as shown here:

```
private void OnAddItemClicked(object sender,
 RoutedEventArgs e)
{
    var itemsCount = lstBox.Items.Count;
    var newitem = new ListBoxItem
                  {
```

```
                    Content = "Item " + (itemsCount + 1)
                };

    lstBox.Items.Add(newitem);
    lstBox.SelectedItem = newitem;
}

private void OnDeleteItemClicked(object sender,
 RoutedEventArgs e)
{
    var selectedItem = lstBox.SelectedItem;
    if (selectedItem != null)
    {
        lstBox.Items.Remove(selectedItem);
        lstBox.SelectedIndex = 0;
    }
}
```

6. Now run the application. You will see the following UI in the screen:

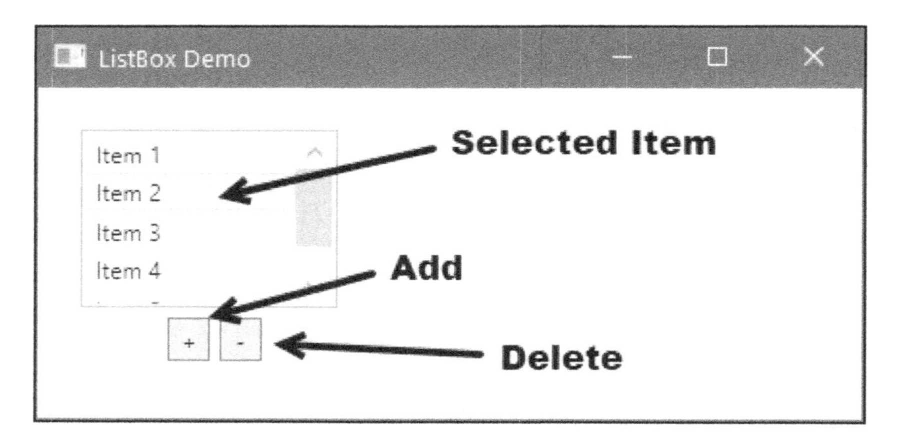

How it works...

In the preceding example, the `ListBox` control contains five items as `ListBoxItem`. When you launch the application, by default, the second item is selected due to its property `IsSelected` being set to `True`.

The two buttons are used to `add` or `delete` items in the `Listbox` control. Click on the + button to trigger the `OnAddItemClicked` event, which will create a new instance of the `ListBoxItem` and add it to the `ListBox` control. Scroll the list to see the newly added entry. As the `SelectedItem` property of the `ListBox` is assigned with the latest item, it will now get selected, removing the previous selection.

Click on the - button to trigger the `OnDeleteItemClicked` event. This will get the current selected item, and, if it is not `null`, it will be removed from the `ListBox` control. The property `SelectedIndex` will set to `0` (zero), to select the first element after deletion.

There's more...

`ListBox` has numerous properties to perform specific actions. Let's learn a few of them. Later in this section, we will also cover how to add a customized `ListBoxItem` having additional UI controls.

Implementing multi selection

`ListBox` supports multi selection. By default, when the `SelectionMode` property is set to `Single`, it only accepts a single selection of items. If you set `SelectionMode` to `Multiple`, it will accept multi selection. The `Extended` mode allows you to perform single selection, but if you press the *Ctrl* key while selecting items, it will act as a multi selection.

Customizing the ListBoxItem with multiple controls

You can easily customize the `ListBoxItem`, by adding additional UI controls to it. Consider the following XAML code snippet, where we have added a `ListBox`, which has four `ListBoxItem`:

```
<ListBox Width="150" Margin="20 10 10 10">
    <ListBoxItem>
        <StackPanel Orientation="Horizontal">
            <Rectangle Width="10"
                       Height="10"
                       Fill="Red"
                       Margin="0 0 8 0" />
            <TextBlock Text="Red (#FFFF0000)" />
        </StackPanel>
    </ListBoxItem>
    <ListBoxItem IsSelected="True">
```

```
                <StackPanel Orientation="Horizontal">
                    <Rectangle Width="10"
                               Height="10"
                               Fill="Green"
                               Margin="0 0 8 0" />
                    <TextBlock Text="Green (#FF00FF00)" />
                </StackPanel>
            </ListBoxItem>
            <ListBoxItem>
                <StackPanel Orientation="Horizontal">
                    <Rectangle Width="10"
                               Height="10"
                               Fill="Blue"
                               Margin="0 0 8 0" />
                    <TextBlock Text="Red (#FF0000FF)" />
                </StackPanel>
            </ListBoxItem>
        </ListBox>
```

If you see the preceding code snippet, each `ListBoxItem` has a `StackPanel` to hold a `Rectangle` control and a `TextBlock` control. If you run the preceding code, you will see the following UI:

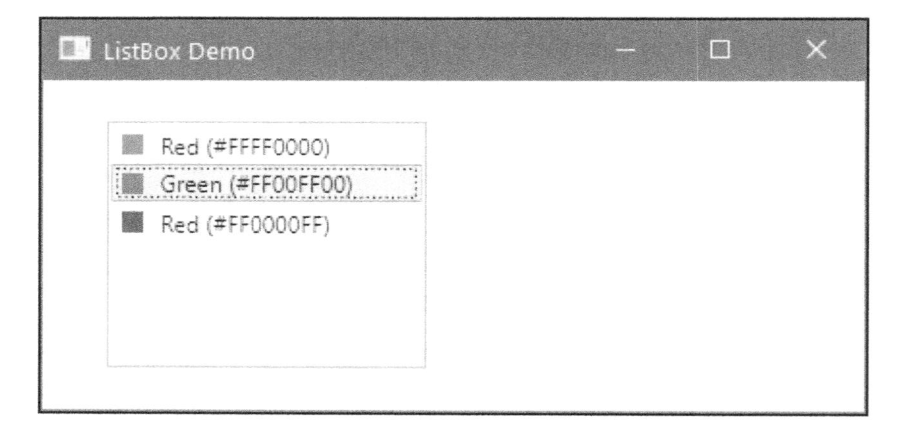

In the preceding screenshot, notice the way the items have been listed. Each item consists of a rectangle to preview the color that is listed as an item. This is more useful when displaying information on an entity.

Generally, this is done using the `DataTemplate` property of `ListBox` control, which we will learn in the later chapters of this book.

Providing options to select from a ComboBox

A ComboBox control is an items control and works like ListBox, but only one item from the list is selectable. A ListBox control by default lists multiple items on screen, but ComboBox control displays the scrollable list only on a user click. Thus, it takes up a lot less space.

This recipe will talk about ComboBox control and how to use it.

Getting ready

Begin with creating a new WPF application project, called CH02.ComboBoxDemo, using your Visual Studio IDE.

How to do it...

Follow these simple steps to add a ComboBox control in your application UI:

1. Replace the default Grid with a StackPanel to host UI controls horizontally stacked.
2. Add the following XAML code, inside the StackPanel, to have a simple ComboBox control with some items in it:

```
<ComboBox Width="150" Height="26"
    Margin="10">
    <ComboBoxItem Content="Item 1" />
    <ComboBoxItem Content="Item 2" IsSelected="True" />
    <ComboBoxItem Content="Item 3" />
    <ComboBoxItem Content="Item 4" />
    <ComboBoxItem Content="Item 5" />
</ComboBox>
```

3. Add another ComboBox to have customized items, as shown in the following example code:

```
<ComboBox Width="150" Height="26"
    Margin="10">
    <ComboBoxItem>
        <StackPanel Orientation="Horizontal">
```

```
                <Rectangle Width="10"
                           Height="10"
                           Fill="Red"
                           Margin="0 0 8 0" />
                <TextBlock Text="Red (#FFFF0000)" />
            </StackPanel>
        </ComboBoxItem>
        <ComboBoxItem>
            <StackPanel Orientation="Horizontal">
                <Rectangle Width="10"
                           Height="10"
                           Fill="Green"
                           Margin="0 0 8 0" />
                <TextBlock Text="Green (#FF00FF00)" />
            </StackPanel>
        </ComboBoxItem>
        <ComboBoxItem>
            <StackPanel Orientation="Horizontal">
                <Rectangle Width="10"
                           Height="10"
                           Fill="Blue"
                           Margin="0 0 8 0" />
                <TextBlock Text="Red (#FF0000FF)" />
            </StackPanel>
        </ComboBoxItem>
    </ComboBox>
```

4. Now run the application, which will look like the following screenshot, with an expandable pop up menu:

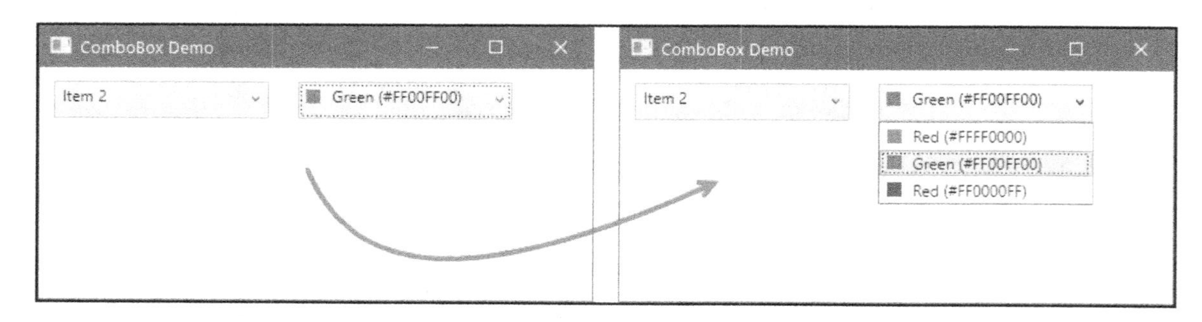

How it works...

Though a `ComboBox` control is like `ListBox`, it does not show the list of items by default. A user intervention is required to display the items. The UI of a `ComboBox` is a combination of three controls:

- A **TextBox**, which displays the selected item
- A **Button**, which is used to show or hide available items
- A **Popup**, which displays a list of items inside a scrollable pane and gives the user the option to select one item from the available list

`ComboBox` contains a collection of `ComboBoxItem`. You can add those to its `Items` property. When you click on the arrow-head, the list of items will pop up in the screen, as demonstrated in the preceding screenshot. To preselect an item from code, set its `IsSelected` property to `True`.

You can also add custom contents to a `ComboBoxItem` to represent a better UI component. The second `ComboBox` in the preceding example, demonstrates how easy it is to customize the UI.

Just like `ListBox`, it also exposes `SelectedItem`, `SelectedIndex`, `SelectedValue` properties to help you to easily set or get the selected item.

There's more...

The `ComboBox` control is not editable by default. But you can control this behavior to provide the user with the option to manually enter the desired value, directly in the `ComboBox` control. The `IsEditable` property is used to add this functionality. Set it to `True`, to change it to an editable `ComboBox`. Consider the following code:

```
<ComboBox Width="150" Height="26"
    Margin="10" IsEditable="True">
    <ComboBoxItem Content="Item 1" />
    <ComboBoxItem Content="Item 2" IsSelected="True" />
    <ComboBoxItem Content="Item 3" />
    <ComboBoxItem Content="Item 4" />
    <ComboBoxItem Content="Item 5" />
</ComboBox>
```

If you run the preceding code, you can see the following UI, where the control now allows you to enter text to it:

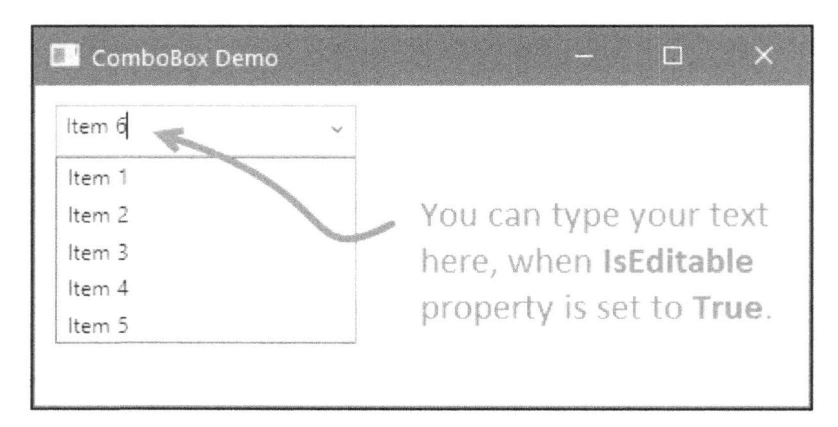

Adding a status bar to your window

The status bar is used to show various information about the current state of the application. You can use this to show cursor position, word counts, progress of tasks, and more. Generally, a status bar is placed at the bottom of the window whereas the menus, toolbars are placed at the top.

In this recipe, we will learn how to add a status bar in a WPF window.

Getting ready

To get started with the status bar, let's create a WPF application project called `CH02.StatusBarDemo`.

How to do it...

Once you create the WPF project, open the `MainWindow.xaml` page and follow these steps to add the `StatusBar` control to the window:

1. Inside the `Grid` panel, add a `StatusBar` tag and set its `Height` to `26` and `VerticalAlignment` to `Bottom`.

2. Now change its items panel template to host a `Grid` with five columns (we will discuss more about grid columns in the next chapter), as shown here:

```
<StatusBar.ItemsPanel>
    <ItemsPanelTemplate>
        <Grid>
            <Grid.ColumnDefinitions>
                <ColumnDefinition Width="Auto" />
                <ColumnDefinition Width="Auto" />
                <ColumnDefinition Width="*" />
                <ColumnDefinition Width="Auto" />
                <ColumnDefinition Width="Auto" />
            </Grid.ColumnDefinitions>
        </Grid>
    </ItemsPanelTemplate>
</StatusBar.ItemsPanel>
```

3. Now, inside the `StatusBar` tag, add the controls that you want to show. Let's add two `StatusBarItem`; one having a plain text content and the other with a `ProgressBar` control. Place two separators in between, as shown in the following XAML snippet:

```
<StatusBarItem Content="Running Process..."
  Grid.Column="0"/>
<Separator Width="1" Grid.Column="1" />
<Separator Width="1" Grid.Column="3" />
<StatusBarItem Grid.Column="4">
    <ProgressBar IsIndeterminate="True"
                 Width="100" Height="15" />
</StatusBarItem>
```

4. Here's the complete XAML code, which you need to place inside the default `Grid` panel:

```
<StatusBar Height="26" VerticalAlignment="Bottom">
    <StatusBar.ItemsPanel>
        <ItemsPanelTemplate>
            <Grid>
                <Grid.ColumnDefinitions>
                    <ColumnDefinition Width="Auto" />
                    <ColumnDefinition Width="Auto" />
                    <ColumnDefinition Width="*" />
                    <ColumnDefinition Width="Auto" />
                    <ColumnDefinition Width="Auto" />
                </Grid.ColumnDefinitions>
            </Grid>
```

```
            </ItemsPanelTemplate>
        </StatusBar.ItemsPanel>

        <StatusBarItem Content="Running Process..."
         Grid.Column="0"/>
        <Separator Width="1" Grid.Column="1" />
        <Separator Width="1" Grid.Column="3" />
        <StatusBarItem Grid.Column="4">
            <ProgressBar IsIndeterminate="True"
                         Width="100" Height="15" />
        </StatusBarItem>
    </StatusBar>
```

5. Once your UI is ready, let's run the application. You will see the following screen:

How it works...

In the preceding example, we have placed a plain text content **Running Process...** as a `StatusBarItem` inside the first column of the `Grid`. The second and fourth columns of the `Grid` contain a `Separator` control, having one pixel width. The fifth column contains a `ProgressBar` control, having an indeterminate state.

When you resize the window, the status bar will follow its parent to resize itself automatically and position it to the bottom of the window. Instead of `Grid`, you can also use `DockPanel` to dock the status bar at the bottom.

Adding a toolbar panel to perform quick tasks

In any windows-based application, you can find a toolbar, usually placed just below the main menu of a window. It contains a set of controls to provide easy access to common functions.

WPF offers you a `ToolBarTray` element to host one or more `ToolBar` controls, containing various UI controls. It provides you with some extra features, such as an automatic overflowing mechanism and a manual repositioning feature.

In this recipe, we will learn how to work with toolbars in a WPF application.

Getting ready

To begin with, open your Visual Studio IDE and create a new WPF application project called `CH03.ToolBarDemo`.

How to do it...

Once the project gets created, follow these steps to add a toolbar in the application window:

1. Open the `MainWindow.xaml` page from the **Solution Explorer**.
2. Now, replace the existing `Grid` with a `DockPanel` so that we can host the toolbar docking to the top of the window.
3. Add a `ToolBarTray` element inside the `DockPanel` and dock it to `Top`.
4. Add a `ToolBar` control inside the `ToolBarTray` and then add a few buttons inside it, as shown in the following XAML markup:

```
<ToolBarTray DockPanel.Dock="Top">
    <ToolBar>
        <Button Content="B" FontWeight="Bold"
                Width="20"
                Click="OnBoldButtonClicked"/>
        <Button Content="I" FontStyle="Italic"
                Width="20"/>
        <Button Width="20">
            <TextBlock Text="U"
                       TextDecorations="Underline"/>
```

```
            </Button>
        </ToolBar>
    </ToolBarTray>
```

5. Add a `TextBox` control inside the `DockPanel`, just below the `ToolBarTray`, so that, it can cover the remaining space of the window. Give it the following name `txtBox`.
6. You can add a multiple toolbar inside a `ToolBarTray`. You can also add other controls inside a `ToolBar`. Let's add the following `ToolBar` with a `ComboBox` inside it. Place it just after the first `ToolBar` control:

```
<ToolBar>
    <ComboBox Width="50">
        <ComboBoxItem Content="8"/>
        <ComboBoxItem Content="10"/>
        <ComboBoxItem Content="12"/>
        <ComboBoxItem Content="14"
                      IsSelected="True"/>
        <ComboBoxItem Content="16"/>
    </ComboBox>
</ToolBar>
```

7. Here's the complete XAML code to take as a reference:

```
<DockPanel>
    <ToolBarTray DockPanel.Dock="Top">
        <ToolBar>
            <Button Content="B" FontWeight="Bold"
                    Width="20"
                    Click="OnBoldButtonClicked"/>
            <Button Content="I" FontStyle="Italic"
                    Width="20"/>
            <Button Width="20">
                <TextBlock Text="U"
                           TextDecorations="Underline"/>
            </Button>
        </ToolBar>
        <ToolBar>
            <ComboBox Width="50">
                <ComboBoxItem Content="8"/>
                <ComboBoxItem Content="10"/>
                <ComboBoxItem Content="12"/>
                <ComboBoxItem Content="14"
                              IsSelected="True"/>
                <ComboBoxItem Content="16"/>
            </ComboBox>
```

```
            </ToolBar>
        </ToolBarTray>
        <TextBox x:Name="txtBox" Text="Sample Text"
           AcceptsReturn="True" TextWrapping="Wrap" />
</DockPanel>
```

8. As we have associated a click event of the first button of the first toolbar, we need to write the event body. Open the `MainWindow.xaml.cs` file, and add the following button-click event implementation inside the class:

```
private void OnBoldButtonClicked(object sender,
 RoutedEventArgs e)
{
    txtBox.FontWeight =
        txtBox.FontWeight == FontWeights.Bold ?
        FontWeights.Normal : FontWeights.Bold;
}
```

9. Once you run the application, you will see the following UI containing two toolbars inside a toolbar panel:

10. Click on the first button (denoted by the character **B**). You will see that the text **Sample Text** becomes bold. If you click the same button again, the text will change the font weight to normal:

How it works...

A `ToolBarTray` can contain one or more `ToolBar` controls. Each `ToolBar` control can contain one or more controls inside it. A `ToolBar` control can also remain empty. When you start adding other controls to it, the toolbar starts changing its size and position, based on the available space.

The controls placed inside a `ToolBar` can have its associated events registered. If you want, you can also use command bindings to have a more granular association between the view and the code.

In the preceding example, the first button, denoted by the character **B**, stands for applying `Bold` weightage to the associated `TextBox`. When you click it for the first time, the `FontWeight` property of the text will set it to `Bold`. When you click it again, it will set to `Normal`. By following the same logic, you can add a `Click` event for other buttons and a `SelectionChange` event for the combobox, as shown in the preceding example.

3 Layouts and Panels

In this chapter, we will cover the following recipes:

- Building a UI layout using a Grid
- Placing elements in uniform cells
- Automatically repositioning controls using a `WrapPanel`
- Placing controls in a Stack
- Positioning controls inside a Canvas
- Wrapping UI elements using a Border
- Creating a scrollable panel
- Docking controls using a DockPanel
- Rescaling UI elements using a `ViewBox`
- Creating a tabbed layout
- Dynamically adding/removing elements in a panel
- Implementing the drag and drop feature

Introduction

WPF provides a proper layout and positioning to provide interactive, user-friendly applications with a suitable container element that helps you to position the child UI elements. The parent container is usually the contents of a window. You can place child level containers and elements with proper margins, paddings, and alignments.

In WPF, `Panel` is the base class that provides layout support. There are plenty of derived panels in WPF that help you to create simple to complex layouts and all of them are defined in the `System.Windows.Controls` namespace.

All `Panel` elements support sizing and positioning defined by the `FrameworkElement`. You can set the `Height`, `Width`, `Margin`, `Padding`, `HorizontalAlignment`, and `VerticalAlignment` properties to design your UI. The following diagram describes these important properties, which you will use everywhere:

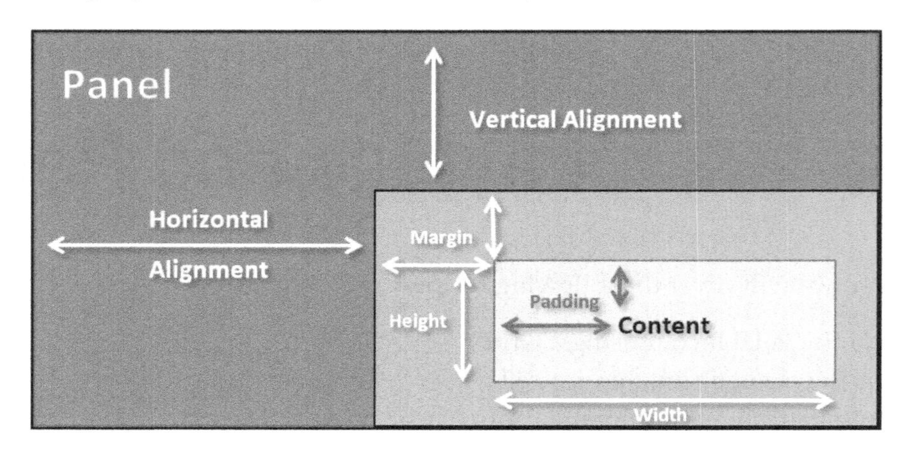

A panel also exposes other properties such as `Background`, `Children`, `ZIndex`, and more. Since a window can contain only one child, a panel is often used to divide the space to hold another control or a panel. Picking the right panel is important to create the layout. In this chapter, we will learn various recipes to design your application layout using various panels.

Building a UI layout using a Grid

A `Grid` panel enables you to arrange child elements in tabular format, represented by cells in rows and columns. This is the default panel that you will see when you create a new WPF project and navigate to the `MainWindow.xaml` file. Visual Studio automatically adds this as the first container inside every window.

It is often useful when you want to represent data in a tabular or matrix form. It is also useful when creating a form layout.

In this recipe, we will discuss the `Grid` panel in detail, so that you can properly use it while designing your application layout.

Getting ready

Let's start with `Grid` as a layout panel, by creating a new project. Open Visual Studio and create a new project named `CH03.GridDemo`, by selecting the WPF application template.

How to do it...

Perform the following steps to create a sample `Grid` layout to host a few rectangles in each cell:

1. Inside **Solution Explorer**, open your `MainWindow.xaml` page.
2. Create a few rows and columns inside the default `Grid` panel, as shown in the following code:

```
<Grid.RowDefinitions>
    <RowDefinition Height="*" />
    <RowDefinition Height="*" />
</Grid.RowDefinitions>
<Grid.ColumnDefinitions>
    <ColumnDefinition Width="*" />
    <ColumnDefinition Width="*" />
    <ColumnDefinition Width="*" />
</Grid.ColumnDefinitions>
```

3. Add six rectangles inside the `Grid`, and place them properly by using the `Grid.Row` and `Grid.Column` attached properties. You can refer to the following sample code:

```
<Rectangle Width="100" Height="60"
           Fill="OrangeRed"
           Grid.Row="0" Grid.Column="0"/>
<Rectangle Width="100" Height="60"
           Fill="OrangeRed"
           Grid.Row="0" Grid.Column="1"/>
<Rectangle Width="100" Height="60"
           Fill="OrangeRed"
           Grid.Row="0" Grid.Column="2"/>
<Rectangle Width="100" Height="60"
           Fill="OrangeRed"
           Grid.Row="1" Grid.Column="0"/>
<Rectangle Width="100" Height="60"
           Fill="OrangeRed"
           Grid.Row="1" Grid.Column="1"/>
<Rectangle Width="100" Height="60"
```

```
Fill="OrangeRed"
Grid.Row="1" Grid.Column="2"/>
```

4. Now run the application and you will see the following UI on the screen:

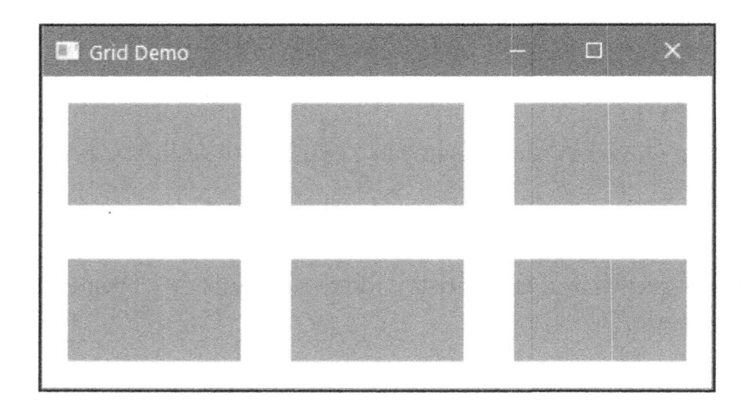

How it works...

Grid works in cells, by creating the rows and columns. `<Grid.RowDefinitions>` and `<Grid.ColumnDefinitions>` define the structure of the Grid. It contains a collection of rows and columns, respectively. Here we have created two rows and three columns (2x3 matrix) using RowDefinition and ColumnDefinition.

When we placed the rectangles inside the Grid, we positioned them in cells by specifying the row and column number by using the attached properties, Grid.Row and Grid.Column. As the index position starts at 0 (zero), the first rectangle placed in the first cell has row index = 0 and column index = 0. Similarly, the sixth/last rectangle has the position Row=1 and Column=2.

You can set the Height of a RowDefinition and the Width of a ColumnDefinition by specifying an absolute value, a percentage value (star sizing), or an automatic sizing. In the preceding example, we used star sizing to define the row and column dimensions.

An absolute value takes an integer to define fixed height/width. Star sizing is a relative based factor, that works like percentage value. When you mark the height/width as *, it takes as much space as possible after filling all other fixed and auto sized rows/columns. When you specify Auto, it takes as much space as required by the contained control.

There's more...

There's more to know about the star sized value. When there are two rows or two columns having height/width defined as *, they will occupy the available space by dividing it proportionally. Thus, in the preceding example, each of the two rows occupied 50% of the available space. Similarly, the three columns equally occupied a total of 100% of the available space.

You can also define them using n*. For example, if a Grid contains two rows, and among them, one of the rows has a height defined as 2* and the other as 8*, they will occupy 20% and 80% of the available space. Let's see this with a simple example.

Create a Grid inside a window and set its ShowGridLines property to True, so that the grid lines are visible on screen. By default, it is set to False. Now divide the entire Grid into five columns. Consider the following XAML code:

```
<Grid ShowGridLines="True">
    <Grid.ColumnDefinitions>
        <ColumnDefinition Width="2*"/>
        <ColumnDefinition Width="Auto" MinWidth="5"/>
        <ColumnDefinition Width="*"/>
        <ColumnDefinition Width="3*"/>
        <ColumnDefinition Width="40"/>
    </Grid.ColumnDefinitions>
</Grid>
```

The width of the second column is set to Auto, which means it will take as much space as the width of the containing element. When the said column does not contain any element inside it, this will have 0 (zero) width. You can specify MinWidth to provide a minimum value.

The fifth column has a fixed width of 40. Both the second column and fourth column width will be calculated first, as they contain auto width and fixed width, respectively.

The other three columns, in the preceding example, will be calculated now based on the available space and will be calculated in the ratio of 2:1:3. The third column in the example will take one-sixth of the space. The first and fourth columns will take 2x and 3x width, based on the width of the third column.

Once you run this UI, you will see the following output. Now resize the window to see how the resizing happens dynamically based on the given inputs:

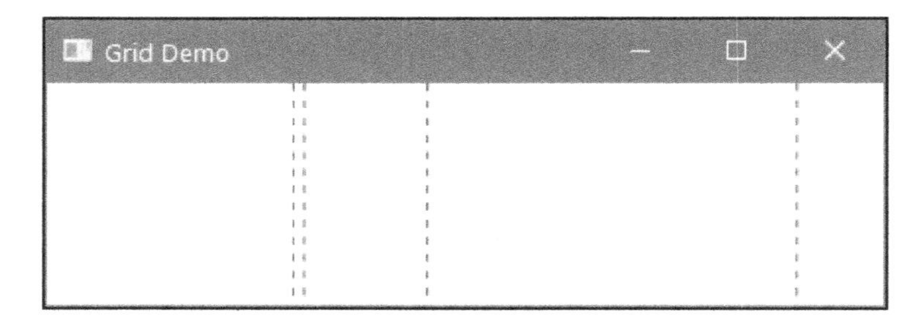

Creating a resizable Grid

It is possible to create a resizable `Grid` in WPF. You can use the `<GridSplitter/>` tag to create a `splitter` control, which can be used by the user to resize a specific column. Let's consider the following XAML code:

```
<Grid ShowGridLines="True">
    <Grid.ColumnDefinitions>
        <ColumnDefinition Width="2*"/>
        <ColumnDefinition Width="Auto"/>
        <ColumnDefinition Width="*"/>
        <ColumnDefinition Width="3*"/>
        <ColumnDefinition Width="40"/>
    </Grid.ColumnDefinitions>
    <GridSplitter Grid.Column="1" Width="5"/>
</Grid>
```

In this example, the `GridSplitter` control has been placed in the second column. When you run the application, you will see a vertical line inside the second column that you can drag to resize the grid column, as shown in the following screenshot:

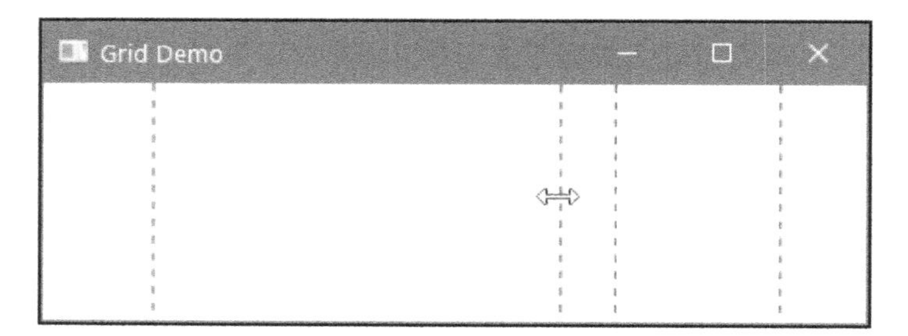

Spanning elements across multiple rows and/or columns

It's not mandatory to place an item in a single cell only. You can span it across multiple rows and/or columns. The attached property `Grid.RowSpan` allows you to span the element across two or more grid row cells. Similarly, `Grid.ColumnSpan` allows you to span the element across two or more grid columns. You can use either or both.

Consider the following code snippet, where the rectangle is spanned across two rows and two columns, starting at the `(0, 0)` cell position:

```
<Rectangle Fill="OrangeRed"
           Grid.Row="0" Grid.Column="0"
           Grid.RowSpan="2" Grid.ColumnSpan="2" />
```

When you run this, you will see the following output:

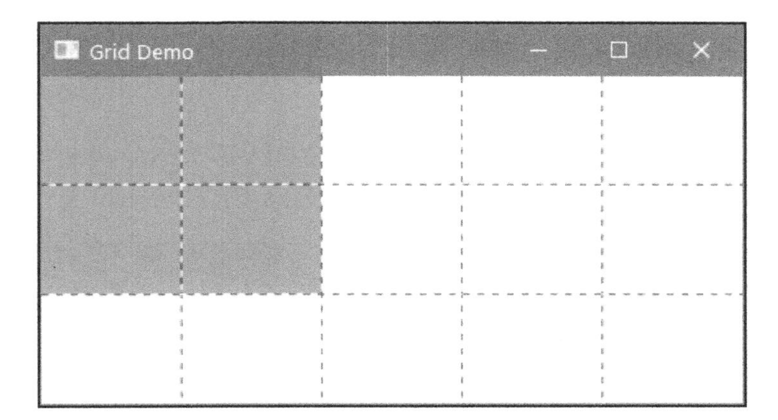

Placing elements in uniform cells

Just like the `Grid` layout system in Windows Presentation Foundation, the `UniformGrid` control also provides the similar layout system, but only with a difference that the rows and columns are of same size. It equally divides the layout into cells, of the same size, based on the number of rows and columns. Thus, you will not have the choice to modify the height and width of the rows and columns explicitly.

In this recipe, we will learn about the `UniformGrid` layout with a simple example.

Getting ready

Let's create a sample application to demonstrate the `UniformGrid` control. Open your Visual Studio IDE and create a new WPF application project named `CH03.UniformGridDemo`.

How to do it...

Now perform the following steps:

1. From **Solution Explorer**, open the `MainWindow.xaml` page.
2. Replace the existing `Grid` panel with the following XAML code:

```
<UniformGrid>
    <Label Content="Cell 1" Background="Yellow" />
    <Label Content="Cell 2" Background="YellowGreen" />
    <Label Content="Cell 3" Background="Orange" />
    <Label Content="Cell 4" Background="OrangeRed" />
</UniformGrid>
```

3. Build the project and run the application. You will see the following output on the screen:

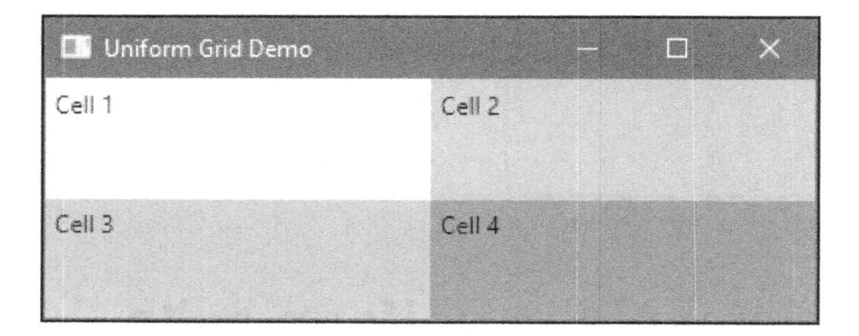

4. Now close the application and add a few more `Label` controls in the same `UniformGrid` as follows:

```
<Label Content="Cell 5" Background="Violet" />
<Label Content="Cell 6" Background="DeepSkyBlue" />
<Label Content="Cell 7" Background="SkyBlue" />
```

5. Run the application once again and you will see that the row and column count automatically changed to accommodate the new elements, as seen in the following screenshot:

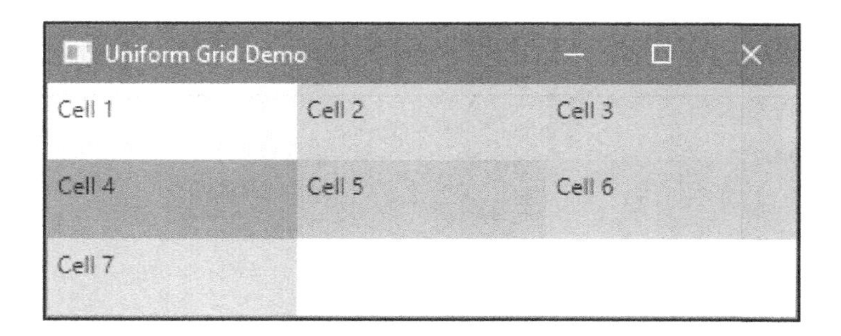

How it works...

When you start placing controls inside an `UniformGrid` control, it automatically calculates the number of cells required to accommodate placing of the added controls. Based on that, it divides the available space into rows and columns to position the child elements sequentially.

When there is a need to place more controls, it again breaks the space into an additional number of equal rows and columns, as shown in the second example.

There's more...

There are many properties that `UniformGrid` provides us with, to customize the UI. We are now going to discuss some of the most important properties.

Setting the row and column count

`UniformGrid` does not have any restriction on setting the number of rows and columns. You can set the numbers by assigning the `Rows` and `Columns` properties. For example, the following XAML will render the elements in a single row only, as we assigned `Rows="1"`:

```
<UniformGrid Rows="1">
    <Label Content="Cell 1" Background="Yellow" />
    <Label Content="Cell 2" Background="YellowGreen" />
    <Label Content="Cell 3" Background="Orange" />
    <Label Content="Cell 4" Background="OrangeRed" />
```

```
        <Label Content="Cell 5" Background="Violet" />
        <Label Content="Cell 6" Background="DeepSkyBlue" />
        <Label Content="Cell 7" Background="SkyBlue" />
    </UniformGrid>
```

The preceding example will have the following output:

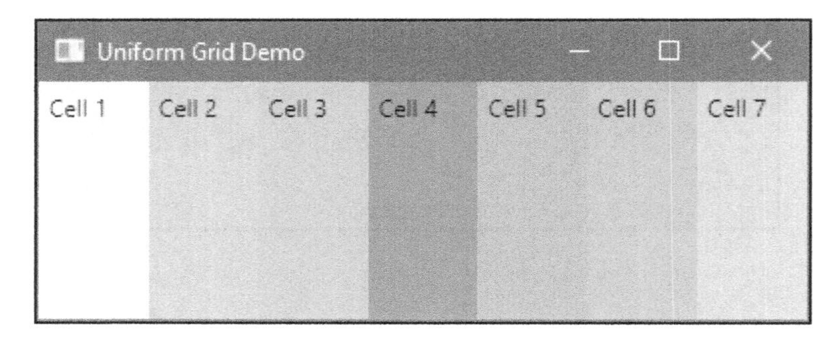

If you set `Columns="2"`, all the elements will reposition themselves into two columns, but in multiple rows. You can also combine both the properties.

Defining the first cell of the UniformGrid

It's a default nature of the `UniformGrid` panel to place the first element at the first cell (Row=`0`, Column=`0`), but it also offers to set the cell position explicitly. The first cell location must be in the first row, starting the index at `0` (zero).

The following example demonstrates how you can set the first element position by assigning the `FirstColumn` property:

```
<UniformGrid Columns="4" FirstColumn="2">
    <Label Content="Cell 1" Background="Yellow" />
    <Label Content="Cell 2" Background="YellowGreen" />
    <Label Content="Cell 3" Background="Orange" />
    <Label Content="Cell 4" Background="OrangeRed" />
    <Label Content="Cell 5" Background="Violet" />
    <Label Content="Cell 6" Background="DeepSkyBlue" />
    <Label Content="Cell 7" Background="SkyBlue" />
</UniformGrid>
```

When you run the preceding example, you will see the following output on the screen, where the **Cell 1** label is positioned at the third column (index position is `2`):

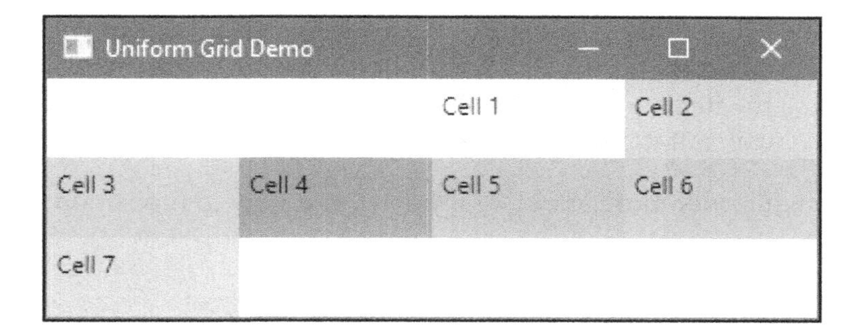

Filling elements from right to left

The default behavior of filling elements in `UniformGrid` is *left to right*. But you can fill them in *right to left* fashion. To do this, set the `FlowDirection` property to `RightToLeft` (the default is `LeftToRight`), as shown in the following snippet:

```
<UniformGrid FlowDirection="RightToLeft">
    <Label Content="Cell 1" Background="Yellow" />
    <Label Content="Cell 2" Background="YellowGreen" />
    <Label Content="Cell 3" Background="Orange" />
    <Label Content="Cell 4" Background="OrangeRed" />
    <Label Content="Cell 5" Background="Violet" />
    <Label Content="Cell 6" Background="DeepSkyBlue" />
    <Label Content="Cell 7" Background="SkyBlue" />
</UniformGrid>
```

When you run the preceding code, you will see a UI similar to the following screenshot:

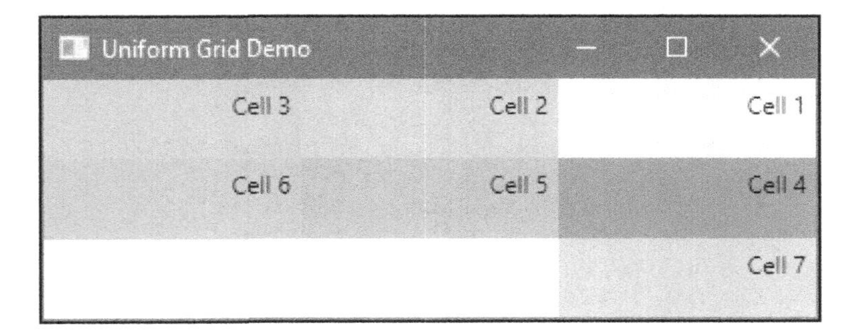

Automatically repositioning controls using WrapPanel

`WrapPanel` in WPF is similar to `StackPanel`, but it does not stack the items in a single line; rather it wraps the items to a new line based on the available space. It also looks like a `UniformGrid` control, but it has odd cell size depending on the item dimension.

In this recipe, we will cover more about `WrapPanel` and how to reposition controls using it.

Getting ready

To get started, open Visual Studio IDE and create a new project named `CH03.WrapPanelDemo`. Make sure to select the WPF app template while creating the project.

How to do it...

Let's look at a simple example to add a few buttons in `WrapPanel`. Perform the following steps to design the UI:

1. From the Visual Studio **Solution Explorer**, open the `MainWindow.xaml` page.
2. Replace the existing `Grid` panel with a `WrapPanel` control and set its `Orientation` property to `Horizontal`.
3. Add a few button controls of diverse sizes. The entire XAML inside the window will look like the following code:

```
<WrapPanel Orientation="Horizontal">
    <Button Content="Button 1" Margin="4"
            Width="100" Height="30"/>
    <Button Content="Button 2" Margin="4"
            Width="100" Height="30"/>
    <Button Content="Button 3" Margin="4"
            Width="100" Height="30"/>
    <Button Content="Button 4" Margin="4"
            Width="208" Height="30"/>
    <Button Content="Button 5" Margin="4"
            Width="100" Height="30"/>
    <Button Content="Button 6" Margin="4"
            Width="60" Height="30"/>
    <Button Content="Button 7" Margin="4"
```

```
                Width="60" Height="30"/>
        <Button Content="Button 8" Margin="4"
                Width="180" Height="30"/>
</WrapPanel>
```

4. Now build the project and run the application. You will see the following output on the screen:

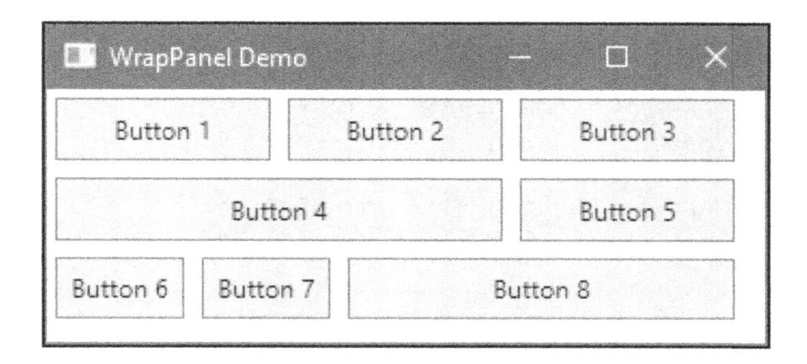

5. Resize the application UI to see how the buttons are placed within the screen.

How it works...

`WrapPanel` works by stacking child elements in a line. Once the line is full and can't hold to add more elements, it wraps there, and adds the new element in the next line and continues. Unlike `UniformGrid`, the `WrapPanel` does not have any fixed width for columns. So, items can be placed based on the available space.

The button controls, which we added as child elements of the `WrapPanel`, get added in stack in the first row. When it's unable to accommodate within the same line, it wraps to the next line to give room for the next elements.

The `Orientation` property of the `WrapPanel` decides whether you want to stack them horizontally or vertically.

There's more...

In the preceding example, we have seen that the items inside the `WrapPanel` have their individual size mentioned along with them. You can also set the size for all the items to a specific value by setting the `ItemWidth` and `ItemHeight` properties, as shown in the following code snippet:

```
<WrapPanel Orientation="Vertical"
  ItemWidth="100" ItemHeight="30">
    <Button Content="Button 1" Margin="4" />
    <Button Content="Button 2" Margin="4" />
    <Button Content="Button 3" Margin="4" />
    <Button Content="Button 4" Margin="4" />
    <Button Content="Button 5" Margin="4" />
    <Button Content="Button 6" Margin="4" />
</WrapPanel>
```

In this case, you won't need to specify the size individually to each child element. When you run the preceding code, you will see the output similar to the following:

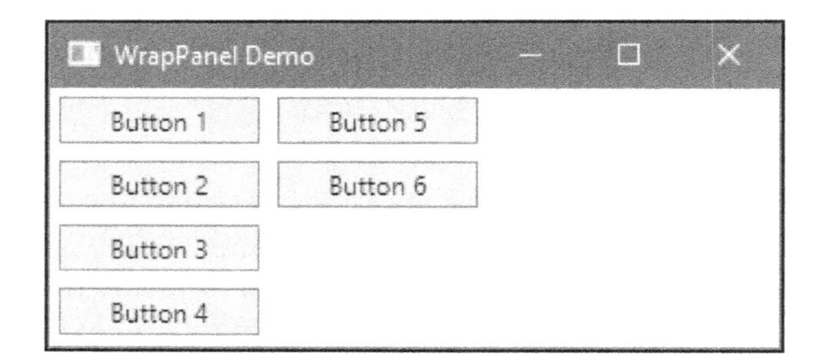

Placing controls in a Stack

Another simple and useful layout panel in WPF is a `StackPanel`. It works almost like a `WrapPanel`, but with a difference that it can't wrap the child elements to a new line. All items added inside it either get placed in horizontal or vertical stacks.

The StackPanel measures its children using either native or relative sizing, keeping the arrangement pass simple by laying out the items in order.

However, the Grid uses complex combinations of child elements when proportional sizing or auto sizing is used. Thus, it makes the Grid layout have a slow to medium performance for the measure pass and the arrangement pass to execute.
Therefore, wherever possible, the StackPanel preferable to over the Grid panel to reduce the rendering overhead.

In this recipe, we will learn how the StackPanel works, by using a very simple example.

Getting ready

To get started, let's open Visual Studio and create a new WPF application project named CH03.StackPanelDemo.

How to do it...

Inside **Solution Explorer**, navigate to the project and perform the following steps to create the sample UI with StackPanel containing a few button controls:

1. First, open the MainWindow.xaml file.
2. Inside the Window tag, replace the default Grid with the following XAML code:

```
<StackPanel>
    <StackPanel Orientation="Horizontal">
        <Button Content="Button 1" Margin="4" />
        <Button Content="Button 2" Margin="4" />
        <Button Content="Button 3" Margin="4" />
        <Button Content="Button 4" Margin="4" />
    </StackPanel>
    <StackPanel Orientation="Vertical">
        <Button Content="Button 5" Margin="4" />
        <Button Content="Button 6" Margin="4" />
        <Button Content="Button 7" Margin="4" />
        <Button Content="Button 8" Margin="4" />
    </StackPanel>
</StackPanel>
```

3. Let's build and run the application. You will see the following output:

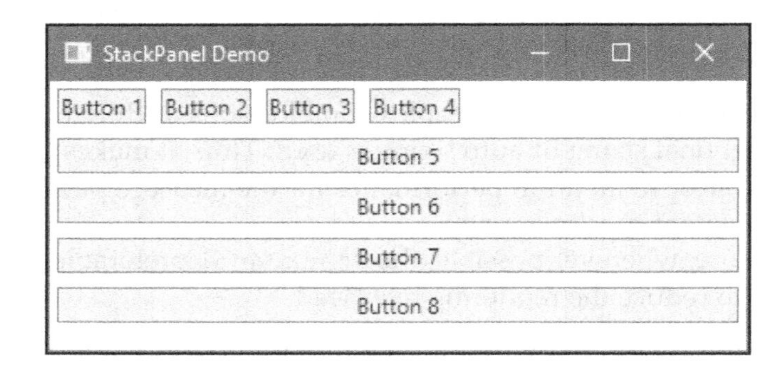

How it works...

The first `StackPanel` is used to hold the multiple inner `StackPanel`, stacked vertically by default. The first inner `StackPanel` control holds **Button 1 - Button 4**. These will be stacked horizontally, as we set the `Orientation` property of the panel to `Horizontal`.

The second inner `StackPanel` holds **Button 5 - Button 8**, stacked vertically, as we set the `Orientation` property to `Vertical`.

Unlike `WrapPanel`, where the default orientation is `Horizontal`, `StackPanel` has its default orientation set to `Vertical`.

There's more...

`StackPanel` stretches its child elements by default, but you can take control of how it will stretch. On a vertically oriented `StackPanel`, you can assign the `HorizontalAlignment` property of the child elements to `Left`, `Center`, `Right`, or `Stretch`, as shown in the following code:

```
<StackPanel Orientation="Vertical">
    <Button Content="Button (Left)" Margin="4"
            HorizontalAlignment="Left"/>
    <Button Content="Button (Center)" Margin="4"
            HorizontalAlignment="Center"/>
```

```
        <Button Content="Button (Right)" Margin="4"
                HorizontalAlignment="Right"/>
        <Button Content="Button (Stretch)" Margin="4"
                HorizontalAlignment="Stretch" />
    </StackPanel>
```

The preceding code example will give you the following output:

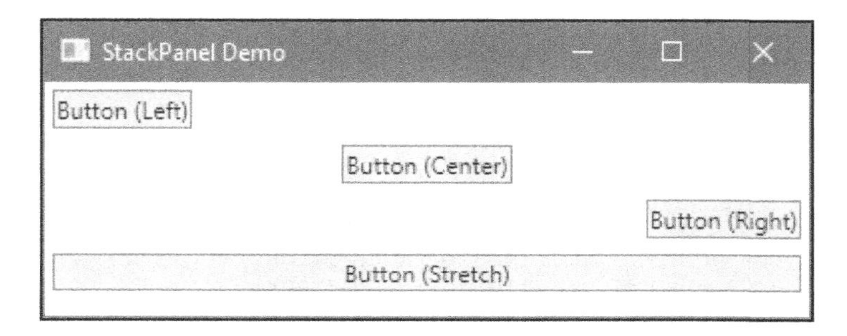

Similarly, you can assign the `VerticalAlignment` property of the child elements, placed in a horizontally oriented `StackPanel`. This property contains the following values—`Top`, `Center`, `Bottom`, and `Stretch`.

Positioning controls inside a Canvas

A `Canvas` is another simple panel in WPF, which allows you to place child elements at a specific coordinate position relative to the `Canvas`. It exposes four attached properties: `Left`, `Right`, `Top`, and `Bottom`, to handle the positioning of controls.

This recipe will help you to understand the positioning of child elements in a `Canvas` panel.

Getting ready

Let's open the Visual Studio instance and create a new WPF application project named `CH03.CanvasDemo`.

How to do it...

Perform the following steps to create a simple `Canvas` panel with a few label controls in it and position them to specific coordinate positions:

1. Open **Solution Explorer** and navigate to the project.
2. Open the `MainWindow.xaml` file and replace the default `Grid` with the following lines:

```
<Canvas>
    <Label Width="100" Height="60"
           Background="GreenYellow"
           Canvas.Left="70" Canvas.Top="40"
           Content="(70, 40)"
           FontSize="20" FontWeight="Bold"/>
    <Label Width="100" Height="60"
           Background="YellowGreen"
           Canvas.Left="220" Canvas.Top="90"
           Content="(220, 90)"
           FontSize="20" FontWeight="Bold"/>
</Canvas>
```

3. Build and run the application. It will show the following screen:

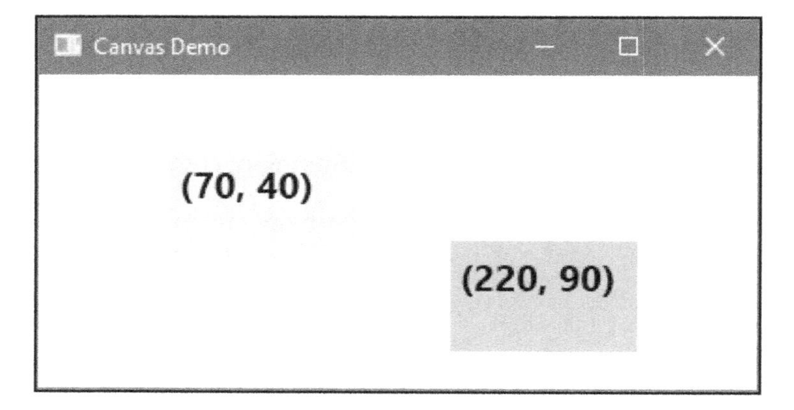

4. Now resize the window and observe the positioning of the labels.

How it works...

The `Canvas.Left` property allows you to assign a value indicating the distance of the child element from the left edge of the `Canvas`. The `Canvas.Top` property allows you to assign a value indicating the distance of the child element from the top.

Similarly, the `Canvas.Right` and `Canvas.Bottom` properties allow you to assign the relative position from right and bottom, respectively.

As you can see in the preceding example, the first label is placed at the coordinate position (`70, 40`), whereas the second element is placed at the coordinate position (`220, 90`). If you resize the window, the position of the child elements will not change.

Points to note are that the vertical and horizontal alignments on child elements do not work. Also, if you set the `Left` property, the `Right` property does not work. Similarly, if you set the `Top` property, the `Bottom` property does not work.

There's more...

The Z-order of a control, placed in a `Canvas` panel, determines whether the control is in front of or behind another overlapping control. You can use the `Canvas.ZIndex` property to play with the positioning of the Z-order.

By default, the `ZIndex` of the first element starts with `0` (zero) and gradually increases by `1` whenever you add a new element on the canvas. But in special cases, when you want to bring an overlapped control to the top, set its `ZIndex` higher than the `ZIndex` of the last element that is overlapping it.

Wrapping UI elements using a Border

The `Border` control in WPF is used as a `Decorator`, which you can use to draw a border around another control. As the WPF panels do not support adding a border around its edges, the `Border` control is used to achieve the same.

This recipe will guide you to add a border to a control. You can also use the same concept to decorate a group of controls placed inside a panel, by wrapping the panel with a `Border`.

Getting ready

To begin with an example, let's first create a new project. Open Visual Studio and create a WPF application project named `CH03.BorderDemo`.

How to do it...

Perform the following simple steps to add a border around `TextBlock`:

1. Open the `MainWindow.xaml` file of your WPF project.
2. Now replace the default `Grid` with a `StackPanel`.
3. Add a few TextBlocks inside it, wrapped by a Border. Here's the complete XAML code:

```
<StackPanel Margin="10">
    <Border BorderBrush="OrangeRed"
            BorderThickness="2"
            Margin="10 4" Padding="10">
        <TextBlock Text="Text surrounded by border"/>
    </Border>
    <Border BorderBrush="OrangeRed"
            BorderThickness="2"
            CornerRadius="20"
            Margin="10 4" Padding="10">
        <TextBlock Text="Text surrounded by border,
        having corner radius = 20"/>
    </Border>
    <Border BorderBrush="OrangeRed"
            BorderThickness="2"
            CornerRadius="5"
            Background="Yellow"
            Margin="10 4" Padding="10">
        <TextBlock Text="Text surrounded by border,
        having a Yellow background and rounded border"
        TextWrapping="Wrap"/>
    </Border>
    <Border BorderBrush="OrangeRed"
            BorderThickness="4 0"
            CornerRadius="5"
            Margin="10 4" Padding="10">
        <TextBlock Text="Text surrounded by two-side border"/>
    </Border>
</StackPanel>
```

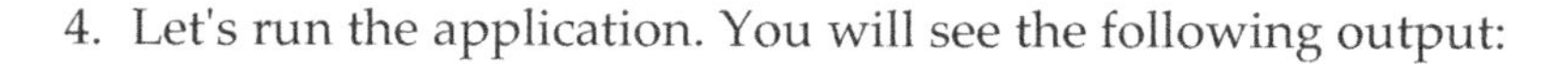

4. Let's run the application. You will see the following output:

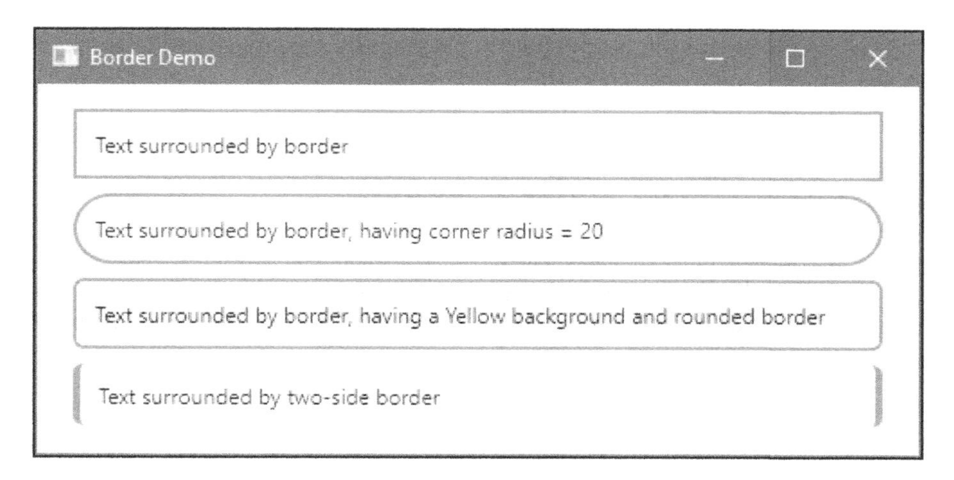

How it works...

The `BorderThickness` property accepts an integer value to draw a border around the control. The property `BorderBrush` adds a color to it. You can use `SolidColorBrush`, `GradientColorBrush`, or any other brush type. The first `Border` control adds a thin `2px` border around the text.

In the second example, the `CornerRadius` property has been set to `20` to add a 20-degree curve around the corners of the `Border` control.

The third example has a border with a background brush to wrap the `TextBlock` control. You can club both the `BorderThickness`, `BorderBrush`, and `Background` properties together to give such a look. Notice the small corner radius of `5` degrees!

In the fourth example, we have provided a border to two sides of the text. The value of `BorderThickness` can have `1`, `2`, or `4` double values. The four doubles (`BorderThickness="5, 3, 5, 4"` or `BorderThickness="5 3 5 4"`) describes the `Left`, `Top`, `Right`, and `Bottom` sides in the same order.

When you provide two double values (`BorderThickness="5, 3"` or `BorderThickness="5 3"`), the first value describes `Left` and `Right`; the second value describes `Top` and `Bottom`, respectively. To provide thickness of the same amount in all the sides, assign only one double to the property (`BorderThickness="5"`).

Creating a scrollable panel

The `ScrollViewer` controls enable scrolling functionality in a WPF application and help you to host other controls. When there are more contents available to show, but the viewable area is smaller than that, `ScrollViewer` is used to help the user to scroll through the content.

In this recipe, we will learn how to use a `ScrollViewer` inside a WPF application.

Getting ready

Let's open Visual Studio and create a project named `CH03.ScrollViewerDemo`. Be sure to create the project based on the WPF application template.

How to do it...

It's a quick step to surround a panel or control using the `ScrollViewer`. Perform the following steps to add a scrolling functionality to an `image` control:

1. Inside the project, add an image named `demoImage.jpg`.
2. Open the `MainWindow.xaml` file from **Solution Explorer**.
3. Now replace the existing `Grid` with a `ScrollViewer`.
4. Add an image pointing to the `demoImage.jpg` file, as follows:

```
<ScrollViewer HorizontalScrollBarVisibility="Auto"
              VerticalScrollBarVisibility="Auto">
    <Image Source="demoImage.jpg" />
</ScrollViewer>
```

5. Run the application and you will see the following window with an image inside a `ScrollViewer`:

6. Use the scroll bars to scroll left-right and/or up-down to see the entire image.

How it works...

`ScrollViewer` exposes two major properties—`HorizontalScrollBarVisibility` and `VerticalScrollBarVisibility`. Both represent an enumeration named `ScrollBarVisibility`, having four values:

- **Visible**: When the property is set to `ScrollBarVisibility.Visible`, the scroll bar will be visible all the time.
- **Hidden**: When the property is set to `ScrollBarVisibility.Hidden`, the scrollbar will not be visible on screen and the user will not be able to scroll to see the complete content.
- **Disabled**: When it is set to `ScrollBarVisibility.Disabled`, the scrollbars will be disabled.
- **Auto**: This is often used to make the scrolling thumbs visible only when they are needed. For this, set the property to `ScrollBarVisibility.Auto`.

Docking controls using the DockPanel

`DockPanel` makes it easier to dock UI elements in the left, right, top, or bottom of the screen. This is often useful, mainly when you want to divide the window into specific areas. For example, a status bar is always kept at the bottom of the window, whereas a menu or a toolbar resides at the topmost position of the window.

This recipe will help you to learn how to dock child elements in an application window.

Getting ready

Let's begin with a new project. Open Visual Studio and create a project named `CH03.DockPanelDemo`, based on the available WPF application template.

How to do it...

Perform the following steps to add a `DockPanel` with a few labels docked into it:

1. From **Solution Explorer**, navigate to the project and open `MainWindow.xaml`.
2. Replace the existing `Grid` panel with a `DockPanel` control.
3. Now add five labels inside it and dock them in various sides of the window.
4. Here's the complete XAML code for reference:

```
<DockPanel>
    <Label Content="Button (DockPanel.Dock='Right')"
           Background="YellowGreen"
           Margin="4" Padding="4"
           DockPanel.Dock="Right"/>
    <Label Content="Button (DockPanel.Dock='Top')"
           Background="GreenYellow"
           Margin="4" Padding="4"
           DockPanel.Dock="Top"/>
    <Label Content="Button (DockPanel.Dock='Bottom')"
           Background="SkyBlue"
           Margin="4" Padding="4"
           DockPanel.Dock="Bottom"/>
    <Label Content="Button (DockPanel.Dock='Left')"
           Background="Orange"
           Margin="4" Padding="4"
           DockPanel.Dock="Left"/>
    <Label Content="Button (None)"
```

```
                    Background="Pink"
                    Margin="4" Padding="4"/>
        </DockPanel>
```

5. Let's run the application. You will see that the labels are positioned in different sides of the window, as shown in the following screenshot:

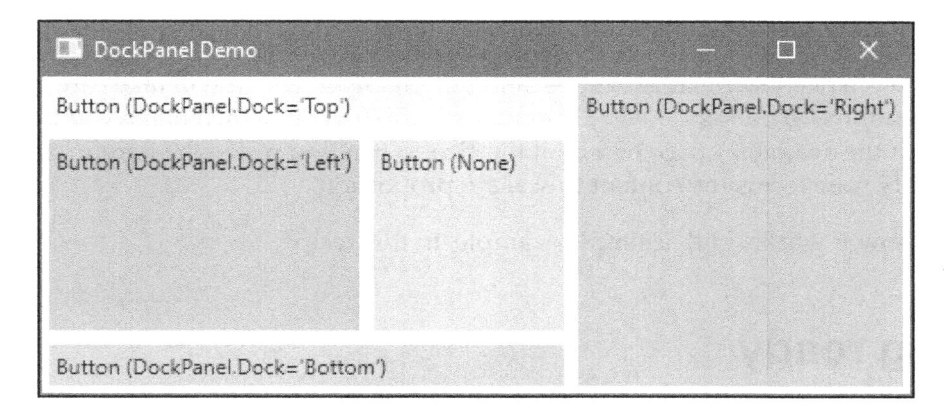

How it works...

The `DockPanel.Dock` property determines the position of the element, based on the relative order. The property is of type `Dock` enumeration and it accepts the following values—`Dock.Left`, `Dock.Right`, `Dock.Top`, and `Dock.Bottom`. If you don't specify the property, by default, the first element will be docked to the left and the other elements will take the remaining space.

In the preceding example, the labels are added inside the `DockPanel` in the following order, having the `DockPanel.Dock` property set to `Right`, `Top`, `Bottom`, and `Left`, respectively. The last label does not specify any `Dock` property and hence it takes the remaining space to accommodate itself inside it.

There's more...

In a `DockPanel`, ordering of dock matters most. If you change the order of the example that we have created previously, you will notice how the `DockPanel` changes the position of the added labels.

Rescaling UI elements using a ViewBox

When you are building an application, you don't know the screen resolution of the system where the application will be running. If you design the UI considering small or standard resolution in mind, the UI controls will look very small in a high-resolution monitor. If you do the reverse, with big screens in mind, the user won't see the parts of the screen, if executed on a low-resolution monitor.

Hence, there is a need to create an auto-scaling mechanism, which will take care of different screen resolutions. `ViewBox` is a very popular control in WPF, which helps you to scale the content to fit the available space based on the size. When you resize the parent, it automatically transforms the content to scale in proportion.

Let's learn how it works, with a simple example, in this recipe.

Getting ready

Open your Visual Studio IDE and create a new WPF application project named `CH03.ViewBoxDemo`.

How to do it...

Please perform the following steps:

1. Open the `MainWindow.xaml` file from **Solution Explorer**.
2. Set a smaller size of the `Window`. Let's set its height to `120` and width to `400`.
3. Replace the existing `Grid` panel with a `ViewBox`.
4. Add text inside it, using the `TextBlock` control as follows:

```
<Viewbox>
    <TextBlock Text="This is a text, inside a ViewBox"
               Margin="10"/>
</Viewbox>
```

5. Run the application. You will see the following output:

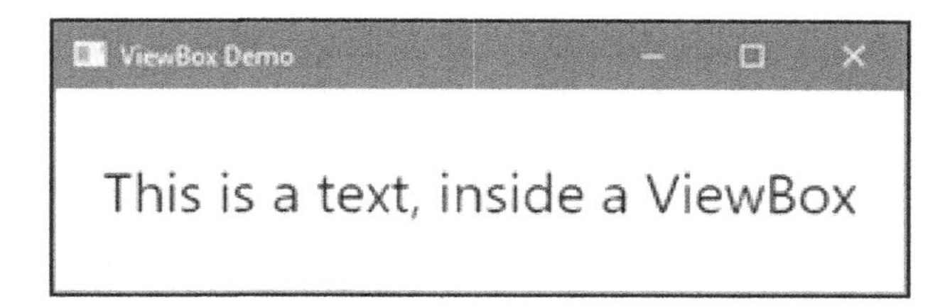

6. Now resize the window and you will see that the text is automatically scaled based on the size of the window:

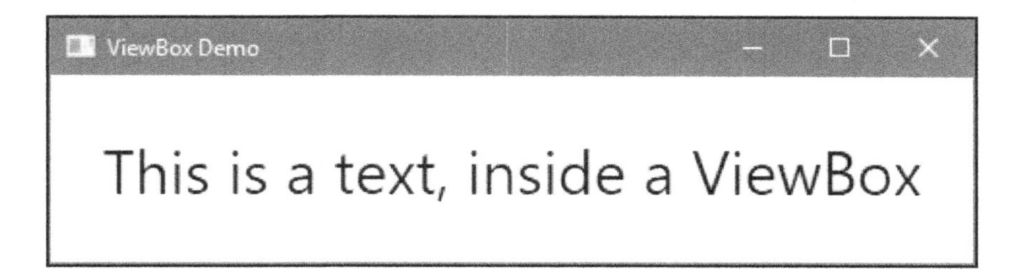

How it works...

The `ViewBox` provides you with a way to adjust the content of a window automatically, based on the resolution of the screen. When you resize the `ViewBox`, it automatically adjusts the size and the relative position of the contents to fit on the screen.

In the preceding example, the size of the window is set to `400x120`. The window has a `TextBlock` control with a text string, wrapped in a `ViewBox`. When you resize the window, the content also resizes by applying scale transform.

But if the aspect ratio of the `ViewBox` window does not fit in proportion, you will see a white space either at the left and right or top and bottom of the content.

There's more...

The `ViewBox` control provides two properties to stretch the content. Those are `Stretch` and `StretchDirection`. When you don't specify the `Stretch` property to a `ViewBox`, it uses the default value for `Stretch`, which is `Uniform`.

When the `Stretch` property is set to `Uniform`, and the `ViewBox` does not match the aspect ratio of the content, it adds a white margin to it. It can be either at the top and bottom or at the left and right sides:

```
<Viewbox Stretch="Uniform">
    <TextBlock Text="This is a text, inside a ViewBox"
     Margin="10"/>
</Viewbox>
```

When it is set to `Fill`, it causes the content to completely fill the space without obeying the aspect ratio. Thus, you may see a distortion in the UI:

```
<Viewbox Stretch="Fill">
    <TextBlock Text="This is a text, inside a ViewBox"
     Margin="10"/>
</Viewbox>
```

When you set the `Stretch` property to `UniformToFill`, it maintains the original aspect ratio and fills the window completely. You will not see any distortion in the UI:

```
<Viewbox Stretch="UniformToFill">
    <TextBlock Text="This is a text, inside a ViewBox"
     Margin="10"/>
</Viewbox>
```

If you don't want to resize the content, set the `Stretch` property to `None`. When you set it as `None`, and resize the window to enlarge, the content will not scale and will remain in its original state surrounded by white space:

```
<Viewbox Stretch="None">
    <TextBlock Text="This is a text, inside a ViewBox"
     Margin="10"/>
</Viewbox>
```

The `StretchDirection` property of the `ViewBox` is used to tell the `ViewBox` to stretch the content based on the `Stretch` property. When the `Stretch` property is set to `None`, the `StretchDirection` property has no effect.

When `StretchDirection` is set to `UpOnly` or `DownOnly`, the content will be resized upward or downward, based on the `ViewBox` size. When it is set to `Both`, the content will be resized in both directions.

Creating a tabbed layout

To accommodate more content in a window layout, tabbed user interfaces are mostly used. They allow users to open multiple pages in a single window. For example, most of the recent internet browsers use tabbed interface to let the user open multiple web pages simultaneously in a single window.

WPF provides `TabControl` to create the tabbed layout. In this recipe, we will learn the basics of tab interfaces, with a simple example to let you understand how it works.

Getting ready

To get started, make sure that you have opened Visual Studio IDE. Now create a new project named `CH03.TabControlDemo`, based on the available WPF application project template.

How to do it...

Let's create the UI interface to host a very basic tab control with a few tab items inside it. Perform the following steps:

1. From the **Solution Explorer** window, open the `MainWindow.xaml` file.
2. Inside the default `Grid` panel, add the `TabControl` with two `TabItem` controls as shown in the following code:

```
<Grid>
    <TabControl>
        <TabItem Header="Tab 1">
            <TextBlock Text="You have selected 'Tab 1'"
             FontSize="30" Margin="4"/>
        </TabItem>
        <TabItem Header="Tab 2">
            <TextBlock Text="You have selected 'Tab 2'"
             FontSize="30" Margin="4"/>
        </TabItem>
    </TabControl>
</Grid>
```

3. Now run this application and you will see the following UI, which contains two tabs inside it:

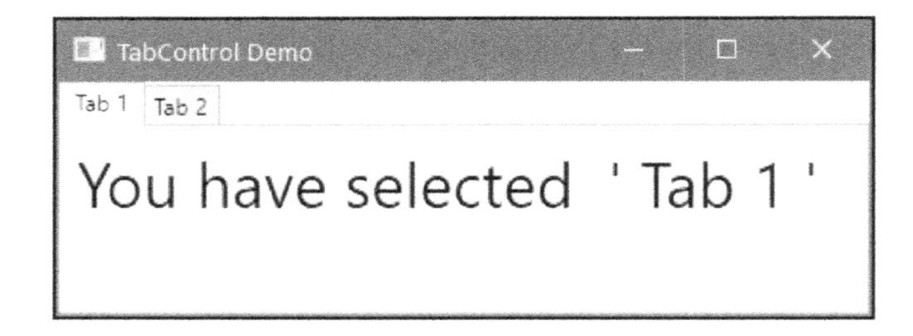

4. Close the application and return to the XAML editor to add another `TabItem` inside the `TabControl`. Let's change the template of the header to contain UI elements other than the plain text. Copy the following XAML after the second tab:

```
<TabItem>
    <TabItem.Header>
        <StackPanel Orientation="Horizontal">
            <Ellipse Width="10" Height="10"
              Fill="Green" Margin="0 1 8 0"/>
            <TextBlock Text="Tab 3"/>
        </StackPanel>
    </TabItem.Header>
    <Border Background="ForestGreen"
            Margin="4">
        <TextBlock Text="You have selected 'Tab 3'"
                   FontSize="30" Foreground="White"/>
    </Border>
</TabItem>
```

5. Now run the application once again and navigate to the third tab. You will see the following UI in the screen:

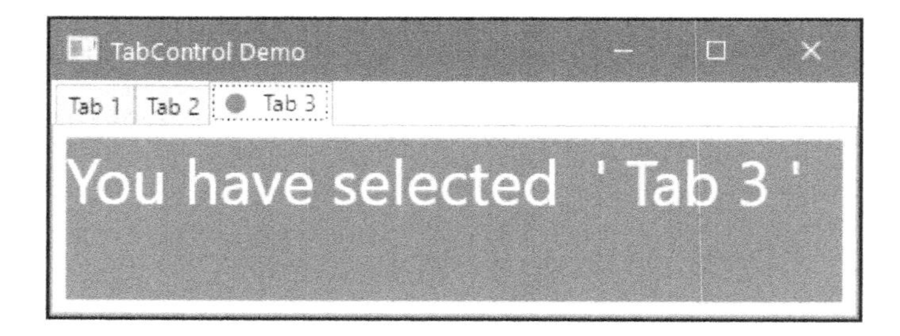

How it works...

The `TabControl` derives from `Selector` to provide you an `ItemsControl` to host elements inside it. You can host only `TabItem` controls, which are actually `HeaderedContentControl` to provide a `Header` to each of the items.

The `Header` property is of type object, which will allow you to put any content inside it, be it a plain text or a different UI element.

In the preceding example, the first two `TabItem` controls contain plain text as headers, whereas the third `TabItem` contains many different `UIElement` to give its header a customized look. When you switch from one tab to another, you will see its associated content, which you can programmatically access through its `Content` property.

Dynamically adding/removing elements in a panel

So far, we have seen how to add static elements/contents in a `Panel` control. But it's not always useful, mainly when you are retrieving data from the backend and populating in the UI or dynamically based on the user interaction.

This recipe will discuss this topic. As all the panels perform similarly to add/remove elements, with a slight difference on the positioning, we will be demonstrating it with a simple `Canvas`.

Getting ready

To begin with the coding, let's create a WPF application project first. Open Visual Studio and create a new project named `CH03.DynamicPanelDemo`.

How to do it...

Let's add a `Canvas` panel inside the window, and dynamically add squares at the current cursor position when the user clicks the `Canvas` panel. Perform the following steps:

1. Open the `MainWindow.xaml` page and replace the default `Grid` panel with a `Canvas`.
2. Give it a name. In our example, let's give the name as `canvasPanel`.
3. Set a background to the canvas panel and register a `MouseLeftButtonDown` event to it. Here's the complete XAML code, for reference:

```
<Window x:Class="CH03.DynamicPanelDemo.MainWindow"
   xmlns=
        "http://schemas.microsoft.com/winfx/
        2006/xaml/presentation"
        xmlns:x="http://schemas.microsoft.com/winfx/2006/xaml"
        Title="Dynamic Panel Demo"
        Height="300" Width="500">
    <Canvas x:Name="canvasPanel"
            Background="LightGoldenrodYellow"
            MouseLeftButtonDown="OnMouseLeftButtonDown"/>
</Window>
```

4. Now open its associated code-behind file `MainWindow.xaml.cs` and implement the event. Alternatively, you can place the cursor on top of the event name and press *F12* to generate the event and navigate to it directly.
5. Inside the `OnMouseLeftButtonDown` event implementation, retrieve the current cursor position and place the element at the same position on the canvas, where the user clicked. Here's the code implementation:

```
private void OnMouseLeftButtonDown(object sender,
 MouseButtonEventArgs e)
{
    var mousePosition = e.GetPosition(canvasPanel);
    var square = new Rectangle
    {
        Width = 50,
        Height = 50,
        Fill = new SolidColorBrush(Colors.Green),
        Opacity = new Random().NextDouble()
    };

    // set the position of the element
    Canvas.SetLeft(square,
```

```
         mousePosition.X - square.Width / 2);
        Canvas.SetTop(square,
         mousePosition.Y - square.Height / 2);

        // add the element on the Canvas
        canvasPanel.Children.Add(square);
    }
```

6. Let's run the application. You will see a blank window with the same background color that we have set on the `Canvas`.
7. Randomly click on the `Canvas` area and you will see the squares popping up on the screen, at the same place where you are left-clicking on the `Canvas`. The UI will look as follows:

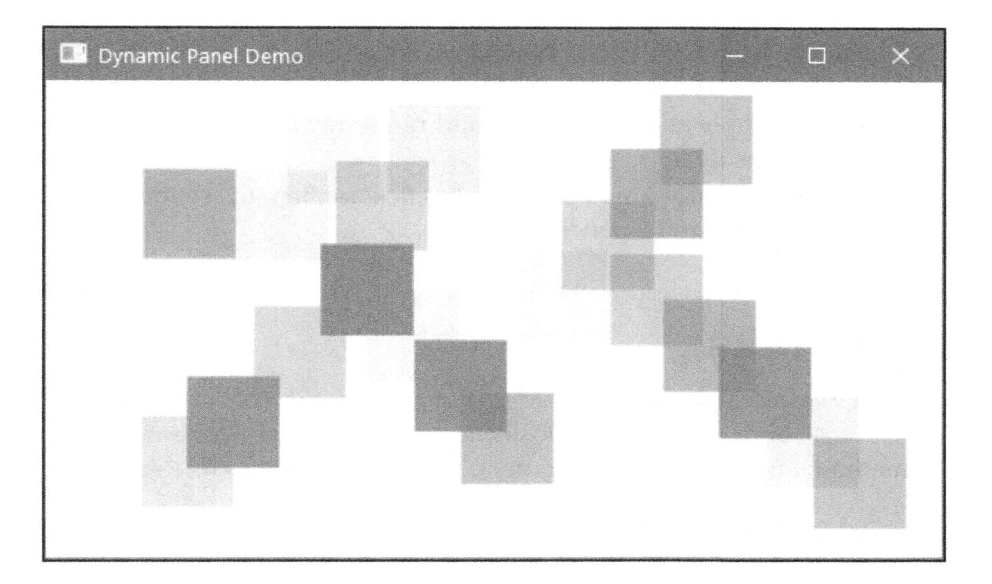

8. To remove the elements from the square, let's register a `MouseRightButtonDown` event in the `Canvas` panel present in the XAML. Close the running application and replace the entire content of the `MainWindow.xaml` page with the following one:

```
<Window x:Class="CH03.DynamicPanelDemo.MainWindow"
  xmlns=
   "http://schemas.microsoft.com/winfx/2006/xaml/presentation"
    xmlns:x="http://schemas.microsoft.com/winfx/2006/xaml"
    Title="Dynamic Panel Demo"
    Height="300" Width="500">
```

```
        <Canvas x:Name="canvasPanel"
                Background="LightGoldenrodYellow"
                MouseLeftButtonDown="OnMouseLeftButtonDown"
                MouseRightButtonDown="OnMouseRightButtonDown"/>
</Window>
```

9. Now navigate to the `MainWindow.xaml.cs` file to add the associated event implementation. Add the following snippet inside the class:

```
private void OnMouseRightButtonDown(object sender,
 MouseButtonEventArgs e)
{
    if (e.Source is UIElement square)
    {
        canvasPanel.Children.Remove(square);
    }
}
```

10. Run the application once again and randomly click inside the `Canvas` to add the squares inside it.
11. Once the squares are in place, right-click on them to see the clicked ones disappear from the panel.

How it works...

Every panel exposes a property named `Children` to hold a collection of `UIElement` as `UIElementCollection`. To dynamically add an element to `UIElementCollection`, use its `Add` method; and to remove an element, pass the element to its `Remove` method.

In the preceding example, when the user left-clicks on the `Canvas`, the `e.GetPosition` method provides the coordinate position (`X`, `Y`) of the click, relative to the panel where it was clicked. The `Canvas.SetLeft` and `Canvas.SetTop` methods are used to position the created element relative to the panel and then are added to it.

Similarly, to delete the element from the panel, the `e.Source` property is used to retrieve the element where the user right-clicked. If it is not `null`, remove it from the `Canvas` by calling the `Remove` method.

There's more...

The coordinate positions are used to place elements in a `Canvas` panel. When you want to place an item in a `Grid`, set the `Row` and `Column` while placing it. For `StackPanel`, `WrapPanel`, and `UniformGrid` panels, you won't need to specify any other property as those will be stacked automatically.

The following example shows you how to dynamically add an element in a `Grid`, at a specific cell position, specified by the `Row` and `Column` index:

```
// set the Row and Column to place the element
Grid.SetRow(element, rowIndex);
Grid.SetColumn(element, columnIndex);

// add the element to the Grid
gridPanel.Children.Add(element);
```

If you want to span the element to multiple rows and multiple columns, you can do so by calling the `Grid.SetRowSpan` and `Grid.SetColumnSpan` methods, as shown in the following code:

```
Grid.SetRowSpan(element, noOfRowsToSpan);
Grid.SetColumnSpan(element, noOfColumnsToSpan);
```

Implementing the drag and drop feature

When you want to provide a rich experience to the user, you may want to use the dragging and dropping feature. You may also want to add a drag and drop feature in your application to access a local resource to upload it to the server.

In this recipe, we will learn the basics of drag and drop implementation in WPF by using a simple example.

Getting ready

Open Visual Studio and create a new WPF application named `CH03.DragAndDropDemo`.

How to do it...

Let's perform the following steps to create a few elements inside a window and provide the option to drag and drop from one panel to the other:

1. First, open `MainWindow.xaml` and replace the existing `Grid` with a `StackPanel`. Set its `Orientation` property to `Horizontal`.
2. Add two `WrapPanel` inside it and set their `Width`, `Margin`, `ItemHeight`, and `ItemWidth` properties.
3. Give a name to both panels. Let's name the first wrap panel `sourcePanel` and the second wrap panel `targetPanel`. We will be using these name later from the code, while accessing them.
4. Add a few labels to the first wrap panel. Set their `Content`, `Background`, and other text formatting properties. Here's the complete markup code:

```
<StackPanel Orientation="Horizontal">
    <WrapPanel x:Name="sourcePanel"
               ItemHeight="60" ItemWidth="100"
               Width="200" Margin="4"
               Background="LightGoldenrodYellow">
        <Label Content="Item 1"
               Background="Olive" Margin="4"
               Foreground="White" FontSize="22" />
        <Label Content="Item 2"
               Background="Olive" Margin="4"
               Foreground="White" FontSize="22" />
        <Label Content="Item 3"
               Background="Olive" Margin="4"
               Foreground="White" FontSize="22" />
        <Label Content="Item 4"
               Background="Olive" Margin="4"
               Foreground="White" FontSize="22" />
        <Label Content="Item 5"
               Background="Olive" Margin="4"
               Foreground="White" FontSize="22" />
    </WrapPanel>
    <WrapPanel x:Name="targetPanel"
               ItemHeight="60" ItemWidth="100"
               Width="200" Margin="4"
               Background="OldLace">
    </WrapPanel>
</StackPanel>
```

5. If you run this application, you will see two panels on the screen. As shown in the following screenshot, one of them will have five labels (**Item 1** - **Item 5**) and the other will be empty:

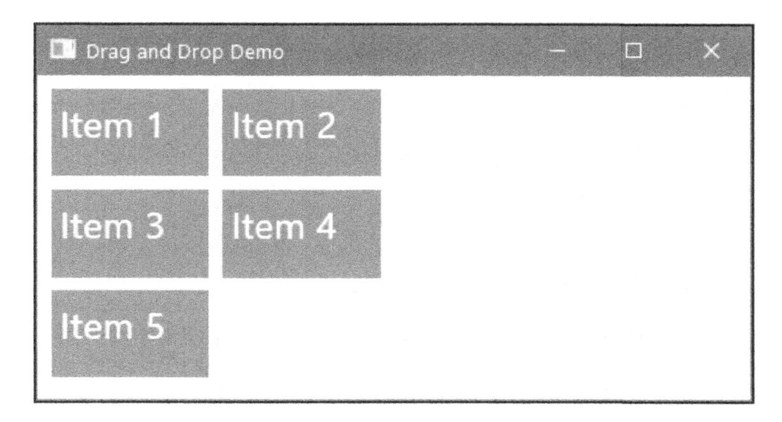

   If you now drag any element from the left panel and try to drop it to the right panel, you will see that it won't work. We have not yet added the drag and drop support.

6. To add the dragging support to the first wrap panel (`sourcePanel`), register its `MouseLeftButtonDown` event property in the XAML as follows:

```
<WrapPanel x:Name="sourcePanel"
           ItemHeight="60" ItemWidth="100"
           Width="200" Margin="4"
           Background="LightGoldenrodYellow"
           MouseLeftButtonDown="OnDrag">
```

7. An `OnDrag` event, registered in XAML, needs to be implemented in the code behind the file. Open `MainWindow.xaml.cs` and add the following event implementation, which will add the dragging support to the `sourcePanel`:

```
private void OnDrag(object sender, MouseButtonEventArgs e)
{
    if (e.Source is UIElement draggedItem)
    {
        DragDrop.DoDragDrop(draggedItem,
                            draggedItem,
                            DragDropEffects.Move);
    }
}
```

8. Now we need to enable the second wrap panel (`targetPanel`) as a droppable target and set its `AllowDrop` property to `True`.
9. Also register its `Drop` event property, so that we can perform the `drop` operation. Here's the entire mark-up for the second panel:

```
<WrapPanel x:Name="targetPanel"
           ItemHeight="60" ItemWidth="100"
           Width="200" Margin="4"
           Background="OldLace"
           AllowDrop="True"
           Drop="OnDrop">
    <!-- This is the DROP Target -->
</WrapPanel>
```

10. Now we need to implement the body of the `OnDrop` event to perform the desired `drop` operation. Navigate to `MainWindow.xaml.cs` once again and add the following code:

```
private void OnDrop(object sender, DragEventArgs e)
{
    var draggedData = e.Data;
    if (draggedData.GetData(draggedData.GetFormats()[0])
                            is UIElement droppedItem)
    {
        sourcePanel.Children.Remove(droppedItem);
        targetPanel.Children.Add(droppedItem);
    }
}
```

11. Let's run the application now. The same screen will appear with two panels. The first panel (left) will have a few elements in it. Position your cursor on one of them, click it to drag it to the other panel (right), and release it there. You will see that the item will be removed from the first and added to the right panel, as shown in the following screenshot:

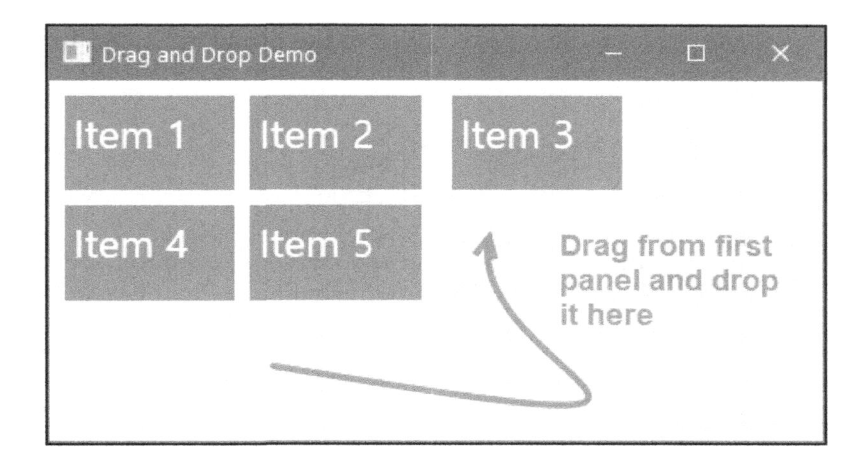

How it works...

The `AllowDrop="True"` property prepares the panel as drop enabled. When you start a drag by clicking on the element, the `DragDrop.DoDragDrop` method written in the `OnDrag` event initiates the drag and drop operation. It takes the first parameter as a reference to the dependency object, that is, the source of the data being dragged. The second parameter is the data object that contains the data being dragged. And the last parameter is a value that specifies the final effect (`DragDropEffects`) of the operation.

In the preceding example, when the element is dropped to the drop target, the dragged data retrieved from the `DragEventArgs` parameter value is first removed from the source and then added to the drop target.

There's more...

Based on your drag-and-drop requirement, you can change the effects by specifying the proper enum value of the `DragDropEffects`. The effects can be of six types:

- **None**: When specified, the drop target will not accept any data and the cursor will change to an unavailable icon:

- **Copy**: When specified, the data is copied to the drop target and during the `drop` operation on the target, the cursor will look as follows:

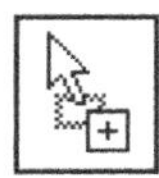

- **Move**: When specified, the data from the source is moved to the drop target. During the `drop` operation, the cursor will change to the following:

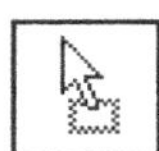

- **Link**: When specified, the data from the source is linked to the drop target. During the `drop` operation on the target, the cursor will change to the following:

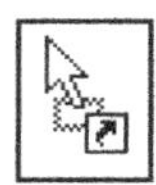

- **Scroll**: When specified, it defines whether the scrolling is about to start or currently happening on the drop target.
- **All**: When specified, the data is copied and scrolled to the drop target after being removed from the source.

4
Working with Data Bindings

In this chapter, we will cover the following recipes:

- Working with CLR properties and UI notifications
- Working with dependency properties
- Working with attached properties
- Data binding to an object
- Data binding to a collection
- Element-to-element data binding
- Sorting data in a `DataGrid` control
- Grouping data in a `DataGrid` control
- Filtering data in a `DataGrid` control
- Using static bindings
- Using value converters
- Using multi-value converters

Introduction

Data binding is a technique to establish a connection between the UI of the application and the business logic in order to have proper data synchronization between them. Though you can directly access UI controls from code behind to update their content, data binding has become the preferred way to update the UI layer for its automatic notification system.

To make data binding work in WPF applications, both sides of the binding must provide a change notification to the other side. The source property of a data binding can be a .NET CLR property or a dependency property, but the target property must be a dependency property, as shown here:

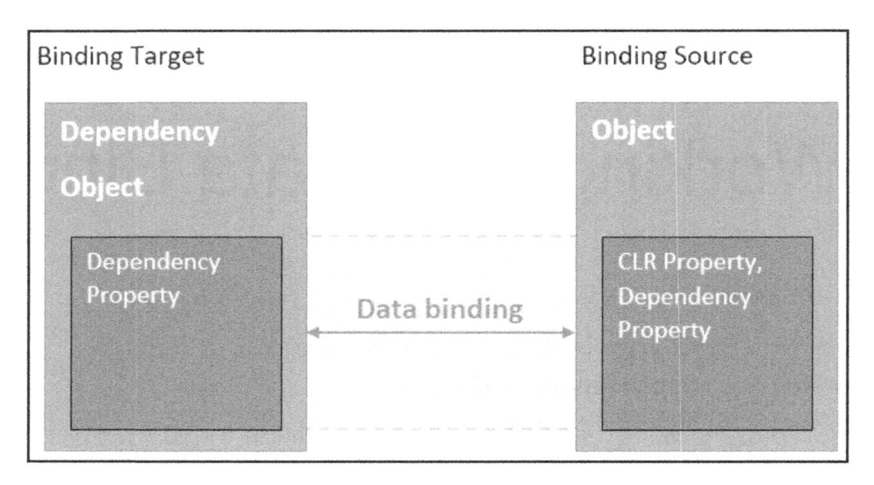

Data binding is typically done in XAML using the `{Binding}` markup extension. In this chapter, we are going to learn more about the WPF data binding mechanism by exploring a few recipes.

Working with CLR properties and UI notifications

The CLR properties are just a wrapper around the private variables to expose getters and setters to retrieve and assign the value of a variable. You can use these normal CLR properties in data binding, but the automatic UI notifications are not possible by default, unless you create the notification mechanism.

In this recipe, we will learn how to perform data binding with CLR properties and then learn how to trigger notifications from the code to automatically update the UI when the value changes.

Getting ready

To get started with data binding with normal CLR properties, open your Visual Studio IDE and create a new WPF application project called `CH04.NotificationPropertiesDemo`.

How to do it...

Perform the following steps to create CLR properties that send notifications to the UI:

1. Open the `MainWindow.xaml` file and give the window a name. For example, name the current window `window` by adding the following syntax to the `Window` tag: `x:Name="window"`.
2. Now divide the default `Grid` into a few rows and columns. Copy the following XAML markup inside your `Grid` panel:

```
<Grid.ColumnDefinitions>
    <ColumnDefinition Width="Auto"/>
    <ColumnDefinition Width="15"/>
    <ColumnDefinition Width="*"/>
</Grid.ColumnDefinitions>
<Grid.RowDefinitions>
    <RowDefinition Height="Auto"/>
    <RowDefinition Height="Auto"/>
    <RowDefinition Height="10"/>
    <RowDefinition Height="Auto"/>
</Grid.RowDefinitions>
```

3. Once the grid has been divided into rows and columns, let's add a few text and button controls inside it. Place these at proper cells, as shared in the following code:

```
<!-- Row 0 -->
<TextBlock Text="Your department"
           Grid.Row="0" Grid.Column="0"/>
<TextBlock Text=":"
           Grid.Row="0" Grid.Column="1"
           HorizontalAlignment="Center"/>
<TextBlock Text="{Binding Department, ElementName=window}"
           Margin="0 2"
           Grid.Row="0" Grid.Column="2"/>

<!-- Row 1 -->
<TextBlock Text="Your name"
           Grid.Row="1" Grid.Column="0"/>
```

```
<TextBlock Text=":"
           Grid.Row="1" Grid.Column="1"
           HorizontalAlignment="Center"/>
<TextBox Text="{Binding PersonName, ElementName=window,
Mode=TwoWay}"
         Margin="0 2"
         Grid.Row="1" Grid.Column="2"/>

<!-- Row 3 -->
<StackPanel Orientation="Horizontal"
            HorizontalAlignment="Center"
            Grid.Row="3" Grid.Column="0"
            Grid.ColumnSpan="3">
    <Button Content="Submit"
            Margin="4" Width="80"
            Click="OnSubmit"/>
    <Button Content="Reset"
            Margin="4" Width="80"
            Click="OnReset"/>
</StackPanel>
```

4. Now open the code behind the file `MainWindow.xaml.cs` and add two CLR properties named `Department` and `PersonName` inside it. The first property (`Department`) always returns a constant string, whereas the second property (`PersonName`) can accept values from the user. Here's the complete code:

```
public string Department { get { return "Software Engineering";
} }

private string personName;
public string PersonName
{
    get { return personName; }
    set { personName = value; }
}
```

5. In the code-behind class, add the following event implementations:

```
private void OnSubmit(object sender, RoutedEventArgs e)
{
    MessageBox.Show("Hello " + PersonName);
}

private void OnReset(object sender, RoutedEventArgs e)
{
    PersonName = string.Empty;
}
```

6. Now build and run the application. As shown in the following screenshot, enter your name in the `TextBox` and click the **Submit** button. A message will be shown to the user with the entered name:

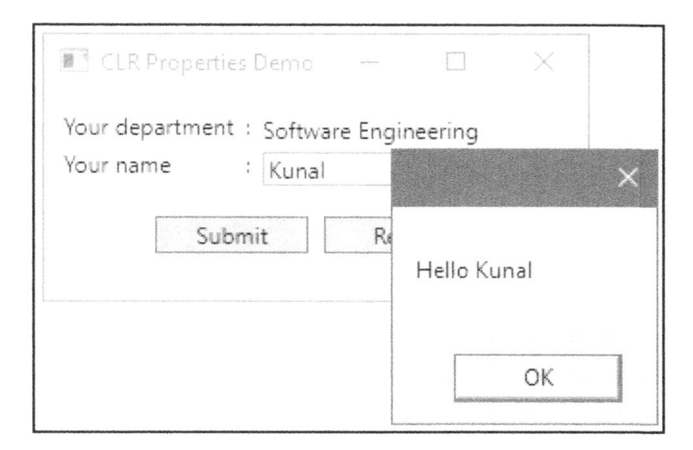

7. Now click on the **Reset** button and watch the behavior. Even though the code has been written to set the property with an empty string, the UI was not modified:

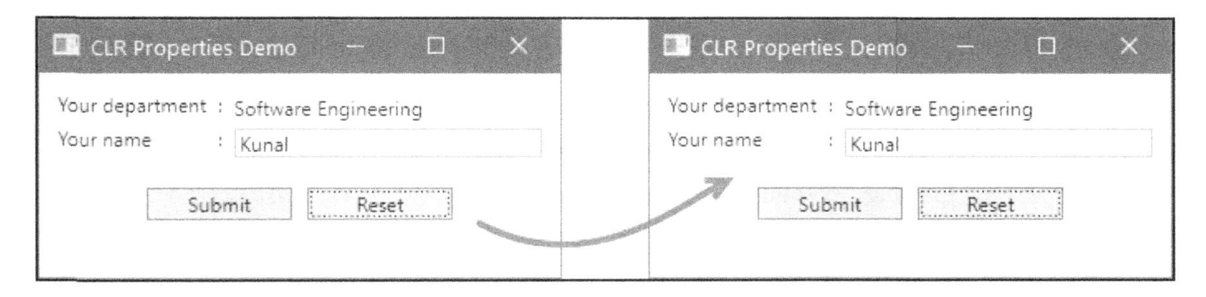

8. To send a notification to the UI when there is a change in the associated property, you need to implement the `INotifyPropertyChanged` interface, present in the `System.ComponentModel` namespace. Open the `MainWindow.xaml.cs` file and add the`INotifyPropertyChanged` interface as defined here:

```
public partial class MainWindow : Window,
INotifyPropertyChanged
```

9. You need to add the following `using` namespace declaration to resolve the build issue:

```
using System.ComponentModel;
```

10. Add the following `PropertyChanged` event implementation inside the class:

```
public event PropertyChangedEventHandler PropertyChanged;
public void OnPropertyChanged(string propertyName)
{
    //in C# 7.0 and above
    PropertyChanged?.Invoke(this, new
PropertyChangedEventArgs(propertyName));

    //prior to C# 7.0
    //var handler = PropertyChanged;
    //if (handler != null)
    //{
    //    handler(this, new
PropertyChangedEventArgs(propertyName));
    //}
}
```

11. Now notify the framework to update the UI when there is a change in the property value. Modify the existing implementation of the `PersonName` property to give a call to the `OnPropertyChanged` event, passing the name of the property as follows:

```
private string personName;
public string PersonName
{
    get { return personName; }
    set
    {
          personName = value;
          OnPropertyChanged("PersonName");
    }
}
```

If you are using C# 6 and above, you can remove the hardcoded strings by using the `nameof` operator.

12. Build and run the application once again. Enter your name in the input box and hit the **Submit** button. You will see the message box mentioning the entered name.
13. Close the message box and hit the **Reset** button. You will see that the text in the `TextBox` initialized to an empty string:

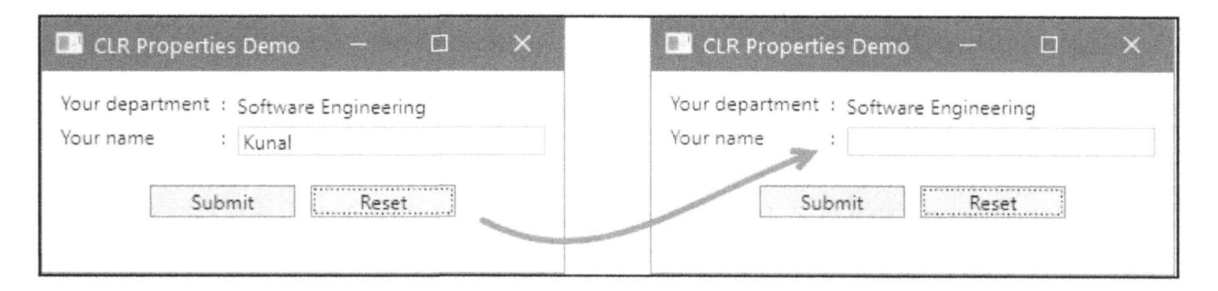

How it works...

In the preceding example, the `Department` property has a data binding with the `TextBlock` control and thus the associated `TextBlock` displays the text returned by the property. Similarly, the `PersonName` property has a data binding with a `TextBox` control. As the data binding has been made to the `Text` property of the `TextBlock` (with `TwoWay` mode), it automatically updates the associated property when the user changes it in the UI.

So, when you hit the **Submit** button, the `OnSubmit` event triggers, and it directly reads the `PersonName` property instead of fetching the text from the UI by accessing the `Text` property of the `TextBox` control.

When you hit the **Reset** button, the `OnReset` event triggers and it sets the `PersonName` property to an empty string. But the UI does not change. This is because the CLR property does not have a notification mechanism to automatically update the UI when a value change happens to it.

To overcome this, WPF uses the `INotifyPropertyChanged` interface, which defines a `PropertyChanged` event to automatically push the UI notification to update the elements in the UI thread. In the example, when you set the `PersonName` property, the `OnPropertyChanged` event fires from the property `setter` and notifies the UI that the `PersonName` has been modified. The UI then sets the value based on the property value.

There's more...

Data binding can be unidirectional (source > target or target > source) or bidirectional (source < > target), known as **mode**, and is defined in four categories:

- **OneTime**: This type of data binding mode causes the source property to initialize the target property. After the binding gets generated, no notifications will be triggered. You should use this type of data binding where the source data does not change.
- **OneWay**: This type of binding causes the source property to automatically update the target property. The reverse is not possible here. For example, if you want to display a label/text in the UI based on some condition in the code behind or business logic, you need to use `OneWay` data binding as you don't need to update back the property from the UI.
- **TwoWay**: This type of binding is a bidirectional data binding, where both the source property and the target property can send update notifications. This is applicable for editable forms where the user can change the value displayed in the UI. For example, the `Text` property of a `TextBox` control supports this type of data binding.
- **OneWayToSource**: This is another unidirectional data binding, which causes the target property to update the source property (the reverse of `OneWay` binding). Here, the UI sends notification to the context and no notification is generated if the context changes.

Here's a simple diagram, describing how the various data binding modes work:

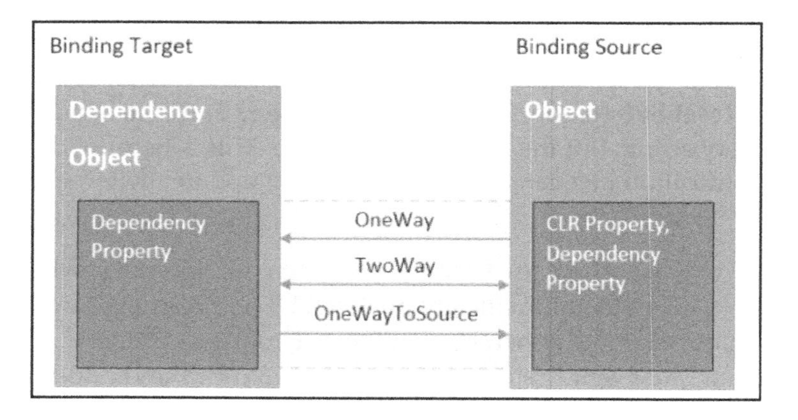

Working with dependency properties

WPF provides a set of services which can be used to extend the CLR properties to provide additional benefits such as automatic UI notifications in the ecosystem. To implement the dependency property, the class must be inherited from the `DependencyObject` class.

A CLR property reads directly from the private member of the class, whereas a dependency property is stored in a dictionary of keys and values provided by the base class. As the dependency property stores the property only when it is changed, it uses a great deal less memory and is accessed faster.

To easily create a dependency property in a `.cs` file, use the `propdp` code snippet. In any class file which is inherited from `DependencyObject`, write `propdp` followed by *TAB* to generate the structure of it. Navigate using the *TAB* key and change the type, name, owner, and metadata details.

In this recipe, we will learn how to use a dependency property to automatically notify the UI that a change has been made in the property value, which will reduce the burden of defining the `PropertyChanged` event from the `INotifyPropertyChanged` interface.

Getting ready

Let's open the Visual Studio IDE and create a project named `CH04.DependencyPropertyDemo`. Make sure that you have selected the WPF application type as a project template. We will use the same example that we have created in the previous recipe.

How to do it...

Perform the following steps to create a dependency property, bind it to the UI, and send notifications from the code:

1. From **Solution Explorer**, open the `MainWindow.xaml` page and use the same UI design that we have used in the previous example. Copy the following XAML markup and replace the content of the `MainWindow.xaml` file:

```
<Window x:Class="CH04.DependencyPropertyDemo.MainWindow"
xmlns="http://schemas.microsoft.com/winfx/2006/xaml/presentatio
n" xmlns:x="http://schemas.microsoft.com/winfx/2006/xaml"
        x:Name="window"
```

```
        Title="Dependency Properties Demo" Height="150"
        Width="300">
    <Grid Margin="10">
        <Grid.ColumnDefinitions>
            <ColumnDefinition Width="Auto"/>
            <ColumnDefinition Width="15"/>
            <ColumnDefinition Width="*"/>
        </Grid.ColumnDefinitions>
        <Grid.RowDefinitions>
            <RowDefinition Height="Auto"/>
            <RowDefinition Height="Auto"/>
            <RowDefinition Height="10"/>
            <RowDefinition Height="Auto"/>
        </Grid.RowDefinitions>

        <!-- Row 0 -->
        <TextBlock Text="Your department"
                   Grid.Row="0" Grid.Column="0"/>
        <TextBlock Text=":"
                   Grid.Row="0" Grid.Column="1"
                   HorizontalAlignment="Center"/>
        <TextBlock Text="{Binding Department,
                          ElementName=window}"
                   Margin="0 2"
                   Grid.Row="0" Grid.Column="2"/>

        <!-- Row 1 -->
        <TextBlock Text="Your name"
                   Grid.Row="1" Grid.Column="0"/>
        <TextBlock Text=":"
                   Grid.Row="1" Grid.Column="1"
                   HorizontalAlignment="Center"/>
        <TextBox Text="{Binding PersonName,
                        ElementName=window, Mode=TwoWay}"
                 Margin="0 2"
                 Grid.Row="1" Grid.Column="2"/>

        <!-- Row 3 -->
        <StackPanel Orientation="Horizontal"
                    HorizontalAlignment="Center"
                    Grid.Row="3" Grid.Column="0"
                    Grid.ColumnSpan="3">
            <Button Content="Submit"
                    Margin="4" Width="80"
                    Click="OnSubmit"/>
            <Button Content="Reset"
                    Margin="4" Width="80"
                    Click="OnReset"/>
```

```
        </StackPanel>
    </Grid>
</Window>
```

2. Now open the code-behind file and add the following CLR property inside the class. We don't need to make it a dependency property, as the value is always constant here:

```
public string Department
{
    get { return "Software Engineering"; }
}
```

3. Now, inside the class, write `propdp` and press the *TAB* key twice. It will create the structure of the property system. By default, `int` will be highlighted. Replace it with `string`.
4. Press the *TAB* key once again and rename the property name from `MyProperty` to `PersonName`.
5. Press the *TAB* key once again to change the focus to the `ownerclass` name parameter of the `Register` method. Rename it to the class name of the owner. In our case, it is `MainWindow`.
6. Press the *TAB* key once again to move the focus to the property metadata. Here you can set the default value of the property. By default, `0` (zero) is selected. Change it to `string.Empty`. Here's the complete implementation of our dependency property, named `PersonName`:

```
public string PersonName
{
    get { return (string)GetValue(PersonNameProperty); }
    set { SetValue(PersonNameProperty, value); }
}

public static readonly DependencyProperty PersonNameProperty =
    DependencyProperty.Register("PersonName",
          typeof(string), typeof(MainWindow),
          new PropertyMetadata(string.Empty));
```

7. Let's add the following event implementations for the **Submit** and **Reset** buttons inside the `MainWindow` class:

```
private void OnSubmit(object sender, RoutedEventArgs e)
{
    MessageBox.Show("Hello " + PersonName);
}
```

```
private void OnReset(object sender, RoutedEventArgs e)
{
    PersonName = string.Empty;
}
```

8. As the code change has been done, let's build and run the application. You will see the application window pop up on the screen. Enter a name in the provided input box and click **Submit**. The message box will be shown, including the entered text:

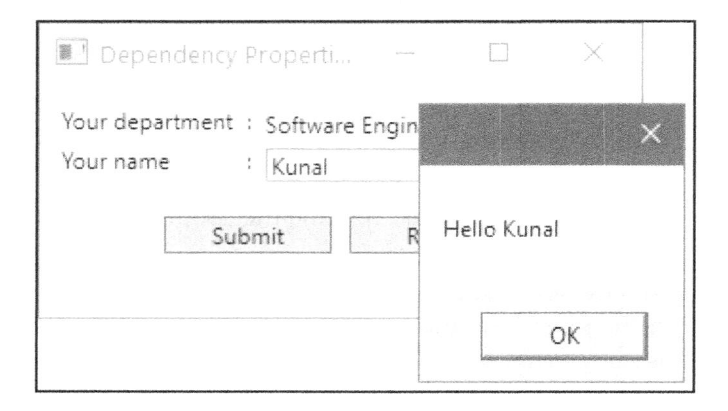

9. Click on the **Reset** button. This will clear the text inside the input box (`TextBox` control):

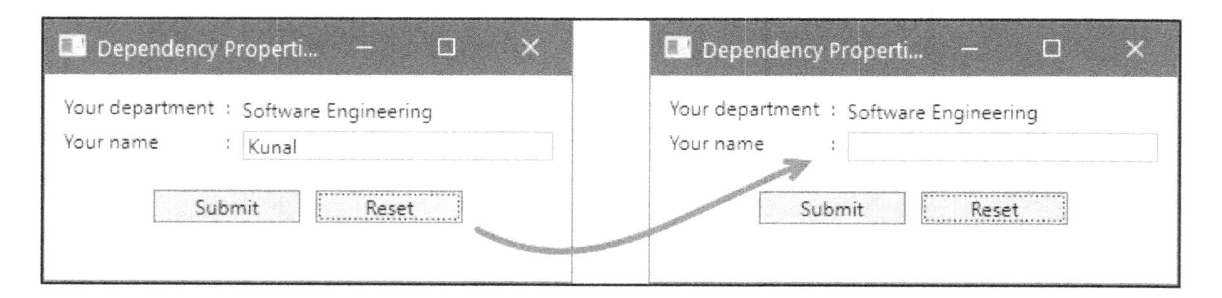

How it works...

The getters and setters work differently in dependency properties. Rather than returning or setting a value from/to its private field (`CLR` property), the dependency property calls `GetValue(DependencyProperty)` or `SetValue(DependencyProperty, value)` from its base class `DependencyObject`. In our example, the name of the dependency property is `PersonNameProperty`.

The static `Register` method of the `DependencyProperty` class takes a few parameters to create the `dependency` property. The first parameter that it takes is the actual `name` of the property. The second parameter is the `type` of the property, the third is the `owner type` which is basically the class name where the `dependency` property is going to create. The next parameter it takes is the metadata information, where you can assign the default value of the property. Here is the complete code:

```
public static readonly DependencyProperty PersonNameProperty =
    DependencyProperty.Register("PersonName",
                        typeof(string),
                        typeof(MainWindow),
                        new PropertyMetadata(string.Empty));
```

When you set a value from the XAML, by providing a data binding with the property, it sets the value which you can pick from an accessible place. Similarly, when you set the value from code, it automatically notifies the UI that a change has been made and performs the same change in the UI. Thus, it reduces the burden of implementation of the `INotifyPropertyChanged` interface and its associated `PropertyChanged` event.

There's more...

The property metadata of the `Register` method can take one to three arguments to it. The first one is the default value that we have seen earlier. The second one is the `PropertyChangedCallback`, which is to be called by the property system whenever the effective value of the property changes. The third one is the `CoerceValueCallback`, which is to be called whenever the property system calls `System.Windows.DependencyObject.CoerceValue` method against the property.

Most of the time, the property metadata is created using one to two parameters defining the default value and the property changed callback. Let's learn with an example demonstrating how this can be written:

```
public string PersonName
{
    get { return (string)GetValue(PersonNameProperty); }
    set { SetValue(PersonNameProperty, value); }
}

public static readonly DependencyProperty PersonNameProperty =
    DependencyProperty.Register("PersonName", typeof(string),
    typeof(MainWindow), new PropertyMetadata(string.Empty,
    OnPropertyChangedCallback));

private static void OnPropertyChangedCallback(DependencyObject d,
DependencyPropertyChangedEventArgs e)
{
}
```

Here, the `OnPropertyChangedCallback` event will be raised whenever you change the value of the property. You can take further action based on the event trigger. You can also call other non-static members from the callback event by accessing the `DependencyObject` "`d`".

You can also validate a dependency property before submitting it to the property system. The fifth parameter of the `Register` method accepts a delegate, called `ValidateValueCallback`. You can implement it to validate the effective value of the `dependency` property. If the value has been validated properly, it will return `true`; if not it will be treated as invalid and will return `false`.

Working with attached properties

An attached property is a kind of `dependency` property which is intended to be used as a global property type and is settable on any object. It does not have conventional property wrapper and can still be used to receive notification of a value change. Unlike dependency properties, attached properties are not defined in the same class where they are used.

The main purpose of using attached properties is to allow different child elements to specify unique values of a property, which is actually defined in a parent element. For example, you can use `Grid.Row`, `Grid.Column` in any child elements of the `Grid` panel. Similarly, the `Canvas.Left`, `Canvas.Top` attached properties are used in any child elements of a `Canvas` panel.

In this recipe, we will learn how to create an `Attached` property and perform the operation from a different class.

Getting ready

First, create a new project called `CH04.AttachedPropertyDemo`, based on the WPF application project type.

How to do it...

Now, perform the following steps to create the `Attached` property named `SelectOnFocus`, to a `TextBox` control, which when enabled will select the text on focus change by using the *TAB* key:

1. Open **Solution Explorer**, right-click on the project, and add a new class by following the **Add | Class...** context menu path. Give the class the name `TextBoxExtensions`.
2. Open the `TextBoxExtensions.cs` file and add the following `using` namespace inside the class file:

```
using System.Windows;
using System.Windows.Controls;
```

3. Inside the class body, type `propa` and press *TAB* twice. This will create the structure of the attached dependency property and the keyboard focus will move to the `property` type, which is `int` by default. Change it to `bool`.
4. Press *TAB* again to select `MyProperty`. Rename it to `SelectOnFocus`.
5. *TAB* it once again to select the `ownerclass` and change it to `TextBoxExtensions`.

6. Press *TAB* to set the property metadata. Set the default value to `false`. Set the `PropertyChangedCallback` parameter to `OnSelectOnFocusChanged`. Here's the complete code, including the callback event:

```
public static bool GetSelectOnFocus(DependencyObject obj)
{
    return (bool)obj.GetValue(SelectOnFocusProperty);
}

public static void SetSelectOnFocus(DependencyObject obj,
 bool value)
{
    obj.SetValue(SelectOnFocusProperty, value);
}

public static readonly DependencyProperty SelectOnFocusProperty
      = DependencyProperty.RegisterAttached("SelectOnFocus",
        typeof(bool),
        typeof(TextBoxExtensions),
        new PropertyMetadata(false, OnSelectOnFocusChanged));

private static void OnSelectOnFocusChanged(DependencyObject d,
DependencyPropertyChangedEventArgs e)
{
    if (d is TextBox textBox)
    {
        textBox.GotFocus += (s, arg) =>
        {
            textBox.SelectAll();
        };
    }
}
```

7. Now open the `MainWindow.xaml` file and replace the existing XAML content with the following one:

```
<Window x:Class="CH04.AttachedPropertyDemo.MainWindow"
xmlns="http://schemas.microsoft.com/winfx/2006/xaml/presentatio
n"
        xmlns:x="http://schemas.microsoft.com/winfx/2006/xaml"
        xmlns:extensions="clr-
        namespace:CH04.AttachedPropertyDemo"
        Title="Attached Property Demo"
        Height="150" Width="340">
    <StackPanel Margin="15">
        <TextBox Text="Normal TextBox Control"
                 Width="200" Height="30"
```

```
                         Margin="4"/>
            <TextBox Text="Select On Focus: Enabled"
extensions:TextBoxExtensions.SelectOnFocus="True"
                         Width="200" Height="30"
                         Margin="4"/>
        </StackPanel>
</Window>
```

8. Now, build and run the application.
9. Focus on the first textbox. It won't have any selection by default. Press *TAB* to move the focus to the second textbox. The entire text of the textbox will be highlighted. Press *TAB* again to focus on the first textbox. There won't be any selection, as the said attached property was added to the second textbox only.

How it works...

Dependency properties are registered by calling the `DependencyProperty.Register` method, whereas attached properties are registered by calling the `DependencyProperty.RegisterAttached` method. It takes four parameters—the actual name of the property, type of the property, type of the owner, and property metadata.

When you set the property to the control, as an attached property (`extensions:TextBoxExtensions.SelectOnFocus="True"`, in our example), in the XAML, it registers it to the WPF property system during the instance load and fires the `PropertyChangedCallback` defined in the `RegisterAttached` method. In the preceding example, the `OnSelectOnFocusChanged` event will be called, which will register the `GotFocus` event on the associated `TextBox` control to perform the selection of the text.

Instead of a specific control such as `TextBox`, you can use `UIElement` to generalize the association. In this way, you can apply it to any control, by registering the attached property in the XAML.

Data binding to an object

Up to this point, we have learned how to create CLR properties with the `INotifyPropertyChanged` interface; we have also learned about the dependency property with a simple data type. There are many instances when you need to bind an object of some class/model to an UI and display its associated properties necessary.

In this recipe, we will learn how to do object data binding to show and retrieve information to and from the user.

Getting ready

Let's open the Visual Studio instance and create a new project named `CH04.ObjectBindingDemo`. Make sure you select the proper WPF application project type.

How to do it...

Perform the following steps to create the model and dependency property, and bind the data to the UI controls, so that, when a change happens in underlying data, it automatically reflects in the UI:

1. First, we need to create a data model. From **Solution Explorer**, right-click on the project and navigate to the context menu entry **Add | Class...** and create a class file called `Person.cs`.
2. Replace the content of the `Person` class with the following three properties:

```
public class Person
{
    public string Name { get; set; }
    public string Blog { get; set; }
    public int Experience { get; set; }
}
```

3. Go to **Solution Explorer** once again and double-click to open the `MainWindow.xaml.cs` file. Create a dependency property named `PersonDetails` and set its data type as `Person`. Also, set its default value to `null` as shared here:

```
public Person PersonDetails
{
    get { return (Person)GetValue(PersonDetailsProperty); }
    set { SetValue(PersonDetailsProperty, value); }
}

public static readonly DependencyProperty PersonDetailsProperty
=
```

```
        DependencyProperty.Register("PersonDetails",
                            typeof(Person),
                            typeof(MainWindow),
                            new PropertyMetadata(null));
```

4. Just after the `InitializeComponent()` method call, inside the constructor of the `MainWindow` class, initialize the `PersonDetails` property and set it as the `DataContext` of the selected class as follows:

```
PersonDetails = new Person
{
    Name = "Kunal Chowdhury",
    Blog = "http://www.kunal-chowdhury.com",
    Experience = 10
};

DataContext = PersonDetails;
```

5. Now, as the backend code is ready, let's open the `MainWindow.xaml` file to design the UI and do the data binding with our model.
6. Replace the existing `Grid` panel with the following XAML markup:

```
<StackPanel Margin="10">
    <TextBlock Margin="0 0 0 20"
               TextWrapping="Wrap">
        <Run Text="{Binding Name}"/> blogs at <Hyperlink
NavigateUri="{Binding Blog}"><Run Text="{Binding
Blog}"/></Hyperlink>, and has <Run Text="{Binding
Experience}"/> years of experience.
    </TextBlock>
    <StackPanel Orientation="Horizontal">
        <TextBlock Text="Enter years of experience:"/>
        <TextBox Text="{Binding Experience, Mode=TwoWay}"
                 Margin="10 0" Width="50"/>
    </StackPanel>
</StackPanel>
```

7. Now compile the project and run the application. You will see the following UI:

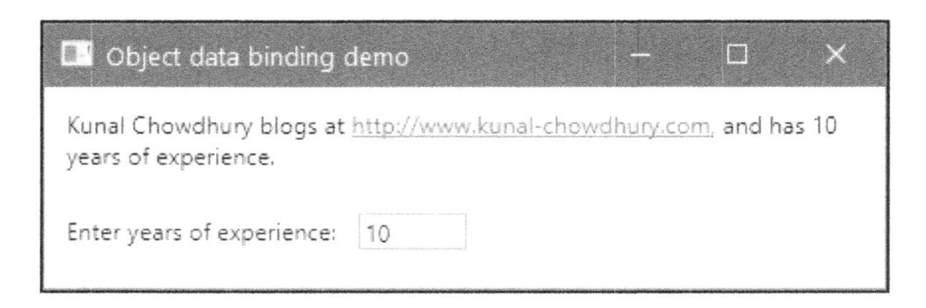

How it works...

The UI of the application has two `TextBlock` controls to represent the data and one `TextBox` to get input from the user. In the first `TextBlock` control, we have multiple `<Run/>` commands to bind the data value from the `Person` class, along with other static texts and a `Hyperlink` to create a link. The data of the UI class is bound to the `DataContext`, which is `PersonDetails` in our case. The properties binded to the UI come from the `Person` class, which is the data type of the `PersonDetails` dependency property.

The `TextBox` control is bound to the `Experience` property, which is again bound to the third `Run` command of the first `TextBlock`. Hence, it is showing `10` in both places. Now change the value of the `TextBox` control to `15` and press the *TAB* key to change the focus. This will trigger the `TextChanged` event of the `TextBox` and modify the underlying property named `Experience`. Due to its nature, the notification will be automatically sent to the UI and the `TextBlock` control will get updated as follows:

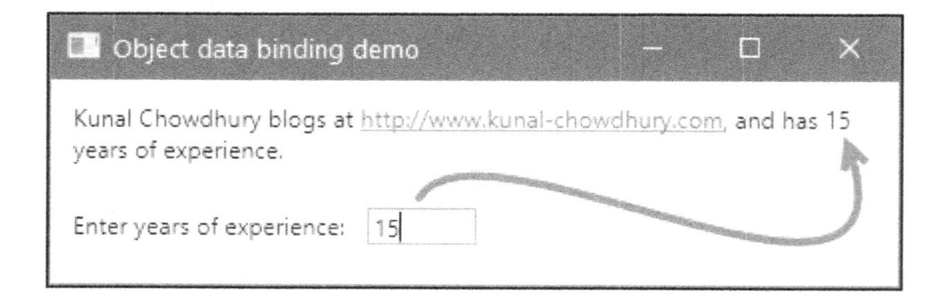

Data binding to a collection

As we learned about object data binding to show a single object on the UI, let's begin with binding a collection of data objects in a UI to display all the records to the user. We will discuss it in this recipe.

Getting ready

Open a Visual Studio instance and create a new project called `CH04.CollectionBindingDemo`. Make sure you use the WPF application project template.

How to do it...

Perform the following steps to create a collection data model and bind it to the UI, using a `DataGrid` control:

1. Inside the **Solution Explorer**, right-click on the project. From the context menu, navigate to **Add | Class...** to create a class file named `Employee.cs`.
2. Open the `Employee.cs` file and replace the class implementation with the following code:

```
public class Employee
{
    public string FirstName { get; set; }
    public string LastName { get; set; }
    public string Department { get; set; }
}
```

3. Navigate to the `MainWindow.xaml.cs` file and add the following `using` statement to define `ObservableCollection` inside the class:

```
using System.Collections.ObjectModel;
```

4. Inside the `MainWindow` class implementation, create a dependency property named `Employees`, of type `ObservableCollection<Employee>`, as shared here:

```
public ObservableCollection<Employee> Employees
{
    get { return
```

```
(ObservableCollection<Employee>)GetValue(EmployeesProperty); }
    set { SetValue(EmployeesProperty, value); }
}

public static readonly DependencyProperty EmployeesProperty =
    DependencyProperty.Register("Employees",
              typeof(ObservableCollection<Employee>),
              typeof(MainWindow),
              new PropertyMetadata(null));
```

5. Now, just after the `InitializeComponent()` method call inside the constructor, write the following code block:

```
Employees = new ObservableCollection<Employee>
{
    new Employee
    {
        FirstName = "Kunal", LastName ="Chowdhury",
        Department="Software Division"
    },

    new Employee
    {
        FirstName = "Michael", LastName ="Washington",
        Department="Software Division"
    },

    new Employee
    {
        FirstName = "John", LastName ="Strokes",
        Department="Finance Department"
    },
};

dataGrid.ItemsSource = Employees;
```

6. Now open the `MainWindow.xaml` file and a `DataGrid` control inside the default `Grid` panel. Create three columns and bind their values to the `FirstName`, `LastName`, and `Department` properties of the `Employee` object. Make sure you set the `AutoGenerateColumns` property of the `DataGrid` to `False`. Here's the complete XAML markup:

```
<Grid>
    <DataGrid x:Name="dataGrid"
              AutoGenerateColumns="False">
        <DataGrid.Columns>
```

```
                    <DataGridTextColumn Header="First Name"
                             Binding="{Binding FirstName}"/>
                    <DataGridTextColumn Header="Last Name"
                             Binding="{Binding LastName}"/>
                    <DataGridTextColumn Header="Department"
                             Binding="{Binding Department}"/>
                </DataGrid.Columns>
            </DataGrid>
        </Grid>
```

7. Now build the project and run the application. You will see the following screen, along with the data inside a `DataGrid`:

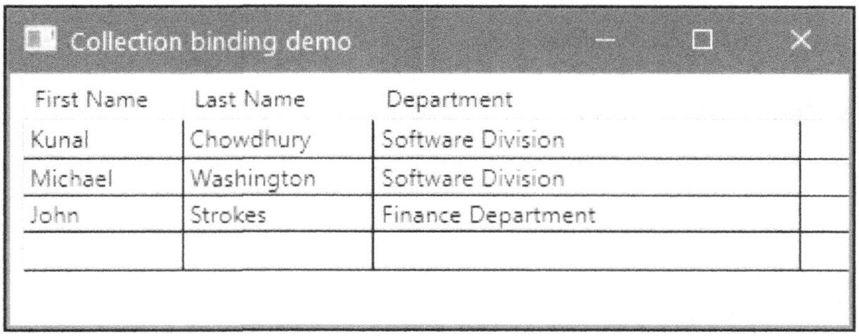

Collection binding demo

First Name	Last Name	Department
Kunal	Chowdhury	Software Division
Michael	Washington	Software Division
John	Strokes	Finance Department

How it works...

When you bind a collection of objects to a `DataGrid`, it creates data grid rows for each object present in the collection. The column defines the properties exposed by the object.

When the `AutoGenerateColumns` property of the `DataGrid` is set to `True` (default), it automatically creates the columns based on the property list. In this example, we have set the `AutoGenerateColumns` property to `False` and defined the individual columns explicitly. Using this method, you can define which column to show or hide. Once you set the collection to the `ItemsSource` property of the `DataGrid`, it populates the rows and columns accordingly.

There's more...

You can also define the binding in the XAML. To do this, first open the MainWindow.xaml.cs and remove the line dataGrid.ItemsSource = Employees;. Now, go to the MainWindow.xaml file and give the window a name (x:Name="window"). Now, set the ItemsSource property of the DataGrid control, as mentioned here:

```
<DataGrid ItemsSource="{Binding Employees, ElementName=window}"
```

Let's run the application once again, by building the project. You will see the same output on the screen.

Element-to-element data binding

In the last few recipes, we learned how to do object-to-element data binding. Though this is commonly used, you will need element-to-element data binding within the same XAML page to reduce the extra lines of codes in the code-behind file. In this recipe, we will learn how to do this.

Getting ready

First, launch your Visual Studio IDE and create a new WPF application project. Give it the name CH04.ElementToElementBindingDemo.

How to do it...

Now perform the following steps to design the UI with a TextBlock and a Slider control. Then we will bind the value of the slider control with the FontSize property of the TextBlock:

1. Open the MainWindow.xaml page and replace the default Grid panel with the following XAML markup:

```
<Grid>
    <TextBlock FontSize="{Binding Value,
     ElementName=fontSizeSlider}"
               Margin="4"
               HorizontalAlignment="Center"
               VerticalAlignment="Center">
```

```
            <Run Text="Font Size:"/>
            <Run Text="{Binding Value,
                   ElementName=fontSizeSlider}"/>
        </TextBlock>
        <Slider x:Name="fontSizeSlider"
                Minimum="10" Maximum="40" Value="20"
                LargeChange="5"
                VerticalAlignment="Bottom"
                Margin="10"/>
    </Grid>
```

2. Now build the project and run it. You will see the application UI on the screen, with a `TextBlock` and a `Slider` control.
3. Now increase or decrease the slider value to see the change in the UI, as shown in the following screenshot:

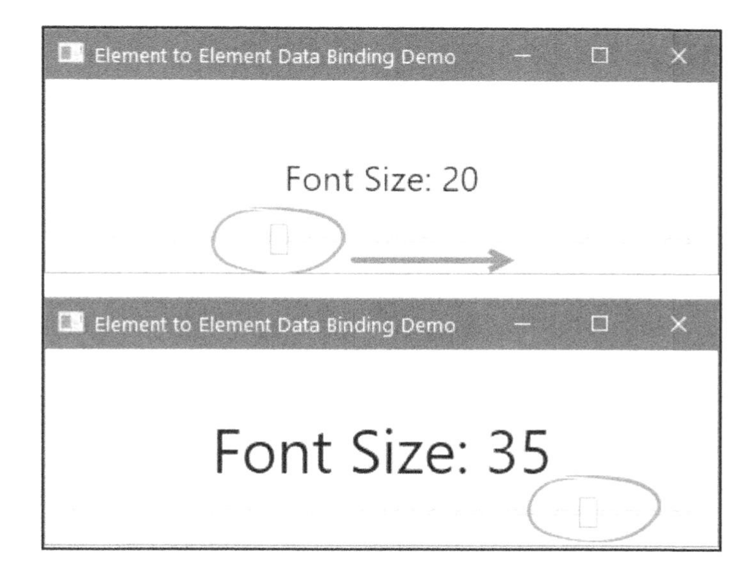

How it works...

When you drag the thumb of the slider, it increases or decreases the value of the slider control (`fontSizeSlider`, in our example). The `FontSize` property of the `TextBlock` control is directly bound to the value of the slider. So, when you drag the slider, based on the value, it increases or decreases the font size.

Similarly, the `TextBlock` has a few `Run` commands. The `Text` property of one of the `Run` commands is also binded with the slider value, and thus, you can see the number (current value of slider) on the screen as the font size.

Sorting data in a DataGrid control

The `DataGrid` control is used to show a number of records in a tabular format. Rows and columns are used to display the data. Along with other common functionalities, the WPF `DataGrid` control offers a default sorting feature. You can also customize this to handle it programmatically. In this recipe, we will learn how to add the sorting feature to `DataGrid` and trigger it on demand.

Getting ready

To get started with this recipe, open your Visual Studio editor and create a new WPF application project, called `CH04.DataGridSortDemo`.

How to do it...

Perform the following to create a data model, populate it, and bind it to a `DataGrid` in the UI. Later, add a `CheckBox` control to customize the sorting functionality:

1. To begin, right-click on the **Solution Explorer**, create a new class file named `Employee.cs`, by following the right-click context menu entry **Add** | **Class...**, and add a few properties in it:

```
public class Employee
{
    public string ID { get; set; }
    public string FirstName { get; set; }
    public string LastName { get; set; }
    public string Department { get; set; }
}
```

2. Open the `MainWindow.xaml.cs` file and add a dependency property, `Employees`, of type `ObservableCollection<Employee>`. Make sure you add the following namespaces, `System.Collections.ObjectModel` and `System.ComponentModel`, in order to resolve the required classes:

```
public ObservableCollection<Employee> Employees
{
    get { return (ObservableCollection<Employee>)
GetValue(EmployeesProperty); }
    set { SetValue(EmployeesProperty, value); }
}

public static readonly DependencyProperty
    EmployeesProperty =
    DependencyProperty.Register("Employees",
            typeof(ObservableCollection<Employee>),
            typeof(MainWindow),
            new PropertyMetadata(null));
```

3. Inside the constructor of the `MainWindow` class, initialize the `Employees` collection as follows:

```
Employees = new ObservableCollection<Employee>
{
    new Employee
    {
        ID = "EMP0001",
        FirstName = "Kunal", LastName = "Chowdhury",
        Department = "Software Division"
    },

    new Employee
    {
        ID = "EMP0002",
        FirstName = "Michael", LastName = "Washington",
        Department = "Software Division"
    },

    new Employee
    {
        ID = "EMP0003",
        FirstName = "John", LastName = "Strokes",
        Department = "Finance Department"
    },

    new Employee
```

```
        {
            ID = "EMP0004",
            FirstName = "Ramesh", LastName = "Shukla",
            Department = "Finance Department"
        }
};
```

4. Now open the `MainWindow.xaml` page and replace the default `Grid` panel with a `StackPanel`. Add a `DataGrid` control inside it and give it a name (let's say, `dataGrid`). Set its `AutoGenerateColumns` property to `False`.
5. Create four data grid columns of type `DataGridTextColumn` and create the data binding with the properties exposed from the `Employee` model. Here's the XAML code:

```
<StackPanel>
    <DataGrid x:Name="dataGrid"
      AutoGenerateColumns="False">
        <DataGrid.Columns>
            <DataGridTextColumn Header="EMP ID"
                      Binding="{Binding ID}"/>
            <DataGridTextColumn Header="First Name"
                      Binding="{Binding FirstName}"/>
            <DataGridTextColumn Header="Last Name"
                      Binding="{Binding LastName}"/>
            <DataGridTextColumn Header="Department"
                      Binding="{Binding Department}"/>
        </DataGrid.Columns>
    </DataGrid>
</StackPanel>
```

6. Now, as the data grid is already in place, assign the `Employees` collection as the `ItemsSource` property of the data grid. You can do this inside the `MainWindow.xaml.cs` file, just after initialization of the `Employees` collection:

```
dataGrid.ItemsSource = Employees;
```

7. If you run the application now, you will see a `DataGrid` control with the records that we have added into the collection. You will be able to sort the records by clicking on the column headers, which is the default functionality of the control:

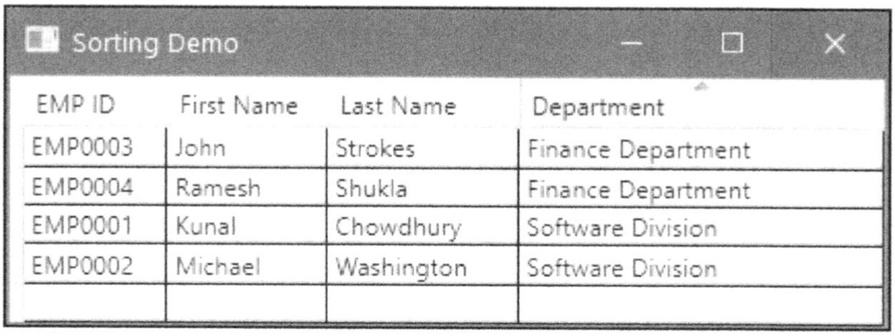

Sorting Demo

EMP ID	First Name	Last Name	Department
EMP0003	John	Strokes	Finance Department
EMP0004	Ramesh	Shukla	Finance Department
EMP0001	Kunal	Chowdhury	Software Division
EMP0002	Michael	Washington	Software Division

8. Now we need to add a `CheckBox` control in the UI to toggle the sort on demand. Let's do this for the `Department` column. Add the following `CheckBox` inside the `StackPanel`, just after the `DataGrid` control:

```
<CheckBox x:Name="sortByDepartment"
          Content="Sort by Department"
          HorizontalAlignment="Right"
          Margin="10"
          Click="OnSortByDepartment"/>
```

9. Navigate to the `MainWindow.xaml.cs` file once again, and add the following event inside the class:

```
private void OnSortByDepartment(object sender,
 RoutedEventArgs e)
{
    var cvs =
    CollectionViewSource.GetDefaultView(dataGrid.ItemsSource);
    if (cvs != null && cvs.CanSort)
    {
        cvs.SortDescriptions.Clear();

        if (sortByDepartment.IsChecked == true)
        {
            cvs.SortDescriptions.Add(
                new SortDescription("Department",
                ListSortDirection.Ascending));
        }
    }
}
```

10. Now run the application again. You will see a new checkbox, under the data grid. Toggle the selection (check status) and observe the behavior on the UI:

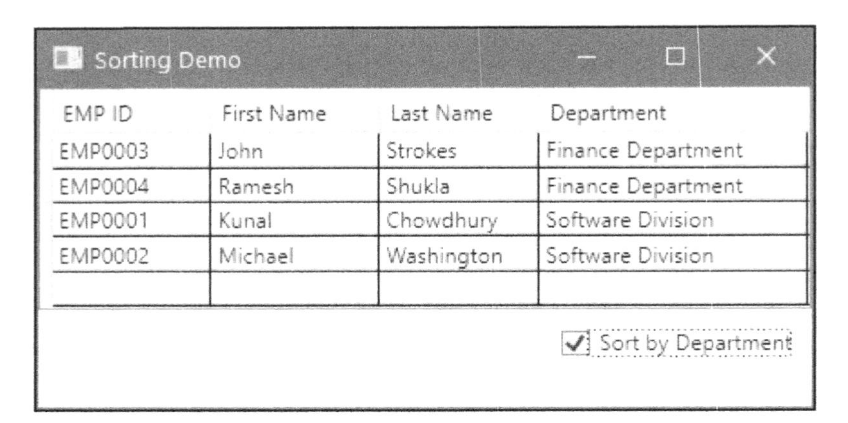

How it works...

Once the `OnSortByDepartment` event triggers, it gets the default view of the data grid and adds `SortDescription` to the `SortDescriptions` property of the default view instance. `SortDescription` takes the property name as the first argument. It defines the column for which you want to add the sort functionality. The second parameter is the `ListSortDirection`, which can be either `Ascending` or `Descending`.

It's not limited to a single `SortDescriptor`. You can add more based on your requirement. At any point of time, when you want to reset the view from the applied sort description, you can call the `SortDescriptions.Clear()` method on the view (in our case, it is `cvs`).

Grouping data in a DataGrid control

The `DataGrid` control also allows you to group the records by field name. In this recipe, we are going to learn how to implement this feature using the `PropertyGroupDescription`.

Getting ready

Let's begin with creating a new project called `CH04.DataGridGroupDemo`. Make sure you select the WPF application template while creating the project.

How to do it...

Perform the following steps to create groups while displaying records in `DataGrid`:

1. Inside the project, create the `Employee` model class and expose some properties, like we shared earlier in the *Sorting data in a DataGrid control* recipe.
2. Create the same dependency property (`Employees`, of type `ObservableCollection<Employee>`) in the `MainWindow.xaml.cs` file and populate the collection with some data records.
3. Now open the `MainWindow.xaml` file and add the attribute `x:Name="window"` to give the `Window` a name, so that we can perform element-to-element data binding.
4. Replace the default `Grid` panel with `StackPanel` and add a `DataGrid` control inside it.
5. Set the `ItemsSource` property of the `DataGrid` to bind the `Employees` collection, exposed from the code behind as a dependency property:

```
ItemsSource="{Binding Employees, ElementName=window}"
```

6. Set the `AutoGenerateColumns` of the data grid to `False`, as we are going to add the columns manually.
7. As shown in the following XAML snippet, add the four columns to the data grid.
8. Also, add a `CheckBox` control, just after the `DataGrid`, to enable it to apply grouping to the records by department name. Here's the complete XAML code:

```
<StackPanel>
    <DataGrid x:Name="dataGrid"
              ItemsSource="{Binding Employees,
                ElementName=window}"
              AutoGenerateColumns="False"
              CanUserAddRows="False">
        <DataGrid.Columns>
            <DataGridTextColumn Header="EMP ID"
                 Binding="{Binding ID}"/>
            <DataGridTextColumn Header="First Name"
                 Binding="{Binding FirstName}"/>
```

```
                <DataGridTextColumn Header="Last Name"
                     Binding="{Binding LastName}"/>
                <DataGridTextColumn Header="Department"
                     Binding="{Binding Department}"/>
            </DataGrid.Columns>
        </DataGrid>
        <CheckBox x:Name="groupByDepartment"
                  Content="Group by Department"
                  HorizontalAlignment="Right"
                  Margin="10"
                  Click="OnGroupByDepartment"/>
    </StackPanel>
```

9. As we are going to add grouping on the `DataGrid` records, we need to design the group style. Add the following snippet inside the `DataGrid`:

```
    <DataGrid.GroupStyle>
        <GroupStyle>
            <GroupStyle.ContainerStyle>
                <Style TargetType="{x:Type GroupItem}">
                    <Setter Property="Margin" Value="0,0,0,5"/>
                    <Setter Property="Template">
                        <Setter.Value>
                            <ControlTemplate TargetType="{x:Type
                             GroupItem}">
                                <Expander IsExpanded="True">
                                    <Expander.Header>
                                        <TextBlock Text="{Binding
                                         Path=Name}"
                                         Margin="5,0,0,0"/>
                                    </Expander.Header>
                                    <Expander.Content>
                                        <ItemsPresenter />
                                    </Expander.Content>
                                </Expander>
                            </ControlTemplate>
                        </Setter.Value>
                    </Setter>
                </Style>
            </GroupStyle.ContainerStyle>
        </GroupStyle>
    </DataGrid.GroupStyle>
```

10. Now we will need to add the `OnGroupByDepartment` event implementation. Open the `MainWindow.xaml.cs` and add the following code:

```
private void OnGroupByDepartment(object sender,
 RoutedEventArgs e)
{
    var cvs =
    CollectionViewSource.GetDefaultView(dataGrid.ItemsSource);
    if (cvs != null && cvs.CanGroup)
    {
        cvs.GroupDescriptions.Clear();

        if (groupByDepartment.IsChecked == true)
        {
            cvs.GroupDescriptions.Add(
              new PropertyGroupDescription("Department"));
        }
    }
}
```

11. Run the application now. You will see that the UI contains a `DataGrid` with some records.
12. Click on the checkbox that says **Group by Department** and observe the behavior:

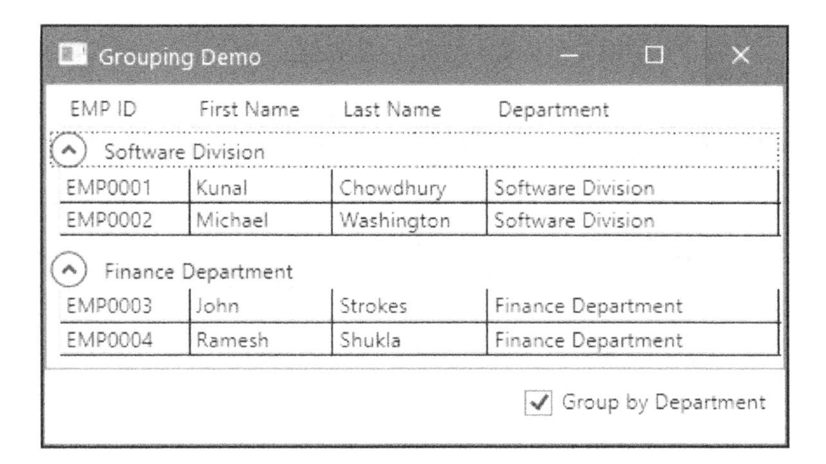

13. Uncheck the checkbox to revert the view to its original state.

How it works...

When you trigger the OnGroupByDepartment event, it retrieves the instance of the default view of DataGrid and applies the group description to it. The grouping applies based on the property name, passed to the PropertyGroupDescription, as shared here:

```
cvs.GroupDescriptions.Add(
        new PropertyGroupDescription("Department"));
```

Based on that, the group style applies to the data grid. The template contains an Expander control with the name of the column to be grouped as the Header:

```
<Expander IsExpanded="True">
    <Expander.Header>
        <TextBlock Text="{Binding Path=Name}" Margin="5,0,0,0"/>
    </Expander.Header>
    <Expander.Content>
        <ItemsPresenter />
    </Expander.Content>
</Expander>
```

You can now expand or collapse the groups and apply sorting or filtering to drill down the data. It helps to find the correct record easily.

There's more...

You can also modify the Expander Header to display the number of records inside a group. The ItemCount property can be used to display the record count. Modify the Expander.Header, as shared here, to customize it:

```
<Expander.Header>
    <StackPanel Orientation="Horizontal">
        <TextBlock Text="{Binding Path=Name}" Margin="5,0,0,0"/>
        <StackPanel Orientation="Horizontal">
            <TextBlock Margin="5,0,0,0"
                       Text="{Binding Path=ItemCount}"/>
            <TextBlock Text=" Item(s)"/>
        </StackPanel>
    </StackPanel>
</Expander.Header>
```

Now build and run the application again. Once the window loads, click on the checkbox to group the records by department name. Observe the item count in the expander, as shown here:

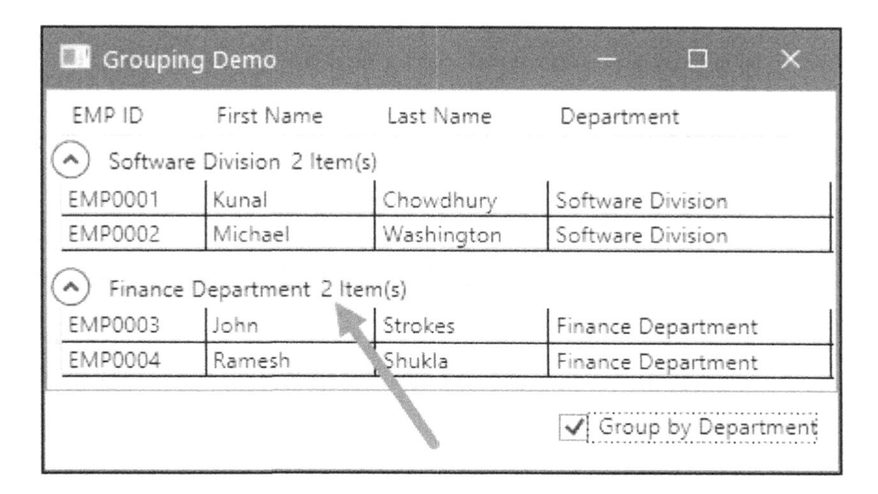

Filtering data in a DataGrid control

When we display a set of huge records in a `DataGrid`, it often becomes difficult for the user to search for and find a particular record from the grid. In such cases, you may want to provide an additional feature to filter the records to a specific search term.

In this recipe, we will learn how to add a search box to filter records in a `DataGrid` control.

Getting ready

Let's start by creating a WPF application project named `CH04.DataGridFilterDemo` in your Visual Studio IDE.

How to do it...

Now perform the following steps to add the search functionality attached to the grid records:

1. Once the project has been created, add a new `Employee` model class inside the project and expose some properties, like we shared earlier in the *Sorting data in a DataGrid control* recipe.
2. Create the same dependency property (`Employees`, of type `ObservableCollection<Employee>`) in the `MainWindow.xaml.cs` file and populate the collection with some data records.
3. Now open the `MainWindow.xaml` file and add the attribute `x:Name="window"` to give the `Window` a name, so that we can perform element-to-element data binding.
4. Replace the default `Grid` panel with a `StackPanel`.
5. Now insert the following horizontal `StackPanel`, containing one `TextBlock` and one `TextBox`, inside the root `StackPanel`:

```
<StackPanel Orientation="Horizontal"
            HorizontalAlignment="Right"
            Margin="4 8">
    <TextBlock Text="Filter records: "/>
    <TextBox x:Name="searchBox" Width="100"
             TextChanged="OnFilterChanged"/>
</StackPanel>
```

6. Add a `DataGrid` control, having four columns inside it. Set the `AutoGenerateColumns` to `False` and add the data binding of the `ItemsSource` property with the `Employees` collection (`ItemsSource="{Binding Employees, ElementName=window}"`). Here's the complete code for reference:

```
<DataGrid x:Name="dataGrid"
          AutoGenerateColumns="False"
          CanUserAddRows="False"
          ItemsSource="{Binding Employees,
           ElementName=window}">
    <DataGrid.Columns>
        <DataGridTextColumn Header="EMP ID"
             Binding="{Binding ID}"/>
        <DataGridTextColumn Header="First Name"
             Binding="{Binding FirstName}"/>
        <DataGridTextColumn Header="Last Name"
             Binding="{Binding LastName}"/>
```

```
            <DataGridTextColumn Header="Department"
                 Binding="{Binding Department}"/>
        </DataGrid.Columns>
    </DataGrid>
```

7. Now navigate to the `MainWindow.xaml.cs` file, and add the following code blocks to implement the `OnFilterChanged` event that gets triggered whenever any text changes in the `searchBox`:

```
private void OnFilterChanged(object sender,
 TextChangedEventArgs e)
{
    var cvs =
    CollectionViewSource.GetDefaultView(dataGrid.ItemsSource);
    if (cvs != null && cvs.CanFilter)
    {
        cvs.Filter = OnFilterApplied;
    }
}

private bool OnFilterApplied(object obj)
{
    if(obj is Employee emp)
    {
        var searchText = searchBox.Text.ToLower();
        return
           emp.Department.ToLower().Contains(searchText) ||
           emp.FirstName.ToLower().Contains(searchText) ||
           emp.LastName.ToLower().Contains(searchText);
    }

    return false;
}
```

8. Let's build the project and run the application. You will see the following UI on the screen:

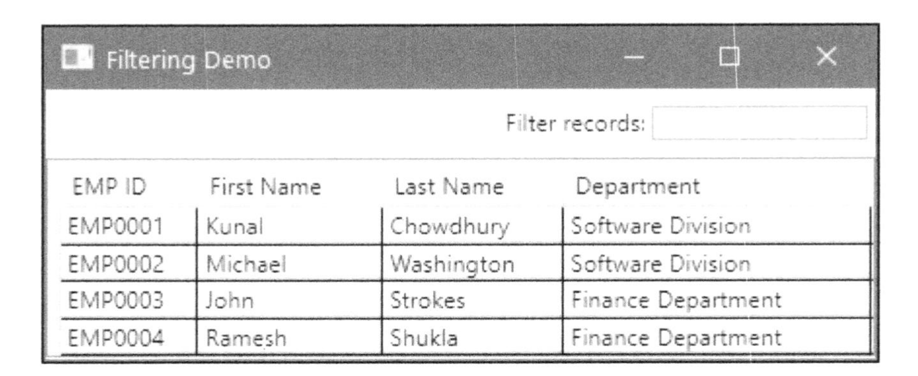

9. Now filter the records by entering some search term in the textbox. Let's enter `Finance` as the keyword and see the behavior:

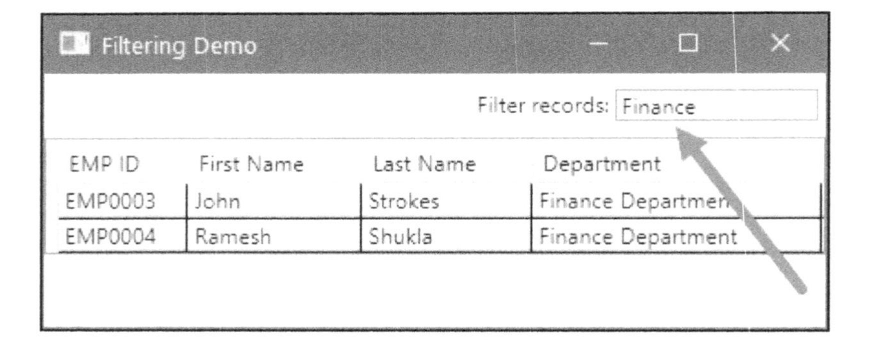

10. If you change the search term to perform the following from the records, it will filter out only those records.

How it works...

When you enter a search term, it fires the event `OnFilterChanged` and retrieves the default view of the `DataGrid`. It exposes a property named `Filter`, which is a predicate. In our example, we assigned the predicate `OnFilterApplied` on the `Filter` property, which, when called, compares the term with `Department`, `FirstName`, `LastName`, and returns `true` if a match is found. Based on the `boolean` value, it shows the said record.

Using static bindings

Often, we use static properties in our applications. Along with WPF 4.5, Microsoft provided us with the option to use static properties in XAML markup, while performing data binding. In this recipe, we will learn how to create such bindings. These can be useful in the next recipes while using Converters, Styles, and Templates.

Getting ready

Let's start by creating a new project, called `CH04.StaticBindingDemo`. Open your Visual Studio IDE and select the WPF application project as the project template.

How to do it...

Once the project has been created, perform the following steps to learn static binding:

1. Open the `MainWindow.xaml` page and add a `Label` inside the `Grid` panel. Give it a background color (let's say, `OrangeRed`) and run the application. This is what we use most often to write hardcoded values inline:

```
<Label Background="OrangeRed"
       Content="Kunal Chowdhury"
       FontSize="25"
       Width="300" Height="60"
       Padding="10" Margin="10"/>
```

2. Now, let's change it to set a background color from the system defined colors. To do this, we need to use `{x:Static}` markup extension to access the static properties. Here's how the code will be changed:

```
<Label Background="{x:Static
  SystemColors.ControlDarkBrush}"
       Content="Kunal Chowdhury"
       FontSize="25"
       Width="300" Height="60"
       Padding="10" Margin="10"/>
```

3. You can also access locally defined resources, within the XAML page or defined in a centralized `ResourceDictionary`. Let's define a color within the same page, under `Window`:

```
<Window.Resources>
    <SolidColorBrush Color="GreenYellow"
      x:Key="myBrush"/>
</Window.Resources>
```

4. Add a `Foreground` property to the label, to assign its foreground color. Let's bind it with the static resource (`myBrush`), that we defined earlier. Here's the code for reference:

```
<Label Background="{x:Static
  SystemColors.ControlDarkBrush}"
       Foreground="{StaticResource myBrush}"
       Content="Kunal Chowdhury"
       FontSize="25"
       Width="300" Height="60"
       Padding="10" Margin="10"/>
```

5. Now let's build and run the application. You will see the colors similar to the following screenshot, where the background will have a light gray color (based on the color set to your system's `ControlDarkBrush`) and the foreground will have a greenish yellow color:

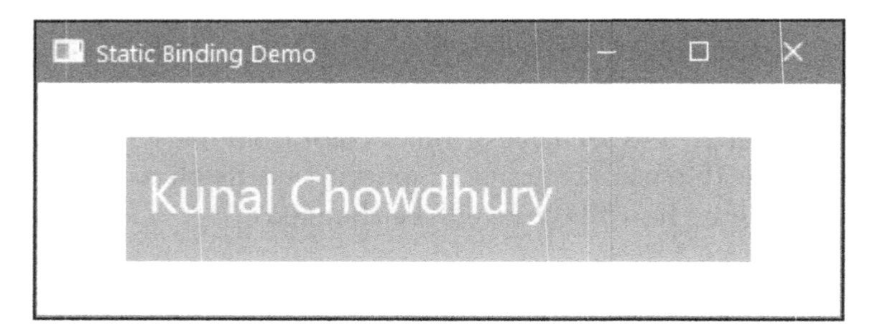

How it works...

A markup extension is a class that derives from `System.Windows.Markup.MarkupExtension` and implements a single method named `ProvideValue`. In this example, we have used the `{x:Static}` markup extension, implemented by the `System.Windows.Markup.StaticExtension` class, which allowed you to access the static property.

Similarly, the `{StaticResource}` is used to access the resource (`Color`, `Brush`, `Converter`, and more), defined in a XAML.

Using value converters

Converters are often useful when you want to perform data binding between two properties that have incompatible types. In such cases, you will need a piece of code which creates a bridge between source and target. This piece of code is defined as a **value converter**.

The `IValueConverter` interface is used to create value converters and contains two methods named `Convert` and `ConvertBack`:

- **Convert(...)**: It gets called when the source updates the target object
- **ConvertBack(...)**: It gets called when the target object updates the source object

In this recipe, we will learn how to create value converters and use them while data binding.

Getting ready

Let's begin by creating a new WPF project. Call it `CH04.ConverterDemo`.

How to do it...

To begin with the value converter, perform the following steps:

1. From the **Solution Explorer**, open the `MainWindow.xaml` file.
2. Replace the existing `Grid` with the following XAML markup, which contains a `CheckBox` and a `Rectangle` inside a `StackPanel`:

```
<StackPanel Orientation="Horizontal"
            VerticalAlignment="Top"
            Margin="20">
    <CheckBox x:Name="chkBox"
              Content="Show/Hide Box"/>
    <Rectangle Fill="Red" Margin="80 0 0 0"
               Width="150" Height="50"
               Visibility="{Binding IsChecked,
                 ElementName=chkBox}"/>
</StackPanel>
```

3. There is a data binding between the `Visibility` property of the `Rectangle` and the `IsChecked` property of the `CheckBox` control. If you build and run the application, you will see that there exists no visible change in the UI when you change the checked state of the checkbox:

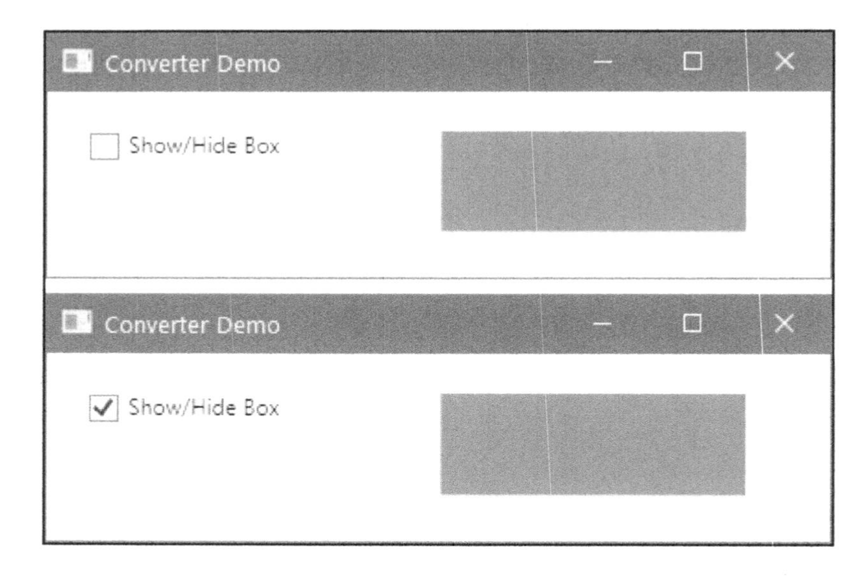

4. As the `Visibility` property does not accept `boolean` values, the `Rectangle` stays always visible by default. Now we will add the converter to it, which will automatically convert the value from `bool` to `Visibility`.
5. Let's create a new class file in the project. Name it `BoolToVisibilityConverter`.
6. Open the `BoolToVisibilityConverter.cs` file and add the following namespaces—`System`, `System.Globalization`, `System.Windows`, and `System.Windows.Data` as `using` statement.
7. Now, mark the class as `public` and implement the `IValueConverter` interface.
8. Add the following two code blocks inside the class:

```
public object Convert(object value,
                      Type targetType,
                      object parameter,
                      CultureInfo culture)
{
    return value is bool val && val ? Visibility.Visible :
    Visibility.Collapsed;
}

public object ConvertBack(object value,
                          Type targetType,
                          object parameter,
                          CultureInfo culture)
{
    throw new NotImplementedException();
}
```

9. Now, go to the `MainWindow.xaml` file and add the following XMLNS namespace, so that we can declare the converter as a window resource:

```
xmlns:converters="clr-namespace:CH04.ConverterDemo"
```

10. Inside the `Window` tag, add the following markup to declare the converter that we have created:

```
<Window.Resources>
    <converters:BoolToVisibilityConverter
       x:Key="BoolToVisibilityConverter"/>
</Window.Resources>
```

11. Now, in the binding syntax of the `Visibility` property of `Rectangle`, associate the converter as `StaticResource`, as shown in the following code snippet:

    ```
    Visibility="{Binding IsChecked, ElementName=chkBox,
    Converter={StaticResource BoolToVisibilityConverter}}"
    ```

12. Once this is done, build the project and run the application.
13. By default, the checkbox will be unchecked and the rectangle will not be visible on the screen. Change the state of the checkbox to checked and observe that the rectangle will become visible on the screen. Unchecking the box will again hide the rectangle:

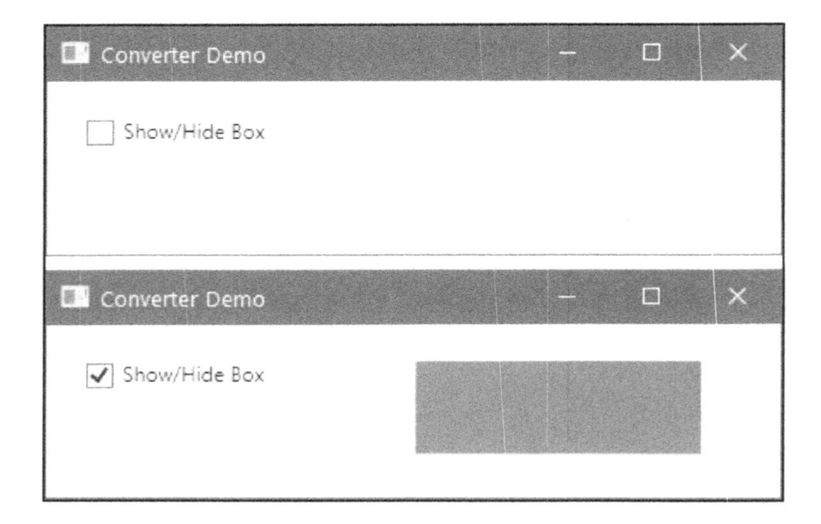

How it works...

A value converter is used to convert one value to another, by implementing the `IValueConverter` interface. The values may be of the same type or different types, but require some transformation that is not possible declaratively. These are often powerful because they are written in code, and hence have more logic to control the functionality.

An instance of the converter is generally created in the XAML page and declared as a resource. Then it sets to the controls by using binding expressions with the `Converter` property.

Whenever the source property changes, the converter returns a different result through the `Convert` method. The `ConvertBack` method is called in a two-way binding mode, where the source and target are reversed. In a one-way binding, there's no need to implement `ConvertBack` and generally we set its body to return an exception, like this—`throw new NotImplementedException()`.

There's more...

You can extend the functionality of the converter by using the converter parameter. Let's modify the `Convert` method to utilize the parameter named `parameter` and reverse the visibility based on its value.

To do so, open the `BoolToVisibilityConverter.cs` and modify the class implementation as shared in the following code snippet:

```
public class BoolToVisibilityConverter : IValueConverter
{
   public object Convert(object value,
                         Type targetType,
                         object parameter,
                         CultureInfo culture)
   {
         var val = (bool) value;
         if (parameter is string param &&
             param.ToString().Equals("inverse")) { val = !val; }

         return val ? Visibility.Visible: Visibility.Collapsed;
   }

   public object ConvertBack(object value,
                             Type targetType,
                             object parameter,
                             CultureInfo culture)
   {
         throw new NotImplementedException();
   }
}
```

Now, open the `MainWindow.xaml` file and modify the data binding of the `Visibility` property of the `Rectangle` to have a `ConverterParameter=inverse`, as shared here:

```
<Rectangle Fill="Red" Margin="80 0 0 0"
           Width="150" Height="50"
           Visibility="{Binding IsChecked, ElementName=chkBox,
           Converter={StaticResource BoolToVisibilityConverter},
           ConverterParameter=inverse}"/>
```

Let's build and run the application. You will see that, this time, the rectangle will be visible by default when the checkbox is unchecked. Now change the status of the checkbox to check, and you will see that the rectangle becomes visible on the screen:

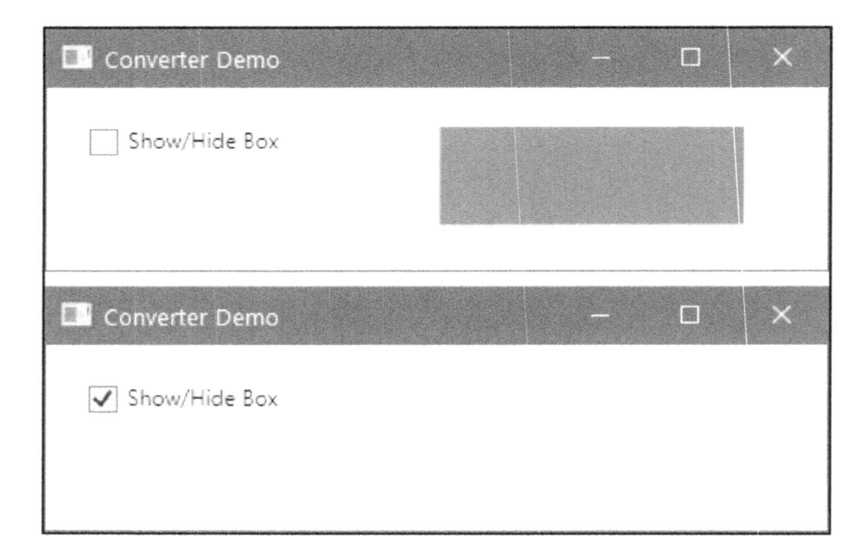

You can, of course, change the implementation and the value of the `ConverterParameter`, based on your business requirement, and use the same converter class to return different values on various conditions.

You can also use `BooleanToVisibilityConverter`, provided by .NET Framework. You can read more about this converter here: `https://msdn.microsoft.com/en-us/library/system.windows.controls.booleantovisibilityconverter(v=vs.110).aspx`.

Using multi-value converters

When you want to change the target value based on multiple values of the same or different types, you will need to use multi-binding. This is done by using a multi-value converter (`IMultiValueConverter` interface).

In this recipe, we will build a sample demo to learn how to work with multi-binding and multi-value converters.

Getting ready

Open your Visual Studio IDE and create a new project called `CH04.MultiValueConverterDemo`, based on the WPF application project template.

How to do it...

Once the project is created, follow these steps to design the UI and do a multi-binding between multiple elements:

1. From the **Solution Explorer**, open the `MainWindow.xaml` page.
2. Inside the default `Grid` panel, create a few rows and columns, so that we can position elements at specific cells. Let's divide the `Grid` into five rows and three columns:

```
<Grid.RowDefinitions>
    <RowDefinition Height="Auto"/>
    <RowDefinition Height="Auto"/>
    <RowDefinition Height="Auto"/>
    <RowDefinition Height="Auto"/>
    <RowDefinition Height="*"/>
</Grid.RowDefinitions>
<Grid.ColumnDefinitions>
    <ColumnDefinition/>
    <ColumnDefinition Width="90"/>
    <ColumnDefinition/>
</Grid.ColumnDefinitions>
```

3. Inside the `Grid` panel, insert the following XAML code snippet to add few labels and input boxes inside the window:

```
<TextBlock Text="Firstname:"
           Grid.Column="0" Margin="2 0"/>
<TextBlock Text="Middle:"
           Grid.Column="1" Margin="2 0"/>
<TextBlock Text="Lastname:"
           Grid.Column="2" Margin="2 0"/>
<TextBlock Text="Fullname:"
           Grid.Row="2" Grid.ColumnSpan="3"
           Margin="2 0"/>

<TextBox x:Name="firstName"
         Grid.Row="1" Grid.Column="0"
         Margin="2 0"/>
<TextBox x:Name="middleName"
         Grid.Row="1" Grid.Column="1"
         Margin="2 0"/>
<TextBox x:Name="lastName"
         Grid.Row="1" Grid.Column="2"
         Margin="2 0"/>
<TextBox x:Name="fullName"
         Grid.Row="3" Grid.ColumnSpan="3"
         Margin="2 0">

</TextBox>
```

4. Build the project and run the application. You will see four input boxes on the screen, along with their associated labels as follows:

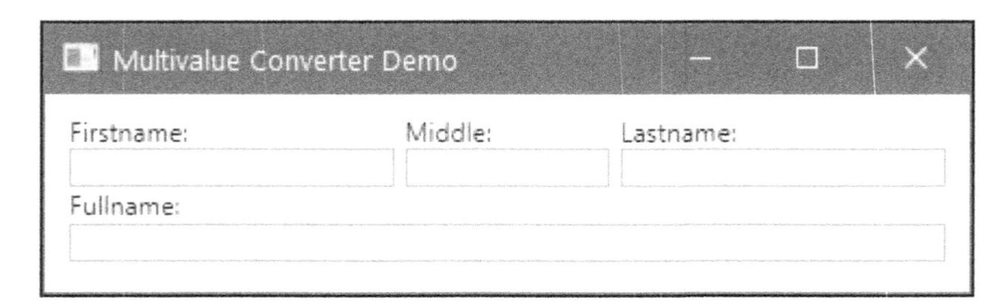

5. Let's close the application and return to the **Solution Explorer**. Create a new class named `FullNameConverter` inside the project.
6. Open the `FullNameConverter.cs` file and implement `IMultiValueConverter` on it.

7. Define the following `using` namespaces in the class file—`System`, `System.Globalization`, and `System.Windows.Data`.
8. Now add the following two methods inside the class, which implements the methods defined in `IMultiValueConverter` interface:

```
public object Convert(object[] values, Type targetType, object
parameter, CultureInfo culture)
{
    return string.Format("{0} {1} {2}", values[0], values[1],
    values[2]);
}

public object[] ConvertBack(object value, Type[] targetTypes,
object parameter, CultureInfo culture)
{
    return value.ToString().Split(' ');
}
```

9. Now navigate to the `MainWindow.xaml` page and add the following XMLNS namespace, so that the converter can be accessible from the XAML markup:

```
xmlns:converters="clr-namespace:CH04.MultiValueConverterDemo"
```

10. Now add the converter to the window resource. To do this, inside the `Window` tag, add the following markup to define the instance by key name:

```
<Window.Resources>
    <converters:FullNameConverter
              x:Key="FullNameConverter"/>
</Window.Resources>
```

11. Now, inside the `Text` property of the `fullName` textbox, define the multi-binding to bind the property with the `Text` property of three `TextBox` controls. Here's the code:

```
<TextBox x:Name="fullName"
         Grid.Row="3"
         Grid.ColumnSpan="3"
         Margin="2 0">
    <TextBox.Text>
        <MultiBinding Converter="{StaticResource
            FullNameConverter}">
            <Binding ElementName="firstName"
                     Path="Text" Mode="TwoWay"/>
            <Binding ElementName="middleName"
```

```
                    Path="Text" Mode="TwoWay"/>
            <Binding ElementName="lastName"
                    Path="Text" Mode="TwoWay"/>
        </MultiBinding>
    </TextBox.Text>
</TextBox>
```

12. Once the binding is done, build the project and run the application. You will see the same UI on the screen. Enter some strings in the `Firstname`, `Middle`, and `Lastname` fields. Observe the value in the `Fullname` field:

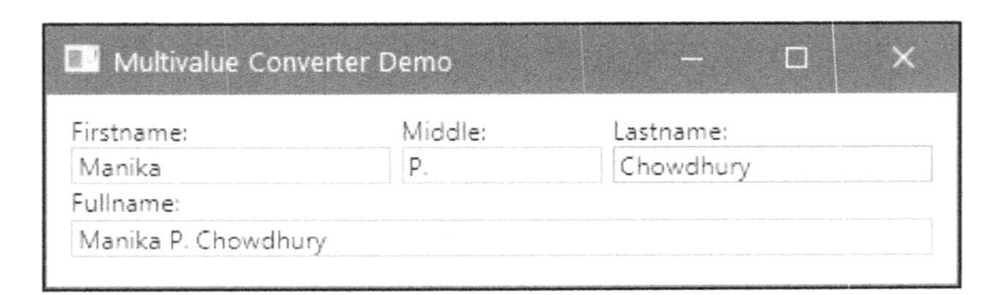

13. Similarly, change the `Fullname` field to hold three strings. Press the *TAB* key once you are done, and observe the value of the other three fields—`Firstname`, `Middle` and `Lastname`.

How it works...

When you use a converter of type `IMultiValueConverter` in a `MultiBinding`, it passes the values defined by the `Binding` tag to the `Convert` method as an object array. In our preceding example, we passed three string values (`firstName`, `middleName`, and `lastName`) to the `Convert` method. The method then concatenated the strings to form a single string, which was the output string of the `Fullname` field as the binding was made with its `Text` property.

Similarly, when we changed the value of the `Fullname` field, the `ConvertBack` method triggered by the binding converter and returned the splitted strings. As per the binding order, those automatically got assigned to the respective fields—`Firstname`, `Middle`, and `Lastname`.

5
Using Custom Controls and User Controls

In this chapter, we will cover the following recipes:

- Creating a custom control
- Customizing the template of a custom control
- Exposing properties from a custom control
- Exposing events from a custom control
- Extending the functionality of a control using behavior
- Creating a User Control interface
- Exposing events from a User Control
- Customizing the XMLNS namespace

Introduction

A custom control is a loosely coupled control defined in a class which derives from the `System.Windows.Controls.Control` class. You may also derive it from a different custom control, depending on your requirement.

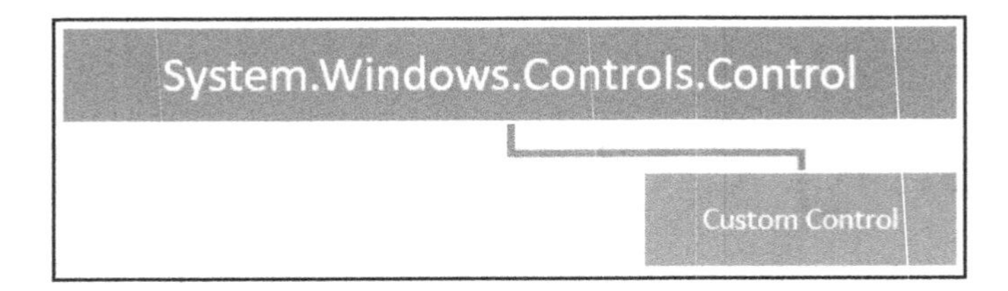

The UI of custom control is generally defined in a **resource dictionary** inside the `resource` file. We can create themes for custom control and reuse them in various projects very easily:

Generally, the **custom controls** are compiled into a `dll` assembly and can be reused in multiple places very easily. You have total control over its code, and thus it gives you more flexibility to extend the behavior. Once you build and add a reference to the custom control in your project, you can find it in the Visual Studio control toolbox, which will allow you to drag and drop the control in your XAML design view and start working with it.

On the other end, **User Control** is nothing but a custom control that you derive to control the UI specific to your project. It derives from the `System.Windows.Controls.UserControls` class, which basically inherits from `System.Windows.Controls.Control`:

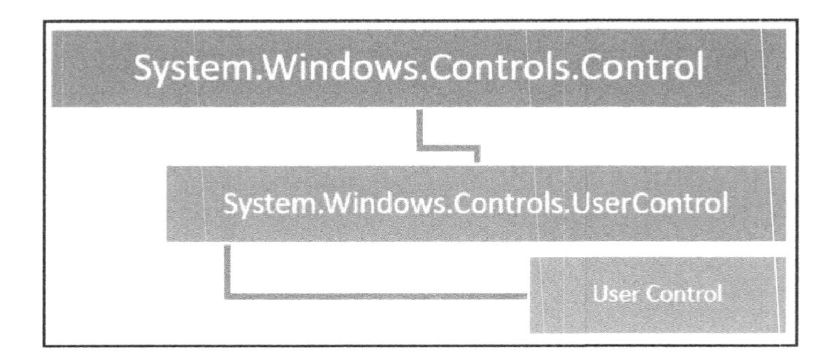

Generally, the User Control gets placed inside a XAML page with tight bonding to its code behind. You can directly access its UI elements from the code behind and do some specific operations.

A point to remember is that you can't create theming support for User Controls but you can style them by creating theme for its child, custom controls. Also, once you create a User Control UI in one project, you can't change it in the other projects.

In this chapter, we will learn how to create custom controls and User Controls, and then customize them based on need.

Creating a custom control

Before working with custom controls, you will need to know how to create custom controls and how to add them to any XAML pages. In this recipe, we will learn these basic operations first.

Getting ready

Let's open the Visual Studio IDE and create a new WPF application project, called `CH05.SearchControlDemo`.

How to do it...

Perform the following steps to create your first custom control, which will contain a text input box and a button to build a search control. At the end, we will add it to the application window:

1. Once the project has been created, right-click on the project, from **Solution Explorer**, and follow **Add** | **New Item...** from the context menu entries. A new dialog window will pop up on the screen.

2. Inside the **Add New Item** dialog window, expand the **Installed** | **Visual C#** | **WPF** tree item, from the left navigation panel, and select **Custom Control (WPF)** from the right screen:

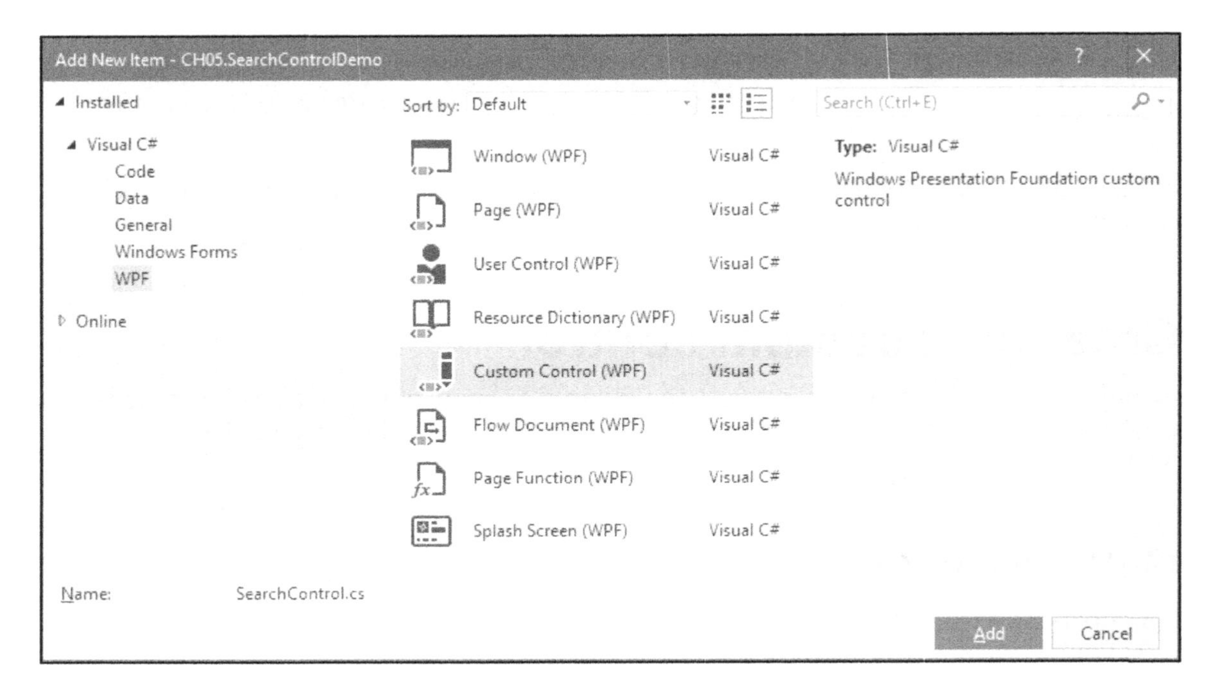

3. Give the custom control a name (let's say, `SearchControl.cs`) and click **Add** to create it. This will create the class file named `SearchControl.cs` inside the project, and a folder (named `Themes`) containing a `Generic.xaml` file.
4. Open the `Generic.xaml` file, which will contain a `Style` for the custom control that we created. This gets generated automatically by the Visual Studio IDE, while creating the custom control from the default template. Here's the default `Style`:

```
<Style TargetType="{x:Type local:SearchControl}">
    <Setter Property="Template">
        <Setter.Value>
            <ControlTemplate TargetType="{x:Type local:
                                 SearchControl}">
                <Border Background="{TemplateBinding
                                 Background}"
                        BorderBrush="{TemplateBinding
                                 BorderBrush}"
```

```
                              BorderThickness="{TemplateBinding
                                    BorderThickness}">
                        </Border>
                    </ControlTemplate>
                </Setter.Value>
            </Setter>
        </Style>
```

5. Now replace the preceding `Style` of the control with the following one, which contains an input box and a button, as the control template inside a `Grid`:

```
<Style TargetType="{x:Type local:SearchControl}">
    <Setter Property="Height" Value="26"/>
    <Setter Property="Width" Value="150"/>
    <Setter Property="Template">
        <Setter.Value>
            <ControlTemplate TargetType="{x:Type
             local:SearchControl}">
                <Grid>
                    <Grid.ColumnDefinitions>
                        <ColumnDefinition Width="*"/>
                        <ColumnDefinition Width="Auto"/>
                    </Grid.ColumnDefinitions>
                    <TextBox x:Name="PART_TextBox"
                            Grid.Column="0"
                            Margin="2"
                            HorizontalAlignment="Stretch"
                            VerticalAlignment="Stretch"/>
                    <Button x:Name="PART_Button"
                            Content="Search"
                            Grid.Column="1"
                            Margin="2" Padding="8 2"
                            HorizontalAlignment="Stretch"
                            VerticalAlignment="Stretch"/>
                </Grid>
            </ControlTemplate>
        </Setter.Value>
    </Setter>
</Style>
```

6. Now open the `MainWindow.xaml` page, and add the following XMLNS namespace:

```
xmlns:controls="clr-namespace:CH05.SearchControlDemo"
```

7. Now, inside the default `Grid` panel, add the custom control that we just created, and optionally set its `Height` and `Width` properties:

```
<Grid>
    <controls:SearchControl Height="30"
                            Width="180"/>
</Grid>
```

8. That's all! Our first custom control has been created and added to the `MainWindow` of the application. Let's build and run the application. You will see the following UI on the screen:

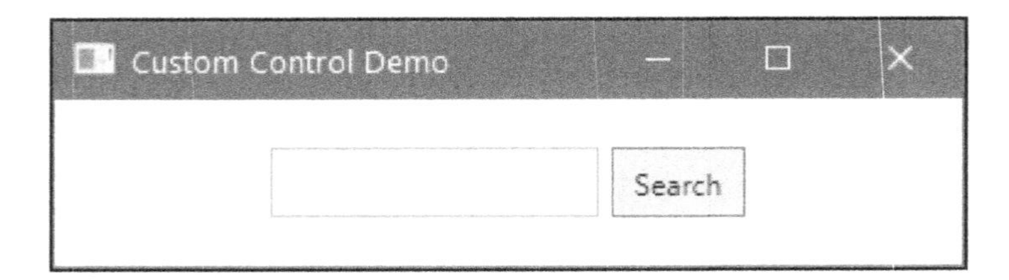

We have just added the UI of our custom control here and hence no functionality related to search will work. We will enhance the functionalities in the next recipes.

How it works...

When you first create a custom control in a project, Visual Studio creates a folder named `Themes`, and places a file named `Generic.xaml`. This file contains all the styles and templates of the custom controls, by default. When you add more custom controls inside the same project, the `Generic.xaml` file gets updated with the styles of the new controls.

The property called `TargetType` defines the type of the control for which we are going to create the style. In the preceding example, `<Style TargetType="{x:Type local:SearchControl}">` defines the style of the custom control called `SearchControl`. To change the UI of the control, we need to update the same style.

The `<ControlTemplate TargetType="{x:Type local:SearchControl}">` defines the template of the control, which generally resides inside the `Style`.

The `Setter` properties inside the `Style` define the default value of various properties of the said control. In the preceding example, we have defined the default value of the `Height` and `Width` properties. You can add additional property values.

There's more...

Before going further with the custom controls, you need to learn and understand some other points related to them. Let's discuss them in the following sections.

XMLNS attribute declaration

When the custom control is present within the same project where you are going to use it, you need to add the XMLNS attribute in the following way:

```
xmlns:controls="clr-namespace:CH05.SearchControl"
```

This is the same way we added it in the preceding example. The `clr-namespace` defines the namespace where the controls are available. A single namespace can have one or more controls.

When the custom control is present in a different project to the one where you are going to add it, you need to add the XMLNS attribute in the following way:

```
xmlns:controls="clr-
namespace:CH05.SearchControl;assembly=CH05.SearchControlDemo"
```

Here, the `clr-namespace` defines the namespace of the controls, whereas the `assembly` defines the fully qualified name of the assembly where the control is present.

Default styling

When you create a custom control, all the default properties of its base class, `Control`, gets assigned to it. You can use `TemplateBinding` to bind the data to a specific control. For example, to change the background color of the input box based on the `Background` property set on the control level, you need to create the template binding in the following way:

```
<TextBox x:Name="PART_TextBox"
         Grid.Column="0"
         Margin="2"
         Background="{TemplateBinding Background}"
```

```
                    HorizontalAlignment="Stretch"
                    VerticalAlignment="Stretch"/>
```

Now, when you change the color of the control, it will change the color of the said input box. Set a color to the `Background` property of our search control inside the `MainWindow.xaml` and observe the change.

Toolbox integration

When you create a custom control within the same project and/or reference a `dll` containing any custom control, you will be able to utilize the **Visual Studio Toolbox** to drag and drop the control directly to the XAML/designer view.

After creating the control or adding the control library in a project, you need to build it first. Now, open any XAML page and navigate to the Visual Studio **Toolbox**. You will be able to find the control, as demonstrated here:

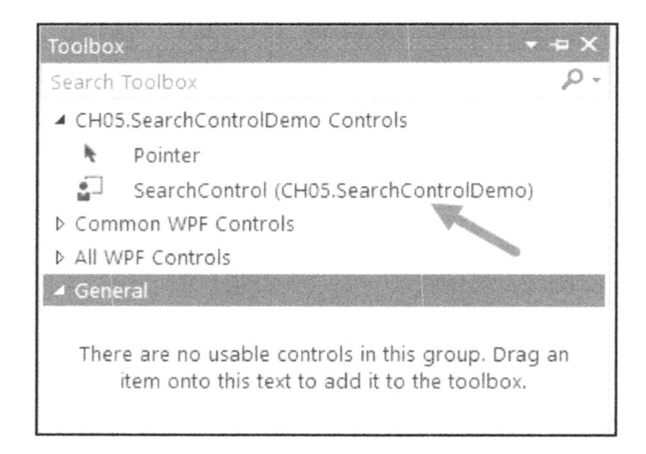

Now you can drag it to the place where you want to add the said control.

Customizing the template of a custom control

The development of a custom control always requires its default template to be changed to give it a proper look and make it ready for theming support. That starts with the customization of the template and its default values.

In this recipe, we will learn how to change the template and use `TemplateBinding` to create a relation with its property values.

Getting ready

To get started, launch Visual Studio, create a project, and add a new custom control in it. For this demonstration, we will be using the existing project, `CH05.SearchControlDemo`, that we created in the previous recipe. So, let's open the project.

How to do it...

As we want to customize the template of the custom control to have a proper template binding, perform the following steps:

1. Open the `Generic.xaml` file, which is present under the `Themes` folder of the project.
2. Now, scroll down to the definition of the `ControlTemplate` as we need to customize the look and feel of it.
3. Search for the `TextBox` control named `PART_TextBox`, and set its `Background`, `BorderBrush`, `BorderThickness`, and `Foreground` properties to have a binding with the control's default properties.
4. Similarly, set the `Background` and `Foreground` property of the button (`PART_Button`) to the same properties of the control, by using template binding. Here's the complete code of the modified control template:

```
<ControlTemplate TargetType="{x:Type local:SearchControl}">
    <Grid>
        <Grid.ColumnDefinitions>
            <ColumnDefinition Width="*"/>
            <ColumnDefinition Width="Auto"/>
        </Grid.ColumnDefinitions>
        <TextBox x:Name="PART_TextBox"
```

```
                              Grid.Column="0"
                              Margin="2"
                              Background="{TemplateBinding Background}"
                              BorderBrush="{TemplateBinding
                                           BorderBrush}"
                              BorderThickness="{TemplateBinding
                                               BorderThickness}"
                              Foreground="{TemplateBinding Foreground}"
                              HorizontalAlignment="Stretch"
                              VerticalAlignment="Stretch"/>
                     <Button x:Name="PART_Button"
                             Content="Search"
                             Grid.Column="1"
                             Margin="2" Padding="4 2"
                             Background="{TemplateBinding Background}"
                             Foreground="{TemplateBinding Foreground}"
                             HorizontalAlignment="Stretch"
                             VerticalAlignment="Stretch"/>
                 </Grid>
             </ControlTemplate>
```

5. You can also assign default values to your control templates, by using the `<Setter/>` tag. You will need to add it inside the `<Style/>` definition. To add default values to the `Height`, `Width`, `Background`, `BorderBrush`, `BorderThickness`, and `Foreground` properties, add the following code block inside the `Style` tag:

```
<Setter Property="Height" Value="30"/>
<Setter Property="Width" Value="280"/>
<Setter Property="Background" Value="AliceBlue"/>
<Setter Property="BorderBrush" Value="LightSkyBlue"/>
<Setter Property="BorderThickness" Value="1"/>
<Setter Property="Foreground" Value="Navy"/>
```

6. Once done, compile your project and run it. You will see the following screen, where the background of the `TextBox` and `Button` controls are painted with `AliceBlue` color. Similarly, the other styles are applied as per the default values specified:

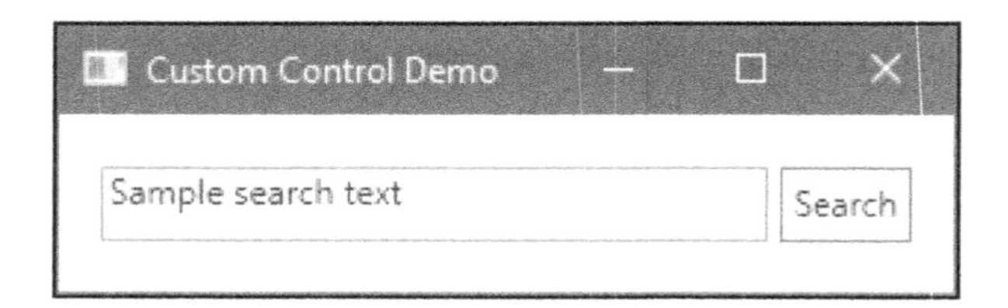

7. You can override the default style values in your application, where you are using the control. To do this, open the `MainWindow.xaml` file and add a custom `Background` color, `BorderBrush`, `Foreground`, and `BorderThickness` to the control as follows:

```
<Grid>
    <controls:SearchControl
        Background="#2200FF00"
        BorderThickness="2"
        BorderBrush="GreenYellow"
        Foreground="Green"/>
</Grid>
```

8. Now, if you build and run the application, you will notice the UI changed as per the custom value that you specified directly to the control:

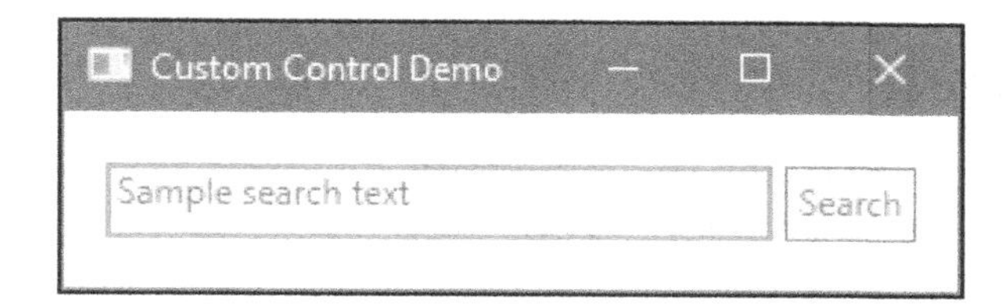

How it works...

`TemplateBinding` is a type of binding used mainly while working with templates. This allows you to replace the visual tree of controls for a completely fresh look and feel, based on the theme or style that you want to use. It also helps you to reference the parent control, read its properties, and apply its values.

When you apply a template binding to a control, present in the `ControlTemplate` of the parent control, it first checks whether the property is present to the parent control. If it is not present, it throws an XAML syntax error.

If it finds the property, it checks whether the value is supplied from the place where the custom control has been used. If it finds no reference, it applies the default value to the property.

Exposing properties from the custom control

Most of the time, while using custom controls, we need to expose additional properties based on the requirement. In this recipe, we will demonstrate exposing dependency properties from the custom control and binding the record to the UI.

Getting ready

Let's extend our previous project to perform these steps. To get started, launch Visual Studio and open the project `CH05.SearchControlDemo`.

How to do it...

Once the project has been opened, perform the following steps to create a dependency property named `SearchTerm` and bind it with the control UI:

1. Let's open the `SearchControl.cs` to create a dependency property. Inside the class definition, type `propdp` and press the *TAB* key twice to create the property structure. By default, it generates `MyProperty` of type `int`.
2. Change the property type from `int` to `string` and press *TAB*.
3. Rename `MyProperty` to `SearchTerm` and press *TAB* again.
4. Now change `ownerclass` to `SearchControl` and press *TAB*.
5. Pass `string.Empty` as the default value to the `PropertyMetaData`.
6. Once these preceding steps are done, your property is ready to use. Now open the `Generic.xaml` page to create the binding to the UI control.
7. Inside the template of the control, find the `TextBox` named `PART_TextBox`.

8. Now, add the `Text` property to it, by using `TemplateBinding`. You will see the dependency property (`SearchTerm`) listed in the XAML IntelliSense, as shown here:

```
<TextBox x:Name="PART_TextBox"
         Grid.Column="0"
         Margin="2"
         Text="{TemplateBinding Sear}"
         Background="{TemplateBi  SearchTerm
         BorderBrush="{TemplateBinding BorderBrush}"
         BorderThickness="{TemplateBinding BorderThickness}"
         Foreground="{TemplateBinding Foreground}"
```

9. Let's complete the template binding as follows:

```
<TextBox x:Name="PART_TextBox"
         Grid.Column="0"
         Margin="2"
         Text="{TemplateBinding SearchTerm}"
         Background="{TemplateBinding Background}"
         BorderBrush="{TemplateBinding BorderBrush}"
         BorderThickness="{TemplateBinding
                          BorderThickness}"
         Foreground="{TemplateBinding Foreground}"
         HorizontalAlignment="Stretch"
         VerticalAlignment="Stretch"/>
```

10. Now navigate to the `MainWindow.xaml` page and add the `SearchTerm` property to the control that we have already added:

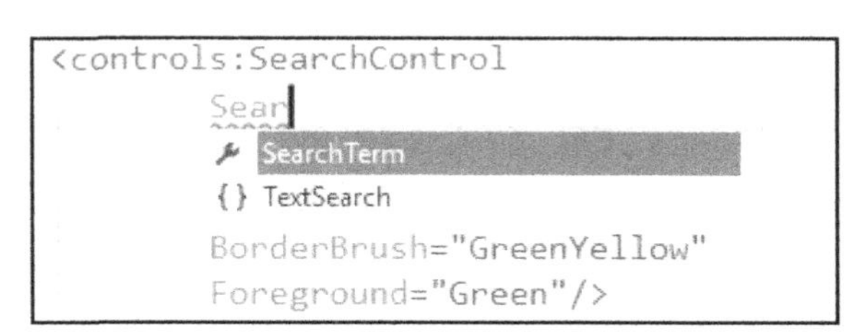

<controls:SearchControl
Sear
SearchTerm
{ } TextSearch
BorderBrush="GreenYellow"
Foreground="Green"/>

11. Set some sample strings to it:

```
<controls:SearchControl
        SearchTerm="my search term"
        Background="#2200FF00"
        BorderThickness="2"
        BorderBrush="GreenYellow"
        Foreground="Green"/>
```

12. Build the project and run it. You will see that the string that you assigned to the `SearchTerm` property of the control, actually assigned the value to the search `TextBox`:

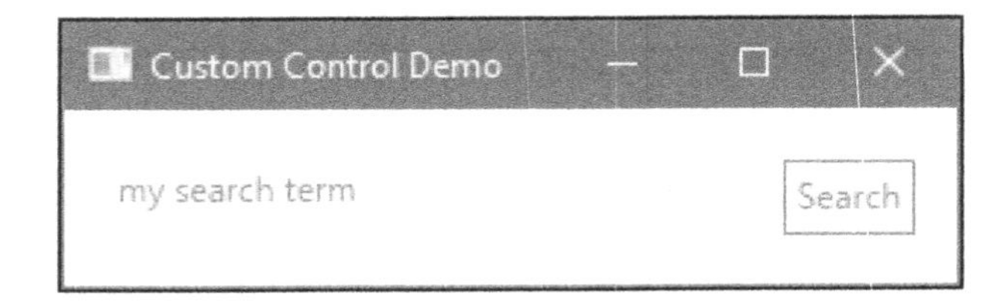

How it works...

Template binding works only with the dependency properties. When you assign a value to the dependency property, it automatically updates the child control where you have created the binding. In our example, when you assign a value to the `SearchTerm` property, it sets the value to the textbox (`PART_TextBox`) control's `Text` property and thus you can see the value provided to it.

Exposing events from a custom control

When you build any custom control, you need to expose additional events, based on the child controls and functionality that you want to expose to the user. In this recipe, we will learn how to expose a custom event from a custom control and perform a specific operation using it.

Getting ready

Let's start with the existing project that we have already used in the previous recipes. Launch the IDE and open the `CH05.SearchControlDemo` project inside Visual Studio.

How to do it...

In this recipe, we will create a public event from the `SearchControl`, so that we can subscribe to the `PART_Button` button event and fetch the user-entered text. To do so, follow perform the following steps:

1. From **Solution Explorer**, create a new class named `SearchEventArgs`, inside the project.
2. Extend the `SearchEventArgs` class from the `EventArgs` and expose a public property (`SearchTerm`) of type `string`. Here's the class implementation:

```
public class SearchEventArgs : EventArgs
{
    public string SearchTerm { get; set; }
}
```

3. Now open the `SearchControl.cs` file. We need to create a delegate and event inside it. Let's add the following inside the class implementation:

```
public delegate void OnSearchClick(object sender,
 SearchEventArgs e);
public event OnSearchClick SearchButtonClick;
```

4. The next task is to associate the button click event with the custom event that we have just created. Pass the `SearchTerm` to the custom event as an argument. To do this, copy the following code inside the `SearchControl` class:

```
public override void OnApplyTemplate()
{
    base.OnApplyTemplate();

    if (GetTemplateChild("PART_Button") is Button
     searchButton)
    {
        searchButton.Click +=
                    OnSearchButtonClicked_Internal;
    }
}
```

```
private void OnSearchButtonClicked_Internal(object sender,
  RoutedEventArgs e)
{
    SearchButtonClick?.Invoke(this, new SearchEventArgs {
      SearchTerm = SearchTerm });
}
```

5. Open the `Generic.xaml` page and perform a slight change to the `Text` property binding of the search `TextBox`. Instead of template binding, let's perform a normal data binding, passing a relative source to it. As we need to take input from the user, we will set the binding mode to `TwoWay`. Here's the XAML code:

```
<TextBox x:Name="PART_TextBox"
         Grid.Column="0"
         Margin="2"
         Text="{Binding SearchTerm,
RelativeSource={RelativeSource TemplatedParent}, Mode=TwoWay}"
         Background="{TemplateBinding Background}"
         BorderBrush="{TemplateBinding BorderBrush}"
         BorderThickness="{TemplateBinding
                                  BorderThickness}"
         Foreground="{TemplateBinding Foreground}"
         HorizontalAlignment="Stretch"
         VerticalAlignment="Stretch"/>
```

6. Once this is done, open the `MainWindow.xaml` and register the `SearchButtonClick` event of the `SearchControl`:

```
<controls:SearchControl
        SearchTerm="my search term"
        Background="#2200FF00"
        BorderThickness="2"
        BorderBrush="GreenYellow"
        Foreground="Green"
        SearchButtonClick="OnSearchButtonClicked"/>
```

7. Open the code behind `MainWindow.xaml.cs` and modify the event implementation to show a message box to the user, with the text that we passed as a search term. You can find it as `e.SearchTerm`, as passed to the event argument. Here's the code for your reference:

```
private void OnSearchButtonClicked(object sender,
 SearchEventArgs e)
{
    MessageBox.Show("You searched for: "" +
     e.SearchTerm + """);
}
```

8. That's all! Let's build the application and run it. As we already have a default value set to the control, click on the **Search** button. You will see a message box with the default search term. Now, change the value to have a different search term. To do so, click on the `TextBox` control and replace the string. Now, click on the **Search** button once again, which will show the new search term inside the message box. Here's a screenshot of the same operation:

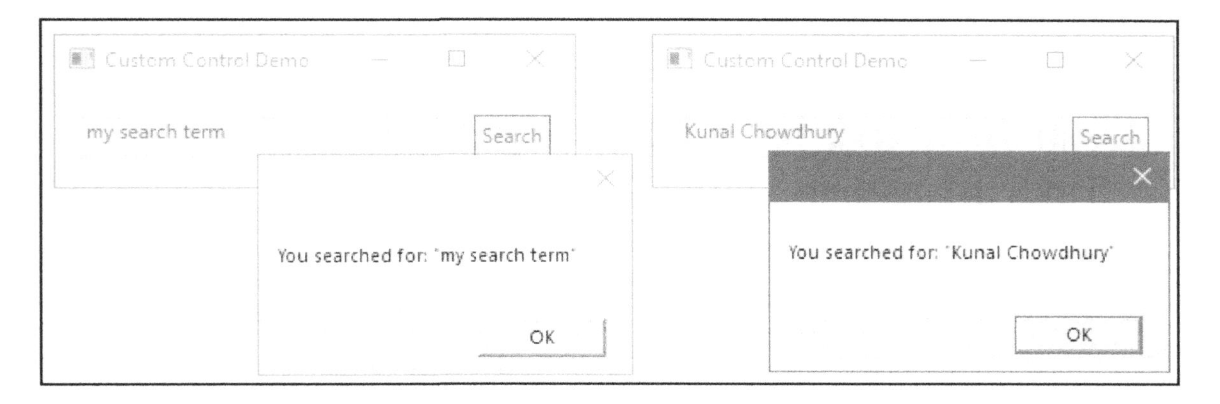

How it works...

When the application loads with the control on the UI, the first thing that it does is to load its defined template and call the `OnApplyTemplate()` method. `OnApplyTemplate()` is a virtual method present inside the `System.Windows.FrameworkElement` class, which gets invoked when application code or internal processes call the `System.Windows.FrameworkElement.ApplyTemplate()`.

As you can see in the `OnApplyTemplate()` method implementation, it finds out the template child named `PART_Button` using the `GetTemplateChild` method call, and registers its associated `Click` event:

```
public override void OnApplyTemplate()
{
    base.OnApplyTemplate();

    if (GetTemplateChild("PART_Button") is Button searchButton)
    {
        searchButton.Click += OnSearchButtonClicked_Internal;
    }
}
```

The `Click` event then invokes the custom event (`SearchButtonClick`), passing the `SearchTerm` as `SearchEventArgs`. Now, when you click on the button in the application UI, it fires the `OnSearchButtonClicked_Internal` event and bubbles up to the application UI. The `OnSearchButtonClicked` event handler then triggers due to its subscription to the custom event and performs the operation. In our case, it shows a message to the user with the search term passed to the search box.

Extending the functionality of a control using behavior

Behavior is a concept to extend the functionality of a control using a reusable component. These components can be attached to any control or a specific type of control to provide designers with the flexibility to design complex user interactions without writing any additional code.

In this recipe, we will learn how to create a behavior and the way to apply it to a control without writing extra code in the code-behind file.

Getting ready

To get started, we need to open the Visual Studio IDE. Create a new project called `CH05.ControlBehaviorDemo`, based on the WPF application template.

How to do it...

Let's start by creating a component which will add a **Size Grow** effect to a `TextBlock` control when hovering over with the mouse cursor. To do this, perform the following steps:

1. To create and/or use behaviors in an application, you will need to set up the project to have a reference to the `System.Windows.Interactivity.dll` assembly file. To do this, right-click on the project and click **Add** | **Reference...** from the context menu.
2. From the **Reference Manager** dialog, search for `interactivity` to find the **System.Windows.Interactivity** assembly in the list of assemblies. Select the latest version, as shown in the following screenshot, and click **OK**. Make sure you verify the added reference in the project:

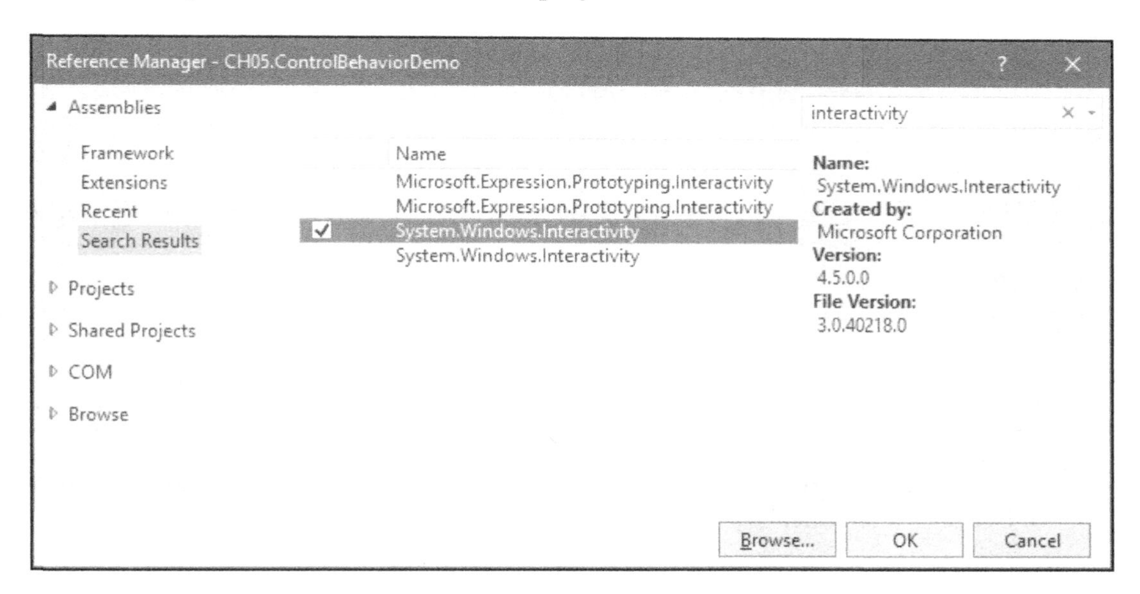

3. Now open the `MainWindow.xaml` page and add a `TextBlock` control inside the default `Grid`. Assign a string to its `Text` property:

```
<Grid>
    <TextBlock Text="Hover to Grow the size!"
               HorizontalAlignment="Center"
               VerticalAlignment="Center">

    </TextBlock>
</Grid>
```

4. If you run the application now, it will have a text in the window. Hovering your mouse on top of that will not have any effect. For that, we need to create the behavior and register it with the `TextBlock` control.
5. Let's create a new class, called `GrowTextBehavior`, inside the project.
6. Mark the class as `public` and extend it from the `Behavior` class. As we are going to create this component for `TextBlock` control, we will extend the class from Behavior<TextBlock>, as shown here:

```
public class GrowTextBehavior : Behavior<TextBlock>
```

7. You will need to add the `System.Windows.Interactivity` namespace as a `using` statement to resolve the class declaration. Alternatively, you can resolve the namespace by clicking the light bulb and selecting **using System.Windows.Interactivity;**, as shown in the following screenshot:

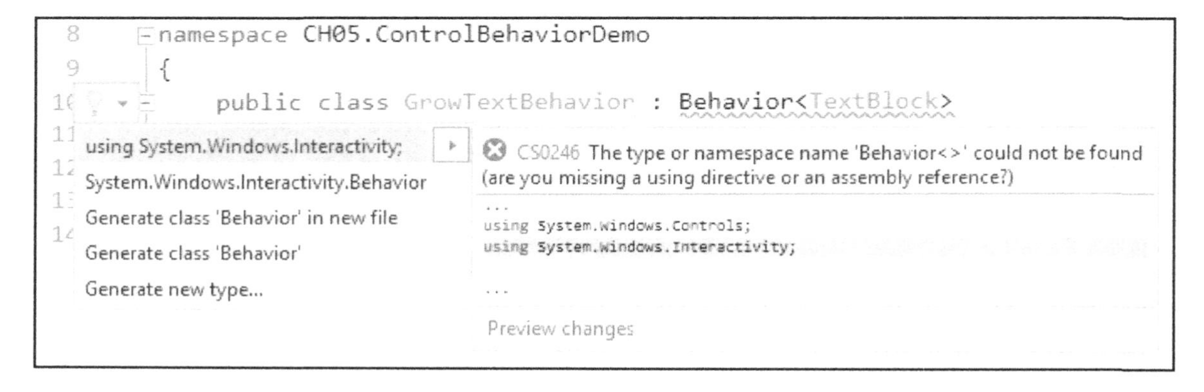

8. Add a `public` property inside the class to take dynamic input of the size to grow by. Give it a name:

```
public int GrowBySize { get; set; }
```

9. Now, inside the class, type `override` and enter a space. From the list of overridable methods, select `OnAttached` and hit the *Enter* key. This will override the `OnAttached()` method inside the class.

10. Similarly, override the method `OnDetaching()` inside the class.
11. Inside `OnAttached()`, register the `MouseEnter` and `MouseLeave` events for the associated object, which is a `TextBlock` in our case. Similarly, inside the `OnDetaching()`, unregister the preceding two events. Here's the code that you may like to take as reference:

```
protected override void OnAttached()
{
    base.OnAttached();

    AssociatedObject.MouseEnter +=
                     AssociatedObject_MouseEnter;
    AssociatedObject.MouseLeave +=
                     AssociatedObject_MouseLeave;
}

protected override void OnDetaching()
{
    base.OnDetaching();

    AssociatedObject.MouseEnter -=
                     AssociatedObject_MouseEnter;
    AssociatedObject.MouseLeave -=
                     AssociatedObject_MouseLeave;
}
```

12. Now it's time to write our logic to grow and shrink the size of the associated `TextBlock` control on mouse over and mouse leave events, respectively. To do so, add the following code block inside the class:

```
private void AssociatedObject_MouseLeave(object sender,
 MouseEventArgs e)
{
    AssociatedObject.FontSize -= GrowBySize;
}

private void AssociatedObject_MouseEnter(object sender,
  MouseEventArgs e)
{
    AssociatedObject.FontSize += GrowBySize;
}
```

13. That ends the implementation of the behavior component for our `TextBlock` control. Now it's time to register it with the control in the UI. To do so, open the `MainWindow.xaml` again and add the following XMLNS namespace declaration:

```
xmlns:i="http://schemas.microsoft.com/expression/2010/interacti
vity"
```

14. Now modify the `TextBlock` control to register the association with the behavior component that we created. Replace the existing markup with the following:

```
<Grid>
    <TextBlock Text="Hover to Grow the size!"
               HorizontalAlignment="Center"
               VerticalAlignment="Center">
        <i:Interaction.Behaviors>
            <b:GrowTextBehavior GrowBySize="10"/>
        </i:Interaction.Behaviors>
    </TextBlock>
</Grid>
```

15. Let's build the application and run it. You will see a text message in the application window. Hover over it to see the growing effect on its size:

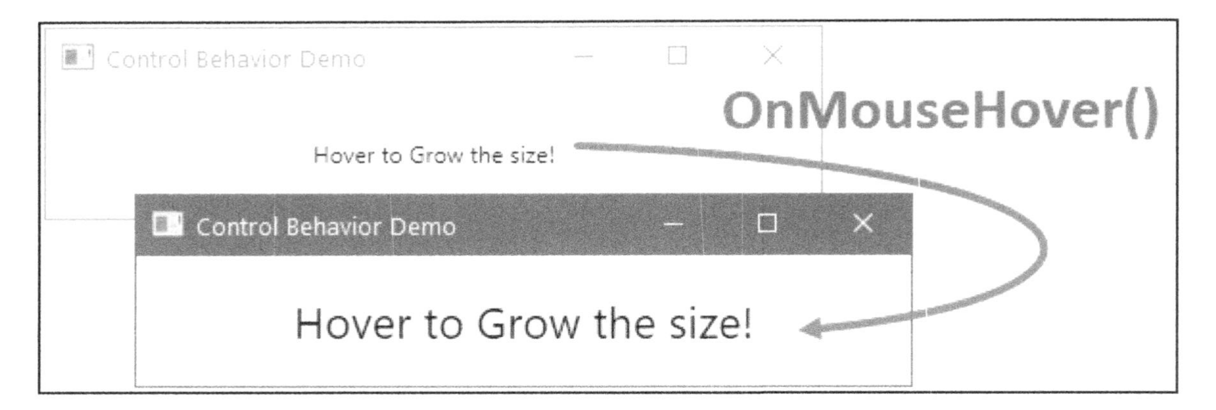

16. Take your mouse away from the text to see how it moves back to the original state.

How it works...

The property, `AssociatedObject`, returns the object to which the `System.Windows.Interactivity.Behavior` is attached. In our case, it's the `TextBlock` control passed as `Behavior` of type `T` (`Behavior<TextBlock>`), which is associated in the XAML code block, as mentioned here:

```
<TextBlock Text="Hover to Grow the size!"
           HorizontalAlignment="Center"
           VerticalAlignment="Center">
    <i:Interaction.Behaviors>
        <b:GrowTextBehavior GrowBySize="10"/>
    </i:Interaction.Behaviors>
</TextBlock>
```

When the association happens between the control and the component, it registers the two events (`MouseEnter` and `MouseLeave`) in our example. Now, when you hover over the mouse on top of the `TextBlock`, it gets the dynamic association of the events and triggers them. This way, it gets notification of the event and performs based on the logic specified.

You can now associate this behavior to any number of controls of type `TextBlock`, without writing additional code behind. The XAML designers can easily pick and associate it with the controls that they want to provide a grow effect on mouse hover.

If you want to associate the behavior to any control, you need to extend it from `Behavior`, instead of `Behavior<TextBlock>`. Similarly, to change the type to any other specific control (let's say, `Label`), change the `T` to `Label` as shown here—`Behavior<Label>`.

Creating a User Control interface

Typically, a User Control is a group of elements and controls joined together to create a reusable component. This is often used to show the same UI in multiple places, either on the same window or in a different window.

In this recipe, we will learn how to create a User Control interface with all its typical features.

Getting ready

Get started by creating a new project. Open the Visual Studio IDE and create a new project based on the WPF application template. Name it `CH05.UserControlDemo`.

How to do it...

To demonstrate the complete use of User Control, we will be creating a color mixer control, exposing some properties from it and binding data using converters. Perform the following simple steps:

1. Once the project has been created, add a new User Control element inside the project. To do this, right-click on the project and select **Add | User Control...** from the context menu entry.
2. From the **Add New Item** dialog, select **User Control (WPF)** as the template to create a blank User Control. Name the control `ColorMixer`. Click on the **Add** button to create a User Control file called `ColorMixer.xaml`:

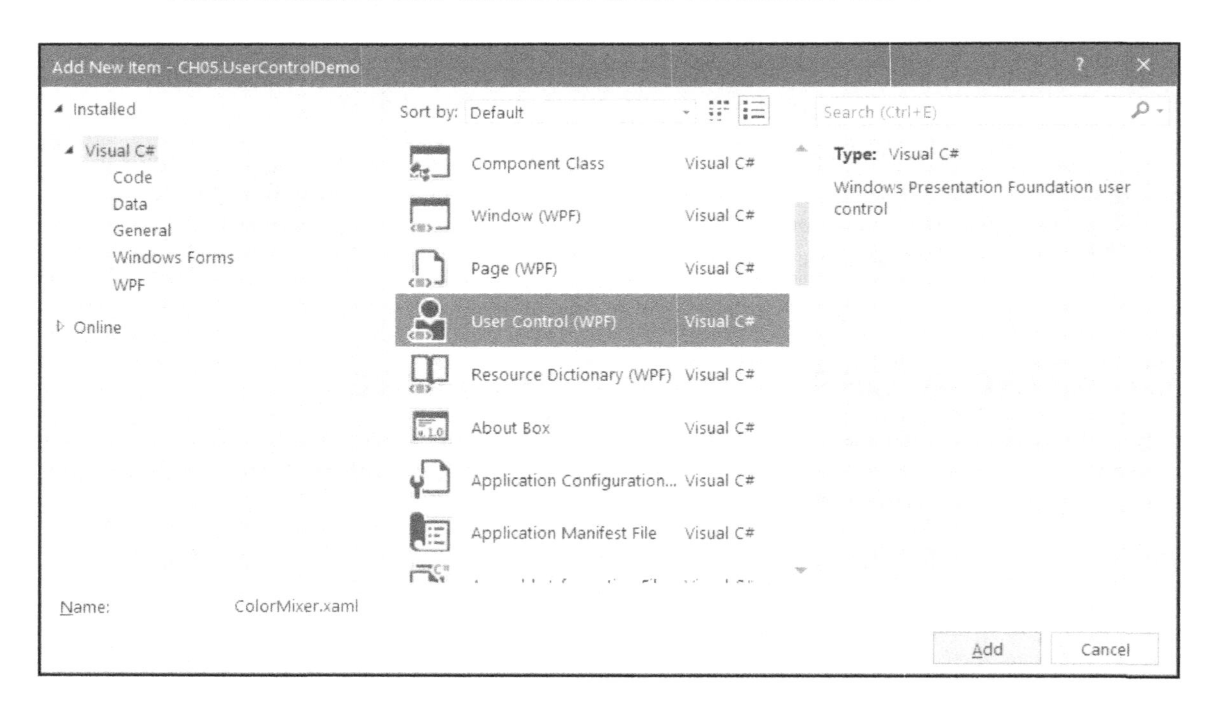

3. Once the User Control has been created, open the code-behind file (`ColorMixer.xaml.cs`) and add a property `SelectedColor` of type `Color` inside it. Give it a default color (let's say, `Colors.OrangeRed`):

```
public Color SelectedColor
{
    get { return (Color)GetValue(SelectedColorProperty); }
    set { SetValue(SelectedColorProperty, value); }
}

public static readonly DependencyProperty
        SelectedColorProperty =
    DependencyProperty.Register("SelectedColor",
    typeof(Color), typeof(ColorMixer),
    new PropertyMetadata(Colors.OrangeRed));
```

4. Let's open the `ColorMixer.xaml` file to provide a UI to the control. We will be adding four `TextBox` controls to assign the color in RGB mode (Red, Green, Blue, and Alpha) and a `Border` to show the output from the RGB mixer.
5. First, give the User Control a name, so that we can easily set its `DataContext` to access its code-behind properties. To do this, add the attribute `x:Name="userControl"` to the `UserControl` tag.
6. Set the `DataContext` of the `Grid` to have an element binding. Add the following attribute inside the `Grid` tag:

```
DataContext="{Binding ElementName=userControl}"
```

7. Now let's divide the default `Grid` panel into a few rows and columns. Copy the following row and column definitions inside the `Grid` tag to create the structure:

```
<Grid.RowDefinitions>
    <RowDefinition Height="*"/>
    <RowDefinition Height="Auto"/>
</Grid.RowDefinitions>
<Grid.ColumnDefinitions>
    <ColumnDefinition Width="*"/>
    <ColumnDefinition Width="Auto"/>
</Grid.ColumnDefinitions>
```

8. Now it's time to add the controls inside the `Grid` to create the UI layout of our User Control. Add a `Border` at the first cell of the `Grid` and bind its `Background` property with the `SelectedColor` property of the User Control that we have created:

```
<Border BorderThickness="1" BorderBrush="Gray"
        Grid.Row="0" Grid.Column="0">
    <Border.Background>
        <SolidColorBrush Color="{Binding SelectedColor}"/>
    </Border.Background>
</Border>
```

9. Now add a `StackPanel` inside the second cell of the `Grid`, which is `Row=0`, `Column=1`. Add four `TextBox` controls and their associated labels inside the panel. Here's the XAML block, which you can copy and place just after the `Border` control:

```
<StackPanel Orientation="Vertical"
            Grid.Row="0" Grid.Column="1"
            Margin="8 4">
    <TextBlock Text="R:"/>
    <TextBox Width="100" />
    <TextBlock Text="G:"/>
    <TextBox Width="100" />
    <TextBlock Text="B:"/>
    <TextBox Width="100" />
    <TextBlock Text="A:"/>
    <TextBox Width="100" />
</StackPanel>
```

10. As the basic UI design is ready, let's place the User Control inside the application window. Open `MainWindow.xaml` and add the following XMLNS attribute to the `Window` tag:

```
xmlns:local="clr-namespace:CH05.UserControlDemo"
```

11. Now replace the default `Grid` panel with a `StackPanel`, so that we can place multiple controls in a stack.

12. Place `<local:ColorMixer />` inside the `StackPanel` and run the application. You will see the following UI on the screen:

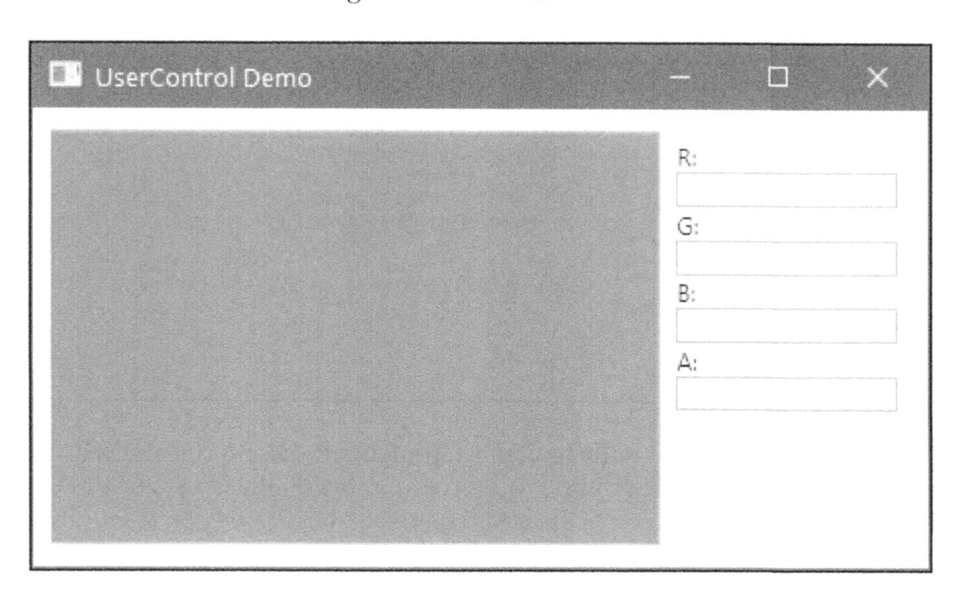

13. The main advantage of a User Control is its ease of use. Creating many instances of it is easy, and there is full design-time support in Visual Studio. Similar to the preceding point, if you place multiple controls of the `ColorMixer` instance inside the `StackPanel`, you will see multiple copies in the UI. Let's not do it, but if you want to try, replace the entire `StackPanel` with the following code block and check out how it places the controls:

```
<StackPanel Orientation="Horizontal"
   Margin="4">
    <local:ColorMixer />
    <local:ColorMixer />
</StackPanel>
```

14. Now let's add the bindings to the `TextBox` controls with the `SelectedColor` property. As the type of the property is `Color`, we will need to create a value converter. So, right-click on the project and add a class by following the context menu path **Add** | **Class...**, name it `ColorToByteConverter`, and hit **OK**.
15. As we need to access the class from the XAML, we will need to mark it as `public`.

16. Now inherit the class from `IValueConverter`, to make it a value converter. Click on the lightbulb icon, as shown in the following screenshot, and resolve the namespace. Alternatively, you can add the `using` statement to resolve the `System.Windows.Data` namespace:

```
public class ColorToDoubleConverter : IValueConverter
```

using System.Windows.Data;
System.Windows.Data.IValueConverter
Generate interface 'IValueConverter' in new file
Generate interface 'IValueConverter'
Generate new type...

CS0246 The type or namespace name 'IValueConverter' could not be found (are you missing a using directive or an assembly reference?)

```
...
using System.Threading.Tasks;
using System.Windows.Data;
...
```

Preview changes

17. Now click on the light bulb again and implement the interface. It will add two methods, called `Convert` and `ConvertBack`, inside the class, as shown in the following screenshot:

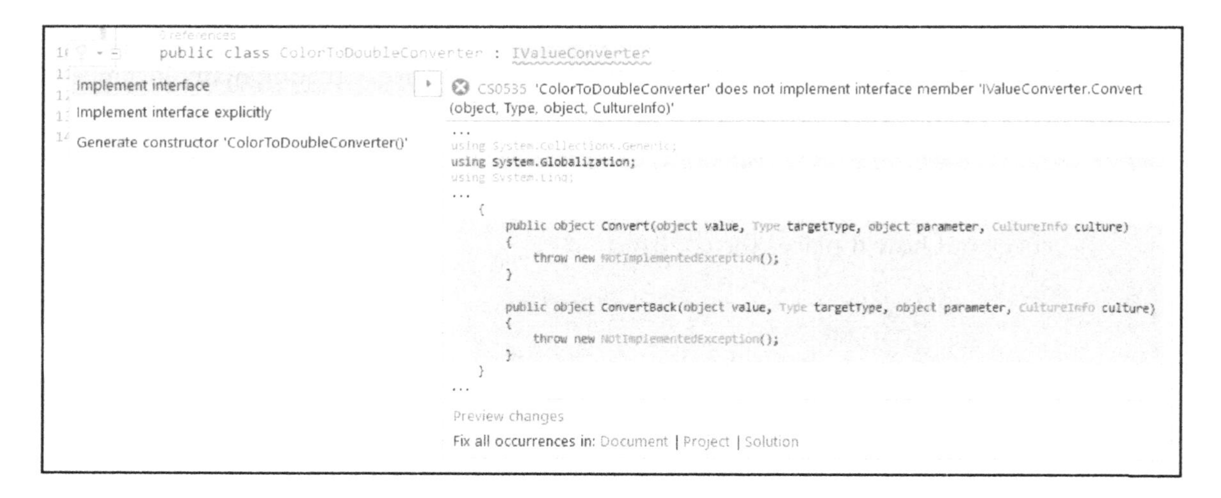

18. Replace the `Convert` method with the following code block, which will break the specified color into an RGBA byte value:

```
public object Convert(object value,
                      Type targetType,
                      object parameter,
                      CultureInfo culture)
```

```
{
    if (value is Color color &&
      parameter is string parameterValue) //C# 7.x syntax
    {
        oldColor = color;

        switch (parameterValue)
        {
            case "r":
                return color.R;

            case "g":
                return color.G;

            case "b":
                return color.B;

            default:
                return color.A;
        }
    }

    return value;
}
```

19. Similarly, replace the `ConvertBack` method to construct the `Color` object from the RGBA values, which you can enter by the `TextBox.Text` property:

```
public object ConvertBack(object value,
                          Type targetType,
                          object parameter,
                          CultureInfo culture)
{
    var color = oldColor;
    var colorValue = System.Convert.ToByte(value);

    if (parameter is string parameterValue) //C# 7.x syntax
    {
        switch (parameterValue)
        {
            case "r":
                color.R = (byte)colorValue;
                break;

            case "g":
                color.G = (byte)colorValue;
                break;
```

```
                case "b":
                    color.B = (byte)colorValue;
                    break;

                default:
                    color.A = (byte)colorValue;
                    break;
            }
        }

        oldColor = color;
        return color;
    }
```

20. Once this is done, open the `ColorMixer.xaml` file and add the following XMLNS attribute under the `UserControl` tag:

```
    xmlns:local="clr-namespace:CH05.UserControlDemo"
```

21. Now create a `<UserControl.Resources>` tag inside the `UserControl` element and register the value converter as a resource. Here's the code that you can copy inside the `UserControl` tag:

```
    <UserControl.Resources>
        <local:ColorToByteConverter
             x:Key="ColorToByteConverter"/>
    </UserControl.Resources>
```

22. Let's modify the `Text` property of all the four `TextBox` controls to have a `TwoWay` data binding with the `SelectedColor` property, and associate them with the converter that we have added. Pass the proper parameter to the converter, as `ConverterParameter`, as mentioned in the following code. You can copy the following code and replace the existing `StackPanel`:

```
    <StackPanel Orientation="Vertical"
                Grid.Row="0" Grid.Column="1"
                Margin="8 4">
        <TextBlock Text="R:"/>
        <TextBox Width="100"
                  Text="{Binding SelectedColor,
    Converter={StaticResource ColorToByteConverter},
    ConverterParameter=r, Mode=TwoWay}"/>
        <TextBlock Text="G:"/>
        <TextBox Width="100"
                  Text="{Binding SelectedColor,
    Converter={StaticResource ColorToByteConverter},
```

```
ConverterParameter=g, Mode=TwoWay}"/>
    <TextBlock Text="B:"/>
    <TextBox Width="100"
             Text="{Binding SelectedColor,
Converter={StaticResource ColorToByteConverter},
ConverterParameter=b, Mode=TwoWay}"/>
    <TextBlock Text="A:"/>
    <TextBox Width="100"
             Text="{Binding SelectedColor,
Converter={StaticResource ColorToByteConverter},
ConverterParameter=a, Mode=TwoWay}"/>
</StackPanel>
```

23. At the end, build the project and run the application. You will see the following UI on the screen, where the rectangular `Border` control has an `OrangeRed` background and the associated `TextBox` control has the RGBA byte value of the color:

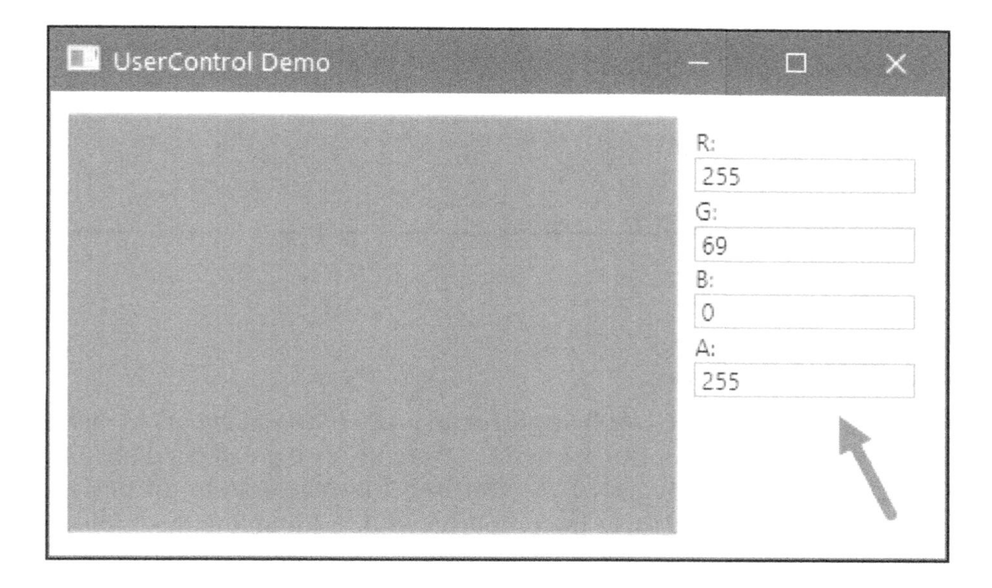

24. Now modify the values of the TextBox controls to have a range (0–255) between 0 to 255 and press *TAB* to reflect the change in the UI. Let's replace the values, Red by 120, Green by 75, Blue by 200, and Alpha by 77, as shown in the following screenshot, which will result in a light violet background color for the Border control:

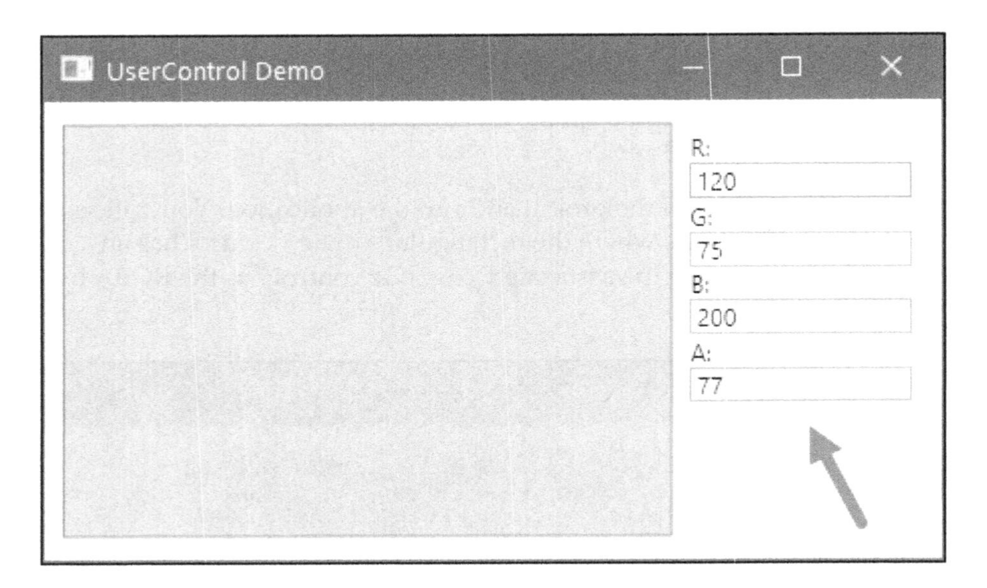

How it works...

A User Control wraps the UI with appropriate properties and events to make it a reusable component. In this User Control, named ColorMixer, we created a dependency property called SelectedColor of type Color. The user (the developer or the designer) can also set a default value to it, by accessing the property, while adding it to the application UI.

The Text property of the TextBox controls, inside the ColorMixer.xaml, is bound with the SelectedColor property. As the types of Text and SelectedColor properties are different, we required the value converter here.

`ConverterParameter` is used to define whether we need to break the R, G, B, or A value of the color composition. The `Convert` method of the converter class breaks the color according to the parameter and returns, which gets displayed in the appropriate `TextBox` control:

```
switch (parameterValue)
{
    case "r":
        return color.R;

    case "g":
        return color.G;

    case "b":
        return color.B;

    default:
        return color.A;
}
```

Similarly, when you modify the value in the `TextBox`, due to its `TwoWay` binding mode, the `ConvertBack` method of the converter triggers. This constructs the color object based on the values available in all the `TextBox` controls and returns, which gets filled in the `SelectedColor` property and reflects in the `Background` property of the `Border` control.

Exposing events from a User Control

In the previous recipe, we learned about User Control, how to create it, and how to expose a dependency property and utilize it. In this recipe, we will learn how to expose events from a User Control, as you will need it in most cases.

Getting ready

Let's open the same project, `CH05.UserControlDemo`, inside the Visual Studio to proceed with this recipe.

How to do it...

To demonstrate the usage of the event, we will add two buttons inside our `ColorMixer` User Control and expose the `OK` and `Cancel` button events from it. To implement the same, perform the following steps:

1. Open the `ColorMixer.xaml` file and add the following `StackPanel` inside the `Grid`, which will place it at row index `1` and column index `0`. The panel consists of two buttons with labels `OK` and `Cancel`:

```
<StackPanel Orientation="Horizontal"
            Grid.Row="1" Grid.Column="0"
            Grid.ColumnSpan="2"
            Margin="4 10 4 4"
            HorizontalAlignment="Right">
    <Button Content="OK" Margin="4"
            Width="50" Click="OnOkClicked"/>
    <Button Content="Cancel" Margin="4"
            Width="50" Click="OnCancelClicked"/>
</StackPanel>
```

2. Open the `ColorMixer.xaml.cs` file and register the button click events (`OnOkClicked` and `OnCancelClicked`) inside it.
3. Inside the `ColorMixer` class, register the following two delegates and events to handle the **OK** and **Cancel** button events from outside the control:

```
public delegate void OnOkButtonClick(object sender,
 EventArgs e);
public delegate void OnCancelButtonClick(object sender,
 EventArgs e);

public event OnOkButtonClick OkButtonClick;
public event OnCancelButtonClick CancelButtonClick;
```

4. Now update the `OK` button and the `Cancel` button event handlers to route the event to the place where the control has been used. Here's the code to replace the button click event implementations:

```
private void OnOkClicked(object sender, RoutedEventArgs e)
{
    OkButtonClick?.Invoke(sender, e);
}

private void OnCancelClicked(object sender, RoutedEventArgs e)
{
```

```
        CancelButtonClick?.Invoke(sender, e);
    }
```

5. To register the associated events, in the application window, open the `MainWindow.xaml` file and register the `OkButtonClick` and `CancelButtonClick` events as follows:

```
<local:ColorMixer OkButtonClick="OnOkClicked"
                  CancelButtonClick="OnCancelClicked"/>
```

6. Navigate to the `MainWindow.xaml.cs` file to implement the associated event handlers. As shared in the following code, show a message box to the UI from the event implementation:

```
private void OnOkClicked(object sender, EventArgs e)
{
    MessageBox.Show("OK button clicked");
}

private void OnCancelClicked(object sender, EventArgs e)
{
    MessageBox.Show("Cancel button clicked");
}
```

7. Let's compile the project and run the application. You will see two buttons on the UI. Click on the **OK** and **Cancel** buttons to see the output:

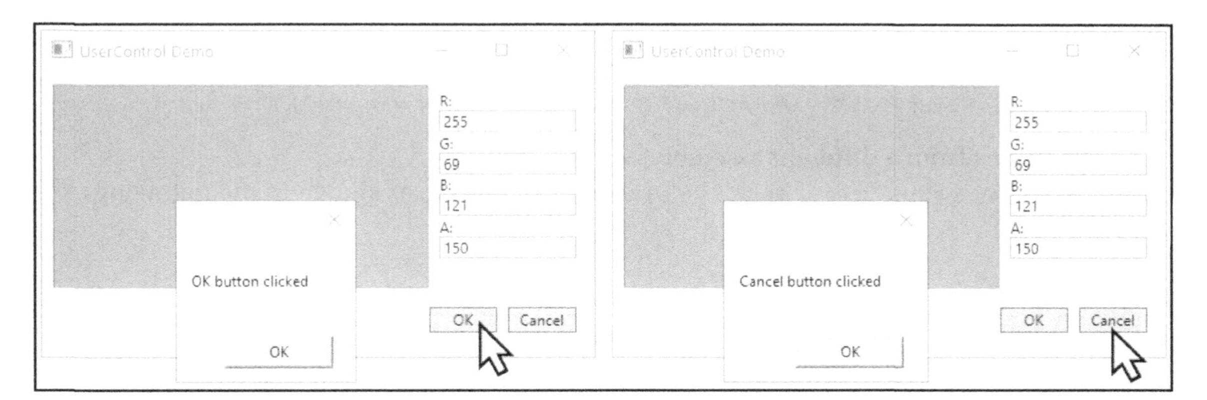

How it works...

When you hit the **OK** button in the application window, it triggers the event associated with the button click. In our case, it's the `OnOkClicked` event, inside the `ColorMixer` class. It then routes the event to the custom event `OkButtonClick`, which gets caught in the originating place. It's the `OnOkClicked` event listener in our `MainWindow.xaml`.

Similarly, when you click on the **Cancel** button, it raises the `Click` event inside the `ColorMixer` class and then routes to the `MainWindow`. If the association is present, it gets called. In our case, it's the `OnCancelClicked` handler in `MainWindow` which triggers the message box.

Customizing the XMLNS namespace

XAML namespace is an extension of XML namespace and conventionally written as `xmlns` in XAML pages. It is used in all the XAML-related technologies to refer to the assemblies and/or namespaces within the XAML page.

Till now, we have seen how to add the XMLNS attribute entry in XAML to refer to custom controls, User Controls, converters, behaviors, and so on, but all that used an assembly/namespace system to define the entry.

For local declaration, we use the `clr-namespace:[namespace]` format, as shown in the following code:

```
xmlns:localBehaviors="clr-
namespace:CH05.NamespaceCustomizationDemo.Behaviors"
```

For declarations from a different assembly, we use the `clr-namespace:[namespace];assembly=[assembly]` format, as shown in the following code:

```
xmlns:behaviors="clr-
namespace:CH05.NamespaceCustomizationLibraryDemo.Behaviors;assembly
=CH05.NamespaceCustomizationLibraryDemo"
```

In this recipe, we will learn how to customize the namespace to give a URL representation.

Getting ready

Let's get started by creating a project called `CH05.NamespaceCustomizationDemo`. In this example, you can either choose a WPF application template or a WPF class library template.

How to do it...

Perform the following steps steps to proceed:

1. Let's create two folders, called `Behaviors` and `Converters`, inside the project.
2. Now create one or more behaviors and converters in the respective folders. These will have `CH05.NamespaceCustomizationDemo.Behaviors` and `CH05.NamespaceCustomizationDemo.Converters` as the namespace for all the behaviors and converters in the respective modules.
3. To create the URL schema for the namespace representation, open the `AssemblyInfo.cs` file present in the `Properties` folder of each project.
4. Now, to create the schema to represent the namespace of the behaviors (`CH05.NamespaceCustomizationDemo.Behaviors`), let's add the following inside the file:

```
[assembly:
XmlnsPrefix("http://schemas.kunal-chowdhury.com/xaml/behaviors"
, "behaviors")]

[assembly:
XmlnsDefinition("http://schemas.kunal-chowdhury.com/xaml/behavi
ors", "CH05.NamespaceCustomizationDemo.Behaviors")]
```

5. Similarly, to define the URL schema for the converters (`CH05.NamespaceCustomizationDemo.Behaviors`), add the following inside the same file:

```
[assembly:
XmlnsPrefix("http://schemas.kunal-chowdhury.com/xaml/converters
", "converters")]

[assembly:
XmlnsDefinition("http://schemas.kunal-chowdhury.com/xaml/conver
ters", "CH05.NamespaceCustomizationDemo.Converters")]
```

6. Navigate to the `MainWindow.xaml` file. To add the XMLNS declaration, you can write `xmlns:behaviors="http://schemas.kunal-chowdhury.com/xaml/behaviors"` instead of `xmlns:localBehaviors="clr-namespace:CH05.NamespaceCustomizationDemo.Behaviors"`.
7. It is a similar case for all the declarations that you have made in the `AssemblyInfo.cs` file to represent the namespace as a URL schema.

How it works...

The `XmlnsPrefix` attribute defines the prefix name that you suggest using in the XAML, while declaring the module namespace. Though it is optional to use the same prefix name, while using the Visual Studio IntelliSense, it automatically adds it.

When you define the XML namespace as URL format, it has multiple benefits over the traditional representation:

- If you follow the same structure, it is easy to remember.
- When you are using custom libraries, you don't have to write the complete namespace and assembly every time in each file. Thus, uses of `xmlns:behaviors="clr-namespace:CH05.NamespaceCustomizationLibraryDemo.Behaviors;assembly=CH05.NamespaceCustomizationLibraryDemo"` can be reduced to `xmlns:behaviors="http://schemas.kunal-chowdhury.com/xaml/behaviors"`.
- You can define the prefix, so that you can follow the same convention in all the files while defining the XMLNS attribute.

6
Using Styles, Templates, and Triggers

In this chapter, we will cover the following recipes:

- Creating the `Style` of a control
- Creating the `Style` of a control based on another `Style`
- Applying `Style` to a control automatically
- Editing the template of any control
- Creating a property trigger
- Creating a multi trigger
- Creating a data trigger
- Creating a multi data trigger
- Creating an event trigger

Introduction

When designing a user interface for an application, you need to ensure the consistency of the look and feel of the controls across the application. For example, if you are using buttons, they should look the same—similar colors, the same margins, and so on.

Styles are objects that hold the `Setter` properties to provide a bunch of settings to elements and controls. Style also provides control templates, which are used to customize the control template to have a distinctive look and feel.

In the Win32/WinForms model, the look and the behavior of the controls were tightly bundled; but in WPF world a control template is created in XAML using designer-oriented tools, and this applies styles to produce a similar look. You can also inherit a style from a different style.

In this chapter, we will discuss styles, templates, triggers, and their relationships with the controls to which they are applied.

Creating the style of a control

Styles provide you with a convenient way to group a set of properties and triggers within a single object and apply it to the elements. You can do this selectively to a set of controls, or you can apply it to all the controls automatically, based on the control type.

In this recipe, we'll begin with the default style of a button and set its various style properties to give it a new look. We will then apply it selectively to set the style of multiple button controls.

Getting ready

Let's get started by creating a new project called `CH06.ControlStyleDemo`. Make sure you create the project based on the WPF application template.

How to do it...

In this recipe, we will get started by creating two buttons inside the application window. Then we will create a style for the button and apply it to both of the controls. Follow these steps to try it on your own:

1. From the **Solution Explorer**, open the `MainWindow.xaml` and replace the existing `Grid` panel by a `StackPanel`.
2. Set the `Orientation` property of the `StackPanel` to `Vertical`, so that we can stack the child controls vertically.

3. Now add a few buttons inside it and assign a content. Here's our markup of the `StackPanel` with two buttons:

```
<StackPanel Orientation="Vertical"
     Margin="10">
    <Button Content="Click Here"/>
    <Button Content="Click Here"/>
</StackPanel>
```

4. Build and run the application. You will see the following UI:

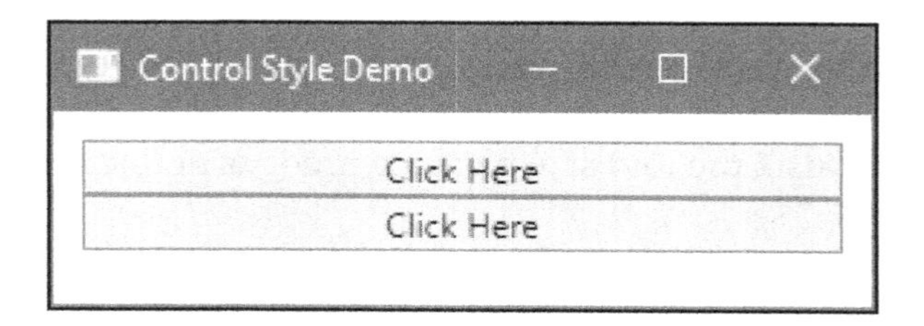

5. Close the application and return to the `MainWindow.xaml` page. Inside the `Window` tag, add `<Window.Resources></Window.Resources>` to add the button style inside it.
6. Copy the following style inside the resources to define a style called `ButtonBaseStyle`, for our button controls:

```
<Style x:Key="ButtonBaseStyle"
       TargetType="{x:Type Button}">
    <Setter Property="Height"
            Value="30"/>
    <Setter Property="MinWidth"
            Value="180"/>
    <Setter Property="FontSize"
            Value="16"/>
    <Setter Property="HorizontalAlignment"
            Value="Center"/>
    <Setter Property="Padding"
            Value="8 0"/>
</Style>
```

7. Now apply the defined style to both of the buttons by adding the attribute `Style="{StaticResource ButtonBaseStyle}"`. Here's the code, for your reference:

```
<StackPanel Orientation="Vertical"
    Margin="10">
    <Button Content="Click Here"
            Style="{StaticResource ButtonBaseStyle}"/>
    <Button Content="Click Here"
            Style="{StaticResource ButtonBaseStyle}"/>
</StackPanel>
```

8. Once this is done, build the project, and run the application again. You will see that the buttons are now shaped properly with some padding between the text and the edge. Also, the font size has increased, as defined in the style. Here's how it looks now:

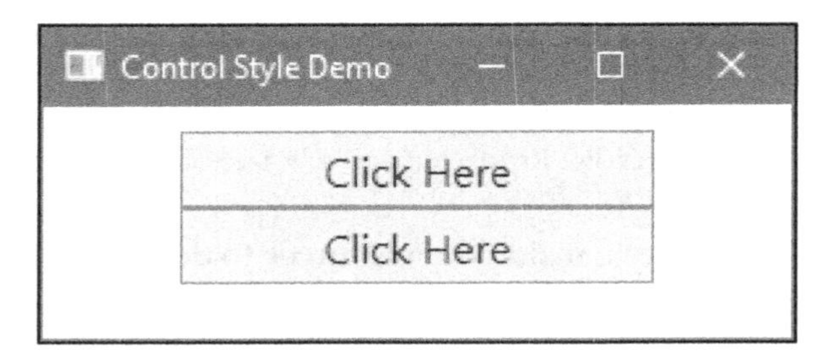

9. Let's add a few additional `Setter` properties to the style. We will now define a `4px` margin, a hand cursor, and a border, as shared here:

```
<Setter Property="Margin"
        Value="4"/>
<Setter Property="Cursor"
        Value="Hand"/>
<Setter Property="BorderThickness"
        Value="2"/>
```

10. Here's the complete style that we have built up to this point:

```
<Window.Resources>
    <Style x:Key="ButtonBaseStyle"
           TargetType="{x:Type Button}">
        <Setter Property="Height"
                Value="30"/>
        <Setter Property="MinWidth"
                Value="180"/>
```

```
            <Setter Property="FontSize"
                    Value="16"/>
            <Setter Property="HorizontalAlignment"
                    Value="Center"/>
            <Setter Property="Padding"
                    Value="8 0"/>
            <Setter Property="Margin"
                    Value="4"/>
            <Setter Property="Cursor"
                    Value="Hand"/>
            <Setter Property="BorderThickness"
                    Value="2"/>
        </Style>
    </Window.Resources>
```

11. Let's compile the project and run the application again. You will now see a better UI with proper styling of the button controls, as shown in the following screenshot:

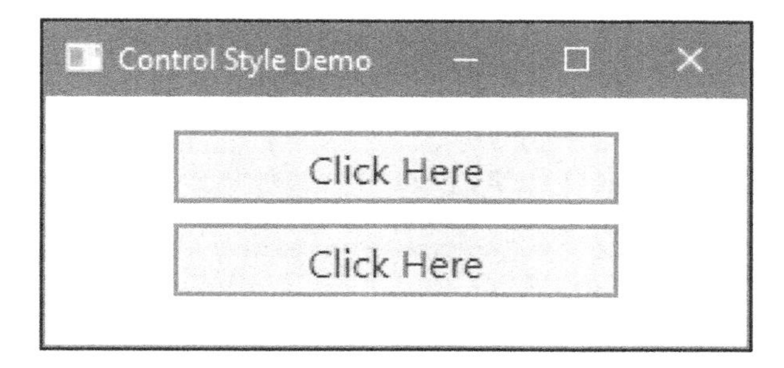

How it works...

When you create a `Style` object, you set a bunch of `Setter` objects to it to define various properties to change the look and feel of the control. This may include the height, width, positions, alignments, colors, fonts, control template, triggers, and more.

The `FrameworkElement` class exposes a `Style` property that can be filled by a `Style` object. Styles are always built as resources, as you see them inside the `<Window.Resources>` tag in our example. It contains an `x:Key` property, which defines the name/key of the style. By using this `Key`, you can perform a binding from any other resources/controls within the scope. The `TargetType` property of a `Style` object is typically set, which makes the `Style` applicable to that type, which can be any type, even a type of a custom control.

In this example, the applied style works on `Button` objects. Trying to apply the same to some other element type will cause a runtime exception.

There's more...

You can omit defining the `TargetType` of a `Style`, but, for that to work, you must define the property with a fully qualified name. For example, the preceding `Style` can be written as shown here to get the same result:

```
<Style x:Key="ButtonBaseStyle">
    <Setter Property="Button.Height"
            Value="30"/>
    <Setter Property="Button.MinWidth"
            Value="180"/>
    <Setter Property="Button.FontSize"
            Value="16"/>
    <Setter Property="Button.HorizontalAlignment"
            Value="Center"/>
    <Setter Property="Button.Padding"
            Value="8 0"/>
    <Setter Property="Button.Margin"
            Value="4"/>
    <Setter Property="Button.Cursor"
            Value="Hand"/>
    <Setter Property="Button.BorderThickness"
            Value="2"/>
</Style>
```

As this makes the property name redundant, to define a qualified name people prefer to use the first one with a `TargetType` defined. Then, what is the use of the second type of declaration? Yes, the question is valid. With this type of styling, by specifying the fully qualified name of the property, you can define a style targeting various types of controls where the said properties are available.

A point to note is that if you explicitly define a property to a control, it will override the property value defined in the `Style`.

Creating the Style of a control based on another Style

Styles support inheritance. That means, you can derive a `Style` from another `Style`. This can be done using the `BasedOn` property, which must point to another `Style` to inherit from. In this recipe, we will learn how to create a `Style` of a button control based on another `Style` of the same type.

Getting ready

Let's get started by creating a project named `CH06.StyleInheritanceDemo`. To do this, open your Visual Studio instance and create a project based on the WPF application template.

How to do it...

Follow these steps to create a base style for a button control and then derive it to create different button styles:

1. Open the `MainWindow.xaml` file and create a `<Window.Resources></Window.Resources>` section inside the `Window` tag.
2. Now, inside the window resources, add the following style definition, which we discussed in the previous recipe of this chapter:

```
<Style x:Key="ButtonBaseStyle"
       TargetType="{x:Type Button}">
    <Setter Property="Height"
            Value="30"/>
    <Setter Property="MinWidth"
            Value="180"/>
    <Setter Property="FontSize"
            Value="16"/>
    <Setter Property="HorizontalAlignment"
```

```
                Value="Center"/>
        <Setter Property="Padding"
                Value="8 0"/>
        <Setter Property="Margin"
                Value="4"/>
        <Setter Property="Cursor"
                Value="Hand"/>
        <Setter Property="BorderThickness"
                Value="2"/>
</Style>
```

3. Replace the default `Grid` to have the following `StackPanel` with four button controls, having the same style that we have created:

```
<StackPanel Orientation="Vertical"
            Margin="10">
    <Button x:Name="baseButton"
            Content="Base Button Style"
            Style="{StaticResource ButtonBaseStyle}"/>
    <Button x:Name="redButton"
            Content="Red Button Style"
            Style="{StaticResource ButtonBaseStyle}"/>
    <Button x:Name="greenButton"
            Content="Green Button Style"
            Style="{StaticResource ButtonBaseStyle}"/>
    <Button x:Name="blueButton"
            Content="Blue Button Style"
            Style="{StaticResource ButtonBaseStyle}"/>
</StackPanel>
```

4. Build the project and run it. You will see the following UI has the same style applied to all the button controls:

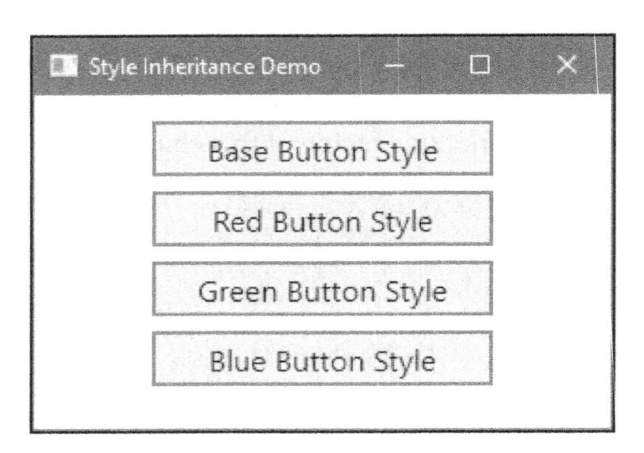

5. To demonstrate the `Style` inheritance, let's create another `Style`, based on the base `Style`. Give it a new `Key` name, `RedButtonStyle`, set the `TargetType` to `Button`, and add a new attribute `BasedOn="{StaticResource ButtonBaseStyle}"` to create the inheritance.
6. Add some additional `Setter` values to the newly created style to define its border, background, and foreground color. Here's the markup for the `RedButtonStyle`:

```
<Style x:Key="RedButtonStyle"
       TargetType="{x:Type Button}"
       BasedOn="{StaticResource ButtonBaseStyle}">
    <Setter Property="BorderBrush"
            Value="DarkRed"/>
    <Setter Property="Foreground"
            Value="White"/>
    <Setter Property="Background"
            Value="OrangeRed"/>
</Style>
```

7. Now change the `Style` property of the `redButton` to point itself to `RedButtonStyle`:

```
<Button x:Name="redButton"
        Content="Red Button Style"
        Style="{StaticResource RedButtonStyle}"/>
```

8. Let's run the application once again, which will have the following UI, where the second button will have a reddish background color and a white font color:

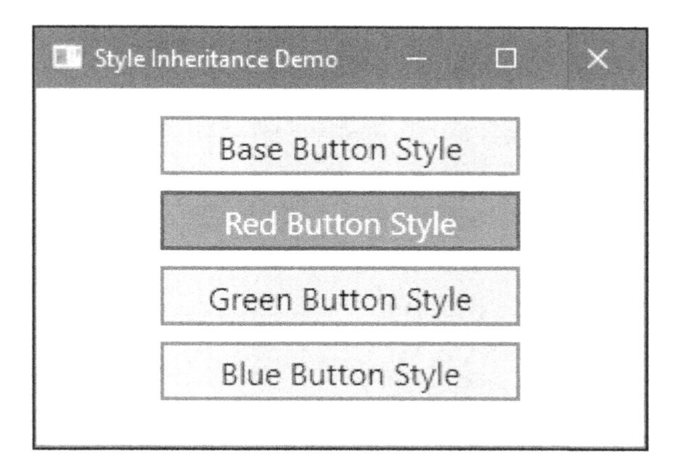

9. Now, add two more styles, based on the `ButtonBaseStyle`, and name them as `GreenButtonStyle` and `BlueButtonStyle`.
10. Set their `BorderBrush`, `Foreground`, and `Background` properties to have a greenish and bluish color, respectively. To do this, copy the following styles inside the `<Window.Resources>` tag:

```
<Style x:Key="GreenButtonStyle"
       TargetType="{x:Type Button}"
       BasedOn="{StaticResource ButtonBaseStyle}">
    <Setter Property="BorderBrush"
            Value="ForestGreen"/>
    <Setter Property="Foreground"
            Value="ForestGreen"/>
    <Setter Property="Background"
            Value="GreenYellow"/>
</Style>

<Style x:Key="BlueButtonStyle"
       TargetType="{x:Type Button}"
       BasedOn="{StaticResource ButtonBaseStyle}">
    <Setter Property="BorderBrush"
            Value="DarkSlateBlue"/>
    <Setter Property="Foreground"
            Value="DarkSlateBlue"/>
    <Setter Property="Background"
            Value="SkyBlue"/>
</Style>
```

11. To apply the preceding styles, modify the `Style` property of the `greenButton` and the `blueButton` as follows:

```
<Button x:Name="greenButton"
        Content="Green Button Style"
        Style="{StaticResource GreenButtonStyle}"/>

<Button x:Name="blueButton"
        Content="Blue Button Style"
        Style="{StaticResource BlueButtonStyle}"/>
```

12. Here's the code snippet for the entire `StackPanel`, which will now have four buttons. Among which the first button is following the base style, whereas the other three buttons are following the new red, green, and blue button styles, respectively:

```
<StackPanel Orientation="Vertical"
            Margin="10">
    <Button x:Name="baseButton"
            Content="Base Button Style"
            Style="{StaticResource ButtonBaseStyle}"/>
    <Button x:Name="redButton"
            Content="Red Button Style"
            Style="{StaticResource RedButtonStyle}"/>
    <Button x:Name="greenButton"
            Content="Green Button Style"
            Style="{StaticResource GreenButtonStyle}"/>
    <Button x:Name="blueButton"
            Content="Blue Button Style"
            Style="{StaticResource BlueButtonStyle}"/>
</StackPanel>
```

13. Time to build the project and run the application. Now, when the application launches, it will have the following UI, but with unique styles. As mentioned earlier, the colors of the buttons will be as per the values we set to the different styles:

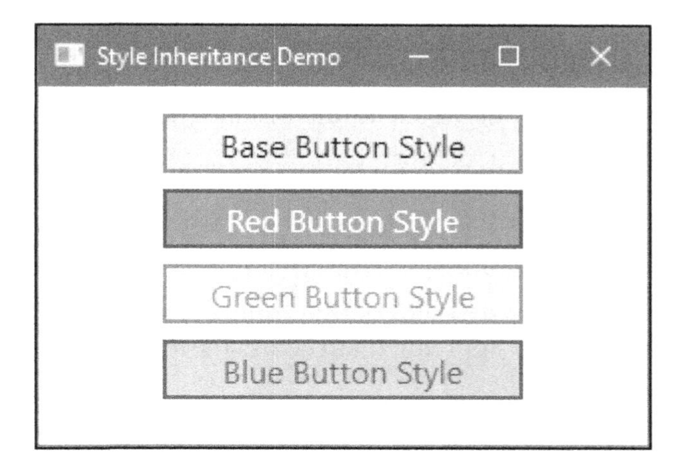

How it works...

An inherited style can have additional `Setter` properties to set, or it can provide a different value for a property that has been set by the base `Style`. In the preceding example, the `RedButtonStyle`, `GreenButtonStyle`, and `BlueButtonStyle` inherit from the first (`ButtonBaseStyle`), and add `BorderBrush`, `Foreground`, and `Background` setter properties to it.

Applying Style to a control automatically

In the previous two recipes, we learned about creating styles and applying them to controls by using the `x:Key` name. It's not always feasible to manually assign the style to a set of huge controls within the same application. For this reason, we need to apply it automatically to all the elements within the scope of a specific window or the entire application.

For example, we may want all buttons within the same app to have the same look and feel. This makes creating new buttons easier, as the developer/designer doesn't have to know what style to apply. If the auto styling is configured, it will make the work far smoother.

Let's see how this can be done with a simple example.

Getting ready

To start this recipe, open your Visual Studio instance and create a new WPF application project called `CH06.StyleUsageDemo`.

How to do it...

Follow these steps to create styles for button controls and apply them to controls within the same window, followed by applying them across the application:

1. Open the `MainWindow.xaml` and replace the existing `Grid` with the following `StackPanel`, containing four button controls:

```
<StackPanel Orientation="Vertical"
            Margin="10">
    <Button Content="Red Button Style"/>
    <Button Content="Red Button Style"/>
```

```
        <Button Content="Red Button Style"/>
        <Button Content="Red Button Style"/>
    </StackPanel>
```

2. Create a `<Window.Resources></Window.Resources>` section inside the `Window` tag and add the following style inside it:

```
    <Style TargetType="{x:Type Button}">
        <Setter Property="Height"
                Value="30"/>
        <Setter Property="MinWidth"
                Value="180"/>
        <Setter Property="FontSize"
                Value="16"/>
        <Setter Property="HorizontalAlignment"
                Value="Center"/>
        <Setter Property="Padding"
                Value="8 0"/>
        <Setter Property="Margin"
                Value="4"/>
        <Setter Property="Cursor"
                Value="Hand"/>
        <Setter Property="BorderThickness"
                Value="2"/>
        <Setter Property="BorderBrush"
                Value="DarkRed"/>
        <Setter Property="Foreground"
                Value="White"/>
        <Setter Property="Background"
                Value="OrangeRed"/>
    </Style>
```

3. Inside the **Solution Explorer**, right-click on the project. Follow the path **Add | Window...** from the context menu entry to open the **Add New Item** dialog window.
4. Enter the name as `SecondaryWindow` and click **Add**. This will create `SecondaryWindow.xaml` and `SecondaryWindow.xaml.cs` files inside the project.
5. Open the `SecondaryWindow.xaml` file and replace `Grid` with the same `StackPanel` to create the UI, having four buttons inside it. Here's the markup that you need to copy:

```
    <StackPanel Orientation="Vertical"
                Margin="10">
        <Button Content="Red Button Style"/>
```

```
        <Button Content="Red Button Style"/>
        <Button Content="Red Button Style"/>
        <Button Content="Red Button Style"/>
    </StackPanel>
```

6. Now, navigate to the `App.xaml` file and remove the `StartupUri="MainWindow.xaml"` attribute, as shown in the following screenshot:

```
<Application x:Class="CH06.StyleUsageDemo.App"
             xmlns="http://schemas.microsoft.com/winfx/2006/xaml/presentation"
             xmlns:x="http://schemas.microsoft.com/winfx/2006/xaml"
             xmlns:local="clr-namespace:CH06.StyleUsageDemo"
             StartupUri="MainWindow.xaml">
    <Application.Resources>
```

7. Now go to its code-behind file, that is, the `App.xaml.cs`, and insert the following code block inside the class implementation to create instances of both the `MainWindow` and the `SecondaryWindow` to show on the screen:

```
protected override void OnStartup(StartupEventArgs e)
{
    base.OnStartup(e);

    new MainWindow().Show();
    new SecondaryWindow().Show();
}
```

8. Once this is done, compile your project, and run the application.
9. As shown in the following screenshot, you will have two windows on the screen. One window (`MainWindow`) will have the styles applied to the button controls, whereas the other window (`SecondaryWindow`) will have the default look and feel:

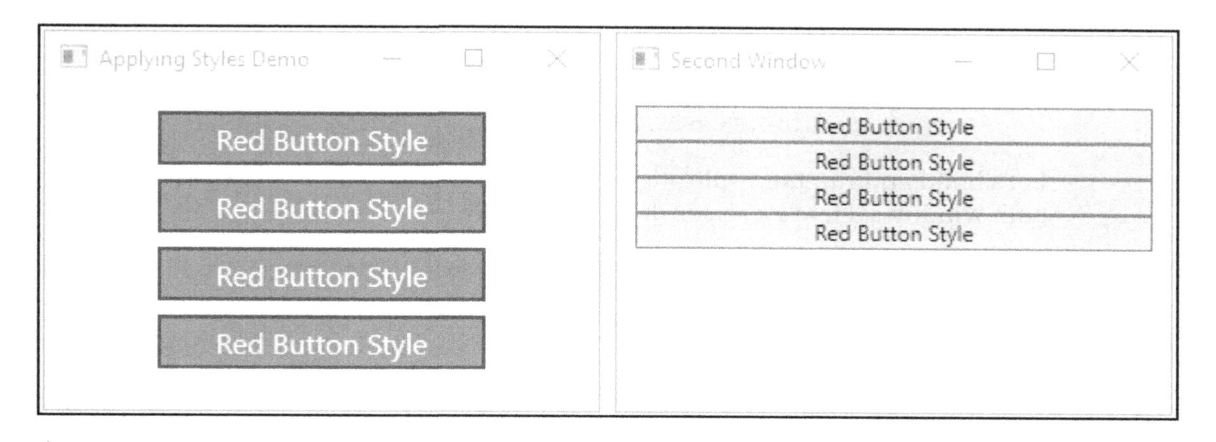

10. Now close the application and navigate to the `MainWindow.xaml` file. Copy the style that we have there and delete/comment the entire `Window.Resources` section.
11. Now open the `App.xaml` file and paste the copied content inside the `Application.Resources` tag, as shared here:

```
<Application.Resources>
    <Style TargetType="{x:Type Button}">
        <Setter Property="Height"
                Value="30"/>
        <Setter Property="MinWidth"
                Value="180"/>
        <Setter Property="FontSize"
                Value="16"/>
        <Setter Property="HorizontalAlignment"
                Value="Center"/>
        <Setter Property="Padding"
                Value="8 0"/>
        <Setter Property="Margin"
                Value="4"/>
        <Setter Property="Cursor"
                Value="Hand"/>
        <Setter Property="BorderThickness"
                Value="2"/>
        <Setter Property="BorderBrush"
                Value="DarkRed"/>
        <Setter Property="Foreground"
                Value="White"/>
```

```
            <Setter Property="Background"
                    Value="OrangeRed"/>
        </Style>
    </Application.Resources>
```

12. Let's build and run the application. You will now see that the styles are applied to both windows. Here's a screenshot of the same:

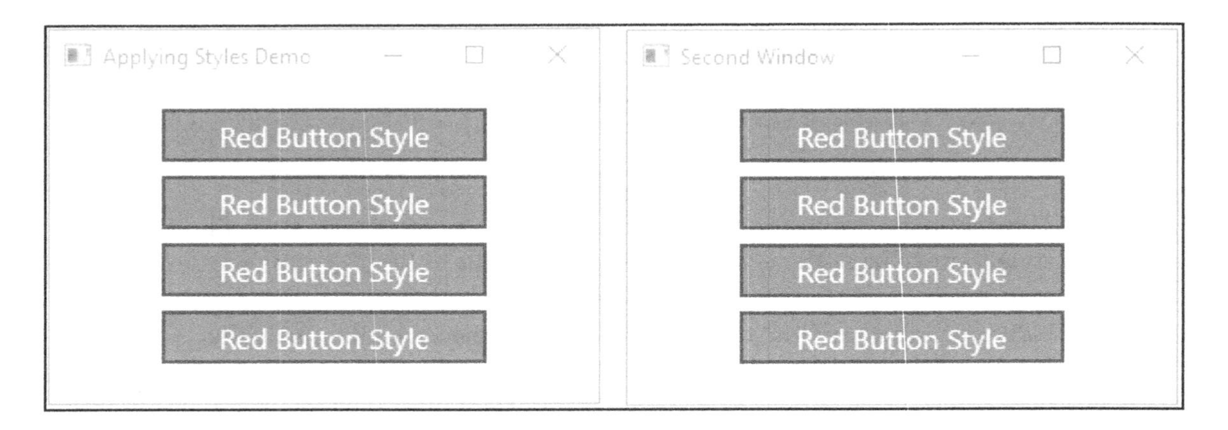

How it works...

The automatic styling works when you create a style without specifying an `x:Key` value. Any element that does not set its style explicitly obtains it automatically.

In the preceding example, we had the buttons in both the windows (`MainWindow` and `SecondaryWindow`), and no `Style` was manually applied to any one of them, but still the controls in the `MainWindow` got the style of **Red Button**, as the `Style` within that window was created without specifying any key (`<Style TargetType="{x:Type Button}">`).

For `SecondaryWindow`, we had no `Style` element defined, and, thus, it applied the default style of the button.

When we moved the `Style` definition to the `Application.Resources` tag in `App.xaml`, it registered the `Style` to the application level. Now, when you run the application, both the windows will receive the style from the application resource, and all controls of type `Button` will apply that style automatically.

If an element wishes to revert to its default style, it can set its `Style` property to `null`. This is generally written as `{x:Null}` in XAML.

Editing the template of any control

WPF allows you to customize the template of any control. Using Visual Studio, you can easily edit any template to meet your requirements. In this recipe, we will discuss how to edit the template of a `ProgressBar` control.

Getting ready

Let's get started with creating a project called `CH06.ControlTemplateDemo`. Make sure you select the right WPF application template while creating the project.

How to do it...

Follow these steps to edit the progress bar template:

1. Open the `MainWindow.xaml` file and replace the default `Grid` control with a vertical `StackPanel`.
2. Add two `ProgressBar` controls inside the `StackPanel` and set their `Height`, `Width`, and `Value` properties, as shared here:

```
<StackPanel Orientation="Vertical">
    <ProgressBar Height="30"
                 Margin="10"
                 Value="40"/>
    <ProgressBar Height="30"
                 Margin="10"
                 Value="60"/>
</StackPanel>
```

3. If you run the application, you will see the application window contains two progress bar controls. Both the controls will have the default style applied to them. Here's a screenshot of the same:

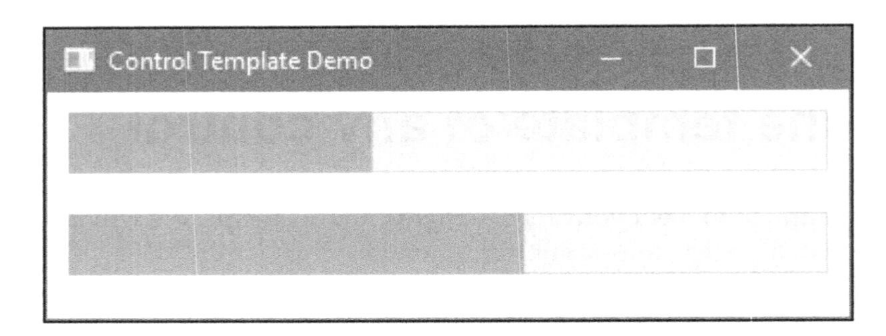

4. Now, we will create a custom template for the `ProgressBar` control and apply it to the second progress bar. To do this, add the following markup inside the `Window` tag to define the template under the `Window.Resources`.
5. Make sure you set the proper `TargetType` and assign an `x:Key` name to it:

```
<Window.Resources>
    <ControlTemplate TargetType="{x:Type ProgressBar}"
                     x:Key="ProgressBarTemplate">
        <Grid>
            <Rectangle x:Name="PART_Track"
                       Fill="AliceBlue"/>

            <Rectangle x:Name="PART_Indicator"
                       StrokeThickness="0"
                       HorizontalAlignment="Left">
                <Rectangle.Fill>
                    <LinearGradientBrush
                          EndPoint=".08,0"
                          SpreadMethod="Repeat">
                        <GradientStop
                                 Offset="0"
                                 Color="Green" />
                        <GradientStop
                                 Offset=".8"
                                 Color="Green" />
                        <GradientStop
                                 Offset=".8"
                                 Color="Transparent" />
                        <GradientStop
                                 Offset="1"
```

```
                            Color="Transparent" />
                    </LinearGradientBrush>
                </Rectangle.Fill>
            </Rectangle>

            <TextBlock FontSize="20"
                       FontWeight="Bold"
                       Foreground="White"
                       HorizontalAlignment="Center"
                       VerticalAlignment="Center"/>
        </Grid>
    </ControlTemplate>
</Window.Resources>
```

6. Now apply the template to the second control by adding the `Template="{StaticResource ProgressBarTemplate}"` attribute value. After doing this, the XAML will look as follows:

```
<StackPanel Orientation="Vertical">
    <ProgressBar Height="30"
                 Margin="10"
                 Value="40"/>

    <ProgressBar Height="30"
                 Margin="10"
                 Value="60"
                 Template="{StaticResource
                            ProgressBarTemplate}"/>
</StackPanel>
```

7. Let's run the application once again. You will see the second control has our custom template applied to it, and it looks like this:

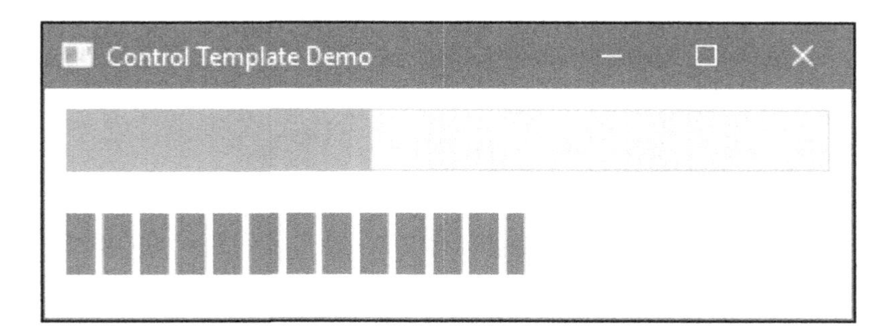

How it works...

When you assign the Template="{StaticResource ProgressBarTemplate}" to the control, it applies the template to the associated control. The progress bar control contains two major parts defined in its template, and they are, PART_Track and PART_Indicator. The first one is used to define the base track of the control, whereas the second one defines the progress indicator.

In our template, we assigned a LinearGradientBrush as the PART_Indicator rectangle's Fill color to design the progress indication in a bar format. GradientStop is used to define the Offset of the selected color, as follows:

```
<LinearGradientBrush EndPoint=".08,0"
                     SpreadMethod="Repeat">
    <GradientStop Offset="0"
                  Color="Green" />
    <GradientStop Offset=".8"
                  Color="Green" />
    <GradientStop Offset=".8"
                  Color="Transparent" />
    <GradientStop Offset="1"
                  Color="Transparent" />
</LinearGradientBrush>
```

Now, when the application runs, because of its repeat behavior (SpreadMethod="Repeat") of LinearGradientBrush, the stacked bars will spread across the control based on the value.

There's more...

It's not easy to remember the default template body of the controls. It is also not possible to remember each control part, defined as PART_Name. Visual Studio provides an effortless way to modify the template.

To do this, right-click on the control and follow the context menu entry **Edit Template** | **Edit a Copy...**, as shown in the following screenshot:

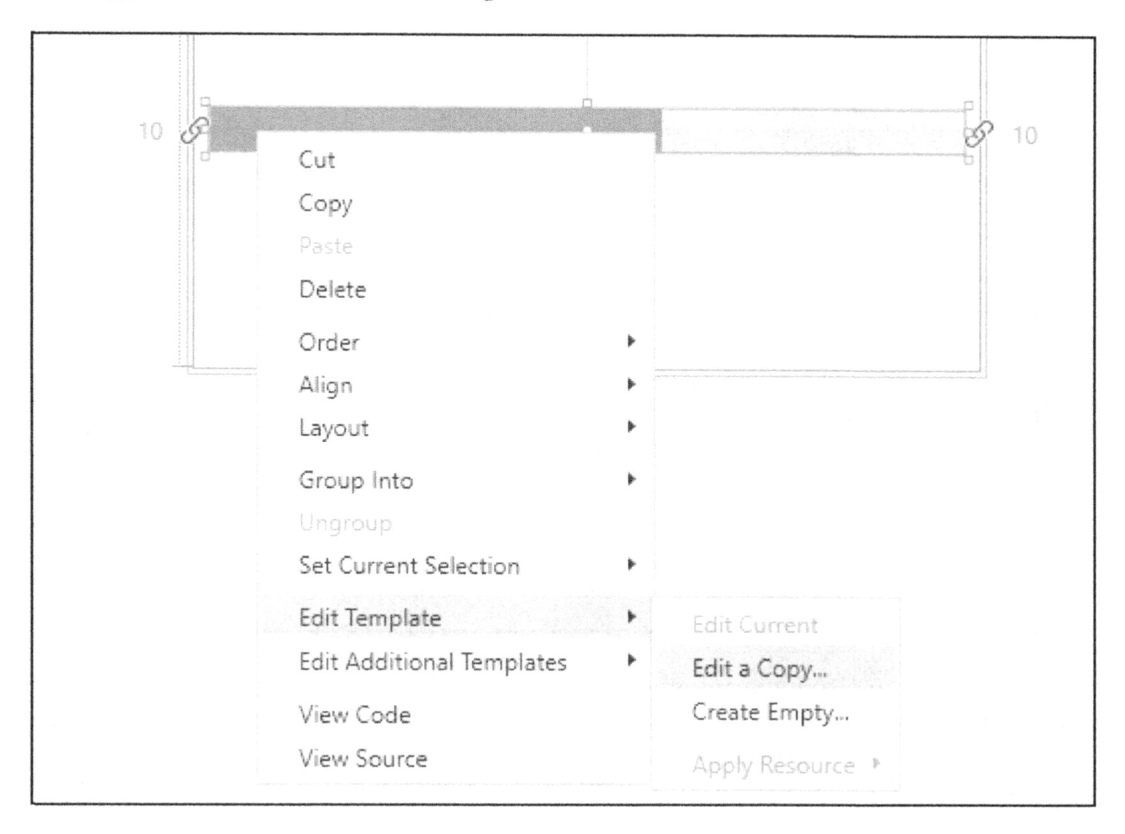

This will open up a dialog window to specify the file where you want to create the style. If you select **Application**, it will be created under the `Application.Resources` tag and will be accessible throughout the application.

If you choose **This document**, it will get created under the `Window.Resources` tag:

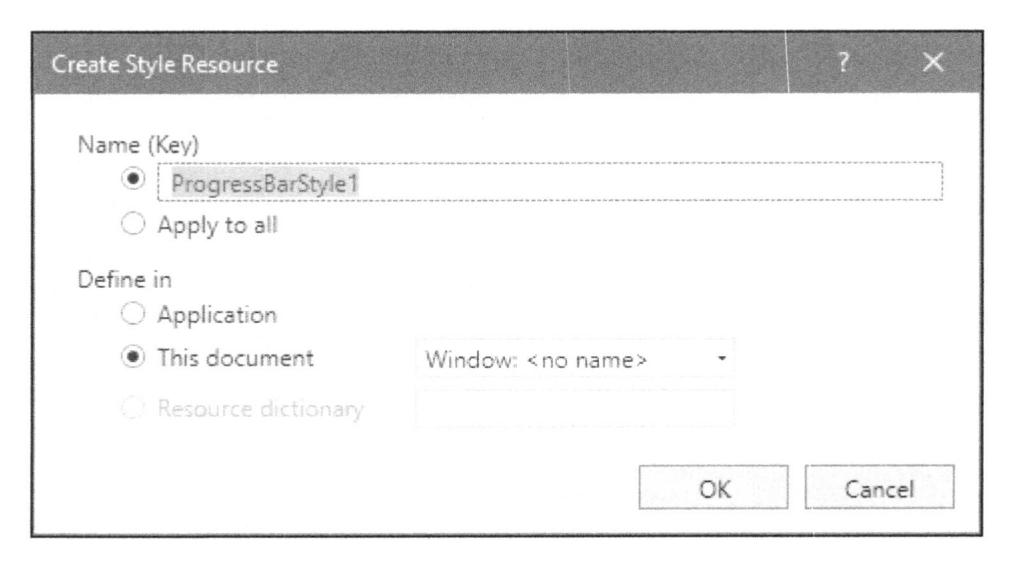

From this screen, you also have an option of whether to create an implicit or explicit style. Select **Apply to all** to create an **implicit style**, and all controls of that type will get the same style within that scope. In another case, give it a **Key** name. Once you click **OK**, it will create the default template in the same XAML. You can customize it based on your requirements.

Never remove any `PART` controls of a template, which is defined by `PART_`, as the controls internally need them.

Creating a property trigger

A trigger enables you to change property values when certain conditions are satisfied. It can also enable you to take actions based on property values by allowing you to dynamically change the appearance and/or the behavior of your control without writing additional codes in the code-behind classes.

The most common trigger is the **property trigger**, which can be simply defined in XAML with a `<Trigger>` element. It triggers when a specific property on the owner control changes to match a specified value.

In this recipe, we will learn about property triggers with a suitable example.

Getting ready

Open your Visual Studio instance and create a new WPF application project called `CH06.PropertyTriggerDemo`.

How to do it...

To work with the property trigger, we will use a `Label` control in this example and trigger the system to change its various properties on mouse hover. Follow these simple steps:

1. Open the `MainWindow.xaml` page and add the following `Label` control inside the grid:

```
<Grid>
    <Label Content="Hover over the text"
           HorizontalAlignment="Center"
           VerticalAlignment="Center"/>
</Grid>
```

2. Inside the `Window` tag, create a `Window.Resources` tag to hold the style of the `Label` control. Create a `Style` inside the resources and set its `TargetType` to `Button`.
3. Add the following trigger inside the style:

```
<Style.Triggers>
    <Trigger Property="IsMouseOver"
             Value="True">
        <Setter Property="FontSize"
                Value="30"/>
        <Setter Property="Foreground"
                Value="Red"/>
        <Setter Property="Background"
                Value="LightYellow"/>
        <Setter Property="Effect">
            <Setter.Value>
                <DropShadowEffect
```

```
                     RenderingBias="Performance"
                     BlurRadius="1"/>
            </Setter.Value>
        </Setter>
    </Trigger>
</Style.Triggers>
```

4. Here's the complete style containing the trigger for the `Label` control, which will change the mentioned properties on mouse hover:

```
<Window.Resources>
    <Style TargetType="{x:Type Label}">
        <Style.Triggers>
            <Trigger Property="IsMouseOver"
                     Value="True">
                <Setter Property="FontSize"
                        Value="30"/>
                <Setter Property="Foreground"
                        Value="Red"/>
                <Setter Property="Background"
                        Value="LightYellow"/>
                <Setter Property="Effect">
                    <Setter.Value>
                        <DropShadowEffect
                             RenderingBias="Performance"
                             BlurRadius="1"/>
                    </Setter.Value>
                </Setter>
            </Trigger>
        </Style.Triggers>
    </Style>
</Window.Resources>
```

5. Now, build the project and run it. You will see a **Hover over the text** label on the application window. Mouse hover on the text to see the effect on the screen, as shown here:

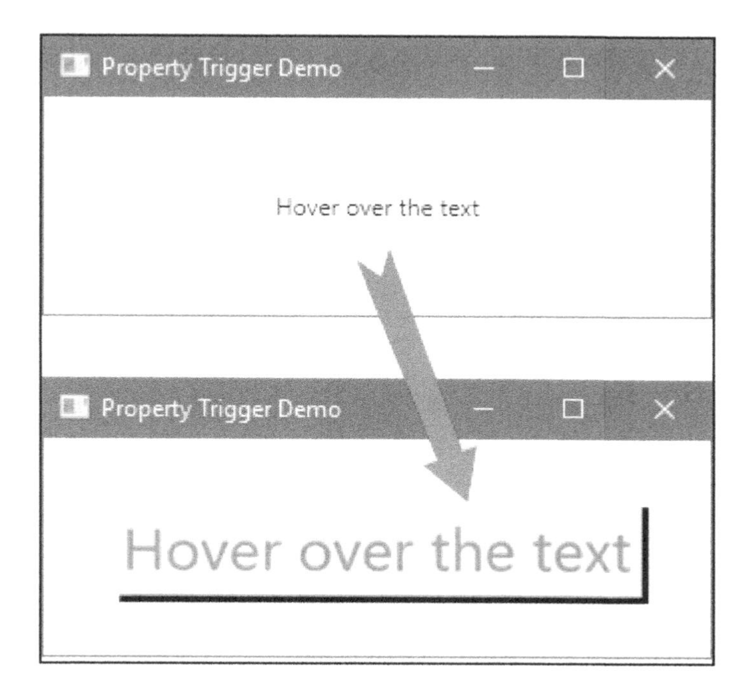

How it works...

The style of the `Label` creates a `Trigger` that fires on mouse hover by checking the `IsMouseOver="True"` property value. When the condition satisfies, it sets the `Setter` properties as defined under it.

When the condition becomes `false`, the setters are logically removed, reverting the properties to their original values. This means that it is not required to provide an *opposite* trigger.

Creating a multi trigger

It is not mandatory to use a trigger to perform only an action based on a single condition. Sometimes you need to create it with a composition of multiple conditions that activate the entire trigger, if all the conditions are met. This is what the **multi trigger** does. Let's see how to create a multi trigger.

Getting ready

Open your Visual Studio IDE and create a new WPF application called `CH06.MultiTriggerDemo`.

How to do it...

In the following steps, we will build a simple application that will create and execute a multi trigger based on some conditions and change the `Foreground` and `Background` properties of the `TextBox` controls:

1. Open the `MainWindow.xaml` file.
2. Replace the default `Grid` panel with a vertical `StackPanel`.
3. Add two `TextBox` controls inside the panel and set their `Text` property to represent some text. Here's the XAML that we will be using in this example:

```
<StackPanel>
    <TextBox Text="Focus your cursor here"
             FontSize="20"
             HorizontalAlignment="Stretch"
             VerticalAlignment="Center"
             Height="30"
             Margin="4"/>

    <TextBox Text="Focus your cursor here"
             FontSize="20"
             HorizontalAlignment="Stretch"
             VerticalAlignment="Center"
             Height="30"
             Margin="4"/>
</StackPanel>
```

4. Now, under the window resources (`Window.Resources`), create a `Style` that targets a `TextBox`:

```
<Style TargetType="{x:Type TextBox}">

</Style>
```

5. Create a style trigger with `MultiTrigger`, based on one or more conditions, and apply the setters, as follows:

```
<Style.Triggers>
    <MultiTrigger>
        <MultiTrigger.Conditions>
            <Condition Property="IsEnabled"
                       Value="True" />
            <Condition Property="IsKeyboardFocused"
                       Value="True" />
        </MultiTrigger.Conditions>

        <MultiTrigger.Setters>
            <Setter Property="Foreground"
                    Value="Green" />
            <Setter Property="Background"
                    Value="LightGreen" />
        </MultiTrigger.Setters>
    </MultiTrigger>
</Style.Triggers>
```

6. Let's execute the application and focus on the `TextBox` controls to see the behavior:

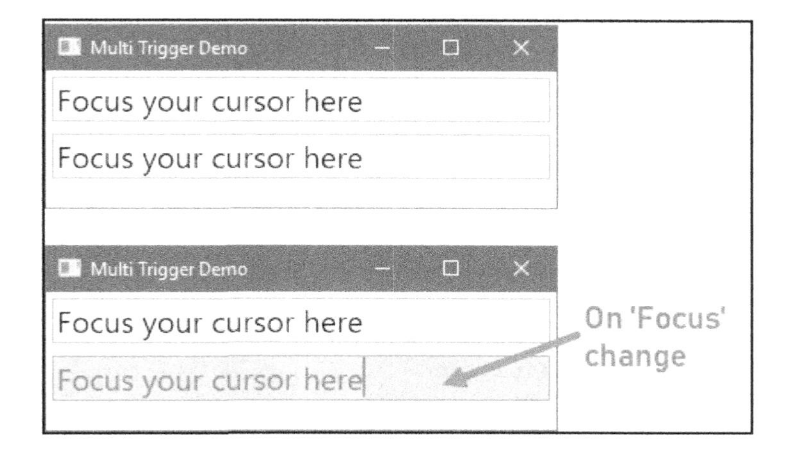

How it works...

This is almost like the **Property Trigger**, but here it is used to set an action on multiple property changes, and will execute it when all the conditions within the `MulitTrigger.Conditions` are satisfied. The `MultiTrigger` object hosts a collection of these `Condition` objects.

Here, in this example, we have `MultiTrigger` associated with `TextBox` controls. When the control is enabled and gets keyboard focus, it changes its `Foreground` and `Background` properties. When either of them is `false`, it returns the property values to its original state.

Creating a data trigger

As the name says, the **data trigger** applies property values to perform a set of actions on the `Data` that has been bound to the `UIElement`. This is represented by the `<DataTrigger>` element.

In this recipe, we will learn how to create a trigger that acts on the underlying data.

Getting ready

Let's get started with creating a new WPF project. Open the Visual Studio and create a project called `CH06.DataTriggerDemo`.

How to do it...

Follow these simple steps to create a data trigger that will act to change the `Background` and `Content` property of a `Label`, based on the radio button selection:

1. From the **Solution Explorer**, open the `MainWindow.xaml` file.
2. Let's divide the `Grid` panel into two columns:

```
<Grid.ColumnDefinitions>
    <ColumnDefinition/>
    <ColumnDefinition/>
</Grid.ColumnDefinitions>
```

3. Now insert a `Label` of `150 x 100` dimension at column `0` (zero) and set its `Foreground` property to `White`:

```
<Label Width="150"
       Height="100"
       Grid.Column="0"
       Foreground="White"
       FontSize="20"
       BorderBrush="Gray"
       BorderThickness="1"/>
```

4. Insert a vertical `StackPanel` at Column `1` and add three radio buttons inside it. Make sure you set their names and the `GroupName`. The `x:Name` property is used to define the name of the controls and the `GroupName="colors"` is used to define a single group for the radios. Here's the complete XAML markup:

```
<StackPanel Grid.Column="1"
            Margin="10">
    <RadioButton x:Name="rdoRed"
                 GroupName="colors"
                 Content="Red (#FFFF0000)"/>

    <RadioButton x:Name="rdoGreen"
                 GroupName="colors"
                 Content="Green (#FF00FF00)"/>

    <RadioButton x:Name="rdoBlue"
                 GroupName="colors"
                 Content="Blue (#FF0000FF)"/>
</StackPanel>
```

5. Inside the `Window.Resources` tag of the window, create a `Style` that targets `Label` control:

```
<Style TargetType="{x:Type Label}">

</Style>
```

6. Insert the following trigger inside the `Style`. The `<Style.Triggers>` contains three `DataTrigger` bound to the checkbox controls:

```
<Style.Triggers>
    <DataTrigger Binding="{Binding ElementName=rdoRed,
                          Path=IsChecked}"
                 Value="True">
        <Setter Property="Content"
                Value="Red"/>
        <Setter Property="Background"
                Value="Red"/>
    </DataTrigger>

    <DataTrigger Binding="{Binding ElementName=rdoGreen,
                          Path=IsChecked}"
                 Value="True">
        <Setter Property="Content"
                Value="Green"/>
        <Setter Property="Background"
                Value="Green"/>
    </DataTrigger>

    <DataTrigger Binding="{Binding ElementName=rdoBlue,
                          Path=IsChecked}"
                 Value="True">
        <Setter Property="Content"
                Value="Blue"/>
        <Setter Property="Background"
                Value="Blue"/>
    </DataTrigger>
</Style.Triggers>
```

7. As the trigger is ready, let's build the project and run it. Change the radio button selection and observe how it works, as shown in the following screenshot:

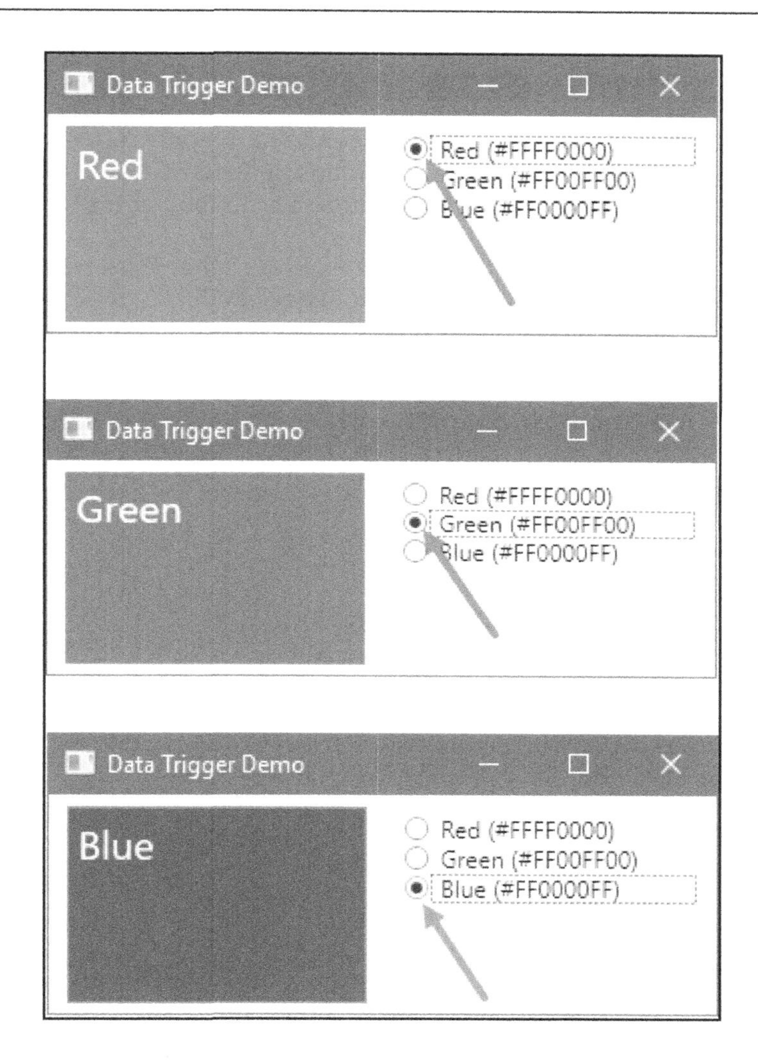

How it works...

When you click on the first radio button (`rdoRed`), it triggers the first data trigger, as it satisfies the `IsChecked` property of `rdoRed` control and modifies the `Setter` properties—`Content` and `Background`.

Similarly, when you change the selection to the second or third radios, the respective `DataTrigger` will fire and update the `Label` control, according to the `Setter` properties.

Creating a multi data trigger

A **multi data trigger** is the same as the **data trigger**, with the only difference being that you can set property values based on multiple conditions defined in the `MultiDataTrigger.Conditions`. Property values are defined in the `MultiDataTrigger.Setters`.

Let's learn about the multi data trigger usages in this recipe.

Getting ready

To get started with the multi data trigger, let's start by creating a project called `CH06.MultiDataTriggerDemo`. Make sure you select the proper project template.

How to do it...

Follow these steps to create a UI with two checkboxes and a button, and then apply a multi data trigger to enable/disable the button, based on the check state:

1. Let's begin by replacing the `Grid` with a `StackPanel`, having two checkbox (`chkLicense` and `chkTerms`) controls and one button:

```
<StackPanel HorizontalAlignment="Center"
            VerticalAlignment="Center">
    <CheckBox x:Name="chkLicense"
              Content="Yes, I accept license agreement" />
    <CheckBox x:Name="chkTerms"
              Content="Yes, I accept Terms &amp; Conditions" />

    <Button HorizontalAlignment="Center"
            Margin="0,20,0,0"
            FontSize="20"
            Content="Register">

    </Button>
</StackPanel>
```

2. Now, modify the `Button` to expose its style, as follows:

```
<Button HorizontalAlignment="Center"
        Margin="0,20,0,0"
        FontSize="20"
        Content="Register">
    <Button.Style>

    </Button.Style>
</Button>
```

3. Add the following button style inside it, which contains a `MultiDataTrigger` to enable/disable the button:

```
<Style TargetType="{x:Type Button}">
    <Setter Property="IsEnabled"
            Value="False"/>
    <Style.Triggers>
        <MultiDataTrigger>
            <MultiDataTrigger.Conditions>
                <Condition Binding="{Binding
                           ElementName=chkLicense,
                           Path=IsChecked}"
                           Value="True" />
                <Condition Binding="{Binding
                           ElementName=chkTerms,
                           Path=IsChecked}"
                           Value="True" />
            </MultiDataTrigger.Conditions>

            <Setter Property="IsEnabled"
                    Value="True" />
        </MultiDataTrigger>
    </Style.Triggers>
</Style>
```

4. Now run the application, which will have two checkboxes and a button on the screen. Change the selections of the checkbox controls to see the behavior:

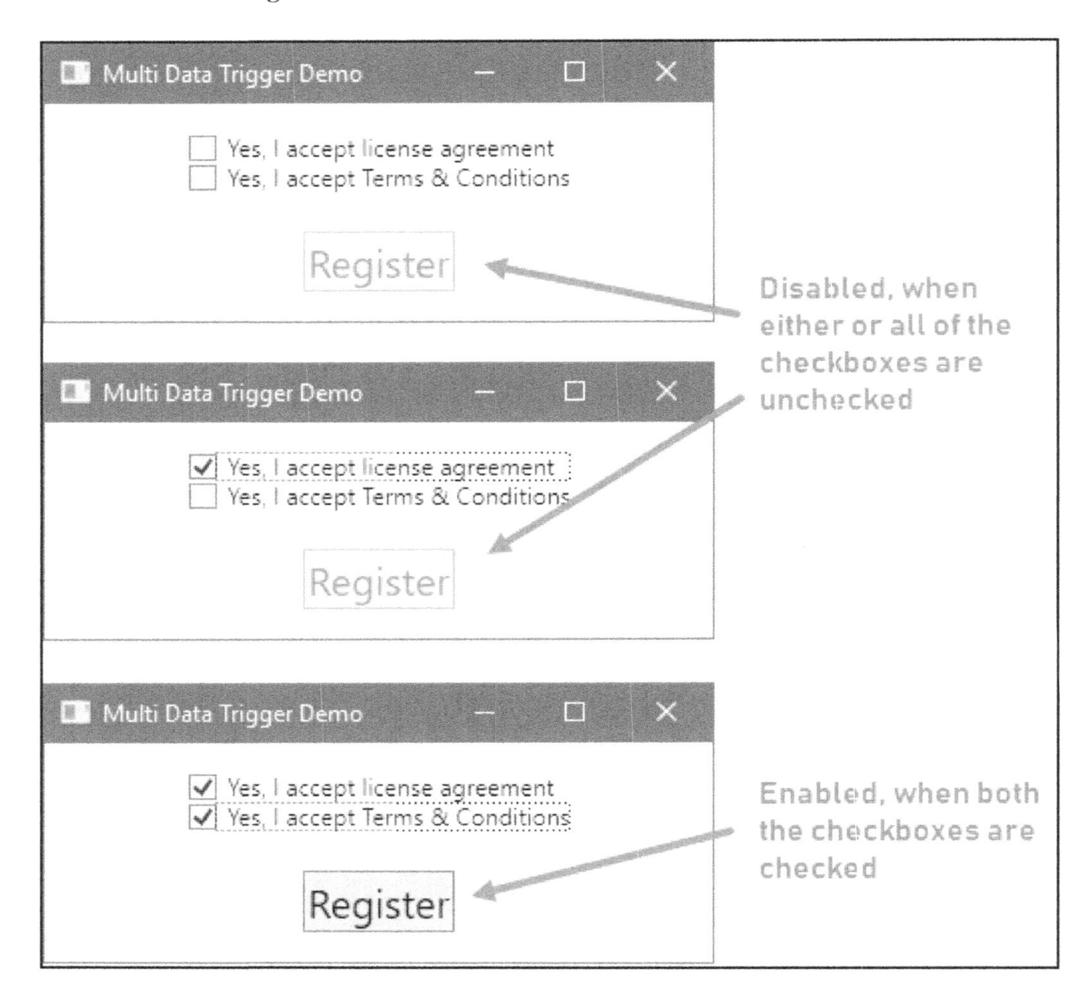

How it works...

A multi data trigger works based on the conditions set to it, which acts on the underlying data. In our example, we have a `MultiDataTrigger` with two conditions.

According to the conditions, if both the checkbox controls are checked, it will trigger and enable the button by setting the `IsEnabled` property to `True`. When any of the preceding conditions are not satisfied, it will automatically set the `IsEnabled` property to the previous value, which is `False` in our case.

Creating an event trigger

Till now, we have seen property triggers and data triggers, which work based on comparing a property to a value. In this recipe, we will learn about **event triggers** which fire when a routed event occurs.

Getting ready

Inside your Visual Studio IDE, create a new project called `CH06.EventTriggerDemo`, based on the WPF application template.

How to do it...

Follow these steps to create a simple event trigger on a `TextBlock` control:

1. Open the `MainWindow.xaml` and add the following `TextBlock` inside the `Grid`:

```
<TextBlock Text="Hover here"
           FontSize="30"
           Opacity="0.2"
           HorizontalAlignment="Center"
           VerticalAlignment="Center">
    <TextBlock.Style>

    </TextBlock.Style>
</TextBlock>
```

2. Add the following style, containing `EventTrigger`, to the `TextBlock.Style` attribute:

```
<Style TargetType="TextBlock">
    <Style.Triggers>
        <EventTrigger RoutedEvent="MouseEnter">
            <EventTrigger.Actions>
                <BeginStoryboard>
```

```
                        <Storyboard>
                            <DoubleAnimation
                  Duration="0:0:0.500"
                  Storyboard.TargetProperty="FontSize"
                  To="50" />
                            <DoubleAnimation
                  Duration="0:0:0.500"
                  Storyboard.TargetProperty="Opacity"
                  To="1.0"/>
                        </Storyboard>
                    </BeginStoryboard>
                </EventTrigger.Actions>
            </EventTrigger>

            <EventTrigger RoutedEvent="MouseLeave">
                <EventTrigger.Actions>
                    <BeginStoryboard>
                        <Storyboard>
                            <DoubleAnimation
                  Duration="0:0:0.500"
                  Storyboard.TargetProperty="FontSize"
                  To="30" />
                            <DoubleAnimation
                  Duration="0:0:0.500"
                  Storyboard.TargetProperty="Opacity"
                  To="0.2"/>
                        </Storyboard>
                    </BeginStoryboard>
                </EventTrigger.Actions>
            </EventTrigger>
        </Style.Triggers>
    </Style>
```

3. Build the application and run it. Hover your mouse on top of the text and you will see that the font size of the text gradually increases, and the visibility becomes `100%`:

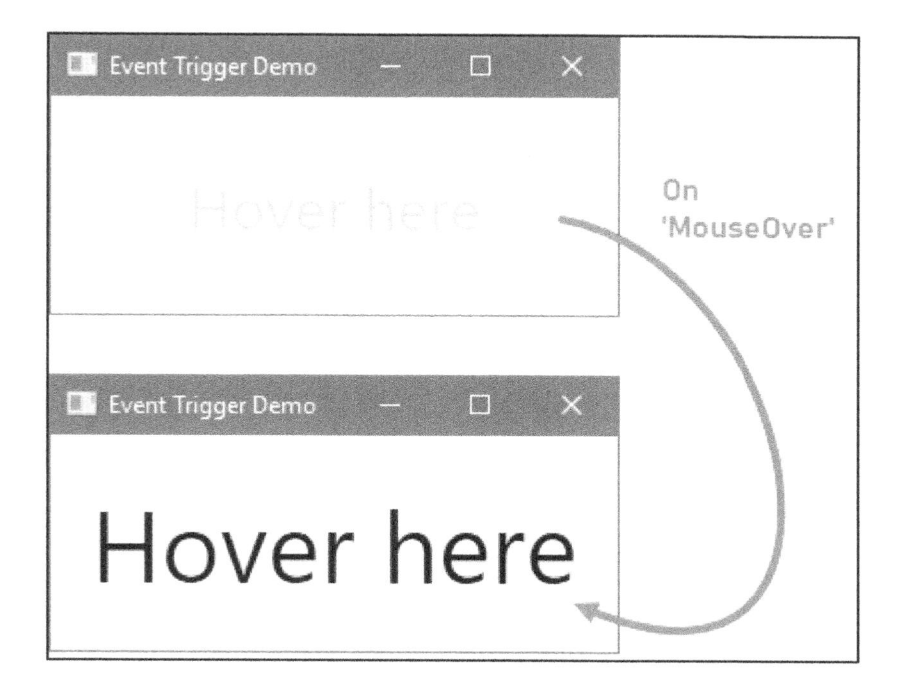

How it works...

The event triggers are generally used to perform actions when the **Routed Events** of the associated `FrameworkElement` raises. This is mainly used in animations to control the look and feel when a certain UI event is raised.

In this example, when you hover over the mouse cursor on the `TextBlock` control, the `MouseEnter` event fires and that triggers `EventTrigger`, which we have defined in the XAML. It then animates the text to have a bigger font size and a higher opacity to give a bigger, better visible content.

When the `MouseLeave` event fires, it reduces the size of the font and brings the control opacity to `20%`. More about the `Storyboard` animations will be discussed in *Chapter 8, Working with Animations*.

7
Using Resources and MVVM Patterns

In this chapter, we will cover the following recipes:

- Using binary resources inside a WPF application
- Using binary resources from another assembly
- Accessing binary resources in code
- Using static logical resources in WPF
- Using dynamic logical resources in WPF
- Managing logical resources
- Using user selected colors and fonts
- Building an application using the MVVM pattern
- Using routed commands in a WPF application

Introduction

While binary resources play a vital role in any application, WPF also provides a different kind of resource, called a **logical resource**. These logical resources are objects that can be shared throughout the application and can be accessed across multiple assemblies. These can be of two types, static logical resources and dynamic logical resources.

On the other hand, **MVVM** (**Model-View-ViewModel**) is a pattern that keeps a separation between the UI and the code, giving the designers and developers the flexibility to work on a single window without depending on each other.

In this chapter, we will first cover binary resources, logical resources, and then move forward to learn building applications using the MVVM pattern. We will also cover how to use **RoutedCommands** to demonstrate the **Command Design Pattern** in WPF applications, which can be invoked from multiple locations.

Using binary resources inside a WPF application

Binary resources are chunks of bytes added to a project with `Build Action` defined for it. Generally, these are images, logos, fonts, files, and so on, which are required by the application and are bundled with it.

In this recipe, we will learn how to use binary resources in a WPF application.

Getting ready

To get started, open your Visual Studio IDE and create a new project called `CH07.BinaryResourceDemo`. Make sure you select the WPF app as the project template.

How to do it...

Follow these steps to add images as binary resources inside a WPF application and load them into the application window:

1. Right-click on the project to add a new folder. Follow the context menu path **Add | New Folder**. Rename the newly created folder as `Images`:

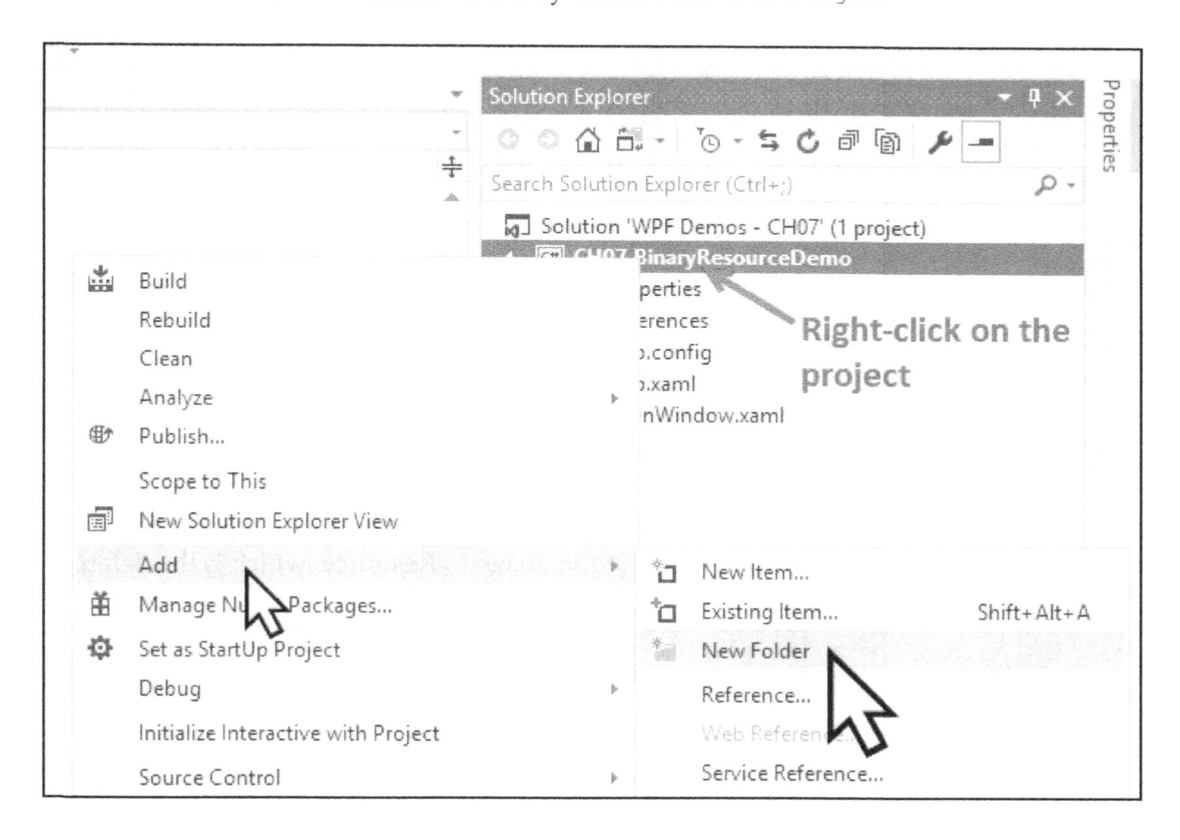

2. Now right-click on the **Images** folder to add a few images. From the context menu entry, select **Add** | **Existing Item...** and add two images of your choice. In this example, we have added two existing images, `image1.png` and `image2.png`, for demonstration:

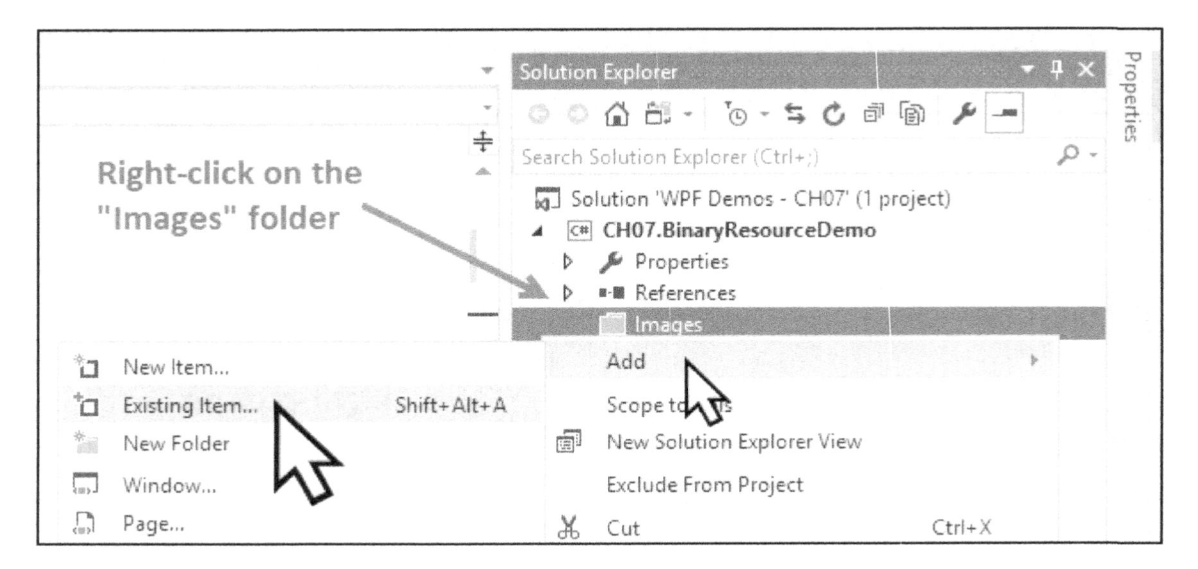

3. From the **Solution Explorer**, right-click on the `image1.png` and go to its **Properties**. Set the **Build Action** of the image to **Resource**, which is the default:

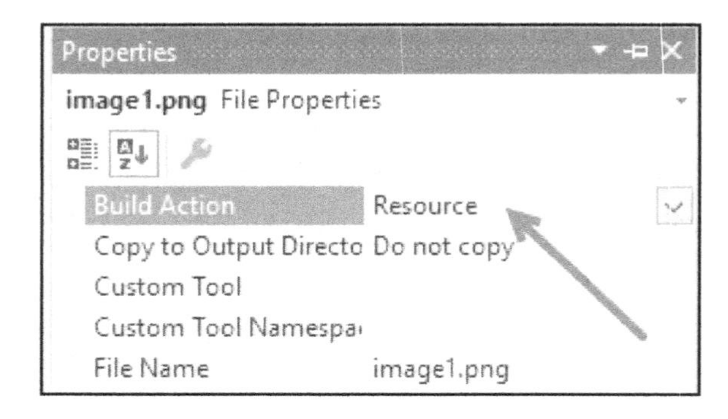

4. Now right-click on the `image2.png` from **Solution Explorer**, and go to its **Properties**. Set its **Build Action** to **Content**.

5. Change the **Copy to Output Directory** to **Copy Always**:

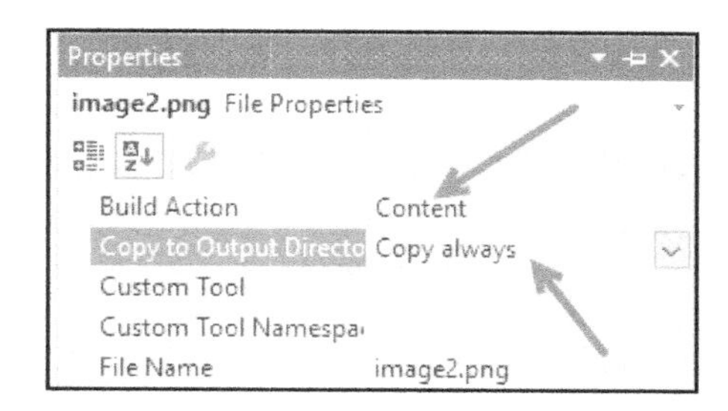

6. From the **Solution Explorer**, open the `MainWindow.xaml` and replace the `Grid` with a horizontal `StackPanel`.
7. Now insert the two images inside the `StackPanel`, and set their `Source` property to `Images/image1.png` and `Images/image2.png`, respectively:

```
<StackPanel Orientation="Horizontal">
    <Image Source="Images/image1.png"
           Width="150"
           Margin="8"/>
    <Image Source="Images/image2.png"
           Width="150"
           Margin="8"/>
</StackPanel>
```

8. Build the project and run the application. You will see the following UI on the screen:

9. Now go to the project's **bin** | **Debug** directory. You will see a folder named **Images** containing the image (`image2.png`) that we defined as `Build Action = Content` and `Copy to Output Directory = Copy Always`.
10. Now replace the `image2.png` with a different image.
11. Run the application now, directly from the **bin** | **Debug** folder, instead of recompiling the project. Observe the output on the screen. You will see that the second image now points to the new image that we have placed in the **bin** | **Debug** | **Images** folder:

How it works...

When the `Build Action` is set to `Resource`, the file is stored as a resource inside the compiled assembly. In our case, `image1.png` was set to `Resource` inside the project binary, which makes the actual image file unnecessary while deploying the application.

When the `Build Action` is set to `Content`, the resource is not included in the assembly. To make it available to the application, `Copy to Output Directory` needs to be set to either `Copy Always` or `Copy if Newer`.

This makes it more appropriate for when the resource needs to change often and a rebuild would be undesirable. If the resource is not available in the output directory, this will render a blank image while executing. If the resource is large and not always needed, it's better to leave it to the resulting assembly.

There's more...

While inserting the image in the XAML, we often use the relative URI (`Images/image1.png`, in our case) as it is relative to the application. You can also assign it more verbosely as `pack://application:,,,/Images/image1.png`, which is generally used while assigning the image source from the code behind.

You can also use the Visual Studio editor to assign the image source. To do so, right-click on the image from the XAML designer view and go to its **Properties**. From the **Properties** panel, click the dropdown arrow, as shown in the following screenshot, to select the desired image from the available items in the list:

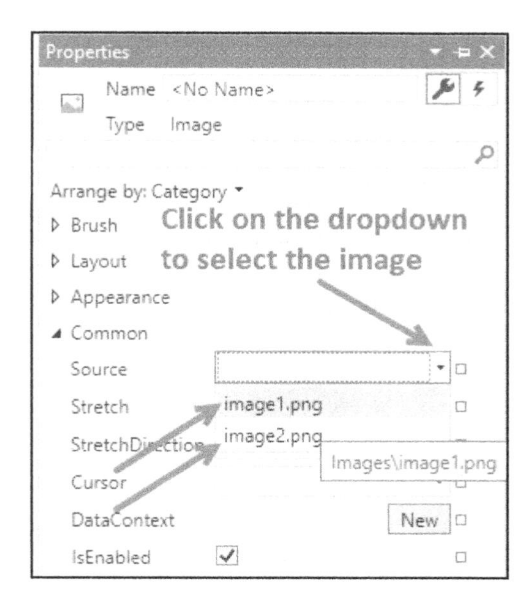

Using binary resources from another assembly

It is not mandatory to have the resources defined in the same assembly where they are going to be used. Sometime, on an as-needed basis, the binary resources are defined in one assembly (generally, a class library), and used in another assembly.

WPF provides a uniform way of accessing these resources defined in other assemblies. To work with this, we need to use the pack URI scheme. In this recipe, we will learn how to use binary resources from another assembly.

Getting ready

Let's begin with creating a new project called `CH07.RemoteBinaryResourceDemo`. Make sure you select the WPF app template while creating this project.

How to do it...

Follow these steps to create a class library to define the binary resource and use it from the application that we have already created:

1. Create another project within the same solution. Let's name it `CH07.ResourceLibrary`, and make sure you select **Class Library (.NET Framework)** as the project template:

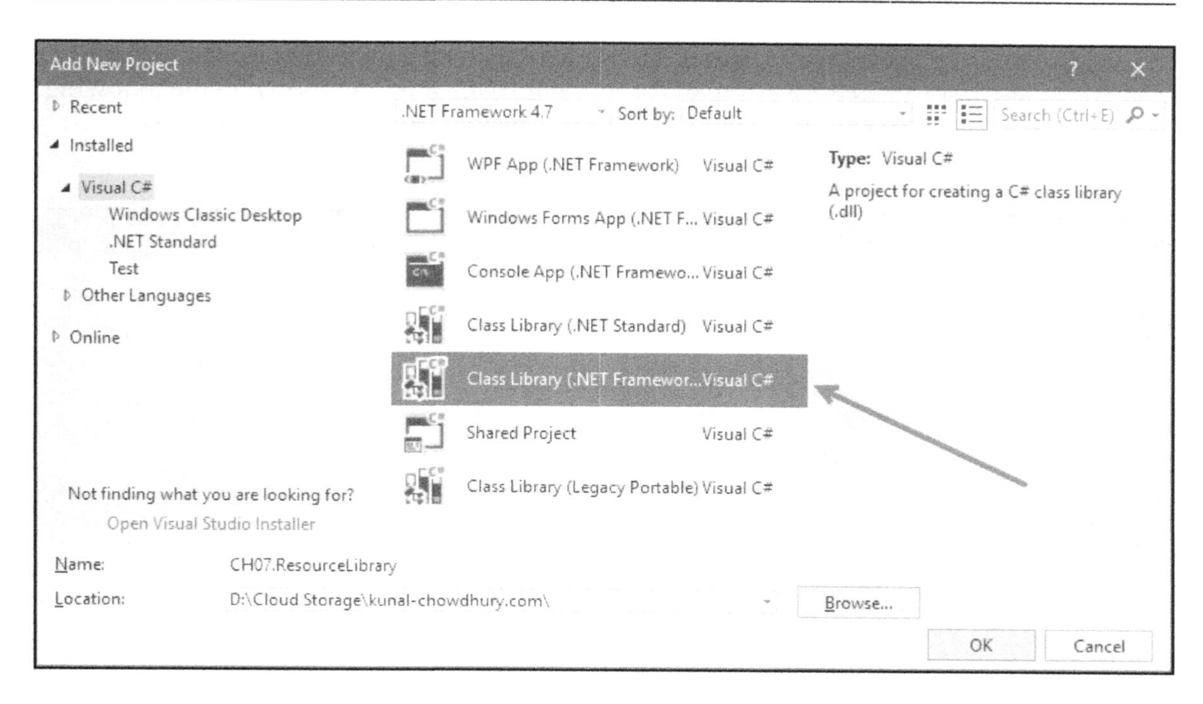

2. Remove the autogenerated class file `Class1.cs`.
3. Now right-click on the project `CH07.ResourceLibrary` and create a new folder named `Images`.
4. Now right-click on the newly created folder and add an existing image (`image1.png`, in our case) into that folder.
5. Then right-click on the image (`image1.png`) and navigate to its **Properties** pane.
6. As demonstrated in the previous recipe, change its **Build Action** to `Resource`. Compile the project `CH07.ResourceLibrary` to make sure that the build is successful.
7. From the **Solution Explorer**, right-click on the other project named `CH07.RemoteBinaryResourceDemo` and navigate through the context menu entry **Add** | **Reference...** to add the assembly reference of the class library in this project.

8. From the **Reference Manager** dialog window, navigate to **Projects** and select the class library (**CH07.ResourceLibrary**) that we created. As shown in the following screenshot, click **OK** once you are done. This will add our class library as a reference to our application project:

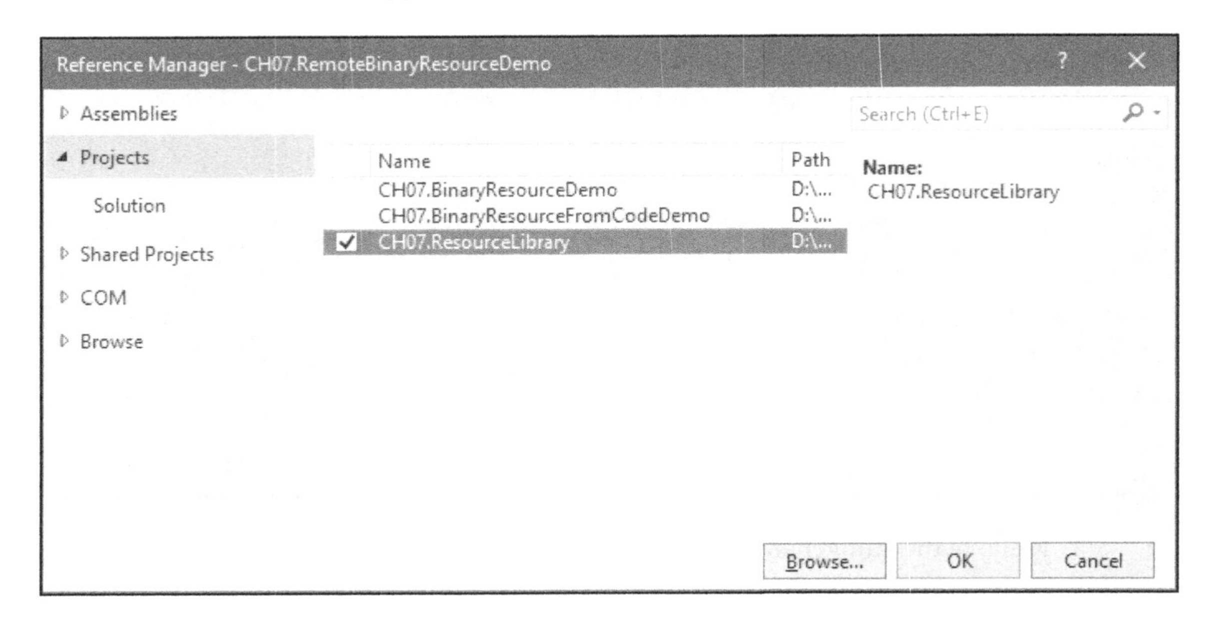

9. Now, from the **Solution Explorer**, navigate to the `MainWindow.xaml` file of the `CH07.RemoteBinaryResourceDemo` project and add the following image inside the `Grid`:

```
<Image Source="/CH07.ResourceLibrary;component/
Images/image1.png"/>
```

10. Let's compile the solution and run the application. You will see that the application window launches with an image, which is present in a different assembly. Here's a screenshot, based on our demo application:

How it works...

When you are using a referenced assembly, the WPF pack URI recognizes it as `/AssemblyReference;component/ResourceName` format. In the preceding example, the **AssemblyReference** is the name of the assembly, which is `CH07.ResourceLibrary` in our case, and the **ResourceName** is the complete path of the resource relative to the project component.

There's more...

An `AssemblyReference` may also include a version and/or the public key token (in case the assembly is strongly named). The version is denoted by prefixing it with a `v`, as shown in the following example:

```
/<AssemblyName>;v<VersionNo>;<Token>;component/<ResourcePath>

"/CH07.ResourceLibrary;v1.0;3ca44a7f7ca54f49;component/Images/image
1.png"
```

This does not work with resources marked with `Build Action` as `Content`. To work with this, we need to use the full pack URI with a `siteOfOrigin` base, as follows:

```
<Image Source="pack://siteOfOrigin:,,,/Images/image1.png" />
```

Please note that the Visual Studio Designer window will fail to load the image when `siteOfOrigin` is used, but this will work fine in runtime.

Accessing binary resources in code

Accessing binary resources in XAML is very simple, but there is an option to read a binary resource from the code behind. In this recipe, we will learn how to read a binary resource in code and set it in the UI. We will be using an image as an example.

Getting ready

Open your Visual Studio IDE. Let's begin with creating a new WPF project called `CH07.BinaryResourceFromCodeDemo`.

How to do it...

Follow these steps to read an image file, embedded as a `Resource`, and display it in the UI:

1. First, create a folder named `Images` inside the project and add an image inside it. Let's name the image `image1.png`.
2. Open the `MainWindow.xaml` file by navigating to **Solution Explorer**.
3. Add an image tag inside the `Grid` panel and name it `img`:

```
<Grid>
    <Image x:Name="img" />
</Grid>
```

4. Go to the `MainWindow.xaml.cs` file and, inside the constructor of the class, just after the `InitializeComponent()` call, create the `streamResourceInfo` from the resource stream of the image. Here's the code to get the stream info:

```
var streamResourceInfo = Application.GetResourceStream(new
Uri("Images/image1.png", UriKind.RelativeOrAbsolute));
```

5. Now we need to create the instance of `BitmapImage` from that stream. Copy the following content and pass the `streamResourceInfo.Stream` to the `StreamSource` property of the `BitmapImage`:

```
var bitmapImage = new BitmapImage();
bitmapImage.BeginInit();
bitmapImage.CacheOption = BitmapCacheOption.OnLoad;
bitmapImage.StreamSource = streamResourceInfo.Stream;
bitmapImage.EndInit();
bitmapImage.Freeze();
```

6. Now set the `bitmapImage` instance to the `Source` property of the image::

```
img.Source = bitmapImage;
```

7. Here's the complete code for accessing the stream and assigning it to the image source:

```
public MainWindow()
{
    InitializeComponent();

    var streamResourceInfo = Application.GetResourceStream(
                              new Uri("Images/image1.png",
                              UriKind.RelativeOrAbsolute));

    var bitmapImage = new BitmapImage();
    bitmapImage.BeginInit();
    bitmapImage.CacheOption = BitmapCacheOption.OnLoad;
    bitmapImage.StreamSource = streamResourceInfo.Stream;
    bitmapImage.EndInit();
    bitmapImage.Freeze();

    img.Source = bitmapImage;
}
```

8. Once done, build the project and run it. You will see that the assigned image is loaded into the application window:

How it works...

The static method `Application.GetResourceStream` provides an easy way of accessing a resource using its relative URI. It returns a `StreamResourceInfo` object. The `Stream` property of the `StreamResourceInfo` object provides access to the actual binary data, which has been set as the image source property by converting it to an instance of `BitmapImage`.

For the `Application.GetResourceStream` method to work, the resource must be marked as a `Resource` in `Build Action`.

If the resource has been marked as `Content` in the `Build Action` property, then the `Application.GetContentStream` method should be used to get the resource stream.

Using static logical resources in WPF

Logical resources in WPF are the objects that can be shared and reused across some part of a Visual Tree or an entire application. These can be colors, brushes, geometrics, styles, or any other .NET objects (`int`, `string`, `List<T>`, `T`, and more) defined by the .NET Framework or developer. These objects are typically placed inside a `ResourceDictionary`.

In this recipe, we will learn how to use logical resources using the binding key `StaticResource`.

Getting ready

Make sure that Visual Studio is running. Create a project called `CH07.StaticResourceDemo`, based on the WPF application template.

How to do it...

Follow these steps to create a logical resource and use it inside the application window:

1. Open the `MainWindow.xaml` file and replace the `Grid` with a horizontal `StackPanel`.
2. Insert a `Border` control inside the `StackPanel`. Set its `Height` and `Width` properties to `80` and `150`, respectively:

```
<Border Height="80"
        Width="150"
        Margin="8">
</Border>
```

3. Let's add a background color to the `Border` control. We will be using a linear gradient brush to decorate the background color. Let's modify it as shared here:

```
<Border Height="80"
        Width="150"
        Margin="8">
    <Border.Background>
        <LinearGradientBrush>
            <GradientStop Offset="0"
                          Color="LightYellow"/>
            <GradientStop Offset="0.2"
                          Color="Yellow"/>
```

```
                <GradientStop Offset=".5"
                              Color="YellowGreen"/>
                <GradientStop Offset="1"
                              Color="Green"/>
            </LinearGradientBrush>
        </Border.Background>
    </Border>
```

4. Copy the same border with the preceding background and paste it inside the same panel. Now the `StackPanel` will have two border controls with the same properties.
5. Let's build the project and run it. You will see two rectangular shapes with a nice gradient color as the background:

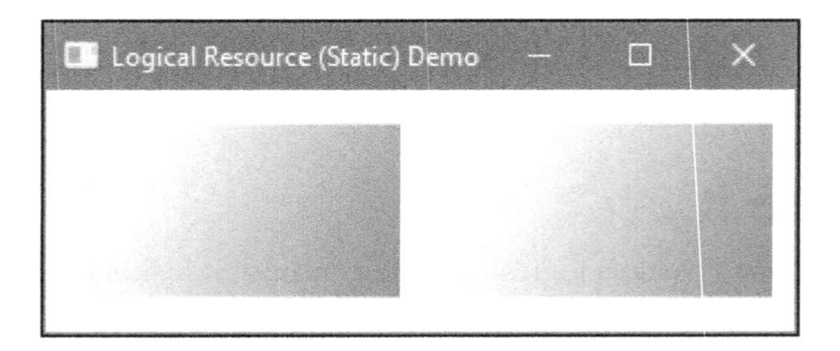

6. As you can see, we have added the same background brush twice to represent the color; it's sometimes difficult to manage, and unnecessarily increases the XAML code as well as the complexity. To resolve this, we can now move the brush object as a logical resource, and access it within the same window or throughout the application. Let's move it to the window level. Insert the `LinearGradientBrush` inside the window resource (`Window.Resources`) and assign a key (`myLinearBrush`) to it:

```
<Window.Resources>
    <LinearGradientBrush x:Key="myLinearBrush">
        <GradientStop Offset="0"
                      Color="LightYellow"/>
        <GradientStop Offset="0.2"
                      Color="Yellow"/>
        <GradientStop Offset=".5"
                      Color="YellowGreen"/>
        <GradientStop Offset="1"
                      Color="Green"/>
    </LinearGradientBrush>
</Window.Resources>
```

7. Now remove the background definition in both the controls and replace it with a binding to the previously mentioned brush. As it is defined within the resource, we will be using `{StaticResource}` to access it. Here's the modified version of the border controls inside the panel:

```
<StackPanel Orientation="Horizontal">
    <Border Height="80"
            Width="150"
            Margin="8"
            Background="{StaticResource myLinearBrush}"/>
    <Border Height="80"
            Width="150"
            Margin="8"
            Background="{StaticResource myLinearBrush}"/>
</StackPanel>
```

8. Let's run the application once again. You will see the same background applied to the rectangular shaped border controls. In this case, we have used just one definition of the brush.

How it works...

Every UI element derived from the `FrameworkElement` has a property called `Resources`, which is of type `ResourceDictionary`. Thus, every element can have resources associated with it. In XAML, we need to define the `x:Key` attribute to the resource to access it, either from the XAML or from the code-behind file.

In our example, we defined `myLinearBrush` as an element of the `ResourceCollection` of the `Window`. Thus, it will be accessible by any control within the same window. If you move the definition inside the `StackPanel`, it will be accessible within that panel:

```
<Window.Resources>
    <LinearGradientBrush x:Key="myLinearBrush">
        <GradientStop Offset="0"
                      Color="LightYellow"/>
        <GradientStop Offset="0.2"
                      Color="Yellow"/>
        <GradientStop Offset=".5"
                      Color="YellowGreen"/>
        <GradientStop Offset="1"
                      Color="Green"/>
    </LinearGradientBrush>
</Window.Resources>
```

To use this resource in XAML, we need to use the markup extension, `{StaticResource}`, along with the resource key provided, `Background="{StaticResource myLinearBrush}"`, which will create the binding between them.

There's more...

It is possible to manage the logical resources from the code behind. You can call the `FindResource` method, passing the resource key to it, to get the instance of the resource. Here's how you can find the resource named `myLinearBrush`:

```
var resource = FindResource("myLinearBrush") as Brush;
```

You can also programmatically add or remove a resource to the collection. Call the methods `Resources.Add` and `Resources.Remove` to add or remove a specific resource, as shown in the following code snippet:

```
Resources.Add("myBrush", new SolidColorBrush(Colors.Red));
Resources.Remove("myBrush");
```

As the `Resources` property is basically a `Dictionary` object, make sure you check whether the specified key is already present before doing any operation, such as `Add/Remove`, on it.

Using dynamic logical resources in WPF

In the previous recipe, we learned how to use logical resources using the `StaticResource` markup extension. In this recipe, we will learn how to use logical resources using the `DynamicResource` markup extension and will also learn the difference between them.

Getting ready

Get started by creating a new project. Open the Visual Studio IDE and create a new WPF application project called `CH07.DynamicResourceDemo`.

How to do it...

Follow these steps to use logical resources dynamically and modify the values of the resource as per the need:

1. Open the `MainWindow.xaml` file and replace the `Grid` with a `StackPanel`.
2. Add a border inside the `StackPanel` and set its dimensions.
3. Add another `StackPanel` inside the panel and add a group of three radio buttons inside it. Label them as `Red`, `Green`, and `Blue`. Here's the complete XAML code:

```
<StackPanel Orientation="Horizontal">
    <Border Height="80"
            Width="150"
            Margin="8"/>
    <StackPanel Margin="10">
        <RadioButton GroupName="colorGroup"
                     Content="Red"
                     Margin="4"/>
        <RadioButton GroupName="colorGroup"
                     Content="Green"
                     IsChecked="True"
                     Margin="4"/>
        <RadioButton GroupName="colorGroup"
                     Content="Blue"
                     Margin="4"/>
    </StackPanel>
</StackPanel>
```

4. Now add a `LinearGradientBrush` to the window resources and set its key name as `myLinearBrush`. Add some `GradientStop` to define a nice gradient brush, as follows:

```
<Window.Resources>
    <LinearGradientBrush x:Key="myLinearBrush">
        <GradientStop Offset="0"
                      Color="LightYellow"/>
        <GradientStop Offset="1"
                      Color="Green"/>
    </LinearGradientBrush>
</Window.Resources>
```

5. It's time to bind the defined brush with the `Border` control. Modify the XAML to have a `StaticResource` binding between them, as follows:

```
<Border Height="80"
        Width="150"
        Margin="8"
        Background="{StaticResource myLinearBrush}"/>
```

6. Register `Checked` events for all three radio buttons, so that we can perform some changes on the checked status change:

```
<StackPanel Orientation="Horizontal">
    <Border Height="80"
            Width="150"
            Margin="8"
            Background="{StaticResource myLinearBrush}"/>
    <StackPanel Margin="10">
        <RadioButton GroupName="colorGroup"
                     Content="Red"
                     Margin="4"
                     Checked="OnRedRadioChecked"/>
        <RadioButton GroupName="colorGroup"
                     Content="Green"
                     IsChecked="True"
                     Margin="4"
                     Checked="OnGreenRadioChecked"/>
        <RadioButton GroupName="colorGroup"
                     Content="Blue"
                     Margin="4"
                     Checked="OnBlueRadioChecked"/>
    </StackPanel>
</StackPanel>
```

7. Navigate to the `MainWindow.xaml.cs` and add the following implementation for all the radio buttons' `Checked` event:

```
private void OnRedRadioChecked(object sender,
 RoutedEventArgs e)
{
    var brush = Resources["myLinearBrush"];
    if (brush is LinearGradientBrush lBrush)
    {
        lBrush = new LinearGradientBrush
        {
            GradientStops = new GradientStopCollection
            {
```

```
                new GradientStop
                (Colors.LightGoldenrodYellow, 0),
                new GradientStop(Colors.Red, 1)
            }
        };

        Resources["myLinearBrush"] = lBrush;
    }
}

private void OnGreenRadioChecked(object sender,
 RoutedEventArgs e)
{
    var brush = Resources["myLinearBrush"];
    if (brush is LinearGradientBrush lBrush)
    {
        lBrush = new LinearGradientBrush
        {
            GradientStops = new GradientStopCollection
            {
                new GradientStop(Colors.LightYellow, 0),
                new GradientStop(Colors.Green, 1)
            }
        };

        Resources["myLinearBrush"] = lBrush;
    }
}

private void OnBlueRadioChecked(object sender,
 RoutedEventArgs e)
{
    var brush = Resources["myLinearBrush"];
    if (brush is LinearGradientBrush lBrush)
    {
        lBrush = new LinearGradientBrush
        {
            GradientStops = new GradientStopCollection
            {
                new GradientStop(Colors.LightBlue, 0),
                new GradientStop(Colors.Blue, 1)
            }
        };

        Resources["myLinearBrush"] = lBrush;
    }
}
```

8. Once this has been done, run the application. You will see a rectangle with three radio buttons. By default, the **Green** radio button will be selected. Change the selection to **Red** or **Blue** to observe the behavior. You will see that the color always stays **Green**, irrespective of the selection:

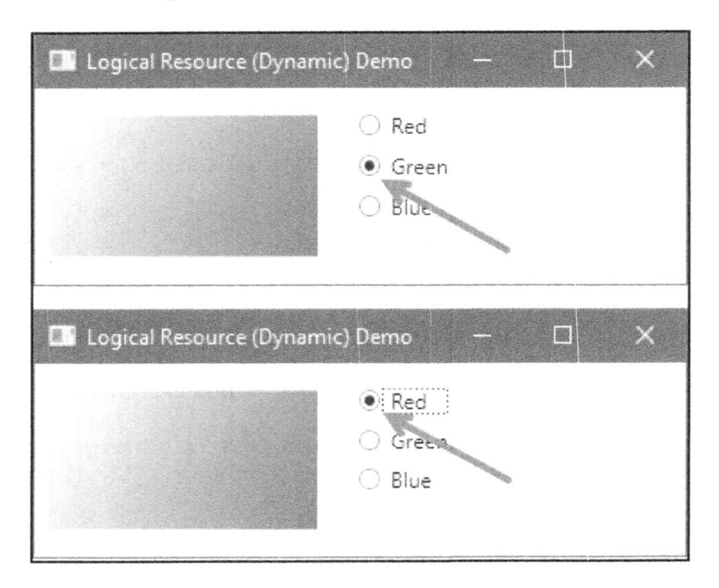

9. Let's close the application and navigate back to `MainWindow.xaml`.
10. Change the `StaticResource` to `DynamicResource`, as shared in the following code snippet:

```
<Border Height="80"
        Width="150"
        Margin="8"
        Background="{DynamicResource myLinearBrush}"/>
```

11. Now, run the application once again. By default, **Green** will be selected, and the rectangle will have a green gradient background. Change the selection to **Red** or **Blue** to observe the color change:

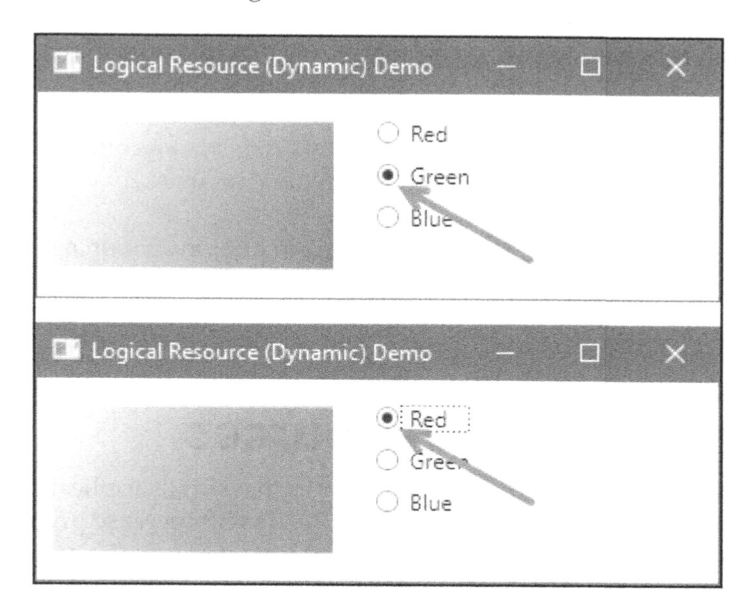

How it works...

When you bind the logical resource as a `StaticResource`, it causes the binding to occur at construction time. On the other hand, the `DynamicResource` markup extension binds to a resource dynamically, only when it is needed.

In the preceding example, when we registered the resource to the `Background` property of the `Border` control as a `StaticResource`, we were not able to see the change reflected in the UI, even though we replaced the resource with a new object on selection of the radio button. But when we changed the binding to `DynamicResource`, the change was automatically reflected. This is because the dynamic resource binding refreshes itself if the object changes. But this is not same with the static resource binding, as it always keeps referencing the old object.

There's more...

The `StaticResource` binding throws an error at design time if the object specified by the `x:Key` is not present. On the other hand, `DynamicResource` does not throw any exception, and displays as blank. Later, when it finds the `Key`, it binds itself with that resource.

`StaticResource` should be used most of the time, unless there is a need to replace resources dynamically. `DynamicResource` should be used by the themes that can easily swap the resources.

Having a large collection of `DynamicResource` on a complex UI can impact the performance of the UI. Wherever possible, mark them as `StaticResource`.

Managing logical resources

There could be several types of logical resources in a single application, and placing them inside a single XAML file (for example, `App.xaml`) will increase problems while maintaining them. To resolve this problem, you can separate the resources of different types into their own respective files and reference them in `App.xaml`.

In this recipe, we will learn how to manage these logical resources with a simple example. Though this will be shown with a single file, you can create separate files and reference them.

Getting ready

Assuming that you have opened Visual Studio, now create a new WPF application project called `CH07.ManagingLogicalResourceDemo`.

How to do it...

Follow these simple steps to create separate resource files and reference them in the application:

1. As we want to create a separate resource file, we need to create a file of type **Resource Dictionary**. Inside the **Solution Explorer**, right-click on the project node and create a new folder named `Themes`.
2. Now right-click on the **Themes** folder and select **Add** | **Resource Dictionary...** from the context menu entry:

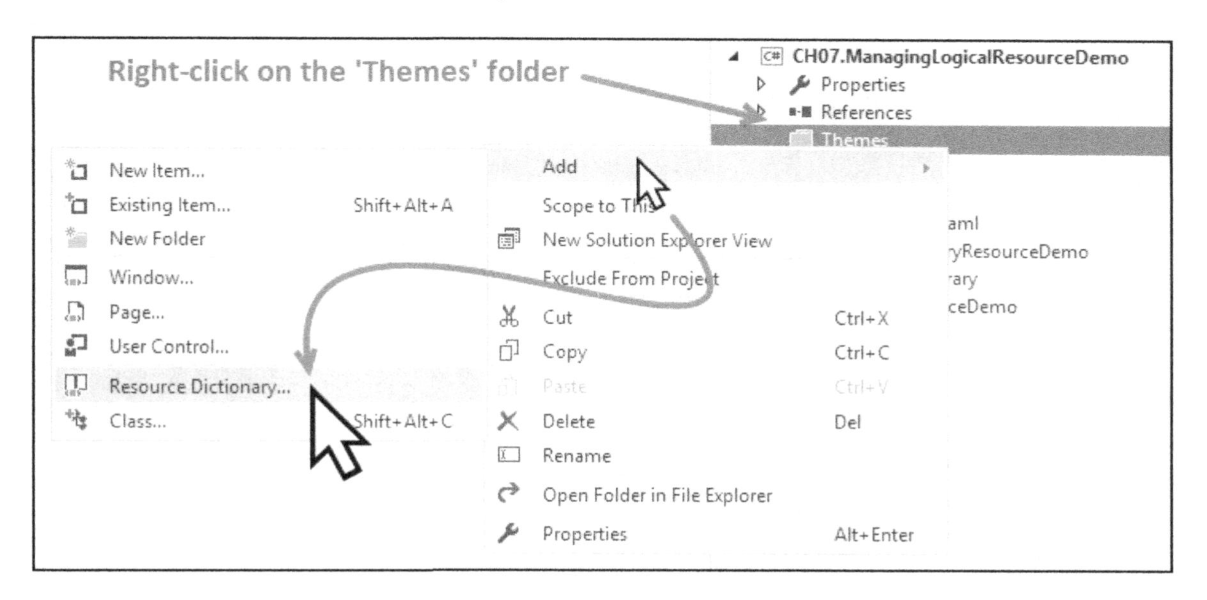

3. In the **Add New Item** dialog, make sure that the **Resource Dictionary (WPF)** template is selected. Name it `Brushes.xaml`, and click **Add**:

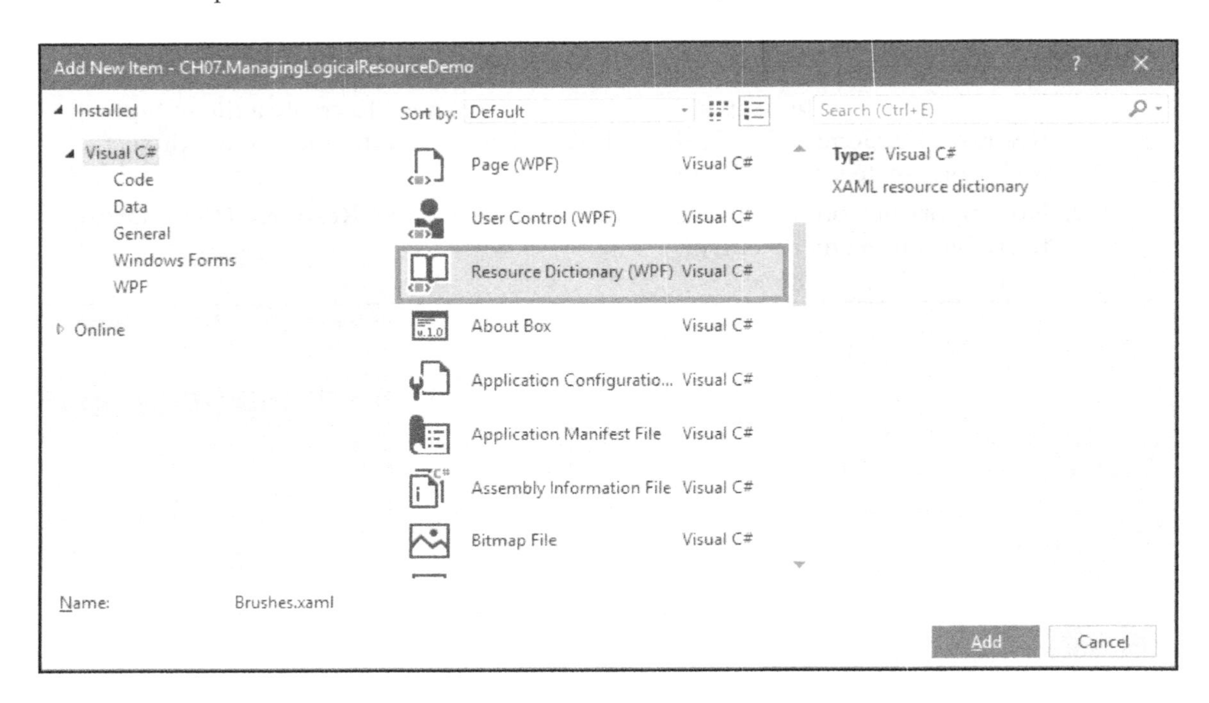

4. From the **Solution Explorer**, open the newly created file `Brushes.xaml` and add the following `LinearGradientBrush` inside the `ResourceDictionary` element with a `x:Key` name of `myLinearBrush`. You can add multiple elements inside the `ResourceDictionary` to have a resource collection. Make sure you assign a unique key name to each one of them:

```
<LinearGradientBrush x:Key="myLinearBrush">
    <GradientStop Offset="0"
                  Color="Yellow"/>
    <GradientStop Offset="1"
                  Color="OrangeRed"/>
</LinearGradientBrush>
```

5. Open the `MainWindow.xaml` and replace the `Grid` with the following markup to have a `Border` control inside it. Set the size of the element and bind the `Background` property with the `myLinearBrush` that we have created:

```
<Grid>
    <Border Height="100"
            Width="280"
            Margin="8"
            Background="{DynamicResource myLinearBrush}"/>
</Grid>
```

6. If you run the application now, you won't see any elements inside the window, because the mapping of the file has not been created yet. As we have the binding as `DynamicResource`, you won't see any error.
7. Let's close the application and open the `App.xaml` file.
8. Inside the `Application.Resources`, add an element named `ResourceDictionary`. Inside this, create another element named `ResourceDictionary.MergedDictionaries` and load the `ResourceDictionary` that we have created. Here's how it will look:

```
<Application.Resources>
    <ResourceDictionary>
        <ResourceDictionary.MergedDictionaries>
            <ResourceDictionary
                 Source="Themes/Brushes.xaml" />
        </ResourceDictionary.MergedDictionaries>
    </ResourceDictionary>
</Application.Resources>
```

9. Now run the application once again. You will see a rectangular shaped border control in the application window with a nice gradient color, which we have created in the `Brushes.xaml` file. Here a screenshot of the application window:

How it works...

A `ResourceDictionary` can load one or more resource dictionaries using its `MergedDictionaries` property (`ResourceDictionary.MergedDictionaries`), which is a collection. It's not always mandatory to have a reference to other resource dictionaries, but it can also have its own resources as well:

```
<Application.Resources>
    <ResourceDictionary>
        <SolidColorBrush Color="Red" x:Key="redBrush" />
        <SolidColorBrush Color="Green" x:Key="greenBrush" />
        <SolidColorBrush Color="Blue" x:Key="blueBrush" />
        <ResourceDictionary.MergedDictionaries>
            <ResourceDictionary
                    Source="Themes/SolidBrushes.xaml" />
            <ResourceDictionary
                    Source="Themes/GradientBrushes.xaml" />
            <ResourceDictionary Source="Themes/Fonts.xaml" />
        </ResourceDictionary.MergedDictionaries>
    </ResourceDictionary>
</Application.Resources>
```

The `Source` property of the `ResourceDictionary` element must point to the location of the `ResourceDictionary`. If that location is within a subfolder, that subfolder must be included.

There's more...

When there exist two or more resources with the same key name that originated from multiple merged dictionaries, it will not throw any error or exception. Instead, it will load the one from the **Resource Dictionary** that was added last in the element tree.

Using user selected colors and fonts

Sometimes, it is useful to use the system theme in an application UI to have a synchronous flow of colors and fonts between the operating system and the application. In these cases, we can dynamically load those values and apply them to our UI elements. This is achievable by accessing some special resource keys within the `SystemColors` and `SystemFonts` classes. In this recipe, we will learn how to use them.

Getting ready

Let's get started by creating a new project called `CH07.SystemResourcesDemo`. Make sure you select the WPF application template from the available list.

How to do it...

We will now build an application that uses system colors and fonts. Follow these steps to proceed with it:

1. Open the `MainWindow.xaml` file and insert the following `Rectangle` inside the `Grid` panel:

```
<Rectangle Height="100"
           Width="300"/>
```

2. We want to fill the rectangle with the color of the desktop brush. Add the following markup to fill the background color of the rectangle `Fill="{DynamicResource {x:Static SystemColors.DesktopBrushKey}}"`. Now the XAML will look like the following:

```
<Rectangle Fill="{DynamicResource {x:Static
SystemColors.DesktopBrushKey}}"
           Height="100"
           Width="300"/>
```

3. Let's run the application now. You will see that a background color for the rectangle has been picked up by the application. This is based on the selection that you have for the `DesktopBrush` in your system:

4. To confirm this, right-click on your desktop and select **Personalize**. If you are using Windows 10, you will see the Settings app navigates to the **Background Settings** page. Check the color that is selected in the **Background** settings and the color applied to your application. Both will be the same:

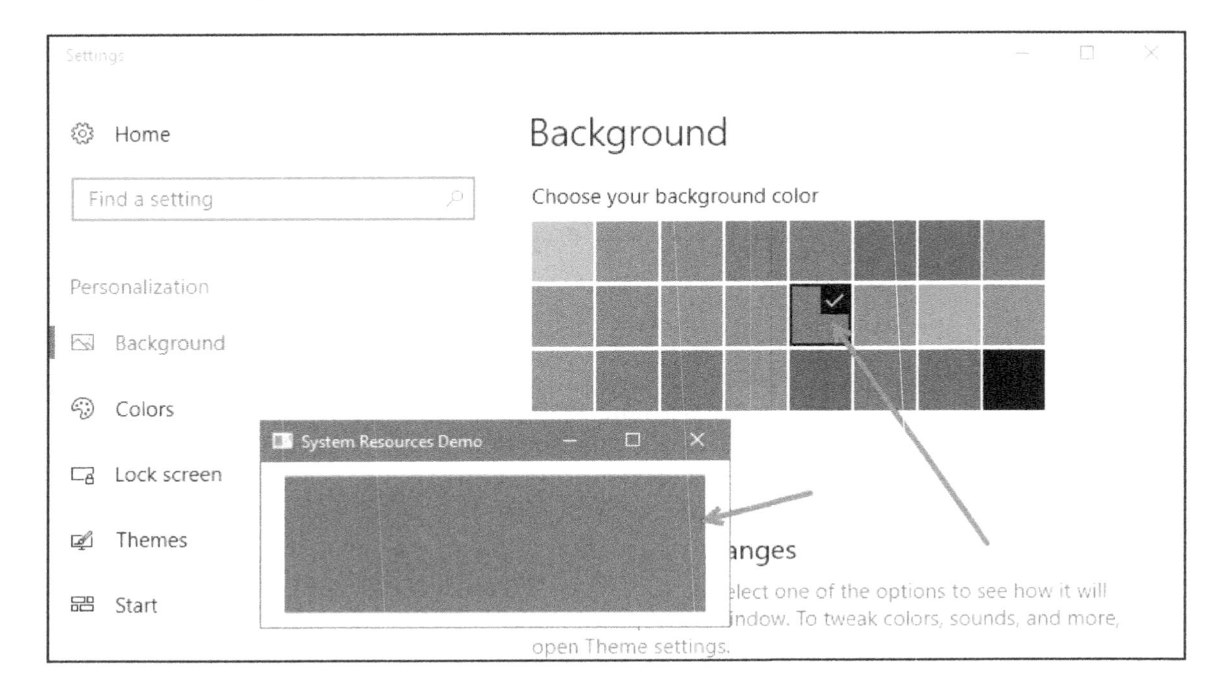

5. Let's select a different color from the **Background Settings**. You will see that the color will automatically get applied to your application:

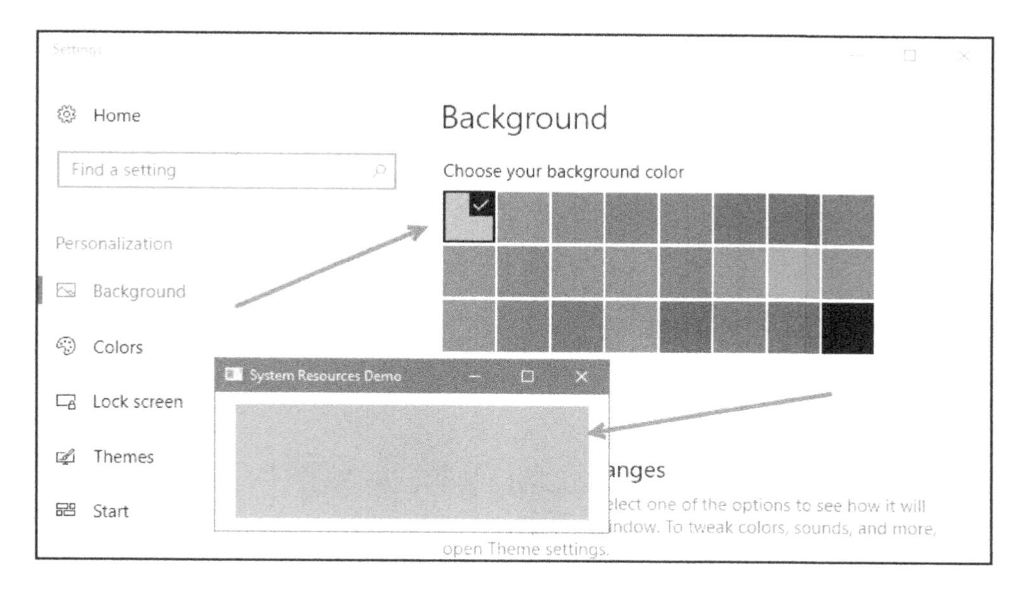

6. Now select the + symbol (**Custom color**) to select another color of the default colors in the palette:

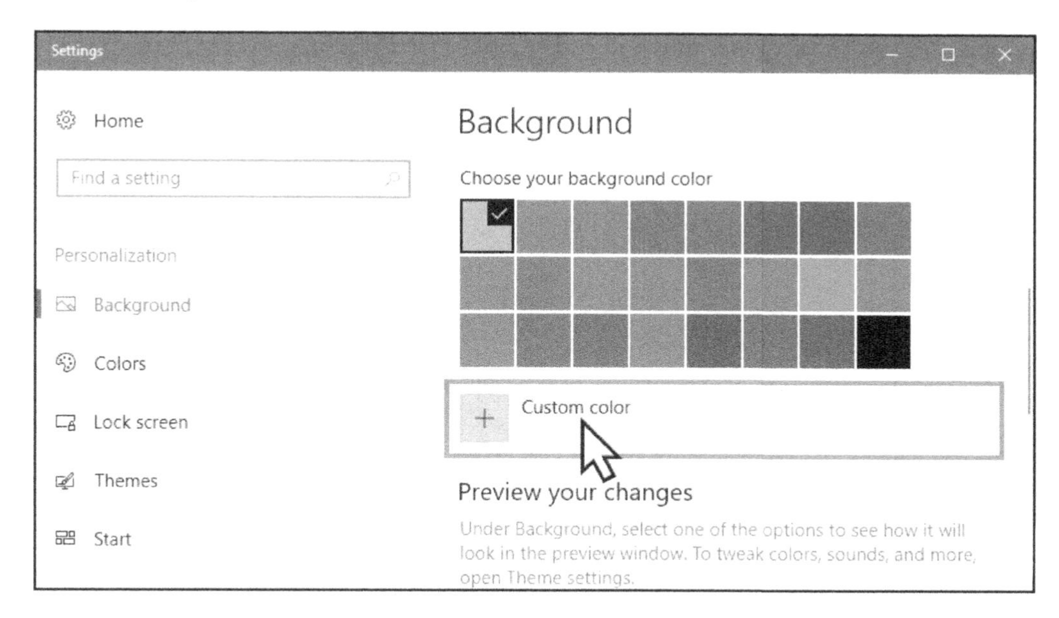

7. As shown here, pick a custom background color for your desktop and click **Done**:

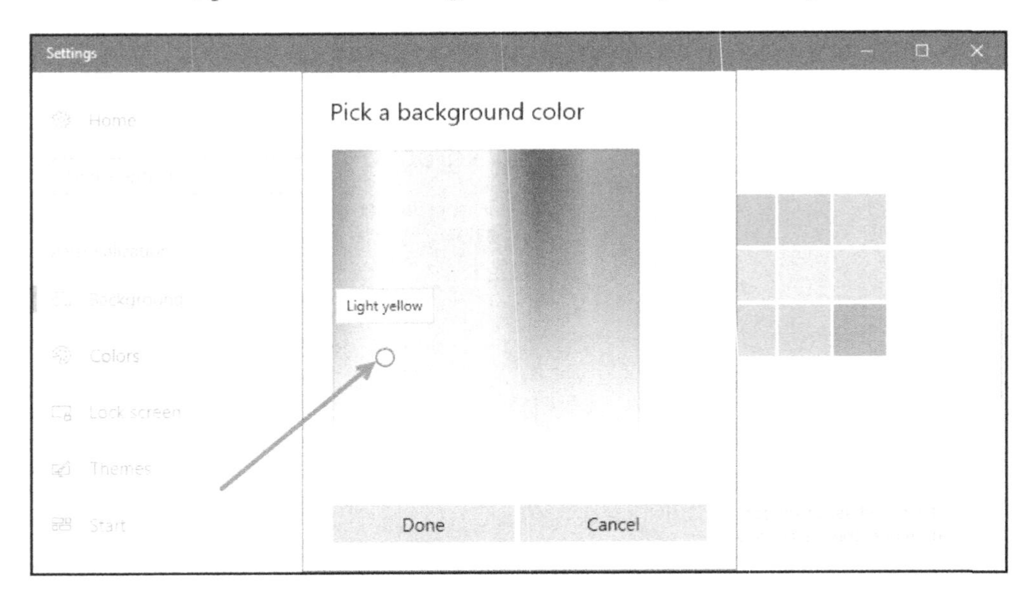

8. Check the application window now. You will see that the color selected on the **Settings** app is applied to the rectangle background. Navigate to your desktop, the same color will be applied there too:

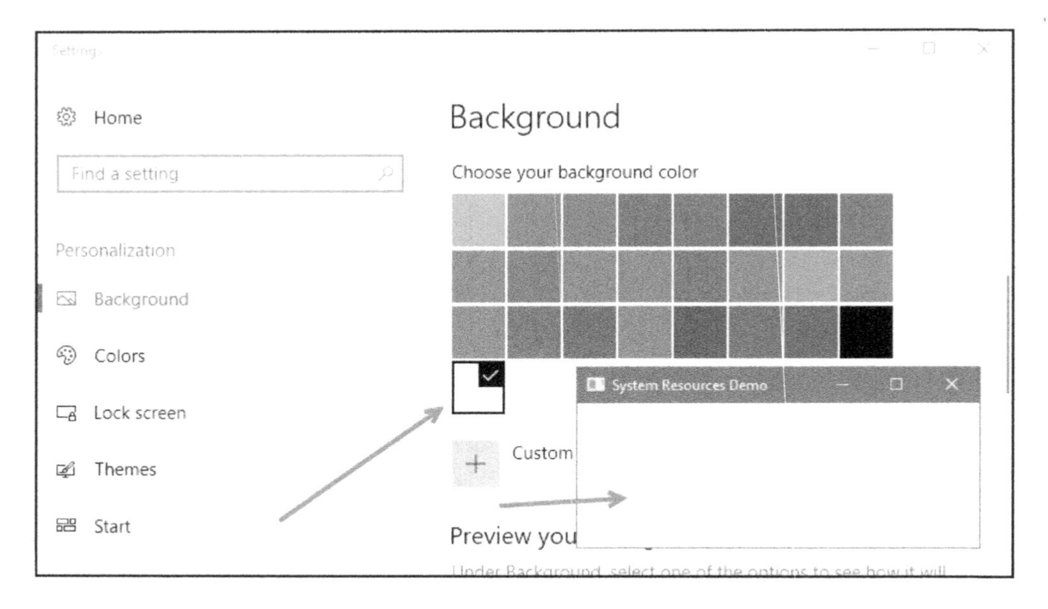

How it works...

It is not mandatory to provide a `string` type key name to a resource binding. You can also provide a static object to the binding. In this example, we used the static value `SystemColors.DesktopBrushKey` in combination with the `{x:Static}` markup extension:

```
Fill="{DynamicResource {x:Static SystemColors.DesktopBrushKey}}"
```

As we have learned about the dynamic resource binding in the previous recipes, this example also follows the same method, and thus you can see the selected color is automatically applied to the rectangle.

There are many static keys under the `SystemColors` class, which you can reference in your design. This is often useful when you want your application to be in sync with the operating system's theme.

There's more...

Just like `SystemColors`, we have the `SystemFonts` class too, which exposes font related static properties. You can define `FontFamily`, `FontSize`, and `FontWeight` styles from the system palette, as follows:

```
<TextBlock FontFamily="{DynamicResource {x:Static
SystemFonts.CaptionFontFamily}}"
           FontSize="{DynamicResource {x:Static
SystemFonts.CaptionFontSizeKey}}"
           FontWeight="{DynamicResource {x:Static
SystemFonts.CaptionFontWeightKey}}"
           Text="Hello World!"/>
```

Building an application using the MVVM pattern

MVVM stands for **Model**, **View**, and **ViewModel**, which is a pattern that facilitates the separation between the **GUI** (**Graphical user interface**) from the business logic. It means that a designer and developer can work together, without any hassle.

In this pattern, the model is the data that gets displayed in the view with the help of ViewModel. In this recipe, we will learn how to create an MVVM application, expose the properties from the ViewModel to the associated view, and display records without writing any code in the XAML code behind file.

Getting ready

Let's open the Visual Studio IDE and create a new project, called `CH07.MVVMDemo`, based on the WPF app template.

How to do it...

Once the project has been created, follow these steps to construct the project for the MVVM standard (not mandatory) and build a sample demo using the MVVM pattern:

1. Each WPF app project has a `MainWindow.xaml`. From the **Solution Explorer**, let's delete the default file.
2. Inside the project, create three folders named `Models`, `Views`, and `ViewModels`. This is just to create a proper structure for all our code files.
3. Now right-click on the **Views** folder, create a new `Window` by following the context menu path **Add** | **Window...**, and name it `MainWindow.xaml`.
4. Open the `App.xaml` file and modify the `StartupUri` to point to the correct file. As shown in the following screenshot, change the `StartupUri` to `ViewsMainWindow.xaml`:

```
<Application x:Class="CH07.MVVMDemo.App"
             xmlns="http://schemas.microsoft.com/winfx/2006/xaml/presentation"
             xmlns:x="http://schemas.microsoft.com/winfx/2006/xaml"
             xmlns:local="clr-namespace:CH07.MVVMDemo"
             StartupUri="Views\MainWindow.xaml">
    <Application.Resources>

    </Application.Resources>
</Application>
```

5. Open the `MainWindow.xaml` file from the **Views** folder and replace the `Grid` with a `DockPanel`.
6. Add two `StackPanel` inside the `Dock` and design the UI, as follows:

```
<DockPanel Margin="10">
    <StackPanel Orientation="Vertical"
                DockPanel.Dock="Left">
        <ListBox Width="180" Height="110">
        </ListBox>
        <TextBlock>
        </TextBlock>
    </StackPanel>
    <StackPanel Orientation="Vertical"
                Margin="4 0"
                DockPanel.Dock="Right">
        <TextBlock Text="Firstname"/>
        <TextBox Text=""/>
        <TextBlock Text="Lastname"/>
        <TextBox Text=""/>
        <Button Content="Add"
                Margin="0 8"/>
    </StackPanel>
</DockPanel>
```

7. If you run the application now, you will see the application window looks like this:

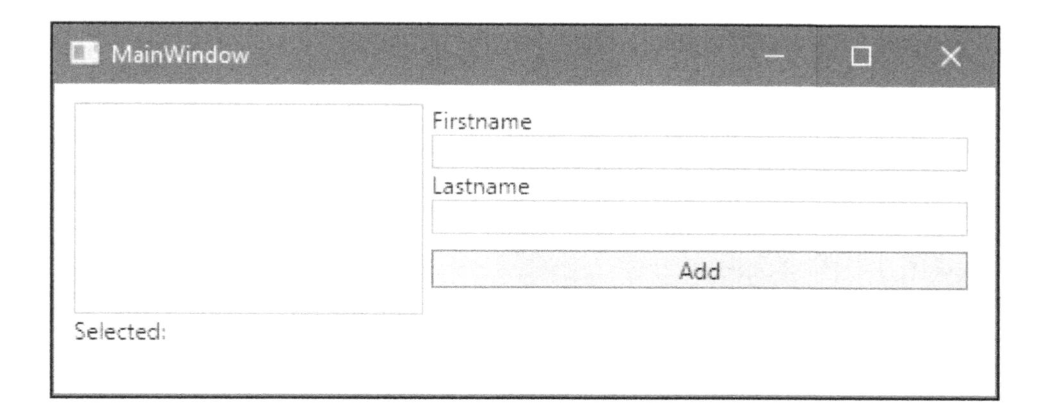

8. Now, right-click on the **Models** folder and create a class file named `UserModel.cs` and modify the class to have two properties of type `string`. As shown here, name them `Firstname` and `Lastname`:

```
public class UserModel
{
    public string Firstname { get; set; }
    public string Lastname { get; set; }
}
```

9. Right-click on the **ViewModels** folder and add another class file. Name it `MainWindowViewModel.cs`.
10. Open the `MainWindowViewModel.cs` file and add the following namespaces inside it:

```
using CH07.MVVMDemo.Models;
using System.Collections.ObjectModel;
using System.ComponentModel;
```

11. Now inherit the `MainWindowViewModel` class from `INotifyPropertyChanged` interface, which is present under the `System.ComponentModel` namespace.

```
public class MainWindowViewModel : INotifyPropertyChanged
```

12. As we already know, the `INotifyPropertyChanged` interface exposes the `PropertyChanged` event handler; we need to register that inside the class. Copy the following code to implement the interface:

```
public event PropertyChangedEventHandler PropertyChanged;
public void OnPropertyChanged(string propertyName)
{
    PropertyChanged?.Invoke(this,
        new PropertyChangedEventArgs(propertyName));
}
```

13. Once this has been done, create two properties inside the `ViewModel`. Name one `SelectedUser`, which is of type `UserModel` and the other `UserCollection`, which is of type `ObservableCollection<UserModel>`. Make sure you call the `OnPropertyChanged(str)` method from both the setters, so that the value change can be automatically reported to the UI. Here are the properties that we are going to refer to in this demonstration:

```
private UserModel m_selectedUser;
public UserModel SelectedUser
{
    get { return m_selectedUser; }
    set
    {
        m_selectedUser = value;
        OnPropertyChanged("SelectedUser");
    }
}

private ObservableCollection<UserModel> m_userCollection;
public ObservableCollection<UserModel> UserCollection
{
    get { return m_userCollection; }
    set
    {
        m_userCollection = value;
        OnPropertyChanged("UserCollection");
    }
}
```

14. Inside the constructor of the ViewModel, initialize the `UserCollection` property with some dummy data:

```
public MainWindowViewModel()
{
    UserCollection = new ObservableCollection<UserModel>
    {
        new UserModel
        {
            Firstname = "User", Lastname = "One"
        },
        new UserModel
        {
            Firstname = "User", Lastname = "Two"
        },
        new UserModel
```

```
            {
                Firstname = "User", Lastname = "Three"
            },
            new UserModel
            {
                Firstname = "User", Lastname = "Four"
            },
        };
    }
```

15. As the `viewmodel` is ready, having all the properties that we need, let's associate it with the view as its `DataContext`. You can do this either from the code behind or from the XAML itself. As our target is to keep the code behind as small as possible, let's do it from the XAML. Open the `MainWindow.xaml` and add the following `XMLNS` entry to it, so that we can access the `viewmodel` that we have created:

```
xmlns:viewmodels="clr-namespace:CH07.MVVMDemo.ViewModels"
```

16. Inside the `Window.Resources` tag, add our `viewmodel` as a resource and define it as `x:Key="ViewModel"`, as follows:

```
<Window.Resources>
    <viewmodels:MainWindowViewModel x:Key="ViewModel"/>
</Window.Resources>
```

17. As the `viewmodel` has been registered as a resource, set the `DataContext` of the `DockPanel` to the `ViewModel` that we defined. The binding needs to be done using the `{StaticResource}` markup extension. Here's how it will look:

```
<DockPanel DataContext="{StaticResource ViewModel}"
           Margin="10">
```

18. Now set the `ItemsSource` and the `SelectedItem` properties of the `ListBox` control to have a data binding with the properties inside our `viewmodel`.

```
<ListBox Width="180" Height="110"
         ItemsSource="{Binding UserCollection}"
         SelectedItem="{Binding SelectedUser}">
```

19. Similarly, set the `DataContext` property of the `TextBlock` to `SelectedUser` and create the data binding, as shown, here to display the selected full name of the user:

```
<TextBlock DataContext="{Binding SelectedUser}">
    <Run Text="Selected:"/>
    <Run Text="{Binding Firstname}"/>
    <Run Text="{Binding Lastname}"/>
</TextBlock>
```

20. Let's run this application now. You will see the following UI, where the values in `ListBox` control will be shown as the fully qualified name of the `model` class:

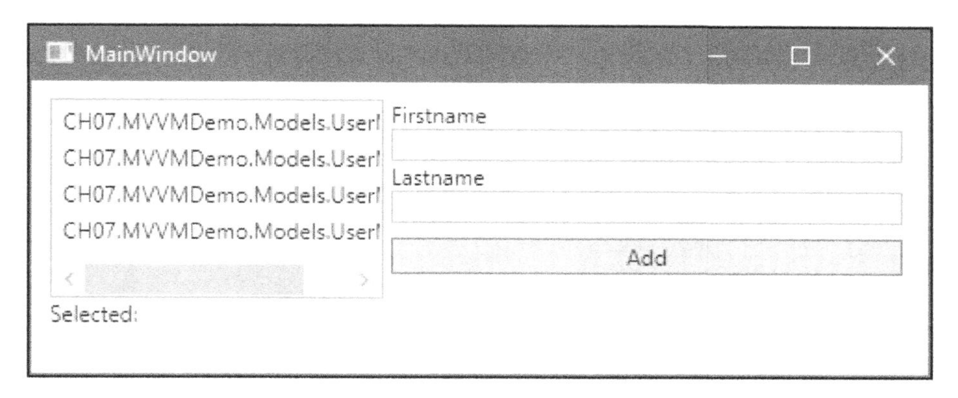

21. To resolve this, we need to create the `DataTemplate` of the `ListBox`. Define the `ListBox.ItemTemplate` as follows, to have a `TextBlock` with the user's full name, by concatenating the `Firstname` and `Lastname` properties:

```
<ListBox.ItemTemplate>
    <DataTemplate>
        <TextBlock>
            <Run Text="{Binding Firstname}"/>
            <Run Text="{Binding Lastname}"/>
        </TextBlock>
    </DataTemplate>
</ListBox.ItemTemplate>
```

22. Once this has been done, the XAML code of the application UI will look similar to this:

```
<StackPanel Orientation="Vertical"
            DockPanel.Dock="Left">
    <ListBox Width="180" Height="110"
             ItemsSource="{Binding UserCollection}"
             SelectedItem="{Binding SelectedUser}">
        <ListBox.ItemTemplate>
            <DataTemplate>
                <TextBlock>
                <Run Text="{Binding Firstname}"/>
                <Run Text="{Binding Lastname}"/>
                </TextBlock>
            </DataTemplate>
        </ListBox.ItemTemplate>
    </ListBox>
    <TextBlock DataContext="{Binding SelectedUser}">
        <Run Text="Selected:"/>
        <Run Text="{Binding Firstname}"/>
        <Run Text="{Binding Lastname}"/>
    </TextBlock>
</StackPanel>
```

23. Let's run the application now. You will see the correct values inside the `ListBox`:

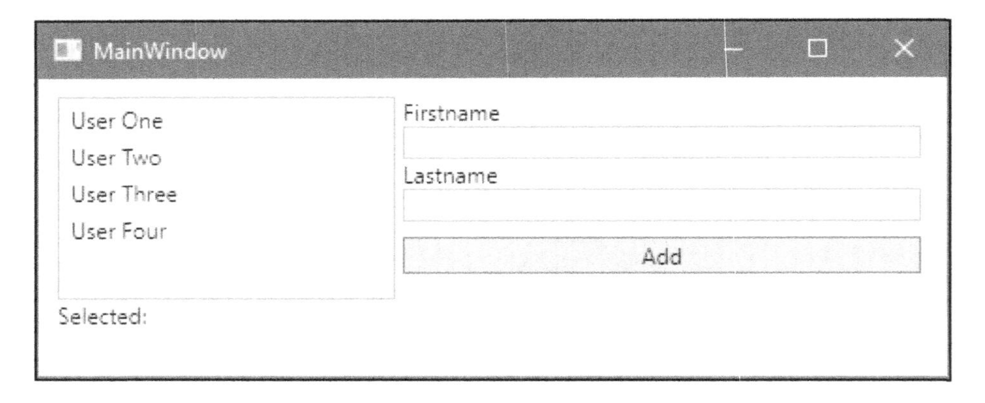

24. Select any of the `ListBox` items to see the selected username in the `TextBox`. Change the selection to update the UI automatically:

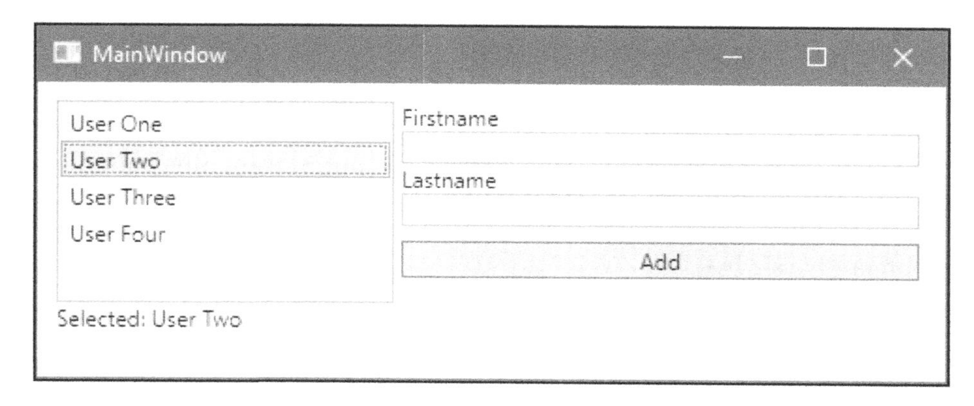

How it works...

MVVM consists of three important parts—**Model**, **View**, and the **ViewModel**. The *Model* represents the data; the *View* is the actual UI, which displays the relevant parts of the model; and the *ViewModel* is the mechanism that hands out the required data to the view. A ViewModel basically exposes properties and commands, and maintains the relevant state of the view.

If we compare the MVVM pattern with a bike (as represented in the following screenshot), the bike **Body** is the **View**, the **Fuel** is the **Model** and the **Engine** of the bike is the **ViewModel**, which moves the View (bike body) by burning/using the Model (Fuel):

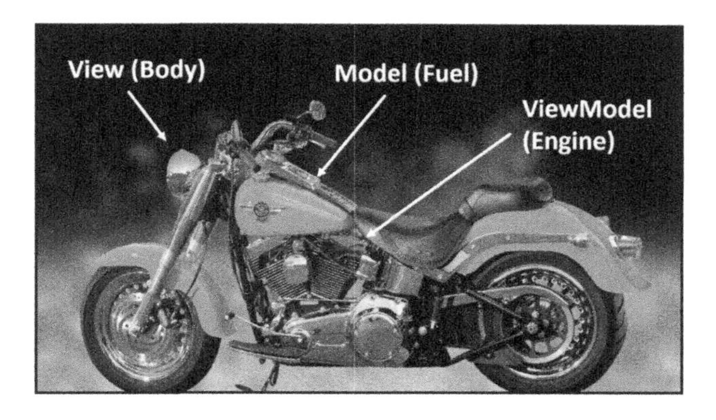

In our application, we used the `DataContext` to define the binding between the View and the ViewModel, which we then used to access the properties. If you now navigate to the `MainWindow.xaml.cs` file, you won't see any additional code except the constructor of the code-behind class.

In the MVVM pattern, our intention is to keep the code-behind file (`MainWindow.xaml.cs`) code free (or less code), so that the direct binding between the UI and the code will be reduced. Note that the MVVM is not a framework, but in using this pattern you can create a framework. For example, the **MVVMLight** (`http://www.mvvmlight.net`) from **GalaSoft** provides a fully customized framework, which you can use in your application to keep the development hassle free.

Using routed commands in a WPF application

Routed commands are used to navigate a route through the element hierarchy. This process is also well known as bubbling and tunneling. The class `RoutedCommand` implements the `ICommand` interface and allows the attaching of input gestures, such as mouse input and keyboard shortcuts, to the target.

In this recipe, we will learn how to use routed commands with a simple example.

Getting ready

To work on this recipe, we will be using the previous MVVM demo application. Launch your Visual Studio IDE and open the project `CH07.MVVMDemo`. In this example, we will be using `RoutedCommand` for the **Add** button click event.

How to do it...

Follow these simple steps to register the routed command to the button click and perform the operation:

1. From the **Solution Explorer**, right-click on the project node and create a folder named `Commands`.

2. Right-click on the **Commands** folder and create a new class named `RoutedCommands.cs` by following the **Add** | **Class...** context menu path.
3. Inside the class implementation, declare a static member of type `RoutedCommand` and name it `AddCommand`. Here's the code implementation:

```
public class RoutedCommands
{
    public static RoutedCommand AddCommand =
                                new RoutedCommand();
}
```

4. Add the following namespace to resolve the `RoutedCommand` class:

```
using System.Windows.Input;
```

5. Once that has been done, navigate to the `MainWindowViewModel.cs` file, present under the **ViewModels** folder, and add a property named `NewUserDetails` of type `UserModel`. We will be using this property to bind with the `Text` property of the `TextBox` controls present in the UI. The property implementation is as follows:

```
private UserModel m_newUserDetails;
public UserModel NewUserDetails
{
    get { return m_newUserDetails; }
    set
    {
        m_newUserDetails = value;
        OnPropertyChanged("NewUserDetails");
    }
}
```

6. Now, inside the constructor of our ViewModel, initialize the `NewUserDetails` property:

```
public MainWindowViewModel()
{
    UserCollection = new ObservableCollection<UserModel>
    {
        new UserModel
        {
            Firstname = "User", Lastname = "One"
        },
        new UserModel
        {
```

```
                Firstname = "User", Lastname = "Two"
            },
            new UserModel
            {
                Firstname = "User", Lastname = "Three"
            },
            new UserModel
            {
                Firstname = "User", Lastname = "Four"
            },
        };

        NewUserDetails = new UserModel();
    }
```

7. Navigate to `MainWindow.xaml` now, which is present under the **Views** folder. Modify the XAML as follows, to set a `DataContext` for the `StackPanel` and create data bindings with the `TextBox` controls. Make sure you set the data binding mode to `TwoWay`, else the code will not receive the updated value received from the UI:

```
<StackPanel Orientation="Vertical"
            Margin="4 0"
            DockPanel.Dock="Right"
            DataContext="{Binding NewUserDetails}">
    <TextBlock Text="Firstname"/>
    <TextBox Text="{Binding Firstname, Mode=TwoWay}"/>
    <TextBlock Text="Lastname"/>
    <TextBox Text="{Binding Lastname, Mode=TwoWay}"/>
    <Button Content="Add"
            Margin="0 8"/>
</StackPanel>
```

8. Now add the following `XMLNS` attribute to the XAML page, so that we can access the classes present under the `CH07.MVVMDemo.Commands` namespace:

```
xmlns:commands="clr-namespace:CH07.MVVMDemo.Commands"
```

9. What next? We need to create the command binding under the `Window` tag. Add the following XAML code block inside the `Window` tag:

```
<Window.CommandBindings>
    <CommandBinding Command="{x:Static
commands:RoutedCommands.AddCommand}"
                    CanExecute="CanExecute_AddCommand"
                    Executed="Execute_AddCommand"/>
</Window.CommandBindings>
```

10. Register the `CanExecute` and `Executed` events, named `CanExecute_AddCommand` and `Execute_AddCommand`, respectively, inside the code-behind class file, which is `MainWindow.xaml.cs` in our case.
11. Navigate back to the `MainWindow.xaml` and associate the command with the `Button` control, as follows:

```
<Button Content="Add"
        Margin="0 8"
        Command="{x:Static
commands:RoutedCommands.AddCommand}"/>
```

12. The complete markup changes will look like this:

```
<StackPanel Orientation="Vertical"
            Margin="4 0"
            DockPanel.Dock="Right"
            DataContext="{Binding NewUserDetails}">
    <TextBlock Text="Firstname"/>
    <TextBox Text="{Binding Firstname, Mode=TwoWay}"/>
    <TextBlock Text="Lastname"/>
    <TextBox Text="{Binding Lastname, Mode=TwoWay}"/>
    <Button Content="Add"
            Margin="0 8"
            Command="{x:Static
commands:RoutedCommands.AddCommand}"/>
</StackPanel>
```

13. Now open the `MainWindow.xaml.cs` file and create a member variable of type `MainWindowViewModel`. Name it `ViewModel` and initialize it as `null`. This will be used to store the reference of the ViewModel from the window resources:

```
private MainWindowViewModel ViewModel = null;
```

14. Inside the constructor, grab the associated `ViewModel` reference from the `Resources`:

```
public MainWindow()
{
    InitializeComponent();

    ViewModel = Resources["ViewModel"] as
                          MainWindowViewModel;
    if (ViewModel == null)
    {
        throw new NullReferenceException("ViewModel
        can't be NULL");
    }
}
```

15. The `CanExecute_AddCommand` event passes an argument of type `CanExecuteRoutedEventArgs`. It contains a property named `CanExecute`, which is responsible for holding a `boolean` value, indicating whether the `System.Windows.Input.RoutedCommand` associated with this event can be executed on the command target. As we have associated the `AddCommand` with the button, `e.CanExecute = true` will enable the button. In other cases, it will be disabled. So, let's modify the `CanExecute_AddCommand` event to implement this logic:

```
private void CanExecute_AddCommand(object sender,
 CanExecuteRoutedEventArgs e)
{
    if (ViewModel != null)
    {
        var userDetails = ViewModel.NewUserDetails;
        e.CanExecute =
        !string.IsNullOrWhiteSpace(userDetails.Firstname) &&
        !string.IsNullOrWhiteSpace(userDetails.Lastname);
    }
}
```

16. Once that has been done, we need to implement the `Execute` command. Modify the `Execute_AddCommand` event handler, as follows:

```
private void Execute_AddCommand(object sender,
 ExecutedRoutedEventArgs e)
{
    ViewModel.UserCollection.Add(ViewModel.NewUserDetails);
    ViewModel.SelectedUser = ViewModel.NewUserDetails;
    ViewModel.NewUserDetails = new Models.UserModel();
}
```

17. Let's run the application now. You will see that the **Add** button is disabled. This is because, as per our logic, the `e.CanExecute` property has been set to `false` as both the `TextBox` fields are empty:

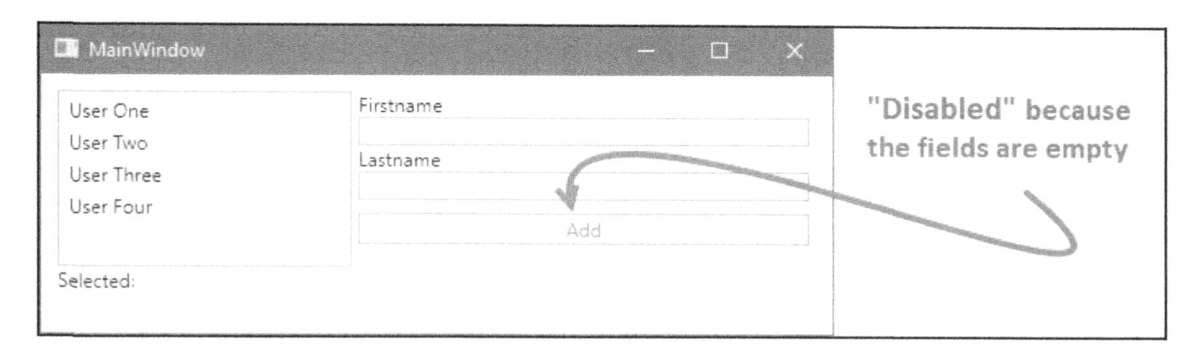

18. Enter some strings into both the `TextBox` fields and press the *TAB* key. It will automatically enable the button control, as follows:

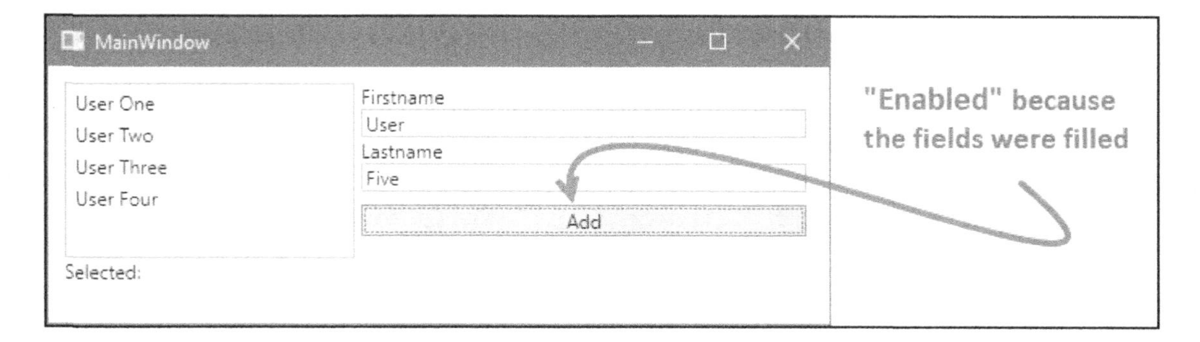

19. Click on **Add**, which will add the entered value to the collection and reset the `TextBox` fields. As soon as it resets the fields to empty, the button will automatically become disabled until the user fills the fields again:

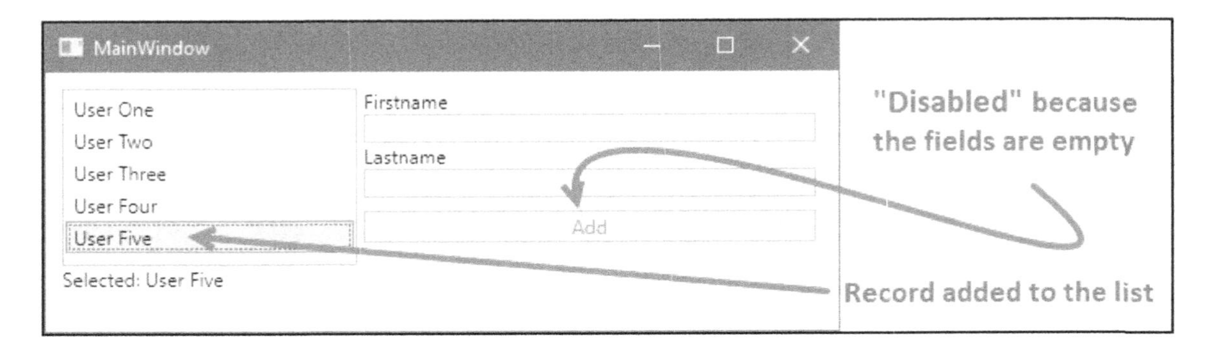

How it works...

The `RoutedCommand` class falls under the `System.Windows.Input` namespace, and provides two methods named `CanExecute` and `Execute`. The `CanExecute` method indicates whether the command is available, whereas the `Execute` method executes the command.

The `RoutedCommand` objects are basically empty shells and can't contain the implementation. For this to work, they look for a `CommandBinding` object from a target element that indicates the handler of the command. It registers the `CanExecute` and `Execute` methods to fire when the command associates with any control.

For example, in this demonstration, the `AddCommand` associated with the `Button` control has a `CommandBinding`, which denotes its `CanExecute` and `Execute` handler as `CanExecute_AddCommand` and `Execute_AddCommand`. When the button fires the `Click` event, it routes to the command binding to execute the associate command interface.

8
Working with Animations

In this chapter, we will cover the following recipes:

- Scaling an element while rendering
- Rotating an element while rendering
- Skewing an element while rendering
- Moving an element while rendering
- Grouping multiple transforms
- Creating property-based animations
- Creating path-based animations
- Creating key-frame-based animations
- Adding easing effects to animations

Introduction

Windows Presentation Foundation (**WPF**) is well-known for its rich **graphical user interface** (**GUI**) and layout features, which enables you to create stunning desktop applications. Animations can be used to create an attractive **user interface** (**UI**) by just animating UI elements, transformations, screen transitions, and more.

In this chapter, we will learn how to create animations using **storyboards**. We will first start with recipes that will help you to understand various transformations, such as `ScaleTransform`, `RotateTransform`, `SkewTransform`, and `TranslateTransform`. Then we will proceed towards recipes to learn various kinds of animations, such as property-based animations, path-based animations, and key-frame-based animations.

At the end, we will learn various easing functions introduced in WPF 4, which can be used to create easing effects on your linear animations to give them a non-linear look.

Scaling an element while rendering

The `ScaleTransform` is used to scale (stretch or shrink) an object horizontally or vertically. The `ScaleX` property is used to specify how much to stretch or shrink the object along the *X* axis, whereas the `ScaleY` property is used to specify how much to stretch or shrink the object along the *Y* axis. Using the `CenterX` and `CenterY` properties, the operations are performed based on the center pointing at certain coordinate points.

In this recipe, we will learn how to stretch or shrink an element using the scale transform.

Getting ready

First, open your Visual Studio instance and create a new WPF App project named `CH08.ScaleTransformDemo`.

How to do it...

Follow these steps to add `Image` controls to the application UI, and apply `ScaleTransform` to scale the image:

1. From the **Solution Explorer**, right-click on the project node and create a new folder. Name it as `Images`.
2. Now, right-click on the `Images` folder and add an existing image from your system. Name it as `image1.png`:

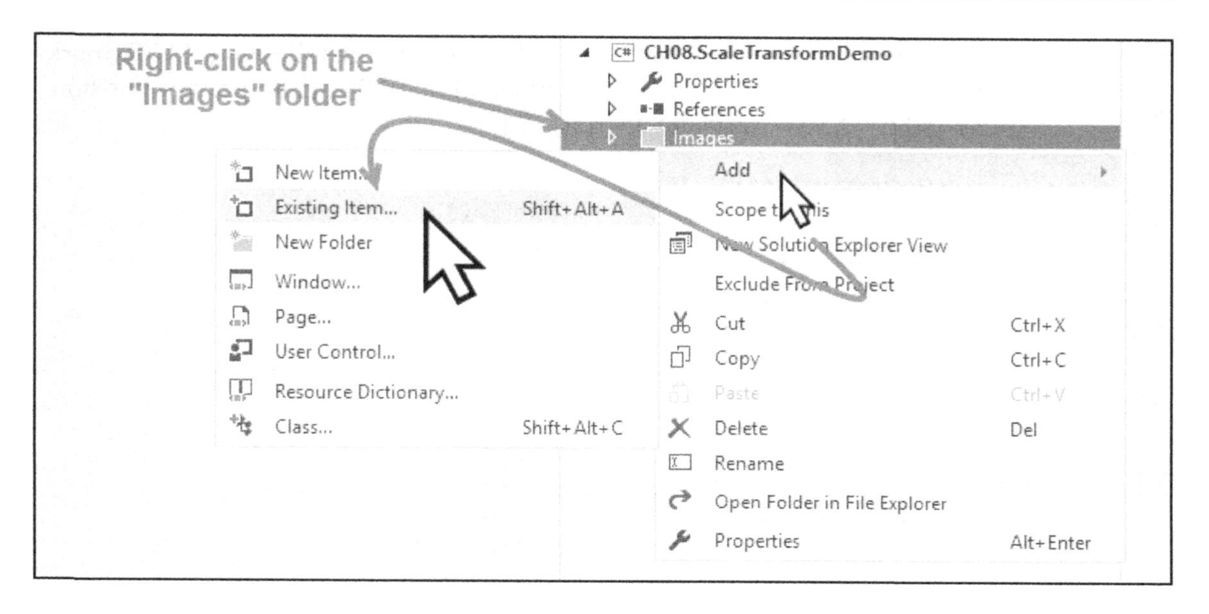

3. Navigate to the `MainWindow.xaml` page and replace the default `Grid` with a horizontal `StackPanel`.
4. Inside the `StackPanel`, add the following `Grid` with two image controls. Both, the image controls should be pointing to the `Images/image1.png` image file. The second image will have a transform set to it to scale the image to 80%, as shown in the following code snippet:

```
<Grid>
    <Image Height="300" Width="260"
           Margin="4" Opacity="0.2"
           Source="Images/image1.png"/>
    <Image Height="300" Width="260"
           Margin="4"
           Source="Images/image1.png">
        <Image.RenderTransform>
            <ScaleTransform ScaleX="0.8"
                            ScaleY="0.8"/>
        </Image.RenderTransform>
    </Image>
</Grid>
```

5. Let's add one more `Grid` inside the `StackPanel` with the following XAML markup, where the two images are scaled to 50% and mark the scaling center position to (`0`,`0`) and (`100`,`100`), respectively:

```
<Grid Margin="110 0 0 0">
    <Image Height="300" Width="260"
           Margin="4" Opacity="0.2"
           Source="Images/image1.png">
        <Image.RenderTransform>
            <ScaleTransform ScaleX="0.5"
                            ScaleY="0.5"
                            CenterX="0"
                            CenterY="0"/>
        </Image.RenderTransform>
    </Image>
    <Image Height="300" Width="260"
           Margin="4"
           Source="Images/image1.png">
        <Image.RenderTransform>
            <ScaleTransform ScaleX="0.5"
                            ScaleY="0.5"
                            CenterX="100"
                            CenterY="100"/>
        </Image.RenderTransform>
    </Image>
</Grid>
```

6. Let's run the application now and check the scaling behavior of the various images on the screen.

How it works...

The `RenderTransform` attribute helps you to set runtime transformation to any UI Element. In this example, we used `ScaleTransform` to scale the image on the application window.

When you run the application, the first one is the default image with an opacity set to 20%, whereas the second one is scaled to 80% with an opacity of 100%. The `ScaleX` and `ScaleY` properties are used to scale an element, which takes a decimal value to represent the ratio. For example, 0.8 denotes 80%, whereas 1.2 denotes 120% of the scaling:

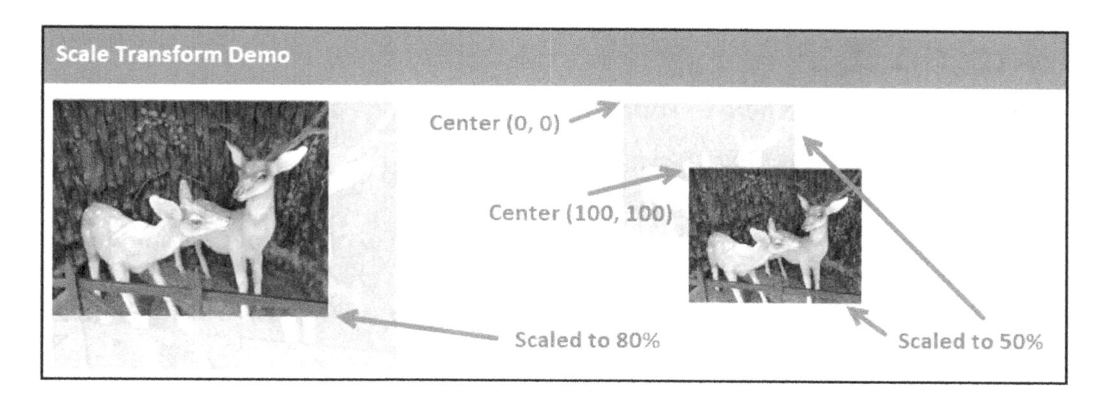

For the third and fourth images, both are scaled to 50%. But, as you see on the UI, the positions of the said images are different. The properties `CenterX` and `CenterY` are used to set the scaling center position. The third image has the scaling center set at (`0,0`), whereas the fourth one has its center position set at (`100,100`):

```
<ScaleTransform ScaleX="0.5"
                ScaleY="0.5"
                CenterX="100"
                CenterY="100"/>
```

Rotating an element while rendering

When you want to rotate an element at runtime, the `RotateTransform` is used. It rotates the element around a center position denoted by `CenterX` and `CenterY`, at an angle in degrees specified by the `Angle` property.

Let's learn how to use `RotateTransform` to rotate a UI element at a specified angle. In this recipe, we are going to discuss this.

Getting ready

Open Visual Studio and create a new project named `CH08.RotateTransformDemo`. Make sure to select the **WPF App** template while creating the project.

How to do it...

Follow the steps mentioned here to apply rotation to an `Image` control:

1. From **Solution Explorer**, right-click on the project node and create a new folder. Name it as `Images`.
2. Now right-click on the **Images** folder and add an existing image from your system. Name it `image1.png`.
3. Open the `MainWindow.xaml` file and replace the existing `Grid` with a horizontal `StackPanel`.
4. Insert the following XAML mark-up inside the `StackPanel` to add two images the application window. The first image will have an opacity set to 20%, and the second image will have a `RotateTransform` set at an angle of 45 degrees:

```
<Image Height="300" Width="260"
       Margin="4" Opacity="0.2"
       Source="Images/image1.png"/>
<Image Height="300" Width="260"
       Margin="4"
       Source="Images/image1.png">
    <Image.RenderTransform>
        <RotateTransform Angle="45"/>
    </Image.RenderTransform>
</Image>
```

5. Let's add one more `Grid` inside the `StackPanel`.
6. Add two more images into the new `Grid` panel. Set the `RenderTransform` attribute of both the images to have a `RotateTransform` set to it at an angle of `45` degrees.
7. As shown in the following XAML snippet, set the center position of the rotation of the images using the `CenterX` and `CenterY` properties. In this demonstration, we will set (`0`,`0`) and (`30`,`30`) as the rotation center of the respective images:

```
<Grid Margin="80 0 0 0">
    <Image Height="300" Width="260"
           Margin="4" Opacity="0.2"
           Source="Images/image1.png">
        <Image.RenderTransform>
            <RotateTransform Angle="45"
                             CenterX="0"
                             CenterY="0"/>
        </Image.RenderTransform>
    </Image>
```

```
        <Image Height="300" Width="260"
               Margin="4"
               Source="Images/image1.png">
            <Image.RenderTransform>
                <RotateTransform Angle="45"
                                 CenterX="30"
                                 CenterY="30"/>
            </Image.RenderTransform>
        </Image>
    </Grid>
```

8. Once this is done, build the project and run it. You will see four images on the screen, which will look like the following screenshot:

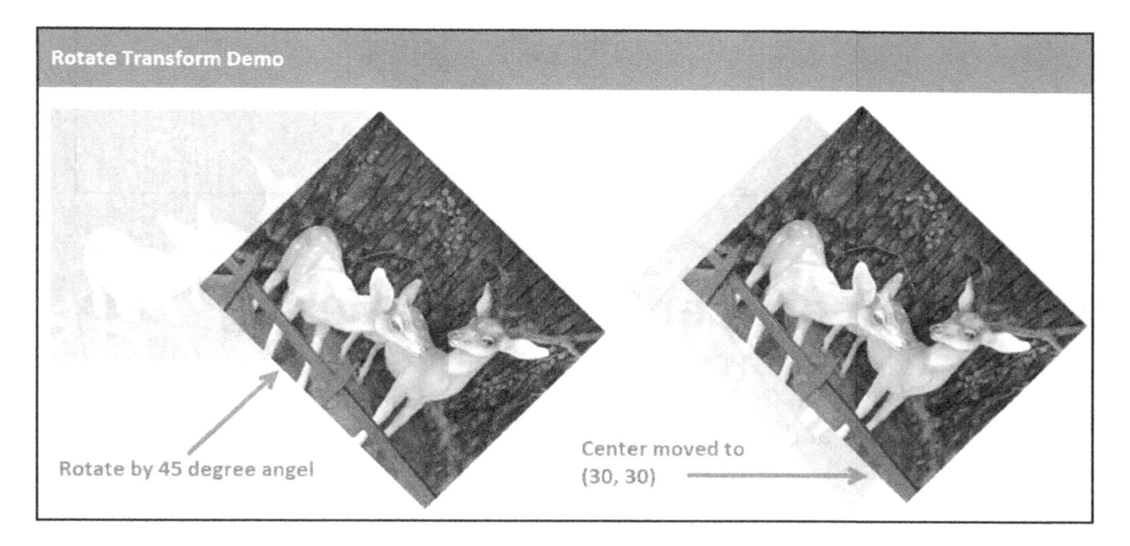

How it works...

`RotateTransform` allows you to rotate an element at a certain degree specified by the `Angle` property. In the first image, no transformation was applied and thus it will look as default. If you compare this with the other images on the screen, the second image is rotated clockwise at an angle of `45` degrees. The third and fourth images are also rotated at an angle of `45` degrees, but with a small difference.

For the third image, the rotation was done at the center position (`0,0`). For the fourth image, it was done at the center position (`30,30`). Here's how the difference will look:

Skewing an element while rendering

`SkewTransform` is used in a WPF platform to shear an element so that it has a 3D look in a 2D plate by adding depth to it. The `AngleX` and `AngleY` properties are used to specify the skew angle of the *X* axis and the *Y* axis, while the `CenterX` and `CenterY` properties are used to specify the *X* and *Y* coordinates of the center point.

In this recipe, we will learn how to apply skew transform to an image.

Getting ready

To get started, open your Visual Studio IDE and create a new project named `CH08.SkewTransformDemo`, based on the WPF application template.

How to do it...

Let's add some images to the application window and apply skew to those at a certain angle and certain center positions. Follow these steps:

1. From **Solution Explorer**, right-click on the project node and create a new folder. Name it `Images`.
2. Now right-click on the `Images` folder and add an existing image from your system. Name it as `image1.png`.
3. Open the `MainWindow.xaml` file and replace the existing `Grid` with a horizontal `StackPanel`.
4. Insert the following `Grid` inside the `StackPanel` to have two images. The first one will have opacity set to 20%, whereas the other will have a Skew applied to it at an angle of `50` degrees and `5` degrees on the *X* and *Y* axes. To set these, use the `AngleX` and `AngleY` properties, as follows:

```
<Grid>
    <Image Height="300" Width="260"
           Margin="4" Opacity="0.2"
           Source="Images/image1.png"/>
    <Image Height="300" Width="260"
           Margin="4"
           Source="Images/image1.png">
        <Image.RenderTransform>
            <SkewTransform AngleX="50"
                           AngleY="5"/>
        </Image.RenderTransform>
    </Image>
</Grid>
```

5. Add one more `Grid` inside the `StackPanel` and insert two images inside the new `Grid`. Set `SkewTransform` to both of the images at the *X* and *Y* axes as `30` degrees and `5` degrees, respectively. For one of the images, set the skew center position at (`0,0`), and for the other image, set the skew center position at (`200,-100`) by specifying the `CenterX` and `CenterY` properties as follows:

```
<Grid Margin="200 0 0 0">
    <Image Height="300" Width="260"
           Margin="4" Opacity="0.2"
           Source="Images/image1.png">
        <Image.RenderTransform>
            <SkewTransform AngleX="30"
                           AngleY="5"
```

```
                                         CenterX="0"
                                         CenterY="0"/>
                </Image.RenderTransform>
            </Image>
            <Image Height="300" Width="260"
                   Margin="4" Opacity="1.0"
                   Source="Images/image1.png">
                <Image.RenderTransform>
                    <SkewTransform AngleX="30"
                                   AngleY="5"
                                   CenterX="200"
                                   CenterY="-100"/>
                </Image.RenderTransform>
            </Image>
        </Grid>
```

6. Let's run the application. You will see images on the screen, such as the following ones:

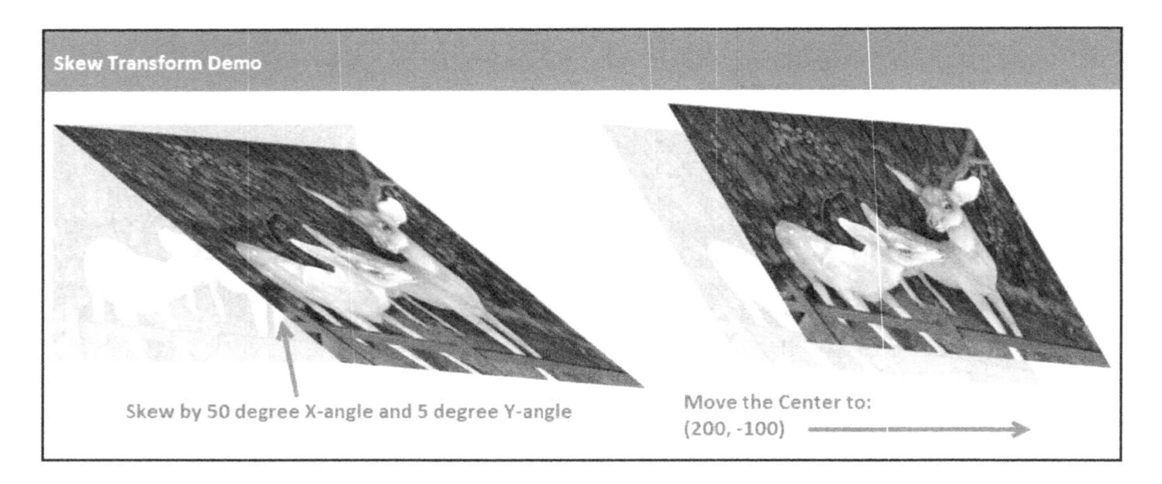

How it works...

When you set `AngleX` and `AngleY` to a `SkewTransform`, the associated element skews/shears counterclockwise from the *Y* axis and the *X* axis, respectively, at an angle specified, which is measured in degrees.

The `CenterX` property is used to set the *X* coordinate of the transform center, whereas the `CenterY` property is used to set the *Y* coordinate of the transform center. In the preceding example, when we specified `CenterX` and `CenterY` to the image, it changed the skew position centered at (`200,-100`) coordinate point, as shown in the following screenshot:

Moving an element while rendering

`TranslateTransform` is used to move an element from one position to another in the 2D interface. The `X` and `Y` properties are used to move an element towards the *X* and *Y* axes. In this recipe, we will learn how to apply this transforming to an element.

Getting ready

Open Visual Studio and create a project named `CH08.TranslateTransformDemo` based on the WPF application template.

How to do it...

Follow these simple steps to move an image from a certain coordinate location specified by the `X` and `Y` properties:

1. Before working on this, we need to add an image file to the project. From **Solution Explorer**, right-click on the project node and create a new folder. Name it `Images`.
2. Now right-click on the `Images` folder and add an existing image from your system. Name it `image1.png`.
3. Open the `MainWindow.xaml` file and add two images inside the `Grid` panel. Set the first one with a transparency of 30%. For the second image, add a `TranslateTransform` to it at a (`300,80`) location specified by the `X` and `Y` properties, as shared in the following screenshot:

```
<Grid VerticalAlignment="Top"
      HorizontalAlignment="Left">
    <Image Height="300" Width="260"
           Margin="4" Opacity="0.3"
           Source="Images/image1.png"/>
    <Image Height="300" Width="260"
           Margin="4"
           Source="Images/image1.png">
        <Image.RenderTransform>
            <TranslateTransform X="300"
                                Y="80"/>
        </Image.RenderTransform>
    </Image>
</Grid>
```

4. That's it! Let's build and run the application.

How it works...

When you run the application, you will see two images on the screen. The first one, which has a 20% opacity level, is placed at the far left of the window. The second image, which was placed on top of it, has been moved to a coordinate point (`300, 80`), as shown in the following screenshot:

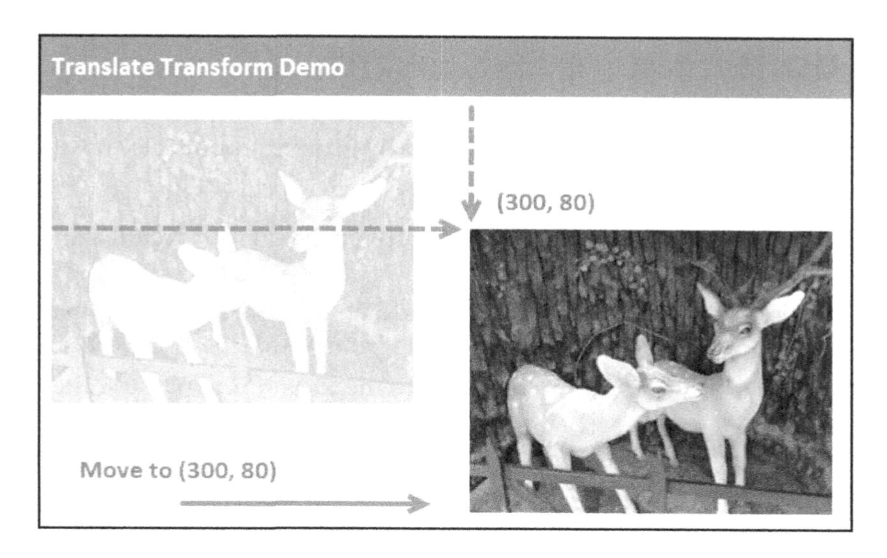

To set the distance to translate along the *X* axis, the `X` property of the `TranslateTransform` is used, which is `300` here. Similarly, to set the distance to translate along the *Y* axis, the `Y` property of the `TranslateTransform` is used. It is `80` in our case.

Grouping multiple transforms

It is not mandatory to have a single transform to a single element. You can group multiple transforms to it, by using the `<TransformGroup></TransformGroup>` tag. In this recipe, we will learn how to group multiple transforms.

Getting ready

To get started, open Visual Studio and create a new project named `CH08.GroupedTransformsDemo` based on the WPF application template.

How to do it...

Let's follow these steps to add two images to the application window and flip the second image to give a reflection effect. This will be done by grouping multiple transforms to that image:

1. First, we need to add an image to the project. To do this, create a folder named `Images` in the project root directory.
2. Right-click on the `Images` folder and add an existing image to it. Name it `image1.png`, which will be accessible from XAML as `Images/image1.png`.
3. From the **Solution Explorer**, navigate to the `MainWindow.xaml` file.
4. Replace the existing `Grid` panel with a horizontal `StackPanel`.
5. Insert two `Image` controls inside it and set their names as `originalImage` and `flippedImage`.
6. Now set the image source of both the controls to `Images/image1.png` and then set their size. This is how the XAML will look:

```
<StackPanel Orientation="Horizontal"
            Margin="10">
    <Image x:Name="originalImage"
           Source="Images/image1.png"
           Height="200" Width="250"/>
    <Image x:Name="flippedImage"
           Source="Images/image1.png"
           Height="200" Width="250"/>
</StackPanel>
```

7. Run the application, which will give the following output:

8. Close the application and return to the `MainWindow.xaml` file.
9. Now we will flip the second image (`flippedImage`) to give a reflection effect. To do so, first set the `RenderTransformOrigin` of the `Image` control to `0.5,0.5`.
10. Now add `<Image.RenderTransform>` to add the transforms mark-up. In this case, as we are going to add multiple transforms, add a `<TransformGroup>` tag inside it.
11. Let's add `ScaleTransform`, `SkewTransform`, `RotateTransform`, and `TranslateTransform` inside the `<TransformGroup>` tag to flip the image. This is how the `RenderTransform` of the `Image` will look:

```
<Image x:Name="flippedImage"
       Source="Images/image1.png"
       Height="200" Width="250"
       RenderTransformOrigin="0.5,0.5">
    <Image.RenderTransform>
        <TransformGroup>
            <ScaleTransform ScaleY="1" ScaleX="-1"/>
            <SkewTransform AngleY="0" AngleX="0"/>
            <RotateTransform Angle="0"/>
            <TranslateTransform/>
        </TransformGroup>
    </Image.RenderTransform>
</Image>
```

Once done with the changes, your XAML will look as the following code:

```
<StackPanel Orientation="Horizontal"
 Margin="10">
 <Image x:Name="originalImage"
 Source="Images/image1.png"
 Height="200" Width="250"/>
 <Image x:Name="flippedImage"
 Source="Images/image1.png"
 Height="200" Width="250"
 RenderTransformOrigin="0.5,0.5">
 <Image.RenderTransform>
 <TransformGroup>
 <ScaleTransform ScaleY="1" ScaleX="-1"/>
 <SkewTransform AngleY="0" AngleX="0"/>
 <RotateTransform Angle="0"/>
 <TranslateTransform/>
 </TransformGroup>
 </Image.RenderTransform>
 </Image>
</StackPanel>
```

12. Let's build the project and run the application again. What did you see? There's a reflection of the first image created by flipping the second image. Here's a screenshot of the output:

How it works...

It works by defining the transformation mark-up inside the `<TransformGroup>` tag. In our example, we applied the `ScaleTransform`, which created a flip effect. The rest of the other transforms that we applied here use default values. You can modify their values and check how this works in the UI.

There's more...

Visual Studio provides you with a straightforward way to add transforms to any UI element. From the designer view, select the element for which you want to apply the transform and navigate to its **Properties** pane. Here, you can find an expander pane with the title **Transform**. This is used to set various values to different transforms available in XAML.

As shown in the following screenshot, you can define `TranslateTransform`, `RotateTransform`, `ScaleTransform`, `SkewTransform`, and `Flip`. Each tab/section consists of different values that it can accept:

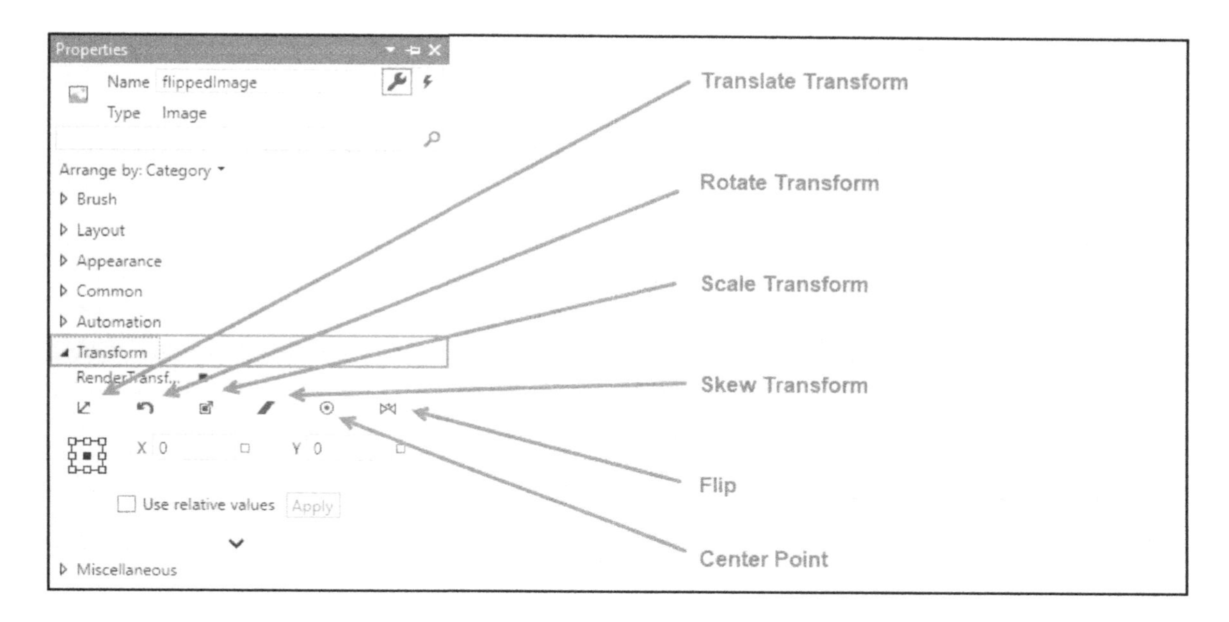

Creating property-based animations

Property-based animations are used to change a dependency property from one value to another in a duration specified. There exists various animation classes under the namespace `System.Windows.Media.Animation`, which includes `DoubleAnimation`, `ColorAnimation`, and `PointAnimation`. These are used to create animation based on the type of property being animated.

In this recipe, we will learn how to create property-based animations. Keep in mind that only Dependency Properties can be modifiable during an animation.

Getting ready

To get started with this recipe, let's first create a project. Open Visual Studio IDE and create a project named `CH08.PropertyBasedAnimationDemo`, based on the WPF application template.

How to do it...

In this demonstration, we will add a square box to the application window. On mouse hover, we will run a storyboard to change the size and color of the box and then reset it to the initial value on mouse leave. Follow these steps:

1. From **Solution Explorer**, navigate to the `MainWindow.xaml` file.
2. Inside the XAML file, you will find a `Grid` panel placed by default. Let's add a `Rectangle` control inside it and set its `Height` and `Width` properties to `100` to give it a square look.
3. Give the rectangle the name `squareBox` so that we can identify it from our `Storyboard`.
4. Add a `SolidColorBrush` to fill the background of the `Rectangle`. Set a color to the brush and name it `squareBoxFillBrush`. Here's the XAML snippet:

```
<Grid>
    <Rectangle x:Name="squareBox"
               Height="100"
               Width="100">
        <Rectangle.Fill>
            <SolidColorBrush x:Name="squareBoxFillBrush"
                             Color="Black"/>
        </Rectangle.Fill>

    </Rectangle>
</Grid>
```

5. As we need to add a `Storyboard` animation to the `MouseEnter` and `MouseLeave` events of the `Rectangle`, let's control these using triggers. As shown, add a `<Rectangle.Triggers></Rectangle.Triggers>` element to our `Rectangle` control:

```
<Grid>
    <Rectangle x:Name="squareBox"
               Height="100"
               Width="100">
        <Rectangle.Fill>
            <SolidColorBrush x:Name="squareBoxFillBrush"
                             Color="Black"/>
        </Rectangle.Fill>
        <Rectangle.Triggers>
```

```
        </Rectangle.Triggers>
    </Rectangle>
</Grid>
```

6. As we will be triggering the animation on `MouseEnter` and `MouseLeave` events, add an `EventTrigger` inside the `<Rectangle.Triggers></Rectangle.Triggers>` element that we have added.
7. Now expand the trigger to have `Actions` to begin a `Storyboard` animation. Modify your XAML mark-up as follows:

```
<Rectangle.Triggers>
    <EventTrigger RoutedEvent="MouseEnter">
        <EventTrigger.Actions>
            <BeginStoryboard>
                <Storyboard>

                </Storyboard>
            </BeginStoryboard>
        </EventTrigger.Actions>
    </EventTrigger>
</Rectangle.Triggers>
```

8. Inside the `Storyboard` animation for the `MouseEnter` event, we will be changing the size and color of the `squareBox` rectangle control. By using `DoubleAnimation`, we will be changing the `Height` and `Width` properties of the rectangle, and by using the `ColorAnimation` we will be changing the `Fill` color. Update the `Storyboard` as follows:

```
<Storyboard>
    <DoubleAnimation Storyboard.TargetName="squareBox"
                     Storyboard.TargetProperty="Height"
                     To="200"/>
    <DoubleAnimation Storyboard.TargetName="squareBox"
                     Storyboard.TargetProperty="Width"
                     To="400"/>
    <ColorAnimation
             Storyboard.TargetName="squareBoxFillBrush"
             Storyboard.TargetProperty="Color"
             To="OrangeRed"
             Duration="0:0:1"/>
</Storyboard>
```

9. Similarly, add another `EventTrigger` to the `Rectangle` control to trigger another `Storyboard` on the `MouseLeave` event to reset the size and the color. This new mark-up will look as follows:

```
<EventTrigger RoutedEvent="MouseLeave">
    <EventTrigger.Actions>
        <BeginStoryboard>
            <Storyboard>
                <DoubleAnimation
                       Storyboard.TargetName="squareBox"
                       Storyboard.TargetProperty="Height"
                       To="100"/>
                <DoubleAnimation
                       Storyboard.TargetName="squareBox"
                       Storyboard.TargetProperty="Width"
                       To="100"/>
                <ColorAnimation
              Storyboard.TargetName="squareBoxFillBrush"
              Storyboard.TargetProperty="Color"
              To="Black"
              Duration="0:0:1"/>
            </Storyboard>
        </BeginStoryboard>
    </EventTrigger.Actions>
</EventTrigger>
```

10. Run the application now. You will see a square with a `Black` background, as shown in the following screenshot:

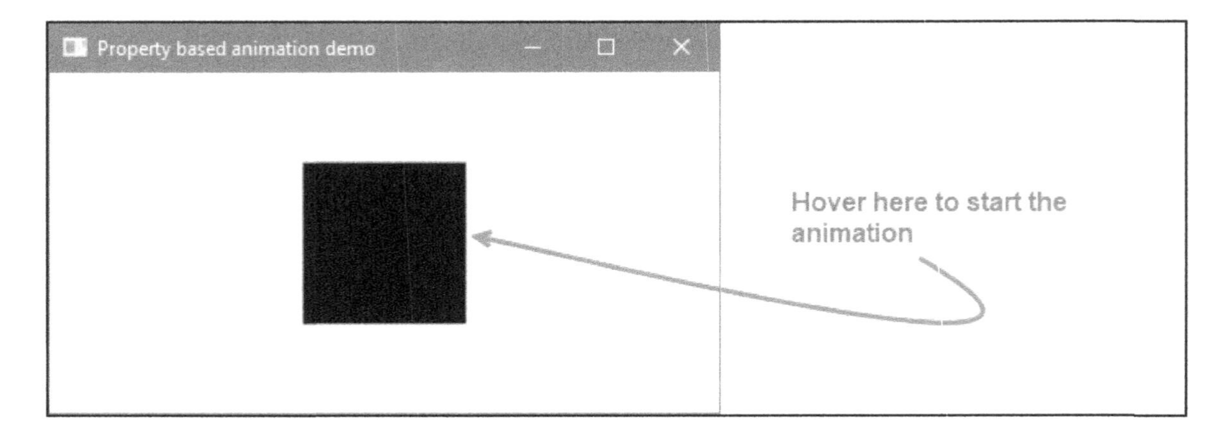

11. Mouse hover on the square. This will resize the square to a rectangle and change the color to `OrangeRed`. Check the transition of the size and color, which will have a nice animation:

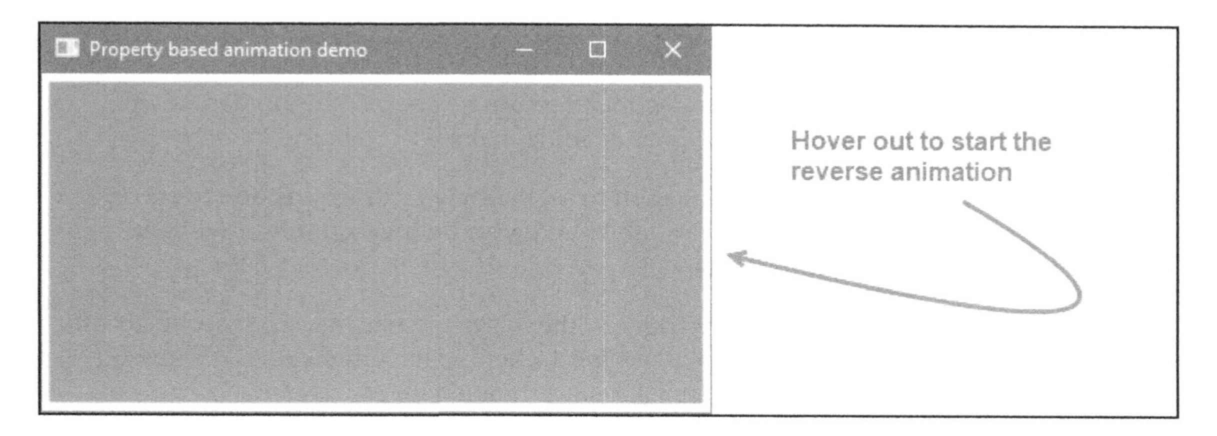

12. Now hover out your mouse cursor from the rectangle. What happens now? With a nice animation, the rectangle will reset back to a square. Also, the background color will change from `OrangeRed` to `Black`.

How it works...

Animations may be created manually by constructing the appropriate animation type, specifying properties, and then calling `BeginStoryboard` on the element to animate. The properties must be of type dependency property, which you want to animate on the animation object.

In this example, when the `MouseEnter` event triggers, the following `Storyboard` animation runs. `DoubleAnimation` and `ColorAnimation` accepts the attached properties, `Storyboard.TargetName` and `Storyboard.TargetProperty`, which allows the `Storyboard` to change the said property of the targeted element at runtime:

```
<Storyboard>
    <DoubleAnimation Storyboard.TargetName="squareBox"
                     Storyboard.TargetProperty="Height"
                     To="200"/>
    <DoubleAnimation Storyboard.TargetName="squareBox"
                     Storyboard.TargetProperty="Width"
                     To="400"/>
    <ColorAnimation Storyboard.TargetName="squareBoxFillBrush"
```

```
                                Storyboard.TargetProperty="Color"
                                To="OrangeRed"
                                Duration="0:0:1"/>
</Storyboard>
```

`From` and `To` properties are used to change the property from a specified value to another. Though it is optional to set the `From` field, you need to specify the `To` field in order to have the change in effect for the `Storyboard`. In the preceding example, the animation will change the `Height`, `Width`, and `Color` from its initial value.

You can also set a `TimeSpan` to the animation to set the time for the transition to occur. You can use the `Duration` property to set the value. In the preceding example, it will take `1` second for the transition to happen from a `Black` color to an `OrangeRed` color.

Similarly, when the `MouseLeave` event triggers, the following `Storyboard` responsible for resetting the value will trigger, which will set the `To` field to its initial value. When the `Storyboard` runs, you will see a nice transitional animation on the screen:

```
<Storyboard>
    <DoubleAnimation Storyboard.TargetName="squareBox"
                     Storyboard.TargetProperty="Height"
                     To="100"/>
    <DoubleAnimation Storyboard.TargetName="squareBox"
                     Storyboard.TargetProperty="Width"
                     To="100"/>
    <ColorAnimation Storyboard.TargetName="squareBoxFillBrush"
                    Storyboard.TargetProperty="Color"
                    To="Black"
                    Duration="0:0:1"/>
</Storyboard>
```

These are some common properties that you will find in most of the animation types:

- `From`: It is used to indicate the starting value of the animation. If you omit the `From` field, it will use the current value of the dependency property.
- `To`: It is the target value of the animation, which you should fill. If you omit it or put the current value, the said animation will have no effect.
- `Duration`: It is the duration of the animation. Apart from a `TimeSpan` type value in `hh:mm:ss.ms` format, it can also contain two special values—`Duration.Automatic` (default value) and `Duration.Forever`. When you specify `Duration.Forever`, it will run for an infinite length. In XAML, `hh:mm:ss.ms` format is mostly used.

- `FillBehavior`: It indicates the animation's behavior when it ends. The default value `FillEnd` asks to keep the last animation value; the previous value, which was used before the animation, will have no effect. The other value, `Stop`, destroys the animation and reverts the property to its value without the animation.
- `BeginTime`: When you want to set a delay before the animation begins, you can use this attribute to define the delay time.
- `AutoReverse`: If you want to automatically reverse the animation, after it ends, you can set it to `true`. The total animation duration will be effectively doubled when enabled.
- `SpeedRatio`: It allows you to speed up or slow down the animation duration.
- `RepeatBehavior`: This attribute specifies the count or the time you want to repeat the animation, after it ends. This is often useful when you set `AutoReverse` to `true`.

Creating path-based animations

Along with property-based animations, which we learned about in the previous recipe, WPF also supports **path-based animations** that run along a path specified by the `PathGeometry`.

In this recipe, we will learn how to use a `PathGeometry` to animate an element along its way.

Getting ready

Let's begin with creating a new WPF application project. Name it `CH08.PathBasedAnimationDemo`.

How to do it...

In this demonstration, we will use a circle to animate it on the click of a button. The animation will be performed based on a path specified by a set of geometry coordinates. Let's build this by following the steps mentioned here:

1. From **Solution Explorer**, navigate to the `MainWindow.xaml` file.

2. A default `Grid` panel will be present inside the file. Let's divide it into two rows by specifying the row definition as follows:

```
<Grid.RowDefinitions>
    <RowDefinition Height="*"/>
    <RowDefinition Height="Auto"/>
</Grid.RowDefinitions>
```

3. Let's place a `Canvas` panel inside the first row. Add an `Ellipse` of `Height="30"` and `Width="30"` to form the circle. Give it a name `circle`.
4. Set the fill color of the `Ellipse` and position it at the (`100, 100`) coordinate location of the canvas. Here's the complete mark-up for your reference:

```
<Canvas Grid.Row="0">
    <Ellipse x:Name="circle"
             Height="30"
             Width="30"
             Canvas.Left="100"
             Canvas.Top="100"
             Fill="OrangeRed"/>
</Canvas>
```

5. We will be using this `Ellipse` to animate inside the canvas along a path. For this, we will need a `PathGeometry` defined. To do so, add the following inside the `Window` tag as `Resources` to define the `PolyLineSegment` points as a collection of coordinates:

```
<Window.Resources>
    <PathGeometry x:Key="animationPath">
        <PathFigure IsClosed="True"
                    StartPoint="100,100">
            <PolyLineSegment Points="150,150 400,200 300,50
200,200 100,100 400,100 50,50 400,150 100,250, 100,50" />
        </PathFigure>
    </PathGeometry>
</Window.Resources>
```

6. Let's add a `Button` control inside the `Window`, which will be used to trigger the animation. Surround the button with a horizontal `StackPanel` and place it inside the second row of the `Grid`:

```
<StackPanel Grid.Row="1"
            Orientation="Horizontal"
            HorizontalAlignment="Center"
            Margin="10">
    <Button Content="Animate"
            Width="100">

    </Button>
</StackPanel>
```

7. Now we need to catch the `Button.Click` event. For this, we will need an `EventTrigger` to define against the `Button` control. And, once the trigger fires, the action is to begin a `Storyboard` to perform an animation. Let's modify the `Button` control to have this trigger set to start a storyboard. Here's the code to refer to:

```
<Button Content="Animate"
        Width="100">
    <Button.Triggers>
        <EventTrigger RoutedEvent="Button.Click">
            <EventTrigger.Actions>
                <BeginStoryboard>
                    <Storyboard x:Name="Animate"
                                AutoReverse="True">

                    </Storyboard>
                </BeginStoryboard>
            </EventTrigger.Actions>
        </EventTrigger>
    </Button.Triggers>
</Button>
```

8. Now it's time to add some path animations to the `Storyboard` that we have added inside the `Button.Click` event handler. Let's use `DoubleAnimationUsingPath` to bind the `PathGeometry` that we added to the `Window.Resources` tag.

9. Set the `Storyboard.TargetName` to `circle` and the `Storyboard.TargetProperty` to `(Canvas.Left)` and `(Canvas.Top)` to create an animation in both the *X* and *Y* axes. Here's the code:

```
<DoubleAnimationUsingPath Duration="0:0:5"
        Storyboard.TargetName="circle"
        Storyboard.TargetProperty="(Canvas.Left)"
        PathGeometry="{StaticResource animationPath}"
        Source="X"/>
<DoubleAnimationUsingPath Duration="0:0:5"
        Storyboard.TargetName="circle"
        Storyboard.TargetProperty="(Canvas.Top)"
        PathGeometry="{StaticResource animationPath}"
        Source="Y"/>
```

10. Let's build the application and run it. You will see the following UI with a circle and a button:

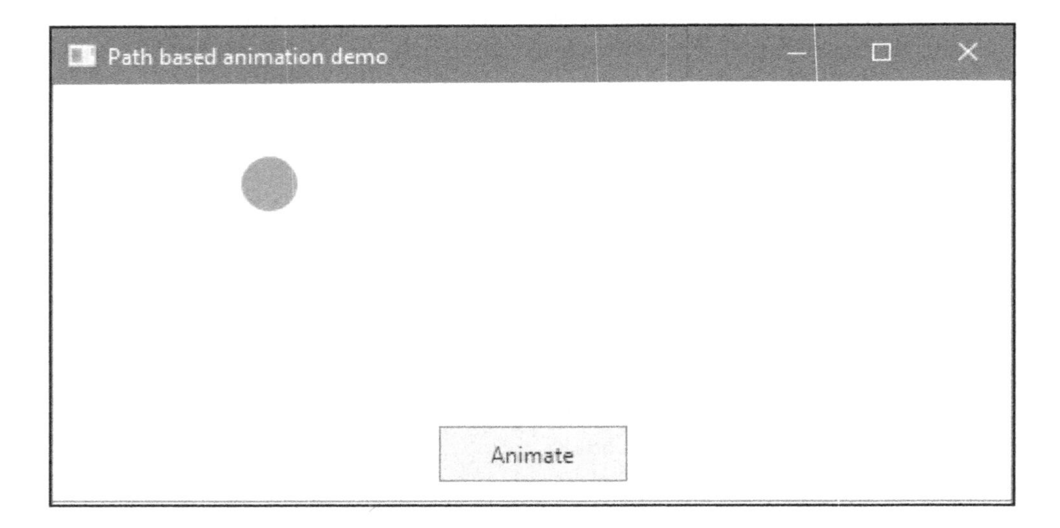

11. Click on the **Animate** button and observe the positions of the circle. You will see a nice animated flow on the screen:

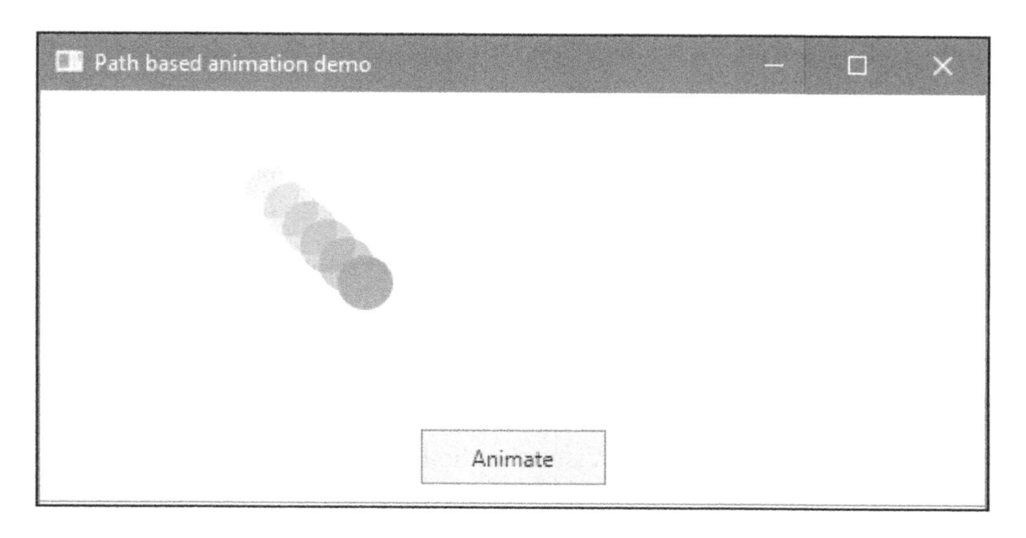

How it works...

The path-based animations use a `PathGeometry` as a path to create the animation. In our example, we defined it under the `Window.Resources` tag as an `animationPath`, which represents the path in a 2D interface as a collection of coordinate points. See the following code snippet:

```
<PathGeometry x:Key="animationPath">
    <PathFigure IsClosed="True"
                StartPoint="100,100">
        <PolyLineSegment Points="150,150 400,200 300,50 200,200
100,100 400,100 50,50 400,150 100,250, 100,50" />
    </PathFigure>
</PathGeometry>
```

The `DoubleAnimationUsingPath` that we used in our storyboard animation uses `Canvas.Left` and `Canvas.Top` as the target properties to animate along the *X* and *Y* axes. When the `Storyboard` plays, the target element moves from one coordinate point to another, having a smooth animation between the two points.

Creating key-frame-based animations

Key frame animations in WPF enable you to animate an element using more than two target-values and control an animation's interpolation method. A key frame animation has no `From`/`To` properties with which we can set its target values.

The animation's target values are described using key frame objects, which you need to add to the animation's `KeyFrames` collection. When the animation runs, it transitions between the key frames that you specified.

In this recipe, we will learn how to create a key-frame-based animation and use it in our application.

Getting ready

We need to create a project first. Open Visual Studio IDE and create a new project named `CH08.KeyFrameBasedAnimationDemo`, based on the WPF application template.

How to do it...

Let's follow these steps to create a key-frame-based animation:

1. Open the `MainWindow.xaml` file.
2. Add two rows inside the `Grid`, by specifying `RowDefinitions`:

```
<Grid.RowDefinitions>
    <RowDefinition Height="*"/>
    <RowDefinition Height="Auto"/>
</Grid.RowDefinitions>
```

3. Add a `Canvas` panel at 0th row of the `Grid`.
4. Insert an `Ellipse` inside the canvas and set its `Height` and `Width` properties to `30`, so that it displays as a circle.
5. Provide a name to the `Ellipse`, and position it to the (`50,100`) coordinate position on the `Canvas` panel, and fill the background with an `OrangeRed` color.

6. Insert a `Button` control inside a horizontal `StackPanel`, and place the panel inside the second row. Here's the complete XAML of the UI that we have generated for this demonstration:

```
<Grid>
    <Grid.RowDefinitions>
        <RowDefinition Height="*"/>
        <RowDefinition Height="Auto"/>
    </Grid.RowDefinitions>
    <Canvas Grid.Row="0">
        <Ellipse x:Name="circle"
                 Height="30"
                 Width="30"
                 Canvas.Left="50"
                 Canvas.Top="100"
                 Fill="OrangeRed"/>
    </Canvas>
    <StackPanel Grid.Row="1"
                Orientation="Horizontal"
                HorizontalAlignment="Center"
                Margin="10">
        <Button Content="Animate"
                Width="100">

        </Button>
    </StackPanel>
</Grid>
```

7. On pressing the button, we need to animate the circle around the application window. To do this, we will be using an `EventTrigger`. Define the trigger for a `Button.Click` event and set its action to begin a storyboard.
8. Set the `AutoReverse` property of the `Storyboard` to `True`. Here's the code for launching the storyboard when a user triggers the button click event:

```
<Button Content="Animate"
        Width="100">
    <Button.Triggers>
        <EventTrigger RoutedEvent="Button.Click">
            <EventTrigger.Actions>
                <BeginStoryboard>
                    <Storyboard x:Name="Animate"
                                AutoReverse="True">

                    </Storyboard>
                </BeginStoryboard>
            </EventTrigger.Actions>
```

```
            </EventTrigger>
        </Button.Triggers>
    </Button>
```

9. Inside the storyboard, we need to define an animation that will run based on the key frame specified. This is done by adding one or more `LinearDoubleKeyFrame`(s) inside a `DoubleAnimationUsingKeyFrames` element. Insert two instances of `DoubleAnimationUsingKeyFrames` inside the `Storyboard` definition.
10. Set the `Storyboard.TargetName` property of `DoubleAnimationUsingKeyFrames` to `circle`.
11. Set `AutoReverse` to `True` and `RepeatBehavior` to `Forever`.
12. For the first `DoubleAnimationUsingKeyFrames`, set the `Storyboard.TargetProperty` to `(Canvas.Left)`. For the other one, set it to `(Canvas.Top)`.
13. Define key frames by adding one or more `LinearDoubleKeyFrame` instances to the `DoubleAnimationUsingKeyFrames`. Set their `KeyTime` and `Value`. Here's the complete code:

```
<DoubleAnimationUsingKeyFrames
        Storyboard.TargetName="circle"
        Storyboard.TargetProperty="(Canvas.Left)"
        AutoReverse="True"
        RepeatBehavior="Forever">
    <LinearDoubleKeyFrame Value="50"
                          KeyTime="0:0:0" />
    <LinearDoubleKeyFrame Value="450"
                          KeyTime="0:0:1" />
    <LinearDoubleKeyFrame Value="450"
                          KeyTime="0:0:3" />
    <LinearDoubleKeyFrame Value="250"
                          KeyTime="0:0:5" />
</DoubleAnimationUsingKeyFrames>
<DoubleAnimationUsingKeyFrames
        Storyboard.TargetName="circle"
        Storyboard.TargetProperty="(Canvas.Top)"
        AutoReverse="True"
        RepeatBehavior="Forever">
    <LinearDoubleKeyFrame Value="100"
                          KeyTime="0:0:0" />
    <LinearDoubleKeyFrame Value="200"
                          KeyTime="0:0:1" />
    <LinearDoubleKeyFrame Value="50"
                          KeyTime="0:0:3" />
```

```
            <LinearDoubleKeyFrame Value="150"
                                  KeyTime="0:0:5" />
        </DoubleAnimationUsingKeyFrames>
```

14. Once done, let's run the application. You will see a circle on the screen at the (`50`, `100`) coordinate point. There also exists a button labeled **Animate**, as shown in the following screenshot:

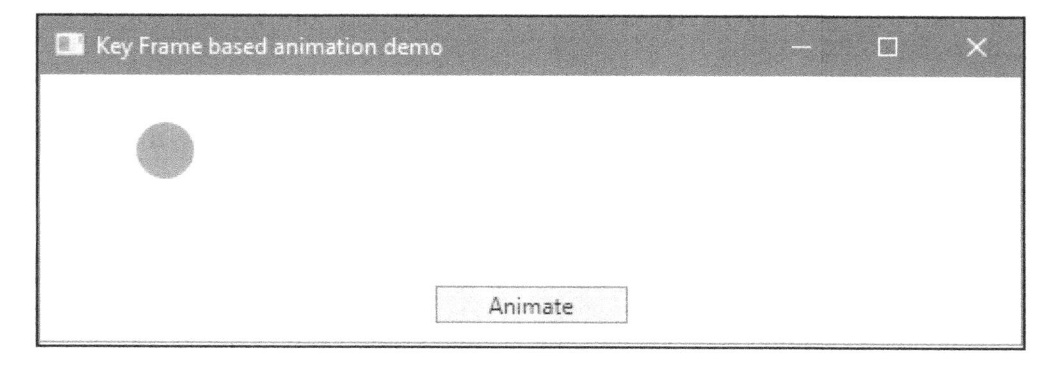

15. Click on the **Animate** button to start the defined storyboard. See the movement and the speed of the circle:

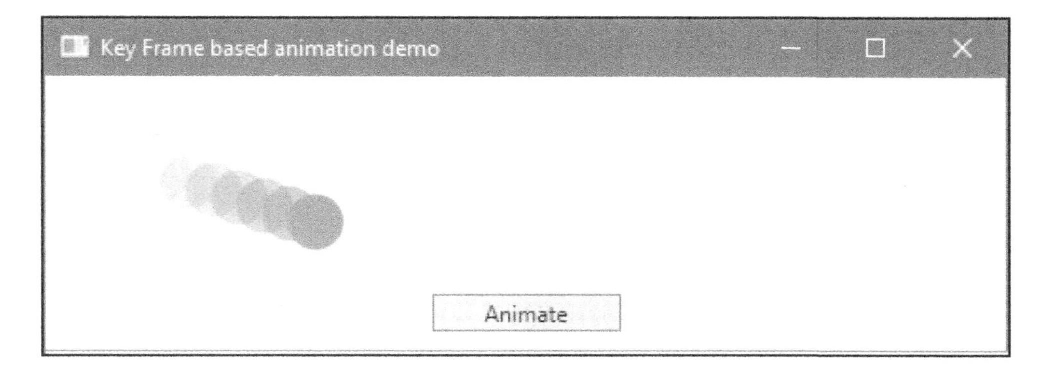

How it works...

When a key frame animation begins, it iterates through the specified key frames in the order they were defined by their `KeyTime` properties. If there exists no key frame at time `0` (initial point), the animation creates a transition between the target property's current value and the `Value` of the first key frame defined in the collection.

If the animation's `Duration` is `Automatic` or set to the time of the last key frame, the animation ends.

In the preceding demonstration, the first key frame (at time `0`) sets the animation's output value to `Canvas.Left="50"` and `Canvas.Top="100"`. In the next key frame (at time `1 sec`), the output value sets to the (`450,200`) coordinate point, and you will see a smooth transition between the (`50,100`) and the (`450,200`) points. Similarly, in the third and fourth seconds, the circle transitions from (`450,200`) to (`450,50`) and then to the (`250,150`) coordinate points.

As the defined `Storyboard` has an `AutoReverse` property set to `True`, the animation will have a reverse transition to move the circle from the end point (`250,150`) to the initial start point (`50,100`) via the (`450,50`) and the (`450,200`) coordinate points.

There's more...

The key-frame-based animation class type is not limited to only `DoubleAnimationUsingKeyFrames`. You can use any of the following key frame animation classes to construct your storyboard:

- Boolean: `BooleanAnimationUsingKeyFrames`
- Byte: `ByteAnimationUsingKeyFrames`
- Color: `ColorAnimationUsingKeyFrames`
- Decimal: `DecimalAnimationUsingKeyFrames`
- Double: `DoubleAnimationUsingKeyFrames`
- Int16: `Int16AnimationUsingKeyFrames`
- Int32: `Int32AnimationUsingKeyFrames`
- Int64: `Int64AnimationUsingKeyFrames`
- Matrix: `MatrixAnimationUsingKeyFrames`
- Object: `ObjectAnimationUsingKeyFrames`
- Point: `PointAnimationUsingKeyFrames`
- Quaternion: `QuaternionAnimationUsingKeyFrames`
- Rect: `RectAnimationUsingKeyFrames`
- Rotation3D: `Rotation3DAnimationUsingKeyFrames`
- Single: `SingleAnimationUsingKeyFrames`
- String: `StringAnimationUsingKeyFrames`

- Size: SizeAnimationUsingKeyFrames
- Thickness: ThicknessAnimationUsingKeyFrames
- Vector3D: Vector3DAnimationUsingKeyFrames
- Vector: VectorAnimationUsingKeyFrames

Adding easing effects to animations

Property-based animations are linear, whereas the key-frame-based animations are non-linear and are used to create **Beizer**-based interpolations. But creation of such effects is not so easy. To overcome this, WPF 4 introduces **easing functions** to turn a linear animation into a non-linear one and add some easing effects to those animation objects.

In this recipe, we will learn how to do this with a suitable example.

Getting ready

To get started with adding easing effects to an animation, let's open Visual Studio and create a new project named CH08.EasingEffectDemo. Select a WPF application template while creating the project.

How to do it...

Let's follow these steps to create an animation with various kinds of easing effects:

1. From **Solution Explorer**, open the MainWindow.xaml file.
2. Divide the existing Grid panel into two columns, by applying ColumnDefinition to it:

```
<Grid.ColumnDefinitions>
    <ColumnDefinition Width="*"/>
    <ColumnDefinition Width="Auto"/>
</Grid.ColumnDefinitions>
```

3. Now, inside the Grid, place a Canvas panel, and set its Grid.Column attribute to 0 (zero).

4. Inside the canvas, add an `Ellipse` (name it as `circle`) and set its `Height` and `Width` properties to `80` to give it a circular look. Set its `Fill` color property, and position it to a (`150,80`) location. Here's the code snippet:

```
<Canvas Grid.Column="0">
    <Ellipse x:Name="circle"
             Height="80"
             Width="80"
             Fill="OrangeRed"
             Canvas.Left="150"
             Canvas.Top="80"/>
</Canvas>
```

5. Now add a vertical `StackPanel` inside the `Grid` and set its `Grid.Column` attribute to `1`.
6. Add three radio buttons (`GroupName="AnimationSelector"`) inside the `StackPanel`, and add a `Storyboard` animation to fire when the `RadioButton.Checked` event is triggered.
7. Add a simple `DoubleAnimation` to move the circle horizontally by setting its `Storyboard.TargetProperty` to `(Canvas.Left)`.
8. Now expand the animation to add an easing effect to it. Insert a `<DoubleAnimation.EasingFunction></DoubleAnimation.EasingFuncti on>` attribute to hold the effect that we are going to add.
9. Let's add a `BackEase` effect to the three radio buttons. This type of effect represents an easing function that retracts the motion of an animation slightly before it begins to animate in the path indicated, and is denoted by the following function—`f(t) = t3 - t * a * sin(t * pi)`. Set the `Amplitude` property of the function to `0.3` and the `EasingMode` property to `EaseIn`, `EaseOut`, and `EaseInOut`, respectively. The complete code will look as follows:

```
<StackPanel Grid.Column="1"
            Margin="10">
    <RadioButton GroupName="AnimationSelector"
                 Content="BackEase - EaseIn"
                 Margin="4">
        <RadioButton.Triggers>
            <EventTrigger
                  RoutedEvent="RadioButton.Checked">
                <BeginStoryboard>
                    <Storyboard AutoReverse="True">
                        <DoubleAnimation
             Storyboard.TargetName="circle"
             Storyboard.TargetProperty="(Canvas.Left)"
```

```
                    To="350">
            <DoubleAnimation.EasingFunction>
                    <BackEase EasingMode="EaseIn"
                              Amplitude="0.3"/>
            </DoubleAnimation.EasingFunction>
                                </DoubleAnimation>
                            </Storyboard>
                        </BeginStoryboard>
                    </EventTrigger>
                </RadioButton.Triggers>
            </RadioButton>

            <RadioButton GroupName="AnimationSelector"
                         Content="BackEase - EaseInOut"
                         Margin="4">
                <RadioButton.Triggers>
                    <EventTrigger
                          RoutedEvent="RadioButton.Checked">
                        <BeginStoryboard>
                            <Storyboard AutoReverse="True">
                                <DoubleAnimation
                    Storyboard.TargetName="circle"
                    Storyboard.TargetProperty="(Canvas.Left)"
                    To="350">
            <DoubleAnimation.EasingFunction>
                    <BackEase EasingMode="EaseInOut"
                              Amplitude="0.3"/>
            </DoubleAnimation.EasingFunction>
                                </DoubleAnimation>
                            </Storyboard>
                        </BeginStoryboard>
                    </EventTrigger>
                </RadioButton.Triggers>
            </RadioButton>

            <RadioButton GroupName="AnimationSelector"
                         Content="BackEase - EaseOut"
                         Margin="4">
                <RadioButton.Triggers>
                    <EventTrigger
                          RoutedEvent="RadioButton.Checked">
                        <BeginStoryboard>
                            <Storyboard AutoReverse="True">
                                <DoubleAnimation
                    Storyboard.TargetName="circle"
                    Storyboard.TargetProperty="(Canvas.Left)"
                    To="350">
            <DoubleAnimation.EasingFunction>
```

```
                    <BackEase EasingMode="EaseOut"
                              Amplitude="0.3"/>
             </DoubleAnimation.EasingFunction>
                               </DoubleAnimation>
                           </Storyboard>
                       </BeginStoryboard>
                   </EventTrigger>
               </RadioButton.Triggers>
           </RadioButton>
       </StackPanel>
```

10. Let's run the application. You will see the following UI on the screen:

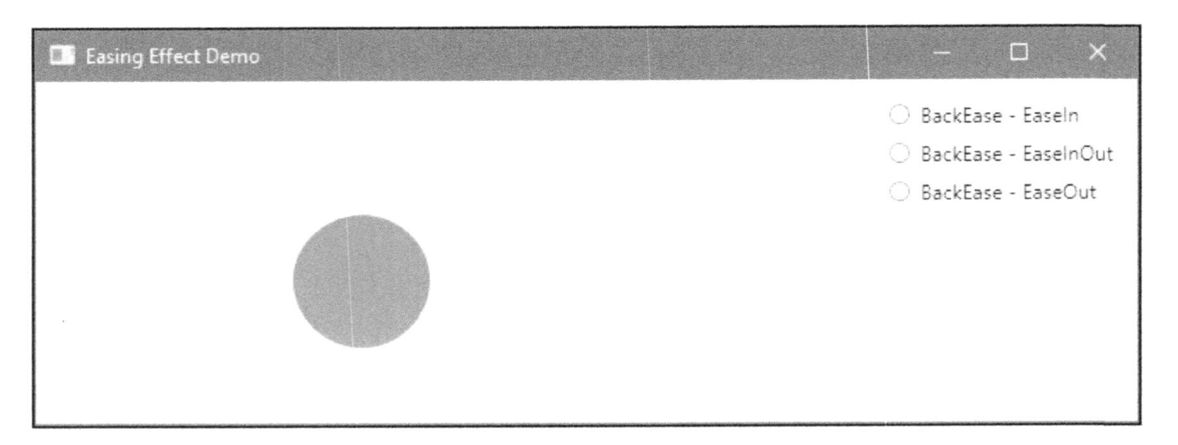

11. Now change the selection of the radios and observe the effects added to the animation of the circular object.

How it works...

Animation easing applies a function to the animation value to alter a linear animation to form a non-linear one. A mode option, defined by the `EasingMode` property, allows you to set when to apply the easing function. This could be at the beginning (`EaseIn`), at the end (`EaseOut`), or both (`EaseInOut`).

In the preceding example, we defined a `BackEase` function to the animation with different easing modes, which will animate when the `Checked` event of the radio buttons trigger.

The following graph demonstrates different values of `EasingMode`, for the `BackEase` effect:

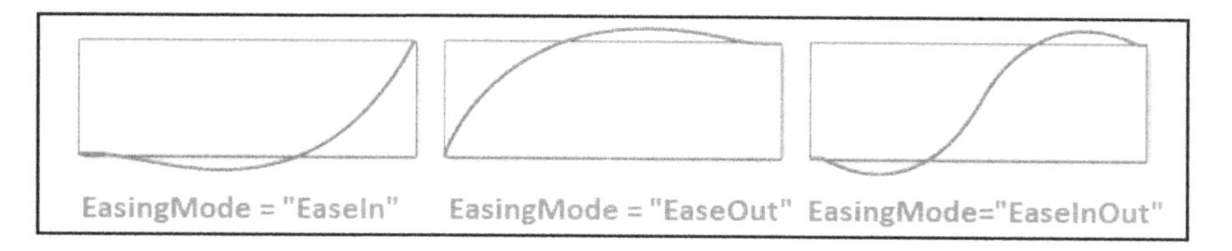

There's more...

It's not limited to only the `BackEase` function, but it can have any of the 11 built-in easing functions defined in WPF. The complete list is as follows:

- `BackEase`
- `BounceEase`
- `CircleEase`
- `CubicEase`
- `ElasticEase`
- `ExponentialEase`
- `PowerEase`
- `QuadraticEase`
- `QuarticEase`
- `QuinticEase`
- `SineEase`

All these listed easing functions derive from the abstract class `EasingFunctionBase`, which implements the `IEasingFunction` interface. It contains an `Ease` method and adds the `EasingMode` property, which indicates whether the function should be applied at the start of the animation (`EaseIn`), the end of the animation (`EaseOut`), or both ways (`EaseInOut`).

Let's modify our existing UI to have some more built-in easing functions added to the animation. To demonstrate this, we are going to add 10 more radio buttons inside the `StackPanel` and apply the easing functions to each one of them, as discussed in the following section.

BounceEase

This type of function creates an animated bouncing effect to the target. The `Bounces` and `Bounciness` properties can be used to control the bounces. The `Bounces` property denotes the number of bounces and the `Bounciness` property defines how bouncy the bounce animation is. The lower the value of `Bounciness`, the higher the bouncing animation; the higher the value of `Bounciness`, the lower the bounces of the animation.

In the following example, let's apply a `BounceEase` function to the `DoubleAnimation` to create a bouncing effect. Let's add the following `RadioButton` inside the `StackPanel`:

```
<RadioButton GroupName="AnimationSelector"
             Content="BounceEase - EaseInOut"
             Margin="4">
    <RadioButton.Triggers>
        <EventTrigger RoutedEvent="RadioButton.Checked">
            <BeginStoryboard>
                <Storyboard AutoReverse="True">
                    <DoubleAnimation
                     Storyboard.TargetName="circle"
                     Storyboard.TargetProperty="(Canvas.Left)"
                     To="350">
                        <DoubleAnimation.EasingFunction>
                            <BounceEase EasingMode="EaseInOut"
                                        Bounces="2"
                                        Bounciness="2"/>
                        </DoubleAnimation.EasingFunction>
                    </DoubleAnimation>
                </Storyboard>
            </BeginStoryboard>
        </EventTrigger>
    </RadioButton.Triggers>
</RadioButton>
```

The following graph demonstrates different values of `EasingMode`, for the `BounceEase` effect:

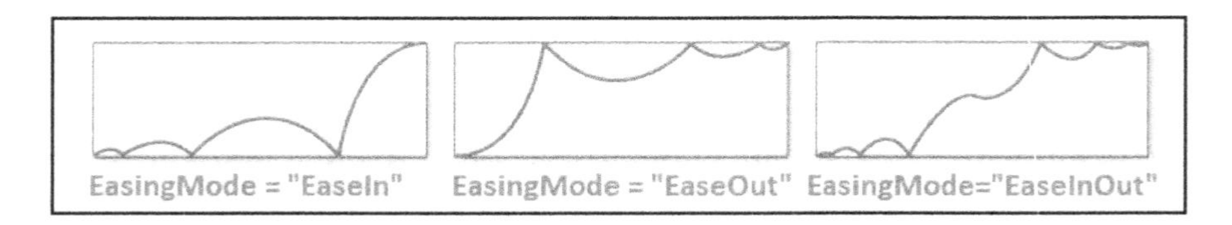

CircleEase

This represents an easing function that creates an animation that accelerates/decelerates using a `circular` function, and is denoted by the following function `f(t) = 1 - sqrt(1 - t2)`.

Let's add the following `RadioButton` inside the `StackPanel` to create an animation with a circular easing effect:

```
<RadioButton GroupName="AnimationSelector"
             Content="CircleEase - EaseInOut"
             Margin="4">
    <RadioButton.Triggers>
        <EventTrigger RoutedEvent="RadioButton.Checked">
            <BeginStoryboard>
                <Storyboard AutoReverse="True">
                    <DoubleAnimation
                     Storyboard.TargetName="circle"
                     Storyboard.TargetProperty="(Canvas.Left)"
                     To="350">
                        <DoubleAnimation.EasingFunction>
                            <CircleEase EasingMode="EaseInOut"/>
                        </DoubleAnimation.EasingFunction>
                    </DoubleAnimation>
                </Storyboard>
            </BeginStoryboard>
        </EventTrigger>
    </RadioButton.Triggers>
</RadioButton>
```

The following graph demonstrates different values of `EasingMode`, for the `CircleEase` effect:

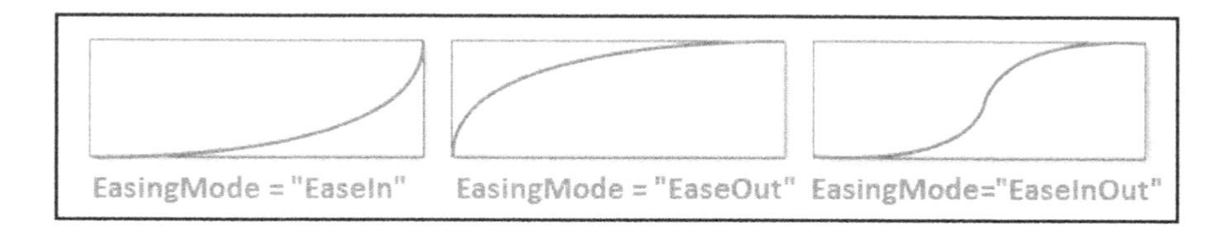

CubicEase

This creates an animation that accelerates/decelerates using the formula `f(t) = t3`, where `EasingMode` can be applied to control acceleration, deceleration, or both, by setting the value `EaseIn`, `EaseOut`, or `EasInOut`.

Let's add the following `RadioButton` inside the `StackPanel` to create an animation with an accelerating `CubicEase` function:

```
<RadioButton GroupName="AnimationSelector"
             Content="CubicEase - EaseIn"
             Margin="4">
    <RadioButton.Triggers>
        <EventTrigger RoutedEvent="RadioButton.Checked">
            <BeginStoryboard>
                <Storyboard AutoReverse="True">
                    <DoubleAnimation
                     Storyboard.TargetName="circle"
                     Storyboard.TargetProperty="(Canvas.Left)"
                     To="350">
                        <DoubleAnimation.EasingFunction>
                            <CubicEase EasingMode="EaseIn"/>
                        </DoubleAnimation.EasingFunction>
                    </DoubleAnimation>
                </Storyboard>
            </BeginStoryboard>
        </EventTrigger>
    </RadioButton.Triggers>
</RadioButton>
```

The following graph demonstrates different values of `EasingMode`, for the `CubicEase` effect:

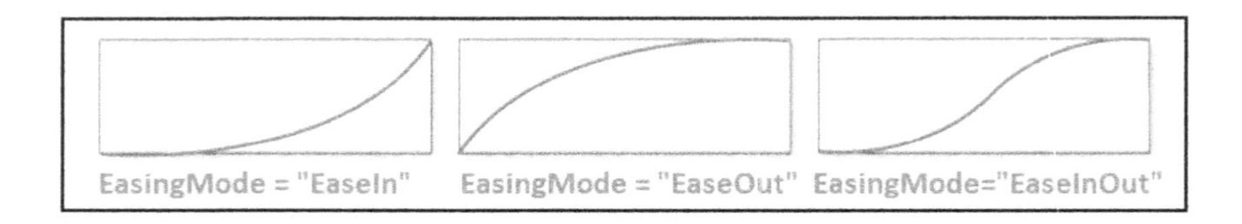

ElasticEase

As the name says, it represents an easing function that creates an animation that resembles a spring oscillating back and forth until it comes to rest. The `Oscillations` property can be used to get/set the number of times the target slides back and forth over the animation destination. The `Springiness` property can be used to define the stiffness of the spring. The smaller the value of `Springiness`, means a stiffer spring in action.

To demonstrate, let's add the following `RadioButton` inside the `StackPanel` to create an animation with `ElasticEase`, having `Oscillations="3"` and `Springiness="1"`:

```
<RadioButton GroupName="AnimationSelector"
             Content="ElasticEase - EaseInOut"
             Margin="4">
    <RadioButton.Triggers>
        <EventTrigger RoutedEvent="RadioButton.Checked">
            <BeginStoryboard>
                <Storyboard AutoReverse="True">
                    <DoubleAnimation
                     Storyboard.TargetName="circle"
                     Storyboard.TargetProperty="(Canvas.Left)"
                     To="350">
                        <DoubleAnimation.EasingFunction>
                            <ElasticEase EasingMode="EaseInOut"
                                         Oscillations="3"
                                         Springiness="1"/>
                        </DoubleAnimation.EasingFunction>
                    </DoubleAnimation>
                </Storyboard>
            </BeginStoryboard>
        </EventTrigger>
    </RadioButton.Triggers>
</RadioButton>
```

The following graph demonstrates different values of `EasingMode`, for the `ElasticEase` effect:

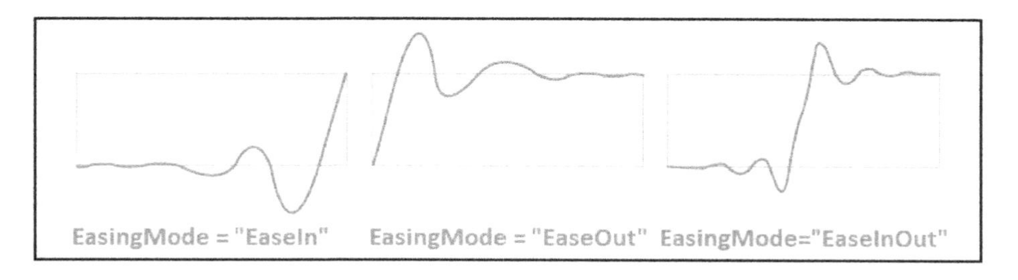

ExponentialEase

This type of easing function creates an animation that accelerates/decelerates using an exponential formula `f(t) = [[e(at) - 1] / [e(a) - 1]]`. The `Exponent` property is used to determine the interpolation of the animation; whereas the `EasingMode` property is used to accelerate and decelerate the animation of the target control.

To demonstrate this, add the following `RadioButton` control inside the `StackPanel`, which will create a decelerate exponential easing effect with the interpolation value `5`:

```
<RadioButton GroupName="AnimationSelector"
             Content="ExponentialEase - EaseOut"
             Margin="4">
    <RadioButton.Triggers>
        <EventTrigger RoutedEvent="RadioButton.Checked">
            <BeginStoryboard>
                <Storyboard AutoReverse="True">
                    <DoubleAnimation
                     Storyboard.TargetName="circle"
                     Storyboard.TargetProperty="(Canvas.Left)"
                     To="350">
                        <DoubleAnimation.EasingFunction>
                            <ExponentialEase EasingMode="EaseOut"
                                             Exponent="5"/>
                        </DoubleAnimation.EasingFunction>
                    </DoubleAnimation>
                </Storyboard>
            </BeginStoryboard>
        </EventTrigger>
    </RadioButton.Triggers>
</RadioButton>
```

The following graph demonstrates different values of `EasingMode`, for the `ExponentialEase` effect:

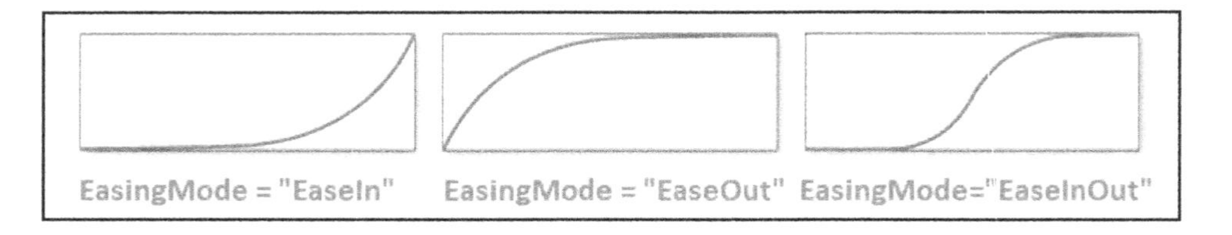

PowerEase

It defines an easing function that creates an animation that accelerates/decelerates using the formula `f(t) = tp`, where `p` is equal to the value of the `Power` property. As with other easing functions, you can add an easing mode to specify whether the animation will accelerate or decelerate.

In this demonstration, add the following `RadioButton` that defines the `PowerEase` easing function to the `DoubleAnimation` specified:

```
<RadioButton GroupName="AnimationSelector"
             Content="PowerEase - EaseInOut"
             Margin="4">
    <RadioButton.Triggers>
        <EventTrigger RoutedEvent="RadioButton.Checked">
            <BeginStoryboard>
                <Storyboard AutoReverse="True">
                    <DoubleAnimation
                     Storyboard.TargetName="circle"
                     Storyboard.TargetProperty="(Canvas.Left)"
                     To="350">
                        <DoubleAnimation.EasingFunction>
                            <PowerEase EasingMode="EaseInOut"
                                       Power="12"/>
                        </DoubleAnimation.EasingFunction>
                    </DoubleAnimation>
                </Storyboard>
            </BeginStoryboard>
        </EventTrigger>
    </RadioButton.Triggers>
</RadioButton>
```

You can use `PowerEase` to substitute `QuadraticEase` [`f(t) = t2`], `CubicEase` [`f(t) = t3`], `QuarticEase` [`f(t) = t4`], and `QuinticEase` [`f(t) = t5`] type of easing functions.

The following graph demonstrates different values of `EasingMode`, for the `PowerEase` effect:

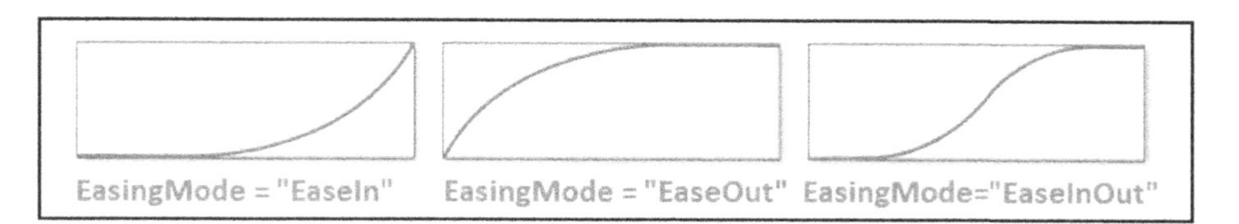

QuadraticEase

It creates an animation that accelerates/decelerates using the formula `f(t) = t2`. You can use `PowerEase` to create the same behavior by specifying `Power="2"`. In this example, we will learn how to add the `QuadraticEase` function to an animation. Add the following mark-up inside the `StackPanel` that we have defined:

```
<RadioButton GroupName="AnimationSelector"
             Content="QuadraticEase - EaseInOut"
             Margin="4">
    <RadioButton.Triggers>
        <EventTrigger RoutedEvent="RadioButton.Checked">
            <BeginStoryboard>
                <Storyboard AutoReverse="True">
                    <DoubleAnimation
                    Storyboard.TargetName="circle"
                    Storyboard.TargetProperty="(Canvas.Left)"
                    To="350">
                        <DoubleAnimation.EasingFunction>
                            <QuadraticEase
                                      EasingMode="EaseInOut"/>
                        </DoubleAnimation.EasingFunction>
                    </DoubleAnimation>
                </Storyboard>
            </BeginStoryboard>
        </EventTrigger>
    </RadioButton.Triggers>
</RadioButton>
```

The following graph demonstrates different values of `EasingMode`, for the `QuadraticEase` effect:

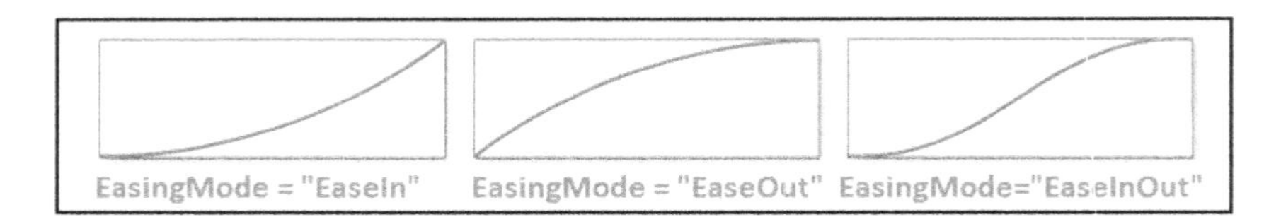

QuarticEase

Like `QuadraticEase`, you can also define `QuarticEase` to create an animation that accelerates/decelerates using the formula `f(t) = t4`. You can use `PowerEase` to create the same behavior by specifying `Power="4"`. Let's add the following mark-up inside our `StackPanel` to define the animation with the said easing function:

```
<RadioButton GroupName="AnimationSelector"
             Content="QuarticEase - EaseInOut"
             Margin="4">
    <RadioButton.Triggers>
        <EventTrigger RoutedEvent="RadioButton.Checked">
            <BeginStoryboard>
                <Storyboard AutoReverse="True">
                    <DoubleAnimation
                     Storyboard.TargetName="circle"
                     Storyboard.TargetProperty="(Canvas.Left)"
                     To="350">
                        <DoubleAnimation.EasingFunction>
                            <QuarticEase EasingMode="EaseInOut"/>
                        </DoubleAnimation.EasingFunction>
                    </DoubleAnimation>
                </Storyboard>
            </BeginStoryboard>
        </EventTrigger>
    </RadioButton.Triggers>
</RadioButton>
```

The following graph demonstrates different values of `EasingMode`, for the `QuarticEase` effect:

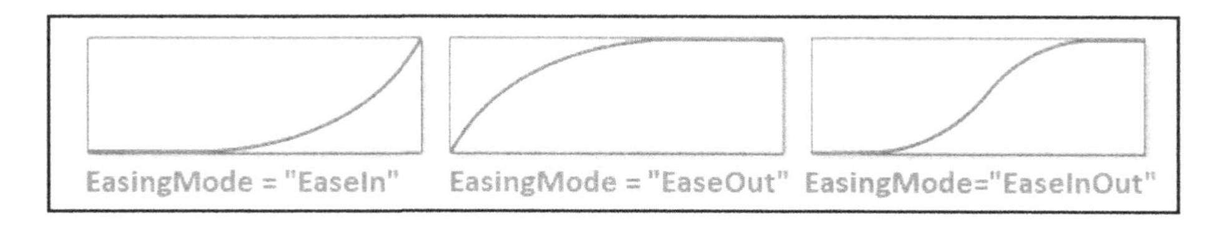

QuinticEase

If you want to add the `QuinticEase` effect to your easing function, add it to your animation. It accelerates/decelerates using the formula `f(t) = t5`. You can use `PowerEase` to create the same by specifying `Power="5"`. Add the following `RadioButton` to define an animation with the `QuinticEase` easing function in our `StackPanel`:

```
<RadioButton GroupName="AnimationSelector"
             Content="QuinticEase - EaseInOut"
             Margin="4">
    <RadioButton.Triggers>
        <EventTrigger RoutedEvent="RadioButton.Checked">
            <BeginStoryboard>
                <Storyboard AutoReverse="True">
                    <DoubleAnimation
                     Storyboard.TargetName="circle"
                     Storyboard.TargetProperty="(Canvas.Left)"
                     To="350">
                        <DoubleAnimation.EasingFunction>
                            <QuinticEase EasingMode="EaseInOut"/>
                        </DoubleAnimation.EasingFunction>
                    </DoubleAnimation>
                </Storyboard>
            </BeginStoryboard>
        </EventTrigger>
    </RadioButton.Triggers>
</RadioButton>
```

The following graph demonstrates different values of `EasingMode`, for the `QuinticEase` effect:

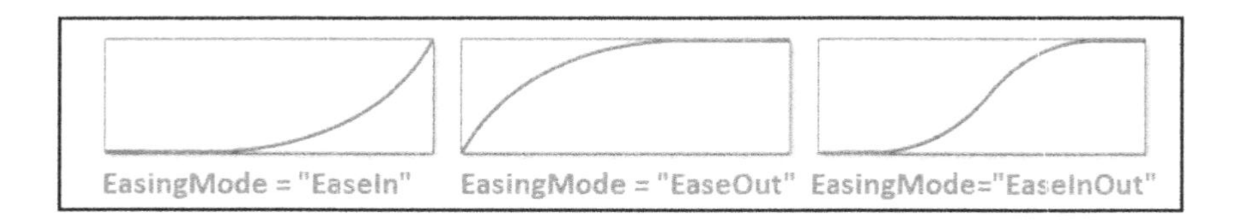

SineEase

This represents an easing function that creates an animation that accelerates and/or decelerates using a sine formula `f(t) = [1 - [sin(1 - t) * [pi / 2]]]`. Add the `EasingMode` property to accelerate and/or decelerate the effect. Let's add the following code inside the `StackPanel`:

```
<RadioButton GroupName="AnimationSelector"
             Content="SineEase - EaseInOut"
             Margin="4">
    <RadioButton.Triggers>
        <EventTrigger RoutedEvent="RadioButton.Checked">
            <BeginStoryboard>
                <Storyboard AutoReverse="True">
                    <DoubleAnimation
                     Storyboard.TargetName="circle"
                     Storyboard.TargetProperty="(Canvas.Left)"
                     To="350">
                        <DoubleAnimation.EasingFunction>
                            <SineEase EasingMode="EaseInOut"/>
                        </DoubleAnimation.EasingFunction>
                    </DoubleAnimation>
                </Storyboard>
            </BeginStoryboard>
        </EventTrigger>
    </RadioButton.Triggers>
</RadioButton>
```

The following graph demonstrates different values of `EasingMode`, for the `SineEase` effect:

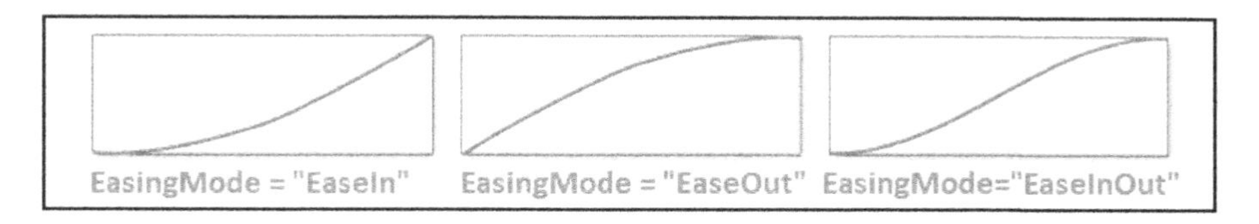

Once you are ready, let's build the project and run it. You will now see the following UI, which contains additional radio buttons inside the right-hand panel:

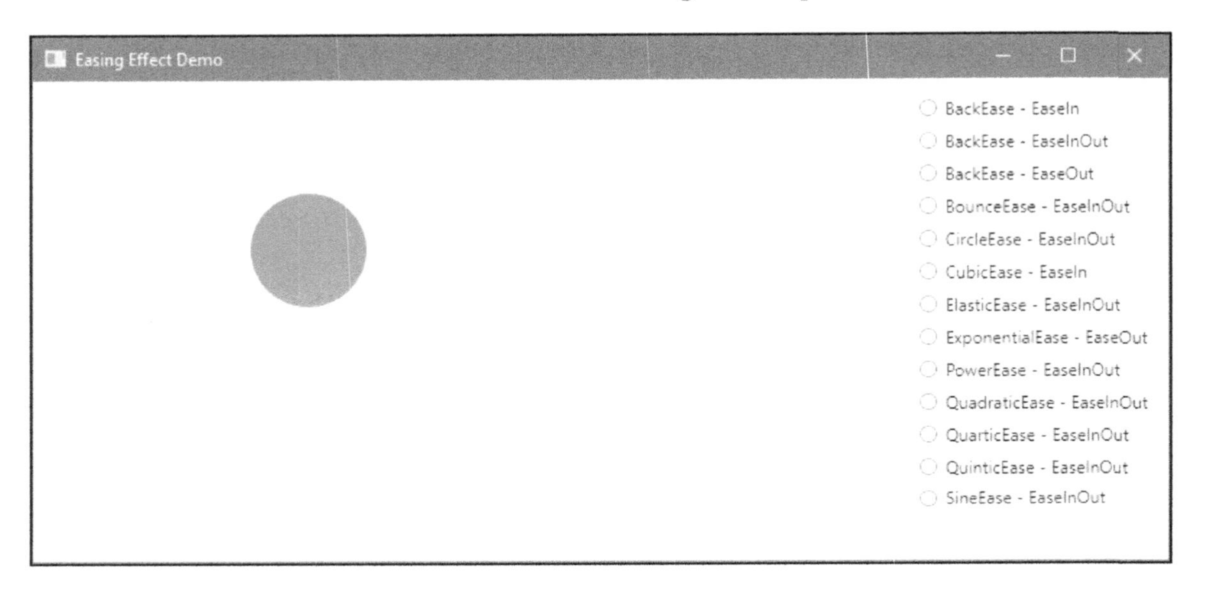

Change the selection of the radios to see the animations for each easing function associated with them.

9
Using WCF Services

In this chapter, we will cover the following recipes:

- Creating a WCF service
- Self-hosting a WCF service
- Hosting a WCF service in IIS Server
- Integrating a WCF service in a WPF application

Introduction

In the modern world, enterprise applications are the key to consumer-centric enterprises. Users access one or multiple devices to connect to the external world. And to succeed at this, the business needs shared services, which can be consumed by all such devices.

The **service-oriented architecture** (**SOA**) is a design principle that enterprises follow to outline well-defined services, using a common set of contracts. Each of these services can be individually modified independently of one another and consumed by the external world.

Windows Communication Foundation (**WCF**) is a framework to build such service-oriented applications. Using WCF, you can send data/messages asynchronously from one endpoint to the other. You can host a service endpoint in IIS, or in an application directly. The messages passed via this service endpoint can be a single character or a word sent as XML, or a complex stream of binary data.

WCF has been widely accepted as a standard to create web services, which offers support to multiple protocols and endpoints. In WCF, there are three important things that you need to remember; these things are generally known as the **ABC of WCF**. The ABC of WCF endpoints defines the following elements:

- **A** for **Address**, which specifies where the service resides. This generally follows the URL format as `schema://domain[:port]/path`, for example `http://www.kunal-chowdhury.com:8080/Services`, `https://www.kunal-chowdhury.com:8050/Services`, or `http://192.168.0.1/Services`.
- **B** stands for **Binding**, which is basically a group of elements that corresponds to the transport and protocol channels located in the channel stack, to define how the messages are handled in the service side and the client side.
- **C** stands for **Contract**, which is nothing but an agreement between the client and the server about the structure (data contract) and content (message contract) being passed through the channel.

In this chapter, we will learn how to create WCF services, host them, and integrate them into a WPF application to give a service call to the defined endpoint. As this book is not about WCF, we will just be discussing basic concepts to get you started with it.

Please ensure that ASP.NET and WCF are correctly installed and registered. To confirm, open the **Visual Studio 2017 Installer**, and make sure that the **ASP.NET and web development** workload, as well as the **Windows Communication Foundation** components, are already installed.

If they're not there already, select them, and modify the installation:

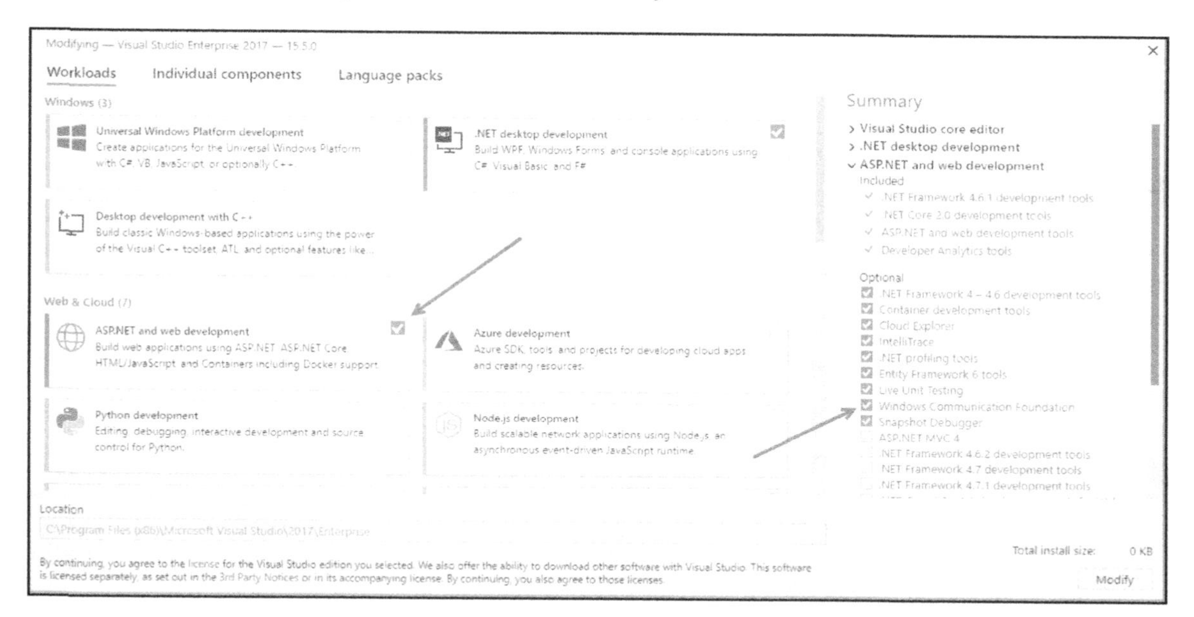

Creating a WCF service

A WCF service is a secure service to process business transactions, which supplies current data to others, exposing a workflow implemented using **Windows Workflow Foundation** as a WCF service. It provides a single programming model to leverage the features to create a unified solution to all distributed technologies. That means you can write the service once and expose different endpoints to exchange messages using any format (default is SOAP) over any transport protocol, that is, HTTP, TCP, MSMQ, Named Pipes, and so on.

SOAP (**Simple Object Access Protocol**) is one of the preferred models, where communication between the server and the client happens by using XML-based data.

In this recipe, we will learn about **data contract**, **data member**, **service contract**, **operation contract**, you need to consider these when creating and connecting to WCF services. When a service reference is taken into an application project, the developer only needs to configure the service with a proper endpoint address. Let's start demonstrating it by creating a simple, basic WCF service.

Getting ready

To get started, open Visual Studio IDE with administrative privileges. This is often useful while deploying the service in a server.

How to do it...

Follow these steps to create a simple WCF service, which we will integrate into a WPF application later in this chapter:

1. First, create a new project named `EmployeeService`. Use the **WCF Service Application** template while creating the project. You can find this under the **WCF** template category, as shown in the following screenshot:

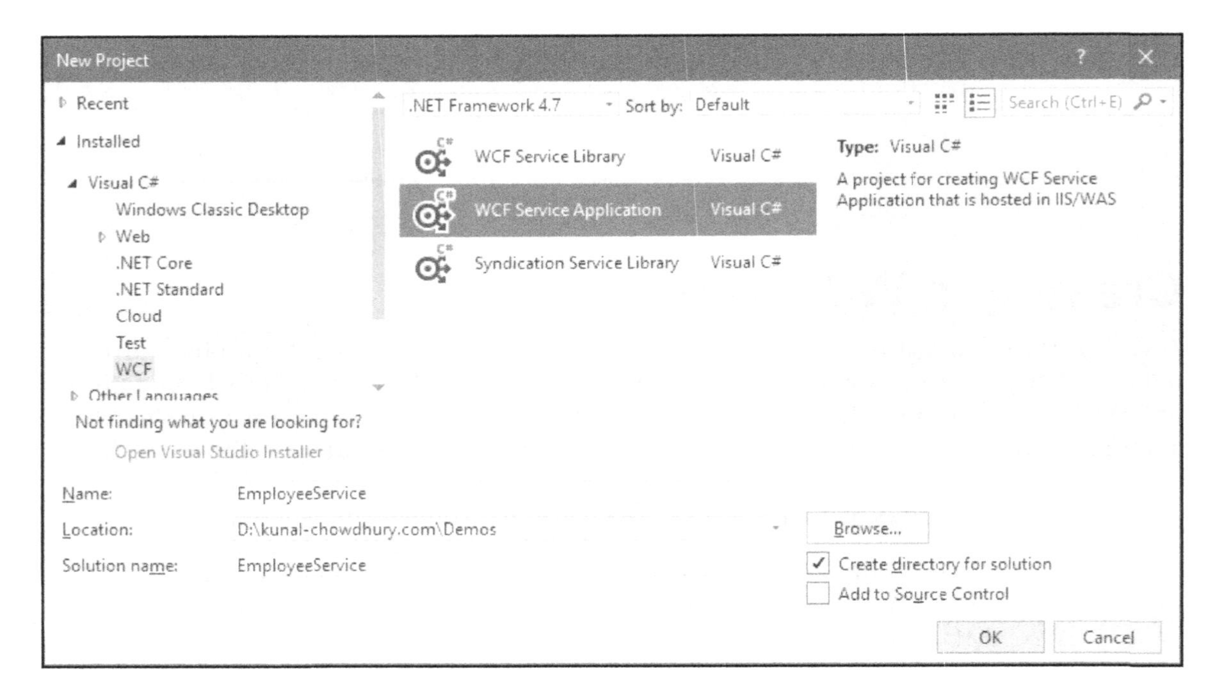

2. Visual Studio, by default, creates three service files (`IService1.cs`, `Service1.svc`, and `Service1.svc.cs`) inside the project. As we will create our own services from scratch, from **Solution Explorer**, let's delete all three of the files:

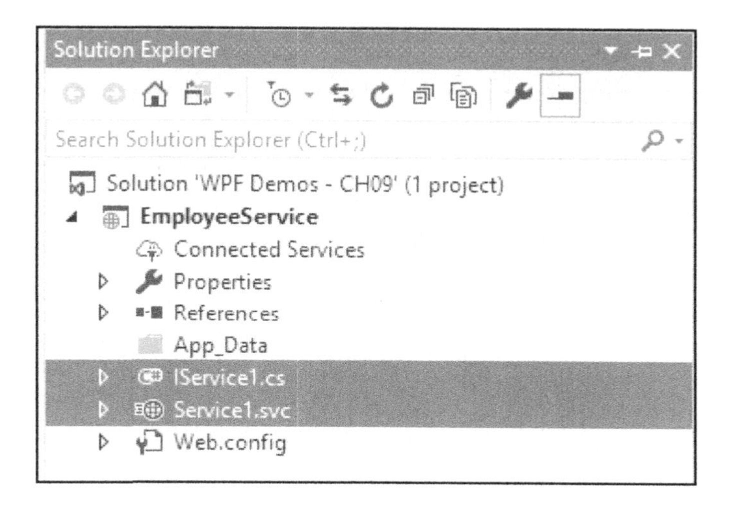

3. Let's create two folders inside the project node and name them `DataModels` and `Services`. This is optional, but it is a good idea to keep the code files organized:

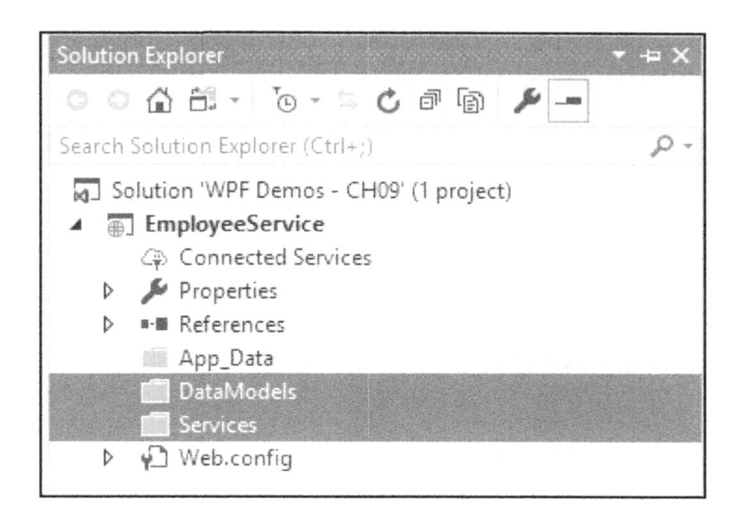

4. Now, right-click on the **DataModels** folder, and follow the context menu entry **Add | Class...** to create a new class file named `Employee`.
5. Inside the class implementation of the `Employee.cs` file, add a few public properties of type `string`, and name them `ID`, `FirstName`, `LastName`, and `Designation`.
6. Set the attribute `[DataContract]` to the class level to specify that the type defines or implements a data contract and is serializable by a serializer, such as `System.Runtime.Serialization.DataContractSerializer`.
7. Set the attribute `[DataMember]` to the properties that you want to be part of the data contract, and mark it to serializable by the `System.Runtime.Serialization.DataContractSerializer`.
8. You need to resolve the namespace `System.Runtime.Serialization`, in order to use the `DataContract` and `DataMember` attributes:

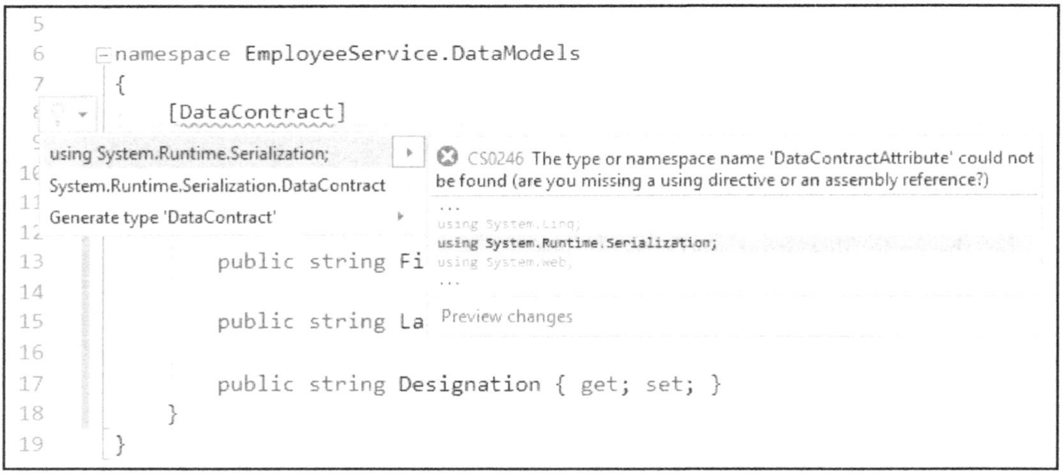

```
5
6   namespace EmployeeService.DataModels
7   {
8       [DataContract]
    using System.Runtime.Serialization;      CS0246 The type or namespace name 'DataContractAttribute' could not
    System.Runtime.Serialization.DataContract   be found (are you missing a using directive or an assembly reference?)
    Generate type 'DataContract'             ...
                                             using System.Linq;
                                             using System.Runtime.Serialization;
13          public string Fi                 using System.Web;
14                                           ...
15          public string La                 Preview changes
16
17          public string Designation { get; set; }
18      }
19  }
```

9. Here's the complete code:

```
using System.Runtime.Serialization;

namespace EmployeeService.DataModels
{
    [DataContract]
    public class Employee
    {
        [DataMember]
        public string ID { get; set; }
```

```
            [DataMember]
            public string FirstName { get; set; }

            [DataMember]
            public string LastName { get; set; }

            [DataMember]
            public string Designation { get; set; }
        }
    }
```

10. Now, right-click on the **Services** folder, and follow the context menu entry **Add | New Item...** to create a new service definition.
11. From the **Add New Item** dialog window, select the **WCF Service** as the template. Give it a name (in our case, it is `EmployeeService`), and click on the **Add** button, as shown in the following screenshot:

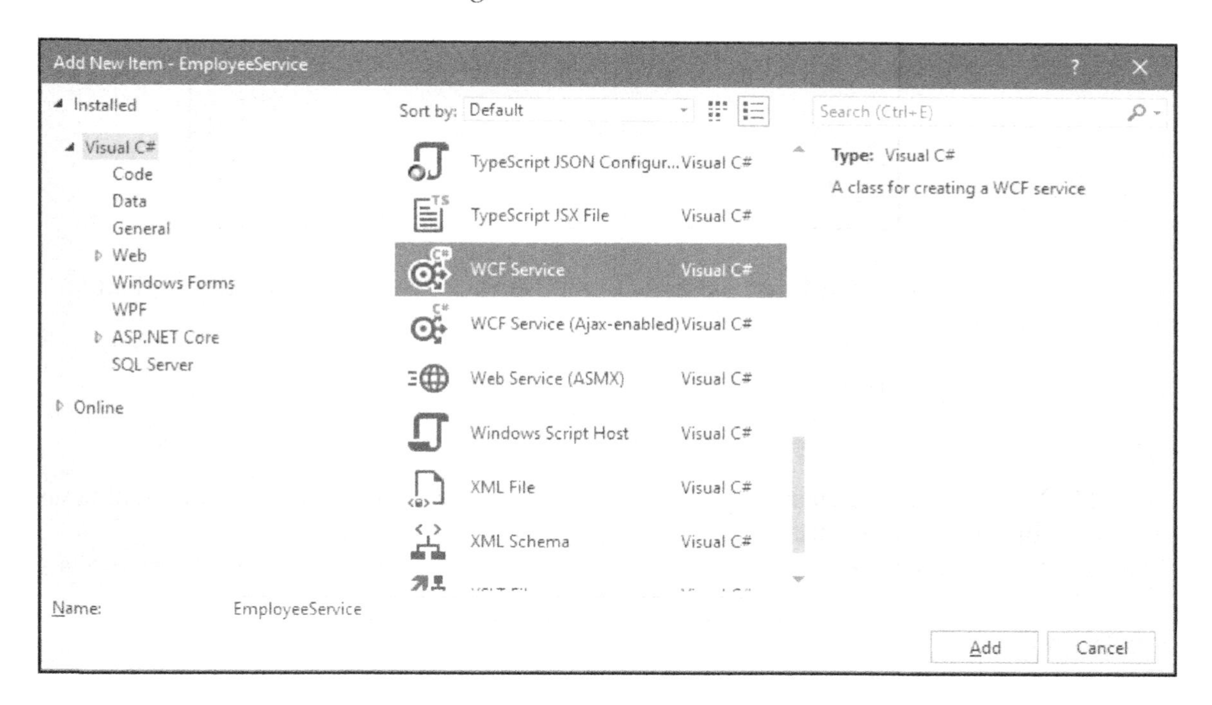

12. This will create three files under the `Services` folder: `IEmployeeService.cs`, `EmployeeService.svc`, and `EmployeeService.svc.cs`:

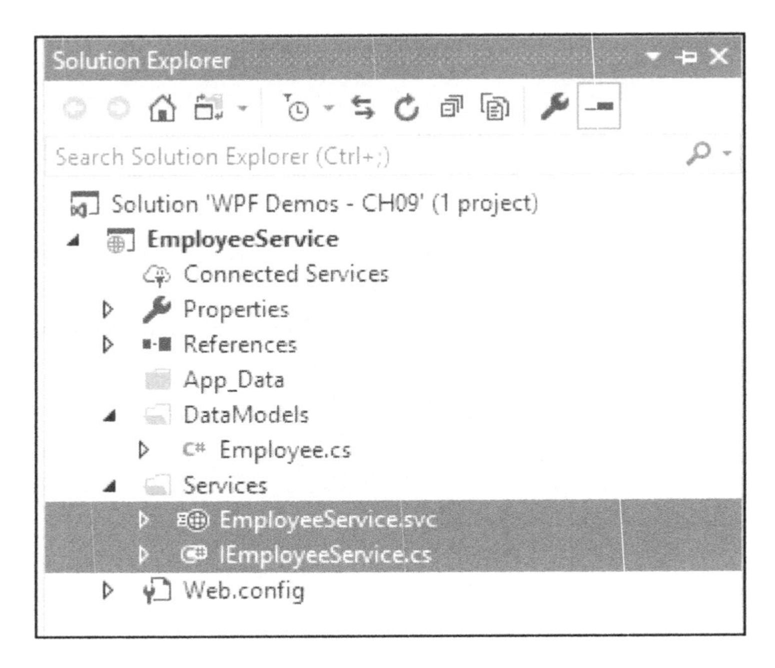

13. From **Solution Explorer**, navigate to the `IEmployeeService.cs` file, and add the following `using` namespace declarations:

```
using EmployeeService.DataModels;
using System.Collections.Generic;
using System.ServiceModel;
```

14. Now replace the class definition with the following code snippet, which will have three operation contracts `GetEmployeeByID`, `GetEmployees`, and `InsertEmployee`. Mark the interface as `[ServiceContract]` and the methods as `[OperationContract]`. Here's the code snippet for reference:

```
[ServiceContract]
public interface IEmployeeService
{
    [OperationContract]
    Employee GetEmployeeByID(string empID);

    [OperationContract]
    List<Employee> GetEmployees();
```

```
        [OperationContract]
        void InsertEmployee(Employee employee);
    }
```

15. Now, from **Solution Explorer**, navigate to the `EmployeeService.svc.cs` file, and create a `static` member variable of type `List<Employee>`. Let's name it `m_employees`, which will be used as a static data source of our demo application:

```
private static List<Employee> m_employees = new
List<Employee>();
```

16. Let's implement the interface `IEmployeeService`, as follows:

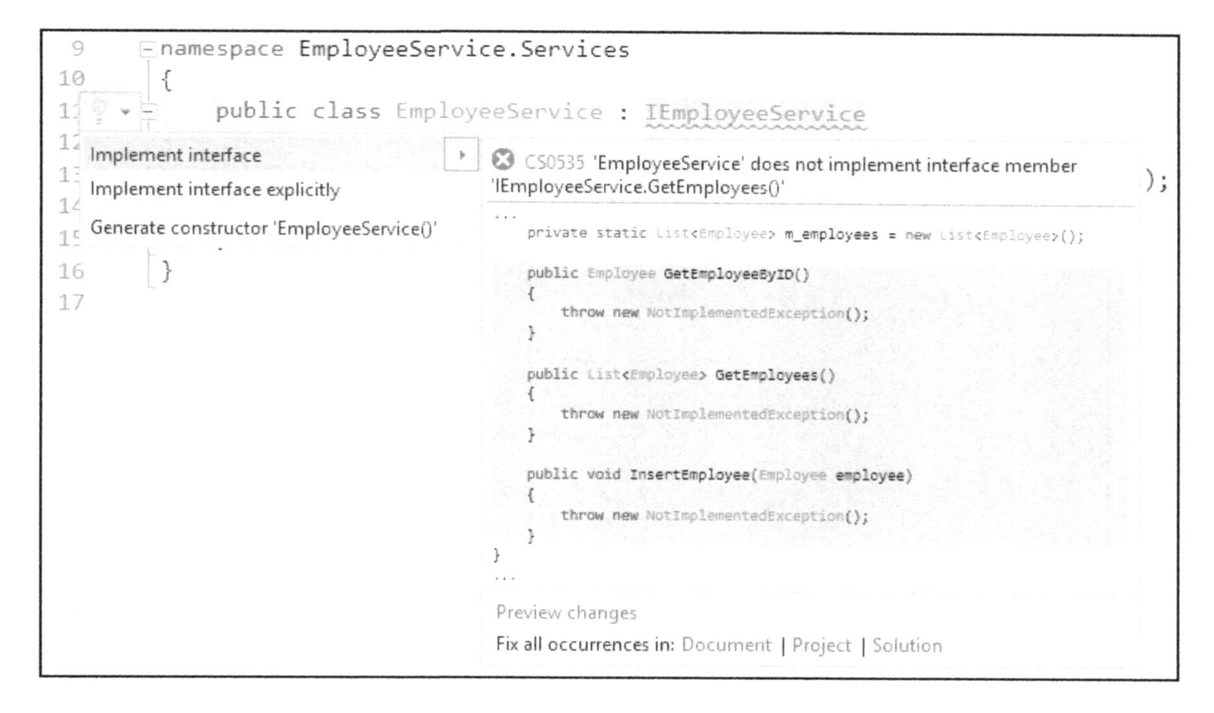

17. Modify the method definitions to perform the operations as per the name/functionality. Let's modify them, which will look like this:

```
public class EmployeeService : IEmployeeService
{
    private static List<Employee> m_employees = new
List<Employee>();

    public Employee GetEmployeeByID(string empID)
```

```
        {
            return m_employees.First(emp => emp.ID.Equals(empID));
        }

        public List<Employee> GetEmployees()
        {
            return m_employees;
        }

        public void InsertEmployee(Employee employee)
        {
            m_employees.Add(employee);
        }
    }
```

18. That's it! Your WCF service named `EmployeeService` is now ready to host, so that applications can consume it. To check whether the service can run properly, build the project and then right-click on the `EmployeeService.svc` file, from **Solution Explorer**, and click on `View in Browser (Browser_Name)`, which is **View in Browser (Firefox)** in our case:

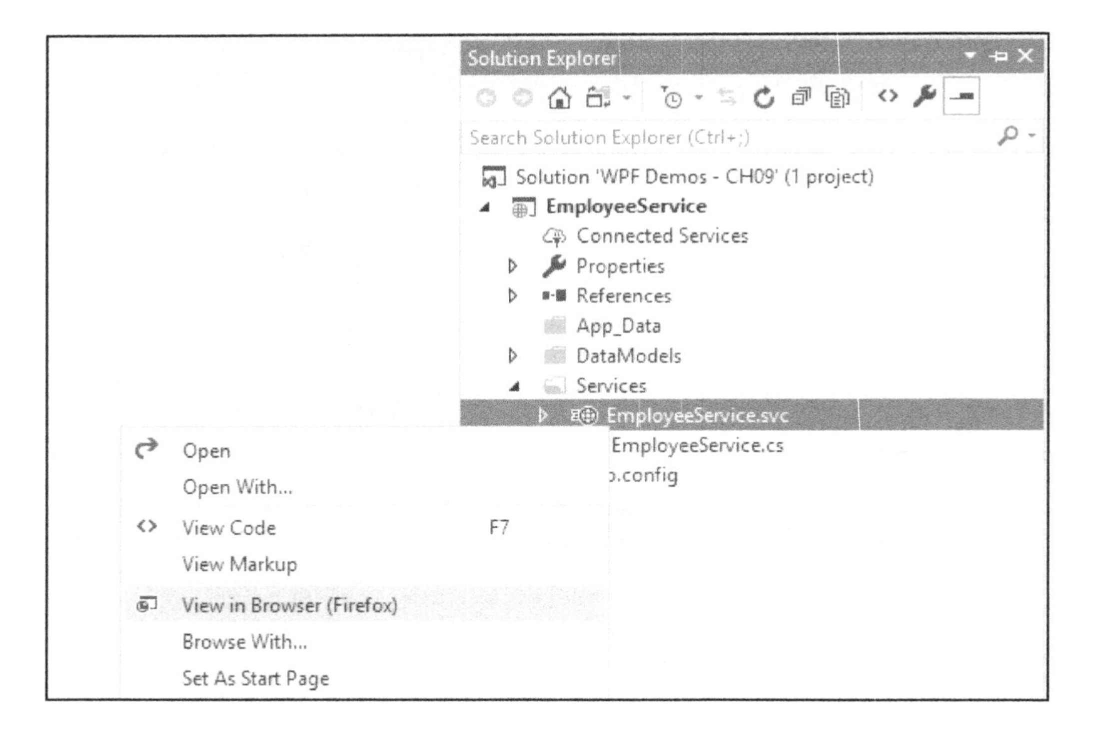

19. This will start the service and show you the message **Service is hosted on the server**.

A point to note is that if you are running the service from Visual Studio, it will require administrative permission to open the specified port and host the service. In case you haven't provided the admin privileges yet, please restart Visual Studio using **Run as administrator**.

20. Once the service has been hosted on `localhost`, this will load the SVC file in a browser window, and it will look like the following screenshot, which tells us that the service is up and running without any issues:

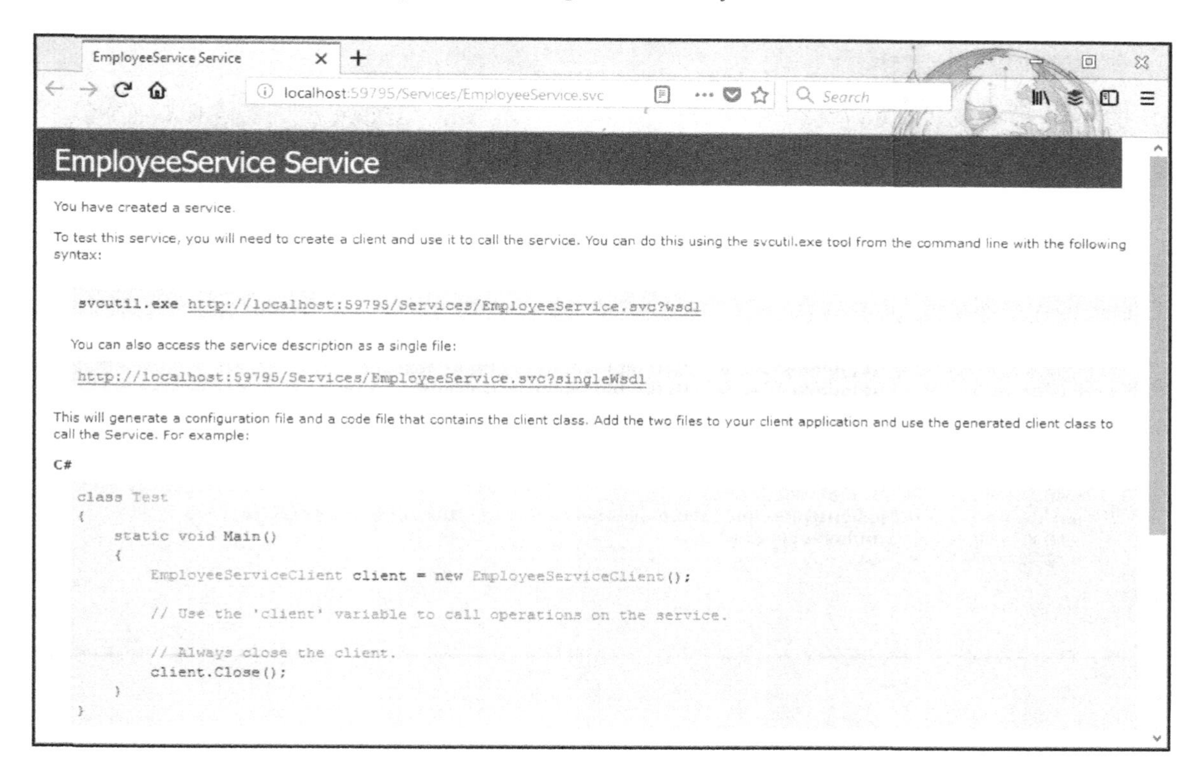

21. Each service provides a **Web Services Description Language** (**WSDL**) that defines the public interfaces including the metadata, which is similar to **interface definition language** (**IDA**). Click on the link to generate the WSDL of the service. In case your browser does not show the generated WSDL on the screen, copy the link, and run it inside the Internet Explorer, which will give you the following XML output:

How it works...

In this simple WCF service, we have used few attributes. Let's learn more about each one of them.

The DataContract attribute

A data contract is a formal agreement between a client and a service that abstractly describes the data to be exchanged. In WCF, this is the most common way to serialize an object and make it ready to be available for passing between client and service. This is done by marking the class with the `[DataContract]` attribute.

It is worth mentioning that the serialization is not restricted to exactly match the class name and/or the property names in the class. You can simply use the `DataContract` and `DataMember` attributes to define their names in serialization. For example, consider the following code snippet:

```
[DataContract (Name = "Employee")]
public class EmployeeModel { ... }
```

In the preceding code snippet, though the class name is `EmployeeModel`, the class will be exposed to serialization as `Employee` as the name mapping has been done using the `Name` property of the attribute.

The DataMember attribute

The `[DataMember]` attribute, on the other hand, specifies that the member is part of a data contract and is serializable by the `DataContractSerializer`. You can use the following properties while defining the data member attribute:

- `Name`: It defines the name of the data member
- `Order`: It sets the order of serialization and deserialization of the member
- `TypeId`: It sets a unique identifier for this attribute in the derived class
- `IsRequired`: This property gets or sets a value that instructs the serialization that the member must be present during deserializing
- `EmitDefaultValue`: When defined, this property value is specified whether to serialize the default value of the data member

You should apply the `[DataMember]` attribute in conjunction with the `[DataContract]` attribute to identify the members of a type that are part of the data contract.

The ServiceContract attribute

The `[ServiceContract]` attribute is used to define an interface that provides the service. A service should have at least one service contract, decorated by the `[ServiceContract]` attribute. The following properties can be used with the `ServiceContractAttribute`:

- `ConfigurationName`: It specifies the name of the service element in the configuration file.
- `Name`: This specifies the name of the contract in the WSDL element.
- `Namespace`: This specifies the namespace of the contract in the WSDL element.
- `SessionMode`: This specifies whether the contract requires a binding that supports sessions. It can have either of the following three values: `Allowed` (specifies that the contract supports the session), `NotAllowed` (specifies that the contract does not support the session), and `Required` (specifies that the contract does not require the session).
- `CallbackContract`: This property specifies the return contract in a duplex conversation.
- `ProtectionLevel`: This specifies the message-level security that an operation requires during runtime. It can be one of three types: `None` (only simple authentication), `Sign` (`Sign` data to help ensure data integrity), and `EncryptAndSign` (`Encrypt` and `Sign` data to ensure integrity and confidentiality of transmitted data).
- `HasProtectionLevel`: This indicates whether the `ProtectionLevel` property has been explicitly set.

The OperationContract attribute

The `[OperationContract]` attribute is used to define the methods of the service contract. This is placed on the methods that you want to include as part of the service contract. The following properties can be used to control the structure of the operation:

- `Action`: This property specifies the action that uniquely identifies the operation.
- `ReplyAction`: This specifies the action of the reply message of the operation.
- `AsyncPattern`: This indicates that the operation can be called asynchronously.
- `ProtectionLevel`: This specifies the message-level security that an operation requires during runtime. It can be one of three types—`None` (only simple authentication), `Sign` (sign data to help ensure data integrity), and `EncryptAndSign` (encrypt and sign data to ensure integrity and confidentiality of transmitted data).
- `HasProtectionLevel`: This indicates whether the `ProtectionLevel` property has been explicitly set.
- `IsOneWay`: This property indicates that the operation consists of a single input message and has no associated output message.
- `IsInitiating`: This specifies whether this operation can be the initial operation in a session.
- `IsTerminating`: This specifies whether WCF will attempt to terminate the current session after the operation completes.

Self-hosting a WCF service

To use a WCF service, you need to host it in a runtime environment, so that the service host can listen for requests from clients, direct those requests to the service, and send responses back to the client. Using the host, you can start and stop the service.

If you want to self-host a service, you must create an instance of the `System.ServiceModel.ServiceHost` class and configure it with endpoints. This can be done in code or in a configuration file. Once the host is ready, any client can access the service by the URL specified.

Self-hosting can be done in any managed application, such as a console application, a Windows service, a Windows Forms application, or a **Windows Presentation Foundation** (**WPF**) application. In this recipe, we will learn how to self-host a WCF service in a console application and execute it.

Getting ready

To get started, let's launch Visual Studio with administrative privileges. Now, open the project `CH09.EmployeeService`, which we created in the previous recipe. Ensure that the project builds successfully, and that the service launches properly in the browser. Mark down the service URL for reference, which we will be using later in this recipe.

How to do it...

Let's follow these steps to create a self-hosted console application:

1. First, add a new project of type **Console Application**, inside the solution, and name it `CH09.SelfHostingDemo`.
2. Now, right-click on the **References** node, and add the project reference of the service (`CH09.EmployeeService`):

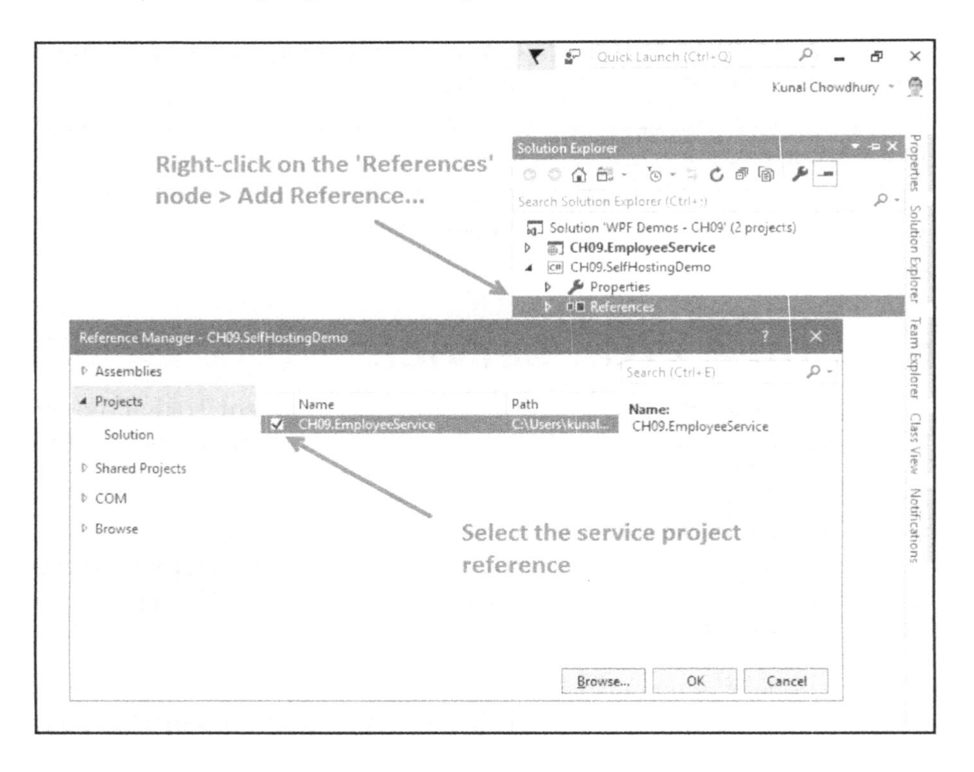

3. Also add the assembly reference of `System.ServiceModel` into the console application project.
4. From **Solution Explorer**, navigate to the `Program.cs` file.
5. Add the following `using` namespaces inside the class file:

```
using CH09.EmployeeService.Services;
using System;
using System.ServiceModel;
using System.ServiceModel.Description;
```

6. Now we need to define the service URL so that we can access it from the host. Create a static member variable inside the `Program.cs` class file, as follows:

```
private static Uri serviceUrl = new Uri(
     "http://localhost:59795/Services/EmployeeService");
```

7. The `Program` class contains a static `Main` method. Replace the definition with the following code block:

```
static void Main(string[] args)
{
    // create Service Host
    using (var serviceHost = new ServiceHost(
       typeof(EmployeeService.Services.EmployeeService),
       serviceUrl))
    {

        // add the service endpoint
        serviceHost.AddServiceEndpoint(
                    typeof(IEmployeeService),
                    new BasicHttpBinding(), "");
        serviceHost.Description.Behaviors.Add(
                    new ServiceMetadataBehavior
                    {
                        HttpGetEnabled = true
                    });

        // start the Service host
        serviceHost.Open();

        Console.WriteLine("Service hosting time: " +
                          DateTime.Now.ToString());
        Console.WriteLine();
        Console.WriteLine("Service Host is running...");
        Console.WriteLine("Press [Enter] key to stop the
host...");
```

```
                Console.ReadLine();

                // close the Service host
                serviceHost.Close();
            }
        }
```

8. Build the solution, and run the console application. You will see the following output in the console output window:

```
C:\WINDOWS\system32\cmd.exe
Service hosting time: 21-12-2017 10:33:04

Service Host is running...
Press [Enter] key to stop the host...
```

9. The service is now hosted through the host process. Press the *Enter* key to stop the service.

How it works...

To host the service, the host application uses the `ServiceHost` class from the `System.ServiceModel` namespace. It gets instantiated based on the type of service that you have implemented. In the preceding example, the `ServiceHost` class creates an object of `EmployeeService.Services.EmployeeService` and removes it from memory whenever the service completes execution.

If you check the `ServiceHost` object in the **QuickWatch Window**, you will notice that the object exposes several properties. The `BaseAddress` property defines the URL of the service, which maintains a runtime socket listener that listens to the port for the created service for any incoming requests. Once it receives any request, it parses the whole message passed to it and calls the service object.

Here's a screenshot of the **QuickWatch Window**, showing the number of properties exposed by the `ServiceHost` object:

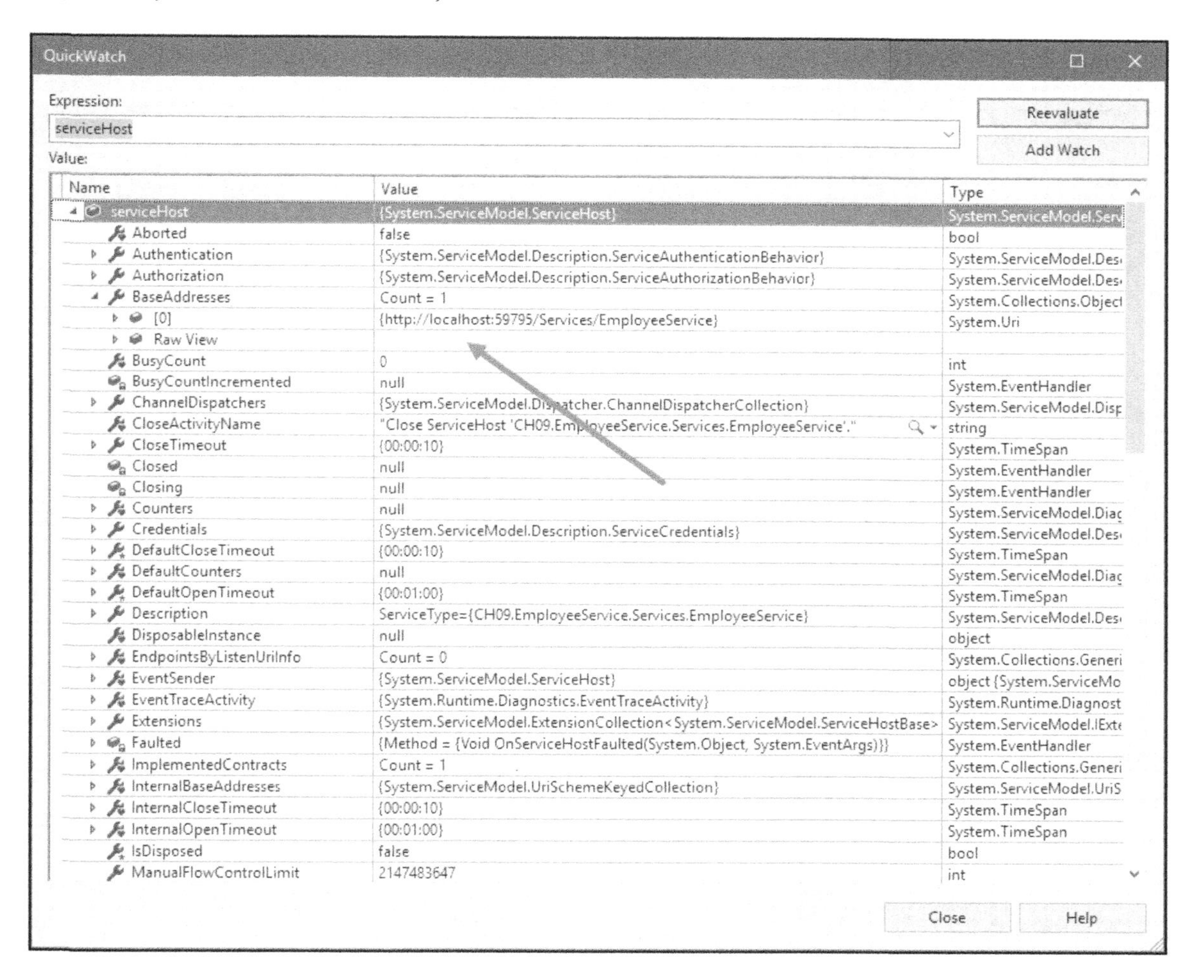

The `serviceHost.AddServiceEndpoint` adds a service endpoint to the hosted service with a specified contract, binding, and endpoint address. You can use any binding type based on your requirement, but here we have used `BasicHttpBinding` to create the service endpoint.

In case of `BasicHttpBinding`, SOAP messages are transferred. The SOAP message contains a well-defined envelop with a header and body of the message inside it. When a client calls the service, the `ServiceHost` class parses the message and calls the service by creating the context.

To see the endpoints used by the `ServiceHost` object, expand the `Description` property in the **QuickWatch Window** and navigate to `Endpoints`. Expand the first endpoint of the service and check the `Address`, `Binding`, `Contract` ("ABC") properties of it. This will look as follows:

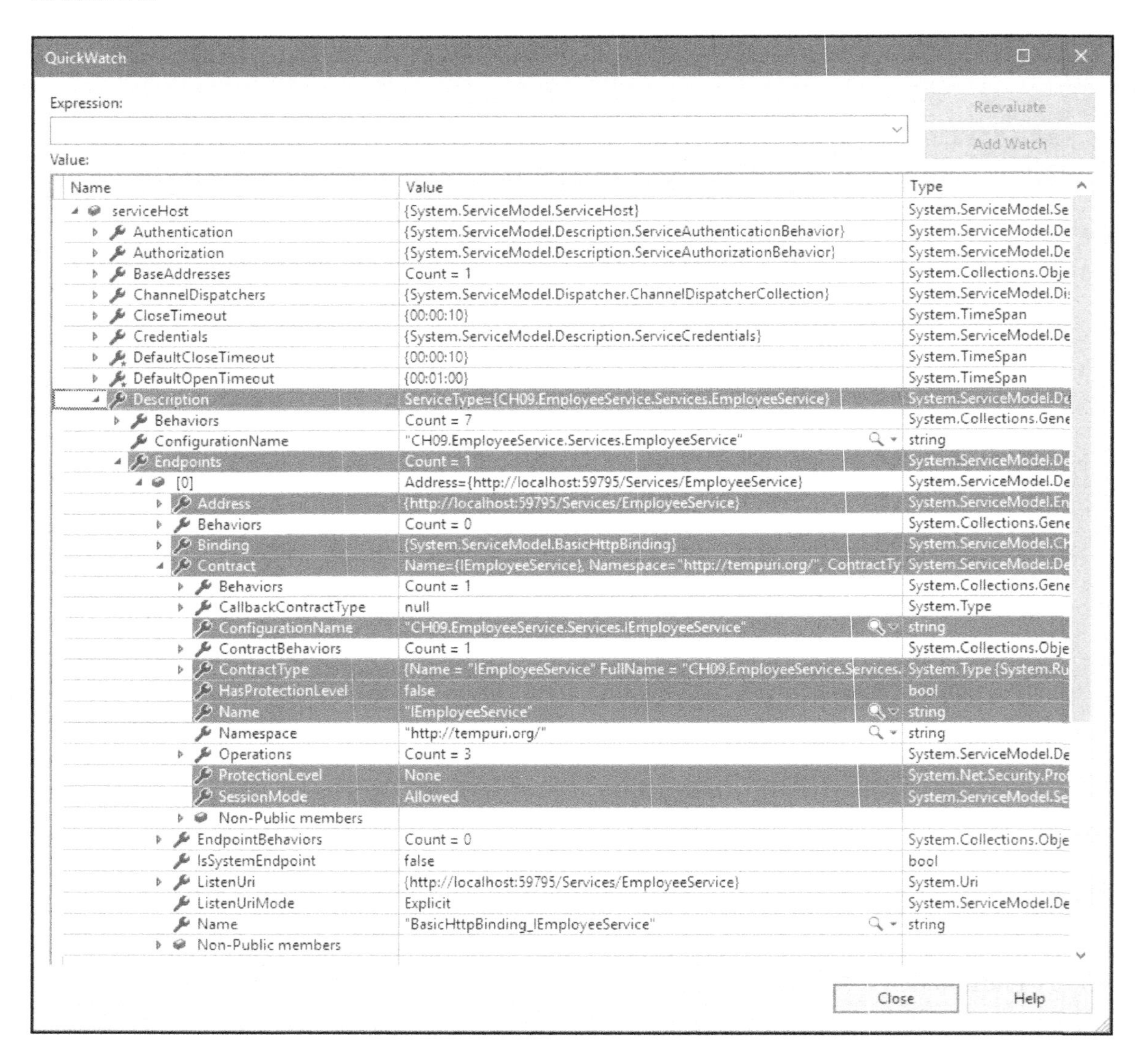

You can see that the `Address` points to the `BaseAdress` of the service, the `Binding` denotes the `BasicHttpBinding` that we created, and the `Contract` exposes service `Name`, `ConfigurationName`, `ContractType`, `SessionMode`, `ProtectionLevel`, `HasProtectionLevel`, and other properties.

When you are ready, the `serviceHost.Open()` method starts the service. It causes the communication object to transition from the created state to the opened state. When you are done, calling the `serviceHost.Close()` method stops the service. This causes the communication object to transition from its current state to the closed state.

In case you want your service object to be reused, you can add a `ServiceBehavior` attribute to the service class, as follows:

```
[ServiceBehavior(InstanceContextMode =
                    InstanceContextMode.Single)]
public class EmployeeService : IEmployeeService
{
    ...
    ...
}
```

When you apply this attribute, it specifies the internal execution behavior of the service contract implementation. The specified `InstanceContextMode` can be one of three types:

- **PerSession**: A new `System.ServiceModel.InstanceContext` object is created for each session.
- **PerCall**: A new `System.ServiceModel.InstanceContext` object is created prior to and recycled subsequent to each call. If the channel does not create a session, this value behaves as `PerCall`.
- **Single**: Only one `System.ServiceModel.InstanceContext` object is used for all incoming calls and is not recycled subsequent to the calls. If a `service` object does not exist, a new one will be created.

There's more...

If you don't have administrative rights on your system, the application will crash with `System.ServiceModel.AddressAccessDeniedException`, saying that the HTTP could not register the URL. The error log will look like this:

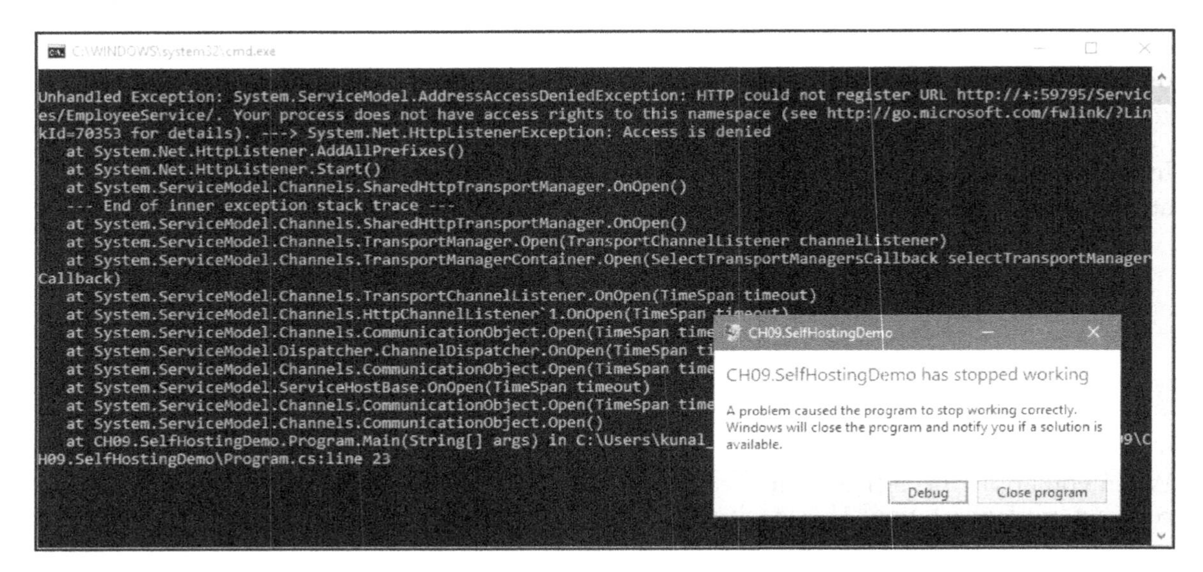

If you encounter this error, run the application under admin privileges. If you are running the application directly from Visual Studio, relaunch Visual Studio with admin privileges. To do so, right-click on the Visual Studio icon and click on **Run as administrator**.

Hosting a WCF service in an IIS server

Another way to host a WCF service is in an **IIS** (**Internet Information Services**). It requires a physical file with a `.svc` extension to host the service properly. Unlike the previous recipe, you won't need to write any code to create the instance of `ServiceHost`. IIS automatically creates it for you while hosting the service.

In this recipe, we will learn how to publish an already created service to host inside the IIS server of Windows.

Getting ready

To get started, launch the Visual Studio IDE with administrative rights. To do so, right-click on the icon and click **Run as administrator**. Now open the existing project `CH09.EmployeeService`, which we have created earlier. Alternatively, you can also open the solution.

To proceed further, we assume that you are familiar with IIS and understand how to use the IIS management tool to create and manage IIS applications.

How to do it...

Let's follow these steps to host our service in an IIS server:

1. First, you need to check whether the **IIS (Internet Information Services)** is already installed on the system, where you are going to host the service. To check this, open the **Control Panel** and navigate to **Turn Windows features on or off**, as shown in the following screenshot:

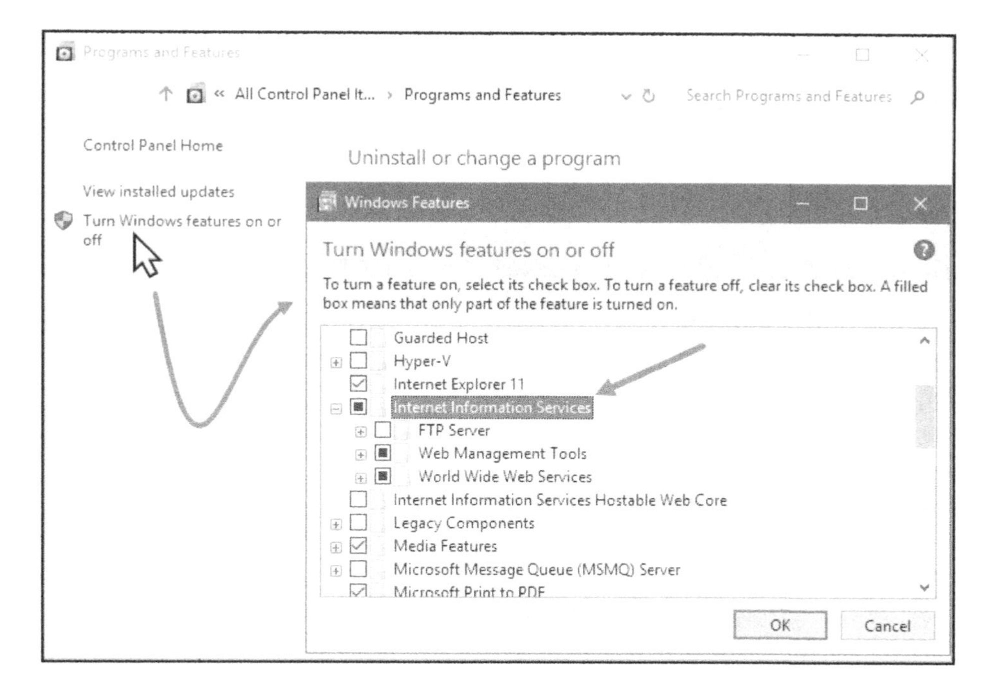

2. From the **Windows Features** dialog, which pops up on the screen, make sure that the **Internet Information Services** feature is checked. If not, check it, and click **OK**. This will install the IIS server on that system.
3. Now, click on Start (⊞), type `inetmgr`, and click the **Internet Information Services (IIS) Manager** app shortcut to launch it. Make sure that the **Default Web Site** is up and running. In the next steps, we will be deploying our service on this website:

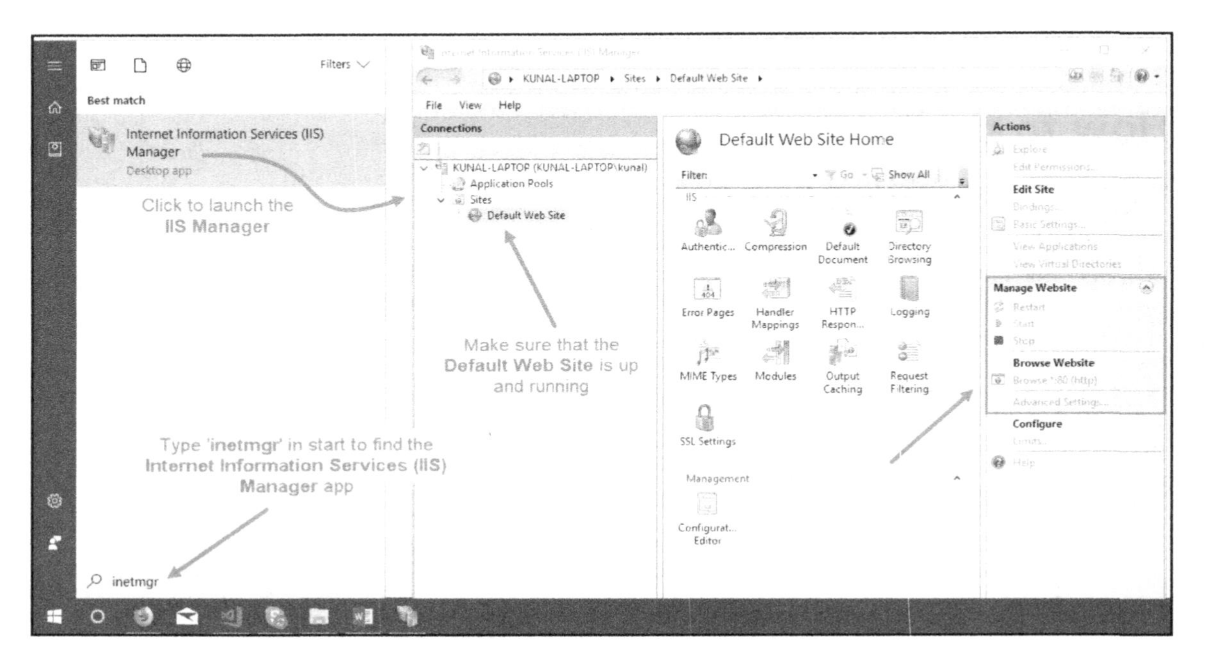

4. Once the IIS is installed (in case it was not already) and the **Default Web Site** in IIS is up and running, navigate back to Visual Studio.
5. From the **Solution Explorer**, right-click on the service project (`CH09.EmployeeService`) node, and click **Publish**:

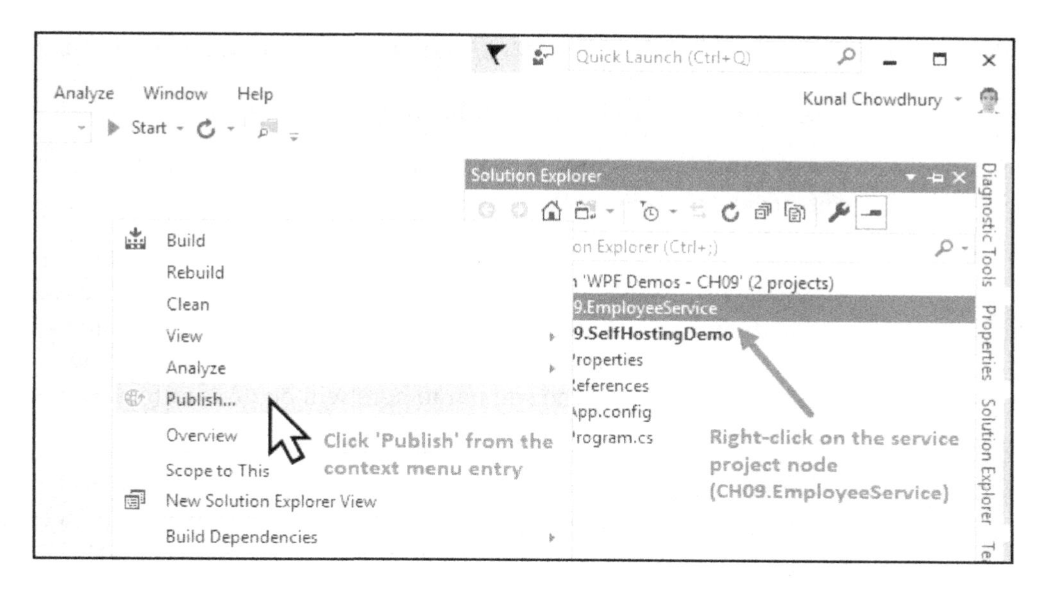

6. This will open the publishing wizard inside Visual Studio. Navigate to the **Publish** tab, select publishing template as **IIS, FTP, etc**, and click the **Publish** button, demonstrated as follows:

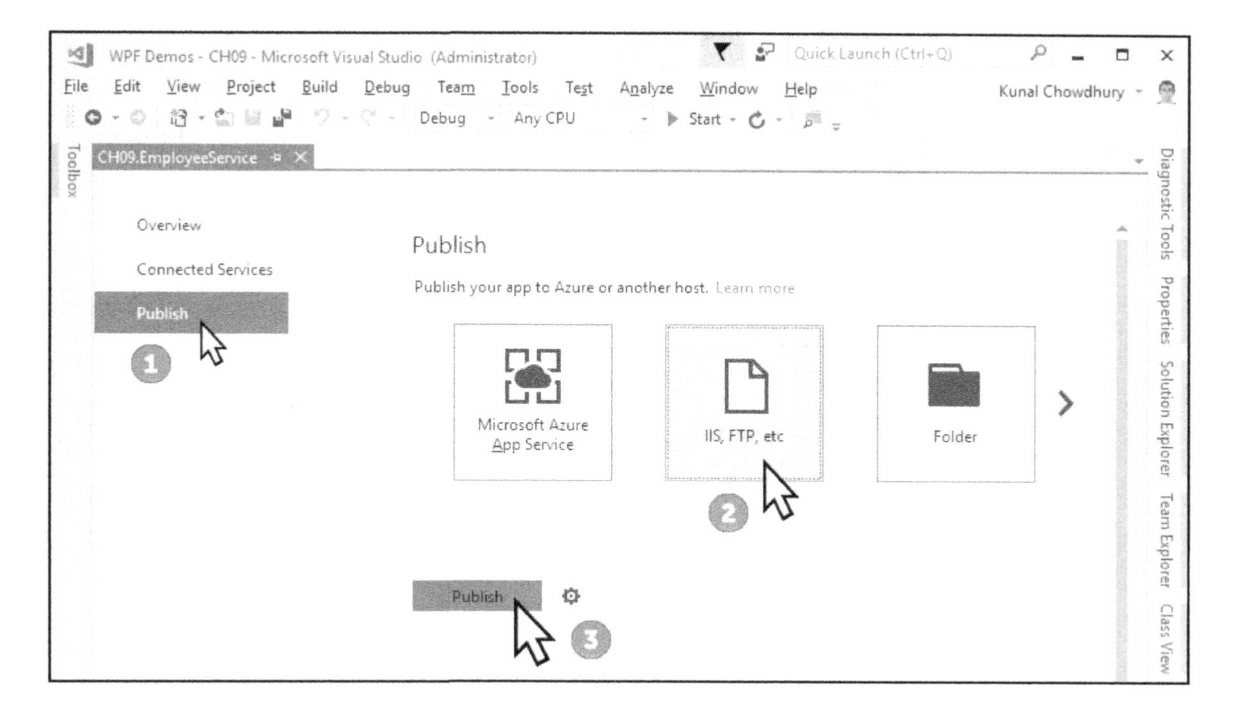

7. This will open the **Publish** dialog. Make sure that the **Connection** tab is selected:

    1. Select **Web Deploy** as the publishing method type.

    2. Enter the name of the server. In our case, as we are deploying it to the same system, it will be `localhost`.

    3. Enter the name of the site where we are going to deploy our service. In our case, it is `Default Web Site`. To deploy it in a specific web app inside the website, enter the name of the web app after the site name. For example, to deploy in the `MyApp` web application inside the `Default Web Site`, the site name here will be `Default Web Site/MyApp`.

    4. Enter the **User name** and **Password** of your web server, where you are going to deploy it. In our case, as it is `localhost`, we will not need to enter any credentials. Those two fields will be by default disabled.

    5. Click on **Validate Connection** to confirm about the publishing details that you entered. On success, you will see a green tick mark beside the **Validate Connection** button.

8. Once done, click on **Next** to proceed to the **Settings** page:

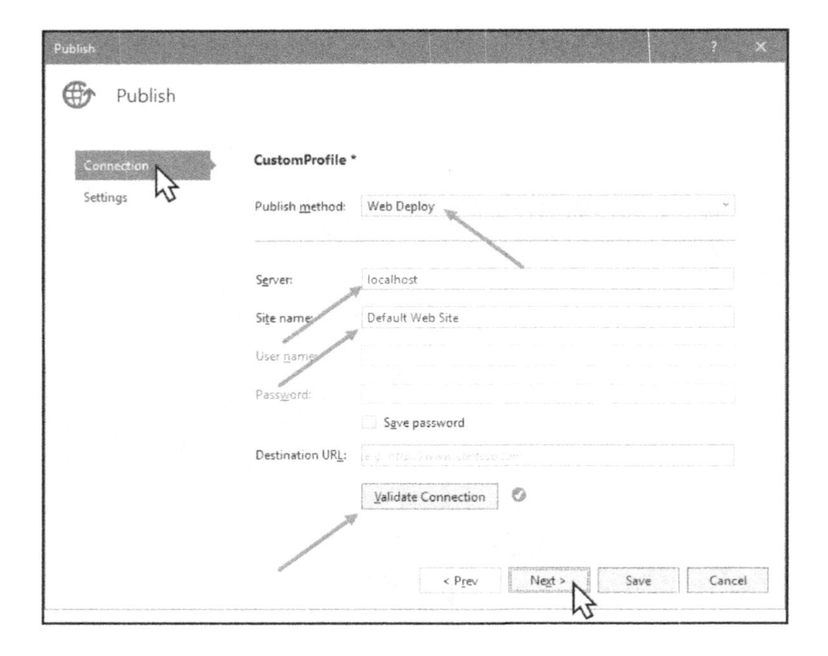

9. Inside the **Settings** page, select **Release** as the **Configuration**. Optionally, select **File Publish Options** based on your requirement.
10. Once you are done, click **Save** to start the publishing:

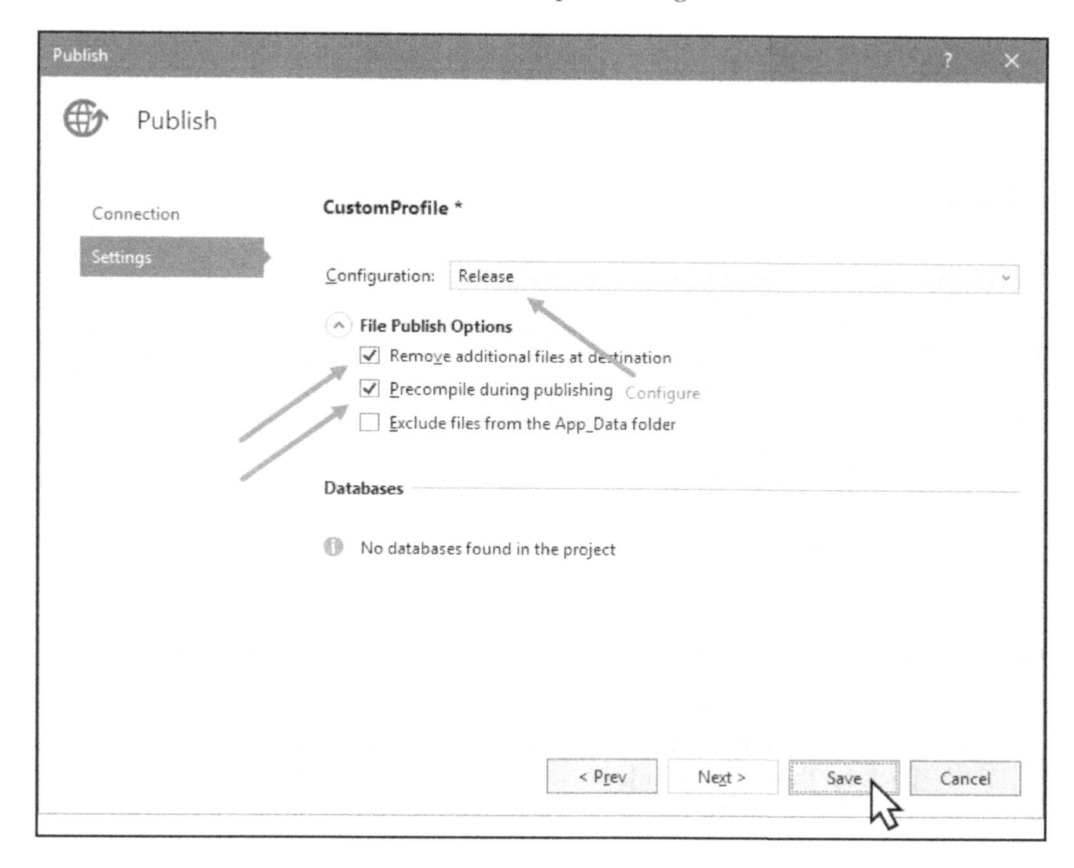

11. Once the Visual Studio IDE builds the solution and completes the deployment to the selected website, navigate back to the **Internet Information Services (IIS) Manager** application (`inetmgr`).

12. Refresh the **Default Web Site** node, which will now list two folders, named **bin** and **Services**. Click on the **Services** folder, and switch to **Content View**. This will list the `EmployeeService.svc` file, which is present inside it. Here's a screenshot of this:

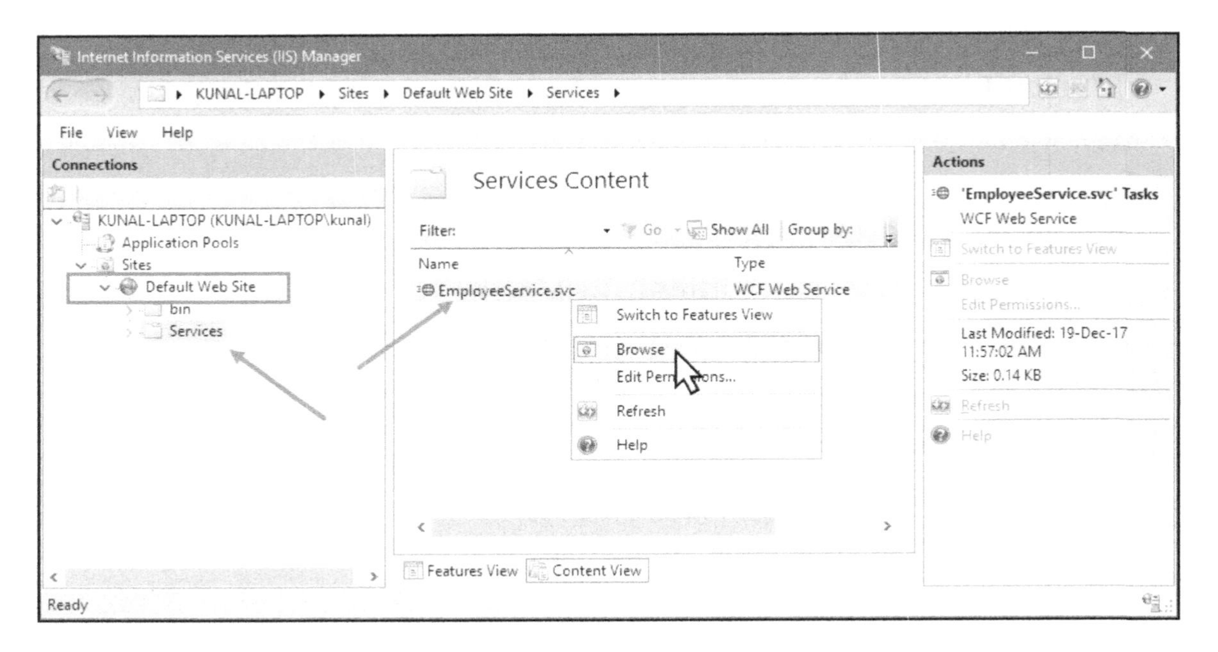

13. As shown in the preceding screenshot, right-click on the `EmployeeService.svc` file, and then click **Browse** from the context menu entry. Alternatively, you can click on the **Browse** link present at the right-side **Actions** pane.
14. This will open the service URL in the browser window as follows:

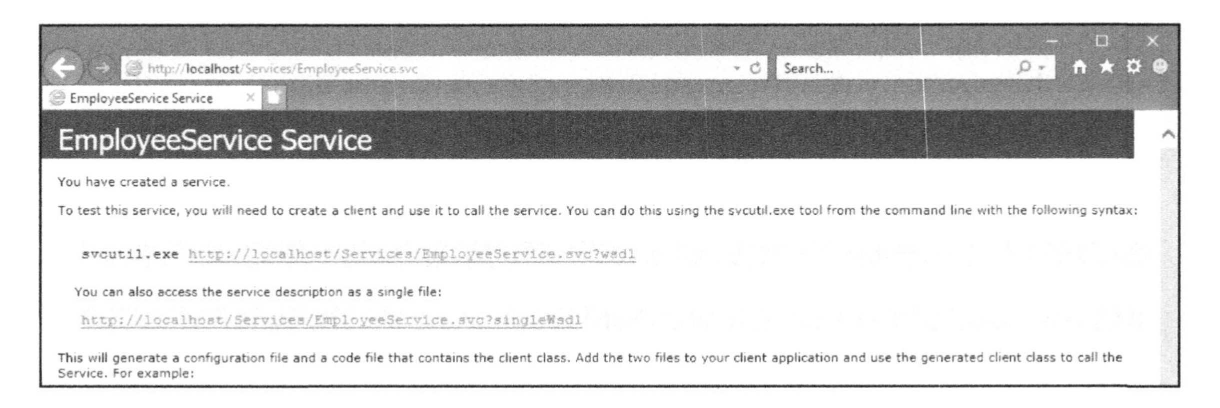

How it works...

IIS hosting is integrated with ASP.NET and uses the features such as process recycling, process health monitoring, message-based activation, and more. IIS also offers integrated manageability, which makes it an enterprise-grade server.

To host a service in IIS, the IIS needs to be configured properly. For hosting in IIS, no additional code needs to be written. The WCF services hosted in IIS are represented as `.svc` files inside the IIS application. A `.svc` file contains a WCF-specific processing directive, that is, an `@ServiceHost`, which creates the service host and allows the hosting structure of the WCF service to activate in response to incoming messages:

```
<%@ ServiceHost
    Language="C#"
    Debug="true"
    Service="CH09.EmployeeService.Services.EmployeeService"
    CodeBehind="EmployeeService.svc.cs"
%>
```

The value of the `Service` attribute is the fully qualified CLR type name (in our case, it's `CH09.EmployeeService.Services.EmployeeService`) of the service implementation. The `CodeBehind` attribute defines the relative path of the code behind the file of the `.svc`, which is `EmployeeService.svc.cs` in our example.

When you deploy a service, the precompiled `.dll` file gets deployed in the application's `bin` directory and updates only when a latest version of the class library gets deployed.

The uncompiled source file gets deployed in the application's `App_Code` directory. When the application gets the first request, these uncompiled source files dynamically load into the memory. Any changes to these deployed source files causes the entire application to be recycled. A fresh recompilation happens automatically when a new request happens to the application.

Integrating a WCF service in a WPF application

Once you create a WCF service, you probably would like to integrate it into a client application. But before that, you will have to create a WCF client proxy, so that you can communicate with the service through the WCF client proxy.

In this recipe, we will learn how to create the proxy client and give a call to the service to pass messages between the service and the client.

Getting ready

Before going into the steps to integrate the service, we need to create a client application. Open your Visual Studio IDE, and create a new WPF project. Name it `CH09.ClientDemo`.

How to do it...

Follow these steps to create the service proxy and integrate the service call in the client application:

1. Right-click on the project node (`CH09.ClientDemo`), and follow the context menu path **Add** | **Service Reference...**, which will open the **Add Service Reference** dialog on the screen:

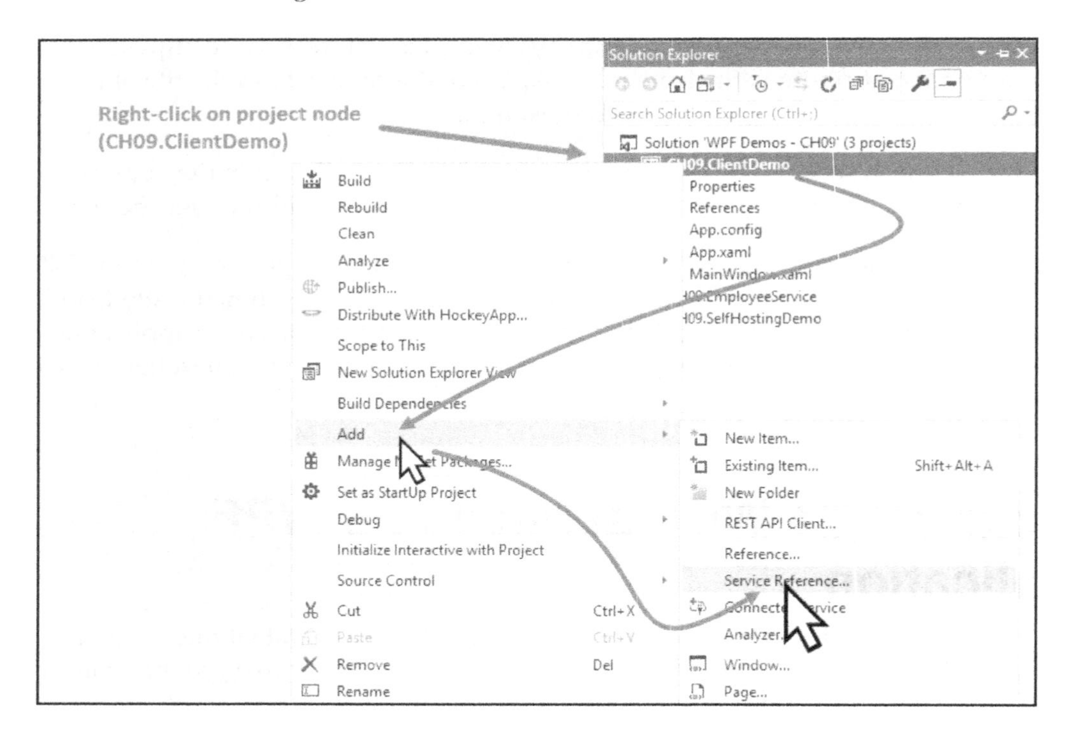

2. In the **Add Service Reference** dialog, enter the service URL (`http://localhost:59795/Services/EmployeeService.svc`) inside the **Address** field and click on the **Go** button:

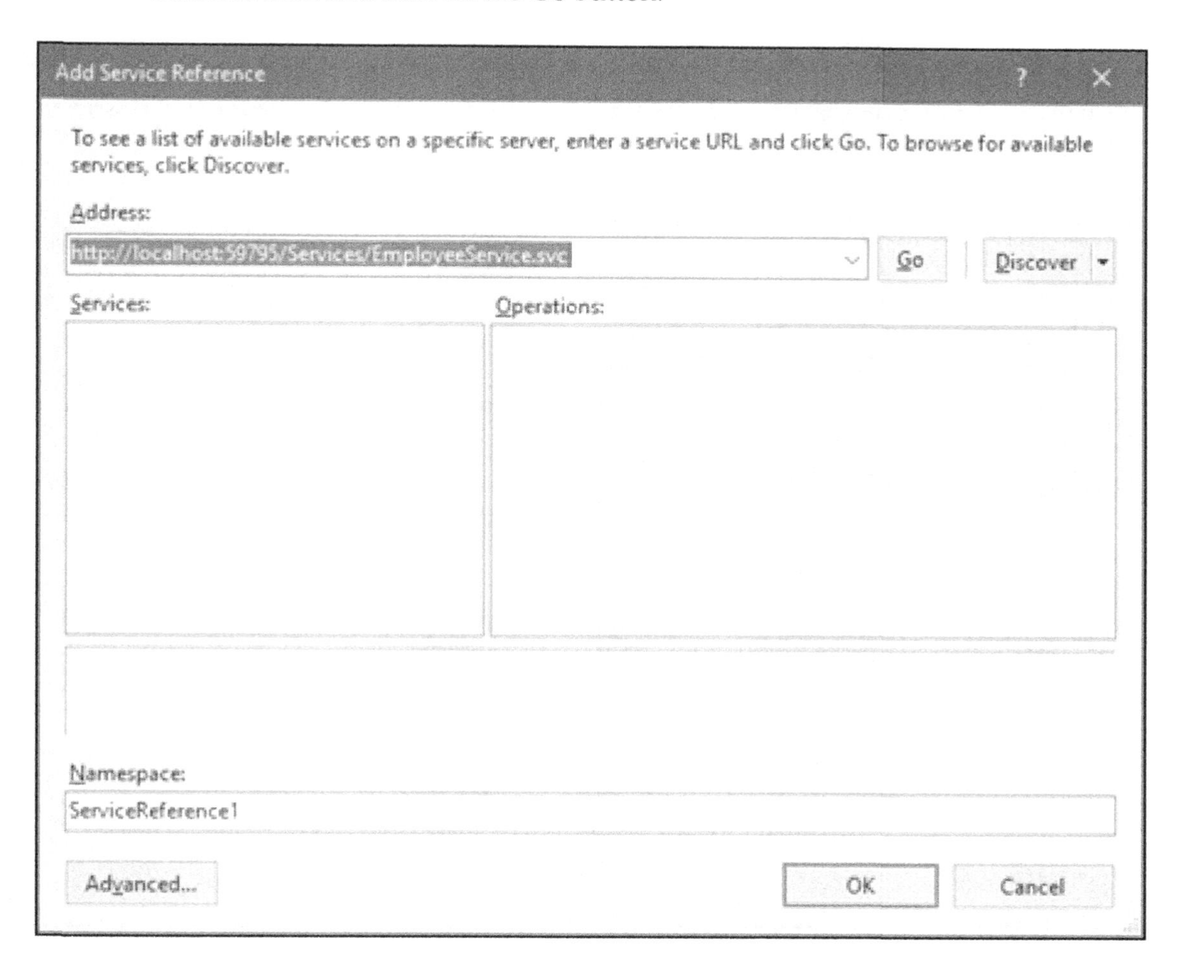

3. This will resolve the service address and show the details about it.

4. As shown in the following screenshot, enter `EmployeeServiceReference` as the **Namespace** for the service proxy and click **OK:**

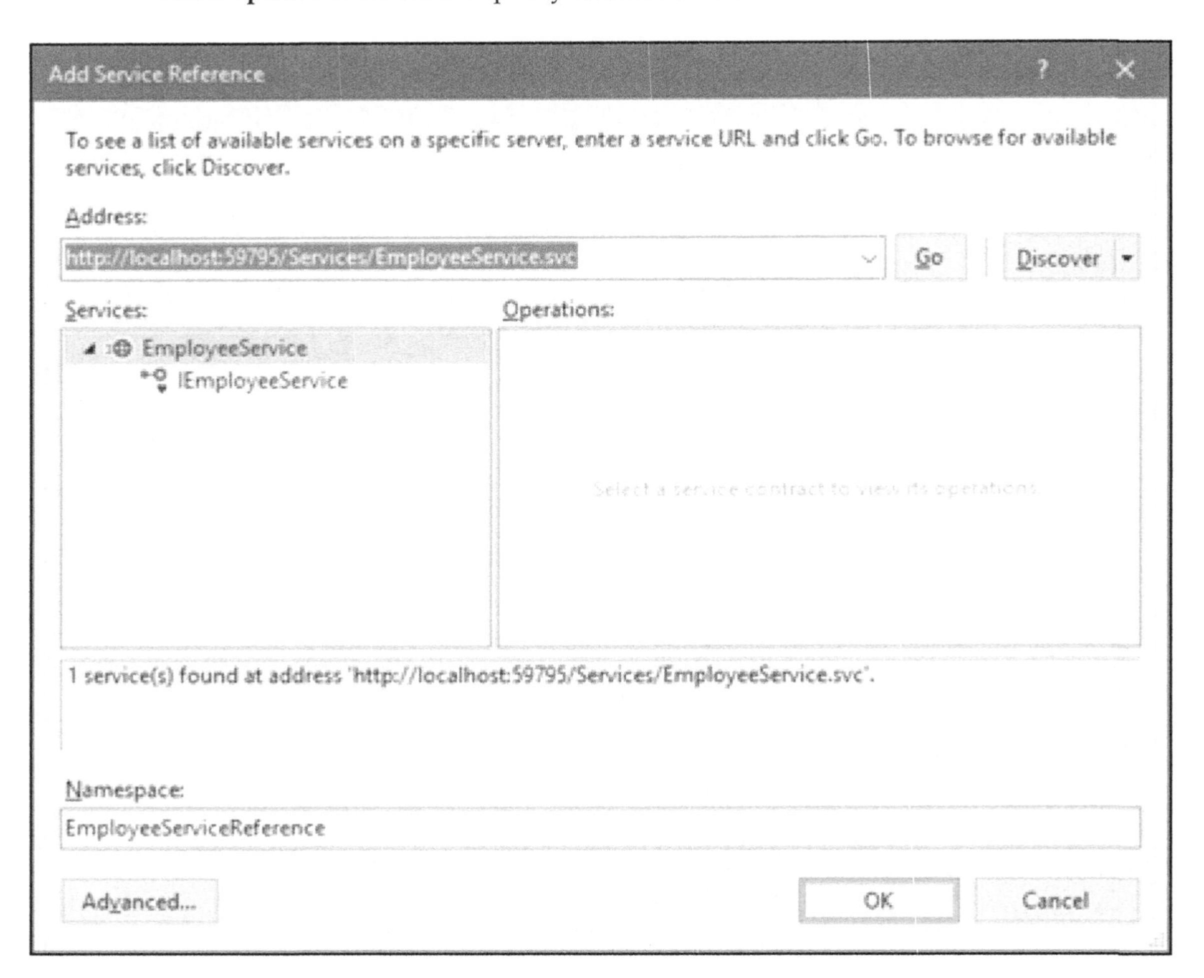

5. This will create the service proxy as **Connected Services** under the project:

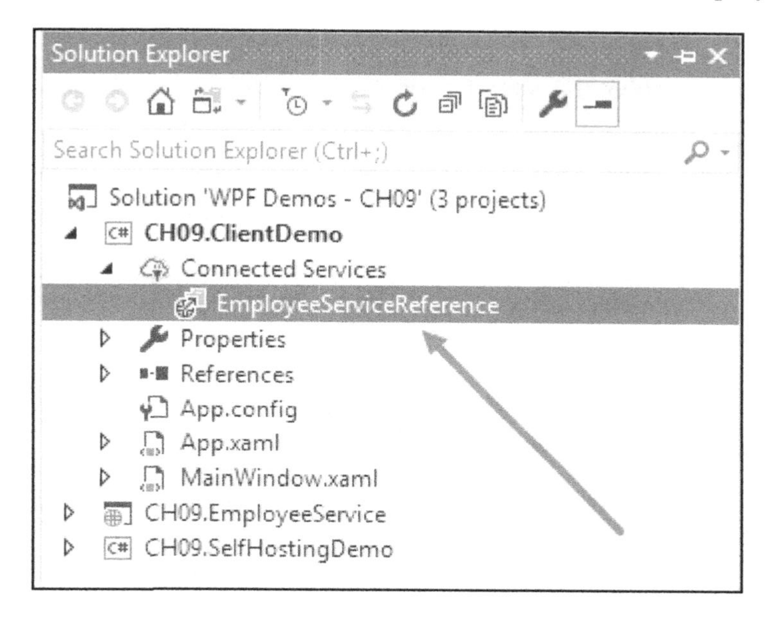

6. Build the project to make sure that there are no compilation issues.
7. Once the build gets succeeded, navigate to the `MainWindow.xaml.cs` file.
8. Create a dependency property of type `ObservableCollection<Employee>`, and name it as `Employees`. The property implementation will look as follows:

```
public ObservableCollection<Employee> Employees
{
    get
    {
        return (ObservableCollection<Employee>)
                  GetValue(EmployeesProperty);
    }
    set
    {
        SetValue(EmployeesProperty, value);
    }
}

public static readonly DependencyProperty
        EmployeesProperty =
            DependencyProperty.Register(
              "Employees",
```

```
                        typeof(ObservableCollection<Employee>),
                        typeof(MainWindow),
                        new PropertyMetadata(null));
```

9. Now, resolve the reference of the `Employee` class, which will add `CH09.ClientDemo.EmployeeServiceReference` as the `using` namespace:

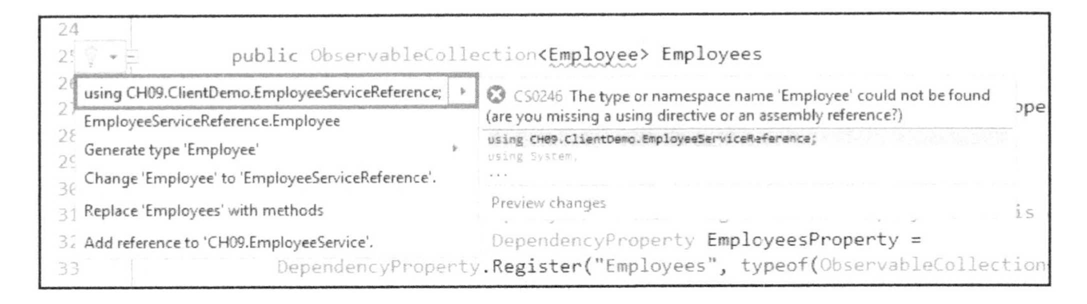

10. Make sure the following `using` namespaces are added to the class file:

```
using CH09.ClientDemo.EmployeeServiceReference;
using System.Collections.ObjectModel;
using System.Windows;
```

11. Inside the class, create the following static instance of the proxy client, so that we can call the service APIs:

```
private static EmployeeServiceClient client =
                            new EmployeeServiceClient();
```

12. Now, add the following two methods inside the class, and make sure that the methods are marked as `async`:

```
private async void RefreshListAsync()
{
    var result = await client.GetEmployeesAsync();
    Employees = new ObservableCollection<Employee>(result);
}

private async void AddNewEmployeeAsync()
{
    var employee = new Employee
    {
        ID = "EMP00" + (Employees.Count + 1),
        FirstName = "User",
        LastName = (Employees.Count + 1).ToString(),
```

```
            Designation = "Software Engineer"
        };

        await client.InsertEmployeeAsync(employee);
    }
```

13. From **Solution Explorer**, navigate to the `MainWindow.xaml` file.
14. Give a name to the `Window` instance by adding the `x:Name="window"` attribute.
15. Split the default `Grid` into two rows, as follows:

```
<Grid.RowDefinitions>
    <RowDefinition Height="*"/>
    <RowDefinition Height="Auto"/>
</Grid.RowDefinitions>
```

16. In the first row of the `Grid` panel, add a `DataGrid`, and create a data binding between the `ItemsSource` property and the `Employees` collection. This will populate the `DataGrid` with the values from the `Employees` collection.
17. Set `AutoGenerateColumns="False"`, `CanUserAddRows="False"`, and `CanUserDeleteRows="False"`, as follows:

```
<DataGrid ItemsSource="{Binding Employees,
                        ElementName=window}"
          Grid.Row="0"
          AutoGenerateColumns="False"
          CanUserAddRows="False"
          CanUserDeleteRows="False">
    <DataGrid.Columns>

    </DataGrid.Columns>
</DataGrid>
```

18. As we have already asked the `DataGrid` not to generate the columns automatically, we need to manually create them, based on the need. In this demonstration, we will only display the `ID`, `Name`, and `Designation` columns in the `DataGrid`. Let's add the following columns, among which, the **Name** column will have a multi-binding with the `FirstName` and `LastName` properties of the `Employee` class to display the full name of the employee. Here's the code for your reference:

```
<DataGrid.Columns>
    <DataGridTextColumn Header="ID"
                        Width="80"
                        Binding="{Binding ID}"/>
```

```
        <DataGridTextColumn Header="Name"
                            Width="200">
            <DataGridTextColumn.Binding>
                <MultiBinding StringFormat="{}{0} {1}">
                    <Binding Path="FirstName"/>
                    <Binding Path="LastName"/>
                </MultiBinding>
            </DataGridTextColumn.Binding>
        </DataGridTextColumn>
        <DataGridTextColumn Header="Designation"
                            Width="150"
                            Binding="{Binding Designation}"/>
    </DataGrid.Columns>
```

19. In the second row of the `Grid` panel, let's add a horizontal `StackPanel` with two buttons in it. Label them as **Refresh** and **Add**. Also, expose the `Click` event of both the two buttons:

```
<StackPanel Orientation="Horizontal"
            Grid.Row="1"
            Margin="8">
    <Button Content="Refresh"
            Margin="4"
            Height="26"
            Width="80"
            Click="OnRefreshClicked"/>
    <Button Content="Add"
            Margin="4"
            Height="26"
            Width="80"
            Click="OnAddClicked"/>
</StackPanel>
```

20. In the code behind the file of the `MainWindow.xaml` (that is, in `MainWindow.xaml.cs`), write the `Click` event implementation for both the two buttons. The `OnRefreshClicked` event will call the `RefreshListAsync()` method to fetch the employees list. The `OnAddClicked` event will call the `AddNewEmployeeAsync()` method to give a call to the service to insert a new employee record, and then call the `RefreshListAsync()` method to fetch the current employee list from the service:

```
private void OnRefreshClicked(object sender,
                              RoutedEventArgs e)
{
    RefreshListAsync();
}
```

```
private void OnAddClicked(object sender,
                          RoutedEventArgs e)
{
    AddNewEmployeeAsync();
    RefreshListAsync();
}
```

21. Let's build the project and run the application. Make sure that the service is already running and accessible.
22. You will see the following application UI on the screen:

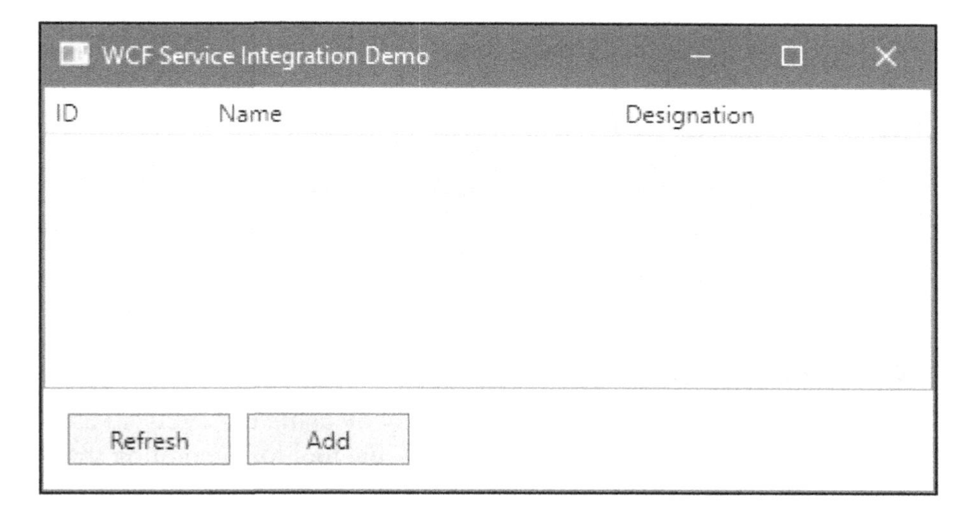

23. Click the **Add** button. This will create a new employee record and pass it to the service to store in the database, which is the static `m_employees` instance in our case.

24. After inserting the record, it will again give a call to the service to fetch the newly inserted details and populate the `DataGrid` in the UI. Clicking the **Add** button multiple times will add the number of records and fill the `DataGrid` accordingly:

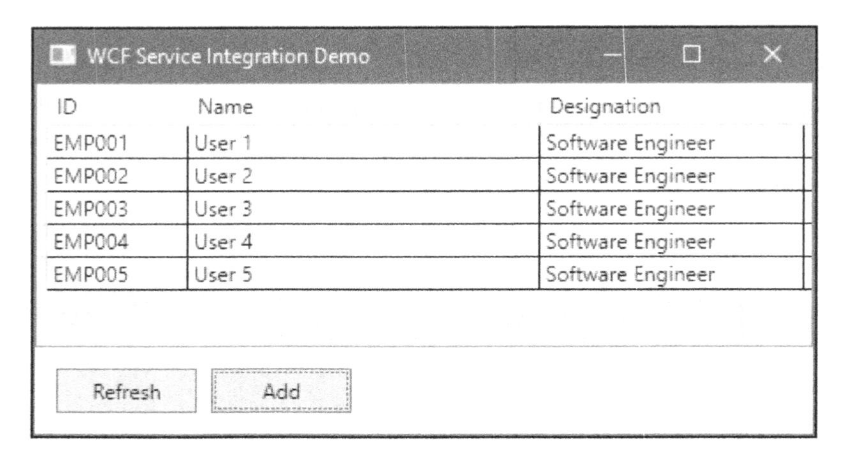

How it works...

The WCF client proxy can be generated manually by using the `SVCUtil.exe` (**Service Model Metadata Utility Tool**). It is a command-line tool for generating the code from the service metadata. The following command can be used to generate the proxy code: `svcutil.exe <Service URL>`.

If you want to create the proxy client for the service that we created earlier, you can enter the following command in a console window:

```
svcutil.exe http://localhost:59795/Services/
EmployeeService.svc?wsdl
```

Alternatively, you can also generate the client proxy from Visual Studio. As demonstrated previously, the **Add Service Reference** feature generates the proxy code automatically. Once you click the **Go** button after inserting the service address, the dialog displays a list of services available at the address specified. It starts generating the code when you click the **OK** button.

In our case, the **Service Model Metadata Utility Tool** and the **Add Service Reference** dialog of Visual Studio (you can use either of them) generates the following WCF client class (`EmployeeServiceClient`) for our service, which inherits from the generic `System.ServiceModel.ClientBase<TChannel>` class and implements the `CH09.ClientDemo.EmployeeServiceReference.IEmployeeService` interface:

```
[System.Diagnostics.DebuggerStepThroughAttribute()]
[System.CodeDom.Compiler.GeneratedCodeAttribute(
 "System.ServiceModel", "4.0.0.0")]
public partial class EmployeeServiceClient :
System.ServiceModel.ClientBase<CH09.ClientDemo.EmployeeServiceR
eference.IEmployeeService>,
CH09.ClientDemo.EmployeeServiceReference.IEmployeeService
{
    public EmployeeServiceClient() {
    }
    public EmployeeServiceClient(string
    endpointConfigurationName)
             : base(endpointConfigurationName) {
    }
    public EmployeeServiceClient(string
    endpointConfigurationName,
           string remoteAddress)
             : base(endpointConfigurationName, remoteAddress) {
    }
    public EmployeeServiceClient(string
    endpointConfigurationName,
           System.ServiceModel.EndpointAddress remoteAddress)
             : base(endpointConfigurationName, remoteAddress) {
    }
    public EmployeeServiceClient
    (System.ServiceModel.Channels.Binding binding,
    System.ServiceModel.EndpointAddress remoteAddress)
             : base(binding, remoteAddress) {
    }
    public CH09.ClientDemo.EmployeeServiceReference.Employee
      GetEmployeeByID(string empID) {
        return base.Channel.GetEmployeeByID(empID);
    }
    public System.Threading.Tasks.Task<CH09.
    ClientDemo.EmployeeServiceReference.Employee>
    GetEmployeeByIDAsync(string empID) {
        return base.Channel.GetEmployeeByIDAsync(empID);
    }
    public CH09.ClientDemo.EmployeeServiceReference.Employee[]
    GetEmployees() {
        return base.Channel.GetEmployees();
```

```
        }
        public System.Threading.Tasks.Task<CH09.
        ClientDemo.EmployeeServiceReference.Employee[]>
        GetEmployeesAsync() {
            return base.Channel.GetEmployeesAsync();
        }
        public void InsertEmployee(CH09.ClientDemo.
        EmployeeServiceReference.Employee employee) {
            base.Channel.InsertEmployee(employee);
        }
        public System.Threading.Tasks.Task InsertEmployeeAsync
       (CH09.ClientDemo.EmployeeServiceReference.Employee employee)
{
            return base.Channel.InsertEmployeeAsync(employee);
        }
}
```

Once the service proxy gets created, you can create the instance of the service client and call the methods of the service. In our example, we created the following service client instance and marked it as `static`:

```
private static EmployeeServiceClient client =
                         new EmployeeServiceClient();
```

The client consists of two API method types for each operation contract that the service has exposed. One of them is a synchronous method, whereas the other is asynchronous. For example, you could see `GetEmployees()` and `GetEmployeesAsync()` methods, as listed in the following screenshot:

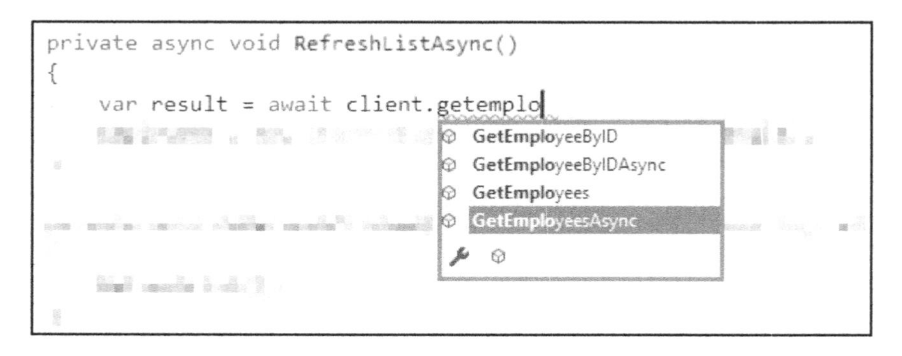

When you want to call the service in a synchronous way, call the `GetEmployees()` method. In case you want to operate in asynchronous mode, call the `GetEmployeesAsync()` method. Similarly, to get the employee details by ID, you can select between `GetEmployeeByID` and `GetEmployeeByIDAsync`, based on synchronous and asynchronous modes. It is a similar case for other service methods.

There's more...

A WCF service client may throw one or more exceptions, which you must handle in your code. Some of the most common exceptions are:

- `SocketException`: This may occur when an existing connection was forcibly closed by the remote host
- `CommunicationException`: This may occur when the underlying connection was unexpectedly closed
- `CommunicationObjectAbortedException`: This may occur when the socket connection was aborted due to an error processing your message, a timeout while processing the request, or an underlying network issue

10
Debugging and Threading

In this chapter, we will cover the following recipes:

- Enabling the UI debugging tool for XAML
- Navigating through XAML elements using Live Visual Tree
- Inspecting XAML properties using Live Property Explorer
- Updating the UI from a non-UI thread
- Adding cancelation support to long running threads
- Using the background worker component
- Using a timer to periodically update the UI

Introduction

When it comes to application development, debugging plays a vital role. It is a process that helps you to quickly look at the current state of your program by walking through the code line by line. While writing the code, developers start debugging their applications. Sometimes, developers start debugging even before writing the first line of code to know the existing logic.

Visual Studio provides us with details about running programs as much as possible and helps you to change some values while the application is running. As a developer, you must already know this. As the focus of this book is on **Windows Presentation Foundation** (**WPF**), we will be discussing XAML UI debugging using **Live Visual Tree** and **Live Property Explorer**.

Later in this chapter, we will discuss **threading** and learn how to update a UI thread from a non-UI thread, a background worker process, and a timer that is used to periodically update the UI.

Enabling the UI debugging tool for XAML

To begin debugging your XAML application UI, you will first need to enable a few settings in Visual Studio. If the settings are disabled, you won't be able to view the **Live Visual Tree** and the **Live Properties** window, which we will be discussing in the next few recipes.

These settings are by default enabled in Visual Studio 2017, but in case are disabled; this recipe will help you to get started with that.

Getting ready

Make sure that you have Visual Studio 2017. Open it to get started with the settings changes.

How to do it...

Follow the steps mentioned here to verify and enable the UI Debugging Tools for XAML in Visual Studio 2017:

1. Inside the Visual Studio IDE, navigate to the **Tools** | **Options...** menu, as shown in the following screenshot:

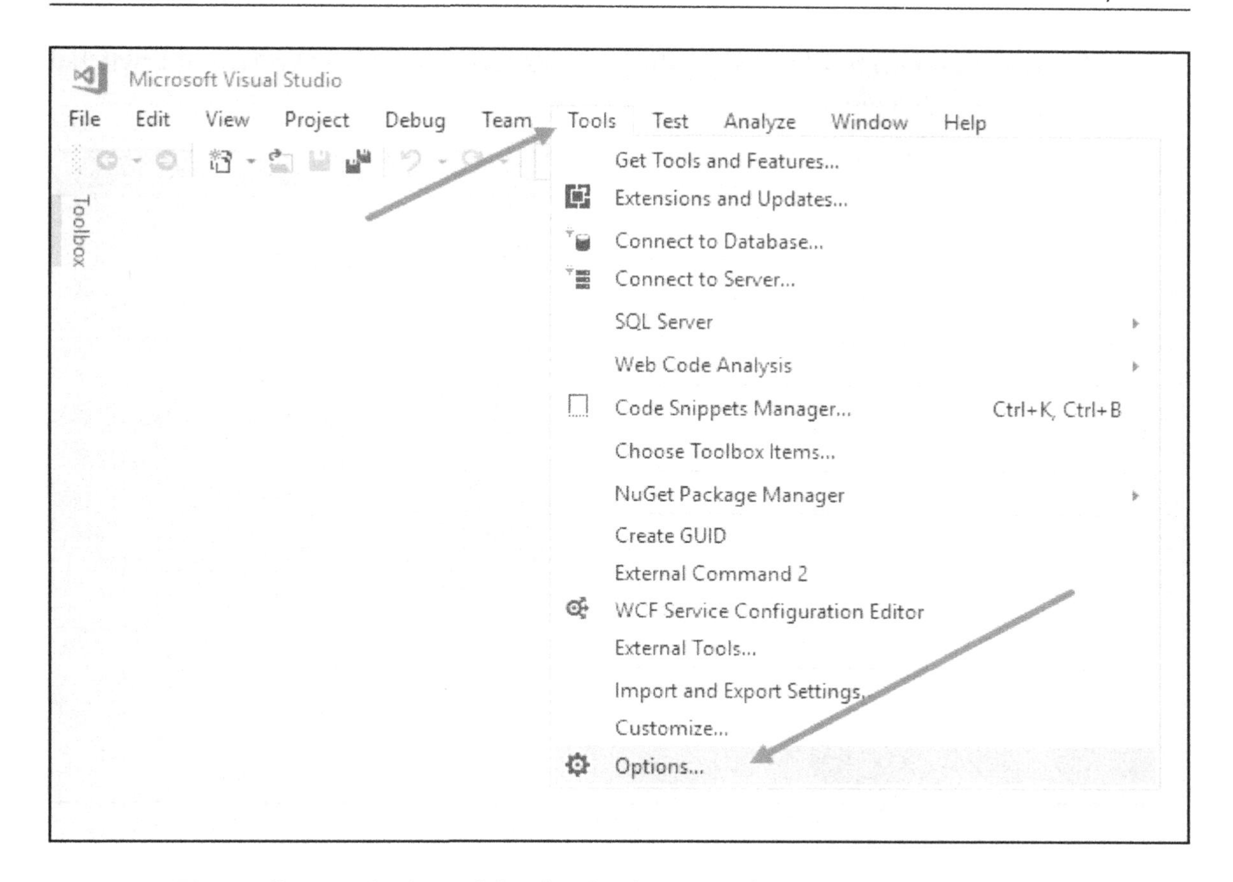

2. This will open the Visual Studio **Options** window. From this page, navigate to the **Debugging** | **General** section.

3. Select the checkbox labeled **Enable UI Debugging Tools for XAML**, and switch it ON if it is not already:

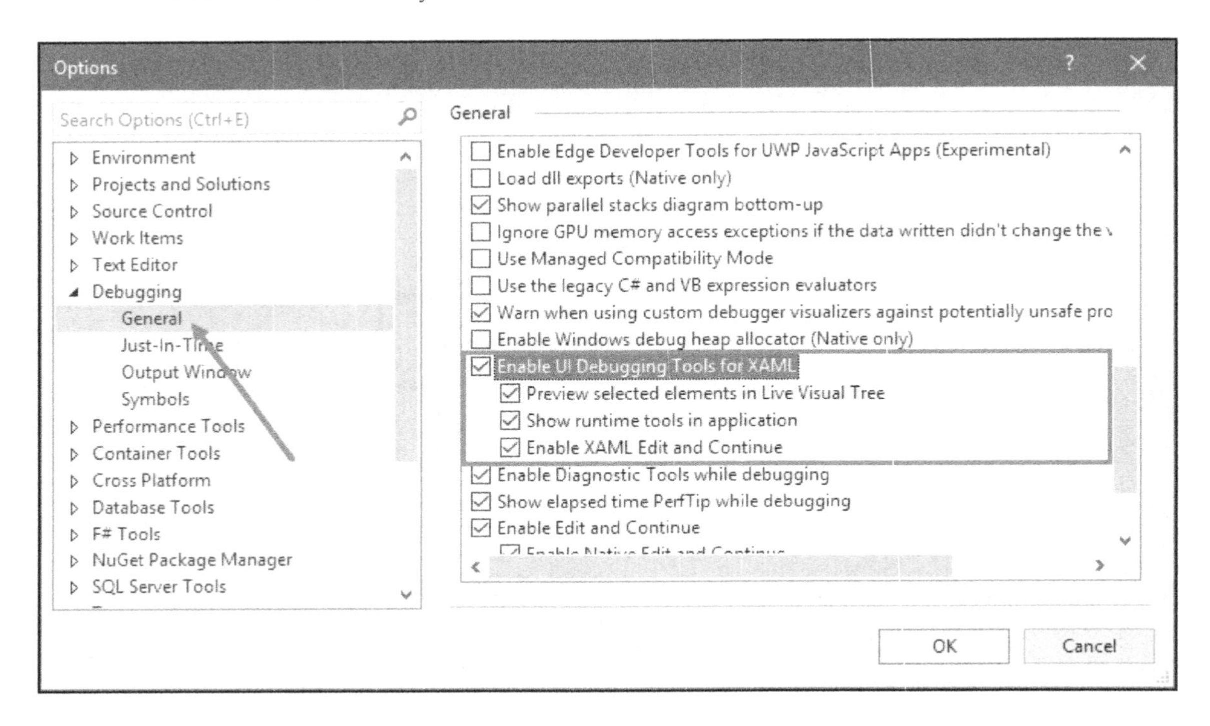

4. Once you switch ON the functionality to debug the XAML application UI, you will enable a few more settings to use the **Live Visual Tree** and modifications of XAML properties when the debugger is already attached.
5. From the same page, select the other checkboxes labeled **Preview selected elements in Live Visual Tree** and **Show runtime tools in application**.
6. To be able to change the XAML elements and their properties when the application is already running in debug mode, check **Enable XAML Edit and Continue**, as shown in the preceding screenshot.
7. Click **OK** to save the changes and restart the debugging process for the changes to take effect. You will now be able to debug your XAML UI.

Navigating through XAML elements using Live Visual Tree

Live Visual Tree is a debugger tool that helps you to perform XAML debugging more easily. Using this, you can inspect the XAML at runtime and visualize the layout to show alignments and space for UI elements.

Basically, Live Visual Tree provides you a tree view of the UI elements of your running XAML application, and provides information about the number of XAML elements inside each container. If the interface changes from one state to another, Live Visual Tree also changes in runtime.

In this recipe, we will learn more about Live Visual Tree and how to use it to visualize the actual control rendering on the UI.

Getting ready

To get started, open Visual Studio 2017 IDE and create a new WPF project named `CH10.XamlDebuggingDemo`.

How to do it...

Follow the steps mentioned here to create our sample demo application and then learn how to use **Live Visual Tree** to navigate through the XAML elements while debugging the application:

1. Let's first design our application UI. Open the `MainWindow.xaml` file from **Solution Explorer**.
2. Divide the default `Grid` panel to have five rows in the following manner:

```
<Grid.RowDefinitions>
    <RowDefinition Height="Auto"/>
    <RowDefinition Height="Auto"/>
    <RowDefinition Height="Auto"/>
    <RowDefinition Height="Auto"/>
    <RowDefinition Height="*"/>
</Grid.RowDefinitions>
```

3. Inside the `Grid`, add the following XAML code block to create a login screen with a few textblocks, textboxes, and button controls. Place them in appropriate rows as follows:

```
<TextBlock Text="Username:"
           Grid.Row="0"
           Margin="0 4 0 0"/>
<TextBlock Text="Password:"
           Grid.Row="2"
           Margin="0 4 0 0"/>

<TextBox x:Name="username"
         Grid.Row="1"/>
<TextBox x:Name="password"
         Grid.Row="3"/>

<StackPanel Orientation="Horizontal"
            HorizontalAlignment="Center"
            VerticalAlignment="Center"
            Grid.Row="4">
    <Button Content="Login"/>
    <Button Content="Cancel"/>
</StackPanel>
```

4. Now, inside the `<Window>` tag, add `<Window.Resources>` and add the following styles for the `TextBox` and `Button` controls to give them a proper look:

```
<Window.Resources>
    <Style TargetType="TextBox">
        <Setter Property="Height"
                Value="24"/>
    </Style>
    <Style TargetType="Button">
        <Setter Property="Margin"
                Value="4"/>
        <Setter Property="Width"
                Value="60"/>
        <Setter Property="Height"
                Value="30"/>
    </Style>
</Window.Resources>
```

5. Once the UI is ready, let's run the application. You will see the following output on the screen:

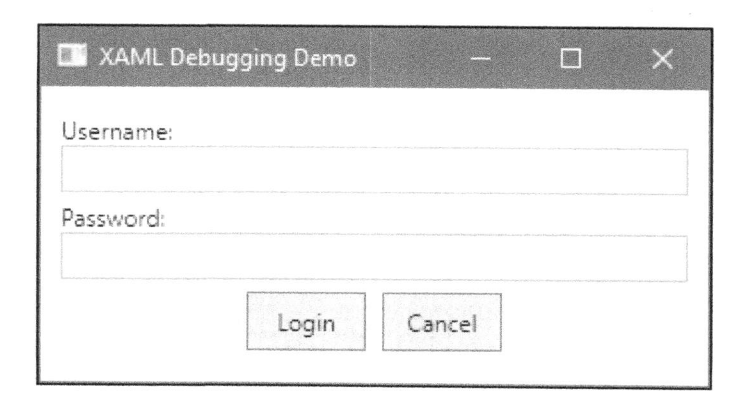

6. Now, close the application and run it in debug mode. To do this, either click on the **Start** button (Start) on the **Visual Studio Toolbar** or navigate to the Visual Studio **Debug** menu and click **Start Debugging**.
7. Alternatively, you can press the keyboard shortcut *F5* to run the application in debug mode.
8. Once the application launches, you will see the following output with a toolbar on the screen:

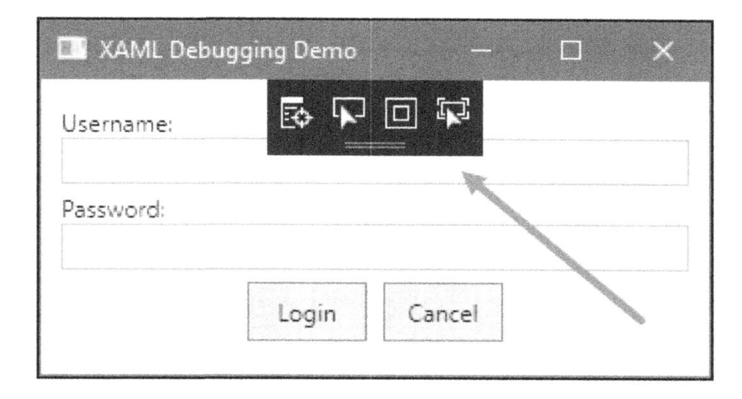

9. In case the toolbar is not present in the UI, navigate to Visual Studio's **Debugging** options and enable **Show runtime tools in application**, as shown in the following screenshot. Also make sure that the other checkboxes (marked here) are already checked:

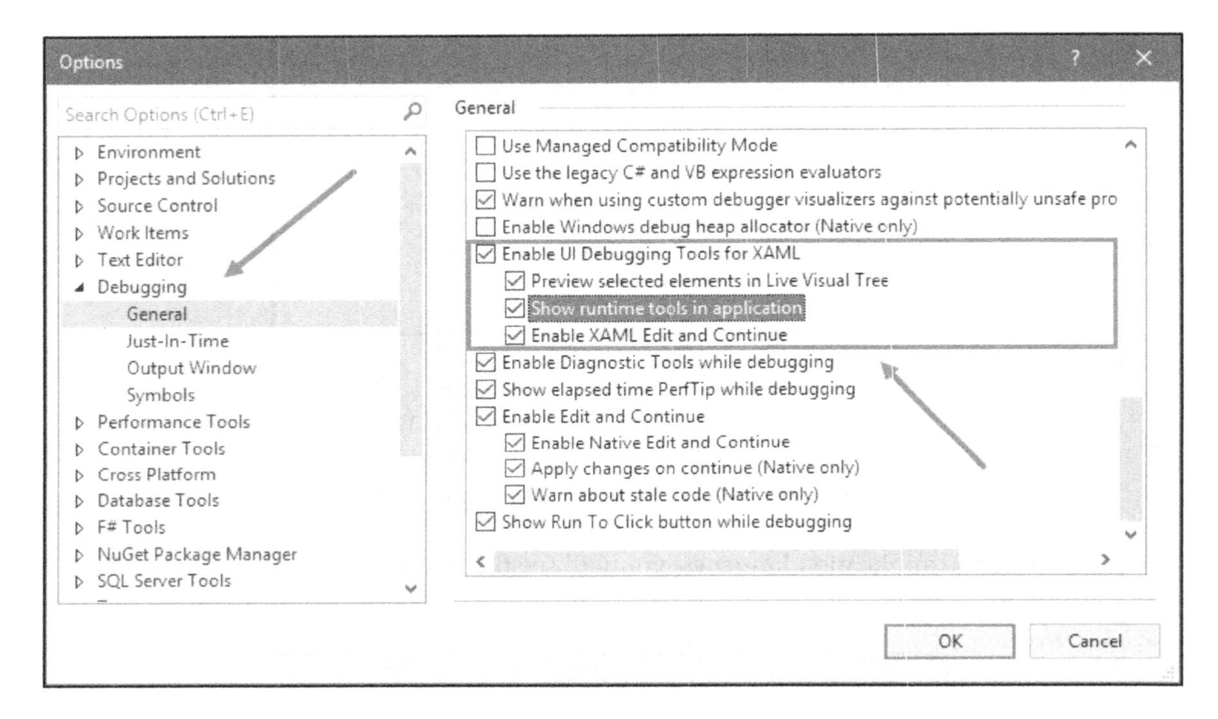

10. When the application is running in debug mode, click on the second button on the runtime toolbar to enable the control selection:

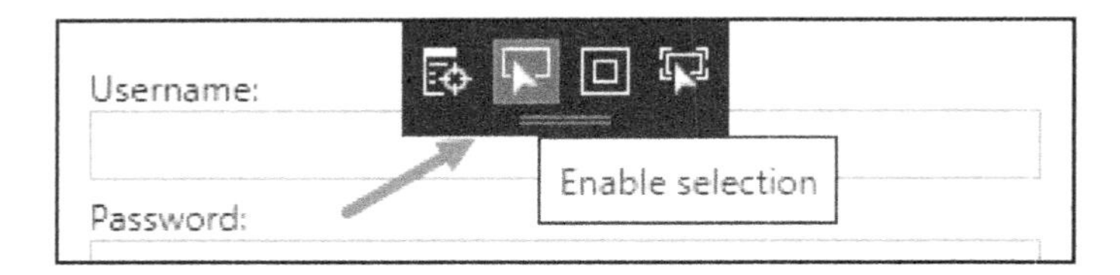

11. Now, hover over on any control on the application UI, and you will see a red dotted border on the hovered control (just like the **IE Developer Tools**), as shown in the following screenshot:

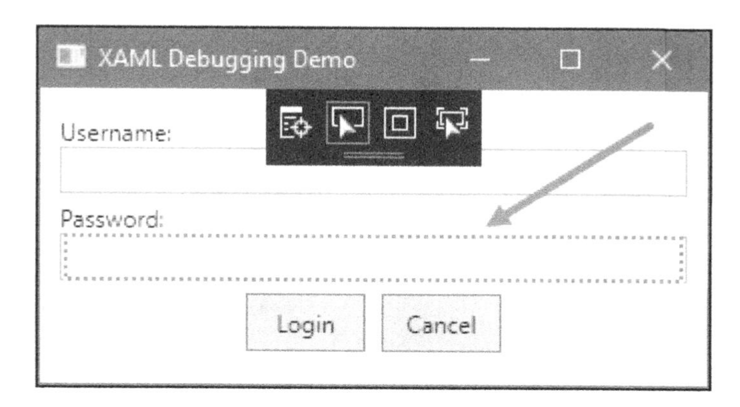

12. Click on any control to open **Live Visual Tree** inside the Visual Studio editor. In case it is not visible, navigate back to the application UI, and as shown in the following screenshot, click the first button on the runtime toolbar to launch the **Live Visual Tree** dialog panel:

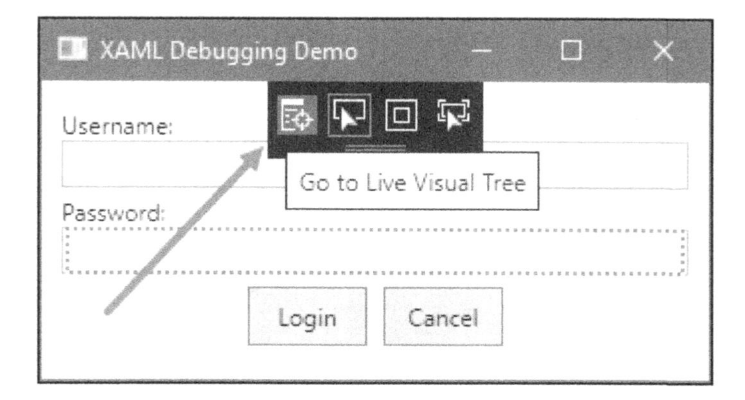

13. Alternatively, you can navigate to the Visual Studio 2017 menu **Debug** | **Windows** | **Live Visual Tree** to launch this dialog window.

14. Click on the input box, labeled **Password**. **Live Visual Tree** will show you the currently selected visual element within the visual tree. Check out the following screenshot:

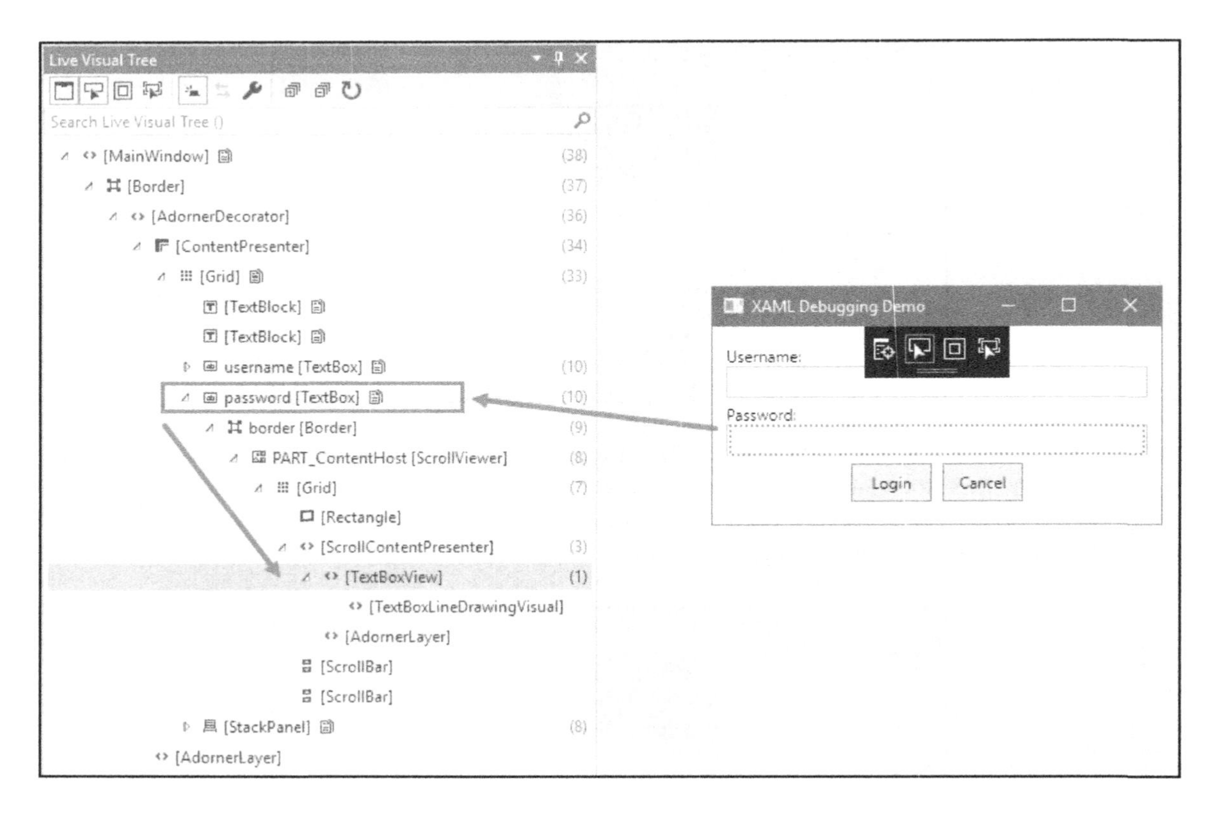

15. Let's click on the button control (labeled **Login**) and, as shown in the following screenshot, the appropriate **Button** control will be automatically selected in the Visual Tree:

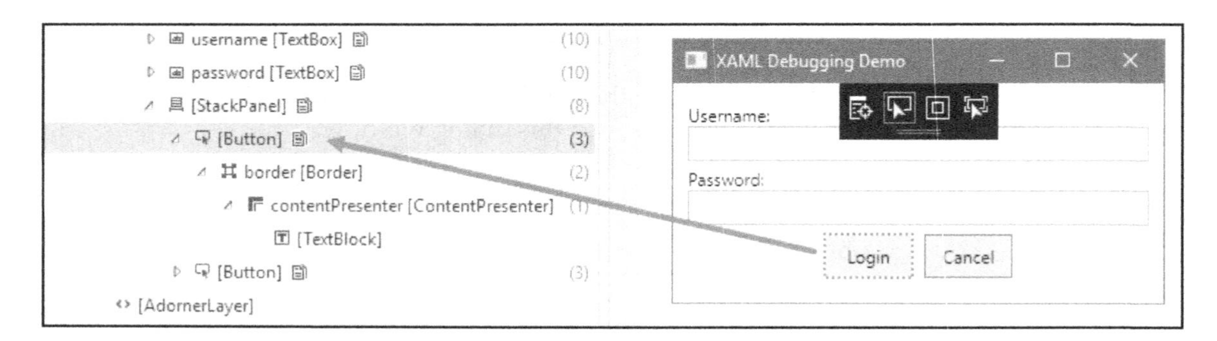

16. Now, click on the **Login** label inside the button. You will see that the `Button` control contains a `TextBlock` element, which is present inside a `ContentPresenter`, wrapped inside a `Border` control:

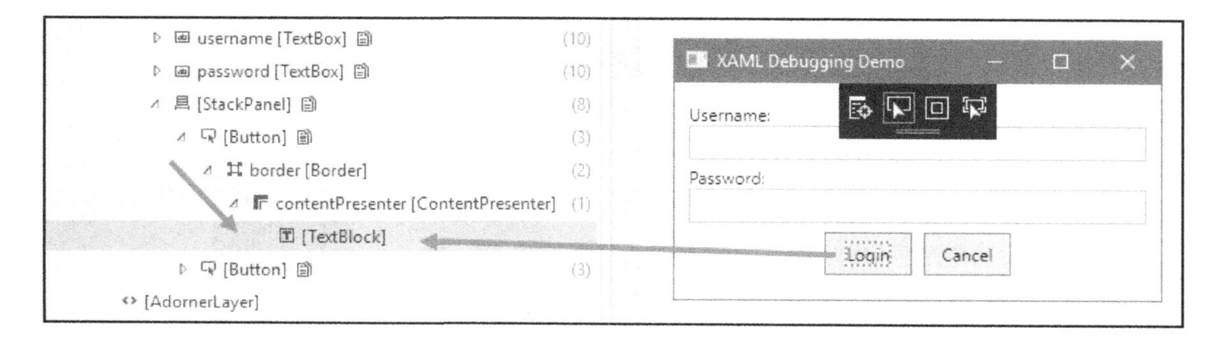

How it works...

When you launch a WPF application in debug mode, the floating toolbar also gets loaded on the screen, which allows you to easily select the element in the running instance of the application and inspect its **Visual Element** in **Live Visual Tree**.

The floating toolbar contains four buttons—**Go to Live Visual Tree**, **Enable Selection**, **Display layout adorners**, and **Track focused element**, as shown in the following screenshot:

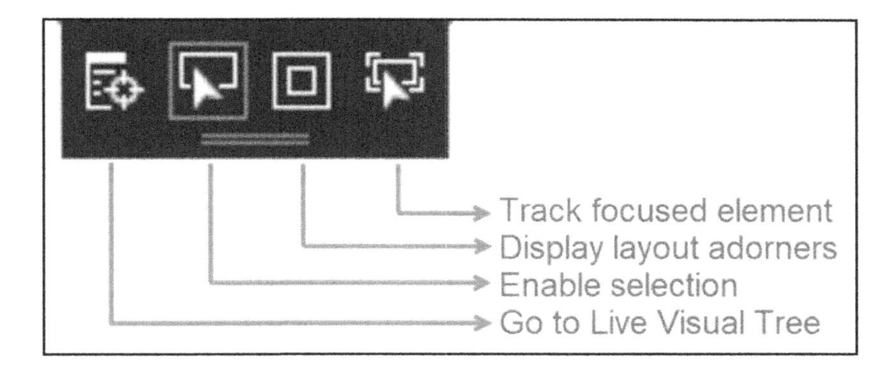

In `MainWindow.xaml`, we have added just the `Button` control inside `StackPanel`, but when you see it on **Live Visual Tree**, you will notice that the `Button` control consists of other UI elements to represent the control. It contains a `Border`, a `ContentPresenter`, and a `TextBlock` to visualize the `Button` content:

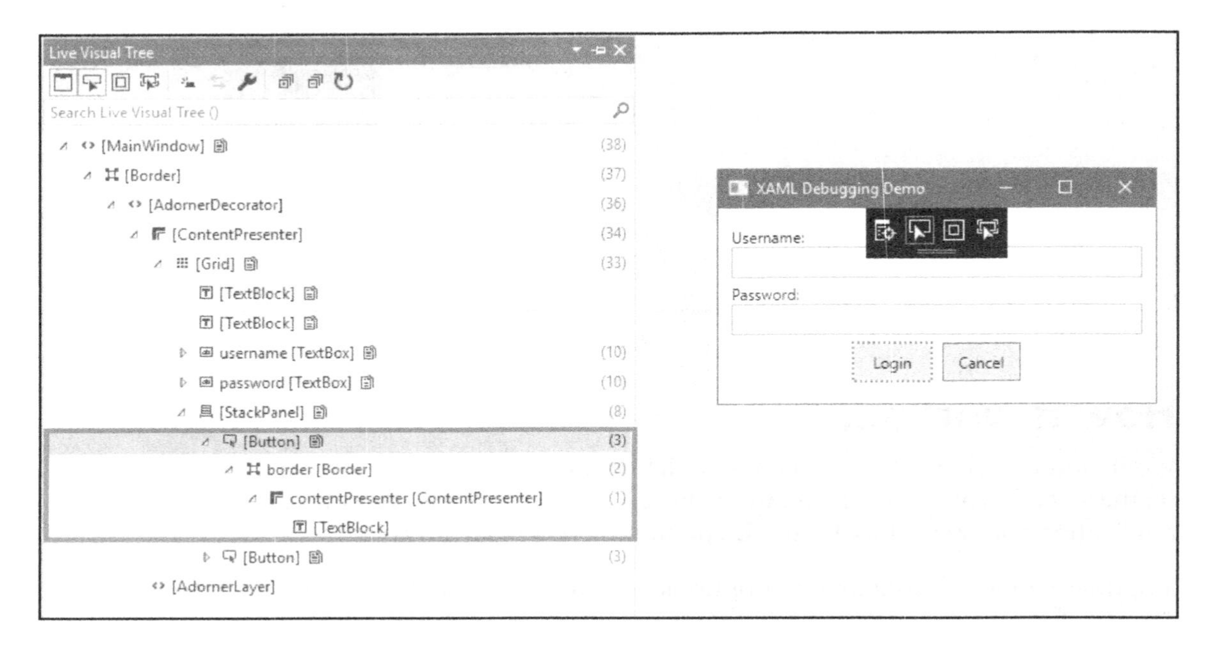

Like this, each UI control consists of one or more UI elements that are only visible in a Visual Tree and can be inspected via Live Visual Tree when the debugger is attached to the application.

Please note that this is how the XAML controls actually render in the UI. The more levels of elements you have in a **Visual Tree**, the more performance issues it may hit. Detecting and eliminating unnecessary elements in the Visual Tree is one of the major advantages of a **Live Visual Tree** debugger window.

Visual Studio 2017 also supports modification of the selected element in the Live Visual Tree window, which we will be demonstrating in the next recipe.

There's more...

You can also ask the XAML debugger to display the layout adorners. While the runtime debugger tool is visible on the application window, click on the third button (as shown in the following screenshot), titled **Display layout adorners**. It will cause the application window to show horizontal and vertical lines along the bounds of the selected object, so you can see what it aligns to. It also displays rectangles showing the margins:

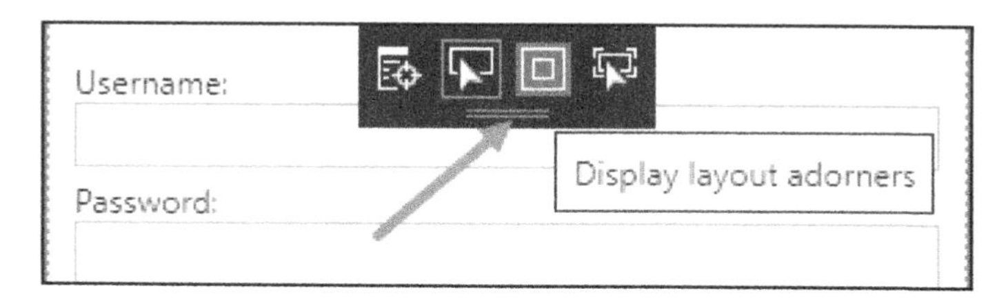

When enabled, hover over or click any UI element on the application window. You will see the layout adorner for that control, as shown in the following screenshot:

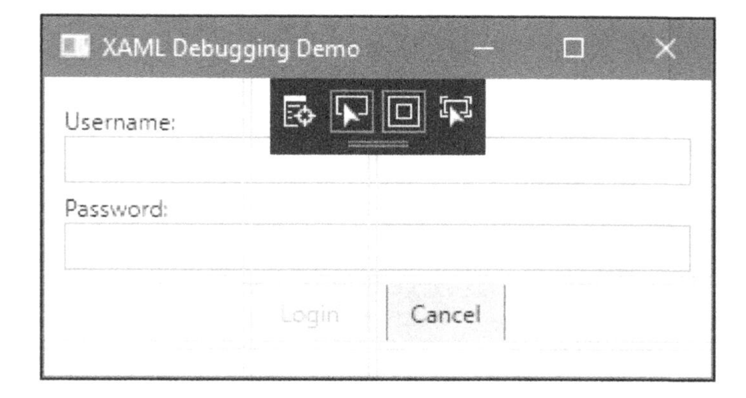

Inspecting XAML properties using Live Property Explorer

In the previous recipe, we learnt about **Live Visual Tree**, which is used to get a real-time view of your running XAML code by inspecting the visual elements. Visual Studio 2015 and above also provide a **Live Property Explorer** window, which allows you to temporarily modify the XAML properties at runtime to see the visual effect.

In this recipe, we will learn about Live Property Explorer. We will use Visual Studio 2017 to demonstrate it.

Getting ready

Let's begin with a demo project creation. Open your Visual Studio 2017 instance and create a new project named `CH10.LivePropertyExplorerDemo`. Make sure to select the WPF application template during project creation.

How to do it...

Follow these steps to design our application UI with a simple button and then utilize **Live Property Explorer** to view and modify the XAML properties at runtime:

1. From **Solution Explorer**, open the `MainWindow.xaml` file.
2. Replace the content of the XAML with the following code to have a basic `Button` with default style:

```
<Window x:Class="CH10.LivePropertyExplorerDemo.MainWindow"
xmlns="http://schemas.microsoft.com/winfx/2006/xaml/presentatio
n"
        xmlns:x="http://schemas.microsoft.com/winfx/2006/xaml"
        Title="Live Property Explorer Demo" Height="150"
Width="400">
    <Grid>
        <Button x:Name="myButton"
                Content="Click here"/>
    </Grid>
</Window>
```

3. Let's run the application. You will see that the button automatically arranges itself to cover the entire application. This is because we have placed the button inside a `Grid` and haven't specified its dimensions and margins, as shown in the following screenshot:

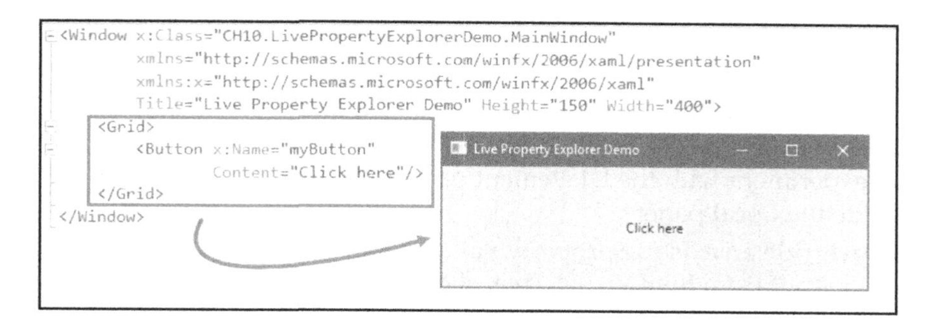

4. Now, close the application and run it in debug mode.
5. Once the application launches in debug mode, navigate to the Visual Studio menu—**Debug** | **Windows** | **Live Property Explorer** to open said explorer window.
6. The **Live Property Explorer** window will look as follows:

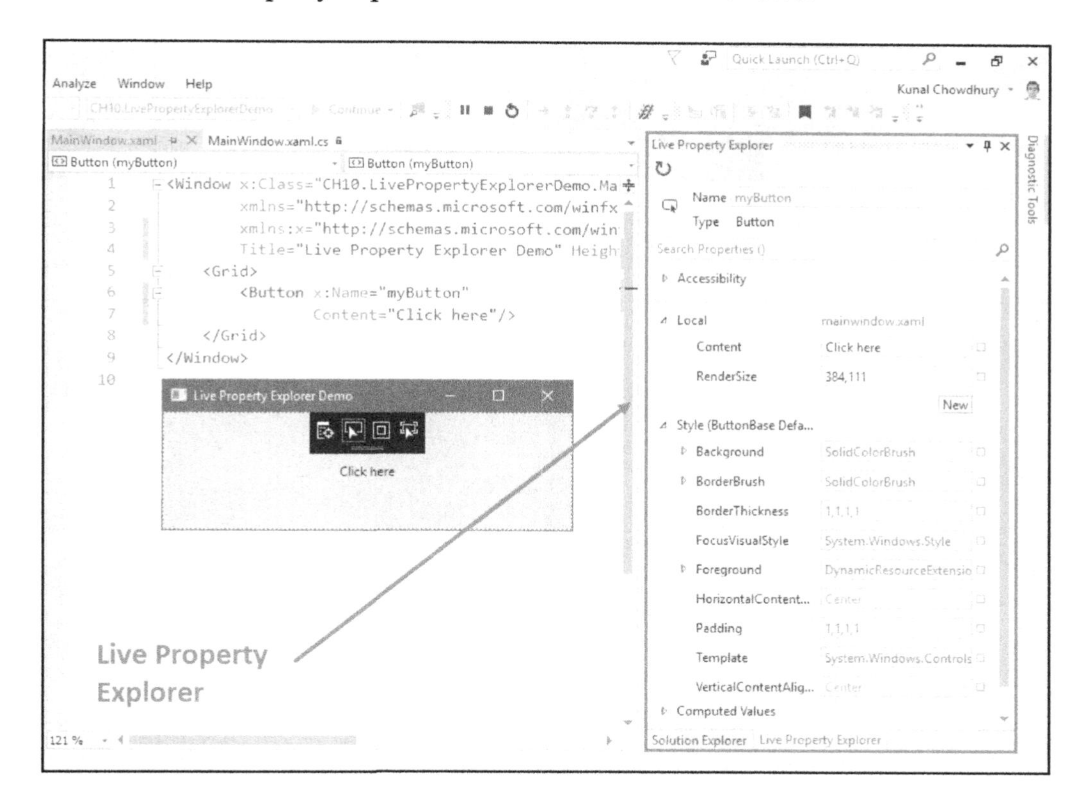

7. As you can see in the preceding screenshot, **Live Property Explorer** is showing the properties of the selected `Button` control, named `myButton`. You will find that most of the properties are disabled. This is because they are either inherited from implicit/explicit styles or have default values.
8. To experiment with the UI element properties, you should modify the properties inside the **Local** panel.
9. To override an existing property value of the selected element (in our case, it is `myButton`) from Live Visual Tree, click on the **New** button, as shown in the following screenshot:

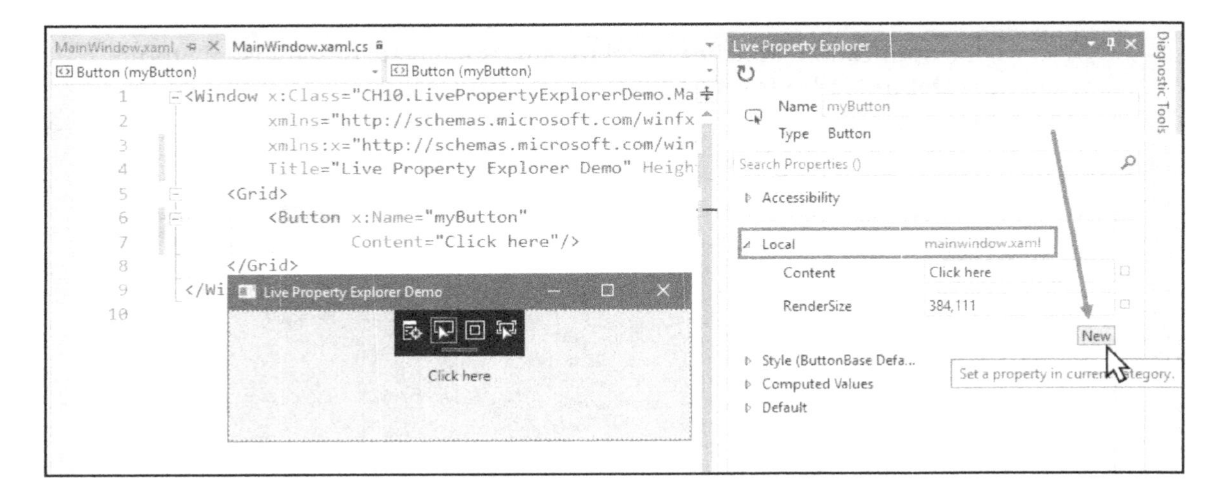

10. This will add a drop-down list in the panel, where you will be able to select the property that you would like to modify. Let's select **Width** from the property list:

11. When you select the property, the panel will get populated with the appropriate property boxes to fill it. Enter `120` as the value against the **Width** property.
12. Notice the running application window. The `Button` control in the window will be automatically resized to a width of 120 pixels.

13. Observe the actual element in the XAML designer window. The change was not performed in the XAML code:

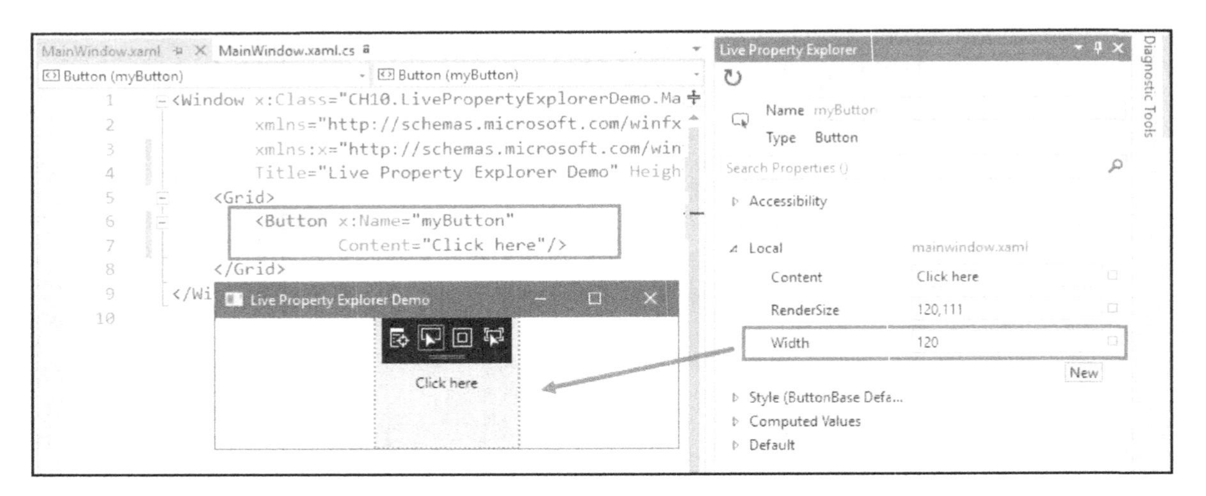

14. Let's modify a few more properties of the `Button` control. Click on the **New** button and select `Height` from the property list. Set its value to `30`.
15. Click on the **New** button once again and select `Background` from the property list. Now enter `Red` as its value. You can alternatively enter `#FFFF0000` to apply a red color as the button background.
16. Once you perform these changes, look at the running application window. The new height and the background color have already been applied to the button:

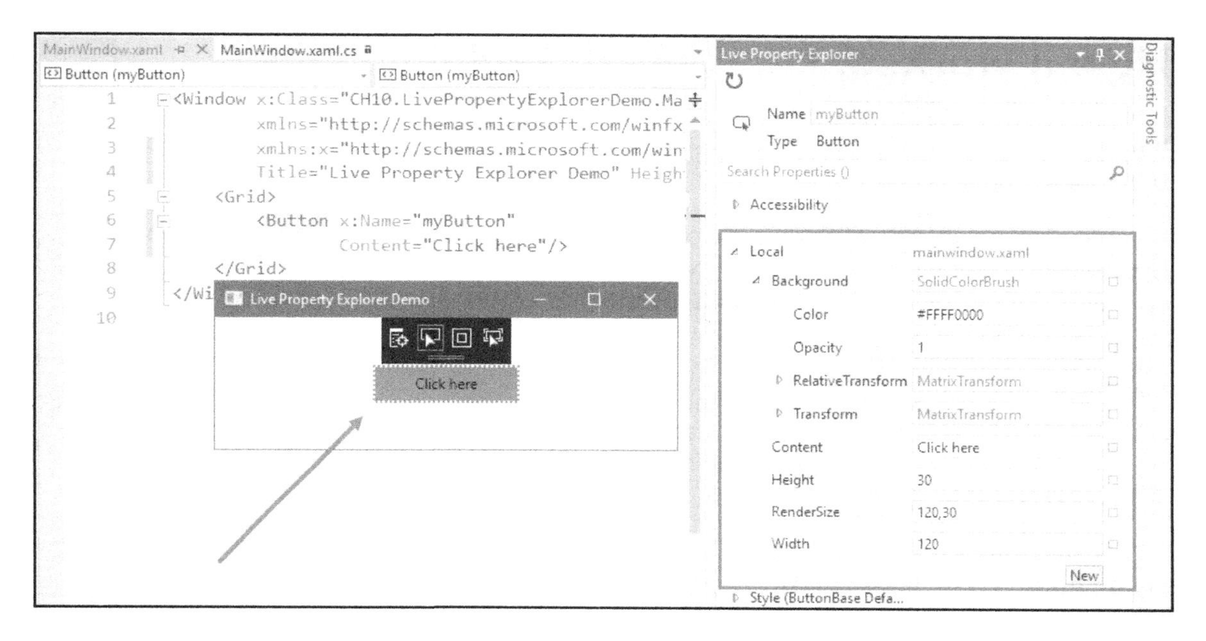

17. Let's change a few more properties. Add the `FontSize` and `Foreground` properties in your local property list. Set their values to `16` and `White`, respectively.
18. Check the application window for the changes. It will now look as follows:

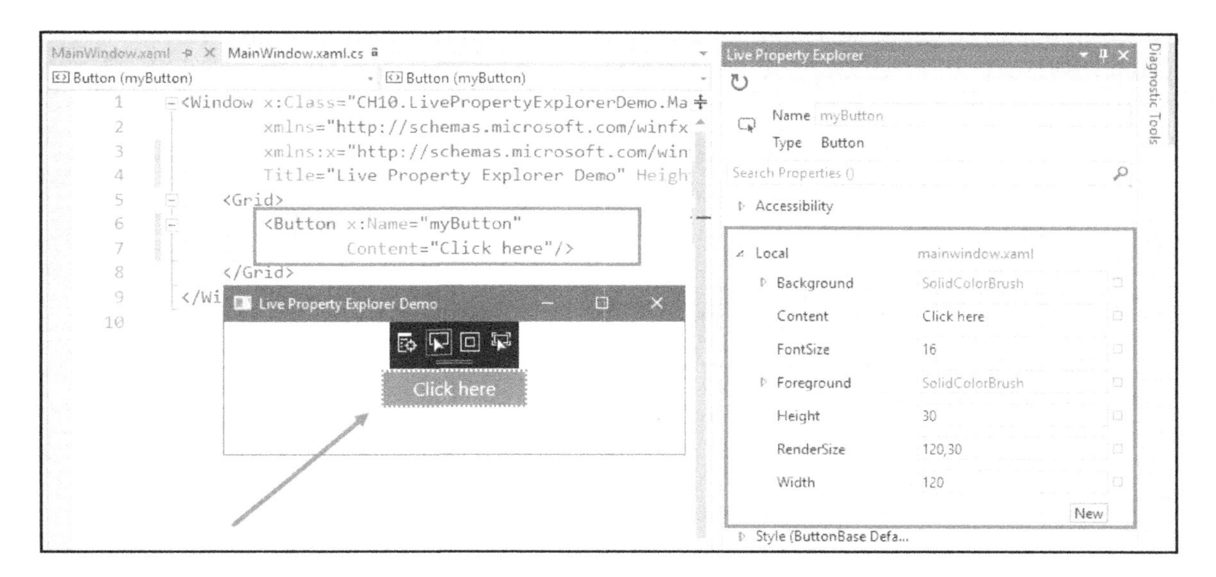

How it works...

Live Property Explorer only gives you a preview of what you want to modify in runtime. Based on that, you can change the original UI in the XAML view or designer view for permanent changes.

If you end the debugging session, the changes that you performed in the **Live Property Explorer** window won't be saved and you will lose those changes. When you restart the application, you will see fresh values as per the default.

This is often useful when you want to see the changes live at runtime for any element inside the Visual Tree.

There's more...

To permanently set the properties of any UI element while the application is running in debug mode, use either the XAML code view or the XAML designer view. The running application will automatically get the update of the style changes.

To modify the XAML code while the application is running in debug mode, make sure that the **Enable UI Debugging Tools for XAML** and the **Enable XAML Edit and Continue** settings are enabled (checked) in the Visual Studio Options window, under the **Debugging** | **General** section.

Let's run the application once again in debug mode and start modifying the control properties directly in the XAML view. Once you have made some changes, check the running application and you will see that it already has been updated with the modified data:

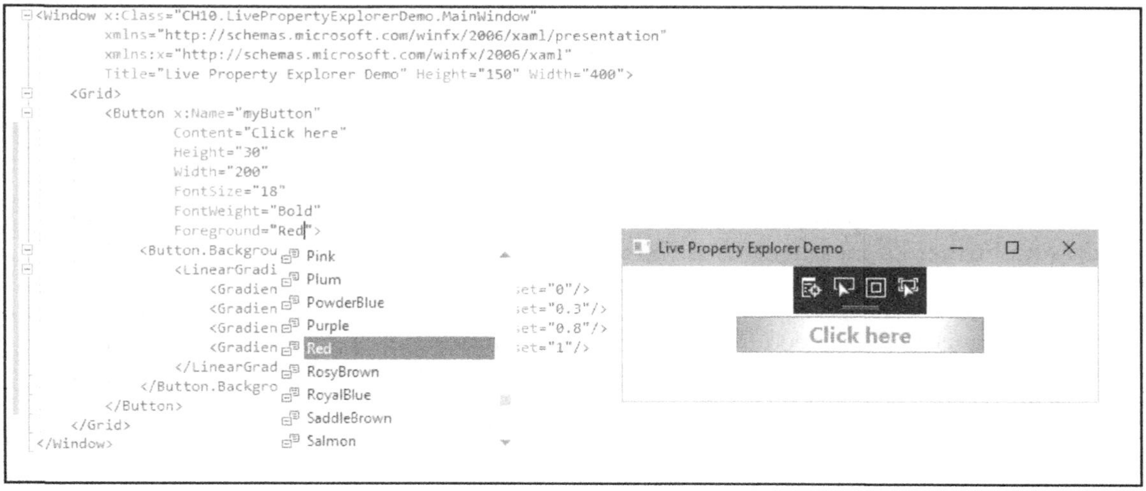

Here's the modified XAML code of the button, which we used in the preceding screenshot. When applied, it will result in the addition of a nice linear gradient color to the button background:

```
<Button x:Name="myButton"
        Content="Click here"
        Height="30"
        Width="200"
        FontSize="18"
        FontWeight="Bold"
        Foreground="Red">
    <Button.Background>
        <LinearGradientBrush>
            <GradientStop Color="#FFFF5454"
                          Offset="0"/>
            <GradientStop Color="#FFFFF754"
                          Offset="0.3"/>
            <GradientStop Color="#FFFFF754"
                          Offset="0.8"/>
            <GradientStop Color="#FFFF5454"
                          Offset="1"/>
        </LinearGradientBrush>
    </Button.Background>
</Button>
```

Updating the UI from a non-UI thread

In WPF, the UI is managed by a single thread, called a **UI thread**, which that creates an instance of a window and processes the UI messages for that window. This is known as **message pumping**.

When the UI thread is performing a lot of operations, it enters in to a wait state and stops processing further UI messages. This causes the application to enter *Not Responding* mode, which is commonly known as **UI freezing**.

To resolve this issue, you need to offload that long running operation into another thread. This keeps the UI thread free and allows it to perform the UI updates and stay responsive.

In this recipe, we will learn how to offload a long running process into a separate thread in a thread pool and perform the UI updates once it completes the execution.

Getting ready

Let's begin by creating a WPF project. Name it `CH10.ThreadingDemo1`. Make sure to select the right WPF App template during project creation.

How to do it...

We will create a simple application that will count odd and even numbers in a numeric range. This will be done on a non-UI thread and once the result is available we will update the UI. Follow these steps:

1. From **Solution Explorer**, open the `MainWindow.xaml` file.
2. Replace the existing `Grid` with the following simple user interface to provide the numeric range, and a button to calculate and display the result:

```
<Grid Margin="10">
    <Grid.RowDefinitions>
        <RowDefinition Height="Auto"/>
        <RowDefinition Height="Auto"/>
        <RowDefinition Height="Auto"/>
    </Grid.RowDefinitions>
    <StackPanel Orientation="Horizontal"
                Grid.Row="0"
                Margin="4">
        <TextBlock Text="From:"
```

```
                  Margin="4"/>
        <TextBox x:Name="fromValue"
                 Text="100"
                 Width="100"
                 MaxLength="10"
                 Margin="4"/>
        <TextBlock Text="To:"
                   Margin="4"/>
        <TextBox x:Name="toValue"
                 Text="1000000000"
                 Width="100"
                 MaxLength="10"
                 Margin="4"/>

        <Button x:Name="calculateButton"
                Content="Calculate"
                Margin="4"
                Padding="8 2"
                Click="OnCalculateClicked"/>
    </StackPanel>

    <TextBlock x:Name="oddResultBlock"
               Grid.Row="1"
               Text="Total odd numbers: 0"
               Margin="4"/>

    <TextBlock x:Name="evenResultBlock"
               Grid.Row="2"
               Text="Total even numbers: 0"
               Margin="4"/>
</Grid>
```

3. Navigate to the `MainWindow.xaml.cs` file and add the following two member-variables to store the total count of odd and even numbers:

```
private int totalOdd = 0;
private int totalEven = 0;
```

4. We will now create a method to calculate the odd and even numbers. Inside the `MainWindow` class, create a method named `CalculateOddEven`, and implement the code block as shown in this following code snippet:

```
private void CalculateOddEven(int from, int to)
{
    for (int i = from; i <= to; i++)
    {
        if (i % 2 == 0) { totalEven++; }
        else { totalOdd++; }
    }
}
```

5. Now, we need to invoke the call. Let's implement the button click event `OnCalculateClicked` to call the `CalculateOddEven` method and display the result:

```
private void OnCalculateClicked(object sender,
                        RoutedEventArgs e)
{
    totalOdd = 0;
    totalEven = 0;

    if (int.TryParse(fromValue.Text, out int from) &&
        int.TryParse(toValue.Text, out int to))
    {
        calculateButton.IsEnabled = false;

        CalculateOddEven(from, to);

        oddResultBlock.Text = "Total odd numbers: " +
                              totalOdd;
        evenResultBlock.Text = "Total even numbers: " +
                               totalEven;
        calculateButton.IsEnabled = true;
    }
}
```

6. Run the application and click on the **Calculate** button. The UI will freeze for some time while the long running operation is in-progress, as it finds out the odd and even numbers between the `100 - 1000000000` range. Once the calculation completes, it will unfreeze the UI and display the result:

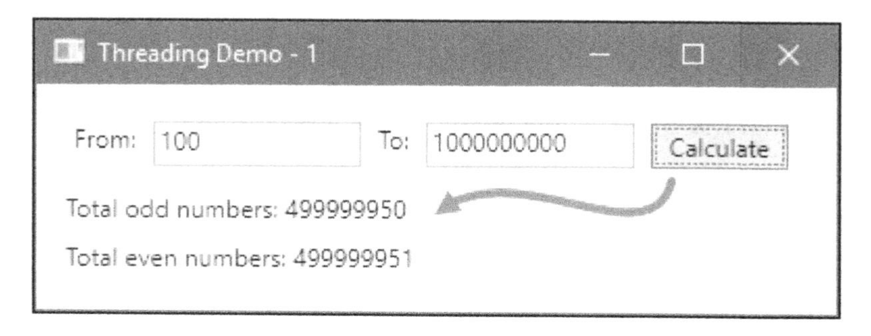

7. To resolve this issue, we should move the long running process to a different thread so that the UI thread keeps responding. We will be using a thread pool to move the process to a different thread. You can also perform this by creating a new `Thread` instance or by using `Task`.
8. In this example, we will be using thread pool. This can be done by calling `ThreadPool.QueueUserWorkItem`, as shown in the following code snippet:

```
ThreadPool.QueueUserWorkItem(_ =>
{
    CalculateOddEven(from, to);
});
```

9. Now, we need to update the UI once the operation gets completed. This can't be done outside the `ThreadPool.QueueUserWorkItem` block, as the operation will run in a different thread. The same can't be done directly inside the `ThreadPool.QueueUserWorkItem` block too, as the update should be performed in the UI thread. For this to work, the `Dispatcher.BeginInvoke` block can be used within the `ThreadPool.QueueUserWorkItem` block, as shown in the following code snippet:

```
ThreadPool.QueueUserWorkItem(_ =>
{
    CalculateOddEven(from, to);

    Dispatcher.BeginInvoke(new Action(() =>
    {
```

```
                oddResultBlock.Text = "Total odd numbers: " +
                                      totalOdd;
                evenResultBlock.Text = "Total even numbers: " +
                                       totalEven;
                calculateButton.IsEnabled = true;
            }));
        });
```

10. Let's run the application once again. Click on the **Calculate** button. You will observe that the UI is responsive while the long running operation is in progress.

How it works...

Each and every element in WPF inherits from `DispatcherObject`, and thus, the UI thread is always associated with `System.Windows.Threading.Dispatcher`. This is the reason why the `Dispatcher` object can be accessed any time by using the `DispatcherObject.Dispatcher` property.

`ThreadPool.QueueUserWorkItem` causes a delegate to execute on the CLRs thread pool. Thus, the operation performed within that delegate never executes on the UI thread.

Once the operation completes, and you need to update the UI, you must update this from the UI thread. The call to `Dispatcher.BeginInvoke` causes the delegate to run on the UI thread and make the necessary changes to the UI.

A point to note is that the dispatcher is also accessible from the UI thread, using the static property `Dispatcher.CurrentDispatcher`.

There's more...

There are two kinds of invocations by `Dispatcher`—`BeginInvoke` and `Invoke`. We have already seen the uses of `BeginInvoke`, which basically invokes `delegate` and returns to perform other operations while `delegate` is still running on the UI thread.

On the other side, the `Invoke` operation does not return until `delegate` completes its execution on the UI thread.

`BeginInvoke` is always preferable unless there is a specific reason to wait for the UI operation to complete.

`Dispatcher` maintains a queue of requests that need to be processed on the UI thread. This is basically handled by setting `DispatcherPriority`. The default priority is `DispatcherPriority.Normal`, but you can set a lower or a higher priority based on the importance of the operation.

Adding cancelation support to long running threads

When you execute a long running process on a different thread, to keep the UI responsive during the operation, you may want to provide a functionality to cancel the operation. This can be done on an on-demand basis.

In this recipe, we will learn how to add cancellation support to the existing long running operation that we have built in the previous recipe.

Getting ready

We will be using the same example that we used in the previous recipe. You can copy the entire `CH10.ThreadingDemo1` project folder and give it a new name, `CH10.ThreadingDemo2`. Launch Visual Studio and open the new (`CH10.ThreadingDemo2`) project inside it.

How to do it...

Follow these steps to update the existing project and to have cancellation support during the long running process:

1. Navigate to the `MainWindow.xaml` file and modify the UI to have a `Cancel` button in it. Add the following button control inside `StackPanel`, and label it as `Cancel`:

```
<Button x:Name="cancelButton"
        Content="Cancel"
        IsEnabled="False"
        Margin="4"
        Padding="8 2"
        Click="OnCancelClicked"/>
```

2. Make sure to set its `IsEnabled` property to `False`.
3. Now, navigate to the `MainWindow.xaml.cs` file and add the following member variable inside the class:

```
private CancellationTokenSource tokenSource = null;
```

4. On the `Cancel` button click, we need to cancel the running operation. Let's modify the `OnCancelClicked` event to perform the same as the following code snippet:

```
private void OnCancelClicked(object sender,
                             RoutedEventArgs e)
{
    if (tokenSource != null)
    {
        tokenSource.Cancel();
        tokenSource = null;
    }
}
```

5. Let's navigate to the `CalculateOddEven` method and modify it to accept a third parameter of type `CancellationToken`:

```
private void CalculateOddEven(int from,
                              int to,
                              CancellationToken token)
```

6. Inside the `for` loop of the `CalculateOddEven` method, check whether the `CancellationToken.IsCancellationRequested` is `true`, and if so, return immediately after setting the `totalOdd` and `totalEven` values to `-1`:

```
for (int i = from; i <= to; i++)
{
    if (token.IsCancellationRequested)
    {
        totalOdd = -1;
        totalEven = -1;
        return;
    }
```

7. For reference, here's the modified code of the `CalculateOddEven` method implementation:

```
private void CalculateOddEven(int from,
                              int to,
                              CancellationToken token)
{
    for (int i = from; i <= to; i++)
    {
        if (token.IsCancellationRequested)
        {
            totalOdd = -1;
            totalEven = -1;
            return;
        }

        if (i % 2 == 0) { totalEven++; }
        else { totalOdd++; }
    }
}
```

8. On `OnCalculateClicked` event implementation, we need to perform some changes. First create the instance of `CancellationTokenSource` and assign it to the `tokenSource` variable.
9. Then, pass the instance to the `CalculateOddEven` method as the third parameter value.

10. Then, inside the `Dispatcher.BeginInvoke` call, modify the code to display **Operation canceled!** based on the value of `totalOdd` and `totalEven` variables. Display the message only if either of them is `-1`. Here's the complete implementation:

```
tokenSource = new CancellationTokenSource();
ThreadPool.QueueUserWorkItem(_ =>
{
    CalculateOddEven(from, to, tokenSource.Token);

    Dispatcher.BeginInvoke(new Action(() =>
    {
        if (totalOdd < 0 || totalEven < 0)
        {
            oddResultBlock.Text = "Operation canceled!";
            evenResultBlock.Text = string.Empty;
        }
        else
        {
            oddResultBlock.Text = "Total odd numbers: " +
                                   totalOdd;
            evenResultBlock.Text = "Total even numbers: " +
                                    totalEven;
        }

        calculateButton.IsEnabled = true;
        cancelButton.IsEnabled = false;
    }));
});
```

11. Once done, let's run the application. Click the **Calculate** button to start the process in a separate thread in the thread pool:

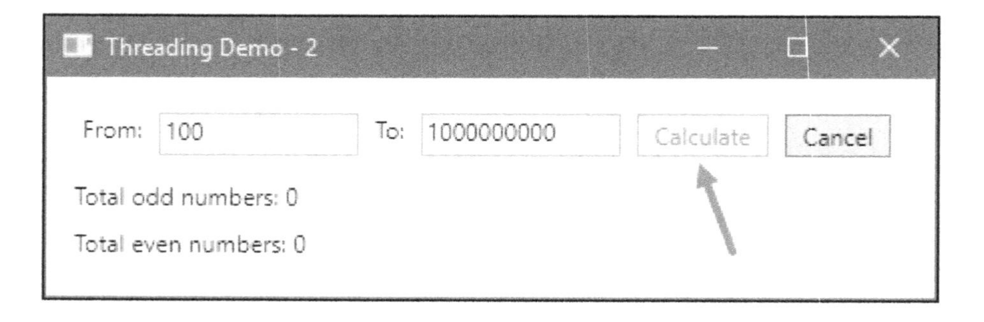

12. While the operation is in progress, click the **Cancel** button. You will see that the process immediately stops and the **Operation canceled!** message gets displayed in the UI:

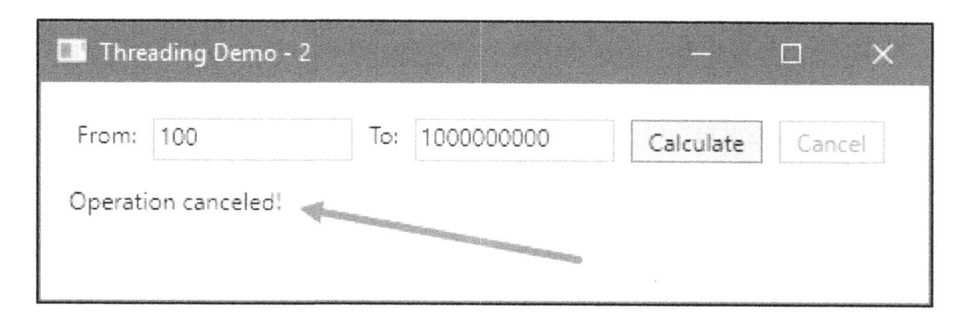

13. Let's click on the `Calculate` button once again and wait until the process ends. What can you see now? It displays the total count of odd and even numbers on the UI.

How it works...

`CancellationTokenSource` represents a logical operation that can be canceled. The `Token` property of `CancellationTokenSource` provides the token object that provides the part of the logical operation.

Whenever the `Cancel()` method gets called on the `CancellationTokenSource` object, all distributed tokens from that source get their `IsCancellationRequested` property set as `true`.

In our example, the `for` loop inside our `CalculateOddEven` method polls the `IsCancellationRequested` property and fills the `totalOdd` and `totalEven` member variables with `-1`, which can be used to understand that a cancellation call was performed. Based on that value, the **Operation canceled!** message gets displayed on the screen.

Using the background worker component

In the previous recipes, we used thread pool to perform long running operations in a different thread. From there, we had to update the UI by marshalling the code to the UI thread, which required additional work.

To overcome this explicit thread pooling and the marshalling of the UI updation on the UI thread, we can use the `System.ComponentModel.BackgroundWorker` class. It provides automatic management of long running operations on a background thread.

In this recipe, we will use that `BackgroundWorker` to do the asynchronous operations without blocking the UI thread.

Getting ready

We will be using the same example that we have used in previous recipes. You can copy the entire `CH10.ThreadingDemo1` project folder and create a new one with the name `CH10.ThreadingDemo3`. Launch Visual Studio and open the new project.

How to do it...

Follow these steps to use a background worker, to perform the long running process, and to count the odd and even numbers within a range:

1. From **Solution Explorer**, navigate to the `MainWindow.xaml.cs` file.
2. Add the following `using` namespace—`System.ComponentModel`, so that we can use the `BackgroundWorker` class.
3. Inside the `OnCalculateClicked` event, instead of calling `ThreadPool` to execute the operation, create an instance of the `BackgroundWorker` class.
4. Register the worker events `DoWork` and `RunWorkerCompleted`.
5. Call the `RunWorkerAsync` method of the background worker by passing the numeric range as an argument. The argument accepts objects, hence, we will use `Tuple<int, int>` as the data type for simplicity. The complete code looks as follows:

```
private void OnCalculateClicked(object sender,
  RoutedEventArgs e)
{
    totalOdd = 0;
    totalEven = 0;

    if (int.TryParse(fromValue.Text, out int from) &&
        int.TryParse(toValue.Text, out int to))
    {
        calculateButton.IsEnabled = false;
```

```
            var worker = new BackgroundWorker();
            worker.DoWork += OnWorker_DoWork;
            worker.RunWorkerCompleted +=
                           OnWorker_WorkCompleted;
            worker.RunWorkerAsync(new Tuple<int, int>(from, to));
        }
    }
```

6. Let's modify the `OnWorker_DoWork` event implementation to extract the argument first. Then, call the long running method (`CalculateOddEven`) by passing the values extracted from the argument:

```
    private void OnWorker_DoWork(object sender,
       DoWorkEventArgs e)
    {
        var argument = (Tuple<int, int>)e.Argument;
        CalculateOddEven(argument.Item1, argument.Item2);
    }
```

7. In the `OnWorker_WorkCompleted` event implementation, release the `BackgroundWorker` instance and then update the UI based on the values. Here's the code for your reference:

```
    private void OnWorker_WorkCompleted(object sender,
     RunWorkerCompletedEventArgs e)
    {
        if (sender is BackgroundWorker worker)
        {
            worker.RunWorkerCompleted -=
             OnWorker_WorkCompleted;
            worker.DoWork -= OnWorker_DoWork;
            worker = null;
        }

        oddResultBlock.Text = "Total odd numbers: " +
          totalOdd;
        evenResultBlock.Text = "Total even numbers: " +
          totalEven;

        calculateButton.IsEnabled = true;
    }
```

8. Once this is done, let's run the application. You will see the same application UI as we saw in the first example:

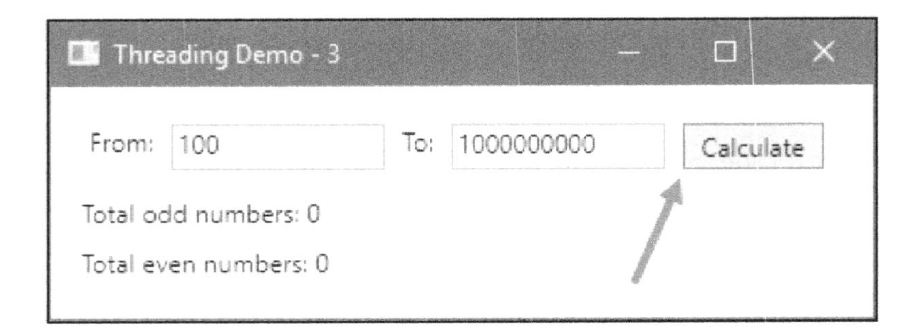

9. Click on the `Calculate` button. You will observe that the application is responding while the execution is happening in the background worker process.
10. Once the execution completes, it displays the result in the UI.

How it works...

`BackgroundWorker` exposes events to coordinate the work. When you call the `RunWorkerAsync` method, the `DoWork` event is raised on the thread pool thread. You can pass an optional `Argument` to the `RunWorkerAsync` method, which can be retrieved from the `DoWorkEventArgs.Argument` property inside the `DoWork` event handler.

As the `DoWork` event handler executes on a thread pool thread, accessing UI controls inside the `DoWork` handler will throw `Exception`. For this reason, pass the value from the UI as an argument to the `RunWorkerAsync` method.

When the `DoWork` event handler completes its execution, `BackgroundWorker` raises the `RunWorkerCompleted` event. This runs on the UI thread, and thus, you can perform UI operations from this event handler. If you have passed any value from the `DoWork` handler, you can retrieve it here from the `RunWorkerCompletedEventArgs.Result` property.

There's more...

To show the current progress indication of the long running background operation, you can raise the `ProgressChanged` event on the worker process and update the UI directly from here. The `ProgressChanged` handler runs in the UI thread and occurs when `BackgroundWorker.ReportProgress(System.Int32)` is called from the `DoWork` handler. For this to work, make sure that you have set the `WorkerReportsProgress` property of the worker to `true`.

You can also check whether `BackgroundWorker` is running an asynchronous operation. The `IsBusy` property will return `true` if it is running the background operation.

In case you want to cancel a running background worker, you can call the `CancelAsync()` method of the worker to request cancellation of a pending background operation. If `BackgroundWorker.WorkerSupportsCancellation` is set as `false`, it will throw `InvalidOperationException`.

Using a timer to periodically update the UI

It is often require to update a portion of the user interface periodically. In that case, a timer object is beneficial to keep the UI refreshed. For example, in your application, you may want to show the current time at some part of the UI. For this, you can use a timer to periodically update the UI without the need to create a different thread.

The `System.Windows.Threading.DispatcherTimer` class can be used to integrate into the `Dispatcher` queue, and can process at a specified interval of time and at a specified priority.

In this recipe, we will use the `DispatcherTimer` class to implement a timer, which will execute its subscribed `Tick` event each time the specified `Interval` is met.

Getting ready

Open Visual Studio and create a new WPF application project. Name it `CH10.DispatcherTimerDemo`.

How to do it...

Follow these steps to create a digital clock experience with a timer:

1. From **Solution Explorer**, navigate to the `MainWindow.xaml` page.
2. Divide the default `Grid` into three rows, as follows:

```
<Grid.RowDefinitions>
    <RowDefinition Height="*"/>
    <RowDefinition Height="20"/>
    <RowDefinition Height="Auto"/>
</Grid.RowDefinitions>
```

3. Add a `TextBlock` control at the `Grid.Row="0"` position and align it to the center:

```
<TextBlock x:Name="clock"
           Grid.Row="0"
           Text="00:00:00"
           FontSize="80"
           HorizontalAlignment="Center"
           VerticalAlignment="Center"/>
```

4. Add a `StackPanel` at `Grid.Row="2"` and insert two buttons inside it. Name the buttons `startButton` and `stopButton`. Also, register the `Click` events for both the buttons as `OnStartTimer` and `OnStopTimer`, respectively:

```
<StackPanel Grid.Row="2"
            Margin="10"
            Orientation="Horizontal"
            HorizontalAlignment="Center"
            VerticalAlignment="Center">
    <Button x:Name="startButton"
            Content="Start"
            Margin="4"
            Height="26"
            Width="100"
            Click="OnStartTimer"/>
    <Button x:Name="stopButton"
            Content="Stop"
            Margin="4"
            Height="26"
            Width="100"
            IsEnabled="False"
            Click="OnStopTimer"/>
</StackPanel>
```

5. Now, navigate to `MainWindow.xaml.cs` to add the code behind the logic.
6. First, add the following namespaces in the class file:

```
using System;
using System.Windows;
using System.Windows.Threading;
```

7. Inside the class, declare a private member variable (`dispatcherTimer`) of type `DispatcherTimer`:

```
private DispatcherTimer dispatcherTimer = null;
```

8. Inside the constructor of the class, let's create the instance of `DispatcherTimer` and raise its `Tick` event to trigger after every `1` second of interval. Here's the code:

```
public MainWindow()
{
    InitializeComponent();

    dispatcherTimer = new DispatcherTimer();
    dispatcherTimer.Interval = TimeSpan.FromSeconds(1.0);
    dispatcherTimer.Tick += OnTimerTick;
}
```

9. Now, inside the `Tick` event implementation, set the `Text` property of the `TextBlock` control (`clock`) to the current time in `hh:mm:ss` format:

```
private void OnTimerTick(object sender,
 EventArgs e)
{
    clock.Text = DateTime.Now.ToString("hh:mm:ss");
}
```

10. When a user clicks on the **Start** button, the `OnStartTimer` event handler will fire. Inside it, let's start the timer by calling the `Start()` method on the `dispatcherTimer` instance. Alternatively, you can also set the `dispatcherTimer.IsEnabled` property to `true` to start the timer:

```
private void OnStartTimer(object sender,
 RoutedEventArgs e)
{
    if (dispatcherTimer != null)
    {
        dispatcherTimer.Start();
```

```
                startButton.IsEnabled = false;
                stopButton.IsEnabled = true;
            }
        }
```

11. When the handler `OnStopTimer` raises, on a click of the **Stop** button we will call the `Stop()` method of the `dispatcherTimer` instance. Here, also, you can set the `dispatcherTimer.IsEnabled` property as an alternate method to stop the timer, but in this case, you will have to set it as `false`:

```
        private void OnStopTimer(object sender,
         RoutedEventArgs e)
        {
            if (dispatcherTimer != null)
            {
                dispatcherTimer.Stop();

                startButton.IsEnabled = true;
                stopButton.IsEnabled = false;
            }
        }
```

12. Now run the application. You will see the following output on the screen:

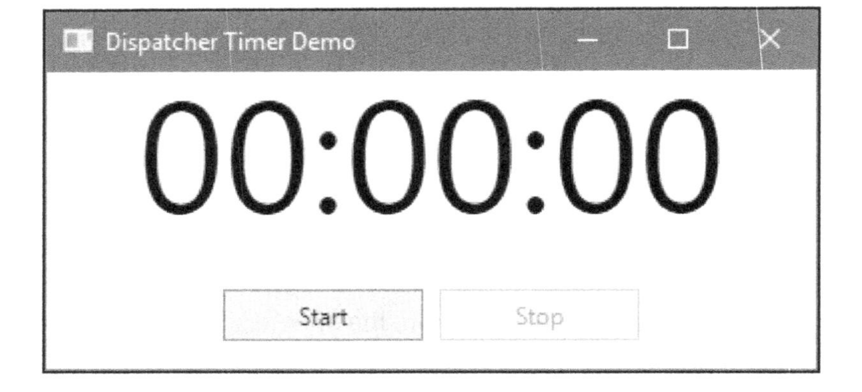

13. Observe the text in the UI, where it is being displayed as `00:00:00`. Now click on the **Start** button. This will now change the text to the current time of your system, and it will refresh after every second:

14. As the time is ticking on the UI, after every second of interval, click on the **Stop** button. This will cause the running timer on the screen to stop.
15. Clicking on the **Start** button again will start the timer and show the current time on the screen. The time displayed on the UI will refresh after every second.

How it works...

When you use a `DispatcherTimer` object, it represents a timer that is bound to the UI thread. The `Interval` property of the `DispatcherTimer` class indicates the period of the timer for the `Tick` event to raise, and continues ticking until explicitly stopped.

To start the timer, you can call its `Start()` method, or set the `IsEnabled` property to `true`. Similarly, to stop a timer, you can call the `Stop()` method, or set the `IsEnabled` property to `false`.

Never perform any lengthy operations in the `Tick` event, as it runs on the UI thread. Long running operations may block the UI from responding.

11

Interoperability with Win32 and WinForm

In this chapter, we will cover the following recipes:

- Hosting WinForm controls in WPF applications
- Hosting WPF controls in WinForm applications
- Calling Win32 APIs from WPF applications
- Embedding ActiveX controls in WPF applications

Introduction

The term **interoperability** describes the capability of different applications to exchange data via a common set of exchangeable formats. It is a characteristic of the product or system, whose interfaces are completely understood, to work with other products or systems.

WPF and Windows Forms present two different architectures for creating application interfaces. The `WindowsFormsHost` and `ElementHost` classes are used to implement the interoperation capabilities between these two.

Similarly, WPF provides interoperability with Win32 programs, which are written in unmanaged C++ code:

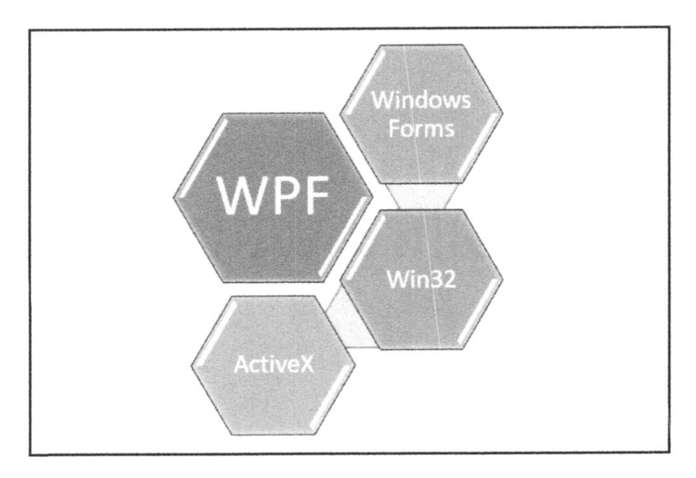

In this chapter, we will start with interoperation between WPF and WinForm, demonstrating the way to host a WinForm control in a WPF application and a WPF control in a WinForm application. Then, we will move forward to learn interoperability between WPF and Win32, followed by embedding ActiveX controls inside WPF.

Hosting WinForm controls in WPF applications

Though **Windows Platform Foundation** (**WPF**) provides a huge set of controls with a rich set of features, there can still be chances of various cases when you have some **Windows Form** (**WinForm**) controls that are not available in WPF. There could be some cases too, when you are porting your WinForm application to WPF, where you have no other choice than reusing existing controls and/or forms, as the reimplementation will burn huge efforts. So, what needs to be done in such cases?

WPF provides a way to reuse existing controls from Windows Forms and host them inside it (whether in a control, a window, or a page). This is called interoperation between the two platforms as they present two different architectures for creating application interfaces.

The `System.Windows.Forms.Integration` namespace provides you with the classes that enable the common interoperation scenarios, whereas the `WindowsFormsHost` class provides you with the capability to implement the interoperation.

When implementing interoperation between the two technologies to host a Windows Forms control inside WPF, the following scenarios may occur applicable:

- One or more WinForm controls can be hosted in WPF
- One or more composite controls can be hosted in a WPF element
- One or more ActiveX controls can also be hosted in WPF
- The WinForm container controls containing other WinForm controls can also be hosted
- You can also host a master/detail form with WPF as master, WinForm as details, and/or WinForm as master, and WPF as details

A point to note is that multilevel hybrid controls are not supported. A **multilevel hybrid control** contains a control from one technology inside a control from another technology.

In this recipe, we will take WinForm's `PropertyGrid` control as an example, which is not available in WPF, and will host it inside a WPF window using the `WindowsFormsHost` control.

Getting ready

Let's start by creating a new WPF application. Open your Visual Studio IDE, and create a new project named `CH11.WinFormInWpfXamlDemo`. Make sure to select **WPF App** as the project template.

How to do it...

Follow these steps to host a WinForm control inside a WPF application window and map its properties:

1. Begin with opening the WPF application window. From **Solution Explorer**, open the `MainWindow.xaml` file.

2. Let's split the default Grid panel to have two columns. The second column will have a width based on its child elements, and the first column will accommodate the rest of the space. Add the following XAML mark-up inside Grid to split it by the specific requirement:

```
<Grid.ColumnDefinitions>
    <ColumnDefinition Width="*"/>
    <ColumnDefinition Width="Auto"/>
</Grid.ColumnDefinitions>
```

3. Place a TextBlock control inside the first cell (0th column) of Grid, name it as txtBlock, and set Hello World! as its Text property:

```
<TextBlock x:Name="txtBlock"
           Grid.Column="0"
           Margin="8"
           Text="Hello World!"/>
```

4. Now, after the TextBlock control, add a <WindowsFormsHost> </WindowsFormsHost> element. When added, this will throw the following design-time error message—**WindowsFormsHost is not supported in a Windows Presentation Foundation (WPF) project**. This is because the required assembly to resolve the WindowsFormsHost element is not referenced in this project:

```
<Window x:Class="CH11.WinFormInWpfXamlDemo.MainWindow"
        xmlns="http://schemas.microsoft.com/winfx/2006/xaml/presentation"
        xmlns:x="http://schemas.microsoft.com/winfx/2006/xaml"
        x:Name="window" Title="Hosting WinForm Control in WPF"
        Height="300" Width="600">
    <Grid>
        <Grid.ColumnDefinitions>
            <ColumnDefinition Width="*"/>
            <ColumnDefinition Width="Auto"/>
        </Grid.ColumnDefinitions>
        <TextBlock x:Name="txtBlock"
                   Grid.Column="0"
                   Margin="8"
                   Text="Hello World!"/>
        <WindowsFormsHost>

        </WindowsFormsHost>
    </Grid>
</Window>
```

WindowsFormsHost is not supported in a Windows Presentation Foundation (WPF) project.

5. To add the dependent assembly references in the project, right-click on the project node and select **Add | Reference...** from the context menu entries.
6. From the **Reference Manager** dialog window, check the following two assembly references (**System.Windows.Forms** and **WindowsFormsIntegration**) and click **OK**, which will add the references in the project:

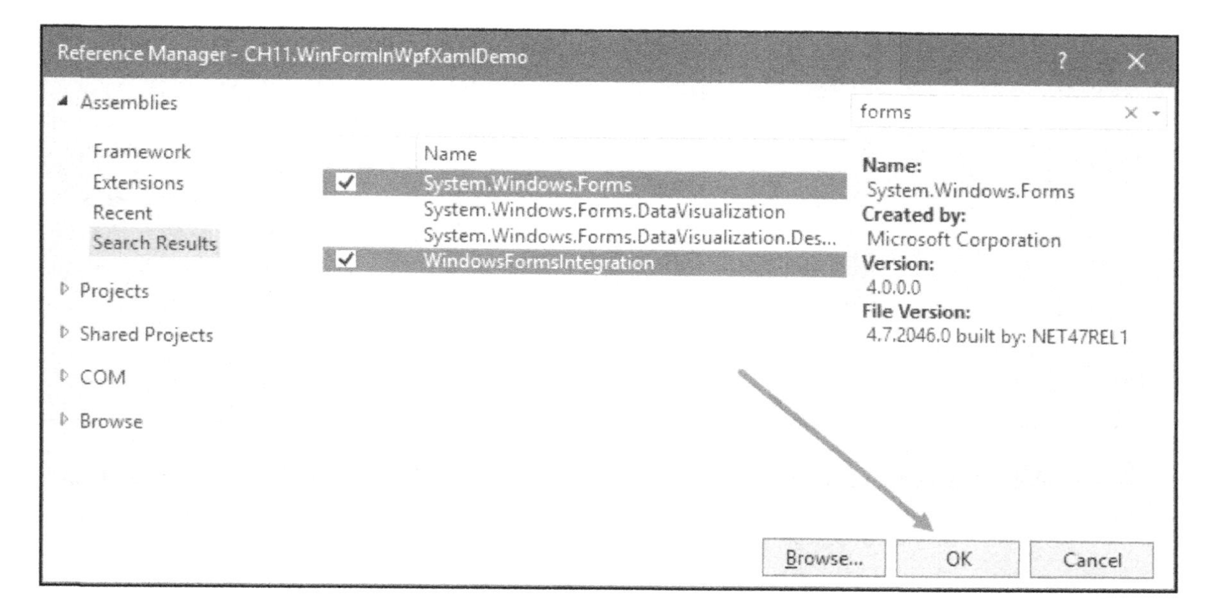

7. Check the XAML file now. The preceding design-time error will now go away, as the required assembly reference has been established.
8. Position the `<WindowsFormsHost>` in the second column (`Grid.Column="1"`) and set its `Width` property to `300`.
9. Now, inside the `WindowsFormsHost` element, place another element of type `PropertyGrid`.

10. You need to add the XMLNS namespace for the `PropertyGrid` to resolve from the `System.Windows.Forms` assembly. As shown in the following screenshot, click the lightbulb icon, or simply press *CTRL* + to add the required XMLNS entry to the `MainWindow.xaml` file:

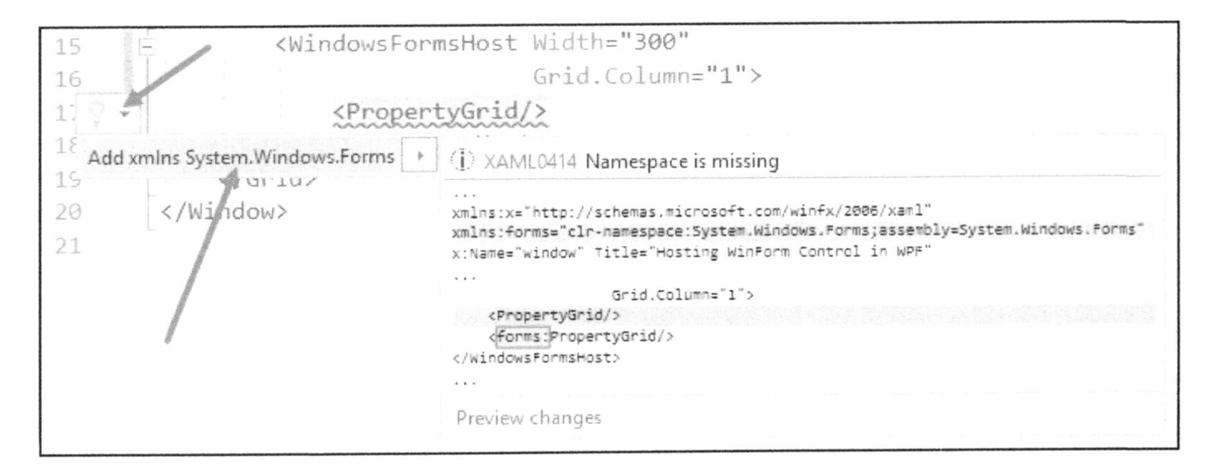

11. Alternatively, you can add the following XMLNS declaration to the `Window` tag:

```
xmlns:forms="clr-namespace:System.Windows.Forms;
             assembly=System.Windows.Forms"
```

12. Add `x:Name="propertyGrid"` to the `PropertyGrid` element to define it with a name. This will be useful later when we want to access it from the code. Here's the complete XAML markup of the `Grid` that we will be using here:

```
<Grid>
    <Grid.ColumnDefinitions>
        <ColumnDefinition Width="*"/>
        <ColumnDefinition Width="Auto"/>
    </Grid.ColumnDefinitions>
    <TextBlock x:Name="txtBlock"
               Grid.Column="0"
               Margin="8"
               Text="Hello World!"/>
    <WindowsFormsHost Width="300"
                      Grid.Column="1">
        <forms:PropertyGrid x:Name="propertyGrid"/>
    </WindowsFormsHost>
</Grid>
```

13. Once done, let's run the application. You will see the following output, having text and an empty property grid:

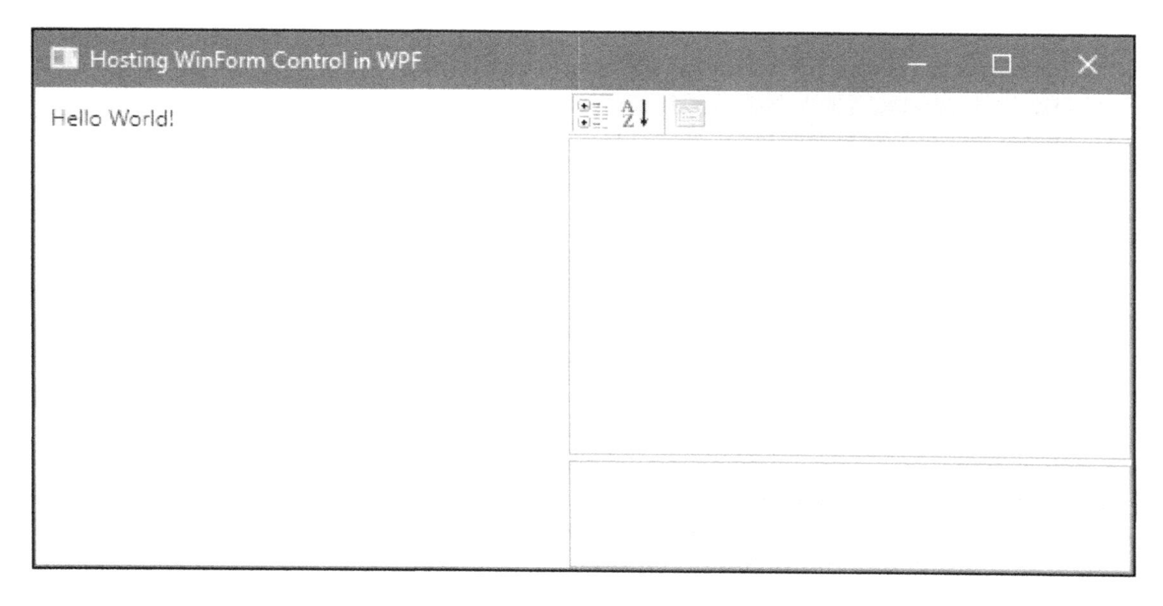

14. Let's navigate to the code behind file (`MainWindow.xaml.cs`) of the application window.
15. Just after the `InitializeComponent()` call inside the constructor of `MainWindow`, add the following line, `propertyGrid.SelectedObject = txtBlock;`, to set the `SelectionObject` property of the property grid that we have already added in the UI. After this change, the code will look as follows:

```
public partial class MainWindow : Window
{
    public MainWindow()
    {
        InitializeComponent();

        propertyGrid.SelectedObject = txtBlock;
    }
}
```

16. Let's run the application again. This time you will see that the property grid contains a set of properties, pointing to the `txtBlock` control placed in the window:

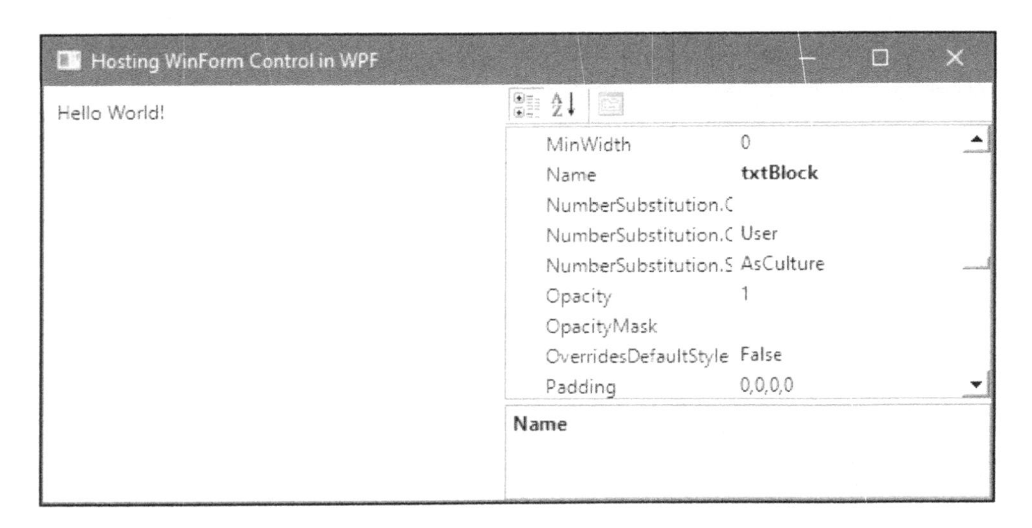

17. Scroll up the property grid and change the **FontSize** property inside the grid to `40`. This will have immediate effect to the font-size of the text that we have added in the UI:

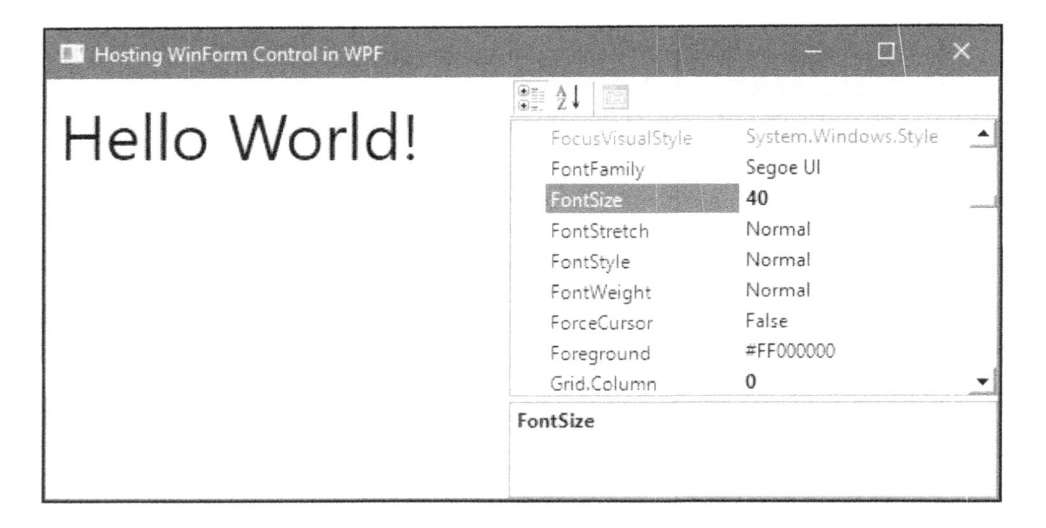

18. Similarly, change some other properties such as **HorizontalAlignment**, **VerticalAlignment**, **FontStyle**, **FontWeight**, **Foreground**, and so on, and see the effect on the screen:

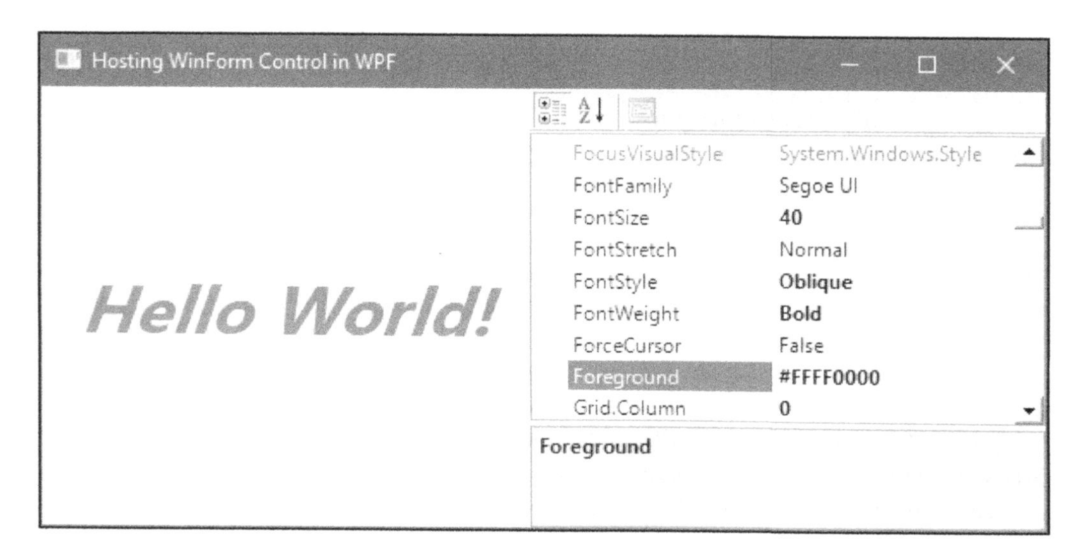

How it works...

The `PropertyGrid` control, part of the .NET Framework, allows you to browse, view, and edit the properties of one or more objects. It uses reflection to retrieve and display properties of any object or type.

Reflection is a technology that allows you to retrieve the type information at runtime.

If you are using WinForm, you will be able to use the `PropertyGrid` control easily from the control toolbar. But, unfortunately, this control is not available in WPF. To use this inside a WPF application, you will need to use the interoperability of WPF and WinForm. For this to work, we need to use the `WindowsFormsHost` class.

The `WindowsFormsHost` class allows you to host a Windows Forms control on a WPF page. It is part of the `System.Windows.Forms.Integration` namespace and it is available inside the `WindowsFormsIntegration.dll` assembly. That's the reason why we had to reference the `System.Windows.Forms` and `WindowsFormsIntegration` assemblies inside the project.

The default location for the `WindowsFormsIntegration.dll` assembly is `%programfiles%Reference AssembliesMicrosoftFrameworkv3.0`, which comes with the other WPF assemblies.

Once the hosting of the WinForm control is successful inside a WPF window, you can then set/get its properties. In the preceding example, we assigned the `txtBlock` control (which is a WPF control) as the `SelectedObject` property of the `propertyGrid` control (which is a WinForm control). Thus, when you run the application, it uses reflection to retrieve all the properties exposed by the `TextBlock` control (`txtBlock`) and populates those inside the `PropertyGrid` with the default values set to each one of them. When you modify a property value at runtime, it changes the associated control based on the selection. Hence, you can see a change in the UI of `TextBlock`, when you change the `FontSize`, `Foreground`, and other properties.

There's more...

Though most of the properties work with `WindowsFormsHost`, there are some limitations with **z-order** and transformations when used in a hybrid application. By default, the `WindowsFormsHost` elements are drawn on top of other WPF elements, and thus there exists no-effect of the z-order property on that.

If you want to enable z-ordering, set the `IsRedirected` property of the `WindowsFormsHost` to `True`, and the `CompositionMode` property to either `CompositionMode.Full` or `CompositionMode.OutputOnly`.

As the WinForm controls do not support proper scaling and rotating features, the `WindowsFormsHost` element does not scale or rotate with other WPF elements. To enable these transforming features, such as z-ordering, set the `IsRedirected` property to `True` and the `CompositionMode` property to either `CompositionMode.Full` or `CompositionMode.OutputOnly`.

Hosting WPF controls in WinForm applications

As WPF provides a rich user interface to applications, you may want to apply the same to your existing applications. But when you have a large Windows Form application project, where you already made a large investment, you won't like to reinvest on the same to scrap it and rewrite the entire project in WPF.

In such cases, WPF interoperation with WinForms is ideal. Using this, you can embed a WPF control inside a form and leverage the additional features of WPF, wherever possible.

In the previous recipe, we learned how to host WinForm controls into a WPF application. But in this recipe, we will learn the reverse, that is, how to host a **WPF composite control** in a **Windows Forms** application. We will learn this by following some simple walkthrough steps. You can extend this procedure later to host more complex applications and controls.

This walkthrough will basically be divided into two logical parts. In the first part, we will build a WPF UserControl, and in the second part, we will host it inside a form window.

Getting ready

Before we start with this recipe to host a WPF control in a Windows Form, make sure that Visual Studio is up and running.

How to do it...

Let's follow these steps to create a WPF composite control and host it inside the Windows Form:

1. First, let's create a **WPF User Control Library** project. To do this, from **Solution Explorer**, right-click on the existing solution and select **Add** | **New Project...** from the context menu.

2. Select **WPF User Control Library (.NET Framework)** as the project template, name it as `CH11.WpfUserControlLibrary`, and click the **OK** button, as shown in the following screenshot:

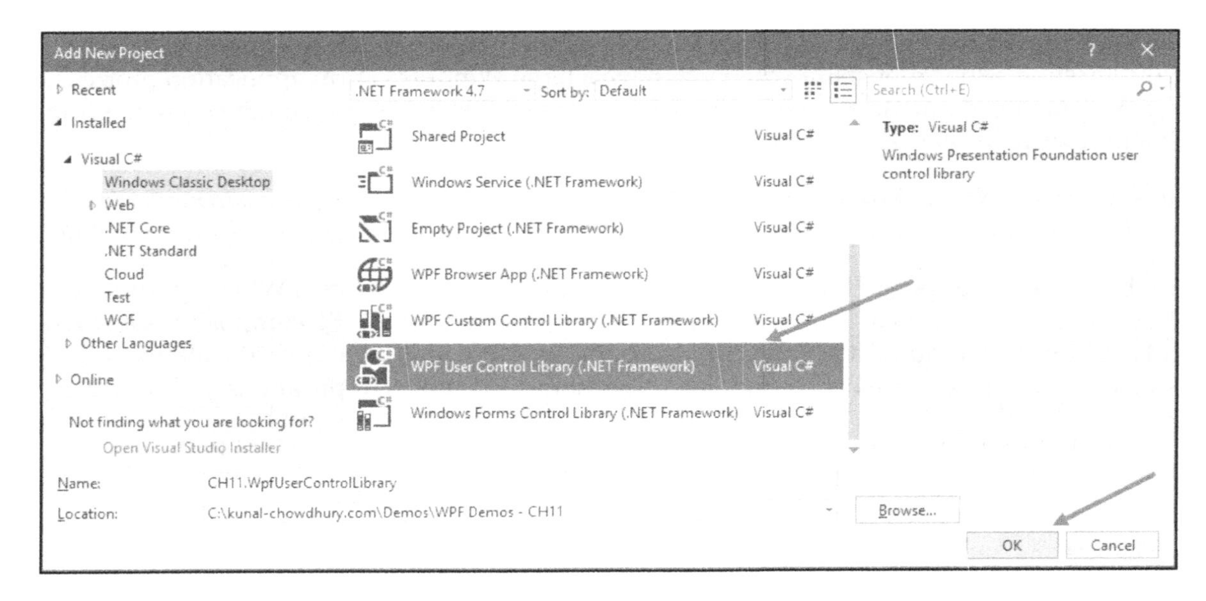

3. Once the project gets created by Visual Studio, you will find a user control named `UserControl1.xaml`, inside the project folder. From **Solution Explorer**, double-click on it to open it.
4. Divide the default `Grid` of the `UserControl1` into two columns. Set the first column as stretchable to occupy maximum available space and set the second column as `Auto`:

```
<Grid.ColumnDefinitions>
    <ColumnDefinition Width="*"/>
    <ColumnDefinition Width="Auto"/>
</Grid.ColumnDefinitions>
```

5. Place a `TextBox` control inside the first column and name it as `searchBox`:

```
<TextBox x:Name="searchBox"
         Grid.Column="0"
         MinWidth="100"
         Margin="4"/>
```

6. Place a `Button` control, named `searchButton`, and place it inside the second column of the `Grid`. Set its `Content` property to **Search** and register its `Click` event with `OnSearchButtonClicked`:

```
<Button x:Name="searchButton"
        Content="Search"
        Grid.Column="1"
        Padding="8 2"
        Margin="4"
        Click="OnSearchButtonClicked"/>
```

7. Here's the complete XAML of `Grid`:

```
<Grid>
    <Grid.ColumnDefinitions>
        <ColumnDefinition Width="*"/>
        <ColumnDefinition Width="Auto"/>
    </Grid.ColumnDefinitions>

    <TextBox x:Name="searchBox"
             Grid.Column="0"
             MinWidth="100"
             Margin="4"/>
    <Button x:Name="searchButton"
            Content="Search"
            Grid.Column="1"
            Padding="8 2"
            Margin="4"
            Click="OnSearchButtonClicked"/>
</Grid>
```

8. Now, press *F7* to navigate to the code behind the `UserControl1.xaml.cs` file.
9. Insert the following event implementation inside the class:

```
private void OnSearchButtonClicked(object sender,
                                   RoutedEventArgs e)
{
    MessageBox.Show("You searched for: {" +
                    searchBox.Text + "}");
}
```

10. Now, it's time to integrate the created user control inside a Windows Form. For this, we need a WinForm project. Let's add the new project inside the solution. To do this, from **Solution Explorer**, right-click on the solution file and select **Add** | **New Project...** from the context menu. Use the following **Windows Forms App (.NET Framework)** template during project creation. Name it as `CH11.WpfInWinFormDemo` and click the **OK** button:

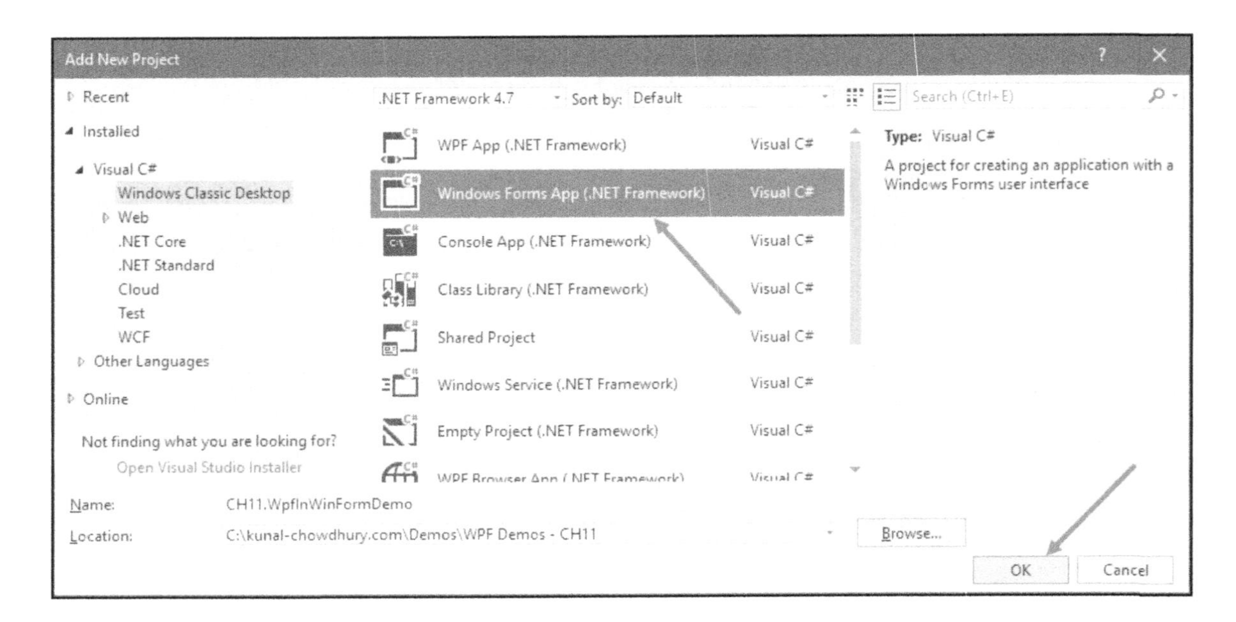

11. Once the project gets created, you need to add the reference of the UserControl Library into this project. To do so, right-click on the **References** node of the `CH11.WpfInWinFormDemo` project and then click **Add Reference...** from the context menu.

12. From the **Reference Manager** dialog, as shown in the following screenshot, expand the **Projects** entry, select the desired library project (in our case, it is **CH11.WpfUserControlLibrary**), and click **OK**. This will add the reference of the library into the project:

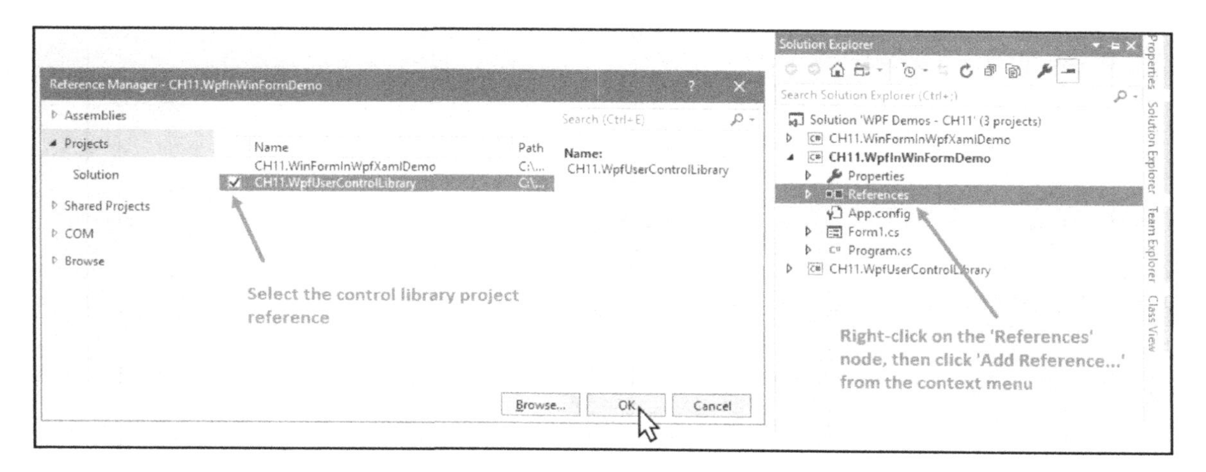

13. Also, add the following assembly references—`PresentationCore`, `PresentationFramework`, `System.Xaml`, `WindowsBase`, and `WindowsFormsIntegration` inside the project. These are required to use WPF controls and host them.
14. Rebuild the solution and make sure that the solution is building without any errors. This step also ensures that the library project gets compiled and becomes discoverable in the main project.
15. From **Solution Explorer**, double-click on the `Form1.cs` file to open it.

16. Now, open the **Toolbox**, and as shown in the following screenshot, drag the **ElementHost** element to the form (`Form1.cs`), from the **WPF Interoperability** section:

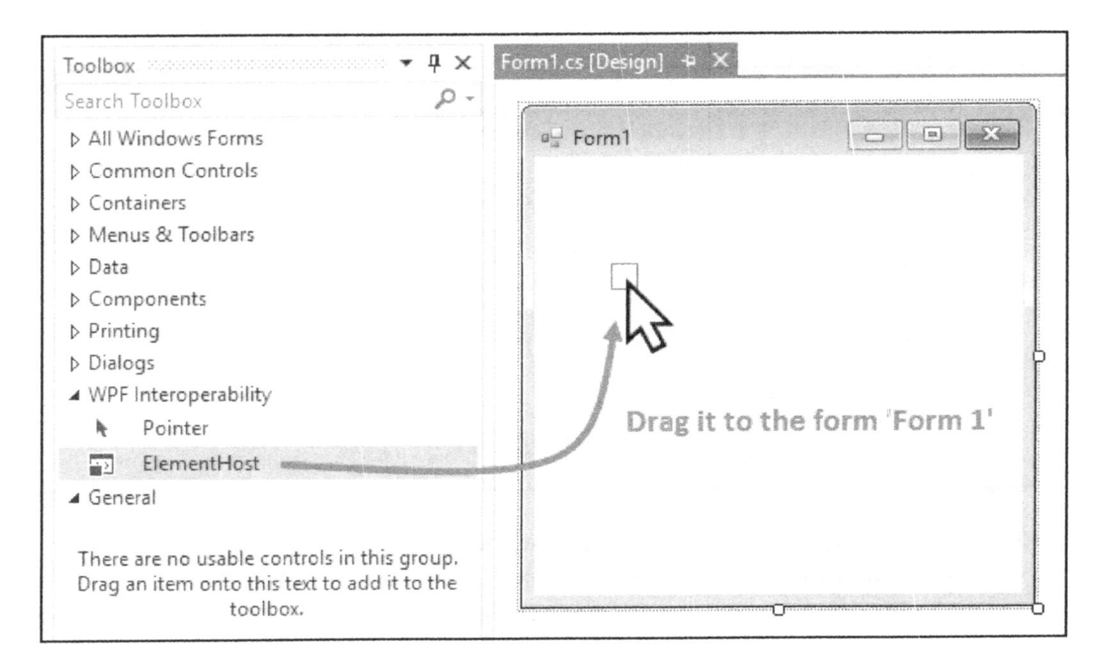

17. Expand the small arrow-head of the `ElementHost` element to select the hosted content. As shown in the following screenshot, click on the **Select Hosted Content** combo and select **UserControl1** to host inside it:

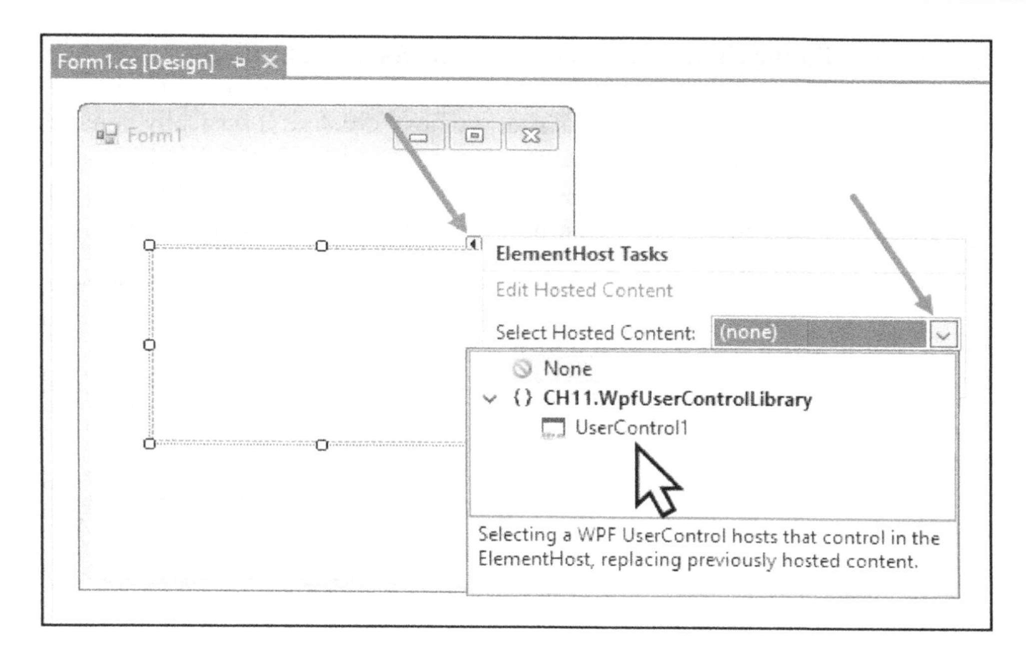

18. Alternatively, you can also drag **UserControl1** from the toolbox. In this case, Visual Studio will add the `ElementHost` and configure it to load the UserControl that you have dragged to the form. Once done, resize the control and position it inside the form:

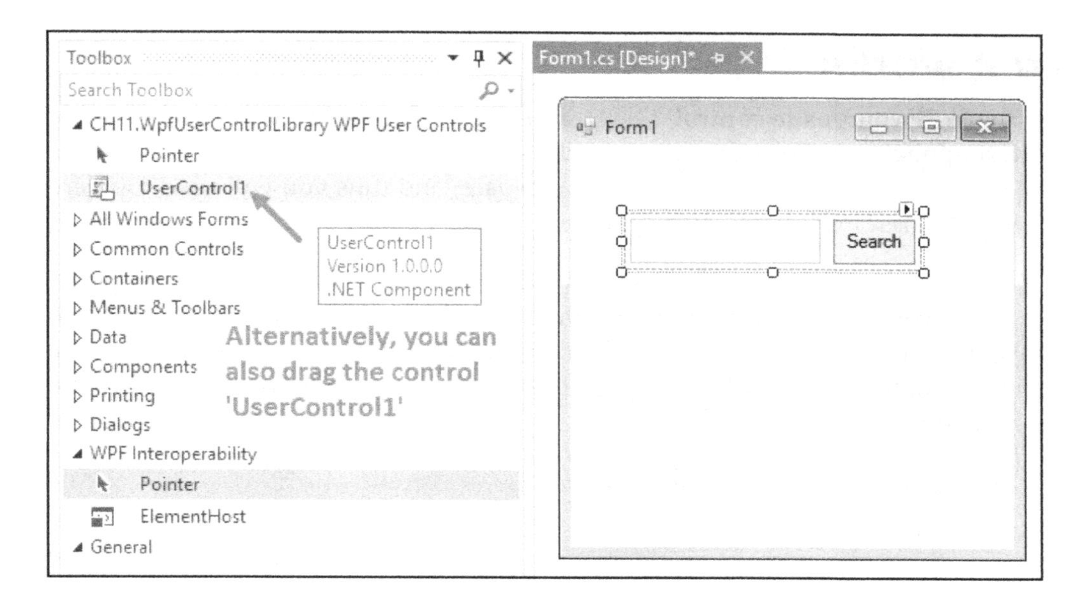

19. Now rebuild the solution again and run the form application (`CH11.WpfInWinFormDemo`). You will see a form window on the screen, containing the WPF UserControl that we have created. It basically consists of a `TextBox` and a `Button`.
20. Enter some text in the search box and click the button. You will see the message box pop up on the screen, containing the text that you have entered:

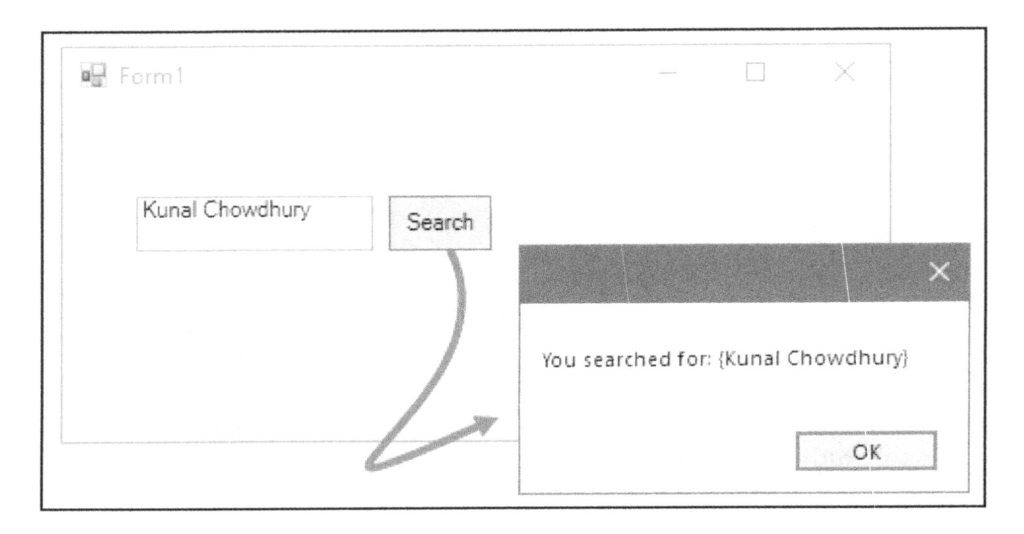

How it works...

To host the **WPF composite control**, the `ElementHost` object is used inside the Windows Forms host application. The `ElementHost` class is part of the `System.Windows.Forms.Integration` namespace, and thus you will need to reference the `WindowsFormsIntegration.dll` in the project.

To host a WPF element in a Windows Form, you must assign it to the `Child` property of the `ElementHost` control. If it is required, use the `PropertyMap` property to assign the custom mappings between an `ElementHost` and its hosted WPF element. Optionally, you can use the boolean `BackColorTransparent` property to set a transparent background to the hosted element.

Calling Win32 APIs from WPF applications

Windows Presentation Foundation and Win32 interpolation can work as different approaches. You can either host a Win32 application in a WPF application, a WPF application in a Win32 application, or call a Win32 API from WPF by importing the specified system DLL. These are often useful when you have already invested a lot in Win32 applications and now you would like to build a rich WPF application by utilizing the existing code.

In this recipe, we will learn how to call a Win32 API from a WPF. We will use a simple example to launch a browser window and then activate/refresh the browser window from our WPF code.

Getting ready

Get started by creating a WPF application. Open your Visual Studio IDE, and create a new project named `CH11.Win32ApiCallDemo`. Make sure to select **WPF App (.NET Framework)** as the project template.

How to do it...

Follow these steps to give a call to Win32 APIs from WPF applications:

1. First, we need to set up the project. Once the project gets created by Visual Studio, right-click on the **References** node of the project.
2. Select the context menu entry **Add Reference...** to add assembly references.

3. From the **Reference Manager** dialog, search for **forms**, and select **System.Windows.Forms** from the list. Click **OK** to add the reference:

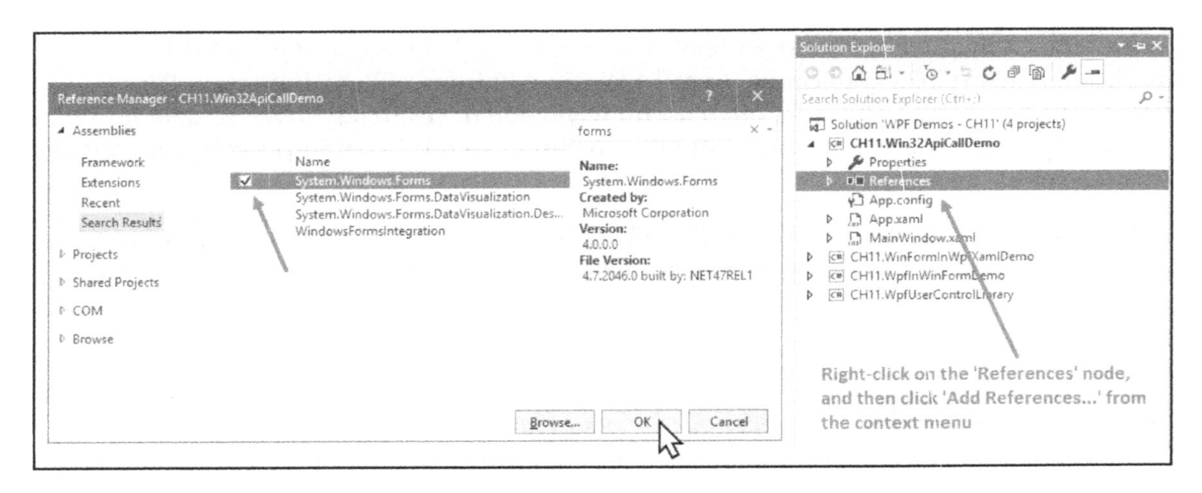

4. Now, from **Solution Explorer**, navigate to the `MainWindow.xaml` file.
5. Replace the existing `Grid` panel with the following markup, which contains a `TextBox` (`address`) and three `Button` controls (`goButton`, `bringToFrontButton`, and `refreshButton`):

```
<StackPanel Margin="10">
    <TextBlock Text="Enter website URL:"
               Foreground="Gray"
               Margin="4 0"/>

    <StackPanel Orientation="Horizontal">
        <TextBox x:Name="address"
                 Text="http://www.kunal-chowdhury.com"
                 Width="250"
                 Margin="4"/>

        <Button x:Name="goButton"
                Content="Go..."
                Padding="8 2"
                Margin="4"
                Click="OnGoClicked"/>

        <Button x:Name="bringToFrontButton"
                Content="BringToFront"
                Padding="8 2"
                Margin="4"
```

```
                    Click="OnBringToFrontClicked"/>

            <Button x:Name="refreshButton"
                    Content="Refresh"
                    Padding="8 2"
                    Margin="4"
                    Click="OnRefreshClicked"/>
        </StackPanel>
    </StackPanel>
```

6. Once the UI is ready, it's time to create the button click event implementations. Press *F7* within the XAML page to navigate to its code behind. Alternatively, you can open the `MainWindow.xaml.cs` file from **Solution Explorer**.
7. In the code behind the file, add the following namespaces:

```
using System;
using System.Diagnostics;
using System.Runtime.InteropServices;
using System.Windows;
using System.Windows.Forms;
```

8. Now, inside the `MainWindow` class, add the following declarations and make sure that the `DllImport` attribute and the `Process` class are discoverable:

```
[DllImport("User32.dll")]
static extern int SetForegroundWindow(IntPtr hWnd);

private static Process process = new Process();
```

9. Let's implement the `OnGoClicked` event handler. Copy the following code to launch Internet Explorer with the specified URL address, which is `http://www.kunal-chowdhury.com` in our case:

```
private void OnGoClicked(object sender,
 RoutedEventArgs e)
{
    goButton.IsEnabled = false;
    process.StartInfo.FileName = "iexplore.exe";
    process.StartInfo.Arguments = address.Text;
    process.Start();
}
```

10. Let's implement the `OnBringToFrontClicked` event handler to bring the launched Internet Explorer window to the front, if it lost its focus. Copy the following code to get the `MainWindowHandle` of the process instance and call the Win32 API method, `SetForegroundWindow`:

```
private void OnBringToFrontClicked(object sender,
 RoutedEventArgs e)
{
    if (process != null)
    {
        var ptr = process.MainWindowHandle;
        SetForegroundWindow(ptr);
    }
}
```

11. Now, let's add the event implementation of the **Refresh** button. Add the following `OnRefreshClicked` handler inside the class file to activate the Internet Explorer window and then call the *F5* key of the keyboard to refresh the said browser window:

```
private void OnRefreshClicked(object sender,
 RoutedEventArgs e)
{
    if (process != null)
    {
        IntPtr ptr = process.MainWindowHandle;
        SetForegroundWindow(ptr);
        SendKeys.SendWait("{F5}");
    }
}
```

12. As the code implementation is done, let's run the application. You will see the following UI on the screen:

13. As the address field of the application is already populated, click on the **Go...** button. This will launch Internet Explorer and will navigate to the address specified:

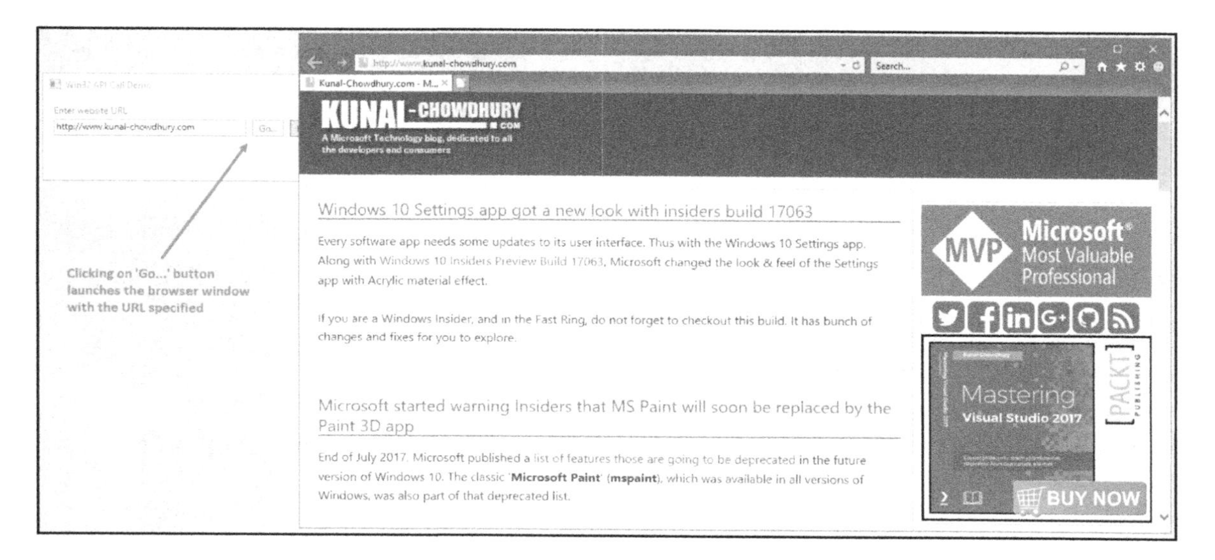

14. Now, click on the application window. This will bring the application to the front.
15. Now click the **BringToFront** button, which will activate Internet Explorer and bring it to the front.

16. Similarly, click on the application window, and then click on the **Refresh** button. This time, Internet Explorer will activate and refresh the content of the window:

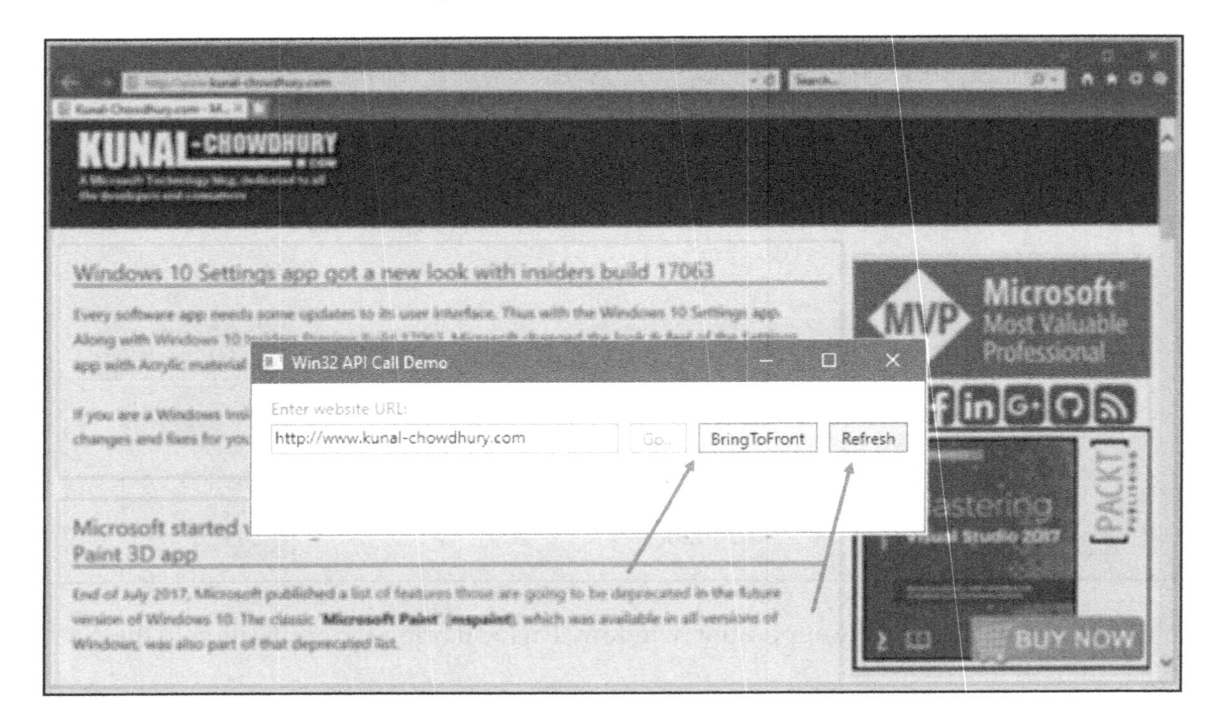

How it works...

When you click the **Go...** button of the application window, this creates the new process of the Internet Explorer (`iexplore.exe`) window and opens the URL specified to the process as its `Arguments`, once we call the `process.Start()` method.

When you click the **BringToFront** button, it retrieves the handle of the main window of the process and passes it as parameter to the `SetForegroundWindow` Win32 API method. The said API method brings the thread into the foreground and activates the window.

A process can set the foreground window only if one of the following conditions is satisfied:

- The process itself is a foreground process
- It was started by a foreground process
- The process is being debugged
- The foreground process is not a Modern Application or the Start screen
- No menus are active

The `DllImport` attribute indicates that the attributed method is exposed by an unmanaged **dynamic-link library** (**DLL**) as a static entry point. In our case, it's the `User32.dll` file.

When you click on the **Refresh** button, just like the **BringToFront** button, it first activates the Internet Explorer window by bringing it to the front. The keyboard input is then being directed to the window.

Note that an application can't force a window to the foreground if the user is working on another window. In this case, the window will flash in the task bar to notify the user.

The `SendKeys.SendWait("{F5}")` method call sends the given key (*F5*, in our case) to the active application, and then waits for the messages to be processed. As we have passed the *F5* key here, it will call the `refresh` method of the browser. Make sure that `System.Windows.Forms` is properly referenced in the project, for the `SendKeys.SendWait` method to work.

Embedding ActiveX controls in WPF applications

WPF also supports **ActiveX**, which you can easily embed in a WPF application. This is not feature specific to WPF, but it works because of interoperability with Windows Forms. The WinForm acts as an intermediate layer between the two.

There are several ActiveX controls present, which can be easily embedded in any WPF application. In this recipe, we will learn how to embed an ActiveX control by following some simple steps. We will demonstrate it using the **Microsoft Terminal Services Control** that ships with Windows.

Getting ready

Make sure Visual Studio is up and running. Create a new WPF project and name it as `CH11.ActiveXDemo`.

How to do it...

Follow these steps to generate the required libraries for the **Microsoft Terminal Services ActiveX** control and embed it inside our WPF application:

1. The first step is to generate the required libraries of our ActiveX control. This is required to get a managed and Windows Forms compatible definition of the relevant type. To do this, open **Visual Studio Developer Command Prompt** and navigate to an empty folder (let's say, `D:libs`).
2. Now, in the Command Prompt, enter the following command to generate the managed definitions of the Terminal Service DLL:

```
aximp c:WindowsSystem32mstscax.dll
```

3. This will generate two DLL files, named `MSTSCLib.dll` and `AxMSTSCLib.dll`, in the same folder (`D:libs`, in our case):

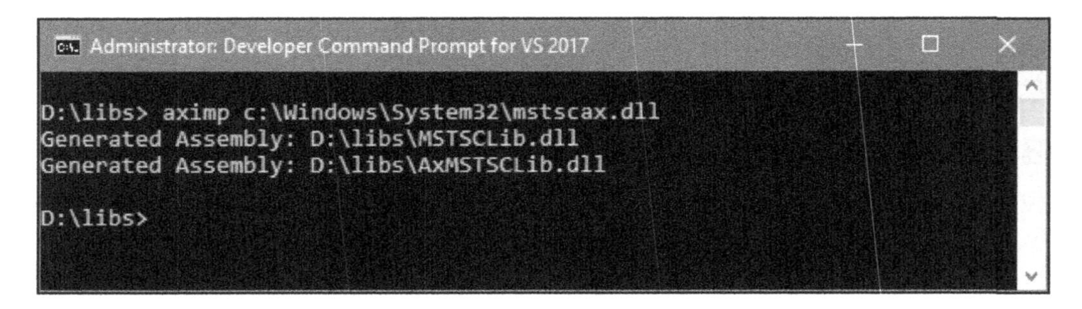

4. Let's copy those DLLs in our project folder. Create a folder named `libs`, inside the root folder of our project, and copy both files there.

5. Now, add the references of those binaries into our project. Navigate back to Visual Studio, and from **Solution Explorer**, right-click on the **References** node. Then, click **Add Reference...** from the context menu.
6. From the **Reference Manager** dialog window, click **Browse...** to add the references.
7. Select both **MSTSCLib.dll** and **AxMSTSCLib.dll**, as shown in the following screenshot and click **Add**, which will add the selection to the **Reference Manager**:

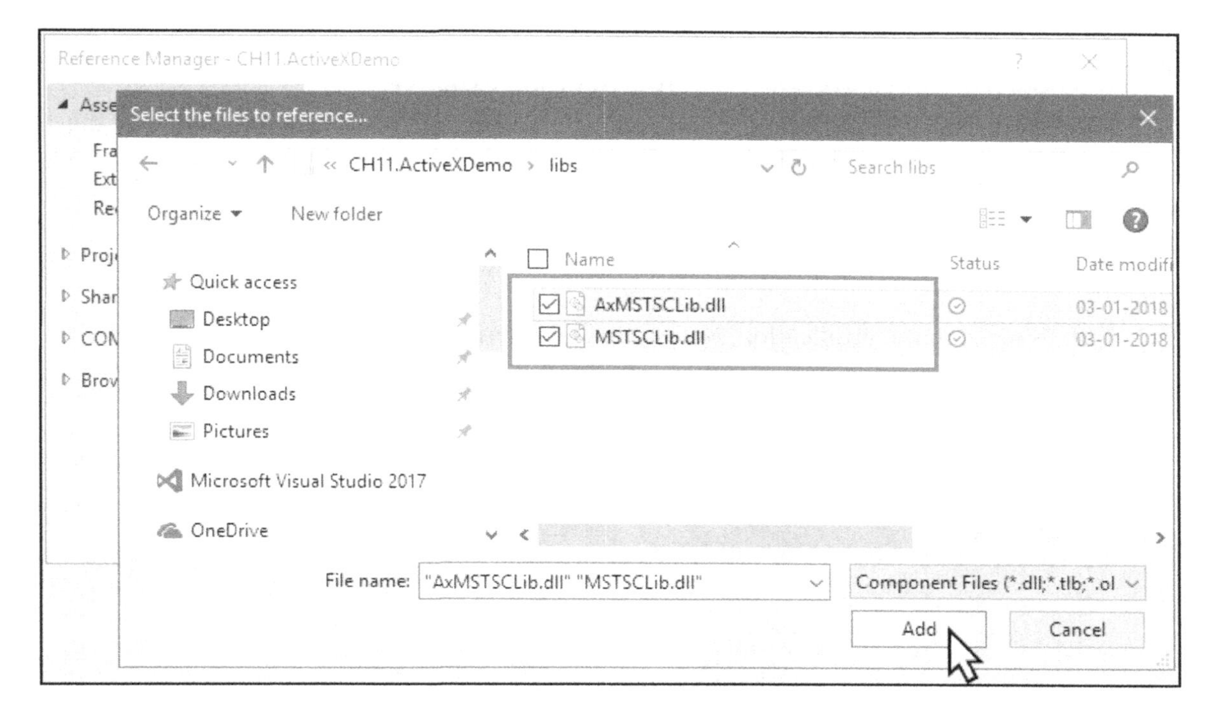

8. Search for `forms`, inside the **Reference Manager** dialog, and select **System.Windows.Forms** and **WindowsFormsIntegration** dlls.
9. Click **OK** to confirm adding the references of the four assembly files.
10. Now open the `MainWindow.xaml` file and add the following XMLNS attribute to it:

```
xmlns:lib="clr-namespace:AxMSTSCLib;assembly=AxMSTSCLib"
```

11. Replace the existing `Grid` panel with the following markup:

```
<Grid>
    <WindowsFormsHost>
        <lib:AxMsTscAxNotSafeForScripting
                                  x:Name="terminal"
                                  Height="500" Width="1000"/>
    </WindowsFormsHost>
</Grid>
```

12. Go to the code behind the file by pressing the *F7* key. Alternatively, you can open `MainWindow.xaml.cs` from **Solution Explorer**.
13. Inside the constructor of the `MainWindow` class, add the following, just after the `InitializeComponent()` method call, and replace the IP with the one that you want to connect:

```
terminal.Server = "192.168.0.10";
terminal.Connect();
```

14. Now, run the application. You will see the terminal host launched in our WPF application embedded inside it, and pointing to the remote machine for which the IP address has been provided as the `terminal.Server` name. Here's how the application will look:

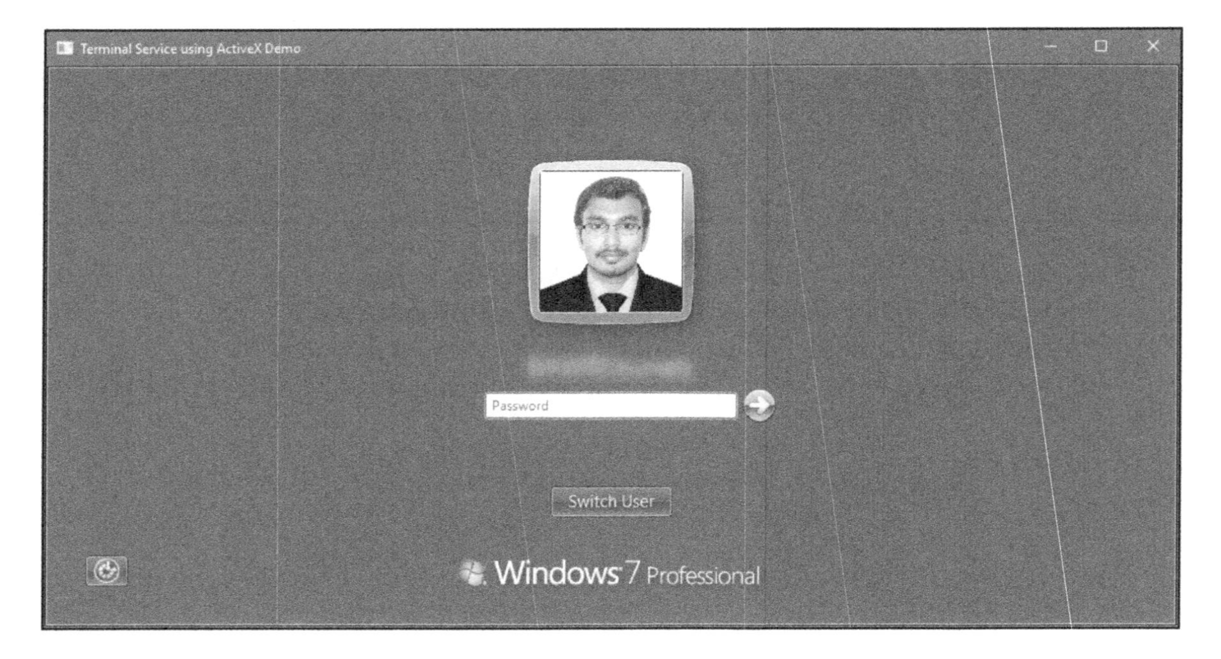

15. Within that application window, you can now log in to the system and access the desktop, files, and programs remotely.

How it works...

The ActiveX DLL for **Microsoft Terminal Services** (the `mstscax.dll` file) resides in the `%WINDIR%System32` directory. The **ActiveX Importer** (`AXIMP.EXE`), which is part of the **.NET Framework component** of the Windows SDK, generates two DLLs (`MSTSCLib.dll` and `AxMSTSCLib.dll`) from that ActiveX DLL.

The first DLL, `MSTSCLib.dll`, contains the managed definitions of the unmanaged interfaces, classes, structures, and enums, defined in the type library contained inside the ActiveX DLL (`mstscax.dll`). This is generally named with the library name from the original type library.

The second DLL, `AxMSTSCLib.dll`, is named the same but with an `Ax` prefix. This contains a Windows Forms control corresponding to each ActiveX class. The Windows Forms representation of the ActiveX control is added to `WindowsFormsHost`.

In our example, the `AxMsTscAxNotSafeForScripting` control is used in XAML, inside `WindowsFormsHost`, to perform the interaction. Its `Server` property, from the code behind the class, has been set to a simple string, pointing to the remote system's IP address or machine name, discoverable from the host.

When you are ready, the `Connect()` call to the instance of the terminal control (`AxMsTscAxNotSafeForScripting`) connects to the remote system. You can additionally provide `Domainname`, `Username`, and other properties to the terminal instance, before calling the `Connect()` method.

Other Books You May Enjoy

If you enjoyed this book, you may be interested in these other books by Packt:

Mastering Windows Presentation Foundation
Sheridan Yuen

ISBN: 978-1-78588-300-2

- Use MVVM to improve workflow
- Create visually stunning user interfaces
- Perform data binds proficiently
- Implement advanced data validation
- Locate and resolve errors quickly
- Master practical animations
- Improve your applications' performance

Mastering Visual Studio 2017
Kunal Chowdhury

ISBN: 978-1-78839-980-7

- Learn what's new in the Visual Studio 2017 IDE, C# 7.0, and how it will help developers to improve their productivity
- Learn the workloads and components of the new installation wizard and how to use the online and offline installer
- Build stunning Windows apps using Windows Presentation Foundation (WPF) and Universal Windows Platform (UWP) tools
- Get familiar with .NET Core and learn how to build apps targeting this new framework
- Explore everything about NuGet packages
- Debug and test your applications using Visual Studio 2017
- Accelerate cloud development with Microsoft Azure
- Integrate Visual Studio with most popular source control repositories, such as TFS and GitHub

Leave a review - let other readers know what you think

Please share your thoughts on this book with others by leaving a review on the site that you bought it from. If you purchased the book from Amazon, please leave us an honest review on this book's Amazon page. This is vital so that other potential readers can see and use your unbiased opinion to make purchasing decisions, we can understand what our customers think about our products, and our authors can see your feedback on the title that they have worked with Packt to create. It will only take a few minutes of your time, but is valuable to other potential customers, our authors, and Packt. Thank you!

Index

D

E

R

S

T

U

V

W

Made in United States
North Haven, CT
07 October 2024